A Tale of Five Cities

BY THE SAME AUTHOR

The New French Revolution

JOHN ARDAGH

A Tale of Five Cities

Life in Europe Today

HARPER & ROW, PUBLISHERS

NEW YORK

Cambridge
Hagerstown
Philadelphia
San Francisco

London
Mexico City
São Paulo
Sydney

1817

To my wife
JENNY

and to my son
NICHOLAS

This book was first published in England under the title *"A Tale of Five Cities: Life in Provincial Europe Today."*

The lines from the song "The Socialist ABC" are quoted by permission of its author Alex Glasgow.

FIRST U.S. EDITION

ISBN: 0-06-010136-9

LIBRARY OF CONGRESS CATALOG CARD NUMBER: 78-22448

80 81 82 83 84 10 9 8 7 6 5 4 3 2 1

Contents

Maps

I
Introduction

This study of life today in five cities of Europe is a pursuit of two separate but inter-related themes. One, it is a voyage of discovery into the soul of the provincial, to see what makes a provincial community tick. Two, it is an enquiry into the differences and similarities between peoples: for this purpose I have chosen towns that as far as possible exemplify their nations, and I concentrate on the local and specific, so that foremost it is the *towns* and not their nations that I am comparing. They represent the four leading countries of the European Community, with Ljubljana added as a postscript to point a contrast.

Using the tools of the journalist, not the sociologist, I have gone into homes and factories, schools and offices, *cafés* and town halls, to try to learn what is this Europe that we belong to and argue about, despair of or take for granted, and what it is we have in common. And I have taken as my terrain the kind of biggish cities that most Europeans today live in. But there is no special connection between these five towns, beyond the fact that I have made them my own and grown fond of them – or most of them.

We know that, superficially at least, the peoples of western Europe have been drawing closer since the war. Some of the old enmities and barriers have been disappearing, and modern life is tending towards a certain material uniformity. As I expected, I found some similar trends in all these towns, especially among the young. The latest fashions could be seen equally in the discothèques of Toulouse or Newcastle, and the same Stuttgart-made cars in the streets of Bologna and Ljubljana; families from Stuttgart or Newcastle were holiday-making on the same Spanish beaches; everyone was watching much the same kind of television, and putting the same brands of Italian refrigerator or Dutch record-player into their trim little flats, in the same kind of high-rise blocks. There is even the gimmick of apeing each others' traditions, as so-called "pubs" appear in Toulouse and Stuttgart, and Newcastle fills up with "bierkellers" and "bistros".

Much of this is superficial. And some towns, notably Bologna, resist these innovations more than others. It would be hateful if we were all to become the same, and I was pleased to find each community preserving a distinctive flavour and temperament beneath the consumer gloss. In fact, their strongest common feature is precisely this: the feeling each has of its own specialness, an exceptional local pride, a cherishing of traditions, a sense of identity that may even have intensified as a defence against modern pressures. I felt this equally at a Newcastle sing-song, a Toulouse rugby match, a Stuttgart *Bierfest*, a Bologna carnival or a Ljubljana poetry festival. This sturdy local patriotism is in many ways fine – but if it includes parochialism, does this inhibit the growth of wider loyalties? Has the development of economic ties in Europe led to any widening of horizons? Have the peoples become more aware of each other, through tourism, the media, or other factors? And if so, has this made them any fonder of each other? Do they feel any sense of belonging to the same European society? – and do they even want to?

I found no easy answer to these questions. I write this book as a dedicated "European", wanting Europe to retain its cultural diversity but also to federate – the two are far from incompatible. I had been encouraged by the seeming progress towards integration until the economic crisis of 1973-4, and have been dismayed by trends since then, as many Governments revert to a narrower national self-interest, and public disillusion with the EEC seems to increase. And so, as I visited these towns, I asked myself: what do they have in common that could ever form the basis of a European union? I met with paradoxes. On one level, their hostility or suspicion seems to be directed more keenly against other areas of the same country, notably the capital city, than against other countries: a Bolognese resents a Roman more than he does a Frenchman. Also, despite their differences of character and life-style, these towns do have far stronger similarities than the mass of their inhabitants realise. But they are separated by mutual ignorance, and language. Perhaps what they have most in common is this: their unawareness of what they have in common.

They are all, in one way or another, involved in the post-war growth of regional feeling. While the nation-states have been groping towards some new unity, there has also been a move in the inverse direction, towards greater regionalism: the two are complementary. This regional trend takes various forms, economic, political, emotional or cultural. In those regions which rightly or wrongly have some sense of their own nationhood – notably Scotland, Brittany, the Basque country – it has even led to separatist campaigns. None of my five towns are in these areas. And yet, in all the five countries featured in this book, and in others too such as Spain, there has been some distinct movement since 1945 towards greater political devolution, whether still embryonic (as in France) or much more extensive (as in Yugoslavia and West Germany). President Tito has found that the best way to prevent his uneasy federation of six republics from flying apart is to give each a real degree of internal autonomy, under the watchful aegis of a centralised Communist Party. It more or less works. In West Germany, also a relatively young nation with no centralised tradition, the eleven *Länder* have been granted even more autonomy than they had before the war. And this too works. In Italy, where the centralist structure imposed after unification was ill-suited to the individualist city-state tradition, a recent reform has finally begun to allow some autonomy to the seventeen regions; and this too is bearing some fruit, despite the disturbed conditions of present-day Italy. In Britain, Parliament has been struggling to decide what kind of devolution to offer the Scots and Welsh, though it remains to be seen how this could be extended, if at all, to England itself. Even in France, the most centralised of countries, the twenty-two economic "regions" have recently been endowed with local assemblies, though their powers remain highly circumscribed.

Moves of this kind are mostly in response to some popular desire for a greater participation in affairs at a local level. The desire may often be vaguely formulated, or felt more keenly by ambitious local dignitaries than by the ordinary citizen; but it does relate to a growing and widely-held feeling that, in biggish centralised countries, national government has become too interfering and bureaucratic, yet also too remote and impersonal, and needs to be balanced by a new tier at regional level, closer to people's lives and better able to provide a sense of involvement. And this trend to regionalism is not at all incompatible with a move towards a federal Europe: in fact, most "Europeans" consider that the two are mutually necessary and complementary. In this view, as the nation-state wanes and some powers are transferred to Strasbourg or Brussels, so the regions must seize their chance, to provide the necessary human-scale counterweights to the new monolith. This at least is the ideal, though still far from realisation. At any rate, all the towns chosen for this book are in one way or another "regional capitals" (the sense of the term varies from country to country). And I returned from these towns a more convinced advocate than ever, both of regionalism and of federalism.

The germ of the idea for this book grew out of my previous one, *The New French Revolution (The New France)*. Researching for that book, I travelled a lot round the French provinces and fell in love with them. I was impressed by the provincial revival of the 1950s and '60s, as cities hitherto enclosed and lethargic became far more prosperous, animated and outward-looking. But though I visited most of the larger French towns, I stayed in none for very long; and I felt that next I should put my enthusiasm to the test by living in one town for several months and making a study-in-depth. But my Paris publisher felt this was uncommercial: "French parochialism is such," he said, "that if you write a book about, say, Caen or Nancy, no one in the rest of France will bother to read it." So my publishers suggested I should compare a French and a British town, which appeared a more promising idea, and then it seemed logical to include a German one too, and then an Italian, to complete the quartet of the larger EEC countries. There we might have stopped, but I was especially interested in Eastern Europe and wanted to add a town in a Communist country as a contrast. Yugoslavia was the obvious choice, for I knew I would be more able to meet and question people freely than in the Soviet bloc. Only Yugoslavia had created its own kind of semi-liberal Socialist society on its own terms, and therefore could present a valid comparison with the West. I was already fascinated by the little I knew of its experiment.

Next came the choice of towns. In agreement with my publishers, I set myself a clear brief. Obviously they must not be national capitals, about which we hear too much: Britain and France, or indeed, say, Austria or Denmark, tend to be assessed too much by foreigners in terms of their glamourised capitals – and yet, Paris is not France. The towns, I felt, should be "regional capitals", even if their status would not be the same in a federal country (e.g. Germany) as in a centralised one (e.g. France). But this contrast might itself be revealing. Next, the towns should not be too large and metropolitan, or they would lack the "provincial" quality I was looking for; nor would I find it so easy to come to grips with them on a visit of a few weeks in each. So I rejected the M-for-a-million-plus places – Munich, Milan, Marseille, Greater Manchester, and such-like. Nor should they be too small, or they might lack sufficient diversity and activity. I settled on 500,000 to 800,000 (with suburbs) as about the right size. I also wanted each town to have some industry, a university, and a varied cultural life. Above all, it must have vitality, tradition and individuality – without being thereby too *un*typical of its country. I knew that no town could be completely typical, yet I wanted places that could be presented as reasonably so. Thus (for diverse reasons) no question of Venice, or Strasbourg – let alone Belfast.

In Germany, a "regional capital" must clearly be a *Land* capital. Munich and Hamburg were too big, some other towns too small, Berlin was out of the question, Frankfurt and Cologne were not *Land* capitals, Bremen was too much of a seaport with no hinterland. Düsseldorf was possible, but too much a world financial centre and also too integrally part of the vast Ruhr conurbation. My final choice was between Hannover and Stuttgart. Either would have done, but I chose the latter as being – so I was assured – the more lively and attractive place. I have no regrets.

In France, of the capitals of the twenty-two so-called "regions", Marseille and Lyon were too big and some other places – Caen, Dijon, Montpellier – too small. Rennes, capital of Brittany, and Strasbourg, capital of Alsace, were obviously untypical. So in different ways were Nice and Grenoble (anyway, they are not capitals). Nantes was a possibility, but a bit too small and dull, so the final choice lay between Lille, Bordeaux and Toulouse. Lille I rejected as too solemn, grey and northern, and too much within the orbit of Paris. Bordeaux could have been a good choice, but I preferred Toulouse as I knew it to be livelier, more diverse, more open-hearted, and providing a more striking example of the post-war transformation of the French provinces. Again, I have no regrets.

In Italy, Milan, Turin and Naples were too big; Genoa also a bit too large and too much a seaport; Palermo (Sicily's capital) too untypical; Trieste likewise, because of its position and history, and anyway too small; Venice and Florence too much museum-towns engulfed by tourism. Pleasant cities such as Verona and Padua were too small and not regional capitals. I toyed with Bari, a lively and prosperous place sometimes called "the Milan of the South", but decided that the *Mezzogiorno* is too much a special case: if Italy is to be compared fairly with Germany, France and Britain, then a central or northern town must be chosen. By a process of elimination this left me with the remarkable city of Bologna, which was not and is not nearly as untypical as its thirty-four years of unbroken Communist local rule might suggest.

In Britain, a non-English town would clearly be untypical, and so I discarded Edinburgh, Glasgow (too large anyway), Cardiff (too small anyway) and inevitably poor old Belfast. Birmingham and Manchester were too big, Liverpool and Sheffield in no sense regional capitals. Bristol attracted me: about the right size, lively, sophisticated, go-ahead. But I felt it was maybe *too* sophisticated, too southern and London-orientated, to be representative of the English industrial provinces: I ought to choose one of the big towns in the Midlands or north. The final was between Leeds, the true metropolis of Yorkshire, and Newcastle, queen of the north-East. And I chose the latter for some of the same reasons that had led me to prefer Toulouse to Lille or Bordeaux: more lively, more full of character, more aware of its regional individuality.

In Yugoslavia, I needed a smaller town, as the country is much smaller in population than the others. Zagreb, the second city, thus seemed proportionately too large, even though it is no bigger than Stuttgart. The next cities are Skopje, Sarajevo, Ljubljana, and of these I chose the last, principally because it is much the most properous and Western-orientated, the least "Balkan" and Turkish-influenced, and therefore best able to provide a meaningful comparison with the West. It may not be fully typical of Yugoslavia, yet I am sure my choice was the right one.

To what extent can my five towns compare fairly with each other? They certainly differ in population:

	municipal area	total conurbation (approx.)
Stuttgart	590,000	1,200,000
Bologna	500,000	620,000
Newcastle	300,000	900,000 (Tyneside, excluding Wearside)
Toulouse	400,000	550,000
Ljubljana	260,000	350,000

These figures may at first seem puzzling. Newcastle is smaller than Toulouse or Bologna as a municipality, yet its conurbation (Tyneside) is much larger than theirs; in Stuttgart's case, too, the total conurbation has more than twice the population of the muncipality. Varying local government structures are a factor: but the principal explanation is that Stuttgart and Newcastle, being at the heart of major industrial areas, have a much larger urban sprawl around them than Toulouse or Bologna, both of them more agricultural by tradition, more geographically self-contained, less close to other towns of any size. In reality Stuttgart and Newcastle are the largest of my towns, followed by Bologna, then Toulouse. And this does roughly correspond to the degree of urbanisation of these countries. As municipalities, Toulouse is the fourth town of France (after Paris, Marseille, Lyon) while larger Stuttgart is only the ninth town of Germany (although Germany's population is a mere 20 per cent more than France's). This merely indicates (a) that Germany is more urbanised than France, and (b) that France's urban population remains heavily concentrated in the Paris area (10 million) whereas Germany for historical reasons has a more even spread of big cities. In sum, these five towns do compare fairly with each other in terms of their respective weighting within each country: each conurbation is the fifth to seventh largest. Stuttgart is the richest and most populous of these towns, just as Germany is the richest and most populous of these nations.

In these European lands with their long histories and strong regional variations, no town is totally typical. I am writing about towns, not nations, and though plenty of national generalisations can be deduced from these chapters, the reader should not carry this too far. I have done my best to choose representative towns. And if in some respects they differ from the national norm, it is usually in exaggerating some common national trait rather than contradicting it. Stuttgart is typical of many aspects of southern Germany: if its natives, the Swabians, tend to be regarded mockingly by other Germans as unusually prudent, thrifty, pious, hard-working and ponderous, are these not frequent German characteristics? Toulouse has a strong meridional personality of its own, yet most of its problems and preoccupations are common to all France: its above-average hostility to Paris is a vivid example of an average French provincial trait. Bologna is a more complex case. This ancient city-state, *sui generis,* regards itself as entirely special – again, an above-average illustration of how most Italian cities feel. Its Communism does not make it untypical. Firstly, this Communism is very mild and "Italian"; secondly, since 1975 most other big Italian cities have come under Communist control too – so

Italy has fallen in step with Bologna! Ljubljana, I admit, is unusually prosperous and sophisticated by most Yugoslav standards; yet it is also very Slav, and it exemplifies the Socialist system of all Yugoslavia. There remains Newcastle, a town of great personality with the typical ruggedness and human warmth of the north of England. But Tyneside is one of the poorer and more depressed areas of struggling Britain, and its natives (Geordies) present in some ways a caricature of British industrial shortcomings and insular attitudes to the world. It has many typical British virtues too. But on reflection I am not entirely sure I was fair to my own country in choosing Newcastle to compete against the heavy guns of Stuttgart.

I made several visits to each town, spending a total of five to eight weeks in each. Toulouse and Newcastle I knew a little already, and their two nations I knew far better than the other three. Stuttgart, Bologna and Ljubljana were new territory to me, though I had been to their countries as a tourist. But in no town did meeting people prove any problem at all. I applied the usual pushy journalistic techniques, my initial introductions snowballed, and everywhere - notably in Stuttgart, Toulouse and Ljubljana - I received a high degree of helpfulness and hospitality, both private and professional. I was invited into hundreds of homes and now have good friends in these towns. Many people seemed to be flattered that their town was to be featured in a book. They were very curious to know what I thought of it - but seldom asked a word about the others!

Who were my initial contacts, and where did I stay?

Stuttgart: A friend at the German Embassy in London introduced me to the city authorities, who provided me with a flatlet at their expense, in the home of a local journalist and his wife who furnished countless contacts. I came with other introductions, too, and the British consulate-general was helpful.

Bologna: A journalist I knew in Paris, Giorgio Fanti, gave me an introduction to his brother, the ex-mayor, and the present mayor, Renato Zangheri. I had some other contacts too. Bologna has a reputation in Italy for openness, but I found it less penetrable and responsive than my other towns. I stayed first in a Catholic seminary outside the city, then in a central *pensione*.

Newcastle: A friend running the local arts association provided numerous contacts, and so did some others. The city authorities were helpful. I stayed first in rather unpleasant digs near the university, then with an elderly widow on a modern housing estate, and sometimes in hotels.

Toulouse: I stayed in a small hotel in the noisy city centre, or with friends. I had good initial introductions, which quickly multiplied. The French have a reputation for inhospitality which, outside Paris, is entirely false: during a five-week stay in Toulouse I was invited to lunch or dinner in the homes of seventeen different French families, in some cases several times. I say this not to show off, but to set the record straight.

Ljubljana: I had some personal introductions, which proved warmly fruitful. I also approached the Yugoslav Embassy in London who introduced me to the Slovene Ministry of Information, and they provided me with lodgings in a family (at my expense) and with numerous contacts. The officials showed a polite interest in whom I was seeing, but did not try to control my movements: I felt just as free as in the other towns to meet whom I wished and talk frankly.

At the end of it all, I like Ljubljana the best of the five; I admire Stuttgart the most and feel most at home there; I understand Toulouse the most intimately; I have developed a strange love-hate feeling towards wayward Newcastle; and I have never come quite to grips with baffling Bologna. And the language barrier? Speaking French, I had no trouble in Toulouse, despite the irritations of the Midi accent. I can get by in Italian; also I found plenty of Bolognesi speaking English or French. My German is poor and my Slovene non-existent, but the people of Stuttgart and Ljubljana are such marvellous linguists that English and French were all I needed. The only town where I had a slight problem was Newcastle – and I am not altogether joking. The Geordie dialect was alien to me, and even a Geordie speaking normal English in his strange accent I found hard to follow.

In each town I followed much the same lines of enquiry, and the chapters that follow are all (except Ljubljana) structured in the same way. This may appear a little too schematic for some readers' tastes, but it does give the book a shape, and I hope it enables the contrasts to emerge. The book can be read either in sequence or, as it were, subject by subject. Thus, if you are specially interested, say, in cultural life, you can read all the five cultural sections, one after the other. But I do not recommend this: it is best to read a chapter right through, maybe skipping.

Each of the first four chapters follows this order:

1 Introduction, scene-setting.
2 History, local character and values, society.
3 Local Government, relations with national government.
4 Town-planning, environment.
5 Civic awareness, community life, daily social life.
6 Cultural life.
7 Standard of living, homes, leisure, food and restaurants, night-life.
8 Education, youth.
9 Industry, labour relations.
10 Foreign minorities, attitudes to foreigners, to the world, and to the rest of the nation; regionalism; conclusion.

The emphasis varies from chapter to chapter, according to relevance and interest. Thus, in Bologna there is much more to say about local politics (fascinating) than about culture (fairly dull); in Stuttgart, conversely, I write at much greater length about the cultural scene (fascinating) than about politics (dullish). And there are some small variations, to suit the points being made: thus social life and party-giving are described in Bologna section (2) but Toulouse section (5). But broadly the pattern is similar throughout, save in the case of Ljubljana which forms something of a postscript and figures little in the constant cross-referencing between towns. In Ljubljana I follow a partially different structure – with special sections on self-management, and freedom of expression – in order best to tackle the central question: what kind of a thing is this strange Socialist society of theirs?

The book has been researched and written in the late 1970s at a time of anxiety in Europe, when faith in ever-rising prosperity has given way to new preoccupations. All these towns are at grips with unemployment and all (save Stuttgart) with high inflation too. All are turning towards a greater concern for quality of life, environment, community, though the approach may differ in different places. All face a malaise in education, and a crisis in city finances, while some have had to come to terms with huge immigrant communities, and over Stuttgart and Bologna there hangs the intermittent threat of new urban terrorism. These are not megalopolises, yet they are becoming just large enough to begin to feel the stresses of modern urban living. They are balanced precariously between an old sleepy *douceur provinciale* and the new excitements and dangers of the big city. As I try to show, each faces up to its new destiny in its own way.

I have lived all my adult life in London and Paris, save for one year in the north of England as a trainee reporter. I have always had a fondness for provincial towns, the ugly ones almost as much as the beautiful ones – as a visitor. I love arriving in an unknown town, armed maybe with a few useful social entrées, and then steadily mapping out the geography and psychology of the place – the sophisticated haunts and the louche ones, the foci of student unrest and bourgeois satisfaction, the pubs and *cafés* where factory-workers meet, or nostalgic expatriates, or cliquish bohemians – and analysing what it is that gives this society its own flavour, unlike any other. Through this book I have got to know Europe far better, and provincialism. I warm to its snugness and human scale, so often lost in large capitals, but I am not impressed by its navel-contemplation. I might enjoy provincial towns less if I did not have an escape route, if I were not a detached outsider, a stranger taking notes. I am glad that the nature of my work obliges me to live in London, or Paris, so that I do not have to test the courage of my province-loving convictions.

II

Stuttgart

The pious millionaires: work, work and build your little house

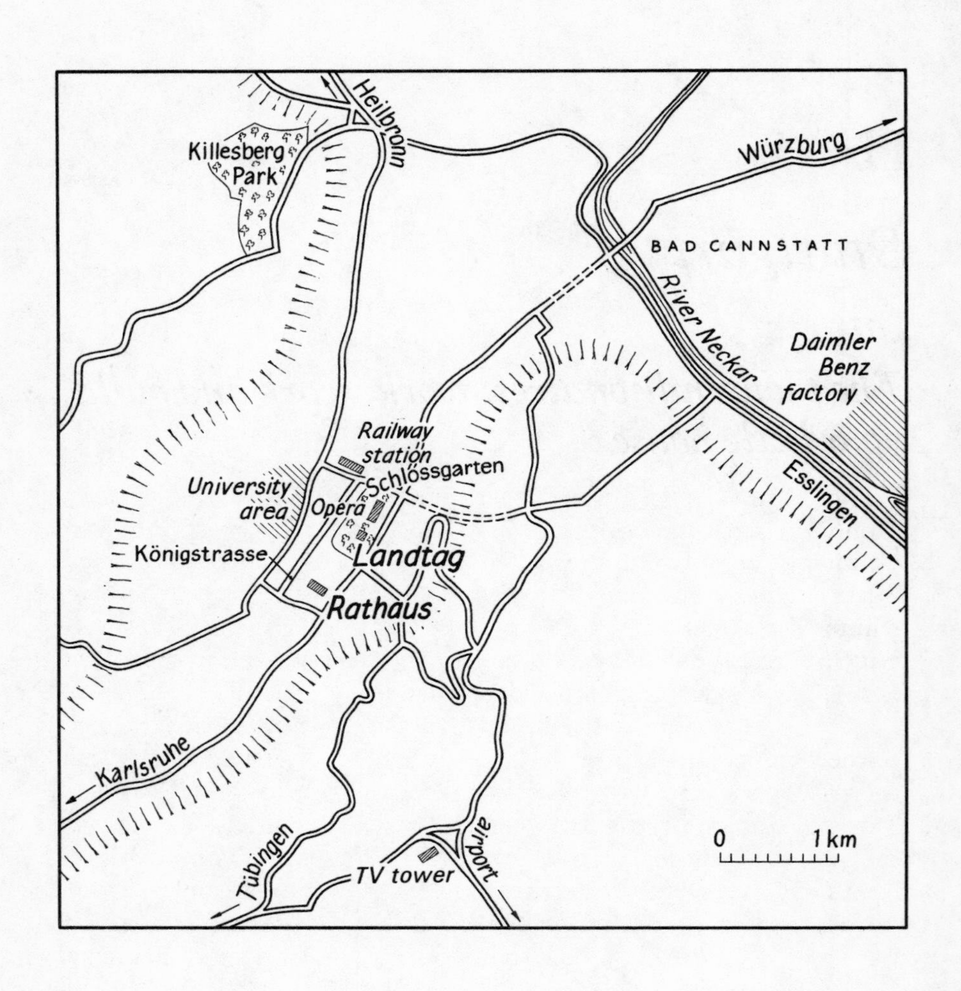

Heilbronn
Killesberg Park
Würzburg
BAD CANNSTATT
River Neckar
Daimler Benz factory
Railway station
Schlössgarten
University area
Opera
Königstrasse
Landtag
Rathaus
Esslingen
Karlsruhe
Tübingen
TV tower
airport
0
1 km

1
Introduction

Cosmopolitan metropolis? – or, as it is often called, "the biggest village in Germany"? Stuttgart is both, and knows it is both.

Though not always the most charming of the five towns in this book, I found it much the most impressive: the largest and wealthiest, also the most self-confident and international, the most modern and best organised, and (on a par with Ljubljana) the town that is the most genuinely a capital. Of course, none of this is very surprising, seeing that Stuttgart is a major centre of German industry and capital of the richest and third largest of the *Länder,* Baden-Württemberg. *"Partner der Welt"* the municipal council has dubbed the town, and this partnership is easily apparent – in the huge foreign population, the international quality of music and ballet, the world-famous car and electrical industries, restaurants of a score of nationalities, and daily jet flights to the main centres of Europe. How Bologna and Newcastle, or even Toulouse, seem enclosed and sluggish by comparison! And yet, the local people, the Swabians, are regarded with a certain mockery by the rest of Germany, as the very prototype of stolid, parochial provincials, seeming to care more passionately about the spotlessness of their front doorsteps – literally – than the fate of the world outside. *"Schaffe, schaffe, Häusle baue"* – "work, work and build your little house" – is their notorious motto. And I found some fascination in this recurrent contrast between the Swabian temperament and life-style, and the busy modern surface of their sophisticated and cosmopolitan city.

There is contrast too in the physical setting of Stuttgart, which hides its metallic heart in a soft green nest of wooded hills. Though the largest and most industrial of my towns, it is also the most leafy and bucolic, and is well known for having the most attractive setting of any big German city. The rebuilt centre lies in a hollow; up the steep hills on either side climb the prosperous suburbs; farther out, other suburbs straggle down valleys or along hilltops amid the undulating forests that enclose the city. Save for a few streets in the centre, nothing is in a straight line: you must climb, loop or zigzag to get from one point to another. Everywhere, there are hazy panoramas and a sense of greenery and elevation, and this helps to make Stuttgart a pleasanter place than some fearsome city of the plain, such as Frankfurt. In some parts of the town, too, are sloping vineyards – one lies just above the central station, others climb down close to the big Mercedes car factory – for Stuttgart produces not only the best cars in Germany but also more wine than any other German commune. Many factory workers own plots of land, and thus are spare-time farmers or vine growers. Small wonder that the late mayor, Arnulf Klett, used to call himself "the greatest village mayor in Germany."

Yet the downtown city centre, largely rebuilt after 1945 and today dominated by the usual assertive blocks containing banks, offices and car showrooms, is an unlovely forest of concrete and neon. Its aura is harsh and metallic. Here and there, a few handsome older buildings that escaped the worst of the wartime bombing have been elegantly restored and are discreetly floodlit; but they are not numerous. The city is highly cultured in its way and pours money into the arts: but its first loyalty is to making that money. The Swabians' mania for hard work, allied to their mechanical genius, has enabled them over the years to build this into a town that rivals Hamburg as the richest *per capita* of the big German capitals. The motor car was invented here – by Gottlieb Daimler, in a garden shed in 1885 – and today the big car factories are still a mainstay of that wealth. Dozens of blue Mercedes signs glitter at night from the rooftops like lode-stars, and they have beckoned into the city more than its share of "guest workers" from southern lands, and of other newcomers to help run the opulent businesses and restaurants. The stolid Swabians still set the tone, but today they are close to being outnumbered by the various immigrants who have arrived in waves since the war – first the Silesians and other refugees from the East, then the workers from Mediterranean lands (euphemistically known as *Gastarbeiter* – "guest workers"), as well as the large foreign business and diplomatic communities.

Each time I arrive in Stuttgart from some other corner of provincial

Europe, my first reaction is to be excited and stimulated by its diversity and energy, its sense of purpose, its aura of sophistication, its ability to make the best of itself, its care for quality and its even-more-than-German thoroughness. These people do not leave things half-finished, as the people of Toulouse sometimes do. Go into the simplest local shop to buy cakes or chocolates, and the girl will expertly wrap them and then twirl the coloured string into fancy shapes – the kind of stylish touch that typifies modern Germany and is generally absent in Newcastle. Attend a *première* at the Opera, or sit in the gaudy Mowenpick *café* on the concrete parapet of the Kleine Schlossplatz, amid the tidy young executives, and you will not feel yourself to be in some provincial backwater. The shopping streets and piazzas are adorned in bright commercial colours: the younger women dress with their own kind of elegance, looking like models from last year's fashion magazines. The city may not always be up-to-the-minute, but it knows how to buy the best. Has it not built up its local ballet company (with the help of choreographers and dancers from abroad) into one of the best in western Europe?

Stuttgart has many of the attributes of a capital. It is the seat of a parliament, the *Landtag* of Baden-Württemberg, housed in a modern glass-and-concrete building in the Schlossgarten, in the heart of town. It is the seat of a regional government, with powers over many matters that in Britain or France would be dealt with from London or Paris. It has more than thirty consulates, even if many are no more than "honorary". The British consulate-general has a staff four times that of a British embassy in a smallish Latin-American country – evidence of Stuttgart's economic importance as capital of a large and rich *Land.* In short, at a time when regionalism is *à la mode* in Europe and several countries are toying with devolution, Stuttgart may seem to illustrate the strengths and advantages of the German federal structure. Yet there could be another side to this coin, as this chapter will explore: paradoxically, may not the lack of a national focus in Germany increase, rather than reduce, the provincialism of a city such as Stuttgart? Add to this the natural self-sufficiency, call it complacency maybe, of the Swabian character. My first reaction on arrival may be one of excitement, but my second is often one of disappointment. In a curious way, Stuttgart seems a little bit less than the sum of its so impressive parts. Its diversity does not quite add up. Fantasy and spontaneity have been tidied away from those neat streets where the pedestrian will never, never disobey a red light (unless, maybe, he is an

Italian immigrant) and where, at least until recently, hippies or buskers might be harangued by strangers in the streets for their lack of *Ordnung*. Even the Swabian writer Thaddäus Troll, very much a local patriot, has written of his town as "more worthy of love than lovable". So who then are these Swabians?

2

The Swabian soul: godliness next to cleanliness

Swabia is a sizeable chunk of south Germany, much of it hilly and wooded like Stuttgart itself. It runs from the Black Forest across to Augsburg and south almost to lake Constance. In the Middle Ages it was an important duchy: today, straddling Württemburg and part of Bavaria, it does not exist as a political unit, but retains its own dialect, customs and cultural identity. Stuttgart, by far its biggest town, began life as a stud farm (hence the name, from *Stuten Garten* – "mares' garden"), founded by the son of Otto the Great in 950 AD. In the Middle Ages it was a lesser town than its royal neighbours, Esslingen and Tübingen. But after 1492 its true history began, for it then became the capital of the rulers of Württemberg who were first counts, then dukes, then (after 1806) kings.

In the 17th and 18th centuries some of these rulers were unpleasant despots who exploited the area: but a number of Swabian towns hit back by forming burghers' associations that forced concessions from the dukes. These civic bodies developed into a kind of parliament, and this is the basis of one of the key features of Swabia today: it has a stronger democratic tradition than most other parts of Germany. Another vital tradition is that of precision industry, in this ill-endowed region where necessity has been the mother of invention. Swabia is without coal, iron or other natural resources, much of its arable land is stony and unfertile, and often in the past there were famines. Many farmers emigrated: but in the 19th century others turned to clock- and watch-making as the best way of topping up their incomes and surviving. This flair for precision work has grown, and is the basis of today's famous mechanical and industrial industries. Thus by their own skill and application the Swabians have pulled themselves up from being one of Central Europe's poorer peoples to become one of its richest.

In 1900 Stuttgart's population was only 175,000, but in the next fifty years it more than trebled, as its industries grew and immigrants flocked in. Between the wars it was the capital of the Free State of Württemberg, part of the Weimar Republic. Fred Uhlmann in his delightful novel *Reunion* [1] gives a picture of the Stuttgart he lived in as a young man, in the 1920s:

> "*Höhenrestaurants* were everywhere, with large terraces where the people of Stuttgart could spend the hot summer evenings, drinking Neckar or Rhine wine and stuffing themselves with enormous quantities of food: veal and potato salad . . . trout from the Black Forest, hot liver and blood sausages with Sauerkraut . . . followed by a fantastic choice of rich cakes topped with whipped cream. If they troubled to look up from their food they could see, between trees and laurel bushes, the forests stretching away for miles and the Neckar flowing slowly along between cliffs, castles, poplar trees, vineyards and ancient towns towards Heidelberg, the Rhine and the North Sea. When night fell the view was as magic as looking down from Fiesole on Florence: thousands of lights, the air hot and fragrant with the smell of jasmine and lilac, and on all sides the voices, the singing and laughter of contented citizens, getting rather sleepy from too much food, or amorous from too much drink. . . . This town of less than half a million inhabitants had more opera, better theatre, finer museums, richer collections and a fuller life than Manchester or Birmingham, Bordeaux or Toulouse."

This idyll of love and laughter ended abruptly in the 1930s, and Fred Uhlmann, a Jew, emigrated never to return. In the war, 60 per cent of buildings were destroyed in 53 air raids: but with typical Swabian energy the city then rebuilt itself faster than any other big German town. First occupied by the French, it then came within the American zone. When the present *Land* structure was set up soon after the war and Baden was annexed to Württemberg, Stuttgart became the capital of a big *Land* with (today) 9 million people. In population it is the ninth city of Germany, but in general importance it ranks about sixth, roughly on a par, let us say, with Cologne and Düsseldorf.

---

[1] Collins, London, 1977.

Is it typical of Germany? Yes and no. In a country with so diverse an historical tradition, no city can be typical – little more than in Italy. By political accident Germany today is divided between East and West: but the truer division, in terms of history, scenery, climate, culture and temperament, is between north and south. And Stuttgart belongs very much to southern Germany, the land of mediaeval cities with half-timbered houses, of woods, vineyards and *Lederhosen,* a land that is gentler and quainter than the north with its wide plains and Prussian dominance where the people are by tradition more militaristic and aggressive, more sinister in a way but perhaps also more glamorous and mercurial than in the south. Yet even this north/south distinction is not entirely valid, for the Swabians with their virtuous Protestant tradition are hugely different in temperament and outlook from their fellow southerners, the Bavarians, who are more Catholic, more fun-loving, but less kindly and more given to extremism. Any generalisation is thus hard. Perhaps it is nearest to the truth to say that the very special characteristics of the Swabians and Stuttgarters, far from being *un*typical of Germany as a whole, are virtually a caricature of some of the features we most often associate with Germans: extreme attachment to orderliness, formality, cleanliness, house-pride, hard work. Stuttgart is thus, if anything, an extreme example of Germanness – shorn of some of the other German excesses of boisterous jollity on the one hand and hardness or brutality on the other.

Ethnically, Swabians are first cousins to the Alsatians and German-Swiss and are often compared to the latter. Like the German-Swiss, the Swabians tend to be thick-set, with big round impassive faces; outwardly a bit solemn and slow to react, but thoughtful, and not without their own humour. Like the German-Swiss they have their own dialect, spoken in a broad sing-song accent and largely unintelligible to a non-Swabian German. It is as much a separate language as the Bolognese dialect, and much more so than the Geordie spoken in Newcastle. The lively existence of these regional dialects is a stronger feature of Germany than of most European countries, and many Swabians are more fluent in their own language than in the standard *Hochdeutsch* of official Germany. All are proud of it. Even educated Swabians who become national figures, such as the former chancellor, Kurt-Georg Kiesinger, prefer to speak this language when on their home ground: it is called "*Honoratioren Schwäbisch*" and is even used for teaching in schools. This is all very different from the situation in Britain or France, where local languages – except one or two Celtic ones, Breton and Welsh – do not have this more-or-less official status. It is one further aspect of German decentralisation: no federal government could, or would dare, impose linguistic uniformity on the nation as has been done, more or less, in France.

Swabian differs from *Hochdeutsch* in many respects. As with many dialects of peasant origin, it shortens words (*"nicht"* is *"net"*). It also has a penchant for diminutives which makes it sound a bit coy: *"haus"* is *"häusle"* ("little house"), even when it is a mansion. This tweeness (as an Englishman would call it) may give one clue to the Swabian character.

The Protestant ethic, which arrived in the 16th century, has helped to mould a people who are cautious, a little puritanical, not easily given to jollity, but as solid and dependable as the Mercedes they produce. The Swabian has something in common with the North-of-Englander, not so much with the chip-on-the-shoulder Geordie as with the confident Yorkshireman: he has the same slow but determined reactions, the same pawky humour. In a theatre, he will get the point of a joke three seconds later than a Berliner, but then laugh just as loud. An Englishman who has lived in several parts of Germany said to me: "These Swabians may be a bit tactless and lacking in suavity, they may sometimes rub you up the wrong way, but they are gentle and reliable. In the Rhineland, where I once lived, people are more lively and sophisticated, their minds move faster, but you never know where you are with them. They can be all over you one day and forget you the next – like Parisians." Swabia has a tradition of philanthropy, and of benevolent paternalism in industry. People show more kindliness and human concern than is usual in Germany. They may be snobbish and conformist, or intolerant on matters such as a neighbour's failure to observe the sabbath: but rarely do they indulge in ideological hatreds or get aroused to political extremism. Significantly, Nazism took root here less than in any other part of Germany: in 1930 Hitler polled fewer votes in Württemberg than elsewhere, and since the war very few ex-Nazis have ever held public positions in Stuttgart. The Nazi period is hardly ever mentioned today: it has all been conveniently buried, and whenever I tried to raise the subject, I found older people ready to talk about their war sufferings in general but not about what had then been their attitude to Nazism. And a younger generation is growing up vaguely curious but still ill-informed. Only now is the Nazi period beginning to be taught in school history lessons.

Swabians have the earnestness often associated with Germans. Once

I called on a group of leading local architects, in the luxury flat of one of them, and found that their way of passing a social evening was to read each other papers on environmental theories, as if at a sixth-form seminar. Swabians are men of ideas as much as of action, and their roll-call of great names includes philosophers, poets and inventors as well as politicians and industrialists. Hegel was born in Stuttgart, and Hölderlin and Schiller not far away. Brecht came from Augsburg, in the Bavarian part of Swabia. Field-Marshal Rommel was a Swabian and his son is today mayor of Stuttgart. And Daimler, perhaps the most influential Swabian of them all, was born only twelve miles from the city.

Swabian hard work, thrift and piety are legendary. Hard work here is a kind of hobby, an end in itself: it is true that many people do also practise sports such as tennis or riding, but often this is less for enjoyment than to keep fit for their work. I could quote dozens of examples of this work mania. For instance, I met a middle-aged man and his wife who owned two tobacconist-shops where each of them worked six days a week, from 7 a.m. to 8 p.m. Though business was thriving, they would never close the shutters and take a holiday, nor hire employees to lighten the load, because of what this would cost – tightness about money being another Swabian hallmark. When the man was asked, "You are fifty-five – when are you going to start living?" he said, "But this *is* my life." Owners of factories will regularly stay at their desks till late at night, and will often refuse to retire even aged eighty or more.

Their money is saved or reinvested. Thrift sometimes reaches comic proportions, and a local motto second to "*Schaffe, schaffe, Häusle baue*" is "*Hund verkaufe, selber belle*" – "Sell your dog and do your own barking". There is a story of how the late Robert Bosch, founder and owner of Stuttgart's world-famous electrical firm, would go around his factory picking up stray paper-clips and complaining, "Look how you waste my money!" The fact that Swabians, at least younger ones, will sometimes tell this kind of story against themselves may indicate a certain self-irony: they may realise that extremes of behaviour that were once solid virtues, in the old days of rural poverty and the fight for survival, have become a little ludicrous amid the new urban prosperity. But they are so conditioned to this behaviour that to change it is not easy.

When they possess wealth, they consider it bad taste to show it. And despite the money that the city and individuals spend on culture, it is still thought a little shameful to lavish money on inessentials. If people want to buy paintings, they will usually go to another town to do so, because they do not want to be seen. Sometimes they will buy modern art as an investment, then keep it stored in the attic rather than display it in their homes. Fortunes are to be made but not seen. I was told of a millionaire factory-owner who kept his huge Mercedes in his garage at home, used it only for out-of-town pleasure motoring, and drove to his office each day in a little Volkswagen "beetle" because he did not want to show off to his workers. This is the status-symbol society turned on its head, and is the very opposite of the situation in Munich, Hamburg or the Rhineland where, as in most countries, a big car or house is an envied prestige symbol.

This puritan dislike of ostentation is closely linked to the famous Swabian *pietismus,* as it is called, a pietism introduced by the Lutherans and taken up officially by the dukes of Württemberg, but today so much second nature that it has become secular as well as religious and is shared even by people who are not church-goers. To enjoy yourself too much is a sin. In the small town of Korntal close to Stuttgart, the stronghold of a leading pietist sect, as late as 1955 it was considered wrong for young people to dance and the authorities took steps to prevent the creation of dance halls. It is also a sin to work on the sabbath, and in Stuttgart more than in most German towns you may find the neighbours protesting if you perform on a Sunday rather than a Saturday the essential rituals of washing the car or tidying the front garden.

Pietism, however, though it remains stronger in Swabia than in most places, has been much in decline in the past ten or fifteen years. Stuttgart has been invaded by modish permissiveness and today has its share of cinemas showing porn films, of sex-shops and even of bare breasts in productions at the *Staatstheater.* Civic elders and others sometimes mutter protests, but there is no serious attempt to stop the tide. The whole matter is shrouded in hypocrisy. Young people may be less libertine than in Hamburg or Munich, but like young people anywhere they have been winning more freedom: and their pietistic elders, instead of merely denouncing them as they used to do, are now beginning to acquiesce in the new morality and question their own values – "Are *we* right, or are *they,* after all?" Yet a certain puritanism still lingers in the corporate sub-conscious, and people are conditioned by it even if not believing in it. A young housewife told me: "Although I think it's nonsense, I still feel reluctant to clean the house on a Sunday. My father was a devout Protestant who held bible-classes on

Sunday afternoons, and he brought me up that way."

But an even worse sin than to clean your house on Sunday is not to clean it at all. In a nation famous for its home-loving, home-polishing virtues, the Swabians are the reigning champions. *Schaffe, schaffe, häusle baue* . . . it is no coincidence that the largest *Bausparkasse* (building society) in Germany has its head office just outside Stuttgart, and many a Swabian father begins to put money into this savings bank for his son at his birth, so that by the time he is thirty the young man may have credit enough to achieve every good Swabian's ambition of having his own *häusle*. This is where much of his income goes, more than on fine clothes or enjoyment – a very different picture from Toulouse. And he will probably select a Swabian wife who can show the necessary zeal in keeping the home spotless. An Englishman living in Stuttgart told me, "While their husbands are shortening their lives through overwork at the office, the women all turn into *Hausfrauen* sooner or later. Our neighbour, aged about sixty, used to be a cultured woman once, but now can talk about nothing but keeping the house clean. She starts her Monday washing late on Sunday night." My own landlady in Stuttgart would feel nervous if I had left one cup unwashed, or if she had not put clean paper in the bottom of the waste-paper baskets and air-freshener in kitchen and toilet. And the outward look of the home is as important as the inside. By law, you may not hang out washing. And by law you must clean the mud or snow from the section of public pavement in front of your house: if you fail to do so, and a passer-by slips and breaks a leg, he can sue you. Rules of this kind are general in Germany but especially strict in Swabia, and the locals obey them unthinkingly.

Swabians are slow to follow the latest world fashions: that is an aspect not only of their caution but of their provincialism. Yet when at last they do adopt them, it is with a characteristic thoroughness. In the late 1960s Stuttgart behaved for two or three years as if unaware of the "pop" influences invading so many European cities: but by 1970, just when others were tiring of this scene, Stuttgart had embraced it massively, and the city was decked out with psychedelic or *art nouveau* posters, with mini-skirts, flowers, beads and the rest of the youth-gear of yesteryear.

"The Swabians," a north German said to me, "have all the virtues, save spontaneity and *joie-de-vivre*." They do not have the uproarious carnivals that you find in the jollier and more Catholic parts of Germany, notably Bavaria and the Rhineland. Recently a few bold spirits tried to organise a carnival in Stuttgart, with floats full of pretty girls and so on. But it was a flop. The inhabitants looked on quietly and failed to join in the fun. Not that Stuttgart is without its own festivals. Every September there is the *Volksfest,* run by the city council and local breweries: four huge beer-tents are set up in a fairground beside the Neckar, in the suburb of Canstatt, and here the population applies itself to jollity with due solemnity of purpose. They consume 1½ million litres of beer, 300,000 chickens and several miles of pretzels, they sing the usual German songs swaying to-and-fro with arms linked, they visit the scores of garish side-shows, and spend more money on fun than they would dare to do in the rest of the year. It is like a muted version of the Munich *Oktoberfest.* Indeed, though the *Volksfest* is local in origin – it was founded 130 years ago by the dukes of Württemberg as a kind of harvest festival – what has struck me on my visits is how much the Stuttgarters have had to sink their pride and borrow from the Bavarians the accoutrements of jollity and folksiness, for lack of suitable ones of their own. The men, from the mayor downwards, wear pointed green Bavarian hats with feathers, and grey Bavarian tunics with high collars and green edges. The waitresses wear Bavarian dirndls with high-busted white puffy bodices. The orchestras in the beer-tents, their musicians noisily extrovert and clad of course in *Lederhosen,* are mostly imported from Bavaria for the occasion. And the Swabians compliantly follow them through the drinking anthems of the big rival city they usually affect to ignore or despise: "*In München Steht ein Hofbräuhaus, Eins, Zwei, Gsuffa . . .*".

On one occasion I attended the opening ceremony of the *Volksfest,* in the middle of the fairground at the foot of the big "fruit pillar", a grotesque priapic column gaudily-painted and stacked with suitable harvest offerings. All the local *Prominenz* were present, including the Prime Minister of the *Land,* senior officers from the local US Army bases, and worthies such as the Honorary Consul of Ecuador, a German businessman who is also chief hunting-master of Baden-Württemberg. The mayor, Dr Arnulf Klett, a figure of immense authority and prestige, emerged dressed up as a beer-steward of one of the leading local breweries, complete with leather apron and black peaked cap. He drank the ritual first frothy litre, guns fired to mark the opening, and horses in gaudy, fancy caparison trotted by, pulling wagons full of huge barrels of beer. Girls and boys in red-and-white Swabian costume danced an innocent maypole dance. I then fought my way through the crowds to inspect the sideshows – past the big-dipper and the men selling *Würst,* pretzels, comic hats and huge clusters of coloured balloons. Many of the sideshows were horrific. It was not merely a-penny-to-see-the-fat-lady but a mark or two to see more morbid things such as waxworks of Siamese twins and of a girl killed by lightning, all garishly advertised. A female dwarf was shouting to the crowd in a squeaky voice to come inside and see her assorted freaks. It was *Struwwel-Peter*-land. But I was relieved to learn that most of the sideshows of this kind were, once again, imported from Bavaria. The Swabians, though they may show a mild curiosity, are not much addicted to this all-too-German genre of Gothic horror.

Inside the big tents, each seating five thousand, the fun goes on all day and half the night over a ten-day period. In one tent, the scene was not unlike a more elaborate version of a Newcastle beer-hall on a Saturday night: vulgar if you like, but democratic and friendly. Scores of chicken-spits were rotating, a whole dead pig was lying by the kitchen door. Girls in sexy bodices came round selling dolls, and heart-shaped gingerbreads with amorous mottoes in icing-sugar. Most people were eating fat sausages with their beer, and I was encouraged to try a typical Swabian speciality, *Schlachtsüssel* (blood-sausages and pork, with *Sauerkraut* and mashed potato) – an acquired taste. There was much noise and laughter, but it all seemed quite decorous. A few Italian *Gastarbeiter* – bolder, and readier to try to "integrate" than the Turks or Slavs – were making after the local girls, and doing what any Italian does to a girl's backside in a crowd. But I was assured that – as compared with the *Oktoberfest* – the general jollity was unlikely to impose any strain on the city's maternity wards next June.

Stuttgart's society in its own little way is almost as fascinatingly varied as that of Paris or London – a society where your neighbour on the tram could be a metalworker from Salonika, a student from Hamburg, a lawyer from Breslau, or a horny-handed vinegrower from a nearby valley. Swabians may tend, like other Germans, to ignore the *Gastarbeiter* in their midst – a crucial topic, to which I shall return – yet in most other respects they are not xenophobic. They have a strong tradition of emigration, notably to the United States where the Swabians today are still the most numerous of any German immigrant group. One aspect of the entrepreneurial Swabian mentality has always been this readiness, despite their devotion to their homeland, to travel far in order to win success. But what they will seldom do is emigrate to other parts of Germany, generally regarded as inferior to Swabia: you are more likely to find a Stuttgarter living happily in Chicago, or even Brazil, than in Hamburg. They will go far, or stay put.

Yet they are welcoming to other Germans who show the good taste of wanting to live in Swabia, and they have assimilated happily and without friction the large numbers of Silesians (some 80,000), East Prussians and others who came here as refugees after the war. The Silesians in particular have made a big difference to Stuttgart: if the town is less parochial, more open-minded and outward-looking than before the war, if pietism is in decline, if there is more contact with other parts of Germany, it is due largely to the influence of these newcomers, mostly Catholic, who can readily be told apart from the Swabians by their accent. Many are of high ability, and have worked their way into key official positions or built up their own businesses. Today they are well integrated into society, and the same is true of the thousands of post-war refugees from other points east such as Czechoslovakia. So Stuttgart, almost as much as Toulouse and far more than Newcastle or Bologna, is a town that has been revitalised by an influx of new population. But there is a difference from Toulouse: the Swabians, so able and confident, have not in any sense allowed themselves to be colonised by the newcomers. They accept their influence, but still set the pace in public affairs. Local government – a subject we shall now examine – is still very much in Swabian hands.

3

Benevolent technocrats in the Rathaus

Manfred Rommel, the mayor, son of the famous old Desert Fox, has a twinkle in his eye and a sly Swabian sense of humour. "I became a general quicker than my father, and I fight better wars in a better cause," he told me, as we sat in his thick-carpeted office in the opulently rebuilt *Rathaus* (town hall). At the age of forty-five he was elected "general" in command of Stuttgart – and the term is not inappropriate, for thanks to the German system of local government he is able to run his city with more power and authority, and probably, too, with more efficiency, than the mayors of any of my other towns.

Like most other larger German cities, Stuttgart is the legatee of a decentralised system dating back many centuries. It was a royal capital, a true metropolis with its own ruling class, and thus it retains a far stronger tradition of civic self-sufficiency and enterprise than tends to be found in a more centralised country such as Britain or France. It is used to taking its own decisions and doing things its own way. And devolution in Germany is not solely a matter of the *Länder* taking over from the *Bund* in Bonn certain key responsibilities (for instance, for education and justice): it operates on the lower level too, so that the *Länder* in turn devolve to their larger towns the control or part-control of a number of matters that in many other countries remain in state hands. It is true that in recent years the influence of the Bonn Government has been increasing, especially over finance. But Stuttgart still has an enviable degree of statutory autonomy, in fields such as health, police, culture, public utilities and many aspects of planning.

It also has men of relatively high calibre in the senior civic positions, thanks to Germany's potent tradition of professional city management. And here, oddly enough, it is the beneficiary of American influence too. The complex German municipal system varies from *Land* to *Land* and was reconstituted just after the war: when the Allies set out to rebuild democracy, each occupying Power saw fit to impose its own model. The British, in the north, set up a British-style system, where the mayor is a figurehead serving a short term. The Americans, in the south, installed something nearer to their own pattern: full-time, fully-salaried mayors, elected for long periods – and this has remained. In Stuttgart, the chief mayor *(Oberbürgermeister)* is directly elected by the people, initially for eight years with options of further twelve-year mandates. He is assisted by five *Bürgermeistern,* full-time salaried specialists who are chosen by the city council but are not members of it. The sixty-member city council can in theory over-rule the mayor but in practice, when he is a strong figure, they play a more passive role. This system puts a strong mayor in a hugely powerful position. He is both chief executive and a political figure. He has a popular mandate and can also devote his full energies to his job, so the city is run in effect by a highly-qualified technocratic oligarchy who see themselves as business managers, more concerned with getting things done than with wheeler-dealing and playing politics. In Newcastle, Toulouse and Bologna, as we shall see, where mayors are either non-salaried non-professionals, or have much greater curbs on their powers, or both, things are very different. In Germany, there is much more professionalism.

The system could be open to abuse under an ineffectual mayor. But both of Stuttgart's post-war mayors have been men of remarkable authority, energy and ability. For twenty-nine years, until his death in 1974, Arnulf Klett ruled the city like a kindly but firm headmaster; and the Swabians, respectful of authority like most Germans, admired him for it and twice re-elected him massively. He was originally appointed by the Allies in 1945 because of his anti-Nazi record: as a young local lawyer he had courageously defended Jews and anti-Nazis in the courts after 1933. After the war, with dazzling energy he got the city rebuilt faster than any other that had been badly bombed – "My first task," he told me, "was to shake people out of the lethargy and daze of defeat. So I took up a shovel myself, literally, and showed them the way. It worked." He was in many ways an archetypal Swabian: son of a Protestant pastor, he had the true local passion for hard work and would frequently stay at his desk till eleven at night. It was finally overwork that killed him, aged sixty-nine. One of his few relaxations was driving his Porsche as fast as possible – "I can touch 220 kph on the autobahn to Frankfurt," he told me proudly. He had a round, bland Swabian face, and a Swabian bluff bonhomie and wry humour; but he had more panache than most Swabians, and was given to wearing dapper bow-ties and filling his office with modernist paintings and sculptures.

Though aloof from party politics, he took pains to cultivate his image. A journalist told me, "He sees to it that he's the best sausage-eater and biggest beer-drinker," and I remember him at the *Volksfest*, demagogically slapping the backs of all in sight and jumping onto the beer-tent rostrum to conduct the orchestra in a thundering chorus. But behind the joviality was also a will of iron, and he ruled the *Rathaus* like a benevolent dictator. He never suffered fools gladly, but was respected for his many qualities which included total integrity: he would tolerate no whiff of corruption. One key to his success was that, being non-party – mid-way between the Socialists (SPD) and Christian Democrats (CDU) – he insisted on keeping party issues out of local government: "We run this city like a modern business firm," one of his assistants told me. For nearly thirty years he *was* Stuttgart – the longest-serving and one of the greatest of post-war German mayors.

Rommel is a Christian Democrat, and when he was elected to

succeed Klett in December 1974, most people expected the holiday from party politics to end. But this has not really happened. Rommel, too, is a remarkable man. He was born in Stuttgart, a Swabian like his famous father but not at all warlike. In fact, he is even more of a moderate than Klett, and for this he has become widely popular, as well as for his energy, good humour and ironic wit. Like Klett, he tried to remain aloof from party politics, and it is often said that he gets on better with the SPD councillors than his own CDU ones. When Stuttgart leapt briefly into all the world's headlines in October 1977, with the suicide in the local Stammheim prison of Andreas Baader and his two fellow-terrorists, Rommel took the controversial step of allowing them to be buried in the same cemetery as the city's greatest heroes and victims of Nazism. This aroused the fury of many Christian Democrats: but Rommel stuck to his guns, pleading that death effaces all past guilt. It was further proof of his liberalism.

The Mayor's relation to the city council is a little like that of an American President to Congress. The council is sovereign, on budgetary matters and for major new projects; but the mayor, by law, is alone responsible for day-to-day administration, where he cannot be interfered with. In practice it is the mayor who initiates many new projects. The council has the right to over-rule him, which in many cities it does. In Stuttgart this has sometimes happened on lesser matters, but usually Klett and Rommel have persuasively imposed their will. The councillors, unpaid and busy with their own professions, are few of them well known to the public, and they generally defer to the mayor and salaried *Bürgermeistern* with their specialist abilities. So in practice the city is run by a benevolent technocracy. But this in no way diminishes the emphasis on welfare: nursery schools, homes for the elderly, and similar services are carefully administered by the oligarchs.

Until 1974, Stuttgart's council was Socialist-controlled, like that of most larger cities. The recent national swing to the Right has now led to a narrow CDU majority: CDU and allies 30 seats, SPD 23, FDP (liberals) 4. The change has in practice made little difference, for CDU and SPD have always got along easily together in Stuttgart, more so than on a national level or in some other towns such as Munich or Frankfurt. This is due quite largely to the placid and pragmatic Swabian character.

Compared with the bitchy intrigues and machinations of local politics in Newcastle and Toulouse, there are two factors in Stuttgart that have always impressed me. One is the apparent absence of scandal or malpractice in civic affairs. In most German towns today, civic corruption is rare – and the fact that affairs are managed by highly paid professionals, not by part-time amateurs, surely has something to do with it. In Swabia, corruption is especially rare. When Daimler-Benz committed the gaffe of offering Klett a carpet worth 60,000 DM as a sixtieth birthday present, there was a public outcry and he donated it to a museum. Councillors, too, are careful not to undertake public work that is connected with their private interests, especially in property development, that familiar graveyard of civic probity. Honesty must not only be done but be seen to be done.

A second factor is the very low key of legitimate controversy on civic issues. Where views differ, the problem is usually settled politely and preferably in private. People seem reluctant to insult each other in public, or to look at local disputes in terms of rival personalities – as they so love doing in Newcastle or Toulouse. One explanation lies in the Swabian temperament: in some other cities, such as Munich, local affairs are indeed more stormy, personalised and politicised. But there may be another explanation too, true of Germany as a whole, relating to a national fear of reviving the excesses of the Nazi past. Even in placid Stuttgart, I felt that many people were still a little fearful of the nation's latent aggressiveness and extremism and were thus holding themselves back, bending over backwards to be outwardly polite, and shying away from controversy as something that might blow up and get out of control. People who know Germany far better than I agree this might be so.

This burial of controversy can carry dangers, for it may also bury the hunting out of injustices. But at least it facilitates a climate of practical efficiency where the city managers can tackle problems on their merits, without too much obstruction from political rivalries. These managers – the mayor and his five *Bürgermeistern* – draw handsome salaries of 100,000 DM or upwards. So it is no surprise that, as in other German cities, the career of *Bürgermeister* attracts men of high calibre and qualifications, and that senior civic officialdom carries much higher prestige than in my other towns. Here I cannot do better than quote a leading expert, David Eversley: in his excellent study, *Britain and Germany: Local Government in Perspective*[1], after stressing that the senior paid officials often have status and prestige at least as high as

[1] A chapter in *The Management of Urban Change,* Sage Publication, London, 1974.

that of *Land* or *Bund* civil servants, he goes on: "Many officials in large German cities simultaneously hold academic and civic appointments. There is nothing even faintly comic, in German popular views, about the man from the town hall, whereas in Britain, local government officers are stock subjects for jokes, being usually equated with inspectors of drains." Mr Eversley goes on, "Because British local government has so few powers, especially financial ones, it does not attract people of high calibre, and because the quality of the decision-makers is not high, British local government tends to be unenterprising." This leads him to a further conclusion: "The German system is geared basically to the idea of action, of positive government. In Britain, the system makes safeguards take precedence over action . . . councillors are elected to safeguard ratepayers' interests. . . . There is in Britain an unwillingness to disturb the status quo which is rarely understood by German administrators . . . [with] their devotion to large-scale public works, roads, public transport, the provision of cultural facilities. . . . In Britain, on the other hand, since the 19th century, large public works have been unpopular."

As we shall see, the German system presents some similar advantages over those of France and Italy too. Not that all is perfect in Germany; one fault, as Mr Eversley suggests, is that "the German system breeds, or so it is alleged, a certain arrogant technocracy of men who do not have to listen too carefully to public opinion, and can spend taxpayers' money on grandiose schemes without worrying too much about their priorities. In Britain, in contrast, rulers may be of lesser calibre but by nature of their origins, training and sensitivity to triennial elections, they are more likely to be receptive about local feelings." We shall see, in Newcastle. In Stuttgart, this charge of technocracy is probably valid: Klett was arguably too much of a technocrat, for all his demagogic manner. Rommel appears to be sensitive to this problem, and is making efforts to consult ordinary citizens much more regularly: every fortnight he visits a different district of the city for the best part of a day, and holds lengthy discussions. It is something that Klett did much more rarely, and it seems to be appreciated. Yet it must also be said that Swabians, like other Germans and unlike the British, tend to acquiesce in a certain paternalistic authoritarianism: once they have elected someone to do a job, they like to leave him alone to get on with it.

And Stuttgart's technocrats have much that needs doing. The city council's autonomy covers a wider range than in my other towns. It is responsible for the three largest city hospitals, as well as for some other aspects of health and welfare services, for many cultural activities, for the police, and for gas and electricity supplies. It also has to pay for much school building. It has 15,000 full-time municipal employees, and an annual budget (in 1976) of 2,180 million DM, of which 631 million DM comes from local taxes. These are formidable figures, but they are not nearly enough to meet all the city's needs, and for many of the most expensive activities the city either receives further grants from *Land* or *Bund* or operates in partnership with them. Thus the *Land* helps pay for school building and shares fifty/fifty the running costs of the Opera House; *Land* and *Bund* pay substantially for new hospitals, and bear 85 per cent of the cost of new road and traffic projects. All this involves a great deal of joint planning and decision-taking, and inevitably there are some frictions. Stuttgart, like other German cities, complains of growing Federal interference in local affairs. The *Bund* is becoming less ready to make cash grants without strings attached: as in Britain and France, the central bureaucrats now insist on determining how their local subsidies should be spent.

Stuttgart's greatest problem today, however, is much less the pressures from *Land* or *Bund* than rivalries with the smaller surrounding communes. This wealthy city is becoming seriously short of finance, simply because its sources of revenue are moving out into the nearby towns – a common problem in many parts of Europe today, and especially acute in Stuttgart. So much of the municipal area is hilly forest that virtually all available building land has been used up and there is no scope for further expansion. Land prices in the centre of town are the highest in Germany: up to 10,000 DM per square metre in central office areas, compared with 1,000 DM or so in a good residential area, and a mere 200 DM or less in places outside Stuttgart. Stuttgarters therefore have been moving out in their thousands, to commuter zones where rents and land prices are lower. Since 1962 the city's own population has fallen from 643,000 to under 600,000, while that of the four surrounding *Kreise* (districts) has risen by 260,000 to reach 1.8 million. The medium-sized towns within a 15-mile radius of Stuttgart – Esslingen, Böblingen, Ludwigsburg and others – have been growing fast.

Industry too has joined the migration. And this is an economic blow for Stuttgart, since a German city's major source of revenue is from the *Gewerbesteuer,* a tax on local industry and business. German towns thus vie with each other to attract new factories and businesses, even more than in France where the situation is somewhat similar. "The mayors round here are always trying to woo our firms away," a Stuttgart official told me, "and often they succeed, for they can offer larger sites, lower land prices, and more plentiful labour." Since 1948 over 200 firms have moved out to new and larger sites, mostly in the vicinity: in 1971 the great Bosch empire itself transferred its head office to nearby Gerlingen. In this way, several of the towns just outside Stuttgart have grown richer *per capita* than the city itself, and have built themselves luxurious new civic centres, theatres, and so on. Sindelfingen has spent 25 million DM on a civic swimming-pool. And many Stuttgarters feel resentful.

In other practical respects, cooperation between Stuttgart and its neighbours works smoothly and sensibly. Public transport, water, sewage and other services are coordinated by regular liaison, and there are not the political or personal clashes or petty jealousies that have frequently obstructed this kind of cooperation in the Toulouse area and on Tyneside. Swabians, cool and pragmatic, know how to work for the common good. Yet Stuttgart increasingly feels that it is being penalised by the present system of local government finance. It wants a reform that will redistribute public revenue or oblige its neighbours to contribute more money to the area as a whole.

Mayor Rommel has made this into a personal crusade, a theme that recurs in every speech he makes. He told me: "Stuttgart is worse off in this respect than any other big German town. In the cases of Munich and Frankfurt, the city is much larger in relation to its suburbs than we are: our suburbs have three times our own population. We are also victims of our geography, since we have this huge 'green belt' of woods within our borders on which, for environmental reasons, we cannot build. In Cologne, the *Land* Government has forced the suburbs to merge with the city in a new 'greater Cologne', and likewise in Hannover. But here, the towns around us have grown too big and powerful for the *Land* to dare impose such a solution. These towns are so proud, they'll fight us every inch of the way to preserve their autonomy. But this is short-sighted, for they need us as we need them: in this huge conurbation, we are the tree and they merely the branches, and they would suffer too if Stuttgart were to rot. Yet we *are* rotting. I'm having to cut public spending on housing, sports centres and so on. The only solution is to find some way of checking this Californian gold-fever in places like Sindelfingen." Rommel has persuaded the *Land* Government to set up a commission to look into the matter. Failing a "greater Stuttgart" solution (in the manner of Tyneside and the other big British conurbations), he would at least like to see some kind of association of communes in the area, whereby some local revenue would be pooled. But politically this will not be easy. In the meantime, Stuttgart's financial difficulties have been posing problems for town-planning.

4
In the heart of the pretty woodlands, a concrete jungle

Stuttgart's peculiar shape, as it straggles along its narrow valleys, sets the modern town-planner an unenviable task. And the city's technocratic rulers, for all their zeal and efficiency, have not always made the best of their opportunities or avoided aesthetic mistakes. At least they have preserved the leafy environment: new parks have been laid out, and no new eyesores have been allowed to pierce the wooded hilltop horizons. But the centre of town, rebuilt after the war with admirable speed and energy, has much the same unadmirable mish-mash of speculators' concrete towers as many other West German cities.

In 1945, most of mediaeval and classical Stuttgart lay in ruins, and the planners had to decide quickly whether to attempt a restoration job or rebuild in a new style. They chose not to try to recreate the pretty half-timbered houses that are such a feature of southern Germany: these hardly exist today in central Stuttgart. But a number of important churches, palaces and other public buildings, dating from the 18th century or much earlier, have been pieced together again in much their original state. So a small area in the heart of the city, around the elegant formal park and lake of the Schlossgarten, has a pleasingly varied ensemble of buildings old and new. The pre-1914 Opera House has the new State theatre on one side of it and the impressive modern glass-and-concrete *Landtag* parliament on the other. Nearby is the handsome Neue Schloss with its late-baroque façade, today housing the offices of some *Land* ministries. Across an irksome arterial road lies the Schillerplatz, the heart of old Stuttgart, and here the beautiful 15th-century Stiftskirche, the Alte Kanzlei with its charming dovecot towers, and the Alte Schloss (a 13th-century moated castle) have all been neatly restored. The pretty Schillerplatz has been made into a paved traffic-free precinct, romantically lit at night with frosted lamps. On some days it houses a flower-market, adding a touch of peasant colour to this workaday city.

But the modern commercial district that lies a few metres away, either side of the Königstrasse, the hideous main shopping street, is little lovelier than rebuilt Frankfurt – or Birmingham. High office blocks predominate. Klett with his shovel may have rebuilt with speed, but it is generally admitted today that he allowed too much leeway to the property speculators, in his anxiety to attract banks and other businesses and thus increase the city's income from the *Gewerbesteuer*. There has never been any inspired master-plan for the central area, and conflicts in the 1960s between city and *Land* on the siting of new ring-roads and major buildings have had unfortunate consequences. For major planning projects the city is not autonomous but has to reach agreement with the *Land* where the latter's financial help is involved: in this case, the *Land* was more conservative while the city wanted bold modern schemes, and the result has been a compromise. Stuttgart in fact has rebuilt its modern quarters less imaginatively than Cologne or Düsseldorf: it has been making some of the same aesthetic mistakes as Newcastle, despite its greater resources and scope.

The most ambitious new structure, completed in 1968, is the Kleine Schlossplatz, a wide concrete platform beside the Königstrasse, raised about six metres above street level. It was intended as a lively social forum in the heart of the new town, and it has been decked out with boutiques, modern sculpture and the coloured parasols of outdoor *cafés*. These provide a certain gaiety: but the concrete parapet is too austere, and it fails in its function as a forum, since its elevation cuts it off from organic contact with the streets below. The broad Königstrasse itself, and some of the narrow shopping-streets nearby, have now been closed to traffic and filled with flower-pots and benches. This is a happy innovation, which has lent a *piazza* quality to the centre of town. But no amount of flower-pots can disguise the ugliness of the buildings that line this main street. Rebuilt central Stuttgart impresses more by its opulence, variety and animation than as an example of inspired modern architecture.

Traffic solutions, too, have been tackled with little inspiration. In this city that spawned the motor-car, the problems of coming to terms with its modern tyranny have at least been eased – as elsewhere in Germany – by wartime devastation. So the carving out of wide modern roads does not pose the same conservationist dilemmas as in mediaeval Bologna or Toulouse. Even so, Stuttgart in its narrow valley provides poor terrain for new urban freeways, and so the solution has been to build underpasses and intersections with confusing clover-leaf shapes, under and around the city centre – so that the motorist frequently finds himself directed to turn right, to reach a point he knows to be on his left. All this is done in the true systematic German manner, with multiple traffic-lanes and complex signposting that you disobey at your peril. Thanks to this system, traffic does move fast most of the time and jams are few. But the pedestrian suffers. Except in the small new traffic-free zone around the Königstrasse, the centre of the city is hell for the pedestrian, since every hundred metres or so there tends to be some arterial road with a metal barrier along its pavement, and a policeman quick to fine you if you climb over. As in most European cities, street parking in the centre has become gradually harder in recent years, despite a fair number of parking meters.

The overall situation has been aggravated since about 1973 by massive central road-works aimed at improving public transport but leading in the shorter term to chaos. Stuttgart is now getting a kind of Metro. A seven-kilometre *Schnellbahn,* part of the Federal rail network and paid for jointly by *Bund, Land* and city, has been built under the centre of town from the main station to the south-west suburbs. Other new tunnels are being carved out for trams, which Stuttgart still prefers to buses as its staple public transport: its ubiquitous yellow trams, fast and modern, are thought to be better suited to the numerous hilly climbs. The *Schnellbahn* is being completed in stages in 1978-9, so Stuttgart now has a fine up-to-date transport system: but for the past five years the acres of muddy roadworks all round the station have been tiresome for the motorist and a horror for the pedestrian in wet weather. When the scheme is ready the heart of the city will be largely traffic-free, with the main networks all below surface. "But," a planner told me, "it is a great pity no one had the foresight to do this work at the time of the post-war rebuilding. Trying to do it in an age of near-saturation of traffic gives us fearful headaches."

Outside the central area, planning is dictated largely by the terrain.

Stuttgart is built on more and higher hills than Rome, and curves away down several deep valleys, housing great factories such as Bosch and Daimler-Benz. On one of the forested hills to the south, dominating the city, is the great spike of the *Fernsehturm*, built by local architects: it was the first television tower of its kind in the world, and at 711 feet is still one of the tallest.

The first priority of suburban planning has been to preserve the green belt and this has been achieved. There would be a popular outcry if it were not, for Stuttgarters adore their greenery. The city contains over a thousand acres of vineyard, more than any other German commune, even the famous wine villages of the Rhine and Moselle; and by local tradition not one vine must ever be destroyed, even though in many cases the land could be better used for other purposes. Trees too are protected by popular sentiment, which rarely allows the city technocrats to cut them down for any new scheme. As a result Stuttgart has the lowest population density of any big German city, and much lower too than Bologna's or Newcastle's: only one-quarter of its land is built on. Some of it is even farmland. This green-belt policy has advantages for the quality of life: the forests are called "our city's lungs" and in summer she would stifle without them, trapped in her cauldron where the climate can be enervating. But the green-belt poses problems for planning and for the city's finances, as we have seen.

As in other cities, several new estates of high-rise blocks, mostly for workers, have been built recently in outer districts of the commune where land has still been available. The work is done, rather as in France, by semi-public housing agencies. These estates are not unpleasing, and the quality of the flats, the siting and the amenities is generally of a higher level than in Toulouse or Bologna. But the average Swabian will always prefer to have his own *Häusle* when he can, and thousands of families of all social levels have been moving out of the city to where they can afford to build or rent their own little house with its garden. Look down on any townlet in the area, and you see an undulating sea of little red roofs, typical of this part of Germany. But this is not the dreary ribbon-development of Britain, for each house is separately conceived: nor is it the anarchy of the pre-war French suburbs, for individualism is tightly checked and you must build to harmonise with your neighbours.

So what kind of community life exists in these neat, affluent suburbs of the new democratic Germany?

5
New tolerance and old snobberies

First question: how open, friendly and egalitarian a society is Stuttgart's? There are some odd paradoxes in a town where a neighbour can be effusively polite and brutally intolerant in the same sentence, and where old-fashioned paternalism co-exists with a certain democratic integration of classes. I was soon aware how much less class division there is than in Toulouse, and how much less class-consciousness than in most British cities. This is true of Germany as a whole, though Swabia may not be entirely typical for it has less of a hard-core proletariat than some areas such as the Ruhr: industry here is more recent, factory workers retain closer rural ties, they are less aggressive as a class and generally feel closer to their employers than in the north. Hence, maybe, their greater acceptance of paternalism. Stuttgart therefore has felt the post-war social revolution less keenly than some parts of Germany, for there has been less impetus for change. Yet in Stuttgart as elsewhere the war and the Nazi period destroyed much of the old order and removed many ancient privileges. Today there are still great inequalities of wealth, but most of the bigger private fortunes are recent. This is something of a *nouveau riche* society, and its social pattern is in many ways closer to that of an American town than to Toulouse or Newcastle.

Workers with their growing affluence have not only been adopting *bourgeois* life-styles, they have also lost much of their class identity and former resentment of the middle classes. The unions' relatively easy cooperation with management, and the low strike level, are both cause and effect. And in a region where most people speak with the same kind of local accent it has become steadily more difficult to tell worker and *bourgeois* apart. They will talk together with few of the complexes and unease still found in Britain, and increasingly, too, they share the same interests. I met several workers' families on one housing estate who took their children to the ballet and opera, went hiking or swimming at weekends, or took holidays in Rumania or Norway, owned expensive modern furniture, and said they felt very little different from their young *bourgeois* neighbours on the estate, with whom they were on friendly terms. And a journalist, an aristocrat by origin, told me: "Our new house in the suburbs was put up by a local building worker, in his spare time. When he'd finished, we invited him and his wife to dinner, as our first guests. They chatted easily and confidently, about their holidays in Greece and Paris, and the football and TV that interested us both. A generation ago, they'd have been much more ill at ease. In fact, the main class barrier today is education. In theory, opportunities are equal. In practice, many working families are still inhibited about sending their children, however bright, into a higher education stream, and will rather urge them to go straight into a job where they can earn good money." As in France.

The same journalist also said: "At the upper end of the scale, too, things have changed. Before the war, a marquess was signalled out at a party as someone really special. Today the apex of the social pyramid is, say, a director of Daimler-Benz." As in all Germany, great respect is paid to official titles and senior positions, political, academic or even managerial: but in this world of status the aristocracy no longer counts for much. As in France, it has withdrawn into its own social ghetto, largely ignored: yet within living memory Württemberg was still a kingdom, and the region still bristles with nobility. The abruptness of the change in climate is to some extent because the aristocracy is seen as part of the bad old past that Germans are trying to forget – not so much the Nazi past (many aristocrats were anti-Nazi including one of Swabia's greatest heroes, Count von Stauffenberg, leader of the bomb plot against Hitler) as the earlier decadent Weimar past. Today noble titles have no civic legality in Germany: a *Graf* is plain *"Herr"* on his identity card.

A young baroness, an elegant girl in yellow hot-pants living in a small modern villa, told me what it felt like to belong to this dispossessed class: "There's still a big annual 'nobility ball' each winter in the city concert hall, and only 'we' can go. It's not mentioned at all by the local Press or radio, while other annual balls – the Press ball, for instance – get columns of print. It's a somewhat melancholy event, with echoes of past glories: the Duke and Duchess of Württemberg, who are still living near Lake Constance, attend it, and people pay them court – old dowagers and counts, much bemedalled, with sad, drooping faces. This aristocracy is mostly rural, and some have held on to enough of their wealth to be able to keep up their castles round here. Others, like my family, have lost their money and have integrated into the middle class, taking jobs in firms – I work for the radio, and my husband and I live like middle-class people. I use my title as little as possible, and get annoyed when I'm addressed by it in public. Some of my radio colleagues tease me about it."

Along with a decline in class divisions has also come a loosening of religious barriers, between Catholics and Protestants. Swabia has been strongly Protestant since the Reformation: the dukes and kings of Württemberg were mostly Lutherans, and alongside this established church there has flourished a multitude of smaller sects, Jehovah's Witnesses and so on, many of them fanatical and puritan. Their strongholds were the mountainous areas, such as the Black Forest, with long hard winters where, as I was told, "If you don't take to drink, you take to religion." The Catholic minority was not persecuted, but it was separate: there were Catholic villages and Protestant villages, and mixed marriages were rare. Then the aftermath of war brought its flood of refugees from the East, nearly all Catholic, so that today Baden-Württemberg is about fifty-fifty in its make up and Stuttgart itself, formerly a Lutheran bastion, is nearly 40 per cent Catholic. Times have changed, oecumenicism is now a world-wide fashion, the moderate Swabians have assimilated and accepted the newcomers – and today, even in the villages, mixed marriages are common. In some Stuttgart suburbs, Catholics and Protestants have built a new church together and hold joint services there. In fact, the main conflict today is not confessional but quasi-political, between "old guard" Christians of whatever denomination and those, mostly younger ones, who want the Churches to concern themselves less with prayer and worship than with radical social action. Militant groups of this kind hold rallies under such slogans as "*Opas Gott ist tot*" – "Grandpa's God is dead."

It is this younger element that has helped to promote the decline of pietism, mentioned earlier. After a cautious delay, Stuttgart now sanctions almost as much permissiveness – in the arts and entertainment, if not in social behaviour – as other Western cities. A pietistic minority may battle against the new fashions, but are generally defeated: when in 1969 the Opera House staged a brilliant production of *The Devils of Loudun*, with the nuns bouncing about bare-breasted, there were murmurs from the city council, but no more. "The city elders were shocked and irritated," a local cynic told me, "but they knew it was great art, so they resigned themselves." In the cinema, there is no official censorship and porn houses are numerous: the

Churches warn their faithful away from such films, but they know that too vigorous a campaign against them would be counter-productive, in box-office terms.

Today Stuttgart even has a Beate Uhse sex-shop, one of a trendy chain that covers a score of German cities. Frau Uhse is a Hamburger who has grown rich by, in her words, "doing good to Germany by making Germans less repressed. Repression led to Nazism." In Stuttgart her shop is not merely tolerated, it flaunts itself: far from being hidden down a side-street, it is right in the Königstrasse, where her illustrated manuals of "a hundred ways of love" decorate its windows in the city's main shopping-street. Inside, varieties of aphrodisiac and stimulant are on gaudy display, and coloured slides explain how to use them. The shop is generally full of customers – not grey men in macs but spruce married couples anxious for advice. Everything is hygienic, commercial: you might be in a beauty-shop or a superior chemist's. The slow and cautious Swabians have proved once again that, if they do a thing at all, they do it thoroughly. But how is such permissiveness accepted? One local comment I heard was: "The pietists despise these things but go secretly to see them. They're hypocrites."

In these moral and sexual matters, Stuttgart may be moving perforce with the times. Yet, looked at from another angle, this society might still appear to the visitor to be steeped in conformism, over-formality, even snobbery. Consider, for example, community living. There is much less casual chumminess between neighbours than you find in Newcastle – or in an American town. Stuttgart in this respect is closer to Toulouse. Yet the great paradox is that the Swabian, while seldom wanting to make friends with his neighbour, will not leave him to his privacy either. Oddity or non-conformity of behaviour, discreetly ignored in Toulouse, is here commented on or even rebuked. It offends against the desire of the German soul for social tidiness. A girl I know who worked late, and then slept till noon with the curtains drawn, had the neighbours shouting at her, "Only lazy people work at night!" And when long-haired hippies, flower-people and girls in mini-skirts made their belated arrival in Stuttgart, for some years older people would accost them in the streets and lecture them. I was even told of a boy and girl, innocently kissing in the street, who were approached by an old lady: "I'd like to see Hitler back: he'd know how to deal with the likes of you!"

Happily, pietism rarely carries such sinister undertones: but it still colours the Stuttgart Sunday. Until very recently, if you were seen washing your car or vacuum-cleaning, or even gardening, on the Sabbath, you could be reported to the police. They rarely prosecuted, but they warned. Since 1977 car washing is no longer illegal. But not long ago a doctor was in fact prosecuted, for gardening. He got himself acquitted only by pleading that he was planting shrubs, given him as a present late on Sunday, that would have wilted by Monday: in the magistrates' hearts, Swabian respect for thrift must have won the day over Swabian pietism! And admittedly there is another side to this coin, as a Lutheran pastor suggested to me: "Should a British kettle call our pot black? Yes, excessive Lord's Day observance is a silly anachronism, but what about Britain? At least we allow professional sports and entertainments on Sunday, far more readily than you do."

Another local obsession, maybe more rational, is over noise. Leases of flats forbid vacuum-cleaning, or similar noises, except between 8 and 11 a.m. and 3 and 6 p.m. One friend of mine found his neighbour threatening to call the police if he persisted in bringing his car back late at night: he had to leave it down the road. Even music is forbidden after 10 p.m. So it is little surprise that most suburbs are dead as the grave after this hour. It is one of the worst forms of cultural shock that the new *Gastarbeiter* must face, and if he attempts to bring the gay midnight spirit of Naples or Piraeus into a residential area, he is quickly slapped down.

This intolerance of neighbours who break rules is of course linked with the Germans' awe of authority and innate distaste for law-breaking. In Stuttgart, as elsewhere, they will stand patiently at a crossing till the pedestrian light goes green, even when no car is in sight. This is less through fear of a hidden cop who might issue a tiny fine than simply because to cross on a red light would make them feel deeply uneasy. Yet a Frenchman or Italian, in jumping the lights, feels he has scored a minor victory. In Stuttgart, if you commit a petty breach such as parking your car in the wrong place, a passer-by will come up and tell you so, very politely. Your offence will have irritated his sense of order. In Britain or France, he will either ignore you, or give a practical warning that a policeman is in the offing.

Respect not only for authority but also for "important" people runs throughout society. And the weakening of class divisions has not removed this snobbery but given it a new slant by creating a meritocracy where, as in America, anyone can be President. An

English couple living in Stuttgart told me they were often struck by contrasts with British society, and the wife said of her charlady: "This good working-class *Putzfrau* is always fuming against the *Gastarbeiter,* getting her views from the popular Press. Yet she is so deferential to the rich and famous. She adores our Royal Family, and hoards old colour-mag articles about them which she re-reads in the evening. When I told her that my husband was a partner in his firm, her eyes glowed with joy: *'Ist Ihr Mann Direcktor? Wunderbar! Ich habe nur prominente Leute!'* ('I work only for prominent people')". My friends added that they moved in a social circle of up-and coming young executives, not all of them Swabians: "We get invited to parties because of my husband's position," said the wife, "and I must dress smartly but inconspicuously. The ideal here is to be 'decent': you see women trying on dull little dresses in shops, and the salesgirl says approvingly, *'Das ist sehr dezent.'* My conversation, too, must not stand out. If I were to break these rules, I would be bitched at behind my back and demoted to the bottom of the peer group but not – thanks to my husband's position – expelled from it. That would happen only if he lost his job. Everyone, too, has the same kind of smart car, usually a Mercedes, and you are classified by the size of your car as well as by your job status." I suggested that this last point did not sound very Swabian. My friend then explained that her group included many people from other parts of Germany, and added, "but even these Swabians, though they think it bad taste to show off their wealth in public, still judge each other by it in private." But surely, I suggested, this *bourgeois* provincial conformism would be just as bad in, say, Leeds or Lyon? – "Maybe, but not, I think, so intolerant. There, if you dissent, you are simply an amusing oddity. Here, it's more like the United States, more tied up with material status-snobbery."

My own landlord, the sweetest and kindest of men and a good Socialist, would automatically divide people into "important" and – dismissively – "not important". He took immense trouble to give me good contacts – he was a journalist too – but I found it hard ever to explain to him that I needed to meet ordinary people and not just the *Prominenz.* All Germans love a title. Once on the *Autobahn* from Munich I was stopped for speeding, and when the policeman found my driving licence had expired he threatened to arrest me. "Can I ring the British consul-general?" I asked, and added, forcefully, *"Er ist mein Freund"* (which happened to be true). He quickly handed back my papers and shooed me on.

It is thus no surprise that in Stuttgart, as in other big German towns, rich businessmen vie with each other to acquire honorary consulships from small Third World countries. Sometimes they even buy these, for 50,000 DM or much more. The titles, however empty in themselves and however footling the work that the post demands, provide an immediate passport to a new world of social respect. And so there exists in Stuttgart a fantasy diplomatic life. Countries as tiny and remote as El Salvador and Tchad, with virtually no contact with Baden-Württemberg, are represented. Of the thirty or so consuls in the town, only five or six are foreign career diplomats; the rest are local Germans with "honorary" status, and I would guess that a third or more of these had bought their posts, in some cases through the agency of the notorious Munich title-broker, Hans Hermann Weyer. A businessman never admits to having bought his title, yet he probably will feel that the large sum has been well spent. He gets no diplomatic immunity, but has perks of other kinds. He may be a small garage owner, or a maker of sanitary fittings or underwear, so the status of "consul" lifts him out of his narrow business rut into the social Olympia. He gets invited *ex officio* to the *Land* President's annual party; he can throw a posh party himself on his country's national day. His "CC" plaque on his car helps him with the German police – needless to say. And his wife, too, enjoys the kudos, in a society where people are addressed by their titles almost every other sentence. There is a touch of the absurd about two Swabian tycoons solemnly calling each other, *"Ja, Herr Konsul", "Nein, Herr Konsul"* – but there it is. One rich and respected local businessman has thought it worth his while to be consul of one of the smallest Third World states. A colleague said of him: "Being a consul does actually help his business – he goes to a score of diplomatic parties a year, and these bring new contacts. He adores putting the national emblem on the firm's gate, and there's one room he can turn into a consular office at an hour's notice." A manufacturer representing an even tinier state told me he had barely heard of it before his appointment. Nor were there any citizens of that state living locally: yet he threw a big consular party each year for 200 guests, in a leading hotel.

Why these aspirations? Germans who have made a lot of money feel inadequate if they have no title to show for it: without a degree they cannot even be *"Herr Doktor"*. So they create this fantasy world, especially evident in more ostentatious towns such as Munich or Frankfurt, but present in Stuttgart too. It is like Genet's *Le Balcon,* where people parade as something they are not. Everyone knows the titles are often bought and therefore void of meaning, yet they still pay extravagant respect to them. No one tries to call society's bluff.

The formality of society takes other forms too. In Germany you are "*Herr Doktor*" even to your friends and, rarely, except to your more intimate ones, "Hans". Anyone from Britain or America is always taken aback at this German avoidance of Christian names. Young typists sharing the same office, of the same age and background, will go on calling each other "*Fräulein*"; close business colleagues of the same rank will remain "*Herr*" to each other. An American woman journalist in Stuttgart, working for a US Army paper, told me that she once wrote a story about a senior German official and, following the style of her paper, had to include his Christian name. So she rang his secretary to ask what it was. "Sorry, I don't know." "Oh, have you only just started to work for him?" "No, I've been with him four years. But he signs his letters with his initials. I've never heard him use his first name." And I recall an incident with my own landlord and his wife in Stuttgart, the Schloskes. We were on cordial terms and they often took me to plays and parties, but I was still "*Herr* Ardagh". Once, after three weeks of this, standing with *Frau* Schloske waiting for her husband at a theatre, I found myself saying without thinking, "I wonder where Werner is." Realising the gaffe I'd committed, I decided to be bold and plunge on: "Look, we know each other quite well now – why not call me John?" She looked at me with alarm, and changed the subject. I never tried again. To this day, I am still "*Herr* Ardagh". But we are true, warm friends. And anyway, what's in a name? – in Newcastle, my landlord called me "John" in his first sentence, and we then proceeded to dislike each other heartily. There are occasions when I prefer German courteous formality to British – or American – indiscriminate back-slapping bonhomie.

Formality, after all, is only a façade. The real question to ask is whether it reflects a cold and unkind society, or whether beneath it people are warm and loyal. This may depend on whether they feel they know each other well enough to trust each other. Swabians, like other Germans, are emotional about true friendship. After a due period of time, when the trust has taken root, a man will suggest to his new friend that they move from "*Sie*" to "*du*" and from "*Herr*" to "Hans": they will then drink on it and embrace, in a ritual that is a kind of wedding. True, young people, especially students, are dispensing with many of these formalities and, as in France, now move more rapidly to "*du*" and first names. But the latter are still used much more rarely even than in France.

This is not to say that Swabians are rude, cold or unhelpful to those with whom they may be on more formal terms. I was impressed by people's politeness and, to an extent, by their hospitality. I found this the most hospitable of the towns in my book, after Toulouse (where, thanks to my French connections, I had a special *entrée*). I was continually receiving impromptu invitations, to lunch or supper, or to tea with large creamy cakes, from people I had not met before, especially younger couples. By French or Italian standards the hospitality was not always very lavish or sophisticated*, but at least it was friendly. And I was struck by the formal courtesy of Swabians, to each other in public: this is the corollary of their snobbery and conformism. Shop assistants are noticeably more polite than in Britain or France. And younger people, as in France, tend to be more polite than older ones – the other way round from Britain.

Also, as in France, people tend to be a little stiff and reserved on social occasions, unless among close friends or family. Anthony Gibbs, an Englishman teaching at the university, noted of his students: "Their idea of a party is to sit round in a neat circle of ten or twelve, and have a single conversation dominated by two or three people. They're not used to the Anglo-American fluid cocktail-party style. When I invited some of them to a party at my flat, and encouraged them to sit on the floor or stroll about, they were shy at first, then got to like it." And other English friends told me of their experience at a Swabian dinner-party, in the home of a rich lawyer and his wife: "There were lots of servants, and our hostess seemed very tense, anxious that all should be just so. We went into dinner in pairs on each others' arms. After the meal, the men made long formal speeches, with toasts, though it was only a private party for ten! We find the people here kindly, but heavy. We miss the sparkle and humour of France, where we lived before."

So what are we to make of this society with its paradoxes of cordiality and prejudice, decency and snobbery? It is still marked by the terrible Nazi past, even if less so than other parts of Germany where Nazism went deeper. If older people are socially reticent and hide behind polite formalities, may this not be because they fear getting too involved with each other, lest the old wounds might be re-opened? Of course, this can only be part of the truth, for rigid formality is a German trait that long

* See page 70-1.

pre-dates Hitler. But friends who know Germany far better than I do have stressed to me that, rather as in France, this is a society where people are kind and loyal to those they know and trust, but less so to a stranger, or at least much less so than in Britain. An Englishman who has lived in Germany for some years summed it up: "This is not really a spontaneously kind society, like Britain's. People have to be *told* here to help each other: witness the notices in the subways, 'A nice man helps a lady up with her pram'. Germans will not go out of their way to help the handicapped: for example, blind people even here in Swabia find it hard to get digs, because people are afraid of being indulgent to weakness. I have a love-hate relationship with this nation. I have many good German friends and individually, in the intimacy of their homes, I find them deeply loyal, generous, rewarding. Those same people, *en masse* or in public, become a different race. Despite his flair for team-work, the German has not yet fully learned to be a social animal."

It follows that the Swabian, like the Toulousain, does not readily indulge in the kind of spontaneous community action that is so common on Tyneside. First, on a human and social level, he does not easily make friends with his neighbours when he moves to a new suburb. The new housing estates are tidy and well-organised, with good amenities, but they tend to be soulless places where people make little effort to get to know each other or forge a living community. At Fasanenhof, a spruce suburb of villas and high-rise flats, one resident, an SPD councillor, told me: "People are far better housed here than in their previous homes, and when they get home they simply shut the door, enjoy their new luxury – and watch TV. They prefer to keep up with old friends in other parts of Stuttgart than make new ones here. This suburb has ten thousand inhabitants, but there's little social or cultural activity. The community association is used mainly as a pressure-group for securing better services from the *Rathaus,* and is no kind of club. The Churches have been trying to get social life going, but they find no great response." A familiar story in many corners of the new Europe.

Secondly, on a civic level, though the Stuttgarter takes enormous pride in his city, he is little concerned to participate through voluntary action in the day-to-day running of its affairs. He prefers to leave his elected rulers to get on with the job. Rommel, as I stated earlier, has been taking steps to consult the citizens more regularly and informally in order to make the technocracy less remote: the citizens may appreciate this, but they do not expect to take the initiative themselves.

In its paternalistic way, the *Rathaus* does its job very well. It operates a wide range of welfare and other services with efficiency and a high sense of social concern. Its homes for the elderly are cheerful and comfortable, it runs numerous youth clubs and summer camps, and it has direct control of a number of hospitals and clinics (health, in my other towns, is not a municipal responsibility). Despite Rommel's problems over finance, this is much the wealthiest of my towns, civic budgets are generous, and many welfare services are exemplary. Some other services are managed, or supported, by local industries or by the Churches. In Germany, firms are readier than in Britain or France to take some voluntary responsibility for the housing and welfare of employees, and this is especially so in Swabia with its tradition of benevolent paternalism. Daimler-Benz, Bosch and other firms have helped to build a number of new housing estates, and share in running their amenities. The Churches, too, both Catholic and Protestant, play a large role in social work, by running clubs and welfare services not only for their own faithful but for the population as a whole.

All this impressive activity is institutionalised, whereas in Britain it is often the result of informal voluntary initiative. Anthony Gibbs noted the contrast: "Even these kindly Swabians do not feel quite the same sense of neighbourly responsibility as we do in Britain. They believe that the role of good Samaritan is the duty of the established authorities, not of the individual citizen. It is hard to imagine any wide support here for a body such as 'Shelter', the voluntary movement that has done so much for the homeless in Britain. When a group of my students, with the sincerest of intentions, held a meeting to discuss how to help handicapped people, all they did in the end was to pass a motion declaring that such help is a good thing. They had little idea of how to pass into action." Recently one or two radical pressure-groups have emerged, to contest the paternalist management of social services by the *Rathaus* and other public bodies. They have tried to stir the citizens into greater participation, into forming action groups either to assist the authorities or to contest them. But their voice has had little influence. Some of them have veered towards Leftist extremism, even sympathy for the Baader terrorists, and this has simply alienated the all-too-silent majority of placid burghers who want the city to be managed as it is, with as little controversy as possible, by a capable and largely middle-class local establishment.

This placidity, and distaste for controversy, find an alibi in the local media – the press, and the regional TV and radio – which do not often stir up lively local debate. Stuttgart has two morning dailies, which merged into financial association in 1972 but retain a certain rivalry. Both are non-party. The *Stuttgarter Zeitung* (160,000 circulation) is solemnly serious in the true German manner; the *Stuttgarter Nachrichten* has a livelier style, yet a smaller circulation. Both, and especially the *Zeitung,* have far fuller local and international news coverage and a far loftier cultural content than the dailies of Newcastle or Toulouse. One reason for this is that in Germany, even more than in France, the leading papers are regional rather than national. Even the greatest dailies, the *Frankfurter Allgemeine Zeitung* and the *Süddeutsche Zeitung* (Munich), are little read in Stuttgart, though both are published less than 150 miles away. So Stuttgart's *Zeitung* is Württemberg's equivalent of the *FAZ* and achieves the same high solemnity and comprehensiveness. It is what earnest Swabians expect of their local paper, and thus is more widely read than the more entertaining *Nachrichten* – how unlike Britain! Both papers cover city affairs in detail and will occasionally launch a crusade on some not-too-inflammable issue: "We fought the *Rathaus* over its slow snow-clearance and forced it to act!" I was told proudly at the *Zeitung,* as an example of its radicalism. Sometimes, it is true, the paper goes further: its campaign against one Swabian dignitary, Eugen Gerstenmaier, ex-president of the *Bundestag,* whom it suspected of corruption, even helped put an end to his political career. But most of the time both papers are cautious in their handling of local controversies.

I once fell victim myself to the *Zeitung*'s curious self-censorship. In 1974, I did a 40-minute BBC radio broadcast on the Arts in Stuttgart. In it, I spoke of my fondness for the town and my admiration for its official culture, but I also expressed – in my script, and through my interviewees – some of the criticisms of Swabians that are made in this chapter: smugness, acceptance of official spoon-feeding, etc. A few days later, I was flattered to see a lengthy commentary on the broadcast, in the *Zeitung.* But when I read it, I felt less flattered. The author, the paper's cultural editor, made one or two oblique references to my criticisms – "Doktor Ardagh produces some home truths about the Swabian character" – while devoting nearly all his space to quoting my praises, and praising those praises. He distorted the sense of my broadcast, perhaps in a very German anxiety to prove that the rest of the world shares the city's high opinion of itself.

Blandness and avoidance of controversy might also be regarded as features of Baden-Württemberg's radio and TV stations, located in Stuttgart. These are a product of the special and complex structure of broadcasting in Germany, which has the effect of imposing an emasculated political neutrality in an honourable bid to achieve fairness and objectivity. Though it derives some revenue from advertising, broadcasting is non-commercial and in public hands – those of the *Länder*. They run one of the three TV networks, and some radio, as a nationwide consortium. In the case of the other TV networks, and most radio, each *Land* produces a variety of programmes just for itself while pooling others nationally. Not surprisingly, in so decentralised a country, this system leads to a much higher proportion of regional programming, geared to regional needs, than in France or even in Britain. And in many ways this is admirable. But after 1945 the Germans, lacking any BBC with its tradition of autonomy plus impartiality, and not wanting to copy the French *étatiste* pattern, were faced with the problem of how to set up public-service broadcasting with a reasonable degree both of independence and political fairness. They devised a system whereby each station is run by a *Land*-appointed corporation and its director is a political nominee who tends to be of the same colour as the *Land* government: but, in order to correct bias of this sort, other senior posts in the station are shared out between the parties in proportion to their strength in the *Landtag*. Thus, if the head of some department is CDU, his deputy will be SPD, and this so-called *proporz* system spreads down through the echelons, so that technical staff and even programme assistants are paired off. Ironically, while this may help to achieve political balance, it also introduces political tensions at a level where they are hardly relevant. It can lead to stalemates harmful to radical broadcasting, for a programme may be shorn of its controversial content in order to balance the rival views of those making it.

This may help to explain the nature of the programmes broadcast from the Süddeutsche Rundfunk station in Stuttgart. It has fine modern studios, and a relatively large budget for serving its wealthy region. The cultural tone of many programmes is lofty, but in current-affairs they are seldom outspoken. One radical-minded producer told me of his frustrations: "The director of current-affairs is careful not to offend the *Land* authorities, to whom he is indebted indirectly for his job. And so it goes on down the line. Producers are worried about getting the sack if they are too critical, and this makes them cautious in covering local affairs. Hard-hitting interviews with local politicians are rare. The reporter is deferential, and if he does dare ask probing questions, the politician will often take it as a personal insult." When a programme deals with social rather than political matters, it is often bolder: a new series made in Stuttgart in 1974 achieved national fame by taking its cameras, for instance, to talk to convicts in their cells about prison reform. But this is a rare case. In general, broadcasting in Stuttgart reflects the local establishment as much as the press does. Neither plays quite the constructive role that it might in civic affairs.

6

The revolt against a "temple culture"

The paradox of a Stuttgart both *"Partner der Welt"* and "the biggest village in Germany" – its own descriptions of itself – is nowhere so apparent as in its cultural life, where the ultra-conservative jostles with the daringly modern. Councillors who admit to hating modern art will readily vote public money for avant-garde exhibitions so that Stuttgart can keep up with its rivals in this field. Yet the city ignores and spurns its most distinguished intellectual, Max Bense, computer-art expert at the university, who calls Stuttgart "a stifling nightmare". Music and ballet are of high international quality: yet one local critic was ready to tell me, "Few of my fellow-Swabians who dutifully attend concerts and operas are true culture-lovers. They go because socially it's the right thing. They are philistines."

Many people spoke to me of a "cultural gulf" – not so much between highbrow and popular as between established and informal: on the one hand, the official prestige culture, lavishly subsidised; on the other, a few little unofficial *milieux,* mostly feeling isolated and impotent. Stuttgart's opera has often in the past decade been better than Paris's; yet the town has no Latin Quarter. The formal subsidised culture is beyond comparison with that of my other towns; only Ljubljana, also a true capital, has the same elaborate institutions, but not the same quality. In a Germany where the metropolitan culture found in London or Paris is shared between several cities, Stuttgart's superiority over Newcastle or Toulouse is unsurprising: it may not be quite in the same class as Hamburg or Munich, but it ranks high, and public spending on the arts is here generous even by German standards.

There are historical reasons for this. The kings who ruled in Stuttgart till 1918 spent lavish sums on its opera, theatres, music and museums; and today city and *Land* authorities see it as their duty to keep up this tradition. They share on roughly a fifty-fifty basis the subsidising of the Württembergische *Staatstheater* (the opera house plus two adjacent theatres) and of other activities. The *Staatstheater* draws about half its revenue from box-office and the rest from an annual subsidy of some 60 million DM, twice that of Covent Garden. The city's own annual budget for the arts, some 58 million DM or 100 DM per head, is several times that of any comparable British town. This "enlightened" policy you could regard as one more good mark for the German system for local government. Or you could see it as a sign of German cities' greater wealth. It also reveals a difference in values.

In Britain, this scale of spending on the arts would soon spark off a ratepayers' revolt. Here it is considered normal. The only dissent is against not the size of the subsidies but the way they are spent: some radicals think the official culture is too élitist and should be brought closer to the taste of ordinary people. Yet many of these "ordinary" Stuttgarters, even if not eager culture-seekers themselves, still feel proud that the city should possess these prestige symbols. They thrill to the ballet company's successes abroad, just as a Geordie thrills to a football cup victory by Newcastle United. And the elders in the *Rathaus* consider that culture is also a valid economic investment, like advertising, a means of attracting new industry. Hans Schumann, city arts officer, told me, "Without the culture that we sponsor, Stuttgart would be a boring place and many dynamic citizens would move away. Besides, we have a duty to cater for Stuttgarters' spiritual needs."

The catering is impressive: top talent is hired from all over the world. The renowned ballet company has a Brazilian director *prima ballerina assoluta* and was founded by the late John Cranko, at one time with Covent Garden. Opera, theatre, music and art all flourish in their varied ways, though quality may vary. As you might expect in this staid town, much of the cultural repertoire is conventionally classical: but in recent years the adventurous and modern, from Stockhausen to conceptual art, has also made its appearance, to a surprising degree. As in most big towns, there are several different publics – and large ones.

Ballet and concert performances are nearly always sold out. Over the year, nearly twice as many people go to the *Staatstheater* as to football matches in the local stadium.

This bright picture leaves some questions unanswered. Who are the various audiences? Why do they go and what does culture mean to them? Does the official diet in fact correspond to public taste? Why do so many artists and intellectuals complain that, in the midst of this *cornucopia,* they are "living in a ghetto"? Why so much spoon-feeding and, relatively, so little of the more spontaneous do-it-yourself activity, whether high or low-brow, that exists in Newcastle? The answers relate to the kind of place Stuttgart is. First, let us look more closely at the official scene.

Opera, ballet and theatre come under the same central management, and their *Generalintendant* is appointed by the *Land* Government. From 1949 to 1972 the post was held by a great personality, Walter Erich Schäfer, who can take more credit than anyone else for Stuttgart's prowess in the arts during that period. This father-figure, genial but tough, cajoled a suspicious *Land* and city into letting him carry through policies that at first they thought wildly liberal. He invited Cranko from London and backed him through his initial troubles. He did the same for Peter Palitzsch, maverick Leftist theatre manager. Schäfer also took personal charge of the opera, and steadily coaxed local audiences to accept a dosage of modern works beside their preferred Mozart and Puccini. It was he who sponsored the provocative *Devils of Loudun.* He was not a producer himself, but as manager built up a fine team, including the Wagnerian tenor Wolfgang Windgassen and the Czech conductor Vaclac Neumann. And so for a number of years the yellowish colonnaded Grosse Haus beside the Schlossgarten was regarded as the home of one of the three or four best opera companies in Germany – perhaps *the* best for Wagner, after Bayreuth.

Today the scene is less brilliant. Schäfer's successor, Hans Peter Doll, is more of a bureaucrat, less of an inspiring crusader. For this and other reasons the opera's quality has fallen (though it still outshines, by far, that of Bologna or Toulouse). Windgassen is dead, and some other bright stars have moved away. Too much emphasis has gone recently on importing star singers and directors, rather than building up a good permanent company. But ups-and-downs of this kind are normal in the fortunes of any company, and Schäfer at least has left a permanent legacy: Stuttgart today accepts modern opera. The company may be falling back again too much on routine productions of the obvious classics: but it can still sometimes rise to the occasion with a fine presentation of a difficult new work – for example, recently, Schönberg's *Moses and Aaron.*

The famous ballet company has managed more successfully to retain its high standards, despite the sudden death of John Cranko in 1973, aged only forty-seven. Cranko, a South African of Polish origin, was a choreographer at Covent Garden before he moved to Stuttgart in 1960. By a coincidence, Stuttgart had been one of the four great ballet cities of Europe in the 18th century, under Jean-Georges Noverre, but this glorious tradition had long since been lost. And it is doubly ironic that Cranko should have had to come to Germany to find the scope and recognition that eluded him in London, and that Stuttgart should again have called in a foreigner to create a great ballet company. Stuttgart and Cranko needed and found each other: the result was stunning, and its legacy remains so. He told me soon before his death: "I've had opportunities here that I'd never have found at the Garden. We do about eighty evenings of ballet a year in this Opera House, and we can stage three new programmes a year – even the Garden can't do that. The authorities have also built us a new ballet school for four million marks. This is a better deal than the ballet gets anywhere in Britain, or in most other German cities." How did it happen? Schäfer, believing in Cranko, patiently persuaded the *Landtag* to vote the money needed to build the company – "It had to be explained to them," I was told, "that a dancer needs more than one pair of new shoes a month." Cranko then set about creating a regular audience, in a town that had virtually forgotten ballet: leaning on the Swabians' passion for music, he succeeded. His genius lay essentially in the re-working of classical ballets in new forms, and this suited Stuttgart's own taste: *Eugene Onegin* and *Romeo and Juliet* were among his master-pieces. But he also created some memorable modern pieces, such as *Poème de l'Ecstase,* written for Fonteyn. "Ballets kept bubbling out of him, and he had this amazing gift of being able to inspire us all," a member of the company told me. He drew together a team from many nations and helped Marcia Haydee, his Brazilian prima ballerina, to become one of the world's great dancers – "the Callas of ballet", *Time* has called her. Equally remarkable, he was able to spot young local talent and create soloists from it, such as Birgit Keil, a Swabian. He became a hero in Stuttgart, even for people with no taste for ballet, and when he died there was sobbing in the streets. He had taken the company on tour to many of the world's great cities, always with acclaim, especially in the United States. But it never visited London until – irony – the year after his death. The welcome then was as fervent as elsewhere – tinged maybe with remorse?

Today the company has lost little of its brilliance. Cranko's successor for a while was Glen Tetley, the American choreographer, but his style did not entirely suit the company, and they parted amicably. Now Haydee herself has taken charge, the first case since Pavlova of a prima ballerina also being artistic director. She has retained most of Cranko's repertoire, and some of Tetley's, and also uses guest choreographers. Above all, through the force of her personality she has maintained Cranko's tradition of inspired teamwork despite the company's diversity: the seventy dancers come from at least a dozen nations. And she has built up the ballet school into the foremost in Germany. There are some critics who detect signs of a decline in the company and say that Hamburg is now the home of Germany's best ballet (under John Neumeier). But when the Stuttgart Ballet came again to London in 1976, more than one critic described it as still the best in Europe. In Stuttgart I was told, "Abroad, this city means first Mercedes and second ballet": small wonder that the politicians in the *Landtag* and *Rathaus* consider their subsidy well spent.

They have not always been so sure about the money spent on the *Staatstheater*'s drama company, which uses a modern twin-auditorium theatre beside the opera house. It may be significant that one of the few features common to all my five towns is that subsidised theatre has led to repeated civic controversy – and nowhere more so than in Stuttgart where, as in Toulouse, it has highlighted a fundamental conflict between two definitions of culture, established *bourgeois* and modern Leftist. In a city so proud of its official culture, this has often led to embarrassment. In 1963 *Generalintendant* Schäfer chose as director of the drama company a certain Peter Palitzsch, a Marxist and former pupil of Brecht in East Berlin, and one of the best-known post-war German theatre producers. It may seem odd that so prudent a town should have picked such a firebrand: but Schäfer wanted to bring in new ideas and put Stuttgart on Germany's theatrical map. Palitzsch, a tall, thin man with long nervous hands, chain-smoking yellow French cigarettes, told me: "I agreed to come to Stuttgart because the public here is not frivolous and modish as in, say, Düsseldorf, but solid and reasonable, and so I felt this would be the right place for breaking with tradition and trying a new kind of experimental social theatre." For several years he got away with it. He gave a Marxist twist to Shakespeare's histories; he staged, brilliantly, the world *première* of Tancred Dorst's *Toller,* about the Left-wing uprising in Munich in 1919; he introduced Stuttgart not only to Brecht but to Brechtian methods, avoiding guest stars and often radically reworking the text of a play in rehearsal, with the author where possible. If Shakespeare was not around to be consulted, too bad. The company's work was uneven, but always interesting. It was an exciting time to be in Stuttgart. Palitzsch drew round him a regular audience, many of them students, very different from the more conventional audiences for opera and ballet: men with beards and girls in duffle-coats would clamber onto the stage after the show and stay there late in animated discussion.

But Palitzsch, arrogant and uncompromising, increasingly fell foul of his main employers, the *Land* government. The *Theaterbeirat,* a *Land*-cum-city advisory board, did not have the right to veto his plays directly but they could and did put pressure on Schäfer, complaining that they found his repertoire too Leftist and his Arden and Pinter productions too erotic. Finally Schäfer tired of fighting his battles for him; Palitzsch, too, grew weary of the feuding and in 1972 moved off to Frankfurt, taking most of his company with him. The theatre then went into a period of decline, and the eager young audiences stayed away. After 1974 a new director, Claus Peymann, from Frankfurt, put it back on the rails again but pushed it in a different direction. A devotee of literary, apolitical theatre, who made his name by promoting Handke who is closer to Ionesco than to Brecht, he offered a serious but eclectic diet that mixed Handke, Wedekind, von Hörvath and Thomas Bernhard with the older classics. Stuttgart is unlikely to risk burning its hands on a Palitzsch again for some time. The change also reflects the decline in West Germany's vogue for political theatre in the past few years. In 1979 Peymann left Stuttgart, after a fairly successful five years.

Three other Stuttgart theatres, privately run, receive civic subsidies. One puts on "*boulevard*" comedies; one battles away with off-beat plays on a shoestring; a third is that near contradiction-in-terms, a Swabian satiric cabaret. This is the Renitenz, devoted to cosy Swabian self-mockery about thrift, tidiness, etc., a place where businessmen safely take their guests for a taste of local *Gemütlichkeit.* Its 1975 show was called "*Playgirls, Snobs und Kaviar*" (sic) and it thinks itself very up-to-the-minute but scarcely reflects the grand tradition of German cabaret. "For satire to rely on municipal subsidy isn't exactly the kiss of life," said one local critic; "true cabaret in, say, Munich and Berlin has in the past decade gone into a bitingly political phase and then out again. The Renitenz is panting along two fashions behind the times."

But if satiric cabaret is hardly Stuttgart's forte, the same need not be said of classical music. The city's musical life is varied and distinguished. Even more than most Germans, Swabians have music in their blood: they are taught it intensively at school, they perform it in their leisure time by joining amateur choirs or chamber groups, and they eagerly attend the concerts and other musical events on which the city council spends some 7 million DM a year in subsidies. This level of municipal and popular support has encouraged a number of music groups of high quality to choose Stuttgart as their home. The Melos Quartet, one of the best in Europe, is based here; so is the famous chamber orchestra directed by Karl Münchinger, who lives in Stuttgart. The town has as many as five symphony orchestras – Toulouse, Newcastle and Bologna have one each – as well as some hundred amateur or semi-amateur choirs of varying quality. The Liederhalle, the large modern concert hall run by the city, is nearly always filled in advance with block-bookings – at least, when the better-known classics are being played. Needless to say, Stuttgart's taste for contemporary music is a few years behind that of some cities: when Stockhausen came recently to conduct his hymns, the hall was only half full. "Endless Beethoven Fifth and Ninth is what people really want," is one comment I heard from a local highbrow; but Swabians do genuinely love their classics and are not going merely out of habit.

The town's relationship with the visual arts is more ambivalent, for this is not a part of the world with a strong artistic tradition. By chance, some of Germany's leading modern architects live and have their offices in Stuttgart, including Frei Otto, and Heinle who designed the Munich Olympic village of 1972: but they have done little creative work for Stuttgart's own modern architecture. Similarly, a number of talented artists with a more than local reputation have chosen to live and work in the town because they like it – the painters Otto Grieshaber and L. M. Wintersberger, and the sculptors Otto Hajek and Kaspar Leck, amongst others. But for selling their work they turn elsewhere, notably to Cologne which is now the main German art market. And so the town's commercial galleries cannot do much to help local artists. Yet this does not mean that Stuttgart is closed to modern art: on the contrary, there has been a breakthrough since the 1960s, due as in the theatre to the arrival of a maverick outsider, able to attract students and others who are eager to attend exhibitions even if they cannot afford to buy. Stuttgart like other big German towns has its *Kunstverein* (Arts Association), an autonomous body handsomely subsidised by the city (800,000 DM in 1978) and *Land.* Its director until 1973 was Uwe Schneede, a young Holsteiner full of bold ideas, and he virtually created a new public for modern art in a town that knew next to nothing about it. To the *Kunstverein*'s handsome premises beside the Schlossgarten he brought controversial exhibitions of that kind of art he believed in – surrealist, abstract, or politically committed – and drew eager responses from a section of the public. The city councillors sometimes took fright and threatened to cut off his subsidy: but Schneede confronted them, with more tact than Palitzsch, and won. For several years – until he moved on to a better job elsewhere – he made this city's *Kunstverein* into one of the most creatively adventurous in Germany. His successor, Dr Osterwold, is likewise showing enterprise. Once again, conservative Stuttgart has shown that it can also embrace the most *avant-garde.*

This brief survey will give some idea of the liveliness and quality of the cultural scene, which is due quite largely to enlightened official paternalism. Yet the sponsors' well-meaning intentions are today under fire from a number of younger radicals, who object to the spoon-feeding and want more "participation". One of their leaders, Klaus Hubner, denounces what he calls "putting culture into temples" and asks, "Is this prestige culture what the public actually wants?" It is not an easy question to answer because, as in any big city, there are several publics: Palitzsch's was not that of *Tosca.* Yet it may be possible to identify an "average" Swabian cultural consumer, middle-class and serious, at whom the official spoon is directed. What does he want? He is generally more self-consciously "cultured" than his English, or even French, counterpart; and he usually holds to a very Germanic concept of *Kultur* as an immutable value system that you learn to receive – like taking Communion – with a view to self-improvement. A Swabian family will not only attend cultural events but also create culture in its own home circle, in a manner that an Englishman might find quaintly Victorian. Anthony Gibbs told me: "Many of my Swabian friends have classical libraries of which they are proud, and they put more conscious effort than an Englishman into encouraging their children to read the right books. *Kultur* is coupled with homeliness. Above all, the tradition of family *Hausmusik* is very much alive: I am often invited round for a social evening where my host and hostess and their teenage children perform quartets for their guests. Maybe the daughter is a gifted pianist and the son plays the flute. It's endearing, and like something out of Jane Austen."

This kind of *bourgeois* family takes its musical tradition as much for granted as its French equivalent takes good eating. The feeling for music, whether in the home or concert hall, is sincerely felt: there are scores of singing clubs, and the choirs rehearsing *Messiah* or Bach oratorios are more prevalent than in Wales. But when it comes to taking a seat in the stalls, especially at the Opera House, for a big professional occasion, other motives may emerge too – motives of pride and prestige. First, there is pride in Stuttgart: some of the Swabians' enthusiasm for culture-going certainly springs from the fact that the product *is* largely home-grown. Touring companies from other cities seldom pay visits: the opera and ballet may import guest stars, but these companies are essentially local, and going to see them is a bit like going to cheer the local football team. The ballet's biggest ever ovation in Stuttgart was for its first performance after returning from a triumphal American tour, and Cranko and his team were a bit put out. It seemed they were being applauded less for their own merits than for having waved the local flag in New York, thus reassuring Stuttgarters that their ballet must be one of the best because the world thinks so too.

Secondly, there is personal pride. In this formal society, people dress up even for routine occasions as they have mostly ceased to do in Britain except for something such as a Covent Garden first night. Anthony Gibbs said: "In Manchester, I could go straight from work to the concert hall in a pullover; here, I'd be made to feel awkward. Not all the culture here is first-rate, and it annoys me to see people coming decked in their jewels and Yves Saint-Laurents to applaud the mediocre." Swabians – if less so than the Bolognese – judge you by how you dress. Another English resident, Jessie Church, had this to say about attitudes behind culture-going: "The average educated Swabian strives to be a good allround cultivated person, and feels it is his duty to be able to speak about music and books. People go to events in order to be seen, yes, but also out of curiosity to see and hear what is being talked about. They want to know about the newest things, things that have already been accepted elsewhere. That's the crux: Swabians will accept the *avant-garde* or provocative, so long as they know it has already won acceptance somewhere else. They have little true judgement of their own, except maybe for music. They absorb the 'right' things without thinking. It is hard therefore to make a reputation here, starting from nothing: but someone already famous can come here, give a poor performance, and be warmly applauded – just because he is well known." And Roderick Klett, a TV producer, commented, "Stuttgart wants to buy the best and may sometimes succeed, but does not always understand what it has bought." He told me how in 1971 the *Land* Government, wanting to do its bit for modern art, spent 50,000 DM on a reclining figure by Henry Moore, whom they knew to be a big OK-name. They planned to put it in front of the *Landtag*. But there was a public outcry, and many burghers denounced Moore as "ill-minded". The authorities, embarrassed, finally hid the sculpture behind some bushes.

All this may seem the quintessence of provincialism. But at least the public is not apathetic. There does exist a kind of "*tout Stuttgart*" in the Parisian sense, a sophisticated *milieu* where the latest cultural events are eagerly discussed, even if the opinions are second-hand. This kind of *milieu* barely exists in Newcastle or Toulouse, where provincialism lacks these metropolitan aspirations. And Stuttgart has noticeably been evolving, over the past two decades, from its previous strictly classical concept of culture towards a new interest in trendiness: in the 1950s, the *Land* would not even have considered buying a Moore. One major influence has been the influx of so many cultivated exiles from Soviet bloc countries, who have brought new ideas and helped to open the Swabian imagination to new horizons. The sheer cultural vitality today is exhilarating. But the biggest contrast with my other towns, and notably with Newcastle, lies in this acceptance as normal of so high a degree of official spoon-feeding. In Newcastle, as we shall see, amenities for the arts are far less lavish yet there is far more spontaneity. Maybe German formality inhibits the growth of a free-and-easy do-it-yourself cultural *milieu* to balance the "temple culture", in a town where most activity is civically sponsored. Once a "happening" was held in the Kleine Schlossplatz: Otto Hajek, the sculptor, painted the terrace in bright colours, and there were balloons, psychedelic lights and electronic music. But it was all neatly organised by the City Museum.

Stuttgart has seen little of any effective "underground" or counter-culture, save on the level of verbal protest and theorising by a few individuals. The non-official scene is atomised. There are the intellectuals, feeling isolated in their little ghettoes. There are the *Gastarbeiter,* who carry on their boisterous folk traditions within the seclusion of their own clubs and *cafés* but are rarely invited to contribute more publicly. And there is Stuttgart's own young generation, badly provided for yet poor at creating its own scene for itself. One trouble is the nature of the university, simply a newly upgraded technical college, without the traditions of Tübingen or Heidelberg. Its students grind their noses into their science text-books, and it is hard to induce them to take part in, for instance, drama groups. On the fringe, one or two non-official youth initiatives have been struggling to the surface, but they sadly lack amenities. A tawdry barrack-like hall is the home of a folk-club, the Laboratorium, which shows the occasional underground film and has lively concerts, but nearly all the songs are Anglo-Saxon or French, and dated – Baez, Brassens, et al. Why is the splendid repertoire of German traditional folk heard so rarely these days? One answer: the Nazis took over the best songs which are thus now discredited. Those lyrical choruses still revive memories of jackboots and the *Hitlerjugend.* The devil always steals the best tunes.

There is not even much modern "pop" in Stuttgart, though hardly for the same reasons. In a town with so rigorous a definition of culture, "pop" in official eyes has little of the respectability it has now won in, say, Britain. What is more, pop can spell trouble. Once the Rolling Stones came to Stuttgart and were graciously allowed to perform in a municipal hall. But the fans got excited, some chairs were damaged – and pop concerts were thereafter banned!

So complete is the municipal monopoly of culture that all the big theatres and halls are in civic hands, and there is no large commercial building that could accommodate pop concerts or other mass enter-tainments. This is a reason for the sparceness not only of pop but of the kind of middlebrow culture that is such big business in Britain: there is no hall for touring musical comedies that might compete with the highbrow diet of the *Staatstheater.* This does not mean that the public are not interested. In fact, nearby Böblingen recently built itself an arts centre that now houses touring shows such as *Hair* and *My Fair Lady* – and Stuttgarters have flocked out in their thousands. But inside the hallowed city walls? Never.

This raises the issue of whether the city's "*bourgeois*" culture excludes the working-class, who generally lack the education for it. The new radicals claim that it does, but possibly they exaggerate. The trade unions have a system of block-bookings at low rates for the *Staatstheater* and concerts, and these are very fully patronised especially for the more popular classics. Now that German workers are acquiring *bourgeois* life-styles, some of them are also adopting the middle-class German's respect for *Kultur*: many working families go readily to Brahms, Puccini, or *Swan Lake,* and I even met a Daimler-Benz skilled worker who is devoted to Brecht and other political plays and reads Böll and Grass. He may not be typical, and even the Puccini-lovers form only a minority of workers, whose mass popular tastes are not catered for by the city spoon-feeders. Nor is much attempt made to prosyletise them – for instance, by applying the policy, now common in Britain and France, of sending groups of actors into pubs or factory canteens to whet appetites with simple, humorous playlets. The drama company's one attempt at this kind of experiment was not a success: maybe formality and over-reverence for *Kultur* were again the stumbling-block. So, despite the exceptions, the mass of workers are among those who stay outside the temple gates, uninitiated.

This entire cultural situation is now increasingly under question, from groups of journalists, teachers, and others. In 1973 the more radical of the local dailies, the *Nachrichten,* ran a series of fifteen articles on the theme, "What's wrong with Stuttgart's culture?" There was much Germanic theorising and airing of vague statements such as "Culture must help to re-animate traditional values": but the debate was also lively, and it revealed a widespread unease. The paper's cultural editor, Hans Fröhlich, wrote, "More and more people are getting fed up with our institutions which do not reach the masses. The opera is only for an élite, and most people have no contact with this culture, owing to lack of educational equality. The authorities admit this, but do nothing." A music critic wrote, "The city's concerts are a conservative institution of the 19th-century *bourgeoisie.* I want talk-in concerts where the composer comes to explain what he is after. Music is to be enjoyed by all, like a sunset." And an SPD spokesman wrote, "The old pub-round-the-corner culture is being lost. We must build new local centres where all can participate."

The most cogent voice in the debate was that of Klaus Hübner, a youngish, shaggy-haired, pipe-smoking Leftish intellectual and teacher, who is the most effective leader of the new crusade against the temple. He wrote, "High society here regards culture as some exclusive asset that you 'have' or 'do not have' – and ordinary people do not 'have' it. I detest this attitude. I want to redefine culture, to throw out hermetic rituals, to get rid of the respectfulness and turn culture upside down so that all can enjoy it. At present, nine citzens in ten cannot appreciate the official culture, and the *Staatstheater* gets far too much of the total subsidy. We must take culture out of the museums and into the streets – but that's not easy when the city is being ruined by new motorways. I'd like to see a big outdoor leisure zone in the centre, with music and 'happenings', and café-theatres at every corner But the *bourgeoisie* are always scared that if something spontaneous occurs the police will turn up. As no doubt they would."

I called on Hübner and his charming wife, Katinka. After plying me with *Würst,* stewed aubergines and pickled mushrooms, and playing eclectically some old Beatles records and Pound reciting his *Cantos,* he told me: "This 'temple' culture is a feudal legacy from the royal days. The municipality has to follow the lead of the *Land* which wants its posh institutions here in the capital so as to boost its feudal image. But the local people are not invited. We should present not only Schiller and Goethe, who have little relevance to modern problems, but another culture that means something to the working class. For instance, plays about 'life in our street'."

Populist views of this kind are the familiar coinage of radicals and Leftists throughout the West these days, and are not always shared by the workers in whose name they plead. In Stuttgart, the blueprints rarely get beyond the verbal stage. But Hübner and a few friends have at least been doing more than criticise: they have been taking practical steps to build their own cultural network. For a start, Hübner has provided Stuttgart with an "art" movie house, something it badly lacked. This town like others in Germany suffers from the appalling national distribution system, which makes virtually no provision for off-beat or foreign-language films. In the commercial cinemas, foreign films are nearly always dubbed; many of the best never arrive at all, or they slip into some fleapit for two or three days, unnoticed and ill-publicised. In all Stuttgart, no full-time cinema has any consistent policy of showing serious films: the university's modest ciné-club is little used by non-students. To fill this gap, Hübner opened a *Kommunaleskino,* modelled on the kind already active in Frankfurt. From a wary *Rathaus* he managed to extract a small subsidy for his civic venture, but for the first four years he had to manage with make-shift premises lent by a bank, where he could show films only at week-ends and only on 16mm. The town's commercial cinemas were furious at the competition, and even tried to get the place closed down for non-compliance with fire regulations. In 1977 the *Rathaus* at last provided him with a more suitable little cinema, in the new civic Planetarium. Here he shows the modern classics, from Bergman and Truffaut to Germany's own "new wave", as well as "underground" or Leftist films of his own choosing.

Hübner also tried to persuade the *Rathaus* to let him take over the great empty shell of the former civic theatre. He wanted to run it as "a leisure and communications forum where workers and intellectuals would feel equally at home, with political debates, experimental crafts, improvised drama". The *Rathaus* at first murmured sympathy for the project, but many city fathers then took fright at the dangers of sanctioning a forum for political protest, and funds were never allotted. However, in the past three years or so the general views of Hübner and his allies have begun to make some practical impact on the authorities. The *Rathaus* has started to decentralise a part of its cultural effort, by building small socio-cultural centres in one or two suburbs, for participatory activities. And since 1974, on two or three evenings each summer there are big popular one-night open-air festivals, known as "Long Nights": in the traffic-free Schillerplatz and Königstrasse, music and dancing goes on till the early hours, together with boozing and *Würst*-eating, and free cabaret shows and other spectacles. The crowds are enormous, up to 300,000, and the innovation marks some attempt to cater for a wider popular taste. But, as usual, the initiative and the planning all come from the technocrats in the *Rathaus.*

Many of Stuttgart's creative intellectuals – poets, philosophers and others – not only oppose the "temple" culture on political grounds but also, in a more personal sense, feel isolated and ignored. They complain that the city is not interested in their work, despite its pride in its literary and philosophical traditions. Hegel, Schiller and Hölderlin were all from in or near Stuttgart, and there were big official celebrations to mark the bicentenary of Hölderlin's birth in 1970. Today the town is a leading centre of German publishing: it has excellent bookshops, and a civic library with 23 branches, 400,000 books and an annual subsidy of over 6 million DM – a library nearly up to Newcastle's standards. Swabians on average buy or read more books than the average Briton, Frenchman or Italian, and they regard themselves as lovers of literature. Why then do so many writers feel they are living in a hostile environment? I once spent an evening with a charming group of novelists and poets, most of them earning their living through radio to supplement royalties, and they said, in sum: "This town is basically philistine, it supports culture for prestige reasons. There is no identifiable intellectual *milieu* here as you find in Munich, or even in Freiburg – no Latin Quarter, no place where artists and writers naturally gather. We feel lonely: in this sprawling city we have to make special efforts to meet, and the authorities ignore us. Here we are in the dark in a provincial town, with all the anonymity of life in Paris or London and few of the advantages." It is true that there is no Latin Quarter, and not more than one or two vaguely bohemian taverns. The only regular meeting-place is a tiny *avant-garde* bookshop run by a Berliner, Niedlichs, who occasionally holds informal discussion evenings and poetry readings in his cheerfully chaotic store piled high with *Astérix* and *Les Temps Modernes.* Yet, if artists and intellectuals fail to create a livelier community, it seems to be partly their own fault. Nothing really prevents them from getting together more effectively, and thus maybe making more impact. They are victims of their own social reticence, typically: even my nice poets, some of them sharing a house, were on *"Frau"* and *"Herr"* terms with each other as if they had just met.

The most notorious case of an intellectual less honoured by Stuttgart than by the world outside is that of Professor Max Bense, distinguished expert on computer art and cybernetics. This is a rarified speciality, and the local burghers can be pardoned for not taking to it as their favourite bedside reading: even so, given Bense's world renown in this field, you would think they might pay some court to him, if only out of pride at the prestige he brings. But no. Bense, like so many other stars of the local cultural scene, is no Swabian: born in Strasbourg in 1910, he spent some years after the war in East Germany, then broke with the Communists, and since 1950 has held a chair at Stuttgart. Here he drew round him a number of *avant-garde* writers and scientists from all over Europe, who for a few years were known loosely – from Tokyo to Hampstead – as the *"Ecole de Stuttgart"*. His influence has been immense, especially in Brazil, Japan, France – and Czechoslovakia, where three books have been written on him. The *Times Literary Supplement* has devoted long articles to him. But in Stuttgart, the Press and other media pay him little attention and he is rarely invited to official functions. It is not so much that his work is too difficult for Stuttgart, more that his behaviour is too disconcerting. He is a whimsical rogue who still makes passes at the girls and enjoys provoking the authorities, especially by asserting his atheism. In 1970 he declared publicly (after the Manila incident) that he admired anyone who tried to murder the Pope, whereupon local bishops both Catholic and Protestant put pressure on the *Land* Government for so wicked a corrupter of youth to be expelled from the university. They almost succeeded.

Bense's faculty office is above a Volkswagen showroom. In one corner is a huge globe-shaped labyrinth which he has built by computer. A short, stocky, bull-faced man, he seems to have programmed himself to radiate energy, with much waving of arms, and as he rattled away to me in bad French, I found his tongue-in-cheek arrogance appealing. "I hate all ideologies, Marxism and Christianity alike. I hate political parties, too. I'm a Socialist, but above all a believer in rational individualism. As for Stuttgart, it's a stifling nightmare: it's only where my body is, not my mind." A friend of his suggested to me later that there might be an element of sour grapes in this: "His non-acceptance here is partly his own fault, but it hurts him. He would like to be asked to play more part in running the university, and to be interviewed on TV and so on. He'd liked to be lionised, as Karl Jaspers is in Frankfurt – though Jaspers' work and ideas are no better understood there than Bense's are here."

Bense, Palitzsch, Schneede, Cranko, Münchinger . . . how is it that such exciting and diverse modern talent was drawn to stolid Stuttgart and flourished there simultaneously for a few years? Officialdom, under Schäfer, certainly played a part: but it was also pure chance that made Stuttgart for a while one of the two or three liveliest cultural centres in Germany. Today, Cranko is dead, Palitzsch and Schneede have left, Schäfer is retired and Bense and Münchinger ageing. These things go in cycles, and maybe Stuttgart's turn will come again. Meantime, the exciting and *avant-garde* has moved on to other towns, leaving Stuttgart with its provincialism again more evident – a theme to be re-examined at the end of this chapter, after next looking at Stuttgarters' affluence and their daily life and night-life (or lack of it).

7

The two-car family eats its frugal "evening bread"

Stuttgart is as affluent a society as you will find anywhere in the EEC: earnings are above average even for Germany. In a period of inflation and shifting exchange rates in Europe, to quote figures may not be very meaningful. But it is possibly true to say that, in 1977, salaries in Stuttgart were on average 60 to 80 per cent higher than in Newcastle and 30 to 40 per cent higher than in Toulouse. Taking into account differences in cost of living (higher in Germany) and in taxation and allowances, this would still leave Stuttgart with a standard of living some 15 to 20 per cent higher than Toulouse's and 25 to 30 per cent above Newcastle's. The gulf between executive and worker salaries is a little greater than in Britain and narrower than in France, and in 1978 a Stuttgart skilled worker was earning some 2,500 DM a month (£8,000 or $15,500 a year), while a middle-rank executive's annual take-home pay, after tax, was £9,000 or more.

Swabians may not like to flaunt their wealth in public, but they enjoy spending their new money, especially on their homes. The consumer boom has been as striking here as anywhere in Europe and is only slightly modified by the post-1973 slow-down. There is more than one car per four people, and the two-car family is frequent. Swabian taste – in furniture, fabrics, décor – may not be so very refined or highly fashionable, yet all the experts remark that with in the the limits of their own preferred styles, the Swabians insist strongly on quality and finish. They want goods to be expensively made: in the shops, the dearer lines sell out more quickly than the cheaper ones. And the big department stores are noticeably more opulent and well-stocked than in my other towns.

In nearly every home, spotlessly tidy, you find the same kinds of modern furniture, comfortable rather than elegant. Antique furniture has no great appeal. Similarly, most people live in relatively modern homes: there is not the middle-class vogue, so common in Toulouse and even in Newcastle, for commuting from some elegantly restored mansion or farmhouse just out of town. One reason is that old dwellings of character are hard to come by: those in the city were mostly bombed to bits, and those outside are still occupied by farmers or the squirearchy. But it also seems that Swabians, rather like Americans, prefer modern to antiquated surroundings – whatever their feeling for local tradition. Trendy young couples live each in the same kind of spruce little modern flats, with their stereo sets and other gadgets; older or wealthier families have spacious villas with gardens on hillsides, where panoramic windows look out over the hills, woods and vineyards – a touch of San Francisco. The solidity and comfort of housing, if not always its taste, is well above that of my other towns.

This applies equally at working-class level. I visited several working families in the suburbs. The first – a joiner aged thirty-eight with a wife and small daughter – lived in a pleasant modern four-roomed flat, with fitted carpet, central heating, refrigerator. The husband's hours were from 7 a.m. to 4.15 p.m. and he earned 1,900 DM a month; his wife worked in a butcher's shop, bringing in another 1,000 DM. "We have a VW 'beetle'," he said, "and an allotment garden out of town where we go a lot at weekends. We also spend our leisure watching the more serious programmes on television, or reading. For our holidays we went to Norway this year, and Holland before that, taking the car and camping."

A second family, a textile worker aged fifty with wife and son, lived in an older pre-war flat, of lower quality. With its poky rooms and aspidistra in the front parlour, I felt I might be in an older quarter of Newcastle. The heating was by coal stove, and the family washed mainly in the kitchen as there was no bathroom save a communal one down the corridor. But the controlled rent was low, only 160 DM a month. The father's monthly salary was 1,300 DM. He said, "For our leisure, we go hiking at the weekends, and to Mozart and Wagner at the opera. I also belong to a singing club and a handball club. We have no car." A third family, more up-market, belonged to the new blue-collar élite: the husband, in his forties, was a technician at Daimler-Benz, earning 3,000 DM. They had a well-built four-room flat, in a new block, with every modern appliance, and everything scrubbed clean including the four well-mannered blond children – a model family of the new Germany. The husband, in perfect English, said, "I work hard, leaving home at 7.30 and getting back after six. But we have a full leisure life. We go hiking and swimming, and get free tickets to the civic pools because we have four children. We go to the ballet and opera too. I get the usual four weeks' holiday, and this year we took a package tour to the Rumanian coast. We get a total of 200 DM a month in family allowances, and I pay 520 DM a month for the flat. Yes, we are happy and prosperous, far more than we could have imagined twenty years ago. But some of our friends are worried about unemployment."

How do Swabians spend their leisure? Rather than just relax, they like to be active and useful. Predictably, the favourite pastime is do-it-yourself improvement of the home: *schaffe, schaffe. . . .* Next in popularity are various cultural pursuits and, of course, TV-watching. Outdoor exercise has become something of a cult, but the accent is less on competitive sports than on long hikes, swimming, gymnastics, even assault-courses in the woods, or other activities with a keep-fit rationale. Sport, like culture or housework, is a tool for self-improvement, and I cannot see Swabians taking to a near-static sport like the *boules* so adored in Toulouse. However, they do also spend some leisure time less earnestly, singing and drinking in wine pubs and beer-halls.

As for eating and restaurant-going – one of my own special sports, therefore given a generous amount of space in this book – I quickly realised that Swabians eat to live rather than live to eat. Gastronomically they are less barbaric than Geordies, but one cannot put it higher than that. As in Toulouse, lunch is still the main meal of the day – often a stew or *Schnitzel,* or some local dish of beef with dumplings and *Sauerkraut.* Mid-morning or mid-afternoon, or both, this is often supplemented with sticky cakes or buns, *Torte* or *Strudeln* – indulgences that help explain the shape of local waistlines. However, the evening meal, *Abendbrot,* is what its name suggests: a light cold supper of bread with sliced meats, cheese, pickles, fruit. Even when entertaining guests, Swabians tend to stick to this formula, that would horrify a Toulousain or Bolognese: at the most lavish and sophisticated dinner-parties I attended, we were offered maybe smoked salmon and Finnish reindeer on the meat-platter, but never anything hot, and never a complicated *hors d'oeuvre* or sweet. Without necessarily meaning to be stingy, Swabians show little refinement about the way they entertain, and even if spending 60 DM a head in a luxury restaurant they will think it bad form to comment on the quality of the meal as a Frenchman does. Or rather, it would not occur to them. A tycoon once paid me the compliment of lunching me in the leading hotel: but he offered me no first course or sweet, just a main dish, and gave me no more to drink than one glass of wine. A Swabian lady who had spent some years in France told me she found these attitudes shaming: "A company director and his wife once asked my husband and me to dinner at home. These gave us cold meat and cheese, and sardines left in their tin. I retaliated by inviting them to a slap-up four-course French meal, which the husband devoured greedily while his wife commented sourly, '*Liebling,* you're never as hungry as that at home.' "

Yet Swabia does have its own speciality dishes, and some restaurants feature them. As in other parts of Germany, the cooking may be too heavy and bland for some foreign tastes, but it has its own subtlety. I enjoyed the ubiquitous *Spätzle* (crinkly flour noodles), as common as spaghetti in Italy and just as delicious when properly *handgemachte*; and I went with pleasure to the *Stüble ('bistro')* in the basement of the smart Zeppelin Hotel, where the décor is folksy and the menu drenched in coy jokes in Swabian dialect ("*Ebbes Warms en Bauch*" – "something hot in your tum") but some of the local dishes are remarkable, for example *Maultaschen* (a soup of spinach ravioli). The best true Swabian cooking is found out of town, in old inns in the suburbs or among terraced vineyards in the winding valleys, and here families drive out for huge Sunday lunches. But there is a hazard: *Sauerkraut* is a local industry, and in autumn when the cabbages have been cut and left to mature on the wide plains, the wind can carry their peculiar acrid stench for miles and spoil any excursion.

In central Stuttgart – as in Newcastle – foreign restaurants easily outnumber indigenous ones. Variety is seldom matched by quality; but at least, if you wish, you can eat Brazilian or Bulgarian, Indonesian or Israeli. Most numerous are the places – Greek, Italian, Spanish, Yugoslav – that are run by ex-*Gastarbeiter* and basically serve those minorities. You can squeeze yourself between large parties of Spaniards to enjoy *zarzuela* or gambas *al ajillo,* or join the Bosnians from Porsche and Bosch with their *djuveč* and *čevapčiči* and never guess you are not in Sarajevo. However, authenticity does not always survive so well. Many young Germans have today decided – like the British – that exotic foreign eateries can be more "amusing" than their staple *Gastätte;* and some immigrant restaurateurs have astutely cashed in on this vogue and adapted to a well-heeled German clientèle – with variable results. At the Pireus "*taverna*", the Greek food has been

Germanised to please local taste – monstrously, for Swabians will not abide garlic and prefer their own mushy salads to a true *horiatiki.* Nor does an Englishman find it appetising to read a Greek menu in German – who fancies *moussaka* when it is called *Exotisches Gericht mit geschnitzelten Schweinfiletspizen, uberbacken*? Yet an Englishman must beware of casting brickbats, for along with the Turks, Serbs and Sicilians, another poor nation from outer Europe has now lent its own *exotische* touch to Stuttgart: yes, there is a Watney's Pub here, complete with piped music and horrible coffee, its décor the same Victorian pastiche as in the so-called "pubs" in Paris.

Stuttgart's smarter restaurants are marked by deftly professional service, slick presentation, large helpings, and cooking that is usually very competent provided it does not fall into the trap of attempting French *haute cuisine.* This, as in Newcastle, is quite beyond local ken, and even if the chef is French he will probably betray his birthright and try to adapt to local taste. Some of the city's luxury restaurants disguise phoney "French" cooking with elaborate frills, and their pretentiousness is comic: at the aptly named Exquisit, I wondered whether professional flower-decorators had been hired to adorn the meat dishes so daintily with their patterns of chopped fruit and vegetables, tasting of nothing. American influences, however, are more assimilable than French; and Stuttgart like other German cities now has its breezy modern-style restaurants, up-dated versions of the traditional *Keller* yet also half-cousins to the Parisian "drugstore", with much the same ritzy décor, soft music, and effusively written menus. The largest and most typical place is the multiple-eatery on the Kleine Schlossplatz run by Möwenpick, the Swiss chain. It is confident and crowded, and has the most metropolitan atmosphere of any restaurant in any of my towns: without stretching credulity, you could imagine yourself to be on the Champs-Elysées. The décor with its pastiche of London street-signs may look like yesterday's imitation of Carnaby Street, and the glossy midatlantic menu may outdo *les drugstores* of Paris in absurdity ("*Big Boy Beefy – Zwei Beefies aus frischem, reinem Rindfleisch, mit goldbraun getoasteten Buns*", etc): yet the food, in its own way, does taste good. And the service, as nearly always in Stuttgart, is brisk but courteous and efficient. Waitresses in Germany look as if they like their job and even know how to do it – a contrast with the sloppy amateurism so common in Newcastle. This professionalism goes down to the simplest level, to the flourish with which you are served *Currywurst*-and-chips from a street-stall, or *Leberkäs* at a quick-lunch counter. The salesmanlike slickness has an American quality: indeed, I am never surprised that Americans tend to feel more at home in modern Germany than elsewhere in Europe, even Britain.

Stuttgart has a plentiful variety of *cafés,* bars and beer-houses with easy licensing laws – for the visitor like myself, a pleasant change after Bologna, not to mention Newcastlle, where it was hard to find anywhere to sit in comfort during the day. Schapmann on the Königstrasse is a large, elegant tearoom/*café-Konditorei* in the true Mittel-Europa tradition, with echoes of Vienna's Sacher or Budapest's Vorosmarty: here the ample ladies of the *bourgeoisie* come in force, in their felt hats and perms, to sit on velvet-upholstered Louis XV-style chairs under the chandeliers and indulge in creamy *Torte* and gossip. Nearby, a few intimate *Weinstuben* have somehow survived the bombing and thus kept intact their old décor of dark wood panelling, and here younger professional people come to drink (at 4 Marks a glass!) the local wines, sweetish, mild and fruity. For the less sophisticated there are the usual large German beer-halls, where the rhythm of the swaying bodies, arms interlocked, grows more intense as the evening wears on, and even the live band is drowned by the bellowing of *"Eins, Zwei, Gsuffa"* from four hundred throats. Munich does this far better, but Stuttgart tries to keep its end up.

Night-life in the Pigalle or Mayfair sense is less active, needless to say. Stuttgart dutifully has its night-spots with such names as Moulin Rouge and Tiffany, and there is even a Casino de Paris, advertising "Striptease und Sexfilms mit non-stop Erotic-Sex Revue". Such places fulfil a need for visiting businessmen, I suppose, but Swabians are not interested, and I doubt any latterday Sally Bowles will ever win world fame here. The one or two late-night bars I visited were empty and dreary. Stuttgart does have one licensed brothel, the Dreifarbenhaus (House of Three Colours), close to the *Rathaus*: prostitutes may also solicit in the foyers of some big hotels, but are banned from the streets. Beyond this, no glimmer of a Reeperbahn exists.

Discothèques too are far fewer than in Toulouse or on Tyneside, and none is even trying to be fashionable. Swabians have other things to do: students and other young unmarrieds usually live with their parents and, like them, are early-to-bed-early-to-rise. The advantage of this low-keyed night-life is that the studenty discothèques that do exist tend to be pleasantly unpretentious and unfrenetic. I grew fond of the Tangente, a small and sympathetic club with a dance-floor in one corner – a place where you can actually see and hear the person you are trying to talk to. Here students and others meet to discuss endlessly such topics as the university malaise, graduate unemployment, and the influence on Swabian youth of the Baader-Meinhof terrorists who died here in a Stuttgart jail. Topics for the next section.

8

Academic reform and student anxiety

The main building of the University lie in the centre of town, and the number of students, 9,500, is little less than at Oxford. Yet you hardly notice them. Stuttgart has almost none of the atmosphere of a university town: indeed, unlike Toulouse or Bologna, it is not one in any traditional sense. The one ancient and famous seat of learning in the area is at Tübingen, 25 miles away: Stuttgart's university is a former technical college, upgraded only in 1967. The accent is on engineering and other applied sciences: arts faculties are small, and some disciplines do not exist at all. Most students live with their parents, work doggedly, and are not very gregarious or politically minded. This university therefore exemplifies less clearly than older, larger or more tubulent ones – such as Frankfurt or Heidelberg – the crisis that over the past decade or so has engulfed higher education in Germany almost as much as in France.

Yet the problems, being largely structural, are nation-wide; and they do exist here too. The noble 19th-century German concept of universities as secluded centres of pure scholarship is being forced to adapt to a more utilitarian and egalitarian age, where escalating student numbers have not been matched by an increase in funds and facilities, and where reforms in curricula and teaching methods have not kept pace with changes in the economy and society. As in many other countries, radical students and conservative teachers are at war over what should be done. In Stuttgart, the noise of this battle is muted, but it can be heard – and I was repeatedly struck by the contrast between the dynamism of industry and local government, and the dispirited, antiquated ambience of the university.

As in all Germany, higher education is the *Land*'s responsibility. The Federal Government provides some of the finance and has recently increased its powers of coordination: but the *Land* remains the effective master, appointing senior staff and dictating how budgets should be spent. German decentralisation thus stops well short of university autonomy, and in Stuttgart there is a running feud between *Land* and university authorities, with the latter complaining not only of inadequate funds but also that "the bureaucrats in the *Kulturministerium* do not understand our problems". One teacher told me, "If I want a new tape-recorder, it has to be approved by the *Landtag*'s finance committee, and that can take months." Fortunately, the university can call on local industry for some of its funding, for research: Germany has a strong tradition of university/industry collaboration, and many students do practical courses in local firms. But most of the budget comes from the *Land* and is plainly inadequate. A new and pleasant campus has now been built in the suburbs, as overspill, but the main down-town campus is a disgrace. Students work cramped together in gloomy buildings, some of them converted Victorian office blocks; there is no hint of grace or greenery. A common complaint I heard was, "This, the richest *Land* in Germany, can spend so much money on opera, hospitals and so on – so why is the university treated as a poor relation?"

One answer is that Germany as a whole is still deciding what it wants its universities to be. How far is the old authoritarian structure to be replaced? Traditionally, professors in Germany are little gods, with huge freedom and prestige: according to one survey, Germans rate them as the most honoured of any profession. Universities have always been run on strict hierarchic lines, and Stuttgart has inherited this system whereby the Rector is a paternal figure, lording it over assistants who do what he tells them. This has recently been modified by a reform setting up a new governing body where junior staff and some students are represented. But old habits do not die easily.

Certainly student-teacher relations have loosened up, in the wake of the 1968 crisis, and they are much easier than, for instance, in Toulouse. There is no English-style tutorial system but more younger teachers are now making efforts to get to know their students individually, and if there is not more contact it is often because students themselves are reticent or senior professors still aloof. In the architecture faculty, which has a good reputation and some famous teachers, a girl student told me, "We are 700, with 10 professors and 70 assistants. We have good links with the latter, but most professors are too busy making money on outside jobs to give us much time. I meet mine briefly four times a year." She and her colleagues worked in a shabby room in a state of matey chaos, and they all complained of lack of guidance and supervision from the senior staff.

Many students also resent what they see as unfairnesses in the selective entry system – a stormy issue in Germany as in many countries. The university has been trying to keep numbers down, in the interests of quality: the *Land*, electorally sensitive to the popular pressure for more places, has been trying to increase them. In the 1960s and early 1970s numbers did rise fast, and matters were aggravated by the liberal German tradition whereby a student, once admitted, can stay as long as he wishes, spinning out a four-year course to six or seven years if he fears exam failure. However, Bonn recently has imposed a national *numerus clausus* system, a little similar to that in Britain: the high school leaving exam *(Abitur)* is no longer the automatic passport to any university, but each faculty can set its own minimum grade for entry and thus to an extent control its numbers. But the British formula has more humane flexibility; Germany's has been criticised, not only by students, for its mathematical impersonality which can lead to injustices, and also for the arbitrary variations between *Länder*. In 1978 controversial new Federal reforms reduced these variations; they also limited the period of study for a degree to four years, and banned student unions and other student bodies from expressing political views. This was greeted with fury, if less in Stuttgart than in many places.

The students are preoccupied with passing exams and preparing their careers – especially now that jobs are scarce – and they are rarely interested in trying to help make the university a livelier place. As elsewhere in Europe, they are now invited to participate formally in its government, and reforms have given them three seats on the Senate: but their role there tends to be passive. Only a small minority of Stuttgart students are politically active, fewer than in most German universities. Leftish militancy flared up briefly, as elsewhere, in 1968-9 but has now died down again. On the fringe there still exist a few extreme-Left groups, Maoists and others, often not on speaking terms with each other. These APOs, as they are known (the terms stands for "extra-parliamentary opposition"), are despised by the main body of students. A young liberal told me, "I used to belong to an APO group, but I found that they talk too much and achieve nothing. They have no positive arguments and are not realistic." A common objection to them is that, while denouncing the entire *bourgeois* world as "fascist", they themselves are highly fascistic in many of their attitudes and methods, and these avowed haters of Nazism are thus the very people who symptomise a revival of Nazi tendencies. Sympathy for the new terrorism has been more limited in Stuttgart than most cities: it was no more than juridical chance that brought Andreas Baader, Gudrun Esslin, Ulrike Meinhof and their friends to be imprisoned in this mild city. When they killed themselves, there was general relief, coupled with anxiety about the possible reopening of old wounds in German society (see below).

Being a new university with no great reputation, Stuttgart attracts relatively few students from other parts of Germany. The student body is made up mostly of phlegmatic Swabians, living quietly with their families, working hard at technical subjects, rather than at those which tend to generate radicalism, such as sociology and economics. Hence university life is neither very political nor very gregarious. Student *cafés* are few; clubs and societies are rarer even than in Toulouse. Once in the Königstrasse I was surprised to see a cohort of twelve students in red-and-black uniforms with swords, singing lustily, marching along with a touch of menace. This, I was told, was one of the traditional German *Verbindungen,* exclusive student fraternities devoted to duelling and beer-drinking. It had come from Tübingen. These bodies still exist, lingeringly, in some older universities, but not in Stuttgart. The new generation is little interested in such reactionary folklore, and the Right is even less present than the Left. Most students keep to little circles of friends they have known since childhood and do not readily make new ones. Thus those who come here from other cities may feel isolated and rejected, unable to find the easy camaraderie and club-life that is such a feature of Newcastle University.

Schools, like universities, are mainly the responsibility of the *Land,* which appoints the teachers and doles out the money. The school world in Germany has been much less agitated since 1968 than in France or Italy: indeed, as far as the academic side is concerned, the average Stuttgart *Gymnasium* (equivalent of *lycée* or grammar school) may seem at first sight to mark a happy medium between the English and French systems. Teachers have higher prestige than in Britain and are much better paid; the teaching is more rigorous, and the curriculum more exhaustive. One group of English sixth-formers on an exchange visit were amazed to find that their Stuttgart counterparts knew more about English history and institutions than they did themselves. At the same time, teaching is more informal and less narrowly academic than in France. A teacher whose *Gymnasium* has regular exchanges with a *lycée* in Nantes told me, "It's a matter of the difference between their deductive methods and our inductive ones, closer to the Anglo-Saxon. In France, the answer is already on the blackboard: here, the teacher leads the class to work it out for themselves." At a girls' *Gymnasium,* where one senior class had exchanges with a *lycée* in Clermont-Ferrand, they were most articulate about the differences, as they saw them: "In French schools, pupils are made to work harder and have to learn more by heart. The *baccalauréat* is certainly more difficult than the *Abitur.* In France, the teacher lectures his class, as at a university; here, we are expected to join in and use our initiative. The teacher will ask us whether we agree with him and even encourages us to interrupt. Teacher/pupil links are certainly closer and easier here than in France, where there is more authoritarianism and also more conflict. Our system is better." I noted too how tidy and orderly the school was, with no graffiti and everyone neatly dressed – so unlike the average *lycée.*

However, the German system has come under growing criticism in recent years. Teaching methods may be modern by French standards, yet many people judge that the subject-matter is too old-fashioned, too rigidly geared to exams. "We are taught about French troubadours but not much about modern France," said one pupil. Many textbooks have not been revised for decades, and their content is in the charge of bureaucrats in the *Land* education ministry who do not always appreciate real school needs. Reform, however, is slow.

Another important contrast is that, compared with Newcastle, though not with Toulouse or Bologna, the average Stuttgart secondary school is a utilitarian place, devoted to academic instruction but not to character-building or extramural interests. The Dillmann *Gymnasium,* Stuttgart's most distinguished, counts Kurt Kiesinger, Klett and Münchinger among its famous old-boys. I found it an orderly place, with a reasonably friendly atmosphere, but with few amenities except academic ones. There was not even any big school hall for concerts or speech days. This, I was told, is because the *Land* government will not pay for "extras", and schools lack their own budgets for such things. All pupils do two hours' sport and two hours' music a week, as part of their studies. Dillmann also has a school orchestra, which is popular, and a small drama group, but there are few other extra-mural activities.

Classes end before lunch, and after this the school is largely deserted: boys do their study at home. A teacher added: "Another contrast with Britain is that, though we teach civics in class, we do not use the school as a community for practical training in democracy. The boys elect their representatives, whom we now allow to discuss with the staff some aspects of school policy – that's new. But we have no equivalent to your 'prefects'. We are closer to the French here."

One world-famous school in Stuttgart has tried, with success, to break away from the traditional German model and create something different. In the 1920s a young Austrian, Rudolph Steiner, came to Stuttgart and founded the Waldorfschule, prototype of the Steiner schools that have since been founded elsewhere in Germany and abroad. Their influence has been world-wide. The Waldorfschule stands on the crest of one of the steep hills above the city centre. It puts the emphasis less on academic work and exams than on culture of all sorts, handicrafts, and group activities. Drama and various forms of free expression are taught in class, and children are encouraged to feel they belong to a living community. There is no streaming of clever children into special classes: an age-group stays together, moving up the school as one class, with the same teacher all the time. The teacher thus becomes a kind of foster-parent who gets to know each pupil closely. This system, so unusual for Germany, is admired by many Stuttgart intellectuals and professional people, who send their children to the school. They claim that it provides a happier and more creative environment than a classic *Gymnasium,* and that this outweighs the possible drawbacks of lack of academic rigour. Many former pupils go into social work, or become artists, doctors or musicians.

In contrast to the Steiner system, in state schools there has been tight streaming from the age of ten, which often determines a child's career for the rest of his life. The tradition in Baden-Württemberg has been that ten-year-olds all take an exam as they leave primary school: those who do well can enter a *Gymnasium,* while others go on to middle or junior secondary schools. Those who leave school at fifteen or sixteen have scope for vocational further education, but only at a *Gymnasium* can one take the *Abitur,* sole gateway to the universities. And it is not easy for a late developer to switch to a *Gymnasium* at fifteen or so. In the light of modern educational theory the system has been criticised for its rigidity, and also for social unfairness: though tuition in *Gymnasien* is more or less free, many workers' families still feel inhibited from sending their children there, however intelligent.

So pressures grew in the 1960s for the introduction of "comprehensive" secondary schools, rather as in Britain. The Brandt Government pronounced in their favour in 1969, and left it to the *Länder* to introduce them at their discretion. The more Left-wing ones did so fairly rapidly. But the more conservative, including Baden-Württemberg, found all kinds of pretexts for delaying the scheme, under pressure from middle-class parents as well as from teachers fearing a decline in academic standards if *Gymnasien* and junior schools were merged. And thus, in 1975 or so, Stuttgart was only beginning to piece together, experimentally, its first *Gesamtschule* (comprehensives). It is a familiar story, in many countries.

And the pupils and students themselves – how do they feel about their education and their future? The spirit of revolt or alienation that informs so much of modern youth today is less acute here than in most parts of Europe, yet it has begun to percolate. For the past decade or so, and notably since the unrest of 1968-9, many young Swabians have begun to question the authoritarian structure of their education, the relevance of their studies, and even the wisdom of their teachers and parents. And since about 1974 they inevitably have become affected by new factors: rising unemployment in Germany, and the much-publicised terrorism of a few young middle-class Germans. Direct sympathy for the terrorists is minimal, yet the malaise that led this minority to such extremism is more widespread. Efficient and prosperous Stuttgart may have suffered less from the employment crisis than almost any other part of Europe, yet even here young people – including graduates – are finding it harder to get jobs. A few turn to political activism: a larger number feel sullen, insecure, isolated, even apathetic. All the experts note that the powerful work ethic which inspired Germans through the post-war decades of recovery and expansion is today much less marked among the younger generation – even in Swabia. Spoilt by their background of comfort and prosperity, this new generation is growing listless and cannot quite share its elders' faith in the values of material progress. It is simultaneously anxious about finding jobs and not quite able to believe in the intrinsic virtues of hard work. All of this is a sadly familiar story in Europe today, and in Stuttgart it must be seen in perspective: young Swabians *are* still more hard-working, more disciplined, more attached to the old values than the average in Germany or elsewhere. Yet they are not immune to outside trends – and who knows how soon this will affect Stuttgart's industrial miracle?

8
The secrets of industrial harmony: co-management and paternalism

The specific Swabian talents are nowhere so evident as in industry. Here the Swabian is most impressively and wholeheartedly himself, and he manages to combine opposite qualities. He is a disciplined team-worker, but also a dynamic individualist; a dogged perfectionist, but also a creative pioneer. This is true equally of the factory manager and the shop-floor technician.

Today greater Stuttgart is the leading industrial area of Germany, after the Ruhr, and in some ways the most successful. Yet its industrial tradition is relatively recent: when Stephenson on Tyneside was inventing the railway-engine, this was still a poor agricultural region with just a few handicrafts. Then, as I described earlier, industry developed out of the sheer necessity of combatting starvation. From the late 19th century onwards their golden age of inventiveness was more spectacular even than Tyneside's had been – Daimler's combustion-engine has influenced the world far more than Stephenson's steam-engine. Zeppelin, Dornier and Messerschmitt, pioneers of the aircraft industry, were Swabians. The electric drill was created in Stuttgart. And a local firm invented the telephone at the same time as Bell: he however was the first to put it to use, and so took the credit.

Little specialised firms of many kinds grew up, in textiles, woodwork, watch-making, machine-tools and other branches of precision machinery. Each patiently developed its own pool of skilled labour. This diversification, plus the stress on quality rather than size, has helped Swabia through periods of recession. It survived the dark 1920s better than most parts of Germany because its specialised products were always in demand and did not depend on mass markets. After 1945, Stuttgart like the rest of Germany found that the destruction of war was something of a blessing in disguise: it gave Swabians the impetus to apply their fierce energy to rebuilding their industries from nothing and making them even better than before. The local factory-owners had mostly avoided joining the Nazi Party, and fewer of them thus suffered confiscation by the Allies than in areas such as the Ruhr. This continuity made recovery easier. Local industry was also given a boost in the post-war years by the arrival of industrialists from East Germany, attracted to the area by its excellent skilled labour. Zeiss, the famous Jena optics firm, was one of the refugee industries that now flourish in Stuttgart and have added to its diversity and skills.

One of the many remarkable aspects of the local industrial achievement is that it has run counter to modern gigantism and has managed to prove that small - or medium-small - is not only beautiful but profitable. In a post-war Europe where so many smaller firms have found survival only through merger with larger ones, Stuttgart has shown a different path to success, based on intelligent specialisation. One thriving local firm is a family concern that exports its liquid level indicators round the world, yet has a staff of only 200. This is not like the Ruhr, a region with huge factories: the only firms in the big league, with 25,000 workers or more, are Bosch and Daimler-Benz. Most of the rest are smallish companies with strong local roots, many still controlled by the families that founded them, basing their success on quality craftsmanship. An Englishman may look enviously at this record, which exemplifies many of the virtues that British industry has lost. How has it been done? One paradox is that it seems to be based on a marriage of two opposing styles of management: paternalism and co-partnership.

The typical local factory is likely to be owned and actively run by a self-made man, or the son of one. He probably works a 70-hour week, lives simply, and is far from the Left's bogey-image of the aloof cigar-smoking tycoon. He may earn 250,000 DM a year, but knows how to turn a lathe or adjust an engine and will readily go to the shop-floor to discuss technical details with his workmen. He wants to avoid his firm becoming too large for his personal daily supervision, and thus less efficient. He cares for profit but also - sincerely - for the welfare of his workers and has closer contact with them than is usual under capitalism. The workers, at least the older ones, respond by accepting this benevolent paternalism. They feel a close identity with their firm: many stay in the same one all their lives.

One such typical firm is Fein, makers of 120 varieties of power drills. Its main factory is near the centre of town. Hans W. Fein, chairman and managing director, sat me down in his ornate office full of vast leather armchairs and outsize silver ashtrays. His Swabian manner was as heavy as his furniture, but with occasional shafts of humour. Across one wall was a huge map of Peru, not a part of his export drive but proof of his social status: he is *Konsul* Fein. "My great-grandfather founded this firm in 1867 and he was a genius: he developed the first automatic coffee-machine, then invented the world's first electric drill and the first telephone" – a local Da Vinci. "Our plant was 80 per cent destroyed by bombing, and then the French removed most of our equipment. So we set to and rebuilt the whole place. Our family and their workers did it together: I remember my father mending windows and plastering walls, while the staff went on over the weekend without extra pay. Today the family still owns the whole firm. I put in a ten-hour day, often including Saturdays. We export 40 per cent of our goods, mainly within the EEC which has helped us a lot." A dynamic attitude to exports has always played a large part in Stuttgart firms' successes.

I asked Herr Fein about his workers. "We have 1,300 in our three factories, 300 of them *Gastarbeiter*. My staff have never been on strike – why should they? I treat them well and we trust each other. Over 150 of them have been with me at least 25 years. My staff work hard – a 42-hour week, from 7 a.m. to 4.15 p.m. Unions play a very small role in my company, but there's a works committee, compulsory by law, and this cooperates with me smoothly over working hours and conditions. I try to be generous: I pay well beyond the statutory six weeks' sick pay. And I take my staff into my confidence: one Sunday I invited fifty of my foremen for dinner in a local pub, where I explained my financial policies and asked for criticisms. Call it paternalism if you wish: but German workers do respond to this approach, more readily than in France or Britain."

One or two firms in Stuttgart are foreign-owned – such as IBM's big plant – but the majority were founded by local initiative, including the two leading ones, Robert Bosch and Daimler-Benz. The latter's origins have acquired the quality of legend. In 1885-6, while Gottlieb Daimler was inventing the petrol engine in a garden shed in Bad Canstatt, by a coincidence Karl Benz was pioneering his own engines at Mannheim, 80 miles away. The two inventors later associated, though their firms did not fully merge until 1960. In the second war, they were making aircraft for the Nazis. Today no members of the Daimler or Benz families are directly involved in the firm, which is now owned by the Deutsche Bank (28 per cent), the Flick financial group of Düsseldorf

(10 per cent), the Kuwait Government (14 per cent) and smaller shareholders. So who on earth was Mercedes? Answer: when in 1900 Daimler built a 35 h.p. family touring car, his sales manager, Emil Jellinek, named it after his daughter, Mercedes. To this day, all the firm's vehicles bear this name.

Daimler-Benz today employs about 100,000 workers in Germany, half of them at its two factories in the Stuttgart area. The firm's boast is that every car is custom-built and that no other make in the world is superior in comfort or safety to the Mercedes, which seems to have outstripped Cadillac and Rolls-Royce as *the* luxury saloon car, with the Pope and Mao among its clients of recent years. In turnover (though not in number of vehicles) Daimler-Benz is now the leading car firm in Europe; 45 per cent of its output is exported; it is the world's largest maker of heavy lorries. What is more, after the outbreak of the energy crisis, this was the only car firm in the world to increase its sales during 1974, and it has since been expanding fast. The management put this down to the fact that motorists now seek a durable car that will last at least ten years. The firm's overall record is certainly very impressive – and the directors and publicity staff never miss a chance to rub it in. Their sublime arrogance takes a lot of beating: to be conducted round the plant by a PR man is like being shown Buckingham Palace by a royal lady-in-waiting, and the visitor criticises at his peril. Other firms are regarded as non-existent: when I asked an executive what he thought of the latest Audi model, he claimed not to have heard of it. This kind of smooth conceit is untypical of Swabia, but indeed few of the directors or senior staff today are Swabians, and the firm no longer makes much contribution to the public or cultural life of Stuttgart as it did in the Daimler family's day. For this it is often criticised.

Daimler-Benz is an excellent employer in its own way, providing high wages, good working conditions, extensive welfare schemes, and a generous system of bonuses and profit-sharing, with incentives for workers to buy shares. The firm also seeks to inculcate loyalty into the staff at all levels: for example it runs apprentice schools and youth camps for junior workers, where organised group-singing and strength-through-joy activities (echoes of the past?) are geared to promoting the spirit of Daimler-Benz togetherness. A firm of this size cannot apply the same kind of family-style paternalism as a smaller concern such as Fein, yet it has been trying to break down the hierarchical divisions that breed class discontent. Assembly-line and clerical workers use the same canteen, shiningly clean and serving good cheap food, and many shop-floor workers own the latest Mercedes models, for one of the fringe benefits is a 21.5 per cent discount on such cars. The firm's strategy has always been to try to win the workers' loyalty with measures of this kind, while at the same time setting its face against an increase of co-management that might give the unions too much control over policy. One architect of this strategy was Hans Martin Schleyer, a full-time director who later became president of the German employers' federation and was kidnapped and killed by terrorists in 1977. Schleyer, a large assertive man with an ox-like face, was famous for his tough line with the unions as the man in charge of Daimler-Benz' personnel policy, and was described to me as "one of the last hard-core warriors of the class struggle". Small wonder that the terrorists later chose him as their principal victim. And incidentally, he was not a Swabian.

Daimler-Benz has a high level of union membership: 90 per cent, compared with the local average of 35 per cent. Yet even in this firm, unions are moderate and cooperative by most British, French or Italian standards. And throughout the Stuttgart area, strikes and other labour conflicts have been even fewer than in most other parts of Germany, ever since the war. So what are the reasons for this exemplary, and envied, industrial harmony? In Stuttgart, we can point to the success of benevolent paternalism, and to the relative absence of an entrenched proletariat as found in the Ruhr, while other factors are common to Germany as a whole. I discussed these with officials at the Baden-Württemberg branch of the German trades union federation, *Deutscher Gewerkschaftsbund* (DGB), where I found myself in an opulent oak-panelled office with a group of smartly-dressed executives. They could have been company directors in a board-room. The ambience was not that of the average trade-union office in Newcastle or Toulouse with its starkness and aura of class bitterness.

One official said to me: "Our trade unions believe that by co-operating with management, rather than fighting it, we have more chance of getting better pay and work conditions. And this has been borne out by results. We do not believe in revolution, we want to reform capitalism from within, and we see the society of the future as a balance between capitalist and social interests. One crucial factor is that German unions realised after the war that their failure to collaborate with the Weimar Republic had been one cause of the down-fall of our democracy. We learned our lesson: this time, we *must* participate. Today we have the most advanced concepts in Europe. We have gone beyond the class-war phase where the French, and especially the British, are still bogged down." I was told later, by an English friend, of a revealing incident. When some British workers came over to set up an Anglo-German exhibition, the British shop-stewards switched off the electric plant at 5 p.m., to prevent their German colleagues from working on through the night to get the exhibition ready in time, as they intended. The British did not want to be shown up. And the Germans were appalled. "A German worker," said my friend, "feels far more responsibility to his job."

The structure of German unions is also a factor behind the industrial harmony. They are not divided on political lines, as in France, nor splintered into hundreds of little craft unions, as in Britain. So they are seldom in rivalry. There are only 16 unions in Germany: thus in many firms all the manual workers belong to the same union, where in Britain there might be a score. At Bosch, in Stuttgart, all the skilled workers are represented by one single union, the metalworkers', one of the largest in the world, and this unity greatly simplifies collective bargaining. It helps to explain the absence of strikes, which in Britain are due so often to jealousies between unions.

The most important consideration of all is that workers, by law, are granted more say in the running of their firm than in almost any other western country. Workers in each factory have the right to elect a works council which has wide powers: employers must seek its agreement for any changes in working hours or conditions, and must consult it over redundancies and dismissals. The council also has the right to decide on welfare matters. In many firms, the council in practice enjoys more influence than the unions, and since strikes and lockouts are forbidden under the laws governing the councils, this is a further explanation for the rarity of strikes. At Bosch I was told, "Wildcat strikes hardly ever get the council's support. In this firm we have not had one for many years."

Since the early 1950s, workers in most larger firms have also had the right to one-third representation on its *Aufsichtsrat,* a consultative board which supervises management and in some cases appoints the managing director. The workers' delegates to this board, who are chosen by the works council and the unions, are privy to confidential information about the firm's finances and policies, which they must guarantee not to pass on to other workers. In practice the system has operated quite well, perhaps surprisingly so, and it does offer the unions a far more real sense of participation than they get, say, in

Britain or France: they have a chance to discuss their firm's commercial policy, even if the final decisions rest with management. The unions thus have a further incentive for siding with the establishment and avoiding strikes – "We are effectively suborned," one union leader admitted to me. In the mid-1970s, a controversial federal law was passed that extends this worker representation to full fifty-fifty parity with management in all firms with a staff of over 2,000, and this began to come into force in 1978 (a similar system has operated for some years in the coal and steel industries). Some of the big Stuttgart employers have expressed anxiety about this innovation, which they fear could lead to stalemate confrontations and hence loss of efficiency. But the unions have been pressing hard for it, and are keen to prove that they will use their new responsibilities in the firm's overall interests. The new co-partnership *(Mitbestimmung),* while increasing the power of the unions, is also likely to make them more than ever the accomplices of capitalist enterprise rather than – as in many other countries – its enemies.

The old family paternalism is gently in retreat, as firms grow larger and worker participation gathers strength. For the moment, Stuttgart appears to demonstrate a happy balance between two opposites – old-style paternalism and new-style co-partnership. But what will the future hold? The economic strains of the past few years have produced signs, notably in other parts of Germany, that the nation's envied *entente* between unions and employers may not last for ever: unions have been growing more demanding, strikes have become less rare. Swabia, as usual, is slower to change, yet here too there are portents. Strikes in Stuttgart's engineering industries, almost unknown in the 1960s, broke out seriously in 1971 and again in 1973 and 1978. This latter strike was for better working conditions: it lasted three weeks, and the employers finally gave in. The rise in unemployment since 1974 has again reduced the strike level, for the usual reason that workers fear losing jobs. But this in turn is a new anxiety. It is true that Stuttgart, because of the structure of its industry, has been able to withstand the employment crisis better than most other parts of Germany: it depends less on sales of mass-consumer products than of capital equipment and luxury and precision goods. By the end of 1977 unemployment was still at only 3 per cent, against a national average of 4.5 per cent. Yet Swabians for many years had grown used to full employment and an easy plethora of jobs. Today, many of them have the feeling that the post-war era has ended and new uncertainties lie ahead.

9

"Partner to the world" – but "guests" are not always invited

The pub was down a dimly lit side-street in a factory district, close to the Bosch works. Owned by a local brewery, it looked from the outside typically Swabian. But from a hundred yards away I could hear the bouzouki music, and inside the noise from the three-piece band was deafening. The place was sparsely furnished, with no more décor than some posters of Athens and of ruined temples by the sea, and notices in Greek (not always obeyed), "Smashing glasses is forbidden". A *doner-kebab* turned on a spit. I was the only non-Greek present. The publican was from Corinth, and his clients, *Gastarbeiter* all, had made the place their own. This Saturday night, they were there in force, mostly young men who had come to Germany without their girls – sad-looking, in a way, for all their boisterous singing and sirtaki-dancing. A large blonde woman who worked in a local piano factory sang something by Theodorakis. Against one wall there sat a family of four generations, from old peasant granny in black to baby son, born in exile. Exchange the Swabian winter fog for a warm velvet night full of stars and cicada, and we might all have been in some Attic village.

I was taken to this pub by a shy young couple from Salonika who had been in Stuttgart for five years. Both worked in the nearby piano factory. The man said, "My old mother has made the sacrifice of leaving my father in Greece and coming to look after our baby girl here, so that my wife and I can both earn. We are saving up to help grandpa pay off his debts so that one day we can all buy a farm near Salonika and settle there. Here we can each earn over 1,500 DM a month, and we save half of it. We've found a small flat in a suburb full of Greeks, with a Greek laundry, a Greek *café* and shops – quite a Greek village. The Germans we meet are polite to us in our work but ignore us socially. We're not unhappy here but we just live for the day we can afford to go back home. Then my wife won't have to go out to work any more. She'll be a lady!"

Stuttgart has thousands of such immigrant families – European exiles in the heart of Europe. This may be in many respects the most outward-looking and international-minded of my towns: it is actively twinned with several cities, from St Louis to Bombay; its daily business links are world-wide; and most of its citizens, if asked, would assure you they believe in some kind of a united Europe. Yet in practice they shun and despise the Europe that is in their midst – the Mediterranean immigrants (some 80,000 here) who give the city its most evident cosmopolitan flavour. You see them everywhere in the centre of town and especially at the main station on Sundays, men and women with the dark complexions of the south, mostly speaking only a few words of German – "guest workers" who have provided the "economic miracle" with its essential manual labour and who benefit from it, yet are kept on the margin of a society that dreads to assimilate them.

Much has been written about the injustices done to the immigrant workers in Europe, especially in Germany where they are most numerous. They are said to be forming a new "sub-proletariat", well-paid, but often badly housed in barrack-like hostels, and culture-shocked by alienation in a land that offers no warmth of welcome to its "guests". There is truth in all this, but it might be worth stressing the positive side too. Socially, the Swabians treat these newcomers with polite indifference rather than active hostility, so there are few of the open conflicts that you find in a land – such as Britain – with a higher degree of integration. The workers come voluntarily and often stay many years, attracted by being able to earn as much in a week as they could in a year in Turkey or Serbia. Some take the menial jobs – as gravediggers, roadbuilders, rubbish-collectors – that the Swabians now refuse to do: but many others, in factories, soon acquire semi-skilled or even skilled positions. And this suits both sides. Local industry gets the labour it needs to maintain its growth. And the governments of the poorer "donor" countries eagerly support the emigration for several reasons: it reduces their own unemployment, it earns foreign currency, and it provides free training. A worker will bring home not only valued Deutschmarks but also, eventually, skills learned in modern factories that he could have never have picked up in his homeland. Therefore several countries, including Spain, Turkey and Yugoslavia, signed official agreements with Germany during the boom years, for organising and stimulating this human traffic. And a Stuttgart firm wanting new labour could, via the Federal Labour

Office, notify its needs to German consulates abroad who would then do the recruiting. In theory no worker can arrive without a job prearranged in this way (except for EEC nationals, most of them Italian, who have free movement); but in reality many people from non-EEC countries, notably Yugoslavia, have come in as tourists, found a job on the spot, and then managed to stay indefinitely.

Since 1974, when unemployment began to rise in Germany, there has been an official cut-back on new recruitment, and some foreign workers have even been sent home. From June 1974 to December 1975 their total numbers in Baden-Württemberg fell from 577,000 to 460,000. But this, the richest of the *Länder,* still has a higher proportion of them than any other. In the Stuttgart area, one worker in five is a foreigner and many bring their families with them. Italians are the most numerous group, closely followed by Yugoslavs, then Turks, Greeks, a few Iberians, and fewer North Africans. The Yugoslavs are regarded by employers as the most educated and intelligent workers; but nearly all *Gastarbeiter* are appreciated for their cheerfulness, willingness and hard work. "A South Italian will work just as hard and well as a Swabian, once he leaves his own *far-niente* environment and joins ours," said one factory owner, who told me of a Neapolitan putting in five hours' overtime a day. Some smaller firms, it is true, try to hire the foreigners at cut rates: but most reputable ones obey the law and offer the same wages and benefits as to their German staff. In larger firms such as Bosch, the immigrants also have their own delegates on the works council, and rarely is there any factory-floor friction with Germans. Herr Fein told me, "Italian women arrive here unskilled and we train them. Many stay ten years or more. They get on with our German staff, but sometimes there is trouble in their own ranks if they come from different parts of Italy." In the main Bosch workshops, where a third of the work force is foreign, I found that all the notices were in Greek and Italian as well as German. Rows of dark-eyed girls were fitting pieces onto car-starters along a conveyor-belt. A *signora* from Trento told me that conditions and pay (400 DM a week) were good, but the work was boring and she felt homesick. A proud-looking Thracian told me she pined for her baby son who was living back home with her parents so that she and her husband could both work and save here.

But it is outside the factory that the *Gastarbeiter* feels his or her condition most keenly – especially the single men, who are the majority. By law an employer is obliged to provide bachelor foreign workers with somewhere to live, and most of the better firms such as Bosch and Daimler-Benz have built hostels which at least are clean, if spartan. But in the case of many smaller firms, especially in the building trade, the workers sleep cramped together in dirty barrack-like dormitories. Several nationalities may share a room, and often there are fights and thefts. Employers sometimes allege that the poor conditions are not their fault, for the men want to save their money and refuse to pay more than the minimum in rent. There is some truth in this: if the immigrant were readier to spend what he earns, his life could be a little less cheerless – but only to an extent. There is not much he can do with his leisure. Very few German girls will be seen in his company, and single girls of his own nationality are not numerous. After work, he returns to his dismal dormitory, or drinks a beer with friends in one of the few pubs that will let him feel at home. On Sundays, hundreds of *Gastarbeiter* comgregate in the big hall of the *Hauptbahnhof* which takes on something of the ambience of a Mediterranean town square. Shops of all kinds are open there all day. The worker can buy his national newspapers, and the trains coming and going from Istanbul, Athens or Naples give a nostalgic hint of home.

About 10 per cent of workers bring their families with them, mostly Italians. They are rarely provided with housing by their firm and often have trouble in finding somewhere suitable, for orderly Swabian landlords dislike letting to noisy southerners. The immigrants tend to move into outer suburbs where rents are lower, and there they group into national colonies, making little contact with German life save that their kids go to the local schools. In some schools more than a quarter of the children are foreign, and this causes some of the same resentments as in parts of Britain: in one case, the neighbours complained so much of *bambini* shouting in the playground that the police came along with decibel measures. The German authorities do at least make some efforts to help their "guests" to adapt to their new environment: there are welfare and advice centres, federally subsidised and most of them run by the Churches. But their influence is not great. Caritas, an international Catholic body, runs a *Centro Italiano* in downtown Stuttgart, a scruffy but friendly place with cafeteria, games room, chapel, and so on. The director, a young Sardinian, told me: "We spend much of our time trying to protect the teenage workers. Often the girls come to Germany to get away from their families and have fun – and they land up pregnant. We are against abortion, so what can we do? To send the girl back to her family, at least if it's the south, might destroy her.

Luckily the Stuttgart authorities pay for the babies to go into foster-homes, in such cases." He went on: "We hold 'socials' in this centre, to try to help Italians to integrate a bit into German life. But it's very hard to get young Germans to come here to meet them. As for the older Germans, I have the feeling that many of them still despise Italy as the wartime ally that betrayed them. They like us less than they do the British or Americans who were merely enemies."

Maybe he was unduly sensitive. It is probably fair to say that the average Swabian accepts the *Gastarbeiter,* of whatever race, as a necessary nuisance, useful to the economy, but to be seen and not heard. The visitor is left alone in peace, so long as his emotional exuberance does not too openly provoke the Swabian sense of order. He is not invited to take part in German social life: this is desired neither by the public nor by the authorities, who consider that moves towards integration could lead only to conflict and the "guests" should thus be treated as birds of passage, even if many of them stay some years. Non-EEC nationals may not, except in special cases, start businesses. *Gastarbeiter* thus make little apparent impact on Stuttgart life: it is the inverse of the situation in New York, where the pressures make it hard *not* to integrate. And it all seems rather a human waste, in a number of ways, for Stuttgart – as Klaus Hübner stressed to me – is depriving itself of the extra cultural variety and vitality that the immigrants could bring. They carry on their lively fiestas in their own little hideaways, but are seldom invited to perform in public.

Against non-Europeans, especially those of dark skin, the feeling is much more overt, and I regret to say that colour prejudice seems to be stronger in Stuttgart than any of my other towns. Africans and Asians, however personable, generally have trouble in finding lodgings. I was told, "You see, people are afraid of what the neighbours will say if they let a room to one of *them.*"

A liberal minority feels indignantly that these attitudes make a mockery of the city's cherished image of itself as *"Partner der Welt".* The city council however prefers to turn a blind eye to the segregation. And meanwhile it goes ahead wholeheartedly with its policy of town-twinnings, more active than in any of my other towns. Dr Klett, the former mayor, told me, "We believe that German cities have a political duty to foster these links with the world, after the tragedy of Nazism." He could have added that, in the post-war years, town-twinning was a means for German cities of regaining respectability. Thanks largely to his efforts, Stuttgart today has no less than eight twins, three of them outside Europe: St Louis, Bombay and Menzel Bourguiba. This last link is less an equal partnership than a form of aid to the Third World, with Stuttgart acting as rich godfather to the small Tunisian town: it has built a technical school there and pays for teacher-training courses. Of the European twinnings, the most successful is with Strasbourg, thanks partly to the proximity (80 miles) and also to the post-war emphasis that both France and Germany have placed on political reconciliation backed by human contacts. Dr Klett himself played a leading part in this national policy, as co-founder of the Franco-German mayors' union. His efforts bore fruit, and today there are some 700 Franco-German twinnings, twice as many as between France and Britain. Most of the initiative has come from the German side: Strasbourg itself resisted Stuttgart's overtures for some years in the 1950s. But today the twinning goes well, with frequent exchanges at a popular level – sporting, cultural and scholastic – as well as the mayoral ones. By contrast, Stuttgart's links with British towns – Cardiff and St Helen's – work less enthusiastically.

In fact, Stuttgart in many ways has closer relations with France – cultural and commercial, as well as civic – than with any other country. Ethnically Swabians are from the same stock as Alsatians, and many of them would say they feel closer in spirit to eastern France than, say, to Prussia. Francophilia in Stuttgart carries a certain cachet. The town has been carried along too by the tide of Franco-German reconciliation. The director of the large *Institut Français* told me: "We are not here just to spread French culture, as we might in Britain: French Institutes in Germany have an added political task too, because of the past. Our language courses, lectures and exhibitions have been geared towards the goal of reconciliation, and I think we have succeeded. There is little sign of enmity any more, except among a few older people. The younger generation have little sense of national frontiers and accept each other easily." With a few nuances, this is my own impression too. The regular French colony in Stuttgart numbers about six hundred, mostly businessmen and their families, while there are thousands of other shorter-term residents. Scores of Swabians have French wives, and most of these marriages work well. One of these wives, who has lived here for thirty years, told me, "There's no doubt that the French and Germans are becoming more similar to each other and want to get to know each other, though of course some of the old clichés linger – for instance, the Swabians believe, until they actually get to know us, that we're all lazy, disorganised and promiscuous. I think Franco-German social relations will finally become like those between Geneva and Zurich, two cities that retain their love-hate rivalries yet collaborate closely."

Stuttgart's youth exchange links are significantly closer with France than with Britain. At the Dillmann *Gymnasium* a teacher told me: "We are twinned with a *lycée* in Nantes, and every year we send a class there for two weeks in term-time and they come here for two weeks in July. I find these visits have an enormous influence: our pupils come back with not only their French improved but all their faculties widened. They exchange drama groups and orchestras too, and many parents have become friends. But we've not had exchanges yet with British schools. There seems less interest for this on the British side, and if we want to send pupils to Britain on visits we find it hard to place them with families." At a girls' *Gymnasium* in Bad Canstatt, German girls speaking perfect French told me of their exchanges with a girls' *lycée* in Clermont-Ferrand: "We enjoy these visits and get on well with the French, though they're different from us. Until sixteen, French girls are noticeably more sheltered and constricted by their parents than we are: then suddenly they become very free, more so than us. French girls are more interested in fashion and pleasure than we are, and less concerned with politics. They're more lively, but also more superficial." This *Gymnasium* too had no links with any British school. The girls told me that the Clermont-Ferrand *lycée* had recently broken off its exchanges with a girls' school in Lancashire, after French parents had complained that their daughters were being corrupted by contact with English permissiveness. There had been pregnancies. But they had no such qualms about sending their girls to safe Stuttgart.

Britain's official cultural presence in the city is slight compared with that of France: the British Council closed its branch some years ago, for reasons of economy, and the Anglo-German Society is none too active, whereas France has two flourishing cultural centres in the area. The sizeable British resident community, of businessmen and others, has good relations with the Swabians, though a most curious problem has arisen on the sidelines in very recent years – that of the British *Gastarbeiter*! In the mid-1970s, Britain's entry into the EEC free labour market coincided with the slump in the British economy, and some thousands of out-of-work Britons went off to skilled or unskilled factory jobs in Germany, attracted by the much higher wages. Some have come to the Stuttgart area. In most cases they get on perfectly well, and there are British technicians at Daimler-Benz who integrate easily. Elsewhere there has sometimes been trouble, either because a few unscrupulous German firms have exploited Britons unaware of their rights, or because Britons have not survived the culture-shock of facing up to German life. I heard stories of Glaswegians and Geordies arriving drunk at Stuttgart station, or objecting – not surprisingly – to being pushed into hostels with Greeks and Muslims where the canteen serves not fish-and-chips but *moussaka* and *dolmades.* A British consular official summed up the problem to me: "The Turk, Serb or Sicilian comes here with a certain humility, he is ready to work very hard, he knows he won't integrate, and he's looked after by inter-Government protocols. The Briton arrives with his usual insular arrogance towards 'Krauts' and other Continentals, he is much less prepared to work hard, and he has no official machinery to protect him, in what is now a totally free market. He can get a job in Stuttgart with as little red tape as in Birmingham, yet he may arrive totally unaware of German conditions and customs. The problem will sort itself out in time. For the moment, it's just one more aspect of the trauma of Britain's espousal of Europe."

As for the American presence in Stuttgart, the US Information Services run an Amerika Haus, one of sixteen such cultural centres in Germany. It is a good deal less active than twenty years ago, when the Americans were still busily "redemocratising" their zone. Today there are still some big US Army bases around Stuttgart, and you see the bored-looking GIs off duty, slouching along the main streets. As elsewhere in the world, US military policy is to keep as low as profile as possible, and the soldiers are encouraged to have minimal contact with the Swabians – so as to avoid incidents. This segregation has now been further encouraged by a new economic factor, the fall of the dollar, so that by an odd irony American forces and local Germans have been virtually exchanging roles since the early post-war years. Initially the Americans came in as rich and well-fed conquerors, finding the Germans eager to scrounge coffee or chocolate. Gradually this has changed, and with the rise of the *Deutschmark,* American service families have become much poorer than the local Germans. Sometimes they cannot even afford to go shopping in the supermarkets that formerly they would have spurned with contempt, and in order to make ends meet some service wives have been taking menial jobs as chars, like the lowest of the immigrant workers. And so the mighty victors of 1945, Americans as well as British, find themselves cap-in-hand as a species of *Gastarbeiter*.

The closest American-Swabian links today are those that spring from the large and long-established Swabian community in the United States that is still closely-knit and keeps up its ties with the homeland. Every year more than a thousand of them fly over by charter to the *Volksfest,* where they make certain to drink the most beer, sing the loudest choruses and wear the silliest hats of all. And they visit their relatives. Herr Single, president of the US Swabians' Society, had come to see his aunt and revisit the cottage where he had spent his childhood: "My father was an artisan and left in the 1920s, when I was twelve, as there was no work here. I'm now editor of the largest German-language paper in the New World, the *New York Zeitung,* selling 50,000 copies a day. We keep up the old traditions: the New York Canstatter *Volksfest* Society holds an annual festival in New Jersey, with imported Swabian beer and lots of song and sideshows – it's more elaborate than the *Volksfest* here. But I come here every year, and have a party with my old schoolchums of fifty years ago. I love Stuttgart."

Any Stuttgarter will claim that he is proud of his city's links with the world. He may point not only to the town-twinnings and the tradition of emigration, but also to the thousand or so foreign students at the university, especially numerous from Asian countries such as Iran. He may have become sceptical about the EEC in practice, but will still claim some faith in the ideal of a united Europe. Yet, though he wants to feel accepted and loved by the world, his actual curiosity about other countries may be less evident. Just as he has little desire for human contact with *Gastarbeiter,* so like a true provincial he is too content with his own way of life to show much real interest in other peoples'. When I was researching this book, Stuttgarters I met were keen to know what I thought of their city but very few asked me for my impressions of the others or what I saw as the differences. Once I arrived hot from Ljubljana, glowing with enthusiasm for the Slovenes, to be met either with total lack of interest or else, in the case of one good lady, with blank incredulity that there could be anything to admire about a horde of Balkan peasants sweating under Bolshevism. A university teacher, not a Swabian, commented to me: "This *Partner der Welt* slogan is really no more than an aspect of Stuttgart's self-regard."

This self-absorption appears even more significant in the context of the city's attitudes towards the rest of Germany. In a nation that has never been centralised, and since 1945 has lost its real capital, Stuttgart today finds there is no other German city whose leadership it acknowledges. Hamburg, Munich and Frankfurt may be larger or more internationally important, but they are certainly not regarded as in any way superior. When I asked Mayor Klett to what other town Stuttgart looks, he said, "In politics, inevitably to Bonn – but Bonn is only a village. Munich we admire for its culture, but it does not influence us." In fact, most Swabians tend to scorn their Bavarian neighbours as dirty, coarse and noisy – "The Balkans begin at Neu Ulm" (just across the *Land* frontier) is a local catch-phrase – and it is true that the villages generally are dirtier across the Danube in Bavaria. With their neighbours to the west, the lighthearted and French-influenced Badeners, the Swabians have a good-humoured rivalry and feel much in common. But north Germany to them is virtually a foreign land, more alien than Austria or German-speaking Switzerland. The Swabians' pull is all to the south, for ethnic and cultural reasons as well as climatic ones – the south is where they go on holiday, pouring across the Brenner or St-Gotthard into Goethe's "*Land wo die Zitronen blühn*". As for the north, it is true that the pre-war hatred and fear of Prussia has waned, now that most of that kingdom has disappeared behind the Iron Curtain and Berlin has been emasculated: and yet, confronted today with a Saxon or Holsteiner, a Swabian will find the dialect incomprehensible (and reciprocally) and the attitudes baffling. A Stuttgart charlady, who had just been to Schleswig for her son's wedding to a girl there, spoke to me as if the man had married a Mexican or Australian.

The post-war decades have seen two contradictory trends. On the one hand, the eclipse of Berlin and the strengthening of the *Länder* after 1945 have lent more power and self-sufficiency than before to *Land* capitals like Stuttgart. On the other, the flood of refugees from the East, the new German mobility and the growth of various modern influences have inevitably tended to bring cities closer to each other, to make them more aware of each other and more similar. It is a trend common to many countries. A Swabian may still feel very different from a northerner: but perhaps it is just because he has more contact that he is now more conscious of the differences. At least this is true of educated people: far more students, executives and so on are moving round Germany than before. In Stuttgart the main new influence, as I stated earlier, has been that of the 80,000 Silesians from the eastern zone, who have now integrated completely – save that few of them have learned to speak that secret local language, Swabian.

The central question is whether Stuttgart's relative degree of self-sufficiency – in local government, in culture, in many social matters and attitudes – is on balance an asset or a disadvantage, compared with the weaker position of the average British or French regional metropolis. In discussions about the future of the European Community it has often been argued that, as Europe moves haltingly towards some eventual integration, and as national sovereignties therefore dwindle, so not only will the regions assume more power and significance, but it will be essential for them to do so in order to provide smaller human-scale units that can balance the anonymity of the new larger one. The more Europe unites, the more important it will be psychologically as well as politically to have strong semi-autonomous regional units that can provide a regional focus for people's need for participation. Thus the German federal system, or indeed that of Switzerland or Yugoslavia, is sometimes held up as a model for Europe; and Italy, Britain and even France are already, in their various tentative ways, moving towards a slightly more regionalised pattern. This federal system clearly gives Stuttgart some advantages over Toulouse or Newcastle. People, perhaps without being greatly aware of it, do feel a little more control over their own destinies. Or at least, bureaucrats in Bonn are not resented quite as much as those of Whitehall or the rue de Rivoli: Stuttgart's lords and masters on the higher rung of government (the *Land*) are at least closely *in situ* within its own walls, in the *Landtag,* and not somewhere remote. Moreover, Stuttgart is large, rich and autonomous enough not only to attract high talent from outside but to retain much of its own (since there is no true German capital to entice it away). An ambitious young Stuttgarter, wanting to make his name in the arts, the media or even business, seldom feels the Julien-Sorel-like desire to move to the brighter lights of Munich or Hamburg, as a Geordie or Toulousain is still powerfully drawn, almost against his will, to London or Paris. If a Swabian wants to make this kind of move, he will more probably feel that no other German city suits him and the answer is to go abroad, to a real world centre such as, yes, London or Paris – or New York. Or he may feel that he can achieve national fame *without* leaving Stuttgart. Take the case of Germany's federalised television system, where each major TV centre – such as Stuttgart's – networks nationally a part of its material. Under this system a gifted and ambitious young producer such as Roderick Klett has been able to achieve national distinction by staying put. "I've reached the top here," he told me, "but why should I move to Munich? I would have no more scope there. And the programmes I make are seen throughout Germany." This is far less true in the case of French or even British television.

But the other side of this coin is that the greater self-sufficiency may tend, oddly enough, to make big German cities *more* provincial, not less. It is a not uncommon view. Since there is no one city in Germany that sets the pace and provides a strong national focus, so there is no city that can set a high metropolitan standard and oblige other cities to look at it. Each one, partly out of pride, falls back on its own resources: Stuttgart refuses to be influenced by Munich, or Hannover by Hamburg. In the arts, we have noticed that there is little touring by national companies, as happens all the time in Britain or France, and a German town may thus build up an exaggerated opinion of its local companies' merits, since there is little point of comparison – except for the ballet company. And this may be true not only in the arts. Germany remains a series of self-contained provincial centres; and Stuttgart, energetic, cosmopolitan, lively, stimulating, remains a big village.

A splendidly impressive village, however. I end by quoting an article by Roger Berthoud, former Bonn Correspondent of *The Times* of London, writing in that paper in September 1978. He said of Stuttgarters: "They give me the impression of striving, individually and collectively, onwards and upwards to improve themselves and their surroundings, towards a more or less clearly-defined goal. Zeal, thrift, cleanliness and efficiency are among the by-products, plus a sense of direction. It makes a change from Britain's sense of (usually) amiable and slovenly drift." Hear, hear.

III

Bologna

Don Camillo and the bourgeois *bolsheviks*

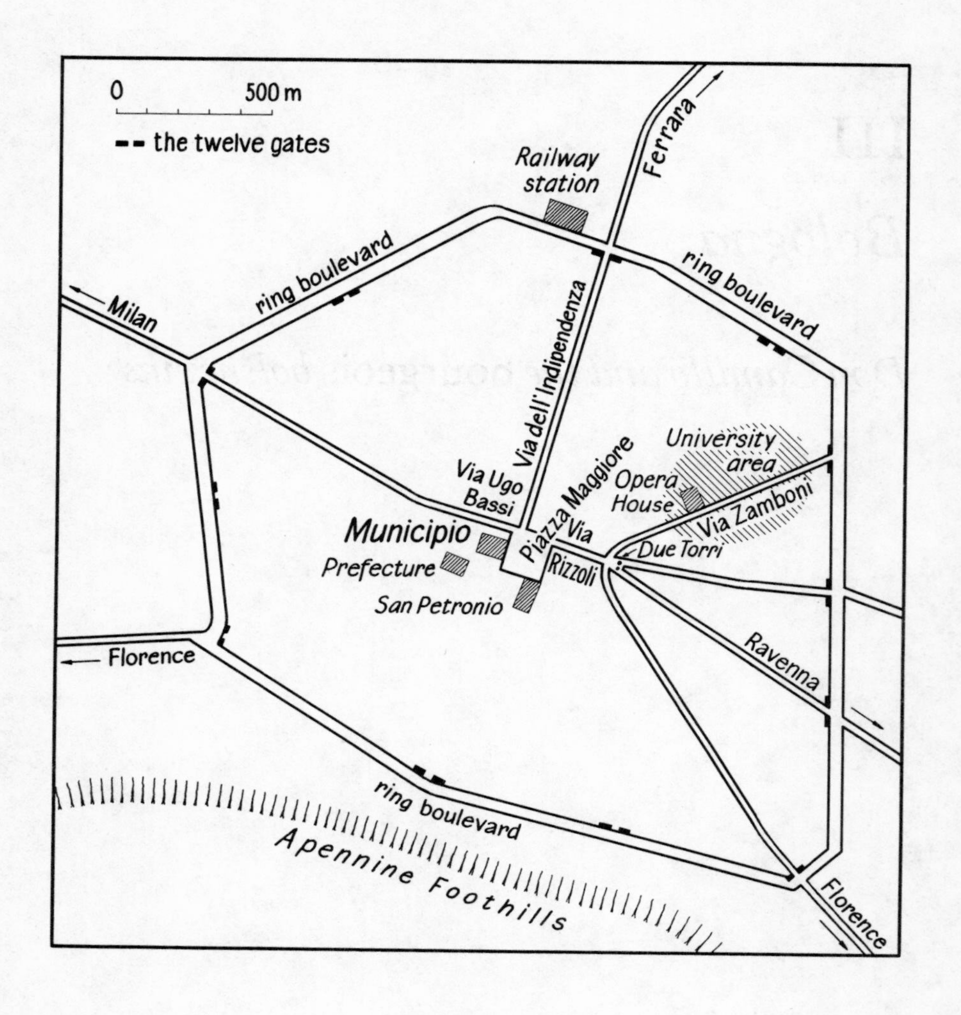
0
500 m
the twelve gates
Railway station
Ferrara
ring boulevard
Milan
ring boulevard
Via dell' Indipendenza
University area
Opera House
Via Zamboni
Via Ugo Bassi
Piazza Maggiore
Via Rizzoli
Due Torri
Municipio
Prefecture
San Petronio
Florence
Ravenna
ring boulevard
Apennine Foothills
Florence

1
Introduction

Dotta, grassa, rossa – learned, fat, red. Bolognese, as much as most Italians, like to think in stereotypes, and these are the three epithets they use to describe their city. "*Bologna la dotta*" because its university, the oldest in Europe, was also for centuries one of the greatest: today it is well past its prime, but it still crams the centre of town with its effervescence of students, 60,000 in all. "*Bologna la grassa*" because this prosperous city is at the heart of one of Italy's richest agricultural areas; and because its *cuisine* is reputedly the finest in Italy and its inhabitants, thereby, the greediest and plumpest. And "*Bologna la rossa*" because of its two strongest identifying features: the redness, or to be more accurate, the pinkness, of its buildings and of its politics. Until thirty or so years ago, "*rossa*" applied essentially to the former, to the russet and orange-pink façades of the buildings in the mediaeval centre, which give the city a deep glow at sunset, a little like Toulouse. Bolognese are justly proud of this beauty. But today "*rossa*" also means something else, about which feelings are more mixed. This is the only large town in the non-Communist world to have been governed ever since the war, without a break, by a Communist-led municipality.

This does not make Bologna untypical of Italy, for its Communism is a typically Italian phenomenon, a world away from Moscow's. It is a reflection of the Italian flair for compromise and paradox. Visiting the city, you would hardly notice it was Communist-ruled. No big banners or slogans or portraits of Lenin: rather, an elegance in the way people dress, and in the boutiques, that vies with Rome or Paris and has little in common with the austerities of Eastern Europe. Many of the local

Communist leaders are mild, cultivated *bourgeois* who collect modern art and give chic little dinner-parties in their homes, served by maids in starched uniforms. They are criticised more often for their conservative policies than for revolutionary excess. And thirty-plus years of Party rule has barely impinged on the comfortable life-style and traditions of the middle classes.

There are some explanations for all this. One is that powers of local government are highly circumscribed in Italy, as in France, and since the war Bologna and other Communist-run cities have merely been "Red" enclaves within a capitalist system with which they must accommodate; another, that the Italian Communist Party (PCI) uses Bologna as a shop-window not only of its administrative efficiency but also of its democratic intentions, and so is careful not to be provocative. This has become even more evident since 1976, as the Party has edged closer to a share of national power. In Bologna, an effective working compromise has been achieved with capitalism, and with the Church. When in the late 1950s the mayor struck up a kind of friendship with the then Archbishop, Cardinal Lercaro, some people compared them to Peppone and Don Camillo, pointing out that Guareschi set his famous stories in an Emilian village not far from Bologna. This parallel was frivolously misleading, for behind the undoubted cooperation has always lain some hostility and suspicion. Even so, many Communist voters are married in church, and some are regular churchgoers. If so many people habitually vote Communist locally, this is partly a reflection of national politics but also because the "Red" municipality has built up an administration that is less corrupt, more efficient and socially just than in the average large Italian town. Bologna is regarded as the least ill-governed city in Italy – for what that is worth. And it has thus managed to insulate itself from much of the chaos that has spread through Italy in recent years. But not from all of it: the very successes of the Communists, and their mildness, have made them a target of the terrorist extreme Left, and briefly in 1977 even Bologna erupted into violence.

But leaving current politics aside, is Bologna typical of Italy or not? No town in this country is typical – this is more true of Italy than of Britain or France. As in Germany, national unity is little more than a century old; and regional differences, especially between north and south, are even sharper than in Germany. And the long history of separate city states has driven so deep into the Italian psyche that, today, cities remain keenly aware of their individuality and separateness – even neighbouring towns with identical cultures and life-styles. Seen from the outside, Naples is patently different from Milan, or Palermo from Venice: but a foreigner might be forgiven for supposing there is little to distinguish, say, Verona from nearby Padua. But let him beware of saying that to the inhabitants! Whereas a Frenchman is particularly conscious of coming from a particular region – say, Brittany or Provence – in Italy with its stronger urban tradition the attachment is more local and precise, and if an Italian moves to another area he continues to wear his town of origin like a badge. He may even be known by the name of his town: a friend of mine in Bari, who mixed in a circle of such "expatriates" from other parts of Italy, told me that someone joining a group of friends in a *café* might be greeted by them with *"Buona sera, Genova!"* or *"Ma ecco Napoli!"* or *"Come sta, Mantova?"* A jocular manner of speech, but with serious undertones.

Bologna represents an extreme example in Italy of this local pride and attachment – perhaps *because* of its highly central position. Being at the main crossroads of north-central Italy, where the rugged peninsula joins the populated northern plain, it has seen so many migrations and invasions treading through or past it, that it has been forced to hug itself within its walls so as to keep its identity. Like many other northern cities, Bologna in the centuries before the unification of Italy evolved its own laws and customs and system of government, and developed a sense of isolation from and also of superiority to its neighbours. Today, the legal and political structures have been unified, but many of the old attitudes remain. Bolognese today not only resent and scorn the Romans and Milanese – that is no surprise – but also look down on neighbours in cities only a few miles away. Accused of being cowardly, a Bolognese might say, *"Non sono Ferrarese"*; of being dishonest, *"Non sono da Modena"* – and it might be more than just a good-humoured joke. Among fellow Bolognese he might make such remarks in the local dialect: *"Am saur briz Frarais"*, he would say. This dialect, *bulgnais,* is as much a separate language as Occitan and even more so than Swabian; yet it is so local that it is not understood in villages a few miles away. Many Bolognese still speak it among themselves; it is one of the exclusive bonds that unite them against the outside world.

This uniqueness of the city and its inhabitants is still marked, though it has begun to dilute in recent years under various modern pressures including that of immigration. The population has risen by 50 per cent since the war; today with suburbs it is over 600,000, making this the seventh city of Italy, ahead of Florence. The bulk of the immigrants have come from the rural hinterland, as farm modernisation has led to the usual surpluses of labour. These people are at least Emilians, and though they have brought their own customs, they have not changed the city's make-up as radically as newcomers from other parts of Italy might have done: in fact, immigration from Sicily and the south has been far less than in Turin or Milan, for there are not the same large-scale heavy industries, nor has this kind of influx been favoured by the municipality. In the professional classes there has been some immigration, notably to the university, but this too is on a modest scale. Bologna does not have the "two populations" of Toulouse or Stuttgart, and remains far more homogeneous than any other town in this book except Ljubljana. It is a town of small shops, artisanal firms and smallish factories, mostly locally-owned, corresponding to the intimate and very personal character of the place – an intimacy that seems to be in part the product of the extraordinary womb-like architecture with its mile upon mile of closely enveloping arcades.

The city lies at the southern edge of the wide plain of the Po valley. On three sides are the flat fertile farmlands, producing grain, hemp, fruit and vegetables. To the south, the foothills of the Appennines slope down to the edge of the suburbs. Drive into the city from any side, and you pass first through the usual higgledy-piggledy mess of Italian post-war urban growth: warehouses and factories, solitary high-rise blocks of flats standing between them on patches of waste ground, children playing on the pavements below garish advertising posters, while belching lorries thunder by and baby Fiats dart out incautiously to overtake them. It is not as strident and ill-organised as many larger Italian cities, nor indeed as Toulouse – the policies of the Red *Municipio* have borne some results in keeping the growth under control – but it is not exactly beautiful. Then, inside the city gates that mark the circuit of the old mediaeval walls, all changes. Within this pentagon shape, roughly a mile by a mile across, you are in mediaeval Bologna, still the focus of all the city's life. This is arguably the best preserved of all larger Italian towns, on *terra firma*. Through traffic is kept away by an elaborate system of precincts and one-way streets; local traffic still proliferates, but in many of the central areas the pedestrian is again king, and he moves against a backdrop that apart from the shopfronts and a few posters has changed little in four hundred years. It is one of the finest mediaeval and Renaissance ensembles in Europe, yet strangely ignored by the heavier tourist cohorts that make for Florence, Rome and Venice. The centrepiece is the Piazza Maggiore, a wide paved area where pigeons bomb and flutter, tourists laze in clusters on the steps of the buildings, and middle-aged Bolognese in tidy suits stand around for hours in groups, talking business, sport or politics. Close to one side of the *piazza* runs the city's main shopping and business street, the Via Rizzoli/Via Ugo Bassi. And all round are the great palaces and monuments with their ochre façades: the Palazzo d'Accursio, dating from the 13th to 16th centuries, that today is the Town Hall; the Palazzo del Podestà with its Renaissance façade, and next to it the 13th-century Palazzo di Re Enzo; the 16th-century Fountain of Neptune with its elaborate sculptures; and the gigantic church of San Petronio, begun in the Gothic style in 1390 and never completed. From here it is a short walk down the arcaded Via Rizzoli to the other famous square of central Bologna, the tiny Piazzo di Porta Ravegnana, in the middle of which stand the *Due Torri* ("Two Towers") that have become as much the touristic emblem of Bologna as the Eiffel Tower is that of Paris. They are two narrow towers of yellowish brick, leaning curiously towards each other as if each trying to rival Pisa: one is 100 metres high and the other, having had its top knocked off in 1351, is less than half that height. Both were built by local patrician families in the early 12th century, and are all that survive of the many towers erected in the city in that period.

From these two squares there splays out on every side a network of narrow ancient streets, many of them lined on one or both sides with deep arcades. It is these arcades that give Bologna its extraordinary secretive quality, almost like the medina of an Arab town – a quality you may find fascinating and protective, or merely claustrophobic. There are 35 miles of arcades, and on the south and east sides they stretch out as far as the old city gates. They afford protection against Bologna's extremes of climate: they are cool under hot southern summers, and in the cold foggy winters of the Po valley they ward off snow and wind. It used to be possible to walk the whole length of the city under these arcades, and even today I know a man who goes on foot the two miles from his home to his office and never needs take an umbrella or raincoat. The arcades are supported by graceful old arches which in many cases bear the weight of buildings. The result is curious, for whereas at street level there is often plenty of wide space, yet the buildings may be so close together across the street that you have to squint up to glimpse the sky and have the impression of being in a vault.

Along these sheltering streets, and in the countless tiny squares, or beside the porticoes of the many lovely mediaeval churches, there takes place an intense and mysterious workaday social life that I found more alien and elusive than that of any of my other towns. In Stuttgart or Ljubljana I was simply in another country; here, in another century.

Returning to Bologna one day in early spring, this was the scene I found. I was impressed, as always, by the elegance - men in velvet-collared coats with expensive, perfectly-knotted ties, girls in furs and swooping wide-brimmed hats, wearing jewellery. Bolognese, even more than most Italians, dress with studied chic whenever they leave their front doors. In the underpass beneath the Piazza Maggiore, a blind man was selling lottery tickets, and a crowd was pressing around a football pools office, for Bologna was about to play Naples in Division A. The open-fronted food shops just off the *piazza* were piled with the usual mind-blowing profusion of *mortadella, osso buco,* peppers, water-melons and every shape and colour of *pasta* - in this, the world capital of good pasta. Bulky saleswomen were joking and bartering with their customers in broad *bulgnais.* Various elderly *bourgeois* men in dark glasses, looking sinister, were dragging little black dogs on leads. Other men were leaning at the counters of innumerable bars open on the street, drinking their minuscule two-mouthful cups of *espresso.* Young girls were peering at the windows of opulent boutiques full of jewellery and furs. As evening fell and the offices emptied, the nightly procession began up and down the Pavaglione, a long colonnade running beside San Petronio where people meet for assignations or merely to show off their clothes to each other. Then, after dark, the floodlighting fell gently on the weathered red brick of the palaces in the Piazza Maggiore; and students in long cloaks, arm in arm, strode whispering and laughing down the shadowy tunnelling arcades of the Via Zamboni, in the heart of the university.

The mood of Bologna is soft and gentle, feminine in a way; not at all metallic like Stuttgart, nor roughly masculine like Newcastle. Bolognese have a reputation for greater openness and friendliness than surly Romans or supercilious Florentines. They smile and laugh a lot, and they look cheerful even when performing dreary tasks such as queuing in government offices. Perhaps the mellow beauty of the architecture somehow rubs off on the inhabitants (just as, in Belgium, I find the people of Bruges nicer than other Flemish). One English lover of Bologna, the TV journalist James Burke, suggested in a BBC talk that whereas in most other towns the people stay at home when the weather is bad or the sun too bright, "In Bologna it's as if there were a giant common house, running the length of the streets, full of people eating, shouting, singing, reading . . . and meeting in a way usually reserved for villagers." Life is just as gregarious as in Newcastle, and more publicly so. I believe also that the arcades have the effect of a cocoon: people feel protected, encompassed within a secret and self-sufficient society where everything is reduced to its human proportion, to gossip, love, barter, joking, the subtle interplay of relationships. "*Una città a misura dell'uomo*" (a city to the measure of man) is the *Municipio*'s slogan, and an apt one. In short, this is a society with its own special rhythms and codes to which it is not always easy for an outsider to adapt, however much he may be made welcome. A society, too, with an intense parochialism.

2

The secret tribal life of the sheltering arcades

Sergio Vacchi, the Bolognese painter, was talking to me one day in a *trattoria*. "In Rome, there's flashiness and decadence. In Milan, they work themselves to death making money. In Florence, they're reserved and snobbish. But here, we have the human scale. Here, this soft, secret glutinous social life goes on throbbing gently, glob-glob-glob-glob-glob – like the deep undercurrents of a slow river." He took another mouthful of creamy *tortellini,* Bologna's richest *pasta.* "It gets under your skin, this place, I can never live happily anywhere else."

Bologna has been glob-globbing away like this since at least the 11th century, when the citizens first formed their own communal government, the leading families built the first towers and arcades, and law teachers first gathered to found the university. Since then, the city has settled deep into its own comfortable, complacent rhythms that are only now being disturbed, finally, by modern life and outside tensions. The people have a comfortable look. They tend to be more robust and of bigger build than the average Italian; the men have large round faces and a jovial manner. Blue eyes and fair hair are common, as often in northern Italy. Bolognese pride themselves notably on their appreciation of rich food and pretty women – indeed, on the beauty of their women. "*Città delle belle donne*" is one local cliché, the title of a song. The cliché is justified, though I doubt the women are lovelier than the high Italian average. They have pale complexions and shimmering hair, auburn, black or gold, and the surprise is that most of them keep such good figures, seeing how much *pasta,* chocolate and *pâtisserie* they eat. Self-abnegation is not the most noted local virtue.

Any other Italian will quickly recognise a Bolognese by his accent, broader and heavier than average north Italian. It comes directly from the *bulgnais* dialect, which is a mixture of French and Latin, with elements of Greek, Etruscan and possibly Celtic. So different is it from ordinary Italian that a simple phrase such as "*ci vediamo domani*" (we'll see each other tomorrow) becomes "*as av dran dman*". *Bulgnais* has its own rich vocabulary of slang and of earthy, vulgar expressions: and even when speaking in Italian, a Bolognese will often express himself with this same earthiness – one of the reasons why the city is called *la grassa. Bulgnais* is a literary as well as popular dialect, and even today plays and poetry are written in it. There have been conscious attempts at revival, as with many regional languages: a local cabaret star, Dino Sarti, has created a vogue with his *bulgnais* songs and sketches. And yet, though most citizens understand *bulgnais,* fewer and fewer of the younger ones use it as their natural vehicle – just as with Breton and Basque. This is one sign of the slow decline of the old uniqueness of Bologna, as outward influences impinge.

The town's class structure is much as in other north Italian cities: a fading aristocracy, less grand than Florence's, living discreetly in its pink palaces in the city centre, as in Toulouse; a tycoon milieu, smaller and less showy than in Turin or Milan; a large, prosperous and self-assured *bourgeoisie,* which includes a strong intellectual element owing to the size of the university; a flourishing artisan and shopkeeper community, many of them warm supporters of the Communists; and the workers, less angrily militant than in many Italian industrial cities. Three decades of Communism have had little influence on this structure, save in ways that must seem paradoxical. The Communists have fortified the semi-Poujadist tradesman class, by wooing it as allies. And their presence may have actually softened class tensions. This is because the workers, on the one hand, many employed in co-operatives, feel some sense of protection through having "their" party in power locally, and this soothes their class hostility; the *bourgeoisie,* on the other, can also feel a certain protection, for the reasonableness of local civic rule has assuaged much of their fear of "Red terror", and they can see that, after all, the mayor and his lieutenants are from their own class and decent enough chaps. Cosy Bologna is no battlefield of the class war – save when infiltrated by the fringe extremist groups.

These and other paradoxes and contradictions are in some cases typical of all Italy, in others specific to this city. As compared with Florentines or Romans, the Bolognese have a reputation for openness and friendliness, not only to each other but to visitors: yet they rarely show much interest in the visitor himself or where he comes from, and if he fails to share their values or their own high opinion of themselves, they will recoil – like Geordies. They are nearly always cheerful in public, and are more charmingly polite to each other than most Italians: shopgirls serve you with a smile, and secretaries are not sour on the 'phone, as in France. Yet the Bolognese can gossip and intrigue ruthlessly behind each others' backs. They are, in most ways, tolerant and easy going, yet can cruelly ostracise someone who is shabbily dressed or breaks social conventions. They have rigorous aesthetic standards about clothes, food and furnishing, and they work hard (Italian *dolce far niente* is a false myth, at least in the north): yet they are intellectually lazy, and uncurious about the world outside their own. They talk non-stop, but seldom above the level of gossip. They are closely involved with their family circle, yet also live a fluid tribal life among groups of friends: they are as gregarious as Geordies, and strikingly more so than Toulousains or Swabians. They do not like to be alone: there is no word in Italian for "privacy".

I can best assess this glob-glob life by describing some of the middle-class dinners and parties I went to, and quoting the people I met. Carmen Licari, a beautiful Sicilian who had moved to Bologna about ten years previously, said: "There's a very personal life here that gets under your skin. When I was a student here, the night-life was very active – I don't mean boring night-clubs, but a life of little bars and *osterie.* We used to drift around in groups of eight or ten friends, with the groups shifting and changing like a kaleidoscope – that's very Bologna. I would never go to bed before about six, then sleep till noon. There were always plenty of places open till dawn, unusual for north Italy – Milan is dead after ten. We went to *osterie,* little old wine pubs used by working people where intellectuals would come too, and sometimes we'd recite poetry. But this life is falling off now, as people move out to the suburbs."

James Burke said, "When I lived in Bologna as a young bachelor, we had just that kind of life. A group of friends would meet in a bar at about seven or eight p.m., then we'd have a long discussion about where to eat, comparing in detail the merits of the different *pasta* in the cheaper *trattorie*. Then after dinner we'd move around from pub to pub till late. We were all more or less intellectuals, but we never seemed to talk about much except food, each other, and girls – or tell long ribald stories in *bulgnais*. You could call it a frivolous life, but it was warm and compelling – under those arcades. Impossible to imagine that kind of society in a modern, spread-out town."

Marisa Galli, a graduate student whose parents live in Modena, said: "I like Bologna because I am free. I'd hate it if my family were here and expected me to live with them. Yet, when we Italian girls break away from our families, we need a substitute and that's why we have the group. I belong to a group of about twenty, mostly older students or unmarried lecturers. It remains fairly stable and self-contained: people drop off as they get married and then others join. There are one or two foreigners, but it's hard for an outsider, even a Bolognese, to join casually, he has to be initiated as it were – over the years we've evolved our own jargon and attitudes, and we like our parties to be just for us. We sit around endlessly in each others' flats. Some parties go on very late, and then begins the polka of who shall take who home, with lots of badinage. But it's innocent: of course we have love-affairs, but discreetly and outside the group, it's totally taboo to have an affair within the group. And the unmarried couple, in public, is not yet accepted in Italy, at least not in a town such as this." She summed up: "I've lived all over Italy, and I like Bologna best, I like its intimacy. Yet also I can't stand it any more, it's too insidious and involving. I just want to get out."

Sometimes I saw this group life in action. One Sunday a girl I knew invited me to join some of her unmarried friends. It might be unkind, though not inaccurate, to describe the day as a cross between Fellini's *I Vitelloni* and a less sophisticated version of Antonioni's *Le Amiche* (from Pavese's novel of listless high-life in Turin, *Fra Donne Sole*). We met after lunch, in the town centre. Everyone was dressed as for Church or a *soirée:* the girls wore furs and jewels. The men were preening themselves with their Alfa-Romeos: they belonged to the *figli-a-papa* set of this well-heeled *bourgeoisie*. After a lot of *ciao*uing, about twenty-five of us drove off in procession to a strange unfurnished flat above a small factory, in industrial waste-land – pure

Antonioni. The flat belonged to a louche-looking character of fifty or so, with dyed hair. Here we mooched around for eight hours, drinking Scotch or Campari, eating open sandwiches, dancing or necking half-heartedly. Everyone was unmarried, save for one couple patently allowing each other licence. The men were mostly *vitelloni* in their thirties or forties, perennial bachelors; the girls, few of them pretty, were husband-hunting but obviously not in the right place. We came home: the non–orgy had not even been erotic. It was not only my sense of cinematic *déjà-vu* that left me with a strong feeling of *ennui*.

This was a very different set from Marisa's young university friends; different too from the young-married groups I met. In Italy, more than in most Western countries, marrieds and unmarrieds tend to form separate social circles: maybe this is because so many unmarrieds still live with their parents and cannot entertain as they wish, and because of the stress put on formal entertaining in the right setting, which requires a home of your own. I was invited to several very similar buffet dinner-parties, each for twenty or so people, youngish university teachers or businessmen, and their wives. We arrived at nine. Everyone shook hands with everyone, and gave his or her name; ladies' hands were kissed. Dress was conventional: many of the women were in neat black dresses, Paris style, and just a few in bright pyjama-suits, then in vogue. The furnishing was elegant but cold: marble floors, upright chairs, fashionable modern paintings (more often bought for show, I was told, than for love of modern art). We sat stiffly round in a circle and were not offered a drink till nearly all the guests arrived, which took us till 9.45. Then maids in uniform brought plates of delicious multi-coloured *pasta* which we ate on our laps. Conversation was less formal than the manners, and often stimulating; and the women entered more actively into discussions about politics or business than would have been likely in pre-war Italy. But it struck me that at each of these parties I was the only foreigner, and rarely was the talk about anything but Bologna. There is much more party-giving in people's homes than in Toulouse or Stuttgart, and the social whirl, though formal, is in some ways closer to the Anglo-Saxon gregariousness. But the fish are whirling in a tiny, enclosed pond.

The *bourgeoisie* live mostly in comfortable villas or flats in the southern suburbs, where the land begins to rise into the hills. A few grander families inhabit older *palazzi,* near the centre, which their ancestors have owned for centuries. This is true also of what remains of the Bolognese aristocracy, far more subdued in its role than in

Florence. The Marchese Gianangelo Salina Amorini Bolognini has a beautiful *palazzo* round a courtyard, which his family has owned and lived in since 1550: today he and his Scottish wife spend most of their time in Rome or France and have little contact with Bologna. I visited another marquis, an elderly recluse living alone in an elegant but gently decaying *palazzo* west of the city, full of signed photos of King Umberto and fine classical paintings. We were served by waiters in livery, but there was no telephone and the place was unheated (in February) and freezing. The marquis told me that his son worked for a US oil company and was engaged to a princess, so maybe the family fortunes will recover. But the old boy seemed fearfully *fin-de-race,* and maybe was sighing for pre-war days when Bologna high society was more fashionable than today. A very personal slant on this was given me by a handsome English lady in her sixties, Mary Colliva Stuart, whose late husband had been *podesta* (mayor) under Mussolini. She has remained in Bologna ever since, a popular figure in *bourgeois* society – even though her views are not everyone's. "Ah, those good old pre-war days! Life was gayer then: this was a garrison town, and the red-and-blue cavalry uniforms lent dash and colour to big public events. Sometimes the *Duce* himself would visit us, and there would be brilliant parties. High society was coherent then, but now it's all dispersed and far less chic. I went to a reception last week at the *Municipio* – so scruffy! The Party leaders' wives looked so dowdy, with no sense of occasion."

This may often be the case at the town hall, as we shall see later. Yet not all the Communist leaders lack elegance in their own lives. Once I was invited to a small after-dinner party in the home of Renato Zangheri, now mayor and then a leading councillor. The stylishly furnished duplex was full of expensive art books and modern paintings, including a portrait of our host by his friend Vacchi. Everyone was smartly dressed, including the wife of the then mayor, Guido Fanti, who wore a bright red trouser-suit. Little trays of liqueur chocolates, *fruits glacés,* and other luxury sweets were passed round repeatedly: but, as at many other Bologna parties, Marxist or not, we were offered little to drink. My one glass of Scotch had to last all evening. On a later occasion I went to a chic dinner-party in the home of one of Mayor Zangheri's friends: four local Communist leaders, their wives, and me. All the men were professors or architects by background. It was the usual formal *bourgeois* Bologna flat, with marble floors, masses of books and an assortment of modern and classical paintings. We began with champagne cocktails, followed by undistinguished food with superb wines, then neat whisky and the usual expensive chocolates. A maid in uniform served. We arrived at nine and stayed gossiping until nearly two. I noted that the wives took part easily in the highly political conversation, they were fully *au fait* with their husbands' work and did not huddle on one side talking children or clothes. But more revealing was the nature of the talk: about politics, but solely on the level of local gossip and personalities. There was some discussion of the value of local intellectual magazines, but none of the arguing about ideas or policies that I would have expected from a French group of this kind, and hardly a single reference to national issues – save a snide remark or two about Fanfani and Andreotti. I was invited to give my views on Bologna but never once asked about Britain. International problems – Spain, Lebanon, Africa – were discussed solely in terms of their impact on the local power game. Yet these were cultivated people of some calibre – more so than the average Newcastle or Toulouse councillor. The evening strengthened my views about Bolognese "narcissism" and lack of appetite about ideas – and maybe said something about local Communism.

As well as this formal home entertaining, there is also as in other Italian towns an exclusively male social life, fluid and casual. There may be less of the organised pub and club activity than in Newcastle: but a man will often, without intending mischief, leave his wife at home after dinner and parade round the bars with his pals. You see groups of middle-aged men in the restaurants in the evenings, or standing in bars or in the streets, often arguing noisily. Above all they congregate in the wide shop-lined subway under the Via Rizzoli, to one side of the main Piazza Maggiore. This is Bologna's *agora*: all the year, and late into the night, little knots of men are standing here, from all classes and professions, altercating about politics, business, sport. Left and Right engage in a non-stop debate that is bafflingly Bolognese. A Communist told me, "Often I have heated discussions, in the subway or in bars, with my friends – some of them Right-wing industrialists. We disagree, but remain friends: Bologna has this easy-going tolerance, more than other Italian towns."

Sometimes men spend part of the evening just roaming about town. An elderly Bolognese told me: "Until recently it was a recreation on fine evenings to *fare i dodici porti* – stroll with a friend round the four-mile ring boulevard that links the twelve gates. But this is less popular now, there is too much noise and smell from cars. People also used to sit outside their doorways in the narrow streets all evening and talk across to each other" – just as in Toulouse – "but this too is being killed by the traffic. Cars are supposed to make social life easier, but in fact they've dealt a blow to the city's night activities. And so has television."

Although men enjoy some social life on their own, this is not to say that they neglect their women. They do not treat them as an inferior species, as the typical Geordie tends to do, nor let them develop into frumpish, manic *Hausfrauen* like the Swabians. They are protective, but also gallant; and although some Bolognese women may hanker for a more total emancipation, they are glad to have their femininity so much appreciated and encouraged. Some feel themselves to be in a happy middle position, between the under-emancipation of southern Italy, where women still have so little freedom, and the situation in some northern societies where women are treated so much as the equals of men that their femininity is not given its due. In daily life in Bologna, there is something of the undercurrent of tingling flirtatious awareness between the sexes that you find in France. Maybe this is a reason why the young women in Bologna seem so relaxed and out-going, and on the whole so happy – as one girl said to me, "We feel admired by men, but also protected, and so we feel sure of our position in a man's world." Peter Nichols in his brilliant book *Italia, Italia,* says that he finds secretaries and shopgirls frequently brusque, wayward and unhelpful, but I wonder if this is not mainly a Roman or Milanese phenomenon – as it is also Parisian. In Bologna, in offices and shops as much as socially, I was struck by the friendliness, gaiety and feminine self-assurance of the women, especially the younger ones. They are nicer than the men.

Until they are married, girls even in northerly Bologna are still treated more strictly by their parents than in Germany or Britain or, generally, in France. I met a graduate of twenty-four, still living with her family, who was expected to be home by 10.30 each evening and not go out two nights running: if she was late, her parents worried. And her father would not let her drive a car. She wanted to leave home and share a flat with a girl-friend but could not face the showdown it would entail. This may today be an extreme kind of case: Bologna may still be conservative, but a girl certainly has more freedom than twenty years ago, when it was still unusual for her to be allowed out late with a man. And Bologna is far ahead of the south: an English girl who had lived previously in Calabria told me of her surprise when she first came to

Bologna and found she could even go into a bar on her own in the evening without causing a scandal.

Beneath its façade of Catholic respectability, Bologna has long enjoyed a reputation for a more vigorous romantic and erotic life than that of most Italian towns. Boccaccio and de Sade have both described their successful pursuit of girls under its arcades, and this tradition continues: most girls have lovers before marriage, and one woman of thirty admitted to me she was laughed at by her friends for being still a virgin. But the romantic game is played with great secrecy and discretion, as in provincial France: lovers do not publicly admit their liaisons as they do in Anglo-Saxon countries, and it is unheard of for a couple to live together unmarried, save in the restricted bohemian milieu. Everyone accepts the promiscuity so long as it hides its face – yes, hypocrisy, maybe. Marisa Galli said, "In our group, we tease so much about love-affairs that one keeps them quiet, and this plus family pressures means that one may have few opportunities for meeting the beloved – but this merely inflames the romantic excitement." And since so many unmarrieds live at home, and flatlets or private bed-sitters are few, a love affair is often a matter of logistics. Students living with their parents may group together to hire some room or flatlet as a *garçonnière* to be shared on a rota basis during the day. Or they borrow a friend's flat – "My students keep asking me for the use of mine," a bachelor lecturer told me. Or they go into the hills or fields in summer, or to out-of-town *pensioni*. Or after dark they use their cars – and in a tiny Fiat 500 this may demand some acrobatic agility. In short, *amore* in Bologna can be an uncomfortable business, but retains a touch of quaint old-fashioned Romeo-and-Juliet passionate romanticism.

Not that true love has driven the professionals out of business: prostitutes make a fair living, though more from business visitors than locals. Organised brothels are illegal, but there is plenty of call-girl activity; and prostitutes lurk at night in the shady avenues near the station, waiting for clients who circle round in their smart cars making their choice. The police turn a blind eye, mostly. This part of town also has a number of bars where queers go for pick-ups. In fact, Bologna's hearty sexuality includes a national reputation for pederasty, and I was told that if a girl says she is from Bologna, a Roman or Milanese may reply, "Poor kid – aren't the men there all gay?" Unjustified, but still. In every respect, Bologna is a very unvicious town. It has little of the underground "*milieu*" found even in Toulouse or Newcastle, and not much of a drug scene either – save in the American student colony, and they, as one of them told me, "try to avoid passing the stuff on to Italians, who tend to talk and give us away." Bologna has less crime than most Italian cities. Recently it has not escaped political terrorism – as we shall see – but has largely been spared the ruthless kidnappings for money that have become so frequent in Milan and elsewhere.

The *commedia dell'arte* of the Bolognese game of love is played out not only against the décor of the mediaeval city but also with the finest and most fastidious of costuming. Elegance and show count for even more than in the average Italian city. The Bolognese carry themselves with physical grace: students in their swirling cloaks go with long easy strides down the arcades, athletically and confidently, as if they really enjoyed walking: so different from the push-and-shove of Toulouse or the slouch of Newcastle. And women and men alike dress as if conscious all the time of being looked at – as often they are. Alone in their homes they may wear tatters, but even the poorest will contrive to buy smart clothes for walking out. The fashions have their own strict conventions, according to season, but do not necessarily follow the latest vogues of Rome or Paris, so that Bologna's chic has an odd timelessness. It is not "pop" in the Carnaby Street sense, nor is there the same gulf as in Britain or France between the clothes of the young and of older people. Colours are bold. During some of my visits to Bologna, the women were wearing bright trouser-suits, very wide-brimmed hats, and maxi-coats with fur linings; fur coats were everywhere. The men would wear immaculate ties and shirts with bold colours, expensive suits, and in winter, coats with fur or velvet collars. A middle-class man will buy two or three new suits a year and several pairs of shoes: an Englishman tends to keep his shoes till they wear out.

This elegance is not mere pride or status-snobbery. One factor is the genuine Italian love of spectacle and drama, which impressed me forcibly during the annual *Carnival dei Bambini*, in Lent. The whole town stops for it: the university closes down for a week. There were several parades, with clowns and floats, and mock races like a small-scale *palio*. One float pelted me with toffees as well as confetti; another, called *"vacanze a Hawaii"*, featured tiny girls doing a hula-hula in brown tights in the February frost. Many adult Bolognese are today scathing about the carnival, saying that it used to be serious and theatrical, with everyone masked as in Germany for *Fasching*, but now it has grown too commercial. Yet the children clearly love it: hordes of all ages were watching, dressed in the most elaborate harlequin outfits, or 18th-century court dress, or as cowboys or astronauts. I saw whole shops devoted to selling these costumes, on which some parents spend a lot of money.

Italians seem to imbibe their feeling for *bella figura* with their mother's milk and it never leaves them. As Peter Nichols has written*, Italian women keep saying to each other, "How do you think I am looking? . . . tell me, tell me . . ." and, to quote him, "An open sports car with a girl in it will as likely as not have a hairbrush behind the windscreen so that she can put herself in order at each traffic light or traffic jam." But not only the fair sex behave like this. Many Bologna factories, under union pressure, are equipped with the finest shower-rooms and changing-rooms, because the workers refuse to be seen in the streets in their dirty work-clothes. How unlike Newcastle, where filthy clothes are a badge of working-class honour! Italian workers leave their factories in neat suits with briefcases, looking like business-men; and if their work happens to be in the street, then they must have smart uniforms. In Milan I once saw a group of men in impeccable sky-blue uniforms and asked if they were airline pilots: no, I was told, these were municipal dustmen. It could happen in Stuttgart: but the Italian care for smartness is not the same as the Swabian mania for cleanness.

As many writers on Italy have noted, it is not only their aesthetic sense that prompts Italians to be so obsessed by *bella figura*. It is also a matter of status, of pride not only in one's own person but in the good name of the family. To dress well is to show oneself worthy of the social status to which one aspires, and to dress badly is to look ridiculous, which Italians hate more than anything. "If I didn't dress well," Carmen Licari told me, "I would be an outcast, I'd no longer be invited to parties. People here stare at you horribly if you are too out-rageously dressed, or go to a party too informally or badly dressed, whereas when I was in London I saw that no one minds at all." It is an odd exception to Bologna's usual spirit of tolerance and kindness. And it puts people under pressure to spend more of their income on clothes than they can really afford. "I hate having to use all my spare money for this keeping-up-with-the-Bologninis," said an English woman; "and I have to keep urging my husband to buy new suits, which he hates." Styles of dress are conformist, and people take care not to be out of step. Thus, they all change together into spring or autumn dress on a given date, irrespective of the climate: one freezing Easter Day, I saw

---

* *Italia Italia,* pages 50 and 77, Macmillan, London, 1973.

men shivering outside a church in their light spring suits which they had put on because spring had officially arrived. Or, if there is a party, then party dress it must be, however impracticable. Some English friends of mine organised a big country picnic; "Our guests came with the women in high heels, the men in stiff suits and the kids with silk shirts and little bow ties. Then they all horse-played around, getting their smart clothes very dishevelled. I think they envied us our slacks, jerseys and flat heels." This formality inhibits neighbourliness of the Anglo-Saxon kind. "There is a charming Italian lady in the flat next to ours," an English woman told me, "and we are very friendly, but I know that I can never knock on her door and ask her across for coffee. She'd expect a day's notice and then come dressed up." Home entertaining can only be pre-planned, whereas the social life of the streets and *cafés,* where everyone is already "dressed", is informal and exuberant.

The social niceties extend to names, titles and manners as well as dress. The kissing of hands is rarer than in Germany but more common than in France. If invited to a meal or party, you bring cakes or flowers with you, or send them in advance. Christian names are not taboo, as in Germany: in fact they are catching on fast, as in France, especially among younger people. But the use of titles, especially in any kind of formal context, persists almost as much as in Germany. Milan has its own fantasy consular life just like Stuttgart's, and I am sure that Bologna would too if it had any consuls (it is too near Milan). But there are plenty of other titles in Bologna, some of them charmingly archaic: the rector of the university is referred to even in informal conversation as "*Il Rectore Magnifico*". Anyone with a degree expects to be addressed by his title – *dottore, professore, ingegnere,* or *avvocato* – and as Dominique Schnapper has noted,* "Titles are such an integral part of the individual that if he is designated without his title, or with an incorrect one, no one will understand whom one is talking about." Titles are also cumulative as in Germany: a newspaper mentioning the President of the Bologna Rotary Club called him "*on. avv. cav. gr. cr.*" and then his name, which meant that he was a member of Parliament, a lawyer, a knight of the Order of Work, and had the Grand Cross.

This is not just a manner of speech. It reveals attitudes, in a society where high stress is put on having the right qualifications. A girl from

* *L'Italie rouge et noire,* Gallimard, Paris, 1971.

Manchester told me, "When I first came to Bologna to teach English, everyone thought I was just a silly little thing in pigtails, but then I gave a lecture on literature at the British Council, and I was mentioned in the local paper as '*Dottoressa*' because of my English Ph D, after which everyone fawned on me." She added: "I adore Italians as individuals, but hate them for their social and public life" – a life that also includes a high degree of nepotism, in a society where you cannot easily get a good job unless you are *recommended* by the right person.

My ultimate impression of Bologna is of a kind of timelessness; in a sense, an imperviousness to modernism. "This place is still pre-1914 in its structures and attitudes", more than one inhabitant admitted to me. But in what does this consist? One can point to the archaism of Italian bureaucracy and public services, affecting banks, schools and hospitals, where staff with crumbling mentalities work to crumbling routines amid crumbling equipment – but matters are worse, if anything, in other Italian cities. One can point also to the specific policy of the Communist municipality which has put the accent less on growth than conservation and has kept the property developers away from the mediaeval city centre – a blessing, in many ways if not all. This we shall look at more closely in the next sections. But maybe this civic policy has its roots in deeper historic traits. Today as in the past, the Bolognese, despite their central position on the map, remain curiously impervious to new trends from outside, much more evidently so than the Milanese or Florentines, or indeed the people of Toulouse or Stuttgart where modernism may provoke mixed reactions but is vitally present. Just as Bologna's sartorial fashion is out-of-time, so its *cafés,* shops and restaurants seem to exist in a kind of limbo somewhere between the 1930s and 1970s; while Bologna's few snazzy boutiques and *avant-garde* art shows impinge only marginally on a society that wants to go its own way in its own time. On two occasions I drove straight from Bologna to Ljubljana, where living standards are lower and the buildings far shabbier, yet I had the impression of travelling forward in time.

Plenty of foreign visitors find this timelessness attractive, in a Western world given over to trendiness. I think I would find it more appealing in a small, sleepy little market town, but in a metropolis of this size I am less sure that it is healthy. Personally I found the city a little too claustrophobic and complacent for my taste, and I met some Bolognese who share this feeling, even while loving their town. Luigi Pedrazzi, a leading intellectual, referred to Bologna's "triumphant, militant narcissism" and "joyous, complacent provincialism", while Romano Prodi, an economist, said, "We Bolognese still see ourselves in terms of the old stereotypes, we believe we are superior in everything, food, elegance, good looks, friendliness – but is it true?" Another writer, Luigi Degli Esposti, felt there was a mediocrity and lack of stimulus in intellectual and social life: he pointed out that Bologna has produced its share of famous people – including Marconi the inventor of wireless, the poet Carducci, the painter Morandi, the film director Pasolini – but no politicians of national rank save one or two Communists. And several people referred to the Bolognese's mental laziness, their shying away from ideas and major issues in favour of the personal and immediate, their lack of curiosity about the world or desire to travel. In my grand tour of European parochialisms that constitutes this book, the Bolognese take first prize. They turn their back on the world even more than Geordies, and with much more self-confidence, without the Geordies' fear of being judged by other values that might after all be superior.

From all I had been told, I half expected to like Bologna the best of my five towns, but I ended up liking it the least. Yet there are many other visitors, Italian or foreign, who stay far longer than I did and after a period of scepticism fall in love with the city and its way of life – with a certain soft civilised gentleness, with the magic of the shifting shadowy patterns of love, gossip and friendship under the protective arcades. "It grows on you, despite yourself," said Carmen Licari; "It's archaic, but now I want to settle here," said Peter Boggis. Bologna may have some obvious affinities with Toulouse, in its architecture, history, climate, culture; but I think the closer parallel is with Newcastle, despite the stark contrasts in life-style and physical looks. The special kind of local patriotism, the fear of change, the sense of conspiracy between those who share the local culture, the initial friendly welcoming of outsiders which may turn sour if they prove too critical: the two towns have this and much else in common. Both are *sui generis* within their nations. And it is a matter of taste whether a newcomer is enchanted or repelled by this very personal, intimate collective life as it goes glob-glob-glob-glob-glob.

3

The Party's "historic compromise" with archbishops and tycoons

The unusual politics of post-war Bologna find their roots in the city's long history – in the 350 years of Papal rule which pushed it towards anti-clericalism and Socialism, and in a tradition of local self-government that stretches back, amid intervals, for nine centuries. The town was founded by the Etruscans as early as 500 BC, and in 189 BC was colonised by the Romans who called it Bononia. After a long period under the Barbarians, it emerged in the 11th century as one of the first Italian self-governing communes, and remains proud of this today. In the 12th century the citizens were electing their own mayor and devising their own constitutional forms: they were helped by the presence of legal experts at the newly founded university, which was attracting lawyers and scholars from all over Italy. After this, in the late 13th century, the city became divided between Guelphs and Ghibellines who fought each other; the Guelphs gained the upper hand and Bologna accepted the sovereignty of the Papacy. The city continued for some time to suffer from the feuds that were common in pre-Renaissance Italy: it fell under the sway of a succession of noble families, notably the Visconti and Bentivoglio, who restricted the citizens' independence but built palaces, towers and churches and opened Bologna to the Renaissance. In 1506 it came under the direct rule of the Popes, like many other towns in this part of Italy, and from then on became more and more closely tied to Rome: it was little more than a municipality, ruled by a Papal legate assisted vaguely by a local senate. Napoleon briefly rescued Bologna from this and made it the second town, after Milan, of the new Kingdom of Italy. But this short period was followed by the Papal Restoration which lasted until the unification of Italy in 1860.

In the centuries when Italy was split into various kingdoms and republics, Bologna was never the capital of a wider area like some other cities – Venice, Florence, Pisa, Turin. Its history was that of an enclosed city-state, separate from its neighbours, and this has decisively influenced its present-day mentalities. Bologna has also been marked by the long years of Papal rule, whose poor administration throughout Emilia bred a spirit of anti-clericalism, sharper here than elsewhere in Italy. People objected not so much to Catholicism itself as to the Church's abuse of its temporal powers, as they saw it. And so churlish were the Bolognese towards the bureaucrats who came from Rome to rule them that this became the most unpopular posting for an official, and the word *sbolognari* entered the Italian language – "to be sent to Bologna", i.e. to be dismissed from the pleasures of Rome and virtually exiled. In modern colloquial Italian *sbolognari* thus means "to be ostracised or given the sack", rather as in France a person is "*limogé*" or in England "sent to Coventry".

After the fall of the Papacy, the discontent continued in the later 19th century, but now it was mainly for economic reasons and was strongest in the Emilian countryside where thousands of poor farmers united against the sharecropping system that made them virtually the serfs of the rich landlords. This is the true origin of the strength of the Left today in Emilia, where the revolutionary tradition is more peasant than urban. Here Italian Socialism was born: in 1861 the first Workers' Society *(Società Operaia)* was formed, and by the turn of the century there were forty of them in Emilia with a total membership of 15,000. Soon the movement spread to the cities, and in 1914 Bologna was one of the first Italian towns to elect a Socialist mayor. After 1918, the division of the town into two hostile blocks, Whites (or Blacks) and Reds, *bourgeoisie* and anti-clerical Leftists, grew more intense: Communism and Fascism were both gathering pace in post-war Italy, and Bologna was one of their hottest points of conflict. The mood was angrier than anything that has been seen since the Second World War (at least until the terrorist outbursts of 1977). Red flags floated everywhere, workers occupied factories and threatened to declare a soviet: the Fascists hit back with violence, burning down union and party offices and workers' cooperatives. For a few brief months in 1921 Bologna actually had a Communist mayor, but this Left-wing régime was swept away in the blackshirt tide the following year. For Fascism, like Socialism, had its roots in Emilia, and was born partly of the reaction of small landowners and tradesmen against the sharecroppers' militancy. Mussolini came from Forli, only 40 miles to the south-east, and Bologna was one of the first Italian towns to elect his movement.

Mussolini quickly made it one of the strongholds and showcases of his régime, and he ruled the town with military swagger. The Left went sullenly underground, while the *bourgeoisie* largely welcomed him: the university does not like to be reminded today that only one of its professors chose to resign rather than swear allegiance.

The war and the rout of Fascism gave the Left its chance to regroup and prepare for a very different future. The Communists with their superior organisation seized the leadership of the resistance movement against the Germans: by 1943, thirteen of the eighteen official partisan battalions in the Bologna area were Communist, and in one popular suburb of the city a workers' republic was set up where no German or Italian Fascist troops dared venture after dark. The partisans were stronger and more effective in Emilia than in any other part of Italy, and this helped give the Communists the prestige they needed for winning and holding power locally after the war. When in April 1945 the Allied forces finally broke through into the Emilian plain, the city was already virtually in the hands of the partisan brigades. The Left controlled the town hall, prefecture and police. It could have set up a "Red republic" in Emilia: but any such venture would have been smashed by American arms, and it was not part of national Communist strategy. So in due course the Party handed back the state apparatus, such as the prefecture, to the national authorities in Rome. But the first municipal elections, in March 1946, gave democratic proof of its strength: with over 38 per cent of the vote it emerged as much the largest party, and together with the Socialists was easily able to form a majority administration.

During over thirty years of rule the Party in Bologna has evolved in its nature and policies, just as Italian Communism as a whole has evolved. In the early post-war years it was tinted with Stalinism, and carried on a bitter local power struggle with the Church: but after 1956, a watershed year, both sides turned to conciliation and co-existence. Gradually the old-style romanticism and ideological fervour of the pre-war Communists, apostles of revolution, has given ground to a new and more pragmatic spirit. A younger generation of Communists now in their forties or fifties has come to power locally, most of them *bourgeois* intellectuals or technocrats rather than working-class militants, and these men – like many of the Party leaders in Rome – can probably be credited with genuinely desiring a democratic rather than a totalitarian society. Revolution as a weapon has been abandoned; ideology's tide has waned, and the stress is on efficient civic administration and social justice. Yet there are some ambivalences. The Party may accept that government should be based on democratic assent: yet within its own organisation, both locally and nationally, it is still secretive and centralist like Communist parties anywhere. The leaders rarely allow their quarrels to emerge publicly, and just as the local politicians are generally subservient to the national Party, so within Bologna the Party operates close control over its 50,000 members through the usual system of cells, indoctrination and discipline.

Above all, it is the municipality's record of good government that has made it popular with many people who might not normally vote Communist. How else to explain that the Party's share of the vote in local elections rose from 38 per cent in 1946 to 45 per cent ten years later and has stayed around that figure ever since, with none of the usual democratic swing against the régime in power? In the Communist landslide victories throughout Italy in the 1975 local elections, the Party even topped 50 per cent in Bologna for the first time, an advance that must have been due to local factors as well as national ones. Italy's four biggest cities – Rome, Milan, Turin, Naples – all fell to the Left that year, thus breaking Bologna's long record of being the largest Communist-run town in the "free" world. But whereas the people of those towns were voting for change and against the status quo, the Bolognese in 1975 were re-electing a régime that they already knew well and, on balance, liked.

The 60-member city council is elected by proportional representation. Until 1975 the Communists had always fallen just short of an overall majority of seats, and ruled in coalition with the Socialists and smaller parties of the Left. Thus in 1970-75 the coalition was made up of Communists (28 seats), Socialists (4), extreme Left (1), in face of an opposition led by the Christian Democrats (14). Today the Left's ruling alliance continues, even though the Party now has a narrow absolute majority (31 seats). But it cannot do what it likes: the controls exercised by the Rome-appointed Prefect are considerable, especially in budgetary matters.

The mayor is assisted by an executive *(giunta)* of fifteen senior councillors *(assessori)* who correspond roughly to Germany's *Bürgermeistern* or French *adjoints au maire.* Usually there are some twelve Communists and three Socialists on this *giunta.* Under State rules, the members each receive a part time salary or "allowance" *(indemnità)* which for the mayor is 450,000 lire a month and 225,000 for each *assessore*: this puts them about half-way between the highly-paid executives of Stuttgart and the virtually unpaid councillors of Toulouse and Newcastle. The *indemnità* does not go far, and I met Communists who complained that this makes it hard for the working man without private means to enter politics. Many *assessori* are therefore professional men who keep their own jobs going, though the Party will find ways of subsidising a poorer man whom it specially wants to see in office.

The mayor for the first twenty-one years after the war was Giuseppe Dozza, son of a local baker and a man with an impeccable Party and partisan background. He was in manner a typical Bolognese, sturdy, jovial, a lover of food and drink, widely popular: but he was also tough and something of a Stalinist, and had to guide the city through the difficult Cold War years when often there were clashes between Party militants and state police. He was a good if over-cautious administrator, and even managed to balance the city budgets which was no mean feat at a time when funds were continually being cut or held up by hostile Ministries in Rome. But he was not a man of ideas and he neglected long-term planning. He was succeeded in 1966 by Guido Fanti, a "new wave" Communist from a more well-to-do and educated background, a smooth tactician who saw the need to liberalise and modernise the Party. It was he who took the boldest steps towards wooing the middle classes and the Church.

When Italy's new regional structure was introduced in 1970, Fanti became president of Emilia-Romagna's new regional assembly and his place in Bologna town hall was taken by the remarkable man who remains mayor today: Renato Zangheri, the antithesis of any crude image of the blinkered, tub-thumping, class-obsessed, totalitarian, proletarian "Commie". Zangheri is handsome, elegant, soft-spoken, a serious collector of modern art, a distinguished academic and – more to the point – a man regarded by his many non-Communist friends as a genuine liberal-minded social democrat. He told me that his ideal of a Communist Italy was a pluralist society where the state would be "ideologically neutral": it would not impose any views save anti-Fascist ones and would limit itself to administration and social justice; it would gradually take over the principal means of production but would guarantee full personal freedoms including that of religion. He said that in Bologna he was trying to prove that a Communist government in Italy would not be anti-clerical, and he added that the nation's electorate must retain its right to vote the Communists out of office if it no longer wanted them. Zangheri's friend Bruno Carnacini, Rector of the university and anything but a Marxist, told me, "I say to Renato, 'you are our Dubček.'"

Born in Romagna in 1925, Zangheri joined the Party after fighting as a partisan. He has been on the directive of its national Central Committee since 1960, and as a leading theoretician played a role in the renewal of the Party in the 1960s and its detachment from blind loyalty to Moscow. In a Communist government he might well be a Minister. He holds the chair of economic doctrine at the university and has written books on capitalism and economic history. He is far less parochial-minded than most Bolognese: he was once a Fellow of Reading University and has many friends among British and American academics. Before becoming mayor, he was *assessore* in charge of the Arts.

Zangheri is a shortish, neatly dressed, mild-mannered man with a proud nose and ready smile. He is widely admired as mayor, and gives local people the impression that he is just as ready to listen patiently to their grievances as to make speeches at them. He has described his aim as to keep as close as possible to the real needs of the city. His home life is that of an average prosperous academic with cultivated tastes, while in the *Municipio* the walls of his smart office are hung with canvases by some of his favourite painters – Guttuso, Sutherland, Jackson Pollock. Zangheri has described Bologna as "a city of contradictions", some of which are indeed apparent at his official receptions in the sumptuous 17th-century salons of the *Municipio,* a *palazzo* that was formerly the seat of the Papal Legate. Once I attended a party for a Communist town-twinning organisation. Mediaeval crucifixes and religious triptychs looked down on the austerely dressed comrades from some of Bologna's twin-towns, Leningrad, Zagreb, Brno. Under marvellous frescoes and rococo stucco-work, an elaborate buffet was laid out, with piles of lobsters and asparagus. The guests, many of them tieless or in casual jerseys, shuffled about looking out of place. Only a few senior clerics in red or purple lent much colour or style to the occasion.

So what have been the true achievements of this curious Communist régime? And what is its real strategy? Certainly it has provided a more efficient and less corrupt administration than that of any other large Italian town. It has carried through some useful social measures and civic innovations, to be described later in this chapter: a chain of municipal pharmacies; a nursery school system that is far the best in

Italy; better cheap housing for workers than in most Italian towns; free public transport at rush-hours and severe curbs on city-centre parking; conservation and restoration of the mediaeval centre; and, most important, the pioneering of a system of neighbourhood democracy new to Italy, by dividing the city into 18 wards each with its local council.

These achievements, while valuable, are none of them especially radical except perhaps the last. Anti-Communist critics allege that the *Municipio*'s successes are outweighed by its excessive boasting about them, and that the main achievement of the régime has been its brilliant public-relations effort, based on a positive but not outstanding record. The critics suggest that Bologna is a town very much easier to govern smoothly than vast industrial centres such as Turin or Genoa with their huge immigrant populations, and that the Communists have been clever in deliberately limiting the city's growth and dissuading immigration. Critics claim, too, that in many matters the *Municipio* is too cautious and conservative and that, given the Bolognese temperament, this is a major reason for its relative popularity.

There may be some truth in all this. But the Communists will reply that, if they are not more radical, it is not their fault: their powers of action are severely circumscribed by officialdom in Rome. And there is a lot of truth in this too. Italy's prefectoral system, like France's, is a Napoleonic legacy: each province has its Rome-appointed prefect, who in the case of Bologna looks after the city and its surrounding rural area of 800 square miles. But Italy, alas, is not France. France's prefectoral system may have its drawbacks but at least, thanks to the strength of its central government and civil service, the prefect and his staff are often able to act as dynamic initiators on a local level: in Italy, where the state is so much weaker, the prefect's role is *de facto* far more negative. He is there to prevent the town councils from overspending or carrying out measures disapproved of by Rome. He can even disband a council on the orders of Rome and call for new elections; and in the tense post-war years this sometimes happened, though it is rare today. Until the recent regional reforms, all municipal projects of more than 3 million lire needed the prefect's approval: and although today, in constitutional theory, the new regional assemblies have taken over the prefect's role of vetting civic budgets, in practice Rome has found ways of holding on to some of its powers, so that a town with its budget in deficit cannot raise money without its authority. The director of services in one town near Bolgna told me that he was having to do all his work by bus or on foot, as the council's budget had followed its politics into the red and the Prefect would not allow him to buy a new car. Prefects, needless to say, tend to be strictest with Communist-run towns. And a town of any political colour must also face the obstacle of bureaucratic delays in Rome, whither the prefect refers most of his decisions for counter-signing by some Ministry. It took Bologna nine years to wheedle a permit out of the government for opening its civic pharmacies, and it was not easy to tell how far this delay was due to political obstruction and how far to sheer Roman muddle. Bolognese Communists hate this kind of control: "We're often the victims of political vengeance," a *giunta* member told me; "they've just cut our nursery schools' budget, and we're sure it's because they are jealous of our success with them." This is easily said. In reality, most unbiased observers would say that prefects in Bologna have rarely exercised their powers unreasonably. The system of vetoes may be tiresome for a council: but without it, many Italian cities would sink into even greater chaos than already. An efficient and responsible council such as Bologna's may not really need such controls: but then, a Christian Democrat government is not going to make an exception for Red Bologna.

In fact, Bologna's real problem today is much less the prefectoral veto than Rome's overall budget cuts. Even more than British or French ones, Italian cities depend on State subsidies for their budgets, since local taxes must be handed over to the State and then redistributed. And in the past few years of economic crisis, the Government has imposed severe cuts in its allocations to all towns, whatever their political colour. In 1975, it reduced Naples' budget by some 105 billion lire and Florence's by 40 billion (both cities were then in Christian Democrat hands). Bologna suffered a 30 billion cut. Its budget, like that of most Italian cities, is saved from heavy deficit only by State aid, and it must also turn to the banks for loans, at high interest. This has led to cut-backs in a number of municipal projects, including, as we shall see, the restoration of the old city.

Of course, the *Municipio* can often use Rome as a convenient scapegoat. The budgetary and other pressures can serve as an alibi for its own conservatism in certain matters – a conservatism that in part reflects local temperament and in part is a deliberate strategy. For many years the Party has used Bologna as a shop-window of Communist virtues, and since the end of the Cold War period in the mid-'50s the *Municipio* has turned increasingly to a policy of broad local alliances and conciliation of local interests. The artisan classes have been wooed, and so have the Party's natural opponents, the Church and the capitalists. Is this an expediency, in order to secure the support of partners who are needed for the Party to stay in power locally, within a capitalist Italy, but who might be swept aside if the Party came to power nationally? Or does it reflect, as Zangheri certainly claims, a genuine acceptance of a pluralist society? This is the central enigma of the Party's national policy of "*compromesso storico*" (historic compromise).

The much publicised love-hate relationship between Party and Church in Bologna is a complex and devious affair that is often misinterpreted. Its sheer oddity quickly strikes any visitor. Before my first visit in 1970, I was given an introduction to Guido Fanti by his brother Giorgio, a journalist in Paris. "Of course you realise," I told Giorgio cautiously, "that as an impartial reporter I must also make contact with your Catholic opponents in Bologna, especially the famous Cardinal Lercaro." He laughed: "No problem – you ask Guido to introduce you, they're great friends." And, lo, on arriving in Bologna I first met Zangheri, at that time a member of the *giunta,* and he said, "I suppose you'd like to meet Lercaro? – OK" – and he went straight to dial a number he knew by heart: "*Buona sera, Sua Eminenza*: I'm bringing you an English journalist." And the next day the mayor-to-be drove me to the ex-Archbishop's home, kissed his hand, and stayed with me throughout a frank interview.

Twenty years previously, relations between the two sides had been rather different. Then the Cold War was at its height in Europe, and in Bologna memories of the Church's collaboration with Fascism were still fresh. Some Catholic leaders were murdered, and Church-going families were harassed by the Party. The Church hit back with an equally virulent anti-Communism; and the man it named Archbishop in 1952, Giacomo Lercaro, then aged sixty, came to Bologna with a reputation as an anti-Bolshevik hardliner – odd as it now may seem, in the light of his later shift. He disapproved of Eisenhower's plans to meet Krushchev, as being likely to strengthen "the Communist myth that coexistence between Catholicism and Communism is possible". In Bologna he set up a squad of "flying monks" to combat the enemy at parish level, and he threw the weight of the Church behind the Christian Democrats in the bitterly fought 1956 local election campaign.

The rout of the Christian Democrats in that election marked a turning-point. Lercaro and others drew the lesson that direct Church intervention in politics was counter-productive: it would be wiser to combat Communism by less direct means and try to understand it better. At the same time the local Communists began to put out feelers towards the Church, following the lead of Krushchev's *détente* and the new softer line of the Party in Rome. Soon after, the accession of John XXIII further influenced Lercaro towards moderation. He and Mayor Dozza actually began talking to each other. And when the mild and modern-minded Fanti took over in 1966, relations became almost cordial. Fanti bestowed honorary citizenship on the Cardinal, and accepted the gift of a prayerbook in return. On a famous occasion, Fanti and the *giunta* went to greet Lercaro at the railway station on his return from a Vatican Council session in Rome. Instead of picking fights, the two sides now began to seek out ground they could safely find in common without either having to yield on its basic ideology. Thus they would support pronouncements against American bombing in Vietnam. The muncipality helped Lercaro find sites for new churches: once it went out of its way to rescue a fine 17th-century church threatened with demolition.

The underlying Communist strategy was clear: it was based in part on the belief, probably correct, that a rapprochement would help the Party to win respect with the middle-classes and would be more likely to seduce some Catholics into voting Communist than lead workers to vote for the Right. What the Church hoped to gain, on its side, is not quite so apparent, and it seems that Lercaro's own complex, emotional and unpredictable personality played a determinant role. He was a Genoese, born of humble parents; small and frail-looking, but a man of great physical strength and work capacity. When I met him, he was seventy-eight and had just retired as Archbishop. I was struck by his piercing blue eyes and gentle, seemingly ingenuous way of talking. "My change of heart after 1956," he said, "was because I realised that Catholics and Communists really have a lot in common, the same concern for the poor and for world peace. I felt I should bow to the verdict of the electorate and collaborate with an efficient administration. But this has never amounted to collusion: I have never approved of the Party's ideals." Lercaro was a flamboyant Archbishop who loved to use all the insignia of the Church, mauve silks, incense, processions; he was also in liturgical matters a radical moderniser. His true concern was with his pastoral mission, and in politics he was really rather naïf. His flirtation with the Communists led him to be hated by many middle-class Catholics who called him "the Red Cardinal". When in 1968 he preached an outspoken sermon in San Petronio against the US bombing in Vietnam, Pope Paul finally stepped in and forced his resignation. He then spent his final years in retirement outside Bologna.

He was succeeded by Cardinal Antonio Poma, a more reserved and orthodox priest who was close to the Vatican's line on the dangers of over-fraternisation. So relations with the *Municipio* are now again cooler and more formal, but with no return to the old hostility. The dialogue remains open, and prelates can still be seen at *Municipio* receptions. Each side finds it prudent to respect the other's interests: for instance, in 1973 a joint commission was set up to decide on the division of responsibilities in private teaching and welfare work. On the local level of ward and parish, the situation varies with the local personalities. Some idealists on both sides believe, with Zangheri and Lercaro, that collaboration in good faith is feasible, for limited practical ends, even if ideologically they can do no more than agree to differ. A Party militant told me, "Often it is easier to get on with priests than with Christian Democrat politicians: they have more human sense. Today, for instance, a Monsignor in this ward came to see me to discuss joint famine relief, aid for Chilean political prisoners, and a joint statement on disarmament" – all safe subjects, far from the nitty-gritty of local conflict. Yet some priests do also collaborate in the practical work of the ward councils, even those controlled by the Left. I visited the *curé* of a working-class parish, a jovial, round-faced typical Bolognese who sat me down to a large lunch. "I am good friends with the ward council chairman, a Marxist, and we work together on welfare and housing problems. But the Church should remain neutral politically and concentrate on spiritual matters," he said, opening a cupboard with 23 kinds of claret and offering me a choice of whiskies and Cognacs. "So I support the Lercaro line. One can approve of individual Communists while rejecting their ideology and leaving that battle to the politicians." Other priests, probably a majority, think this indulgence dangerous. "We should beware of condoning Communism through joint activities with them," said one, "for that in itself is a political gesture."

Inevitably the Church is uncertain on this issue, here as elsewhere in Italy. It has been losing ground, while the Party has been gaining. In Bologna one person in five goes to Mass on Sundays, a higher figure than in France but only half the average for Catholic Italy. The Church has been losing contact with the workers, less than 5 per cent of whom attend mass regularly, and parts of the town are dechristianised, with organised social life and welfare in the hands of the Party and the parish halls almost empty. Yet – and how very Bolognese! – many people see no incompatibility between practising Catholicism and voting Communist. Even non-churchgoers still cling to the main rituals of the Church: over 90 per cent of Bologna's Communist voters were baptised and a majority still have church weddings and funerals and get their children baptised. It is quite usual for Communist officials to be married in church, followed by a reception at the local Party-run *Casa del Popolo*. And in answer to a questionnaire, "Can one be a good Communist and good Catholic?", as many as 71 per cent of Communist voters said "yes," and a mere 8 per cent "no". Even 23 per cent of CD voters said "yes" to the same question.

Does this mean that the Bolognese have abandoned Marx? Or that, still half-believing in a hereafter, they are hedging their bets? A typical explanation, if not quite rational, was given to me by a small shopkeeper: "I am not interested in what Marx may have said, I vote for the Communists because they are the most effective political force around here, and I'd like to see them get the chance to do nationally what they've already done locally. At the same time I go to Church sometimes and have my kids baptised because, well, it's part of our social tradition. The Church is still a kind of family for us, as the Party is too, for many people. I still believe in God, more or less, and I don't think that the Communists, if in power nationally, would prevent the practice of religion." Certainly they would not: the Church would be likely to retain at least as much freedom as in Poland, probably more. But the present situation certainly benefits the Party, politically, more than the Right. The Communists' soft-sell strategy has succeeded in persuading quite a number of Catholics that a Left Government would not be too anti-clerical and need not be feared.

Conciliation with the Church has been part of a wider policy of wooing non-Communist interest groups. Togliatti had preached that Communism and small-scale private enterprise were compatible; and, taking its cue from this, the *Municipio* after 1956 set about attracting Bologna's large class of shopkeepers, artisans and small businesses – the town has some 10,000 self-employed craftsmen. The creation of supermarkets was blocked by the withholding of building permits, with the twofold aim of pleasing the small tradesmen and protecting the Party's own cooperatives from competition. Artisans and small manufacturers were encouraged to group together and helped with loans, with the result that today a large part of this class votes Communist and considers the city council its best shield against take-overs by larger firms. Electorally, the Party relies heavily on this. It has even gone farther and sought accommodation with Bologna's few larger industries – what Robert Evans* has called "a kind of gentlemen's agreement with the capitalist class based on the theory that good business will win as much for the workers as agitation". The aim appears to be to prevent the kind of friction and unrest that could spoil Bologna's reputation as haven of order and consensus. The most notorious case is that of the *Municipio*'s peculiar dealings with Attilo Monti, the leading industrialist in the area, owner of petrol and sugar refineries, hotels and newspapers. Monti is a national figure, a man of extreme-Right sympathies who has backed Almirante's neo-Fascist party. He owns *La Nazione* in Florence and *Il Giornale d'Italia* in Rome, two outspokenly Right-wing papers. He also owns the leading Bologna daily, *Il Resto di Carlino,* which makes strident anti-Communist noises in its coverage of national and world affairs but is strangely silent when it comes to criticising the local administration in any detail or making enquiries into local Communist activities. Why? Though it is denied on both sides, there appears to have been some kind of a deal. Monti has been granted various facilities, including permits to build new plant in "green belt" areas around Bologna: in return, he has undertaken to avoid press attacks that could be embarrassing, and has also agreed to defer certain factory closures that would have led to unrest. Or so it was alleged to me by a number of liberals, who deplored this "cynical pact".

Il Resto di Carlino sells 240,000 copies daily and is much the largest paper in Emilia. Its curious name dates from the days when a *carlino* was a small coin, named after Charles V, that would buy a cigar in a tobacconist's with enough change left over *(il resto)* for a copy of the paper too. Today the paper cannot be said to have any great influence on Bolognese affairs, though it is read by almost as many Communist voters as read the regional edition, printed in Milan, of the national Party paper, *l'Unità.* The *Carlino*'s editor told me: "Fanti and

---

* *Coexistence: Communism and its Practice in Bologna, 1945-1965,* Notre Dame University Press, Notre Dame, Ind., 1967.

Zangheri are wonderful at getting the workers to keep quiet, thus avoiding unrest. I say they're worth two battalions of police – but I won't write that in my paper! I like the local Communists, who are innocuous and have a good record. The Prefect stops them from doing anything wild. But it would be very different if they were in power nationally – then I'd be scared stiff." This is typical of the attitudes of many of the local non-Communist *bourgeoisie.* Some, including the university Rector and a few industrialists, are on cordial dinner-party terms with Zangheri and his cultivated colleagues. Mario Cagli, a lawyer, said, "Some of our friends think we are crazy to do this – but why? Zangheri speaks our language, he's our social equal, and he's sensitive to all problems." In fact the *bourgeoisie* have little to fear. Though the Communists claim to have narrowed differentials by easing the tax burden on the poor, this seems little more than face-saving propaganda: the controls exercised by Rome allow them little freedom of action, and the rich here are no more heavily taxed than in other towns.

Yet this smiling face that the Party turns towards the outside world is balanced, within its own ranks, by a discipline and secretiveness that are almost as marked as in other Communist *milieux.* This is not an easy matter for an outsider to assess, since it is hard to know just what goes on behind the scenes. The Communists do not air their quarrels in public, as other parties do, and they seem to resort to a good deal of Soviet-style "democratic centralism" within their ranks, for all their liberal pronouncements on the future of society as a whole. The Party has 50,000 paid-up members in Bologna itself, by far the highest level in Italy; 30 per cent are women. They are carefully supervised from the Party's efficient head office in the mediaeval centre of the town, a grand old palace with stuccoes and painted ceilings. The town is divided into cells, where members are screened for their orthodoxy; new recruits are indoctrinated, and some are sent to the local Party school. Some working-class parts of the town are effectively under Party control, and a non-Communist there must show some readiness to cooperate. In short, the Party in Bologna is an immensely powerful and tightly-organised force, deriving its funds not only from its large membership but from its affiliates, notably the large and prosperous cooperatives* and the Communist-led trade union, CGIL.§ And the *giunta* has installed a computer centre in the *Municipio* which it claims

* See page 178. § See page 177.

to be the first venture of its kind in Europe: every detail of the population is recorded there. Of course, it is pointed out, this is merely to help with routine civic administration... but what a useful prototype it might prove, if the Party were in power in Italy and needed to keep a central check on 55 million citizens!

Within the Party, there is free and frank discussion behind closed doors, but once a decision has been arrived at, no one breaks ranks in public. Local officials are supposedly elected by the rank-and-file, but in practice the candidate proposed by headquarters is generally the one adopted. This is "democratic centralism", which relates also to the delicate question of how far the Bolognese Communists are obedient to Party policy laid down in Rome. Fanti and Zangheri, both members of the national directorate of the Party, are men of much the same liberal persuasion as Berlinguer and Amendola, the national leaders: so policy clashes are not likely. Even so, though Bologna is allowed to take its own decisions on routine matters, on major ones it defers to the Party in Rome, as far as one can tell. And there is no doubt that the Party leadership fears the strength of the Bolognese and Emilian Communists and does not want them to secure too much power. In 1973, Fanti and Zangheri laid plans to start a Communist daily paper in Emilia, to rival the *Carlino* which sells eight times as many copies locally as *Unità*. But the Party in Rome said no. Was it that *Unità*, fearing loss of sales, put on pressure? Or, more probably, that the Central Party feared local Communists winning too much power and authority through possessing their own paper? Central discipline prevailed, and the project was dropped.

This discipline at all levels is one of the secrets of the success of Communist government in Bologna. There is patently less corruption than in most large Italian cities – but this does not mean there is none at all. In the awarding of public contracts, the *giunta* understandably tends to favour the Communist-led cooperatives, who in turn give funds to the Party. And one hears rumours of under-the-counter deals with private firms, as in the case of Monti. But if bribes are accepted, at least they go into Party funds and not into private pockets as in many other towns, and the Party would justify this milking of capitalism as fair sport. I heard of only two cases of individual councillors accepting money for themselves. The notorious system of *sottogoverno* – rule by nepotism, graft and intrigue – that is the common currency of so much Italian political life, both local and national, is far less in evidence here in Bologna where one factory-owner said, "I don't have to bribe or tip people, as in the rest of Italy." Bologna may be less shiningly uncorrupt than Stuttgart, but it would seem to compare favourably with Toulouse and certainly with Newcastle – and that, by Italian standards, is saying quite a lot.

This mixture of Party discipline and civic efficiency and probity has preserved Bologna from most – but not all – of the chaos that has crept over Italy during the 1970s, as the slow disintegration of the state, and of public confidence in the state, has led to the growth of anarchy and violence in many cities. Until the 1977 riots, extremists of Right and Left alike did not seem to regard Bologna as suitable terrain. The Party has its own trained police force, which operates in liaison with the state police when trouble threatens, and is expert at dealing with agitators; the Party can also count on the obedience of the unions. So in the mid-1970s there were few of the angry demonstrations common in other cities, and this calm in the heart of a chaotic country added to the sense of protectiveness already given to the Bolognese by their womb-like arcades. An industrialist was quoted in *The Sunday Times* in 1975: "Here one feels a bit sleepy because things work and one doesn't feel the pulse of the nation. The darling comrades make us live inside a comfortable nest of cotton wool. Red cotton wool."

Yet beneath the surface, unrest was growing. When the national Party moved into *de facto* support of the Government after the 1976 general election, the small extreme-Left groups in Italy stepped up their campaign against the Communists, denounced as "traitors to the working-class" and "lackeys of *bourgeois* capitalism". And understandably they selected Bologna, the PCI showpiece, as one of their targets. They began by exploiting the students' agitation over poor study conditions and lack of job outlets.* On 11 March 1977 a medical student was killed by the police during a student riot, and the next day armed urban guerrillas moved into action in the mediaeval city, throwing incendiary bombs at public buildings, smashing shop windows, overturning buses to form barricades. They battled with 1,000 armed police, who used tanks to clear the area. The guerrillas then quietly disappeared. Most of them belonged to extreme-Left anti-Communist factions, possibly including the notorious Red Brigades. Few were Bolognese: most had probably infiltrated from elsewhere. Yet they gave the complacent citizens a nasty fright, and it was some weeks before social life in the city centre returned to normal.

---

* See pages 164-171.

The incident has left a permanent mark by creating a new undercurrent of unease. Kidnappings and other individual acts of violence may be far less common than in some other cities such as Milan and Turin; yet, as in those cities, the rich are now taking care not to mark themselves out as targets by flaunting their wealth. Very often they avoid driving their Rolls Royces or Mercedes through the streets late at night, or they will not let their children come home late on their own. And in a more general sense, the national crisis of the past few years has begun to stir the Bolognese from their easy-going complacency and induce many of them to requestion their basic values. The local political comity is being disturbed by matters more dangerous and fundamental, such as the anarchists' threat to the stability of the Italian State. So Bologna, whether it likes it or not, is being forced to take more account of the rest of Italy. It is a less snugly enclosed place than ten years ago.

After the 1977 riots the Christian Democrats joined the Communists in denouncing the terrorists and there was a huge public rally in support of Zangheri and his law-and-order policy. So, in a real sense, the affair strengthened support for the *Municipio* and drew Communists and Catholics closer together. Yet the Party's *compromesso storico* policy has also been causing disquiet within its own ranks since 1976, locally as well as nationally. Some younger militants within the Party share the views of the extremists that the price paid for civic respectability has been too high. In order to retain the wider support it needs, the Party has compromised with the capitalist establishment and, as Robert Evans puts it, "has been forced to adopt the very methods it condemns, to become, apparently, as conservative as many political parties which operate in the Western world it rejects". This is resented by some younger workers and intellectuals who want the Party to resume the class struggle. Their influence for the moment is limited, probably not extending beyond 10 per cent of members: the leadership has the rank-and-file in hand, and in Emilia the latter may want a better Italy but it does not want revolution. So what of the future of Bolognese Communism? This will depend on many factors, national and even European, outside the scope of this book. For the moment, the enigmas remain. Is the Party's own tight discipline really compatible with the open democratic society to which it subscribes? Is its mildness and conciliation a necessary expediency, within the present Italian context, or part of its real nature? Behind all the persuasive propaganda and glossy brochures, how sincere and effective have its local policies been? A closer look at its record in town planning and community affairs may give a further clue.

4

"Conservation is Revolution!" — but a slow one

The *Municipio*'s reputation rests as much as anything on its town-planning policies. It has won a gold medal from UNESCO for its conservation plans for the historic centre, and a prize from the World Traffic Conference for limiting private traffic in the inner city. Elsewhere in Italy, the splendour of the architectural heritage is frequently matched by the uninspired level of modern planning, but Bologna is often quoted as an exception. It has put the emphasis on conservation rather than on development – there are no modern buildings of any distinction – and has sometimes been criticised for this "museum" approach. But, seeing how much there is in Bologna that needs to be conserved, the policy seems justifiable. At least the authorities have prevented the developers from tearing down old buildings to put up new office blocks, as is happening all over Europe.

The expansion of population and industry has been slower than in most other north Italian cities, or than in Toulouse which has comparable problems of conservation. So there has been no great influx of southern immigrants, demanding housing and creating ghettoes, and this has relieved the planners of some pressures and left them more free to concentrate on their stated ideal: to rescue the mediaeval centre from dilapidation, for social as well as aesthetic reasons. Their aim is for this to remain a residential district with a mixed class structure. Their dual policy, of limiting the growth of the city and discouraging workers from moving out into new suburbs, may include obvious electoral motives, as is alleged. But their conservationism also has a large measure of sincerity and accords with the temperament of townsfolk who have a long Latin tradition of centre-city living and who wish to remain within the protective comfort of the arcades.

The strategy was elaborated in the late 1960s. As a first step, traffic was banned in the Piazza Maggiore and some other central squares. Then an expensive public relations campaign was launched, to canvas support for tackling a problem that can be defined as follows. Bologna has the largest mediaeval complex in Europe after Venice. Parts are in good condition and many *palazzi* are well kept by their rich owners. But other areas are derelict: the graceful colonnaded façades are peeling and crumbling or conceal fearful slums. Many houses were bombed and still stand empty or gutted; others are the squalid homes of the poor, with communal toilets and no running water.

The *Municipio*'s ambitious aim is to avoid pulling down these historic houses but to renovate them, stage by stage, over an area of nearly two square miles with a current population of 70,000. The area includes 48 empty monasteries. In 1974 a modest start was made in five small pilot areas, at a cost of 5,000 million lire. But the project is running far behind schedule, owing to budget cuts that are not the *Municipio*'s fault.

The municipality buys the properties, helped by a new compulsory purchase law that enables this to be done cheaply. It rehouses the inhabitants temporarily elsewhere and then, when restoration is finished, it puts them back in their old homes. At first this aroused protests. Artisans and other poor people objected to being dislodged, as slum-dwellers so often do. Some of them even went to Party HQ and angrily tore up their cards. So the *Municipio* was forced to back-track for a while, while tempers were soothed and efforts were made to explain that there would be proper rehousing, on the same spot.

The project is in the hands of Pier Luigi Cervallati, an enthusiastic young Communist architect and member of the *giunta*. He launched the slogan, "Conservation is revolution!" he said to me, "In Rome and Paris only the rich can afford to live in the centre any more. Here we want all classes to coexist, in comfortable homes in the warm environment of the old city. It's inhuman to shift working people out to impersonal suburbs." He claims that it is also actually cheaper to restore houses than build new ones in the suburbs, if only because public utilities already exist in the centre. But inevitably Cervellati has been criticised by non-Communists. Is not this buying up of old property a clever take-over bid by the council to bring the old city under public ownership? The blocking of new residential development has pushed land and housing costs to the highest Italian levels – is this fair? And is there not rather too much effort towards prestige, and the winning of international prizes for blueprints, while the actual work of restoration has done no more than nibble at the problem in a few tiny areas? True, the scheme still exists largely in blueprint: the actual restoration has not got very far. By 1979 only 221 dwellings had been restored, and one larger building to be used as a student hostel. But the *Municipio* has been subject to such heavy state budget cuts for this project that it has no alternative. It has been forced to turn to private capital for help. And most of the restoration of the mediaeval centre since 1974 has been done by private owners at their own cost.

In the city as a whole, outside the historic centre, the housing situation is far from perfect – but this again is not primarily the municipality's fault. In Italy, the building of popular housing is the concern of the state and is carried out by a semi-autonomous national agency backed by state funds, usually very inadequate. The role of the municipalities is to provide the land, and here Bologna has managed better than most cities. Its cooperatives have also done a good deal of building. There is no real shortage of housing in Bologna today, but the low subsidies force rents and prices to be absurdly high: a worker may spend 25 per cent of his income on rent, against 8 per cent average in Britain. Most housing is still privately built and for sale. All round the edge of Bologna you see post-war blocks of flats with severe reddish façades, perhaps ten storeys high, built of local clay brick. The quality of the flats is quite good, but the siting is ill-planned. Bologna's post-war housing record may be well above the appalling Italian average; but it compares poorly with my other Western towns.

The town's record in dealing with traffic has been much more remarkable, even revolutionary by Italian standards. Since 1972 the mediaeval centre has been closed to through traffic, except buses. If you want to drive across the city, you must take the ring road by the gates: it is still possible to penetrate close to the centre by car, but for access only, and if you try to get across you are caught in a maze of one-way alleys from which there seems to be no exit. You quickly realise that in this relatively small area it is quicker to go on foot. Hundreds of new buses have been put into service, and bus transport is free from 5 to 9 a.m. and 4 to 8 p.m., while pensioners can travel free all day and students get cheap all-day passes. All this costs the council over 1,000 million lire a year, but has led to a 40 per cent increase in passenger use of buses, while the council claims that the saving on petrol used by private cars is as much as 4,000 million lire a year. So the Communists are using their own budget to help the Government with its energy import bill!

It is now possible to stroll around the city centre without having to face the honking, seething traffic that plagues many Italian cities. Bologna has become almost a landbound Venice. Parking regulations have been tightened too, though they are variably applied. For aesthetic reasons there are still no meters, but officials in peaked caps will sometimes come up and demand 100 lire. Some streets with "no parking" signs are lined all day with cars which disappear only when a notice goes up saying the street will be cleaned that night. Yet the tow-away trucks can also sweep arbitrarily and cars with foreign plates are not immune. Of all my five towns, this was the only one where my car was towed away - twice - and I had to pay 10,000 lire each time to recover it.

In its overall approach to town planning, Bologna shows an interesting contrast with Toulouse, a town with some similar problems. It has been rather more successful in preserving the quality of life in the historic centre: there is less noise, dirt and traffic than in Toulouse. But in planning for the conurbation as a whole the authorities have shown little enterprise, beyond building a ring motorway to link with the national network. Bologna's expansion has not been phenomenal, yet its population has grown 50 per cent since the war and it has not received the new infrastructure to match. There is a lack of modern public buildings, which could easily have been placed in the outer districts without harming the mediaeval centre's harmony.

Vague and grandiose projects are announced, then indefinitely delayed. Around 1960 the council put forward a plan for a much-needed new administrative and business centre, in the north-east suburbs. Soon afterwards the Japanese architect Kenzo Tange was hired to draw up detailed plans, at a fee of 100 million lire, and this he did amid fanfares of civic publicity. But only in 1975 was the business centre finally built, while other aspects of the project were tacitly abandoned, notably the scheme to build a new suburb nearby to house 6,000, a kind of Bolognese equivalent of Toulouse's Le Mirail. The delays and back-trackings can be put down partly to shortage of finance, Prefectoral vetoes, or, as one industrialist suggested to me, "the sheer lack of organising experience in Italy for this kind of large operation - the *giunta* wouldn't know how to take decisions on this scale. They draw up grandiose schemes for prestige purposes, that's all." But *Assessore* Cervallati had a different explanation: "In the past five years we've decided against this type of expansion and are putting all our efforts into revitalising the centre. In line with this, we've dropped an earlier project for giving the university a site for a new campus east of the town: instead we are helping them to expand round their traditional site by buying up old buildings in the centre. It's important for town and gown to keep in close organic contact, in the centre, as they have for seven centuries. And we want to keep the human scale in Bologna: we must fight against the gigantism that has spoilt many towns." Noble-sounding sentiments. Of course it may be, as the critics suggest, that the *Municipio* has electoral motives, too, in wanting to limit shifts of population that might lose them voters, either through workers moving to new homes outside the civic boundaries, or through an influx of new immigrants who might not be amenable to the Party. Conservation thus has a double meaning. But in public affairs, motives are always mixed. If the Party has its own subtle strategy, this does not prevent cultivated men like Cervellati and Zangheri from being perfectly sincere in their desire to preserve the city's unique heritage, for the benefit of the Bolognese. Their trumpeted restoration schemes may for the moment exist more on paper than in practice. But at least they have succeeded in preventing desecration.

5

A new link between town-hall and citizen

The Bolognese pride themselves on possessing more civic sense and community feeling than most Italians. It goes deep into their history. And without this tradition, the *Municipio* might not have found such fertile soil for one of its more notable innovations: the division of the city into 18 wards or districts, each with its own council. The aim has been to decentralise some municipal activities and give the citizen a closer sense of involvement.

The idea came originally from the Christian Democrats. But the Communists took it over and put it into practice, in 1964. Each ward is presided over by a delegate of the mayor, and he and his council of 20 are appointed by the *Municipio*: but all parties are represented in proportion to their strength in the city, and the CD and other opposition groups have accepted to collaborate with the scheme rather than spoil it through boycott. Of course it would be more democratic if each council were directly elected by the ward's inhabitants: but this would require special legislation in Rome, which the Government for many years refused. Could it be – as the Communists allege – that Rome did not want the experiment to work too well?

The ward councils play a limited but useful role. They select entrants for the nursery schools, which are always over-subscribed; they run information bureaux and carry out some social welfare; above all, they are closely consulted by the *Municipio* on planning and budgetary matters and generally act as a filter for grievances and a link between citizen and town hall – useful in a large town. In most wards the system works smoothly, with a pragmatic spirit of collaboration between Communists and other council members (including a few priests). Sometimes trouble arises when local Communists try to politicise ward activities, for instance by staging "anti-imperialist" rallies. But this happens rarely, and is not encouraged by the *Municipio.*

Some Communists have been afraid that the system might weaken their control over the city, especially as devolution and open discussion run counter to the Party's own centralised and disciplined structures. But the "liberals" led by Zangheri must be credited with a genuine concern for democratic government by consent: "It is essential," the mayor told me, "for the *Municipio* to have a regular two-way dialogue with citizens of every opinion. Therefore we must decentralise." Zangheri patently believes in pluralist democracy, but of course he has an eye on public relations too. The ward councils fall within the broad Communist strategy of conciliation and using Bologna as a showcase. "The scheme helps to legitimise their rule, in the eyes of the middle classes," a Socialist told me, while in 1975 a Christian Democrat added more cynically, "The Communists know they are not risking too much, since Rome has not allowed devolution to go very far. How embarrassed they might be if Rome *were* to allow the councils to be directly elected." However, the Government did finally allow direct elections, which are due for the first time in the spring of 1980. We shall see whether this serves to strengthen the Communist rule, or to encourage opposition to it.

Bologna's scheme has since been followed by some other cities (including Milan and Venice), but there it has not worked so well. The Bolognese suggest this is because other towns lack their civic spirit. One ward chairman, a Socialist, showed me his headquarters where a small staff of paid and voluntary workers were busy on welfare activities. "These councils," he said, "help to reduce the divisions between social groups. One of our jobs is to explain to the citizens what the *Municipio* is doing, and to the *Municipio* what the citizens are feeling, and this is important in a country where normally things are done in great secrecy. On this council, Communists and others work easily together." So in Bologna there is more effective contact between the town hall and the population than in Toulouse or Stuttgart. But the initiative has come from the town hall: as elsewhere in Italy, there are very few of the privately created residents' associations that flourish on Tyneside and are now appearing in Toulouse.

The social and cultural life of the popular suburbs is actively promoted by the Communist Party. Every ward has at least one *Casa del Popolo,* an informal social centre run by the Party but freely open to anyone. I visited one in working-class Corticella: large, inelegant premises, with older people playing billiards and younger ones playing cards or dancing to a juke-box in a brightly lit bar. Some of the activities are politically oriented: debates on Marxism, or concerts and shows by artists such as Theodorakis and the Left-wing actor Dario Fo. But there are also dances and sports, and a banqueting hall for hire by anyone including the Christian Democrats. The Church has its own social hall in the ward, smaller and much less active. In these suburbs, Church and Party co-exist in fairly good-humoured rivalry. Nor is there any very sharp antagonism between the social classes. Workers and *bourgeoisie* of course remain distinct, as anywhere in the West, and class divisions are more evident than in Stuttgart; but as workers pick up *bourgeois* habits, so the gulf has been narrowing. In some other parts of Italy matters may be much less cosy; but here in Bologna, all is smoothed over not only by the Communist's affability but by the temperament of the people, their easy-going gregariousness, their sense of solidarity, of belonging first and foremost to the secret society of this compelling city rather than to any particular class. We shall see the same phenomenon on Tyneside, and to a lesser degree in Toulouse.

Another achievement of the *Municipio* has been the creation of a nursery school network unique in Italy, attended by 75 per cent of all three- to six-year-olds. Elsewhere, these schools tend to be run by religious or other voluntary bodies, with limited funds, and their capacity is far lower: in Turin only 25 per cent of small children are in nursery schools, and in Rome 20 per cent. Bologna's schools are funded by the municipality, with grudging aid from the state. The *bourgeoisie* at first treated the scheme with inevitable suspicion, but today most of them gladly let their children attend, and in the average school you find children from all classes.

The *Municipio* has had success with two other ventures unusual for Italy: a network of municipal pharmacies, and a system of "day hospitals" and home care for the elderly. This is valuable, in a country where the inefficiency of the state medical services is notorious. The Italian national health service suffers from all kinds of deficiencies: neglect of preventive medicine, bad hospital management, severe lack of hospital space so that beds overflow from wards into the corridors. Hospitals are crowded out with elderly people whose families try to dump them there; also, a doctor in Italy is legally responsible for any consequence of failing to admit a patient, so the hospitals fill up with people suffering from minor ailments. Doctors within the state system are under-staffed and overworked, and sometimes a doctor will see 200 patients in a day. No wonder so many people, including poor people, feel obliged to spend their savings on seeking private care.

Since medicine is a state concern, the *Municipio* has neither the funds nor the legal means to do more than offer a few palliatives, such as the care for the elderly. The same applies in other social fields. To an extent, but only to an extent, can the municipality protect its citizens from the chaotic jungle of state bureaucracy and welfare services. The legal and prison systems are gravely archaic, and so is bureaucracy in general, as heavy, slow and legalistic as in many less advanced Latin countries. There are at least 2,000 different health insurance funds, a crazy and costly proliferation. According to one estimate, Italy has some 60,000 useless or anachronistic institutions, including one for helping orphans of the First World War (none of them now under sixty). Yet these bodies still receive state aid. And as the economic and social chaos of Italy was aggravated in the mid-1970s, other nuisances developed: the postal services became more and more erratic, and the waning of confidence in the currency led to a hoarding of coins, so that today it is often impossible to get small change. If you offer 200 lire in a shop or *café* for something costing, say, 170 lire, you are liable to be offered toffees or a box of matches as change. The Italians' good humour, and their flair for improvisation and cutting corners, enable them to put up with these manifold ills. And in Bologna at least the civic utilities work well. But the citizens are not totally immune to the world outside, to the steady erosion of organised Italian society.

6
Cobwebs over a grand cultural tradition

If you want some clue to the nature of the cultural scene in Bologna, visit the central public lending library. It is housed in a superb early 18th-century baroque palace, and the lofty main hall where the books are kept is covered with brilliant frescoes. The building breathes harmony and refinement: its organisation as a library does not. The books seem to be incidental, arranged in any old order with no proper catalogue, and I could find none in foreign languages except some French *livres de poche*. There are only 5,000 ticket-holders and on a Saturday the place was almost deserted. Italians, as is well known, do not read much – perhaps because they are too busy talking.

Bologna values the visual arts more than literature, of course: but the real point I am making is that Italy's marvellous artistic heritage is the backdrop for a contemporary cultural life that staggers along, half-crippled by fusty bureaucracy, lack of funds, and a degree of public indifference. This is true in Bologna as elsewhere. The *Municipio*'s effort for the living arts has been noticeably less striking than its planning and social policies, and is especially mediocre in the fields of theatre and music. True, it is at the mercy, as usual, of state intervention, for the prefect can (and sometimes does) forbid it to spend its own money on a given project. The *Municipio* complains that this prevents it from making the most coherent use of the 3,000 million or so lire (under 2 per cent of its budget) that it spends each year on the arts. Its critics reply that the *Municipio* could do much more if it tried: far from forcing a Leftish diet on the Bolognese, it has not been bold enough, and in an effort to please all tastes it has ended up with a policy based on woolly compromise.

The opera house *(Teatro Communale)* is run by a semi-autonomous board of various local government delegates, with the mayor as chairman. The manager is appointed by the state. Although the operas and concerts play to 80 per cent capacity, only 15 per cent of the revenue comes from box-office, while the rest – over 1,000 million lire a year – comes from state, region and city. "The prefect has just ordered the city to cut its subsidy by half," complained the manager when I saw him; "I'm so short of money I don't know how I'm going to pay the staff." The company is often teetering on the edge of insolvency. It struggles to maintain a full-time orchestra of 100 players, a chorus of 70, and a small ballet troupe: this absurdly heavy paraphernalia is the status symbol normally expected of any large town in this nation with its grandiose opera tradition, but it is becoming something of a façade. Bologna suffers from the malaise affecting opera and music in many parts of Italy.

The opera house is quite small and very traditional, a mini-La Scala. I went to see *Il Trovatore.* Ushers in red-and-gold livery were attending on a *bourgeois* audience of mainly older people. The scene was much as we shall see in Toulouse, save that dress was much smarter: I even saw a few dinner-jackets. The singing of the main parts (by imported stars) was competent, but the production and décor had an un-Italian heaviness and the chorus line, most of them fifty if a day, signally failed to convince as rollicking Spanish students. They seemed to be repeating mechanically some role from their distant youth – like the opera house as a whole. I was surprised to learn that the Bolognese's favourite operas are Wagner's, preferred even to Verdi – "You see," I was told, "Verdi came from a rival Emilian town, Parma, so there's a certain antagonism." The town has recently got round to accepting modern opera, in small doses.

The opera company sometimes goes on tour in Emilia or even abroad, but it never visits the other major Italian cities nor do their companies come to Bologna: municipal jealousy is the reason, much as in Germany. The resulting lack of true competition has an effect on standards, as it does in Germany – and more so, seeing the general level of quality is so much lower. However, in the case of orchestral music there is less parochialism. The *Teatro Communale* runs a season of concerts, usually sold out, that include visits from leading foreign orchestras or chamber groups, for instance, Boulez with the BBC Symphony. The theatre's own orchestra is not of very high quality – "Certainly not as good as the Bournemouth Symphony," said an English music-lover in Bologna: "there are excellent visiting artists, but the calibre of the town's own musical life is dismal. There is little of the good amateur activity – choral societies and chamber groups – that you find in Germany and many parts of Britain. Music is hardly taught in schools, the local conservatory is feeble, and even the vast university has little music performed by students. In Bologna as elsewhere, Italy's music tradition seems to be dying on its feet."

The situation of the city's theatre is little better. It typifies the general crisis of drama in Italy, where even famous companies like the *Piccolo Teatro di Milano* have been losing audiences and running into hardship. Bologna has two small theatres which take touring shows. One, the Ribalta, very small, lives off a subsidy from the Province and shows mainly experimental plays done on shoe-string budgets: it is often near-empty. The other, the Duse, larger and more commercial, is popular with middle-class audiences: it takes whatever is available from the national tour networks, maybe Goldoni one week, Brecht or Anouilh the next. But Bologna alone of the towns in this book has no civic repertory company of its own; and attempts to set one up in the 1960s revealed the problems that this kind of venture tends to face in Italy. The *Municipio* formed a company in 1962, but for the next five years it staggered from one failure to another, constantly changing directors and policies, and finally closed. The experiment has not been repeated. The *Municipio* put the blame on the state, for refusing to authorise adequate subsidy, but there were other factors too. The company never had a home of its own and had to use make-shift premises: nor did it have a coherent policy. The repertory was chosen by a municipal board who, anxious to conciliate and avoid trouble, would select first a play to suit the Communists, then one for the Christians, and so on. Wesker was followed by some Right-wing Catholic piece. "The Communists' placatory strategy may be fine for local government, but it's death to culture," was a comment I heard. At first a worthy attempt was made to attract working-class audiences by touring the *Case del Popolo* with excerpts as "trailers"; but this was done too sporadically, and failed. And the company's middle-class audiences, mostly students, lost interest too. Today Bologna is left with no locally-produced drama, save for an interesting venture by the university's Theatre Institute which sends experimental Brecht-style student productions round the *Case del Popolo.*

For cinema and the visual arts, Bologna fares much better, as at least you would expect in Italy. In addition to the commercial places there is a flourishing municipal cinema – the first of its kind in Italy and possibly the best – that shows a good selection of the best new films: German, Japanese and so on. The *Municipio* gives a small subsidy, but most receipts come from box-office. The Bolognese thus have a far fuller choice of serious films than Geordies or Stuttgarters. Since the ending of the State broadcasting monopoly in 1976, a few local private TV and radio stations have emerged, none other than mediocre.

As befits the Italian tradition, the visual arts are taken very seriously by the city council – especially by Zangheri, a noted art-lover – and standards are certainly higher than in the case of theatre or music. There is a *Biennale* of classical art, often featuring the Bolognese school: it is subsidised mainly by the state and is of good quality. There are frequent exhibitions of modern art too, run by an active local association with municipal backing. These sometimes lead to conflict, for the *avant-garde* ideas of the promoters do not always suit public taste, mainly conservative. Yet the Bolognese are sufficiently alert to modern art for the town to support some fifteen private galleries – one of them distinguished – as well as a large new civic museum of modern art.

The museum will sometimes, for example, hold an exhibition of Arab art "in solidarity with the struggle of the Palestinian people": but this is a fairly rare instance of a civic attempt to give culture a directly propagandist flavour. Generally the *Municipio* acts more subtly: culture is part of the strategy of conciliation and image-building in Bologna and must not be too sectarian. "The council is terrified of losing support," said one critic; "they wouldn't put on Brecht, lest it annoy the Church. No wonder the repertory venture failed." Yet the shortcomings of cultural policy must also be blamed on the state's control of all finance: the modern art museum and cultural centre, first projected in 1960, was not completed until fifteen years later owing to a succession of vetoes by ministerial bodies in Rome.

Since Zangheri took office, the town's cultural policy has become a little more vigorous and imaginative. He has been influential in raising standards at the opera and improving the modern art exhibitions. He has installed a group of modern sculptures outside one of the best-loved mediaeval churches – to the fury of conservatives – and has inaugurated free outdoor performances of ballet and folk-dancing in the Piazza Maggiore. These are highly popular. Zangheri's policy is also to take culture into the suburbs and encourage working people to share in it, and the *Case del Popolo* are enlisted for this purpose. The municipal cinema and even the opera company now put on shows in the suburbs, where new branch libraries have opened too.

From all this it must be evident that the level of official spoon-feeding is almost as great as in Stuttgart, albeit organised differently.

People tend to accept passively what they are given. Save to a small degree in student circles, there is little of the spontaneous cultural activity to be found on Tyneside: nor did I see much evidence of counter-culture, nor even of local folk arts. In former days there was a lively tradition of folk-song and dialect theatre in *bulgnais,* and of local polka-type dancing *(balli alle filuzze),* but this suffered heavily from the post-war impact of television. However, as elsewhere in Europe, a new generation, mostly students, has been making some self-conscious bid to revive the old traditions, and a young cabaret singer, Dino Sarti, has become popular locally with his songs and sketches in *bulgnais.*

Bologna has a small but active *milieu* of writers, artists and intellectuals, most of them eminently Bolognese in their passionate attachment to the town and in their easy gregariousness. They integrate with the town's life, and do not feel resentfully that they are living in a ghetto – as is the feeling in Stuttgart. Many work at the university, where they belong to a glorious tradition: Giosuè Carducci, one of the great Italian writers of his day, taught here for many years in the late 19th century, when Bologna was one of the leading intellectual centres of Italy. Today the scene is less brilliant. Many of the brighter talents have emigrated since the war, to Rome or elsewhere; painters especially find a need to be near their dealers and buyers, and Bologna offers little as an art market. But there are some who feel too intense a loyalty to desert the town like this: Morandi, born in Bologna, lived here until his death in 1964.

The town's most distinguished intellectual creation since the war has been the monthly review *Il Mulino,* founded in 1951 by a group of political theorists, sociologists and economists, mostly liberal Catholics or Socialists. It soon won a national reputation and in the 1950s and early '60s had some influence on the ideas of the centre-Left in Italian politics. It helped to introduce American sociology to post-war Italy, and provided intelligent criticism both of the Communists and the Right. *Il Mulino* is still edited from Bologna, and although in today's changed political climate it has lost some of its impact, the group of young idealists who founded it have stayed together across the years. One of them said to me: "In another town, *Il Mulino* might not have survived: its founders would have quarrelled or split up. It is helped here by the slow, easy rhythm of life and the lack of trendy pressures."

There are novelists and poets too in Bologna, some of them – such as

Giuseppe Raimondi – with a national reputation. They no longer sit so much in *cafés* together, for most of Bologna's old *cafés* have disappeared, but they still keep up the quaint local custom of using bookshops as meeting-places. Carducci in the 1890s used to hold an informal *salon* amid the bookshelves of Zanichelli, the leading bookstore, and this tradition survives. A writer told me: "At the end of an afternoon's work I go along to Zanichelli or Capelli in the hope of meeting my friends. We just stand there and chat. You can't do that in Milan, where the shops are too crowded." Bologna possesses more and better bookshops than any of my other towns save Stuttgart. But they have a low turnover except in educational textbooks: as the statistics show, the Italians are not a great nation of readers, and the Bolognese are no exception. Perhaps if their public libraries were better stocked, and were run in a less fusty and bureaucratic way (there was no shelf access till very recently), the public might read more. But the Bolognese, though artistic, are intellectually lazy. As is common in Italy, their culture is above all visual, and expresses itself in dress, design, décor, care for architecture and love of spectacle, more than in books, ideas, theatre or even music. Frankly, I found the cultural scene less lively and more limited than in any of my other towns, taken all in all. Archaic structures, cobwebby administration, and severe lack of funds may be largely to blame. But possibly, in the land of Dante and da Vinci, there is also a certain public complacency and lack of response.

7
Pasta, siesta, bella figura

The post-1973 economic crisis has hit Italy harder than most European countries, and has led the Bolognese like other Italians to make some cuts in their comfortable living standards. Middle-class housewives have been buying fewer filet steaks and more rabbit or pork; families have been economising on petrol and even on their favourite luxury, new clothes. Yet this is still a prosperous town, as much so as almost any in north Italy. In fact, since its wealth is based on small-scale industry and agriculture, it has not felt the recession as keenly as towns more dependent on vulnerable heavy industry, such as Turin.

There are few of the millionaire fortunes to be found in Milan or Turin. Nor is the average family's standard of living nearly as high as in Stuttgart: but it is very close to that of Toulouse, and probably above Newcastle's. And the Bolognese have a remarkable flair for making the most of their resources, or at least showing them off to the best advantage. This is part of the *bella figura.* They keep their homes scrupulously clean (it is an Anglo-Saxon misconception that Italians, being undisciplined southerners, are thereby dirty). The *bourgeoisie* favour classical rather than modern furniture, but also vie with each other in hanging chic modern paintings on their walls: unlike Swabians, they are not ashamed to flaunt their possessions, and moreover they do so with taste. Marble is relatively cheap in Italy, and even at lower-income level a high percentage of homes have marble floors, bare save for the occasional rug. The result may be aesthetically pleasing, but is not cosy.

Once I was invited to lunch in the home of a skilled worker, a Communist militant. His spruce modern flat had the expected marble floors, and contemporary furniture of good quality. We ate our way through a huge meal, of superb home-made *lasagne* and various kinds of meat. Oddly, the large television set in one corner remained on throughout the lunch, counterpointing our political discussion with a pop music show from Rome. My host told me he spent 25 per cent of his income on rent, and I found that this is quite usual in Bologna where some workers, if they want decent housing, will go up to 40 per cent. The middle classes have to pay out too: a university lecturer told me he paid 150,000 lire a month, about a third of his basic salary, for an old five-room flat on the fourth floor with no lift, and he said this was not untypical.

Given this high cost of accommodation and of some other items, at first sight it may seem a mystery how the Bolognese manage to make both ends meet on their earnings and still enjoy such a pleasant standard of living – eating and dressing so well, running a car (or sometimes two) and yet having money to spare for private school and medical bills to offset the deficiencies of the state systems. One explanation is that Bologna is still a town of rural immigrants, where perhaps nearly half the population retain some property in the nearby countryside or at least have relatives there. "Take my concierge, a factory worker," said an English resident; "every weekend he drives out to see his parents, farming people, and brings the car back laden with eggs, fruit and local wine. That slashes food bills." The Bolognese also are canny bargain-hunters, especially over clothes: they find out where to track down the new fashions at cut prices, or they know some seamstress who for a modest sum can turn an old coat to make it look new. Thus the rigorous requirements of *la bella figura* can be met without the need to pay the absurd prices of the smart dress shops.

Yet a number of expensive boutiques manage to do good business. They have the kind of jokey English names (Pull Shop, John & Johnny) that are now common throughout Europe – even Bologna has succumbed to this vogue. I found Bang Bang Baby doing a nice line in chic velvet coats for six-year-olds, while Bang Bang Lady next door was full of exclusive French leather and Scottish cashmere. The manageress, in her early twenties, wore a shammy-leather miniskirt with frilly strips round the bottom.

One secret of Bolognese budget-squaring is that they spend a good deal less than the French or Germans on costly foreign holidays or the more expensive sports such as sailing or skiing. Like most Italians, they tend to be highly unadventurous about holidays, and usually settle for the Adriatic resorts, sixty miles down the *autostrada*. Riccioni in summer becomes Bologna-*plage*: middle-class families go back year after year to the same villa or modest hotel, and often stay for the full three months of the school holidays, with the husband joining his family at weekends. And they seek out not only the same villa but the same parasol and square metre of sand, so as to be sure of finding themselves next to the same acquaintances and not to any interlopers from Munich or even Milan. I was told of a woman who each year would telephone the lido months in advance to reserve "parasol number 57". Such families will never consider changing to another resort, let alone going abroad. And the children, even when adult, are under pressure to come too, rather than accept invitations to, say, Paris or London.

During the rest of the year, the Bolognese divide their leisure between gossiping, eating, and watching football or TV. They are as habit-bound over favourite TV programmes as any people in Europe, and I was told that one mindless quiz-game became so popular that the cinemas were empty on the night it was screened, so some managements replied by installing TV equipment and interrupting their main film when the show started. Active sports are becoming more popular, but there is a serious lack of facilities for them, especially for swimming. The *Municipio* quoted me the usual excuse: "It's scandalous that we have only one public pool for this big town – the private ones are so expensive – but what can we do? Each time we plan to build one, the Prefect says 'no'."

Like most Italians, Bolognese work hard and eagerly – the idle Italian steeped in *dolce far niente* is just one of those foreign myths. Yet in their daily work and leisure routines Bolognese do seem to have imposed on themselves, a bit irrationally, a sub-tropical life-style that is not quite suited to this town with its more-or-less north European climate. They love to go to bed late, then they get up early without enough sleep, so that after their heavy lunch they need a *siesta* – and many of them take it. In order to cater for this rooted habit, some public offices close for the day at 2.0 p.m. Others stagger on after lunch, with lowered productivity – "You see people in offices sitting upright without moving," I was told: "they've learned to sleep with their eyes open." This *siesta* habit, sensible under the heat of a Sicilian summer, seems a bit absurd amid the winter fogs of the Po Valley: but the conservative Bolognese will not be prevailed upon to change. Significantly, the leading department store, Omnia, closes for nearly three hours at lunch-time: even Toulouse has brought itself up to date a little better than that.

The heavy lunch that precedes and necessitates the *siesta* is a central factor in the life of Bologna *la grassa,* where people take eating as seriously as in Lyon – and *more* so than in Toulouse. A Bolognese who is not a hearty and enthusiastic eater is considered a feeble sort of fellow, and this can even have political consequences: the Communists are always among the first to parade their love of fat living, and it has been said that one of the main factors behind Mayor Dozza's defeat of his Christian Democrat rival, Dossetti, in the 1956 elections, was that Dossetti made the error of showing himself something of an ascetic, while the jovial Dozza exploited this by eating lavishly in the best restaurants and warning that his rival was planning to condemn the Bolognese to bread and water. Floating voters soon made up their minds.

You overhear people, in streets or *cafés,* endlessly comparing different recipes or restaurants. And housewives spend hours preparing food at home, especially for lunch. One Bolognese told me: "My mother starts on the lunch at 8.30, peeling onions, making *pasta* and *ragù,* and it takes her all morning. Eating is a ritual here, and nearly every business discussion ends up round the dining-table. But the young are showing less interest in food – my wife will never spend the time on cooking that my mother does."

All Bolognese are convinced that, just as their women are the loveliest in Italy, so their *cuisine* is the best. Certainly it is the richest, with a calorie content that would horrify any slimmer. But whether Bologna can really justify its claim to be the nation's leading gastronomic shrine must remain a matter of taste. Unquestionably it is the world capital of *pasta,* in all its succulence and variety. But man cannot, except at some risk, live on *pasta*-and-cream alone, though I do happily admit that in some restaurants I fell to the temptation of taking *tortellini* as my first course, followed by *lasagne* or *tagliatelle verde* as a main course – and hang the consequences. This was because I found the main meat dishes, with one or two exceptions, as boring as usual in Italy.

The *pasta* comes in every shape and colour, always enriched with eggs and often with spinach which turns it pale green, or else it is stuffed with mince of pork and *mortadella.* One leading restaurant offers thirty-six kinds of home-made *pasta.* The supreme local delicacy is *tortellini,* little navel-shaped pockets of *pasta* which are filled with mince, then tossed in cream, with polenta, egg-yolk and scraps of meat. There are two local theories as to the origin of this navel shape. According to one, the inventor was inspired by the navel of Venus, who had come down to reveal herself to the city of love. The other legend, no less Bolognese, is that the cook of a 15th-century noble fell in love with his master's wife and would peer through her key-hole as she undressed each night: finally he copied her navel in pasta as a memorial to his hopeless love. Whether this happened or not, the Bolognese still make *pasta con amore.* Through the windows of little shops you see plump matrons carefully kneading and rolling the yellow lumps, or neatly dabbing *ravioli* onto big sheets of *pasta* at amazing speed. To make the best *pasta* is a highly skilled business that may take years of practice. It is also laborious, and so it is no surprise that machines in some places are now doing the work of women, to the detriment of flavour. But at least in Bologna even the cooperative self-service cafeteria still has its *pasta* hand-made, like the best *handgemächte spätzle* of Stuttgart.

Most restaurants offer a kind of *hors d'oeuvres variés* of different *pasta* on the same dish – a galaxy of pale greens and pinks. Or you can order *capriccio di Venere,* a polychromatic concoction of *pasta* with truffles and *béchamel,* topped with a *soufflé* – perhaps a little too heavy on the stomach to be effective as an aphrodisiac, even if accompanied with the local *pétillant* red wines, San Giovese and Lambrusco. Bologna has a large number of solid, traditional restaurants full of dedicated eaters, reminiscent of the French provinces. The most famous, Pappagallo, serves arguably the best *lasagne* in the world. In many places there are big trolleys of the assorted boiled meats that are among Bologna's specialities. The local *cuisine* also has interesting ways with turkey and with pigs' trotters. But too often – especially in private homes – the meat course is simply the eternal *vitello,* beaten so white and hard that it has lost its taste, or else smothered in a too-rich parmesan sauce. I concede that Bologna, not Toulouse, has the best food of the towns in this book; but it is a heavy *cuisine,* of limited range.

The Bolognese are as parochial and conservative in their eating as in other matters. You will not find restaurants here serving the dishes of other regions of Italy. Nor are there foreign restaurants, except for one or two inevitable Chinese. Modern trendy places, in the style of Stuttgart's Möwenpick or Toulouse's "drugstores", have not yet penetrated into staid Bologna: the only equivalents are a few not-very-comfortable *pizzerie,* popular with students. Yet in commercial terms Bologna is the scene of an astonishing catering enterprise. One of the largest and most flourishing of the town's many Communist-dominated cooperatives is CAMST *(Cooperativa Albergo Mensa Spettacolo e Turismo).* This was founded in 1945 by a group of barmen and waiters, who set up a much-needed municipal canteen in the austerity period. Gradually CAMST has grown into a large and lucrative empire covering – as its name implies – a range of leisure and catering activities. In and around Bologna it owns cinemas, hotels, food factories and shops, a hostel for old people, a travel agency, a factory canteen service, numerous large modern restaurants, as well as holiday camps as far afield as Sicily. It does the catering for the *Municipio*'s receptions, and probably provides some money for Party funds; but it might be wrong to consider it as simply an adjunct of the Communist Party. CAMST is run on ordinary business lines and all its services are open to the public. Its package tours will take you to Budapest or Leningrad, but also to Lourdes for Easter. And though some of its centres – such as the Adriatic holiday camp for workers' children, or the spa hotel for miners with chest trouble – have a respectable "socialist" basis, CAMST is not above operating one of the smarter hotels in the town, popular with visiting capitalists. In gastronomic terms, CAMST has managed to apply modern mass-catering techniques to Bologna's traditional *cuisine* without too much loss of quality: my prize for the best cheap self-service restaurant I have ever visited goes without a doubt to the CAMST in the Via Ugo Bassi.

Bologna has no shortage of good restaurants, yet I was bewildered to find an almost total absence of pleasant *cafés* or drinking-places. *Café*-going, in the French or the Central European sense, is not an Italian habit, or at least not in north Italy. The *cafés* that you see in towns such as Florence or Venice are there mostly for tourists. In Bologna, most of the *cafés* that existed before the war have since been taken over by banks or offices, and few are left today save Zanarini and Viscardi, two stiffly formal little places, more like tearooms than *cafés,* frequented by the *bourgeoisie.* Apart from this, there are the numerous narrow little bars where men stand gossiping at the counter as they sip a glass of *grappa* or a minuscule two-mouthful *espresso*: there is no room for more than a perfunctory chair or two, and the comfort is minimal. Some of these bars have small rooms at the back, dim and drably furnished, which are used mainly by amorous couples in search of the privacy that is hard to come by in Bologna: but I found them frequently deserted, even by lovebirds. It seems strange that the Bolognese, who love to chatter endlessly, should not have created a more cosy environment for this: but they seem to prefer to stand around in casual groups, under the arcades or in shops or bars, or else they do their talking over a leisurely meal. As a visitor, I was frequently in search of somewhere comfortable to spend an hour or so, writing notes or reading, and watching the world go by: only Newcastle (hampered by the English licensing laws) seemed to me more deprived and uncivilised than Bologna in this respect.

Bologna has four or five conventional night-clubs with floor shows, patronised by visiting businessmen or prosperous Emilian farmers. And there are equally conventional discothèques, frequented by the more well-to-do students or *figli a papa.* "Night life" in this sense does not scintillate – and why should it? Yet one of Bologna's firm convictions about itself is that it is a town very lively at night, more so than Florence or even Milan. In a sense this is true, but not in the night-club sense. People do stay up very late, eating in restaurants, drifting from bar to bar, or just standing in the street in summer. Some bars and restaurants stay open till 3.0 or 4.0 a.m. "I never go to bed before two, and then I'm up at eight," a middle-aged Bolognese told me. "In summer I often dine at midnight. Many people have two dinners, a main one at seven or eight, then a snack very late in a restaurant." At midnight, you see groups of young men and girls striding down the arcades, singing in chorus at the tops of their voices, like they do in Newcastle when the pubs close. It is most unlike early-to-bed Stuttgart. And it is all part of that strange tribal life of Bologna which even other Italians find mysteriously hard to penetrate.

8

Europe's "most ramshackle" education system

The profound crisis in Italian education, and the school and university system that has been called "the most ramshackle in Western Europe", is a complex and depressing subject that spreads well outside the scope of this book. All I shall attempt here is a few vignettes of the situation, as I saw it in Bologna. Since education is run largely by the state, the local Communists have not been able to do much to insulate the Bolognese from its ill-effects – save with their nursery schools* (these are outside the State system), and by using their influence to mollify Left-wing student extremism. With this they succeeded quite well (at least until the 1977 riots): for many years Bologna has been the least agitated of larger Italian universities.

Yet there has always been discontent beneath the surface, and not surprisingly, for this once-so-glorious university presents the spectacle common throughout Italy of grotesque overcrowding, crippling lack of funds, staff malaise, out-of-date teaching methods, and so on. And so do Bologna's schools. This national tragedy has two main causes: a feudal structure has not been reformed to meet the new needs of an industrialised society; and all decisions still depend on the centralised bureaucracy in Rome, which is mostly incapable of decision and whose only reforms have been *ad hoc* palliatives made with short-term political motives. This centralisation is especially ill-suited to Italy – where it would be far better if education could reflect the strong local

* See page 146.

individualisms of the city-state tradition – and it is one of the more unfortunate of Napoleon's legacies to this land. In fact, Italy's post-1968 crisis in education has much in common with France's. The difference is that things are much worse in Italy. Also, the French in their contentious way have at least been applying a certain zeal and initiative to the search for solutions: the Italians have reacted with good-natured shoulder-shrugging.

The rot runs all the way from the primary schools to post-graduate research. In schools, the worst problem is sheer overcrowding, due to paucity of State funds for new building. In Bologna in 1945-70 only five new middle and secondary schools were built, although the population nearly doubled in that time. Many schools are full to capacity twice over, so that the children have to attend in shifts, like factory workers, one in the morning and one after lunch. Shortage of teachers is not quite so serious: but this poorly paid profession tends to recruit from the dregs of the so-called "educated" classes, and at all school levels the quality of teaching has been falling so low that a high proportion of parents – including workers who can ill afford it – hire part-time tutors for their children to ensure that they pass their exams. This provides useful pocket-money for university students or junior lecturers to supplement their meagre grants or wages: but it is hardly a rational way to run a state education service.

There are plenty of reasons why the teaching profession is unattractive to Italians, one being the military discipline of its career structure. You are a civil servant and must go where you are posted, even to the other end of Italy, on pain of dismissal. I knew a girl teacher living alone with her elderly invalid mother in Bologna. Suddenly the grey men in the Ministry transferred her to a school near Rimini, sixty miles away. "I couldn't uproot my old mother, so I had to get up at five and face four hours in the train each day. The only other offer they made was Viterbo, near Rome. Or I could have resigned. I couldn't plead compassionate grounds, for my sick mother is worth only 'two points' on their scale, whereas to bend their rules you need about twenty points, based on seniority and good headmasters' reports. Are they not human, these bureaucrats?" The system operates at university level too, and can split marriages. One Bolognese was posted to Cagliari University in Sardinia, but his wife did not want to give up her Bologna job. Devotedly, he spent most of his salary on flying home to her each weekend. If he had declined the Cagliari job, he would have forfeited his place on the academic ladder.

Italian schools may be archaic and inefficient, but they are not such unhappy places as you might expect. The chaos is generally cheerful. When visiting Bologna's *licei (lycées)* and *scuole medie* (junior schools for eleven-to-fourteen-year-olds), I was always impressed by how happy and relaxed the children looked, the girls in their tidy black smocks, the boys informally but neatly dressed; and by every account there is less authoritarianism and teacher-pupil tension than in the average French or German school. It says something for the easy-going cheeriness of local temperament that children and staff are able to maintain this atmosphere in premises that are usually so dingy and lacking in facilities, and in face of such dreary academic routines. But then, Italian children do not expect much from their school. As in France, it is no more than a marginal focus for their loyalties and emotions, compared with the family.

The curriculum is still classically inclined, and modern scientific and technical schools are few. In Bologna's leading *liceo classico,* every one of the thousand pupils learns Latin *and* Greek, yet no modern languages at all are taught in the three senior years. No wonder Bolognese tend to be poor linguists: if a number of them today do speak passable English or French, it is usually thanks to private tuition or adult classes. The Ministry has recently gone through the motions of reforming and updating the curriculum, but this has mainly taken the form of lightening the burden of written exams and of making it easier to pass the *maturità* which, like the *bac* in France, provides automatic university entry. Candidates now have to sit only two written papers instead of four, and are examined orally in only four subjects instead of ten. Pupils of course like the change, but most teachers have denounced it as a threat to academic standards. "It's pure demagoguery and political expediency, typical of our weak Government," one headmaster told me; "the purpose is simply to appease the handful of student *contestatori* and keep the classrooms quiet."

Clubs, sports and other extra-curricular activities are even scanter than in France, and so is the teaching of the arts. Shortage of funds and premises is one factor: another is Italian schools' hostility to anything not strictly academic. In one classical *liceo* I found at least a kind of debating society and a rudimentary newspaper produced by the pupils, but there were no school plays – "It is impossible," said the headmaster, "to persuade teachers to organise such things: they all want to go home as soon as classes are finished." He told me that art history was taught for one hour a week, but there were no practical classes in either art or music. (This in *Italy*! – I hope Michelangelo and his friends are turning in their graves.) I found the school's library locked and deserted: there were a few ancient books in glass cases, but hardly any modern ones. "We have no library budget of our own," explained the headmaster; "we depend entirely on the Ministry in Rome who send us some books direct. Some years they cut our supply altogether. We have classical texts here, but hardly any novels." Then I visited a large new scientific *liceo*: it had pleasant modern buildings but no school plays or concerts, no clubs, not even a recreation room where the pupils might improvise such things. "This school was built for 600 pupils and now has 1,950," I was told: "we've had to turn part of the gymnasium into classrooms – so how do you expect us to have a music or art room?" I was shown what was left of the gym, where girls in their ordinary clothes were processing lackadaisically over a "horse". The instructress, in high heels and a chic dress with pearls, was sitting at a desk as if teaching them Latin.

This *liceo* like others in Bologna has been hit by occasional waves of pupil unrest since 1968, led by little groups of *contestatori* who extend their grievances against the school system into wider criticisms of society and distribute tracts, "Let's destroy our *bourgeois* curriculum" or "teachers are repressive colonels". Sometimes there are strikes or sit-ins. But it is all more innocuous than in many Italian cities. One headmaster told me, "We are in a period of transition from the old authoritarianism, to a new system not yet worked out. There's far less discipline than before: pupils walk out of class when they feel like it, and smoke if they want. We don't try to punish them, it's best not to provoke." Most teachers are mild, kindly old buffers who feel passive and powerless, caught between the fires of the Ministry's rigid structures and the new pupil effervescence. Just as in France, there is none of the Anglo-Saxon tradition of school democracy and entrusting discipline to senior pupils: thus there is nothing that could be used as a basis for harnessing the new pupil demands for responsibility. After 1968, some schools tried to set up an embryonic system of pupil delegations, but these mostly remained a dead letter. Another problem is that parents traditionally are excluded from the life of the school. Parent/teacher associations have no legal basis and exist only marginally: most headmasters prefer not to meet parents unless a pupil is involved in a serious crisis. A school thus exists in its own enclosed world, cut off from everyday life, its only duty being to inculcate academic virtues.

All this began to be changed in 1975 when the Ministry, in one of its rare flashes of positive action, decreed a new system of elected councils to help in the running of all primary and secondary schools. Parents, senior pupils, teaching and administrative staff, local authorities and trades unions, and others, now elect or appoint their own delegates, to form a council with certain powers of control over the finances and daily running of each school, the selection of text-books and classroom equipment, and so on. The system seems to have made a fair start, and marks some kind of honest attempt at decentralisation and participation, and at opening stuffy classroom windows to admit a breath of reality and contact with the outside world. But many people think that the reform does little more than scratch at the surface of the real problems. So long as funds remain so short, and so long as the curriculum and teaching methods and the whole academic ethos remain so out of touch with today's needs, it is hard to see how young Italians, in Bologna as elsewhere, can receive the education that a modern society needs.

The malaise in the schools finds its counterpart in the universities, where matters are if anything worse, or at least more confused. The university of Bologna could be compared to a fine piece of antique furniture riddled with woodworm. Along the Via Zamboni in the heart of the old city, the rectorate and other main buildings still stand where they have stood since the Middle Ages, a succession of elegant halls and palaces with high ceilings, fine murals and sculptures. These interiors are kept in good repair, but the Big Hall – equivalent of the Sheldonian at Oxford – is now a set of offices full of typists and filing-cabinets, a typical symptom of the desperate overcrowding. And a university that once was Europe's leader in many branches of scholarship is now, in the words of one professor, "little better than an outsize *liceo* in much of its academic quality".

The university maintained its eminence until the early part of this century, when the faculties of law and medicine were still among the best in Europe: it was here that a young research student, Guglielmo Marconi, made his first experiments with radio. The physics faculty still has some distinction, but the university has seen a general decline over the past fifty years and can no longer claim even to be among the three or four best in Italy. At least it can generally boast of being one of the quietest, in terms of student unrest; but it is just as badly afflicted as others in Italy by the archaic structures of a system that has not been modernised to keep pace with the dramatic post-war changes in the nation's economy and society. Weak governments in Rome endlessly discuss reform, but little has yet been done, even though the student rumblings since 1968 have finally focused attention on the gravity of the situation. Over-crowding and under-funding are the two most obvious problems, which in theory could be solved simply by a massive injection of public money for new buildings and more staff. But even if this were done, and in Italy's present economic state it is hardly conceivable, there would remain the tougher obstacle of academic feudalism, harder to reform because this is a matter of tradition, attitudes and privilege. While the university as a whole has little autonomy and depends almost entirely on the Ministry, yet within each faculty or department the individual "full professor" has tended to be the complete little despot, and the members of this mandarinate are nicknamed *i baroni.* Until the system was modified in 1974, a professor once appointed could do virtually what he liked, drawing a sizeable salary yet teaching for maybe only a few hours a year. Staff and students would go in dread of him, and any advancement usually depended on ingratiating yourself with the right professor. The gulf was immense, in terms both of earnings and of privilege, between these "little gods" and their juniors in the hierarchy, the *incaricati* or "non-established" staff, who had little security of tenure. And by a scandalous practice the most junior teachers, the *assistenti,* would sometimes receive no salary at all, or a pittance of five or ten thousand lire a week: young graduates from well-to-do homes, often girls waiting for their wedding bells, would eagerly accept these jobs simply for the glory of being a university teacher, and the Ministry cynically exploited this snobbery as a neat way of saving itself money.

One of the rare post-war university reforms of any effectiveness came into force in 1974. One of its aims was to limit the powers of the individual baronies by creating thousands of new professors, thus devaluing the title by making it less exclusive: Bologna's quota was to rise over the next three years from 150 to about 400. At the same time junior staff were given more security and status, and the racket of unpaid assistants was abolished. In tune with the new post-1968 vogue for "participation", democratic "councils" were set up within each faculty, representing all levels of staff, plus a few student delegates: these have some powers of decision over administrative matters, selection of junior employees, and so on. The new system appears to be working quite well in Bologna, in a cheerfully haphazard way, and has mollified some of the grievances of the junior staff. But the *baroni* are fighting hard to retain as much as possible of their old privileges, and those with strong personalities still effectively rule the roost in their faculties. The professorship is still a prize worth seeking, and the path to it involves intensive lobbying. With a few exceptions, a university does not elect its own professors: these are chosen by a national committee of senior professors who enjoy hugely the petty power this gives them and the game of intrigue and nepotism that it involves.

The 1974 reforms may have improved slightly the situation inside the faculties, but they have not given the universities more autonomy. This remains the most stupidly over-centralised university system in the EEC, and there has been no parallel to the post-1968 Faure reforms in France.* The pro-Rector told me: "We get 99 per cent of our budget from the Ministry, which lays down precisely how we must spend it. And it allows us very little for research." University research bodies have to scrounge their funds where they can, either from other government sources or from local firms. I did come across one or two successful examples in Bologna of this kind of university-industry collaboration, for instance of a local pharmaceutics firm giving research commissions to the chemistry faculty. But liaison of this kind is on a feeble scale compared with most advanced Western countries – even France – and Italian technology suffers as a result. It would be hard to imagine Bologna today producing another Marconi: he would not find the resources.

Yet the university does not live entirely within an ivory tower. The Rector is assisted by a board that includes representatives of the Chamber of Commerce and local unions, as well as the *Municipio,* the province and region, and of course the Ministry. In practice the *Municipio*'s influence over the university is slight compared with that of the Ministry, which holds the purse strings. Yet the Rector does need to retain the good-will and cooperation of the city council, since he is dependent on it for his building permits. "These conservationists!" he complained to me, "they won't let us alter a window or add an annexe to a laboratory without endless tractations." The university has wanted to ease its overcrowding by expanding onto a new campus east of the city, where it bought some land for the purpose. But the council opposed this. The Communist town-planners' argument is that if historic Bologna is to be conserved, then

---

* See section on education in Toulouse, page 343-9.

the university, so integral a part of it, must stay where it is, and that to shift the students to some dull campus in the suburbs – as has happened in Toulouse and so many towns – would impoverish the city's life. This makes good environmental sense, though it may not have been the *Municipio*'s only motive. Possibly it did not want the university to elude its influence any further or set itself up as a rival force. For this university is certainly not Communist: at most, 10 or 15 per cent of the teaching staff support the Party. Yet, despite occasional frictions, relations between town and gown are generally amicable, and it is part of the Communists' strategy of alliances that they should remain so. The Rector, Bruno Cervellati, an easy-going liberal, is a personal friend of the mayor, and typifies what was described to me as "the local *bourgeoisie's* flirtation with the Party".

Students in Bologna learn to adapt themselves with cheerful resignation to the poor teaching and poorer conditions. The Rector told me: "This place is equipped to cope with about 5,000 students: by 1965 we had 19,000, and today 35,000. But what am I to do about it?" I heard of one department that had a single lecture room for a thousand students, part of it screened off to make into a professor's study, while a teacher in an arts faculty told me, "I give lectures with students literally sitting on my shoes. Outside class, they have almost nowhere to go to relax or study, and if they want to hold a political meeting, they use the corridors. Once I found my seminar invaded by gate-crashers, and when I asked what they were doing, they said, 'It's raining outside'."

Everyone crowds into the faculties, hoping to win the prestige of becoming *dottore,* gateway to so many careers. For the *maturita,* like the *bac* in France, is of little value itself as a job qualification. And not only has this exam been made easier, but for equally demagogic reasons a number of other and simpler secondary-school diplomas have recently been included with it as automatic entry permits to any university. So the student numbers go on swelling uncontrollably. Most professors would like to see some *numerus clausus* system, as operates in Britain and to an extent in Germany: but, as in France, this is alien to the national tradition. The students are especially hostile, so it is considered politically impossible. Yet the victims are the students themselves. There has been no comparable increase in staff, and one young teacher commented to me, "We are asked since 1968 to do more to help the students and get to know them – but how can we, when their numbers swell faster than ours? Most teachers are middle-aged reactionaries who feel they cannot cope with all the new problems. They either have breakdowns, or retire to an Olympian seclusion."

You might therefore expect the university to present the same atmosphere of angry frustration or demoralised dowdiness as many another European campus. Outwardly it does not, for this is elegant, happy-go-lucky Bologna. The premises, though certainly congested, are spectacularly tidy and clean by the standards of Toulouse, and even of Newcastle. The students, relaxed and well-dressed, give the impression that they are not going to let tedious academic chaos interfere with their absorbing and very special social life. It is the familiar Bolognese enigma. Between teachers and students there is usually a casual mateyness and jocularity, with lots of *ciaou*-ing, yet mostly it remains superficial: "Our professor jokes with us, even lets us tease him," said one group of students, "but he never tries to get to know us personally." Some younger teachers are now trying to become friends with at least a few of their students, as is normal in Britain. But the older ones can rarely be bothered, or they are put off by the sheer numbers. They come to give their lectures, then go home. And the faculties are not places where much work actually takes place. "It's the fault of the system," one *assistente* explained; "look, it's February, yet the academic year's teaching has hardly begun. The year is a succession of little exams and holidays. The students have exams when they arrive in October, then more in November interspersed with holidays such as All Saints' Day, then it's time for the Christmas break, then there's carnival-time, then more exams in March, then the Easter break, then more exams in April and May, then come the summer holidays. How can we teach under these conditions?" There are very few written exams, and the term is broken up into a series of "orals": a student must pass twenty or thirty during a three-year course. The effectiveness of this system depends largely on the professor, and it is open to abuses. Some professors take their examining conscientiously, others do not. One pretty girl student told me that when she went before her examiner, he said, "You've got a good record, you look an intelligent girl, let's not bother to test you, I'll give you 30, that's a fair mark." It is only at MA or post-graduate level that a full written exam, including a thesis, is required – and here the professional thesis-writers flourish, more especially in southern Italy but in Bologna too. You see advertisements in the papers, where these academic ghost-writers offer to do a student's work for him, charging maybe 500,000 to 800,000 lire.

Students get a poor deal in many ways. Tuition itself is cheap, usually less than 70,000 lire a year, but the system of grants for living expenses is woefully inadequate, much worse even than in France. There are modest grants for the children of poor families: but most middle-class students must rely on their parents' generosity or else, in many cases, they pay for their studies through taking part-time jobs, usually giving private lessons to schoolchildren. So it is no surprise that there is a vast army of "phantom" students, not taking their studies very seriously and hardly bothering to attend lectures. The Italian drop-out rate of those enrolling but not getting degrees is as high as 75 per cent. It is also possible to protract one's course indefinitely: I met a woman in Bologna who had been attending university for eighteen years but did not yet feel herself ready to attempt her final exams. The system is over-liberal to the point of anarchy.

Unemployment among young graduates has been rising fast in recent years, and is now a major Italian problem, more so than in most EEC countries. Many students, especially in the sciences, feel that the over-theoretical curriculum and methods do not fit them for work in industry or commerce, and this view is shared by employers who find that a graduate needs to be retaught before he is any practical use. "There is hardly any practical work in universities," a physics student complained to me, "and there are few of the technical colleges at university level that you have in Britain." How is it, then, that Italy has so many brilliant engineers and such advanced industries? The answer may lie in native flair and adaptability, and in the clever use of imported technology. But lucky those few graduates who can find élite posts in the good firms. Many have to accept jobs well below their qualifications, maybe as commercial travellers, part-time translators, or minor clerks in banks or offices.

As in France, the students' discontent sparked off the revolt of 1968 which at least had the merit of focusing public attention on their problems. The Government reacted by passing a curious law which liberalised the hitherto ultra-rigid curriculum. A student could now choose his own courses, subject to the formal approval of his professor. He could, for instance, combine biology with languages; or an engineering student could add sociology or fine art to his study of hydraulics. This was yet another demagogic measure aimed at appeasing discontent. It has had only partial success because students, remote from their professors, are seldom given adequate practical guidance in what assortment of courses to choose. And it seems to have led to a further decline in academic standards. The Ministry also introduced a seminar system. A teacher in Bologna commented: "The Left-wing students had been pressing for this, but now they seem not to like the results and have even staged strikes to prevent the seminars from working. It seems they dislike having to work harder in seminars, or they fear losing face if they have to speak in front of a small group. When I give a dictation, at once all the boys in the class get up and leave the room, for they don't want to be shown up in front of the girls if they make mistakes. There's Italian *brutta figura* for you!"

Another result of the 1968 revolt was to make the university authorities begin to take student welfare more seriously. The Ministry actually provided new funds which have enabled the Rectorate's welfare office to create facilities decidedly more elegant than anything I found in Toulouse or Stuttgart. It has converted a lovely old *palazzo* into a leisure centre, where grandiose Renaissance murals preside over the pin-tables and ping-pong. The *mensa* provides excellent meals at low prices, under the eye of a 16th-century Madonna, ten foot high. The welfare office also runs four small hostels for poorer students from other parts of Italy: the one I visited had marble floors and neat modern furniture and, like the *mensa,* was impeccably clean. In Italy, things are done either with fastidious elegance or not at all. And the whole operation is highly paternalistic: the student unions do not run their own social centres, as in British universities.

Since the vast majority of students live at home with their families, in Bologna or nearby towns, they are in no great need of these services. They lead their own absorbing semi-tribal social life, described earlier, and for them the university as a community hardly exists. As in Toulouse, there is little of the organised student life of cultural or sporting clubs that is so highly developed even in a lesser British university such as Newcastle. Once I attended a folk-club in a crowded Bologna cellar, where a tall youth with floppy hair sang movingly a lament for Dubcek – "*Una speranza c'era a Praga*"; but the evening was organised, significantly, by the American student colony, and most of the songs were Baez or Dylan. The university runs an excellent series of concerts by visiting artists; but there is no student orchestra. The academic theatre institute puts on occasional experimental plays; but there is no student drama club. A middle-class student of physics living with his family told me: "I have plenty of friends here, many of them other students, and we are endlessly going to parties, dance-halls or discos – but it's nothing to do with the university."

For the student, especially the poorer student, who has come from some other part of Italy and has no ready-made circle, life can be less fun. Unless he is lucky enough to find a place in one of the few hostels, he will have to go through the sad rat-race of looking for lodgings, most of them over-priced, and there is no university service to help him. Then, between lectures, he will not easily find anywhere to study in peace, for libraries and reading-rooms are in very short supply. Many students take to doing their work in *cafés, faute de mieux*. Once, when I was chatting to someone in one of the few dingy little *cafés* near the university, a girl at the next table called out to us, "Will you please stop talking, I'm trying to work." This may help to explain the paucity of animated *café* life in Bologna.

The only student organisations that pack much punch are at the extremes: the little groups of Leftist activists, mostly Maoist; and the exclusive and traditional fraternities of *goliardi* with their mock-mediaeval rituals and uniforms, Italian counterparts of the German *Verbindungen*. Associations of *goliardi* – the term means a carousing, practical-joking student-vagabond – have existed in Italy for centuries. Bologna's fraternity is called the *Ordine del Fitone,* as was explained to me by its *Gran Maestro,* an arrogant young man with a long black beard who took the whole charade utterly seriously. His fraternity consists of about 50 *bourgeois* students, *commendatori* and *cavalieri,* who dress up in their gaudy costumes for regular dinners and balls. Each spring they organise a carnival, the *Festa della Matricola,* where traditionally the students in their thousands take over the town and go on a cheerful rampage. It is fairly harmless, though a few windows and street-lamps may get broken or cars overturned, and once a student died after being forced to bathe nude in a fountain. But in the past few years the carnival has gone into decline, victim of the new politicisation. The *Ordine del Fitone* is mildly aristocratic and has always seen itself as apolitical – therefore, in the eyes of the new Leftists, it is "fascist". There have been clashes between the two elements, and the *Ordine* has been pushed into taking up a more overtly Right-wing position, against the Leftists, while the police and city council have put some restrictions on the carnival so as to prevent trouble.

Conflict of this kind between Left- and Right-wing students has generally been much rarer than in most big Italian cities. In the months after the 1968 uprisings, the local Communists managed to gain effective control of the main radical student body, the *Movimento Studentesco,* and were thus able to calm it down, to suit local Party strategy. So this movement is now almost as prudent as the *Municipio* itself: sometimes it will stage a march or strike, against some government measure, but always with perfect discipline. To its Left are the real *gauchistes,* mostly Maoists or Trotskyists belonging to national revolutionary bodies such as *Potere Operai* or *Lotta Continua.* As I explained earlier, these groups have again become much more belligerent since 1976, and it was they who played a leading part in the riots of March 1977, when they managed to rally to their support about 5,000 students exasperated by their study conditions. Since then, the university has relapsed into an uneasy calm. The graffiti and tatty posters of the Leftists are everywhere, but the membership of these groups is probably no more than two or three hundred. Only briefly did they manage to fire Bolcgna with the same student political ferment as you find in Rome or Milan.

The mass of students and teachers are less concerned with agitation than with coming to terms individually, as best they can, with the malaise of university life. Each seeks his or her own way of making the system tolerable. One young lecturer gave me a view that is common: "The revolt of 1968 gave us a brief moment of hope that things might be changed radically, but today they are simply worse than ever. The students are mostly apathetic, they don't seem to want to work. I just go to the faculty to give my lectures, then come home again, I try not to get involved in university problems as they only upset me. This may sound selfish, but what else can one do?" Most people agree that the government's few piecemeal reforms have not brought a solution, and that only a radical overhaul of the entire structure can provide real results. An intelligent reform bill was prepared by the Government in 1978, including the much-needed introduction of a *numerous clausus*; but it then fell victim to the political crisis of 1978-9, and has been shelved.

When I asked a woman professor whether she felt that matters were better or worse than pre-1968, she said: "Better, in that there's a little more democracy and participation, the students are now more outspoken and critical, which is healthy. Worse, in that entrance is easier, too many students are flooding in, we just cannot cope, and so the general cultural level is falling, the university is becoming a utilitarian degree-factory." And the solution? She gave an Italian shrug: "It's impossible to reform education without first reforming the whole Italian nation."

9
The creative flair of a self-taught shoemaker

In its preference for the personal, small-scale and stylish, rather than the huge and ultra-modern, Bologna's industry is very Bolognese, you might say. Today this is quite an important industrial town, but you will find no giant factories as in Turin, and no firms anywhere near the size of Daimler-Benz (Stuttgart), Aérospatiale (Toulouse) or the Tyne shipyards. Nearly all the more successful firms are locally owned family-run affairs, relying more on a flair for design and craftsmanship than on modern management techniques. Many, as in Swabia, lean towards a benevolent paternalism. The highly politicised Italian unions do not react to this quite as the German ones do, and local firms have not been immune from the waves of national strikes of recent years – after all, this is Italy. But it is also Bologna: in many cases, capitalists and Red union militants have found their own *entente* in this city of discreet *ententes.*

The industry is recent, even more so than in Toulouse. Before the war there were few factories any larger than the little craft workshops that you still find in back-streets, turning out furniture, pottery, textiles. But since the 1950s Bologna has been caught up willy-nilly in the industrial "miracle" of north Italy, its factories fed with local immigrant peasant labour as the farms modernise. In the province of Bologna, agriculture's share of the working population has dropped since the war from 57 to less than 20 per cent, a mutation as striking as that in the Toulouse area. Farming has also changed its nature: the old feudal share-cropping system has largely disappeared, the large capitalist farms have grown larger and wealthier while the numerous smallholders have been grouping into cooperatives. As much as in the past, this remains one of the most fertile, prosperous and efficient farming regions of Europe, and Bologna is second only to Milan as an Italian market centre. Yet the growth of other sectors has been so great that agriculture today accounts for only 9 per cent of Bologna's economy. Even so, the old rural mentalities subsist, as they do also in

Toulouse: it is often said that the character of local industry – its cautiousness, its dislike of large units – derive from the area's agricultural background.

Is there another potent factor behind the absence of large-scale private firms – the colour of Bologna's politics? It is a question often asked. One answer is clear: a distinction must be made between pre- and post-1956. In the tense Cold War years, the town's "Red" image may well have discouraged some big companies, Italian or foreign, from setting up plant here, and Fiat is said to have been one of these. But ever since 1956 the Communists, in line with their broader strategy, have done nothing to discourage capitalist enterprise, at least in manufacturing. I have already referred to the curious deal with the leading local tycoon, Attilo Monti*. In addition, several factories are owned or part-owned by American interests, and they claim to find Bologna as satisfactory a location as non-Communist cities – in fact, better than many, because Communist discipline ensures that labour relations are less than averagely turbulent. Only in commerce has the *Municipio* tried to limit large-scale private ventures; due to its opposition, the town still has very few large supermarkets. But this is not a matter of ideology: the aim has been simply to win over the small shopkeepers.

If Bologna's industry is a matter of "small is beautiful", this is largely a reflection of local temperament. Factory-owners are not jet-setting tycoons from fashionable families, as they tend to be in Milan. Many are self-made men who started on the shop-floor, or whose fathers were artisans or small farmers. They have built up their firms through hard work, technical ingenuity and a certain flair for salesmanship, and many of them remain close to their workers, not afraid to roll up their sleeves and turn a lathe. They have something in common with Swabian family firms, though the development here is more modest and recent, and they lack the Swabians' organisational genius or long tradition of precision work. Yet a number of enterprises, each employing some 300 to 1,000 people, have built up a solid prosperity since the war, specialising in various kinds of machinery, textiles or shoes.

The most brilliant example, and entirely characteristic, is that of Bruno Magli, whose high-fashion women's shoes are world famous. Son of a railway worker, Magli began as an apprentice at twelve, and as

---

* See page 135.

a very young man started designing his own shoes and shoe-making machinery. Entirely self-taught, today he has four factories in Bologna, employing 1,000 people and turning out 3,500 pairs of shoes a day, a third of them for export. There are Magli boutiques in London, Paris and New York. Magli, now in his mid-sixties, is a dapper man with a taste for elaborate clothes, and he still works with fantastic energy. Like some Renaissance painter with his *atelier* full of disciples, he has drawn round him a team of designers who work for the *maestro* with awed dedication – and the atmosphere, passionate, artistic, informal, is less like that of an ordinary factory than of some laboratory, theatre workshop or design studio, led by a man of genius. The firm creates about a thousand new models each year, and sells at top prices. Magli described himself to me as a typical Bolognese, loving food, girls and fun as well as hard work, and he admitted there might be a link between his firm's creativity and the innate elegance of the Bolognese – "the best-dressed people in the world". He added: "I know all my workers individually. In Bologna, a firm succeeds if it stays at the size where the owner can retain personal control. If it gets too big, it fails."

Considering the faults of the Italian education system, and the relative inadequacy of technical education, it is remarkable that firms such as this can achieve such high technical proficiency. There seems to be some innate aptitude for precision work, which may be an inheritance from the old days when Bologna was a centre of the silk industry. And it exists at all levels, so that the shop-floor worker will learn and apply his craft with just as much flair and skill as the engineer or designer. It is an Italian victory of inspired improvisation over modern methodology. But the Achilles' heel of many of these firms is poor organisation. An industrial economist summed up the problem for me: "These factory-owners have technical ingenuity and they *love* their products, as an artist loves his paintings. And they can inspire their staff. Relations are friendly but not very functional, for most of these bosses do not know how to delegate authority or establish proper liaison between departments. So if the boss goes away or falls ill, or allows the firm to get too big, very soon there is trouble – and often the firm can be bailed out only by some kind of takeover." Several of Bologna's larger enterprises have thus fallen under outside control. Ducati (electronics) is owned by French and American interests and by the Italian State giant, IRI; SASIB (tobacco machinery) is US-controlled, and so is Sabiem, which makes lifts and, with 2,500 employees, is the town's largest manufacturing company.

An English consultant, working for one of the larger local firms, was forthright to me in his diagnosis: "Comparing Italy with Britain, I'd say that Italians at all levels work harder and with more pride in their work; and the unions although politicised are in practice less obstructive. So productivity is higher. But management, except in the small firms, is riddled with inefficiencies. Liaison is poor, so sales and service departments are not kept properly informed of technical changes. In smaller firms there's too much nepotism, and in the larger, more bureaucratic ones, too much insistence on the right paper qualifications: in either case, people are not chosen for their abilities and too many key posts are filled with duds. One trouble is the lack of modern management and business schools in Italy, as compared with France or Germany. And only the giants such as Fiat send their executives to train in America." So Bolognese firms are having to make a brutal choice, between trying to remain at cottage-industry level, or allowing themselves to be absorbed into the modern world of corporate colossi. The local pattern of smallish specialised firms with a strong export base has enabled Bologna's economy to face up to the post-1974 crisis better than most parts of Italy: but by 1966-7 many firms were feeling the squeeze and some were forced to close. It seems that local industries will be obliged to modernise their methods, if they are to survive.

One day I drove into the suburbs to visit Giorgio Longo, who had been described to me as typical of Bologna's old-style benevolent paternalists. His spruce modern factory employs 500 people making plastic piping, and office equipment such as rubber bands, inks and pens. He greeted me in flamboyant style, with the Union Jack flying in my honour at his gates; then he showed me round the plant, teasing and back-slapping his staff in a matey yet headmasterly way. He was a big man of sixty with an ox-like face and arrogant manner, and soon launched into a tirade about his problems: "I built this place up with my own hands. I increased productivity 30 per cent last year, and now I export 45 per cent of my goods. But at this size it's hard for a firm to be competitive internationally unless it's highly specialised, like Magli. So I'm forced to look for a merger. The trouble is, government and unions are both against me. The former pours money into the *Mezzogiorno* where it's wasted, yet penalises firms in north Italy. As for my workers, my own relations with them are friendly, but they're being incited against me by union leaders from outside. Last year the

Communists and the Maoists sent in pickets to stop my men from working. Now, Renato Zangheri happens to be my best friend, and I just don't see how he can approve these rough Red tactics, stopping people from doing their job." He then told me with pride what he was doing for his workers: "I've built them a leisure centre, with a swimming-pool as well as a bar and restaurant, but it's taken me years because the local commune, Communist-controlled, has repeatedly held up my building permits. You see, they're jealous. They don't want *me* to be the one to help the workers."

This is one individual's slant on a local industrial climate that is as full of paradoxes as so much else in Bologna. Kindly paternalism may go down quite well with the tolerant Bolognese worker, but it will not prevent him from being also a loyal union member; and his Communist-led union may simultaneously be preaching class struggle and obeying local Party dictates to play that struggle cool. Italian unions, like French ones, are organised on political rather than craft lines. In Bologna as elsewhere the most powerful is the CGIL, Communist-dominated but including a minority of Socialists and others. Next comes the CISL, more-or-less Catholic. Italy's level of union membership, nearly 40 per cent, is much higher than that of France and not far behind Britain's; and in Bologna, owing to the popularity and discipline of the Communists, it is higher than average, maybe 50 per cent, with the CGIL in a commanding position. This union can thus provide the *Municipio* with crucial support, and it uses its power scrupulously. It has led plenty of strikes in the past few years, but they have generally been less bitter and prolonged than in non-Communist towns.

As a result of the heavy wave of strikes in the autumn of 1969, unions at last won the right – a year later than in France – to official status inside each firm, where they could now set up offices and hold mass meetings. In contrast to the German unions, they have set their faces against proposals for worker participation in management, which they see as a capitalist snare. And they are also cool towards the long-established works committees (*commissioni interne*) which have certain rights and duties in matters of welfare and of liaison with management. But in the late '60s and early '70s the unions fought hard for improvements in wages and working conditions, and with some success – so that, by the time the energy crisis put an end to the boom years, the average Bologna worker was doing at least as well as his counterpart in Toulouse, and probably better than the average Geordie. And Italian employers had emphatically moved ahead of British ones in the quality of the amenities – shower-rooms, reading-rooms, canteens with good food – provided for the staff.

In fact, by the early 1970s the unions were turning their main attention from wages and factory conditions to the disastrous state of public welfare services in Italy (health, housing, pensions, and so on), matters much more the fault of government than of employers. When I talked to a group of activists at the Sabiem plant in Bologna, I was surprised to find they seemed less indignant against their employers than over the crowded hospitals, bad schools and high rents – a different priority from that of British or French unionists. And in 1974 the Italian unions pressed home this point by hammering out with the major state and private companies a social contract that committed employers to themselves making up for government negligence by paying towards certain welfare services.

In Bologna there is less bitterness and agitation on these matters than in most towns. It is not only that the CGIL, as a matter of policy, discourages the kind of violent demonstrations that might prejudice the Party's local image. More significantly, workers do feel some sense of protection through the presence of a Left-wing local government. A CGIL militant told me: "Here in Emilia we, the working-class, have seized a few strategic positions that enable life to be made less difficult for workers. The overall framework is still capitalist, nor can we do much about things that are totally under state control, such as hospitals and secondary schools. But the housing situation is much better than average: it's easier than in most cities for a worker to buy his own house – and we Communists are not against private property on that level. And there are civic nursery schools and other civic welfare services, while the cooperatives help to keep prices down and to protect small producers from exploitation. So here in Emilia, we have plenty of cause to feel a little less bitter than most other Italians."

The cooperative movement is stronger here than in other parts of Italy, and is no less important than the CGIL as an auxiliary of the Communist Party. Cooperatives have been established in Emilia since the mid-19th century: even the Fascists were unable to suppress them. Today there are some 300 in the province of Bologna, employing over 160,000 people, and especially strong in agriculture, the building industry, and the retail and service trades. Their links with the Communist Party are not easy to define. After the war the Communists systematically infiltrated the Emilian cooperative movement, and as late as the mid-1950s the Party was defining cooperatives as "an auxiliary instrument in the class struggle for the emancipation of workers". Today Communists are in key positions in most of the co-operatives though by no means all, and in many cases there is a mixed membership: I visited a *pasta*-making cooperative where the president was a Socialist, the vice-president a Communist, and some members of the board were Christian Democrat. The Party almost certainly does receive direct funds from the cooperatives that it controls, however much it may deny this officially. At least, it receives benefits in kind. The *Municipio* awards nearly all its contracts to cooperatives – for example, to the CAMST for its catering – rather than to private firms. And the Party regards the cooperatives as a useful means of limiting the influence of capitalism and of controlling a large part of the labour market.

Many of the cooperatives, such as CAMST*, are powerful and efficiently-run, with a cheerful and relaxed working atmosphere. I visited a brick-making cooperative in the suburbs, whose nine-man board of directors was elected entirely from among the 220 employees. The president was a simple worker driving a trolley. I was told: "We also have an ordinary hierarchy of job positions, so that you may find the paradox of a foreman giving orders to a member of the board. But, with a little good-will on both sides, discipline is kept. The board changes every two years, so nearly everyone has his turn." Everyone seemed to be in a jolly, joking mood. On the walls of one workshop, photos of *Playboy* nudes were pinned up alongside posters of Lenin, Che, Dubček and Solzhenitsyn – "When Soviet comrades visit us," said my host, "they're horrified – but more by the nudes than by the dissidents. They find us decadent." He laughed.

The factory had a *crèche*, full of tots in neat blue smocks, and a smart canteen where a political meeting was in progress. I was told that most, but not all, of the employees were also members of the cooperative: you must pay 250,000 *lire* to join. But there are no dividends: profits are re-invested or used for welfare purposes, while some are passed on to the local cooperatives federation (from where a percentage finds its way discreetly into Party coffers). The employees/members decide on the rhythm of production and how jobs should be shared out – and it was claimed to me that productivity is higher than in the private sector. This was clearly a "model" cooperative, run on genuinely egalitarian

---

* See page 158.

lines: not all are quite so democratic. Some of the larger ones, such as CAMST, are rather more authoritarian, run by an oligarchy that may include "associate" directors from outside the enterprise, and in these cases the individual worker may not have much more say than in a private firm. But there seems little doubt that the Bolognese cooperatives operate more efficiently than the parallel Yugoslav worker-management system which I studied in Ljubljana, perhaps for two main reasons. First, they are voluntary, not imposed uniformly by the state: since nothing obliges a worker to join a cooperative, he will do so more willingly. Secondly: the Bolognese cooperatives are in competition with private enterprise, and this forces them to keep alert. The Bolognese example of peaceful co-existence between diverse socio-economic systems seems to have much to commend it – if only the Welfare State were not such a defaulter.

10
A wider role for the self-absorbed city-state?

It is rare in Bologna to meet a foreigner at a party, save in some university *milieux*; there are no consulates here, and few foreign businessmen. Despite its architectural splendours, Bologna does not even attract foreign tourists on any massive scale. In short, for sheer boring lack of cosmopolitanism – in its society, its outlook, its links with the world – this proud and sizeable city runs blinkered Newcastle a close second.

You will find some obvious explanations, in local temperament and history, in the absence of big international firms and of foreign immigrant workers (owing to Italy's own employment problems). There is also a simple factor of geography: Milan is so close (130 miles up the *autostrada*) that consulates, airlines and other such bodies generally find it more rational to serve Bologna from there. The town has only a local, not an international airport, so that to fly abroad you must first go to Milan, Florence or Venice, whereas Toulouse, a smaller town than Bologna, is so much farther from any major metropolis that it more easily becomes a metropolis itself. The

Bolognese will hate you for saying so, but in logistic terms their town is little more than an outer suburb of Milan.

Such cosmopolitanism as does exist is thanks largely to the unusual international-mindedness of Mayor Zangheri, and also to the curious open-door system of Italian universities. Of the 8,000 foreigners in Bologna, over 90 per cent are students, mostly Greeks, Arabs, Israelis and Americans, for any foreigner with the rough equivalent of the *maturità* has the same right as an Italian to enrol in any faculty; and many do so, despite the awful study conditions, since exams are so easy to pass in Italy. Most of these gate-crashers are thus the less bright students who have failed entry to their own national universities where the rules may be tighter. And Bologna is a favourite venue. The system has been criticised as "a racket in back-door degrees" and moves have been made on a European level to end it. Some Italian universities have tried also: but when the Rector of Bologna threatened a tightening-up, the large Greek student colony invaded his office for a sit-in, and he climbed down.

The foreign students add a pleasing touch of diversity to Bologna. You notice their presence if only from the slogans on the walls of the Via Zamboni – *Studenti Persiani contro il terrore del Shah*! The Greeks came in hordes during the colonels' regime: in 1973 there were over 1,200, many of them political refugees. They are fewer, now that Greece is free again, but there are still plenty of rejects from the Greek *numerus clausus* system.

The most curious phenomenon is that of the American medical students, about 600 in all, or 1,000 including wives and children. Everywhere in the streets you see their old Fiats or VWs, with US number-plates. A young man from New Jersey with a droopy moustache explained to me their situation: "After Mexico City, Bologna has the largest US medical student colony outside the States. We come not by choice, but because we must get a degree somehow – and German and French medical schools, and all Anglo-Saxon ones, are so hard to get into unless you have graft or are clever, which I'm not. Why Bologna? – there's a certain medical tradition here, and life's cheaper and easier than in Rome or Milan. We don't have to attend lectures: some students even study on their own in the States, and do no more than register here and fly over once a year for the exams. But that's rare, for we are examined in Italian and need to be here to learn it. Language *is* a problem, but Italian at least is quite close to the Latin medical vocabulary we all have to learn anyway. And Italian examiners are indulgent towards our linguistic mistakes - unlike German or French ones."

My informant added that after getting a degree in Bologna it was then easy to practise in the States - "A bit of a racket, yes, but why not make use of it?" He took me along to the Wolf Bar which the American students had adopted as their social centre, a bizarre little *trattoria*-cum-snack-bar with mock-Western décor, old American posters, a notice-board covered with ads for flat-sharers, baby-sitters, cheap lifts to Rome, and a jokey menu scrawled in coloured chalk on a blackboard - "Frappé Awful-Awful 450 1", etc. A student group were chatting up the waitresses in slang Italian. My friend commented: "About half of us adapt to Italian life, pick up the lingo and enjoy Bologna; the others are miserable, and time-serve to get their degrees. Many of us are married; we have private means, for of course we get no grants. We live apart from the local *bourgeois* society which is hard to penetrate: so we fall back on the more open working-class *milieux*. It's easy to get Bolognese girls if you try, but you have to work for it: they don't say 'yes' right away, like American girls."

A strange cold war exists between this medical fraternity and Bologna's second American student community, the Johns Hopkins University, of Baltimore, whose European branch is here. This local college has some 80 students, half of them Americans, doing six-month courses on Italian or European politics, history and economics. The college has a reputation for aloofness and secretiveness, and is rumoured to be a clandestine breeding-ground for CIA agents who come to study the PCI at close quarters. Whether or not this is so, the Johns Hopkins *alumni* look down on the medicos as intellectually inferior (which they mostly are); "But," one medico assured me, "what they really resent is that we steal their girls. The Italian JH girls go out with us, not them: they find us more mature."

This transplantation to old Italy of the jealousies of an aspiring Ivy League campus is the most enternaining feature of an otherwise dull international landscape in Bologna. Small colonies of businessmen and teachers, French, Germans, British and others, exist each within their own little circle, but forming no proper *milieu*: the Germans and British each number about 80. In addition there are British, French and German cultural institutes, each housed in an elegant old *palazzo*, with a library and reading-rooms, and a programme of lectures, concerts and film-shows. Their appeal is to modern-language students at the university and to lonely expatriates. The British institute, affiliated to the British Council, is a venue for Bolognese anglophiles, mostly elderly single ladies, and English girls dabbling in art; and here there flourishes, as in Florence only much more modestly, that traditional Anglo-Italian cultural love-affair with its distinctively genteel, bookish, dilettante, Victorian flavour.

The impetus on the Bolognese side for links with the outside world is left largely to the *Municipio*. The town has been actively twinned for some years with other Communist cities – Zagreb, Leipzig, Kharkhov Cracow – while the council has shown its support for various brands of Communism by sending non-military aid both to Frelimo and the Viet-cong during their "liberation" struggles. More recently, twinnings have developed with Western towns, notably Coventry, Valencia and Mannheim, in line with Party strategy. Bologna's annual children's book fair is the leading event of its kind in the world. And Zangheri has made special efforts to attract international conferences on such matters as town-planning: a major Council of Europe symposium on conservation was held there in 1974. It is easy to raise the charge of prestige-hunting, yet these operations do also reflect Zangheri's genuinely international outlook, and here he is well ahead of most of his fellow-citizens, including his fellow-councillors. I have already commented on various aspects of the Bolognese's insularity, which covers all age-groups. Teenagers travel abroad a good deal less than their counterparts in Stuttgart or Toulouse, even though some frontiers are a mere three or four hours' drive away; not only are family holidays rarely taken outside Italy, but school exchanges and group visits abroad are even rarer than in Newcastle. One *liceo* teacher told me: "Italian schools get no funds for this, nor is there much demand from parents, whose sole concern is for their kids to pass exams. The families would have to pay for any foreign visits, thus only the better-off children could go, and this would be unfair. Our *liceo* has no contact with any foreign school. Once we did try to organise a visit to Scotland, but it was cancelled through lack of interest."

Yet this parochialism must not be mistaken for xenophobia, of which there is very little. A foreign visitor is made welcome, so long as he accepts Bologna on its terms. Above all, there is very much less colour prejudice than in Stuttgart (admittedly, there are far fewer coloureds to be prejudiced against), while African or Asian students are made to feel at home more readily than in Toulouse. As for "European" feeling, the EEC is not a divisive issue as in Newcastle:

nearly all Bolognese including the Communists consider themselves pro-European and pay some lip-service to the ideal of a United Europe, even if few of them care or know much about the EEC in practice. The British and French are regarded with respect, mixed in the latter case with some jealousy and half-buried Italian feelings of inferiority towards France. Above all, attitudes towards Germany have evolved remarkably. In this town so proud of its anti-Fascist and partisan record, the Germans after the war were hated, but today this feeling has largely vanished and Germans are just as popular as French or British. Most foreign tourist visitors are German, and they are treated with courtesy and welcomed for their custom. I was told that football has played a key role in this *rapprochement*. The German professional Helmut Haller, for some years the leading star of Bologna's team, was a friendly, humorous extrovert who became a local idol, and in a town where football counts for so much, he proved the best possible ambassador for his country.

In fact, if the Bolognese feel any hostility towards outsiders, it is directed less against foreigners than against other Italians. The city-state mentality persists, and I met few Bolognese who wanted to live in another Italian town. Rome and Milan they treat with special scorn: whereas the resentment of London or Paris felt by a Geordie or Toulousain is mixed up with grudging feelings of envy and inferiority, a Bolognese actually despises Rome for its muddle and decadence, and he ignores it as far as he can. "We don't understand the Romans," said one girl, "they think and talk differently from us. And Rome has nothing to offer that we don't have already." Milan is positively hated: the easy-going Bolognese, who work hard but affect not to, mock the Milanese for their work mania. Like other north Italians, they also affect to despise southerners and especially Sicilians, though in practice the small immigrant community from the south is easily accepted. I met Sicilians and Neapolitans, working in local factories, who mostly seemed quite happy: "We keep apart from the Bolognese, but they don't trouble us," said a young man from Palermo; "We stick together, with our Sicilian style of cooking, our Sicilian songs, and apart from the climate we've little to complain of in Emilia." Yet they remain *Gastarbeiter* in an alien land, almost as much as they would in Stuttgart. And if Bologna had the same large southern colony as some other northern cities, the co-existence might not be so peaceful.

Given these strong regional differences, the case for effective decentralisation of government in Italy has for long been a powerful one. The nation is as diverse as Germany and has been unified for no longer: it could clearly benefit from a move away from tight Napoleonic centralisation, towards something a little nearer to the German federal system. This was the thinking behind the 1970 regional reform, which was welcomed by all the major Italian parties – and by other Europeans – as a step in the right direction. Under this reform, each of Italy's 17 regions is now, in theory, autonomous in matters of economic planning, transport, agriculture, tourism, culture, health and adult education. Each region has its own directly elected assembly, and several of these are in Left-wing hands, notably Emilia-Romagna (whose capital is Bologna). Needless to say, this has thrown up all sorts of tensions. The Ministries in Rome have used every constitutional device for blocking or slowing down the scheduled transfer of powers to the regions, so that in 1978 a struggle was still taking place as to who controls what; and though the reform had stipulated that the regional assembly should take over the prefect's powers of budgetary control, Bologna like other cities was still in practice under a degree of prefectoral supervision.

It has just not proved possible, during a period of acute crisis in Italy, to carry through these regional reforms as was hoped – and that is no surprise. However, if and when Italy emerges from crisis, the new regional system may yet prove effective, for its structure has been legally established. And already, Bologna is beginning to assume a new role: for the first time in its history, it is no longer a city-state but the administrative capital of a wider unit, and one that is of the same political colour as itself. This gives it an added potential stature. Its future, of course, depends on that of Italy as a whole, notably on whether the Communists enter power nationally. If they do, it could provide the conservative, inward-looking Bolognese temperament with a significant new challenge. Bologna would cease to be an enclave, assiduously protecting itself from the disorders of the rest of Italy: with its Communist experience, it would be called upon to play a more positive role in reshaping the nation as a whole. I am not prejudging whether Communist rule would be good for Italy – it might well not be – but it could shake the Bolognese out of themselves a bit. Bologna might become less "special", and in the eyes of many people, it might lose some of its charm. It could also become less hermetic. Or will the secret glob-glob-glob life of those arcades survive Red revolution in Rome, as it survived Mussolini and everything else?

IV

Newcastle

Keep your feet still, Geordie, hinny, the bad old days were best

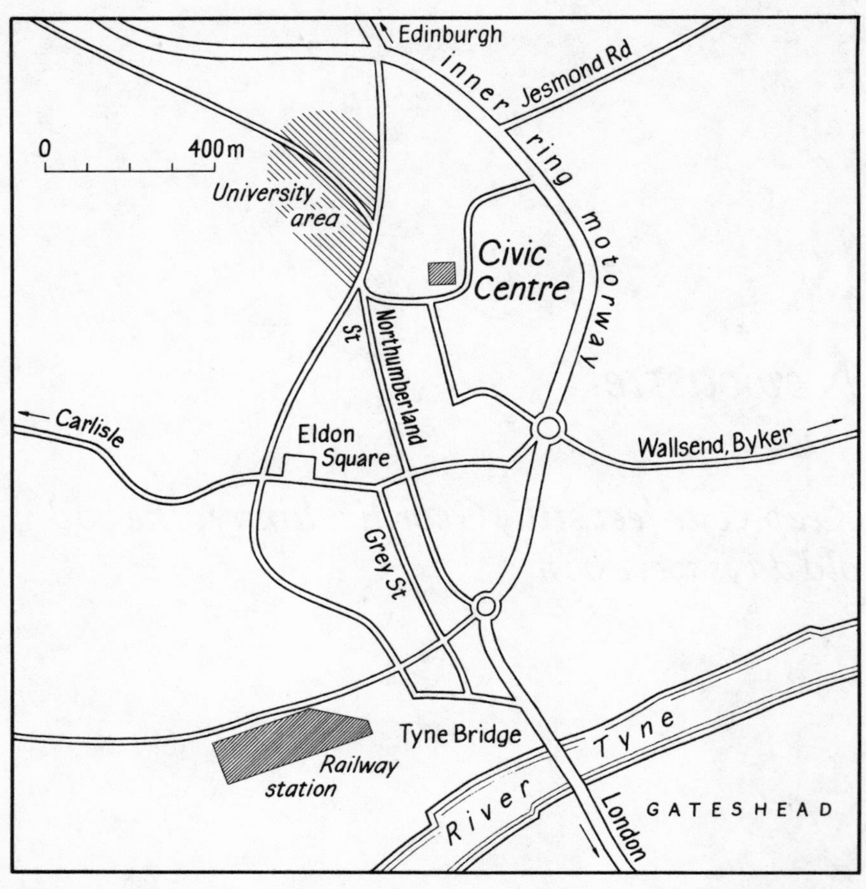
Edinburgh
Jesmond Rd
inner ring motorway
0 400 m
University area
Civic Centre
Northumberland St
Carlisle
Eldon Square
Wallsend, Byker
Grey St
Tyne Bridge
Railway station
River Tyne
London
GATESHEAD

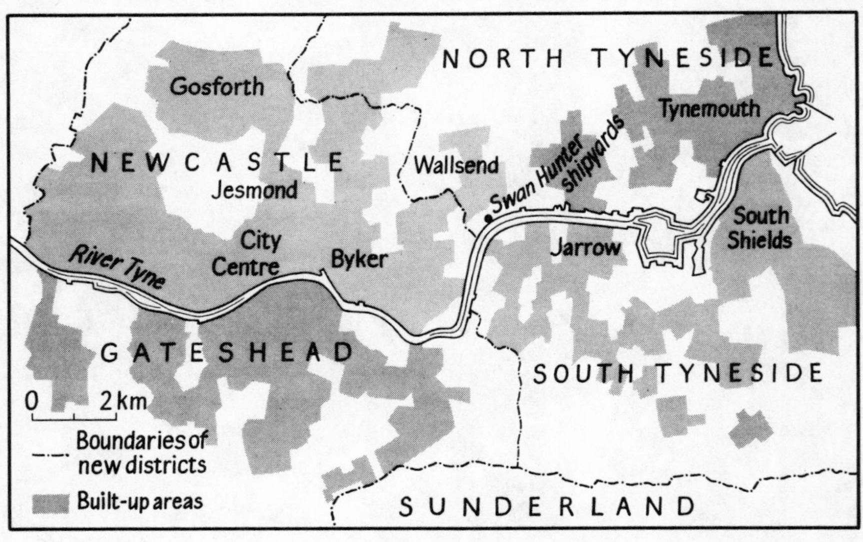
NORTH TYNESIDE
Gosforth
Tynemouth
NEWCASTLE
Jesmond
Wallsend
Swan Hunter shipyards
City Centre
Byker
Jarrow
South Shields
River Tyne
GATESHEAD
SOUTH TYNESIDE
0 2 km
Boundaries of new districts
Built-up areas
SUNDERLAND

1
Introduction

"We Geordies, we know we're the salt of the earth, we're God's chosen people, aren't we?" said the master-of-ceremonies, a bearded Falstaffian figure in doublet-and-hose. "Yes! yes!" thundered a hundred diners-out, raising their goblets of Lindisfarne mead. "We've been through hell here, so we just laugh at life, don't we?" "Yes!" they roared again, delighted – neatly dressed young couples, most of them, who did not look as if they had seen hell. Then ten bonny girls in Chaucerian dress came into the big hall with its mock-mediaeval trappings, and led us in the usual boisterous ritual of Tyneside dialect songs – "Geordie hinny", "Cushie Butterfield", and the local national anthem:

"Thor wis lots o' lads an lasses there, aal wi' smillin faces,
Gannin alang the Scotswood Road, te see the Blaydon Races."

This was one of those "mediaeval" banqueting frolics, newly popular, that pass for sophistication in these parts: hardly a genuine example of traditional Tyneside folk culture, but a modern up-market extension of it, with much the same exuberant vulgarity and radiant togetherness. And it was on this kind of occasion that I finally managed to enter into the spirit of this strange self-absorbed tribal civilisation in this remote region of England.

I confess right away that I find it harder to write fairly about Newcastle than my other towns – just because I *am* from England, or rather, from its south. Arriving here from London, with my Oxford and public-school background, my "posh" accent and class prejudices, I felt ill-at-ease in an area so assertively dominated by working-class values, effusively friendly in its way yet resentful of anyone coming to judge it by outside standards. In Toulouse or Stuttgart I felt more at home! But here in the north-east I was a victim, like the Geordies themselves, of Disraeli's "two nation" syndrome.

There are many things I like and admire, even find inspiring, about Newcastle, and I do not deny it has a stronger personality than any other big English town. But there are other things I find objectionable, even frightening. Sometimes, in the back-streets of slums, amid football crowds, or in dismal pubs with their beer spilt on the tables, and workers talking a language I could not follow, I even felt something of that *Angst* in the presence of an alien, vaguely menacing culture that I have felt in Moslem lands such as Iran or Algeria. (After all, Geordies treat their women in an almost Muslim manner!)

Newcastle is in some ways an archetype of the great blackened cities of the northern half of England, pioneers of the industrial revolution – Leeds, Nottingham, Stoke-on-Trent and others. It is an extreme example: its heavy industries are older and more crisis-ridden than average, its working-class manners rougher and warmer, its resentment of London fiercer. And it has a quite exceptional sense of local pride and identity: not a city-state mentality as in Bologna, but something shared with the region as a whole. It is the metropolis of a wide area, from the Tees to the Scottish border, known sometimes by its ancient name of Northumbria but more often just as "the north-east" – an area that feels itself to be, and therefore is, quite different from the rest of England. At its centre is Tyneside, a conurbation of nearly a million people astride the lower Tyne: Newcastle (population 300,000) is the largest and most historic of the towns that make up Tyneside and the centre of government of its new "metropolitan county". And city and wider conurbation are so bound up with each other that this chapter will be almost as much about Tyneside as Newcastle itself – pronounced locally "New-*cassel*", with the accent on the short "a" as in "tassel". If you call it "*New*-castle" with a long "a", in the southern manner, you are at once marked out as a stranger by Tynesiders, themselves always known as "Geordies". This nickname derives probably from their support for Georges I and II in the 18th century, though according to another theory it comes from the safety lamp, known as a "geordie", devised for local miners by George Stephenson. Geordies have their own dialect, less removed from the standard national tongue than *bulgnais* or Swabian, let alone Occitan; but nonetheless one of the most distinctive of English dialects.

The city looks distinctive, too. Its old mediaeval nucleus clambers up a cliff on the north bank of the Tyne, to surmount the brown, swirling, polluted river. Here, linking Newcastle to its historic rival on the south bank, Gateshead, are five bridges at different levels: the best known is the Tyne Bridge with its curving arch of steel rising to 170 feet, which served as a model for the similar-shaped but larger Sydney harbour bridge. Rising thus in tiers above the river, Newcastle gives a dramatic impression of elevation: it is one of the more imposingly situated of large English towns and sometimes dares compare itself with Edinburgh. The impression is also one of blackness. As Toulouse and Bologna are pink, so Newcastle is grey-black: its older stone buildings, such as the mediaeval castle and the fine churches, are most of them darkened and grimed by two centuries of industrial smoke and coaldust. Some have recently been given a clean. But the blackness is considered so much a part of the city's male Nordic *persona* that façades of new offices are required by the planners to include black or grey parts.

The central district, on a plateau above the river, has one or two elegantly curving streets in the best early Victorian style – famous Grey Street with its Theatre Royal and its towering monument to Earl Grey. Beside this is a gigantic indoor shopping-centre, opened in 1976, looking from the outside like some vast warehouse, and close by is a new inner motorway – two developments that have been much disputed as spoiling the city's character. Newcastle in fact (like Birmingham) has been having its old heart torn out and refashioned to almost the same degree as Stuttgart, but without the necessity of healing wartime wounds, for the town was hardly touched in the war. Yet is there really so much worth preserving, outside a tiny perimeter near the river? Tyneside as a whole presents a picture of mile upon mile of crumbling industry and Victorian urban drabness, under usually grey and chilly skies: a scene that may have a sombre beauty for those who find poetry in pitheads and shipyard cranes, but hardly helps promote the new official image of this area as a delightful one to live in.

To the north of central Newcastle lie the residential districts of Jesmond and Gosforth, where a not-very-assertive middle class lives in its solid stone Victorian houses or newish brick villas, sipping its gin-and-tonics. To the east and west, nearer the river, sprawl the working-class districts: the old insanitary slums of mean red-brick terrace houses, essentially English, many still awaiting demolition, and also the neat new estates and council flats, some – notably at Byker – of inspiringly original design. Here live the shipyard and factory workers, swilling their Newcastle Brown Ale. Further out, most of it beyond the civic boundaries, is the heavy industry, the miles of shipyard downstream towards the sea, the older engineering factories and the newer chemical ones. And further out still are the mines. Many today are wearing thin or have closed, and you have to go a few miles from Newcastle itself to find collieries still working. But coal, once the basis of Tyneside's wealth, is still at the core of its folklore and philosophy. "You can't understand this place till you understand coal," I was told by Sid Chaplin, a leading local novelist and himself an ex-miner.

In its architecture, climate, cuisine and life-styles, Newcastle may seem at an opposite pole from Toulouse or Bologna. Yet it really has far more in common with them than the inhabitants of any of these towns might suppose. The Geordie's attitude to London, an ill-thought-out atavistic mix-up of jealousy and contempt, is much the same as the Toulousain's to Paris. His devotion to the warm womb of his own tribal community, shutting off the world outside, is as strong as the Bolognese's – though with two differences. One, the womb here is an area, not just a city. Two, while the Bolognese is deeply confident that he is every bit as good as the Roman or Milanese, probably better, the Geordie at one level has qualms that London may after all be superior, so the less he sees of it the better. Hence his constant assertion that "Newcassel is the finest city on earth": it just has to be. His terror of being judged by outside values is at the root of his narcissistic parochialism. By nature hospitable, he will warmly welcome any newcomer, but on his own terms: at the first hint of being patronised, he can turn very nasty. And so big is the chip on his shoulder that he is quick to sense slights. Once a local acquaintance offered to take me to a workingmen's club, shrine of all Geordie culture. The day we were due to go, the local paper published an interview with me in which I had said Newcastle was backward in many ways compared with Stuttgart or Toulouse and too ready to accept mediocrity. My friend rang up in huffed embarrassment: "Sorry, I'm much too busy after all to take you this evening. . . .no, I don't know when I could manage it. Goodbye."

These attitudes go back into history. Tyneside has for centuries felt isolated from the rest of the country. This may have made sense in the days of horse travel, for this is the farthest from London – 275 miles – of any big English town. Today, when the motorway journey can be done in four hours, it seems a little silly. With rather more justification, they have long felt neglected and exploited too. In the Victorian industrial heyday, Geordies through toil and inventiveness earned the nation a large part of its wealth: but little of the money stayed in the north-east, it went into the pockets of mine and factory owners living mainly in the south. Then came the inter-war depression, hitting Tyneside harder than the rest of England. It was the poverty of all those decades that forged the strong sense of brotherhood and community concern that is still a dominant local feature. The miners, horribly exploited since Victorian times, were the greatest sufferers; and they remain in memory as folk-heroes, though their descendants today are far fewer and more affluent. This is the basis of the curious *urban* folk-culture of Tyneside that has hardly an equivalent in Europe, save maybe in Naples: most folk-cultures, Basque or Greek for instance, are rural. Today this culture is still vividly alive, and has even infiltrated the middle class which is here less assertive and influential than in other parts of England. So on Tyneside the dominant ethos, the "establishment" if you like, is – rarity! – working-class. The result is a rough spontaneity, a rejection of the airs and graces and despised "civilised" criteria of the south.

After the war, in Britain's boom years of the late 1950s and 1960s, even Tyneside was carried along by the surge of national prosperity and began to change. The old poverty has waned (even though living standards are still well below the north European average, and fell very slightly in the mid-1970s). Smart new hotels, shops and civic centres have appeared, and Tyneside's official publicists and leaders have been trying to shake off the so-called "cloth-cap image" of a dour, depressed, backward-looking area. New influences, like it or not, have been making their impact, as television opens new windows on the world and the workers' clubs exchange sawdust-on-the-floor for plush new carpets. But the Geordie reacts to all this with mixed feelings. He likes his new relative affluence, yes, and is a hearty spender. But he does not want his traditions to be eroded, and he even keeps a nostalgia for the comradeship of "the good old bad old days". An exasperated executive from the south once said to me: "This area's backwardness is partly its own fault. People won't adapt to new circumstances – the miners won't leave their villages to work elsewhere when their pits close, and people accept poor conditions or low standards almost wilfully. They don't, or won't realise how far ahead the rest of the country is." Fair? We shall see.

2

Defiant nostalgia – "a classic case of alienation"?

Tyneside entered history in Roman times. Wallsend, a town just east of Newcastle, is so named because here the Emperor Hadrian set one end of the great wall he built across northern England in about 122 AD, to protect his colony against the wild Scots. Newcastle itself did not yet exist, nor did it in the Dark Ages when Northumbria was a kingdom and a stronghold of early Christianity: the Venerable Bede, "father of English historians", lived and wrote in the great monastery at Jarrow in the 8th century. Newcastle was born in 1080, when William the Conqueror built his "new castle" on the heights above the river – where it still stands – to control the unruly countryside and ward off the Scots. And the town that soon grew up round the castle might have remained in history as little more than a garrison post were it not for two other factors: its position as a port near the river mouth, and the discovery of huge coal deposits in the area.

For many centuries the history of Tyneside has been that of its industry. Coal was mined here even in Roman days, and by the 13th century Newcastle was exporting it massively, mostly by sea to London and Europe. According to one early record, in a single three-week period in 1378, 134 foreign ships left the port with cargoes of coal. There were mines all over Tyneside, even in what is now the city's central park, the Town Moor. Thus in the Middle Ages, despite attacks by Scots and other marauders, Newcastle steadily built up its position as commercial capital of the north-east. It had important guilds and powerful merchant families, and in the 17th century was the fifth largest town in England, after London, Norwich, York and Bristol. So this city is no recent creation of the industrial era, like Birmingham or Sheffield: it has a long and proud history – as any Geordie will remind you.

Above all, this was virtually the cradle of the world's industrial revolution. As Stuttgart invented the motor-car, so Tyneside some decades earlier had pioneered the steam-engine, and this led later to the building here of the world's first railways, the first steamships, and many other inventions.* Through the boom years of the Victorian era, Tyneside led the world in technology, and so fast was expansion that Newcastle's population, a mere 28,000 in 1800, was ten times more by 1900. Immigrants arrived from all parts of the British Isles to find work in the Eldorado which became something of a gold-rush society, but a typically ruthless one. The industrialists made fortunes, but took most of the money away to the sunnier south, while miners and other workers toiled in appalling conditions. Men and boys worked ten- or twelve-hour days in the mines at bare subsistence rates; in the squalid slums, cholera and other epidemics were frequent in the earlier part of the century. Finally the first trade unions were formed, strikes were organised, and gradually rates of pay and conditions improved. But the old hardships, and the battle against callous or neglectful employers have left deep scars. This sense of having been exploited for so long in the past is a reason for Tyneside's continuing legacy of bitterness today.

The economic decline began even before the 1914-18 war. It was due partly to a failure to diversify from dependence on a few heavy industries, or to face the challenge of newer industrial nations. When the Depression came after 1929, Tyneside was hardest hit and Geordies felt they were again being exploited and made the first to suffer. By 1933 over 80 per cent of shipyard workers were on the dole. J. B. Priestley in his *English Journey* reported, "wherever we went there were men hanging about, not scores of them but hundreds and thousands." There was no money for buying new shoes, or jackets to protect against the cold northern winters, and children were saved from starvation only by the setting up of soup kitchens. This was the background to the notorious "hunger march" of October 1936 when 200 men walked from Jarrow to London to draw attention to Tyneside's plight and demand the right to work. The miseries, and also the emotional solidarity they bred, are still within living memory and are passing into a kind of tribal memory. They go a long way to explain why Tyneside is what it is today.

By the late 1930s the employment crisis was already easing, and then the war brought a kind of boom to the Tyne whose industries worked flat out to provide munitions and warships. Since the war, Tyneside has

* For fuller details, see page 266.

been going through a material transformation like so much of western Europe. Much of the old poverty – though not all – has been smoothed away, as the Victorian slums are replaced by comfortable new housing; and improved medical services, better schools and higher pensions make life easier at last for the working class. Though the mines are declining and the shipyards face recurrent crises, some new industries have arrived and wages at least till the mid-1970s have more than kept pace with inflation. Go into the supermarkets, the bingo halls and the workers' clubs, and you see that today's builders and miners have money to spend. Yet the new prosperity remains precarious, as the past few difficult years have shown. Tyneside has not yet really succeeded in making its "second industrial revolution": too many of its firms are still dependent on out-of-date equipment and attitudes. Its economic problems present an extreme example of the malaise of Britain in the 1970s. Why has British industry lost so much of its old prowess? More especially, why has Tyneside lost the pioneering inventiveness and dynamism of its heyday? Neither question is easy to answer. Today, if Britain sneezes, Tyneside catches bronchitis, and unemployment is often at twice the national average. No wonder the population of Tyneside has been falling steadily since the war, as young people reluctantly are forced to seek jobs elsewhere.

So let me try to analyse this Geordie society, described to me by a Marxist as "a classic case of alienation". A world away from the tidy, bourgeois, Europe orientated south-east, it of course has far more in common with the rest of the industrial north: yet here too there are differences. Geordies lack the glib, self-confident, mercantile thrustfulness of the Mancunian or Yorkshireman. They are more stoical, less assured, much less commerce-minded, and for all their rough speech and dress they are a gentle people. Full of contradictions, too. The heritage of poverty has made them penny-wise, so that in buying clothes or food they will go for cheapness rather than quality: yet in their own way they are hedonistic, and rather than save they will blow their spending-money on their own pleasures of boozing, gambling, dancing. They have an unrivalled sense of community concern for the weak, the aged, the handicapped; yet their public life in recent years has seen some of the worst corruption in Britain, and this among Socialists! Their strong comradeship does not easily extend between the sexes: traditionally they are shy of women and prefer to exclude them from their jolly social evenings (but this is now changing). They sing together a great deal - in the pubs and clubs, and along the streets - but they are not great talkers, or at least their talk is not what a Londoner or Parisian might think rational. It can be fruity and even poetic, spiced with vivid anecdote and metaphor, but I have seldom found it easy to induce even the more literate to pursue a coherent line of argument. A Londoner living here agreed: "The critical and intellectual spirit is despised, in favour of earthiness." Everything is seen in human, concrete terms, and far higher store is set on personality than ideas: a common British trait, but especially pronounced up here. People adore bitchy gossip and are cheerfully candid even to strangers: on my first meeting with one Tory councillor, I mentioned a colleague of his, also Tory, and he said, "Oh, that shit!" I can imagine hearing that in Toulouse, but hardly in Stuttgart. In fact, one trait that Geordieland unknowingly shares with Toulouse and also Bologna is this directness and parading of personality. The place swarms with colourful, jokey, braggart "characters" - so similar to some I found in Toulouse.

One such is Arthur Grey, whom I first met when he was Tory Leader of the Council, *de facto* equivalent of a French or Italian mayor - tall, elderly, pipe-smoking, very bluff. At short notice he spared me three hours of his time in his thickly carpeted and panelled office in the Civic Centre, where he poured me several whiskies and an inconsequential stream of wry, self-justifying anecdotes. . . "You see, our cocker-spaniel's just died of cancer, my wife's had four miscarriages, we're sorry we've never had children but there you are, well, I left school at fourteen, worked with Irish navvies, walked miles to work each day in the '20s 'cos I couldn't afford trams, but it didn't harm my health, anyway. I now have sixteen suits and run a Ford Capri, I joined an advertising firm and worked my way up to be manager, I'm brilliant, you see, no, my poverty didn't make me Socialist, just keen to get ahead - oh, thanks, pet, good-night" - this to his secretary, Poppy, who had popped in - "and where was I? - oh, yes, I made myself Alderman a few years ago, mind you old Dan Smith and I we got on quite well although he was Labour, we'd meet and chat here in the gents while having a pee together, and in public he praised my brilliant leadership, of course I know all those people in London, Wilson, Heath and co, know 'em well, yes I admit I've a sharp tongue and I'm not popular, and maybe we do lack social graces up here, but Tyneside's changing. . . ." How very unlike my initial interviews with the mayors of Stuttgart and Bologna.

Another Geordie character I met was Norman Cornish, a handsome man in his fifties who is now a respected local artist. Son of a miner, he went into the pits himself at fourteen and stayed there full-time right up till his mid-forties, long after he had made his name nationally through painting in his spare time. "The mines were a university of Life so I was hesitant to give them up, and I still feel emotionally tied to them." His views on the north-east? – "What I object to are the so-called 'authorities' who tell us we are backward and must get with-it. No, John, I *won't* be dictated to by Carnaby Street, or Coronation Street – but this doesn't mean I've an *assegai* and grass-skirt." Then, contrarywise, "The aborigines in Australia are more advanced than Europeans. I agree with Browning, man's reach must exceed his grasp – but alas, John, Newcastle is being ruined by modernisation, we're all becoming ra-ra-ra New York. And it's sad to see the old colliery world dying. I'd like a few pitheads to be kept as memorials, like the Pyramids or Dutch windmills." Like most Geordies, he kept calling me "John" at our first meeting. And like so many others, he seemed totally uncritical of Tyneside. He, Grey and others are examples of what a professor from the south called "the lively, intuitive, but untrained north-east mind". The area produces brilliant young people, but the best tend to emigrate. Those who stay have many human qualities: intellectual clarity is rarely one of them.

I must come back to class distinctions, a topic that the British often find it in bad taste to discuss honestly, just because it obsesses them so much – like sex in Victorian days. Much more than any of my other towns, even the two Communist-run ones, and more probably than any other large English town, Newcastle is dominated by working-class values. The middle class here keeps a low profile and lacks a distinctive personality: in fact, I have heard the absence of strong middle-class leadership alleged as a cause of Tyneside's backwardness. With affluence, the working class has come to share some *bourgeois* luxuries – cars, colour TV, and so on – and in some cases to send its children to university, but without trying to ape *bourgeois* social values or change its own defiant ethos. Rather, it is the middle class that pays lip-service to workers' values. Hence a pervasive inverted snobbery, fashionable in all Britain today but nowhere so much as here. Local businessmen or politicians preserve a man-of-the-people manner and are careful not to distance themselves from the respected élite that works with dirty hands, prefers beer to gin, and is dedicated to football and dominoes. Geordies who win success in professions such as teaching or the media remain ostentatiously proud of their working-class heritage: one of them, typically, wrote an article in a national paper comparing the city's "unreal" middle-class suburban life with the "real" world of the workers' terrace-houses. And when I visited a workers' club, my host kept yelling at me, "John, these are *real* people, nothing phoney about 'em – fair comment?" – as if afraid I might not agree. "Phoney" tends to equal "cultured *bourgeois*". Yet this clash of values is not transferred into political terms, as it would be in France: it is merely human. And the middle classes accept their situation.

Strangely enough, the result is a society freer from class tensions than in most parts of England, notably the south-east. Perhaps it is that the working class, being locally in such a position of strength, feel less resentment against this passive middle class in their midst: their anger is directed outside the area. Many newcomers comment on this: a Londoner living here told me, "There's much less of the social-climbing and status-snobbery of big cars or lavish parties that you find in some other areas. People are friendly and genuine, provided they feel accepted." And there is far less flaunting of wealth than in the *Room-at-the-Top* world of West Yorkshire. Tyneside has the feel of one big chummy family, with little of the compartmentalisation of Toulouse, the formality of Stuttgart, or the *bella figura* of Bologna. Honorary consulships would never win you much kudos here.

Newcastle no longer has old distinguished families within its borders, as does Toulouse. The merchant families that ruled it in the 18th century, such as the Ridleys, now form part of an aristocratic "county" set that lives out in the Northumberland countryside, uses Newcastle only for shopping and other amenities, and makes little impact on its life. Nor is much impact made by another educated minority – the youngish immigrants from the south or midlands who come for a few years to do a university job or an executive stint in their company's local branch, so as to earn promotion. These "foreigners" rarely integrate.* They are the counterparts of the "new Toulousains", but are far less numerous: Newcastle cannot hope to exert the same appeal for such *cadres* as sunny Toulouse. Tyneside in fact has not enjoyed the same massive influx of a new intelligentsia as either Toulouse or, in its different way, Stuttgart, and this lack of new blood has been a serious handicap to its progress.

A London girl teaching in a secondary school in a rough area said, "I

---

* See page 280.

feel in a foreign country here, what with the strange, horrible things they eat – pease pudding! – and the obscure dialect. The kids regard me as foreign, and tease me for my posh accent, but good-humouredly. They call everyone 'man', even me – 'Hey, Miss, man!' " This dialect has a broad twang, less abrasive than a Toulousain's, but almost as irritating to my ear at least. It is virtually a language of its own, with many words in common with Norwegian: "gannin hyem" means "going home", and "I don't know" is "Aa divven knaa." Working-class Geordies use this tongue among themselves much of the time; but can speak "polite" English too, when they wish: they are bilingual, like Swabians. Like Yorkshiremen, they use endearments with strangers, which some southerners find over-familiar: go into a shop and you will be called "pet" or "hinny" (Geordie for "darling"). Even "bugger" is a term of admiration, not insult: "yer bugger" (rhyming with "sugar") means "clever old you". And many older men *do* wear cloth-caps, as sensible protection from the cold winters: the often-resented "cloth-cap image" has some reality.

The true citadel of Geordie hedonism and comradeship is the workingmen's club of which there are hundreds on Tyneside, some small and spartan as in the old days, others large, plush and modernised. People spend an evening here as much to satisfy their strong gregarious instincts as for the specific amusements of beer, games or music: Geordies feel an almost physical need for a snug togetherness with a crowd of their own kind. One winter night I visited a typical larger club. The vast main drinking-saloon, for men only, was full of rough-faced Geordies in their working clothes, playing dominoes, cards and darts, drinking pints of Newcastle brown ale, making a lot of noise. The lounge bar next door, where ladies are graciously permitted, had a very different ambience, more genteel, with opulent gilt-and-chrome décor of impressive vulgarity, cosy chairs, and a lot of youngish couples in their going-out finery – it could have been the saloon of any modern road-house. Upstairs, in the large concert hall, a "go-as-you-please" was in progress – the club's amateur talent contest where members mount the platform to sing their own solos, and maybe win a small prize. Men with strong baritone voices sang the old music-hall favourites and some newer "pop", while the packed audience joined loudly in the choruses, clapping wildly, stamping their feet. It was all so very north-of-England. Such "real" people.

This club, like many others, hesitantly began to admit women members a few years ago. But they are still barred from the "men only" saloon, and must be the wives of other members: the club is afraid that admitting single women as members would turn the place into a forum for pick-ups and spoil its comradely spirit. Many clubs still allow no women to join, for the notorious old *machismo* of Tyneside dies hard. One personification of this is "Andy Capp", famous caricature-hero of a comic strip-cartoon in the London *Daily Mirror* – a boorish little man who wears a large cloth cap and baggy clothes, boozes too much and bullies and enslaves his exasperated wife. The portrait may never have been quite fair: yet till recently there *was* a good deal of wife-beating, and women were expected to keep out of clubs and pubs and stay in the kitchen waiting on hubby subserviently. Behind the scenes they held a certain power, including the purse-strings: but socially they accepted their "inferiority" and could often be seen giving up their seat to a man in a bus.

Today Tyneside is no longer quite so much the Marrakesh or Palermo of the north. A younger generation of Geordie women, having heard of Women's Lib, will not tolerate the old ways and have persuaded their spouses to help them with the chores and take them to the clubs. A new law in Britain since 1976 makes any sex discrimination, in working life or in public places, illegal: this does not apply to the private clubs, which can still do what they like, but it has broken the unwritten "men only" rules of the pubs – at least in theory, if not always in practice. After the law came into force, a few combative girl journalists in Newcastle decided to test it by entering the male pub saloons. They were made to feel so unwelcome that they did not try again, nor did they dare take the publicans to court as they could have done.

This anachronistic sex-war, typical of Tyneside, is not really much fun for a modern girl. Judith Hann, a Geordie journalist writing in *Cosmopolitan* in 1975, quoted a friend living in the poor quarter of Byker: "In a place like this, couples marry very young. The women are housebound and they hardly see their men. They lead a completely different social life, and there's little communication between them at any level." Miss Hann commented: "Probably because of this gulf there are strong friendships between women. They spend evenings out together in the pubs – groups of women dressed up to the nines. . . . The extended family, with an ever-strong commitment to mother, is often blamed for causing the separate social lives and limited contact between married couples. When a girl marries she often moves only one street away from her mother." The strength on Tyneside of the matriarchal extended family, generally a facet more of Latin than Nordic countries, was stressed to me by quite a number of people.

Archaic this society may in some ways be, but any visitor is also impressed by its friendliness – too effusive for some tastes – and its very real human concern. If you are in any sort of trouble, however minor, people will go out of their way to be kind and helpful, to a degree rare today in a big town. Ring a secretary, with a request to see her boss or some query, and whether she knows you or not she will do all she can, with many a "yes, pet" and "of course I will, luv", and "don't you worry, dear" – so unlike France. And though people may initially have a sharp tongue, they are sensitive enough to feel worried if they have caused offence. Once, parking my car clumsily, I brushed against a pedestrian and he yelled out, "What the fuck. . . . ?" but then hung around until I had left the car, clapped me on the back and grinningly apologised.

The old hard years have forged a wonderful spirit of caring that suffuses all local life. Family ties may be strong but they are not, as often in Toulouse, in conflict with community ones. And this warm little world, with its limited horizons but fierce traditions, exerts a lasting pull of loyalty on those cleverer Geordies who leave to seek success in the big world but do not forget. Sophisticated journalists such as Alan Brien of *The Sunday Times* (born in Sunderland) pour out articles in lyrical praise of every aspect of Geordie low-life and folk culture. And Geordies are recomforted. But the intensity of this tribal feeling, Tyneside's strength, is also its enemy: may it not be a haven that protects Geordies from facing up to the outside world? An inward-looking self-pitying nostalgia, a parochialism that seeks to exclude the world, a fear of cosmopolitan values, an ignorant acceptance of low standards – these are Geordie traits I have never managed to find attractive.

The workers' sufferings of the Victorian age and the Depression have left so deep a scar that a tribal folk-memory of them persists. Hence the obsessive harping over "the bad old days" in so much of today's popular culture, in the stream of new songs and plays that extol the martyrdom of the miners, that glorify the pit-lamps and club beers as proud symbols of their culture, and crusade bitterly against past wrongs that by now have largely been righted. In the hugely successful local play, *Close the Coalhouse Door,* written in 1968 and described by its author Alan Plater as "an unqualified hymn of praise to the miners", a girl from the south asks, "Are they always like this? – living in the past," and a miner answers, "Well, we've had a bigger ration of the past here than in most places." And a southerner commented to me, "There's a wistfulness here for the Depression as the time of greatest warmth and togetherness, hence a feeling that adversity is the noble and correct thing and success is wrong. I've met people who clearly do not *want* to lose their bitterness against the old injustices - or what could they still believe in? This popular gut-reaction gets exploited, of course, by the militant Leftists." Admittedly the old hardships were great and the injustices unforgiveable, and no one should minimise them: but for Geordies to continue thus to brood over them is dangerously near to self-pity and to a masochistic narcissism - like a young man with an unhappy childhood who goes through life feeling that the world has done him a wrong, and so never quite grows up. Few people can ever have cherished quite so lovingly the outsize chip on their shoulders. "We, you see, are the Blacks of Britain, despised and exploited," said one Geordie, quite seriously. If he finds out one day that he is white, and not exploited except by himself, how will he ever cope?

Parochialism is common enough anywhere, and the towns in this book are chock-full of it. Geordies make of it a fine art. On a typical news page in the local daily, a fire on Tyneside injuring two people got a much larger headline than an air crash in the Caribbean killing sixty. And Graham Turner in his fine book *The North Country* quotes amusingly the case of an appointments board for a senior managerial job in local government, interviewing a candidate with Oxford and Sorbonne degrees and a brilliant subsequent career. The man is asked whether he has any relations on the local council, whether he is a Labour Party or union man, and whether his wife shops at the Co-op. He replies "no" in each case, adding, "We go to Harrods, actually." When he has left the room, the chairman asks, "Who put that bugger on the short-list? - he's got nae qualifications at all."

One Geordie journalist told me, "I see no virtue in this place becoming more cosmopolitan or open to outside influences. Why should it improve us, say, to go off to eat Spanish food in Spain and talk Spanish, rather than have good British food here? And if we tried to set our sights by London standards, this could spoil the character of the north-east. We don't want the gin-and-tonics arriving from the south: let's drink our beer in our own way." In Bologna, this smug insularity comes from an assurance of superiority: on Tyneside, it is part of the inferiority complex, of a fear of being judged by other values and found wanting. For example, Geordies are rightly proud of their small Northern Sinfonia orchestra, which they know to be one of the best in the provinces. But when it planned a European tour there was some local opposition, less because of the cost than through fear of its being criticised by world standards. This Geordie complex is almost a caricature of the general British distaste for having to reassess themselves in the light of foreign values – the crux of the whole dilemma of joining the EEC.

This rejection of the outside world leads inevitably, on Tyneside, to an easy acceptance of mediocrity in life-styles, in matters of taste and elegance. People do not know any better, or they do not want to know. "Geordies are easily satisfied with their shops, food, décor staying the same way," said one critic; "they lack a sense of style, and like many other British people they make a cult of amateurism and fear the slickly professional." Hence food that is dismal even by English provincial standards. And, coming from neat Stuttgart, my first impression in Newcastle has often been one of sloppiness – cracked cups in cheaper *cafés,* spilt beer lying unwiped on pub tables, incompetent waitresses, fish-and-chip wrappings in the gutter, peeling shop-façades in poorer streets. When I stayed in one small hotel (AA recommended!), the bathwater was barely tepid, the electric shaving-point did not work, the skylight had no curtain so that I was woken by the sun at 6 a.m., and the coffee was muddily undrinkable: yet the staff were all charming and obliging, and I felt they just did not notice these things and would have been surprised if I had complained. Ignorance therefore is part of the trouble – but also a wilful, blinkered chauvinism: "We are proud of our smoke," said one elderly local mayor. The famous Federation Ale, the beer brewed locally and sold in all the clubs, is flat, insipid stuff, as most non-Geordies would agree. Judith Hann writes categorically, "It is Britain's best beer." No true Geordie would for a moment think otherwise.

In the past years, a few of the more go-ahead local public figures have come to realise the harm that Tyneside does to itself through these attitudes. Public money and efforts have been spent to promote new links with the outside world and to attempt to provide the area with a new, more up-to-date image, in the hope of thus enticing the new industry and new outside talent that are so much needed. "Making the north-east a better place to live in" has become the great slogan. Materially there has been some progress, as we shall see. But the old attitudes do not change easily, and local government is in some respects a reflection of them. It is time to look at the astonishing success-and-failure story of T. Dan Smith – the man all Britain knew in the 1960s as "Mr. Newcastle".

2

Visions and intrigues of "The New Brasilia"

How much autonomy in civic affairs does Newcastle enjoy, compared with my other towns? The quick answer is: less than Stuttgart, more than Toulouse or Bologna. But, as a result of Britain's local government reforms of 1974, Newcastle (population 308,000) is now a "district council" within the new "metropolitan county council" of Tyne-and-Wear (population 1,200,000), and this new two-tier system makes the real answer more complex. We shall return to it, after first examining some other features of local politics.

One of the most obvious of these is that a British town has no real mayor in the Continental or American sense. Newcastle has a Lord Mayor but the post is little more than an honorary one, rotating annually among senior councillors. It involves some pomp and prestige, for the mayor in his chains of office must preside and speechify at public functions, but he has virtually no power. The real political control, if anywhere, is in the hands of the "leader of the council", a man chosen by the majority party or group on the council, for a longish term. This leader, if he has the right political gifts, is in a position to wield as much power as a French or Italian mayor: but in practice he seldom does. This is because he usually lacks the stature: a criticism often made of Tyneside politics is that the best men refuse to enter the game and most councillors whether Labour or Tory are mediocrites, of limited education and outlook, some of them small businessmen attracted to the town hall by the useful "contacts" it can bring them. This may be true in many towns – Toulouse, among others – but is especially so in this little world of intriguers and wheeler-dealers. Tyneside has a notable tradition of petty corruption: once in the 1930s three former mayors were up before the courts in the same year.

The notorious T. Dan Smith, who dominated the north-east in the 1960s, is a tragic-heroic figure whose paradoxical career broke all the rules. He typified the worst extremes of local corruption, yet also showed a reformist zeal and international vision that were untypical of Tyneside, to say the least. It is rare in Britain for a local politician to achieve national prominence, for we have neither the German system of long-ruling professional mayors, nor the French tradition whereby a big-town mayor is usually also a well-known deputy or senator. Dan Smith, in his heyday of untarnished glory as "Mr. Newcastle" (before his seamier side became known), has represented much the most striking post-war exception to this British norm.

He was born at Wallsend in 1915, the son of a miner. He left school at fourteen and spent much of the 1930s on the dole: this shared suffering has marked him profoundly. A brilliant youth, he was early attracted to Leftist politics, and became a Trotskyist, pacifist, and passionate soap-box tirader against the moderate Labour Party. But after the war he was persuaded to join the party and became a Newcastle councillor in 1950. After 1958, when Labour regained control of the council from the Tories, Dan's hour came, and two years later he was elected Leader of the Council and chairman of its housing committee. His politics were by now less rebellious and more pragmatic than in his youth, but still idealistic, and he rapidly set out on a rousing crusade to transform stagnating Newcastle into a golden city of the future. If he never quite managed this, his achievements were nonetheless remarkable. He tore down many of the worst old slums and replaced them with hygienic modern blocks. He bullied a hesitant council into letting him engage famous planners and architects from London and abroad to redesign central Newcastle as a worthy metropolis for the north. He instigated the setting up of an arts association and a development council for the north-east that together would revitalise the region's economy and make it "a better place to live in", with Newcastle as its jewelled hub. He spoke of the city repeatedly as "the New Brasilia", and though many people smirked at the hyperbole, he was probably justified in using it, for he knew that Geordie rhetoric was needed to fire a lethargic city with some sense of modern purpose. He made his mistakes, but few people doubted the sincerity of his vision at that time, behind all the verbiage. No original thinker, he had a gift for activating the ideas of others and firing people with his own enthusiasm. He shook Newcastle up, as no one has ever done before or since.

I met him first in 1970 – a tall, pale man with a beaky nose and wispy hair swept back. He talked fast and excitedly, with no false modesty, using grandiloquent phrases in the Geordie manner but with no lack of coherence. "I've always been an internationalist, I've felt that to become a true regional capital Newcastle must open its gates and take ideas from the world. But I had a job to persuade my fellow-councillors, Labour even more than the Tories. They usually compared Newcastle with its local rival, Gateshead: I wanted to compare it with Rome and Athens."

His rhetoric may have seemed fanciful, yet there was sincerity in his desire to break Tyneside of what he called "our besetting sin of parochialism" and link it with a wider world. In this, as in the dynamic calibre of his leadership, he was a rare kind of Geordie. In fact it surprised some people that he chose to remain in local politics when by the mid-1960s he was a national figure, controlling the Labour Party in the north-east. But his ambitions were to promote a new kind of regionalism, and soon afterwards he left the city council to devote himself to the chairmanship of the Northern Economic Planning Council which he had helped to create. However, the Labour Government never allowed this new body to win the influence he had hoped. He began to become disillusioned. A few years later, the rumours of his shadier practices that for long had been circulating in private came suddenly into the headlines: in 1973 he went on trial for corruption. It had long been known that from his first years on the city council he had run a network of "public relations" firms, parallel to his official work, and he coupled this with a mildly flamboyant style of life – running a Jaguar with the number-plate "DAN 68", and retaining a hired suite at the luxury Carlton Tower Hotel in London for his high-level "contact " work. At his trial in Leeds, it was proven that he had misused his public posts – on the city council and later the NEPC – to award building contracts to big national firms from whom he took large sums of money as commission. He used the cover of his PR firms to make the contacts, and worked closely with the notorious Yorkshire architect John Poulson, jailed in 1971. Thus Smith made himself thousands of pounds – but smashed his own career for ever. In 1974 he was given six years in jail. Was this the "New Brasilia", to make Newcastle politics look thoroughly Latin American?

It is a sad and enigmatic story of how power corrupts. Many Geordies today talk regretfully of Smith as "a good man who went wrong", and they believe – probably rightly – this his earlier work for the city was in good faith, whatever misuses he later made of it. He himself stated at the time of his trial that he did not see anything so awful in making a little money for himself on the side, in return for all he had done for Newcastle as an unpaid councillor; he saw men around him making millions in property development, and was it so wrong to seek a tiny share of the cake? So there may well be truth in the view that his moral fall dates from the time when his city planning work brought him into regular contact with London and its glamorous world of wicked tycoons: this seduced him, and some flaw in his humble upbringing made him unable to resist. Is this morality tale not unconnected with Geordies' famous mistrust of London, their fear that if they compete with it, or are tainted by it, they are sure to come out the worse?

Another judgement on the affair is that it points an argument against the British system whereby councillors receive very little pay for their hard work, and also in many sectors are free from close state supervision. If Smith had been drawing a handsome salary, like the mayor of Stuttgart and his adjutants, would he have been so prone to temptation? If he had been subject to the same Prefectoral controls as in Toulouse, could he have got away with it? This latter point is not so easy to argue, for Toulouse has also known corruption – on a lesser scale – and in Britain too the state has checks on civic housing projects. But on the question of salaries for elected local leaders, it seems that Britain could learn a lot from Germany. In Smith's day, a senior councillor received only a minor indemnity and some expenses: today he can draw some £2,000 a year, but this is still peanuts compared with the long hours he will probably put in, and it means that a councillor without private means or other profession may find it hard to earn a decent living. Hence the temptations remain.

The Tories won back control of the council in 1967, under Arthur Grey. It may be asked how on earth Newcastle, with the working-class basis I have described, can ever throw up a Tory majority. There are explanations. One, the city itself has sizable middle-class areas and is much less proletarian than adjoining districts such as Gateshead. Another, the Tory party here takes some of its colouring from the Tyneside ethos, it is relatively "populist" in its style and make-up – led by such as Arthur Grey – and is not the same as it is in the Thatcher heartlands of shire and stockbroker-belt. Anyway, since 1973 the city has been back in Labour hands, under the unremarkable leadership of Tom Collins. Of the 78 councillors, most are trade-unionists, artisans, shopkeepers and the like. If Newcastle today is reasonably well administered, it is due less to these men than to the capable team of fully-salaried officials they have hired from outside – men like the chief executive, Ken Galley (a Yorkshireman), and the housing director, John Dixon (from Essex). Professional civic management at this level is seldom as good in Britain as in Germany – as we saw in Stuttgart – but it compares favourably with France.

One of Smith's achievements was to bring in this kind of talent. He appointed Britain's first "city manager". Traditionally in Britain the senior civic officer is the Town Clerk – and dully clerical, in the lay sense, he often is. Smith set a new trend, soon to be copied elsewhere, of trying to run the city more on business lines, and for this he hired a man with a modern managerial outlook, and gave him a higher salary and grander title. He chose Frank Harris, a thrusting, cultivated southerner, from the Ford Motor Company, who stayed on through the first two years of the Grey régime, till he finally resigned in frustration. He was an impatient, sharp-tongued man, nick-named "the fastest slide-rule in the north", and his wrist-watch carried an alarm which he would sometimes set to go off during one of Grey's interminable speeches in committee! He fought hard to speed up and modernise the wheels of civic routine, and did succeed in cutting by more than half the man-hours spent by the council's 65 committees: but needless to say he made himself unpopular with the slow-minded worthies who objected to being treated like board members of an American car firm. One of the few Tory councillors sympathetic to him told me: "Of course he was right: much public money is wasted in muddle and palaver. But try to bring in business methods, as he did, and you hurl yourself against vested interests. The old boys enjoy their endless intrigues, their petty chairmanships of sub-committees, they feel that's what they're in the game for. However, Dan and Frank did make some progress: the city *is* run more efficiently than before their day."

But how much autonomy does it have? Like most larger towns, Newcastle until the 1974 reforms was a "county borough", separate administratively from the county of Northumberland to which it belonged geographically, and with a degree of independence – subject to government supervision – in such matters as education and planning. But on Tyneside there were 16 different councils, most of them mere "urban districts" attached to the far-flung counties of Northumberland and Durham; and the conurbation, astride these two counties, had no central body to coordinate its planning and public services. This led to problems just as great as in the Toulouse and Stuttgart areas – especially as Tyneside has a long legacy of local rivalries. From mediaeval until very recent times Newcastle's neighbours, notably Gateshead and Tynemouth, feared her attempts to dominate or exploit them. And Geordies, for all their solidarity in face of the outside world, still keep alive these internal feuds, half in jest but half seriously. This has hampered local government. David Bean * reports that just before the war "the principle of non-cooperation was so bad that the Urban District of Gosforth, which is in effect a posh northern suburb of Newcastle, spent unnecessarily large sums of money sending its sewage a long detour, including an unnecessary ninety-foot rise to get over a watershed, which of course needed pumps, all to avoid passing over Newcastle territory, which lay in its natural drainage-path". Even by 1970 there was little joint sewage disposal on Tyneside, and though progress had been made towards voluntary coordination of planning and transport, various jealousies persisted: for example, Newcastle – just like Stuttgart – resented being expected to subsidise the central amenities on its territory, such as theatres and swimming-pools, which the other districts used but did not pay for, while these districts took most of the overspill population and new industries, and thus the lion's share of new revenue from taxes.

Matters were much the same in other parts of England and Wales. A reform of local administration was clearly needed, and in the early 1970s the government pushed this into force despite varied opposition. The main feature of the new system is that each of the six largest English provincial conurbations (around Birmingham, Leeds, Liverpool, Manchester, Newcastle and Sheffield) is now under a single authority, rather as Greater London has long been. Previously each bestraddled various boroughs and parts of counties, with no coordination. At least in principle the change is a logical and sensible one, to take account of the need of a big modern urban area for cohesive central planning; and Britain here has acted with a radical boldness, compared with the very slow and tentative French and German steps in this direction.

Tyneside and adjacent Wearside (the big shipbuilding town of Sunderland and its suburbs) are now regrouped as the "metropolitan county" of Tyne-and-Wear, made up of five "districts" each of 200,000 to 300,000 people. Newcastle is the largest but has no juris-

---

* *Tyneside: a biography,* page 4, Macmillan, London, 1971.

diction over the others, save that the new county offices happen to be within its borders. Nor are the districts under the control of the county: they answer direct to London. The two local tiers of command divide between them the various spheres of responsibility, and of course must liaise: but there is no organic link. In a nutshell, the county deals with strategic matters, and the districts with practical services to individuals. Thus Newcastle district retains its former responsibilities, as a county borough, for housing, social services and public education, while the county is in charge of transport, planning and infrastructure. One typical example: the district deals with refuse-collection, a very local matter, and the county with refuse-disposal, which requires much wider organisation. These are statutory matters laid down in the Act, but there are some spheres where the local bodies can themselves decide on the carve-up that suits them best; and in Tyne-and-Wear, county and districts have agreed to share responsibility for the arts and leisure services. The overall budgetary arrangements are very complex: in outline, county and districts each draw a large part of their revenue from local taxes (rates) – a much higher proportion than in France – and this is topped up by the government with special funds for the costlier services, notably transport schemes (county) and education (district).

The new system has had serious teething troubles, not surprisingly. The demarcation line between planning (county) and housing (district) is proving a shadowy one, and this has led to confusion and frictions. Who finally decides on the details of new buildings and local roads? – this is not clear under the Act and usually has to be hammered out case by case. Newcastle has seen its civic boundaries extended to include Gosforth and some other suburbs, and thus its population rose overnight in 1974 from 221,000 to 308,000: but at the same time it lost control over some matters, notably the right to plan within its own borders, and this has put its proud nose out of joint (Dan Smith today could never have carried through his great planning schemes as leader of Newcastle council: he would first have had to capture County Hall). This is one cause of complaint, while a more serious one is the alleged duplication of functions. Ken Galley, Newcastle's chief executive, told me in 1977: "The appallingly confused situation is not the fault of individuals – we have excellent personal relations with the county – but with the system. The division of labour is crazy: why should they control all transport, when much of it is purely our local concern?" These views were echoed to me by the county's chief executive: "The government has given us the worst kind of two-tier system – a political compromise, with no logic in the division of some functions." Yet many other local figures believe that it will all get sorted out in time, in the usual pragmatic British manner. Frictions there may be between the tiers, but inevitably there is now better cooperation between the different parts of Tyneside: Gosforth, no longer master of its own sewage, could not obstruct as it did in the 1930s. Tyne-and-Wear in fact is said to be running more smoothly than some of the other new metropolitan bodies, and one reason may be that the county and the five district councils are today all in the hands of the same party, Labour. This is accident, and could change. But in general, whatever its imperfections, the new British system offers a sensible blueprint for joint planning and sharing of resources. *Oberbürgermeister* Rommel told me how much he envied it. It could prove a model for solving the squabbles of the Stuttgart and Toulouse conurbations.

The question still to be examined is how far county and district are subject to Government interference and supervision in the daily running of their affairs. There is no prefect here to parade openly the power of London: yet, discreetly, each Ministry has its own regional branch and this in practice exerts many of the same state controls over local spending as in Toulouse, or Bologna. For in Britain, too, a local council depends heavily on state funding of its projects, and the money is not given without prior approval of how it is to be spent. Tyne-and-Wear's budget from its own sources cannot possibly meet the cost of its larger projects: its new "Metro", now being built, is 75 per cent financed by the state which therefore supervises every detail. Even when the council takes a loan from a third party, such as a bank, it still needs clearance from a Whitehall that wants to control the level of public borrowing in Britain.

In the case of Newcastle city council, it is hard to draw a fair balance-sheet of a complex subject. Certainly Newcastle has less autonomy than Stuttgart. In some ways it may have more than Toulouse or Bologna: it derives a far larger *per capita* budget from direct local taxes (rates on property), and has powers of initiative in important fields where they have none or little. Notably, it has much more control over local housing and social services than the equivalent in Toulouse or Bologna, and is responsible for school education which in France and Italy is run by the state. Yet this relative autonomy can be deceptive. The council is in a sense acting as agent for the state in these matters and is under its supervision. Thus Newcastle builds its own schools and pays its teachers – with funds from its own and state sources – but must follow overall Ministry policies. It can initiate its own housing schemes, but must seek detailed approval of them from the state, provider of most of the funds. Government involvement in local affairs has in fact been on the increase in Britain in recent years, for a number of reasons. One is that Labour, until recently in power nationally, believes in state control. Another, that in a period of belt-tightening Whitehall has grown more anxious to check local over-spending (it persuaded Newcastle to cut its planned 1977 budget by £3.9 million).

Geordies, needless to say, have not always taken kindly to this growth of London's power. There are frequent grumbles over Whitehall's delays in granting planning permission for renovation schemes. These delays may seldom be politically motivated, as so often in Toulouse and Bologna: they are none the less irritating to local planners. The Ministry of Housing took four years to agree to some of Dan Smith's big schemes for rebuilding the heart of the city. But there are many Geordies today – as we shall now see – who wish that the approval had never been given.

4

Eldon Square and Byker Wall: renovation or conservation?

Down by the quayside you find 17th-century half-timbered houses, and narrow ancient alleys known as "chares" that rise in steep steps and have such names as Dog Leap Stairs and Pudding Chare. Higher up the hill are some fine mediaeval churches and friaries, as well as Georgian mansions made of local stone, and a smattering of Gothic revival and *art nouveau*: Grainger Street and curving Grey Street are lined with some of the noblest Victorian buildings in Britain. Newcastle in its austerely dignified way has a stronger heritage of interesting architecture than almost any other large English provincial town; but the diverse styles and epochs are all jumbled together, as in

Rome, and between and around them lie acre upon acre of drabness and squalor - a mish-mash of warehouses and parking-lots, grimy office blocks and mean little shops and pubs, reaching their worst in the wasteland panorama of shacks, stacks and decrepit factories around Byker Bridge.

So this city presents the modern planner with peculiar difficulties. How is he to sweep away the worst, and preserve and restore the best, when the two are so bound up together? A policy based on conservation, as in Bologna, would not make much sense when the historic centre lacks harmony and has so much that does need rebuilding: on the other hand, to tear down the central area and start again, as some English cities have done, could destroy much of value. The city planners have been trying to compromise. While conserving the Grey Street and quayside areas, they have recognised that some radical redevelopment of adjoining areas is essential. Central Newcastle, with its new urban motorways and mammoth shopping-centre, has thus altered more dramatically in the past decade than any other of my towns, even Toulouse where the development has been mainly in the suburbs. But the changes in Newcastle have been heavily contested, by conservationists and others. The public debate has been loud and long.

There was not much coherent post-war planning before the arrival of Dan Smith in 1960. A few office blocks were thrown up piecemeal. The only interesting new building was the Civic Centre (town hall), begun in the 1950s: this controversial creation has marble façades, modern sculptures in glass and bronze, luxurious office suites, floodlit fountains and terraces, and a tower lit up with a lurid blue at night, whose mechanical carillon plays local tunes such as *Blaydon Races*. Altogether, a flamboyant addition to the city's diversity of styles.

When Smith arrived, he proceeded to promote what he called "the mediaeval walled city concept". Urban ringways would divert through-traffic so that the central area could become partly a pedestrian precinct, and the main road entrances to it would be under modern arched buildings, giving the feeling of entering an old fortified town. The elegant Grey Street area would be cleaned up and restored, and a modern complex built next to it. Smith's main objective was to preserve the city's centripetal character and prevent the dispersal, as in Toulouse, of its central services into far-flung suburbs. He wrote, "I wanted to see the creation of a 20th-century equivalent of John Dobson's masterpiece" (Grey Street) "and its integration into the historical framework of the city. If this could be achieved, I felt, then our regional capital would become the outstanding provincial city in the country." To help him realise this grandly styled vision, Smith appointed as Chief City Planner a man of high talent, Wilfred Burns, a Lancastrian who had helped design the new Coventry. Nearly twenty years later, their vision has been partly fulfilled – if not quite as they planned it.

One of Smith's first objectives was to keep the student quarter close to the centre so that – as in Bologna – it could enrich, and be enriched by, the rest of the city's life. He was opposed to the building of a new campus in the suburbs. He fought hard for this, and won. And so today the university (admittedly, tiny by Continental standards) and the polytechnic and other colleges have been given space to expand in their existing areas: they form a "precinct of learning" right next to the new commercial zones. The result, though a little cramped, has strong advantages. However, Smith's two major schemes – for the new Eldon Square shopping complex and the urban motorways – have come into being only through constant compromise in face of constant criticism.

In the case of Eldon Square, Smith's plan was to renovate a largely decrepit ten-acre area between Grey Street and the university, by installing a super-modern shopping-centre to serve the whole north-east, together with leisure amenities and a mammoth much-needed hotel. Some of the inspiration came from foreign schemes of this kind, such as Parly Deux west of Paris: roofed-in pedestrian shopping-*boulevards* on two levels, with access from car-parks beneath. Smith intended the city to finance and run the scheme itself, with the help of a loan: good Socialist, he did not want private developers to take over, as they had in some other big British cities. But matters were still at planning stage when the Tories won back the council in 1967, and they preferred to farm out the project to a London development company, who put the accent on features that would make the quickest profit. The imaginative plan for a 28-storey hotel, a shining tower of aluminium, designed by Arne Jacobsen, was abandoned because the future managers, Forte, felt it would not pay. Some £150,000 had been wasted in architects' fees. But despite this and other setbacks the main shopping-centre went ahead, and when Labour returned to power it was too late to modify it again. Costing well over £20 million, it finally opened in 1976. It has five department stores, 104 smaller shops, rest-aurants, a two-tier network of walkways with local folksy names (Sidgate, High Friars), and up in the roof an attractive recreation centre. Frequently crowded, the complex is pleasing in a ritzy bazaar-like way, and in commercial terms is quite a revolution for Newcastle. It certainly makes shopping easier – but it cannot earn many marks for design. It consists of two titanic buildings linked by a footbridge, and their monolithic windowless façades give them the look of aircraft hangars or warehouses, out of scale with their surroundings. This has caused local indignation. The biggest outcry has been over the eclipse of Eldon Square itself, an elegant ensemble of stone-fronted mansions designed by Dobson and built by Grainger in 1825-31: part has been knocked down, and part preserved as an enclave, a kind of museum piece, within the two wings of the complex where it is virtually invisible.

The east-central urban motorway, finally completed in 1976, has also come in for heavy criticism. Newcastle under Smith was one of the first English cities to pioneer the urban motorway concept, which he believed was essential for his "walled city". His mile-and-a-quarter eastern ringway today links the Tyne bridges with the main road to Edinburgh, thus diverting north-south through-traffic from the centre. This is useful: but its critics claim that it has also erected a barrier between the city centre and the smart suburbs, and ruined an attractive park in the process. So in the early 1970s this and other schemes became the chief targets of a broad-fronted conservation campaign against the Tory council and its Smithian legacy. The Northumberland gentry attacked "the *folie de grandeur* of Smith's planning and his quality-of-life nonsense" (as Lord Ridley put it); the Geordie populists, led by novelist Sid Chaplin, cried out that Newcastle was being "ruined by the tyranny of the car". The TV screens hummed with the debate. By 1972 a conservationist body called SOCEM was active – Save Our City from Environmental Mess. It was too late to save Eldon Square or stop the east ringway, but SOCEM did have some influence in the decision after the 1974 energy crisis to postpone further motorway schemes. However, motives were mixed. A city planner complained to me, "Many of these SOCEM crusaders are interested parties, middle-class Jesmond people who principally are fighting to protect their own property. And it's stupid of pedestrians to feel menaced by an urban motorway, whose purpose is to protect them from traffic." Now that the outcry has died down, more people are coming to accept this.

Tyneside as a whole has coped quite well with its traffic problems, though admittedly the task has been easier than in Toulouse or Bologna since the streets are less narrow. In the city, traffic generally moves at a steady pace thanks to strict enforcement of parking rules and other measures. New trunk roads have been built all over the conurbation, as part of the Government-backed campaign to modernise the region's economy. By 1973 work was about to begin on an urban motorway from the city to Tynemouth and a western inner ringway to link with the eastern one: but then came the oil crisis, fashion swung against the motor-car, and the new Tyne-and-Wear council quietly shelved these projects under pressures both economic and ecological. Instead, the accent is now on improving public transport, notably with an ambitious £160 million project for a so-called "Metro". This is remarkably similar to Stuttgart's new transport system, since it is also based on the use of fast modern trams above and below ground, linking with an existing rail network and requiring a new tunnel below the city. This, three miles long, is today being driven under central Newcastle from Jesmond to the Tyne where – so deep is the river valley – the tramway will cross by a new bridge, to burrow again under Gateshead. Along both sides of the river it will adopt Tyneside's existing surface rail network, suitably modernised. The "Metro", due to open in about 1980, will carry fast yellow electric trams along its 36-mile track, running every four or five minutes. The inspiration for this "re-invention of the tram" comes largely from modern Germany, but the pioneering of it in urban Britain is here on Tyneside – and the ecologists are delighted at what they see as a blow to motorway mania.

Whatever the merits or defects of the numerous innovations on Tyneside, at least one can be impressed by the liveliness and seriousness of the public debate on environment. This is in the best British tradition, where the individual citizen not only cares but feels that his voice can have some influence on the planners: spontaneous unofficial campaigns against official policies carry more weight than they do in Toulouse or Stuttgart. Recently the conservationists have gone into battle to preserve late-Victorian piles: they were angry at the pulling down of the former town hall and central library to make room for redevelopment, and they want no more of this. How far one sympathises may depend on one's view of Victoriana: personally I find the campaign too sentimental, too bigoted in its hatred of all modernism, and based on an over-estimate of the buildings' aesthetic merits. Yet it is also true that the authorities until recently did not take conservation seriously enough. Now, under some public pressure, they are doing restoration work on a number of interesting mediaeval and 18th-century buildings, and they have scoured the grime from some façades (including Dobson's much-admired central station) to restore the yellow-brown of the original stone. Newcastle's famous blackness is beginning to disappear.

The one big failure has been to do anything positive with the quayside, which is no longer used as a port and cries out for transformation into a promenade with lawns and trees. This was the aim of Smith and Burns who planned to make it "as pleasant as the waterside of Hamburg", and to encourage *cafés,* restaurants, night-clubs. But the money was never voted. The quayside has a lively traditional Sunday flea-market, and a few *"bistrots"* and art-galleries have opened in the streets behind, to present the hint of a Latin Quarter. But the riverwalk itself is still no more than a series of sheds and parking lots. Newcastle has shown itself even slower than Toulouse – as we shall see – at making imaginative use of its great river.

In sum, Smith's vaunted renewal has gone off at half-cock. His original plan included some inspired ideas but also muddled thinking, and was then distorted by compromises. However, it may be fairest to suspend judgement until the various traffic-schemes have been completed and the mess cleared up (in 1977 they were still carving out a Metro station in Grey Street). The central area is only now ceasing to be one vast building-site, and it is this temporary upheaval – as in Stuttgart – that has annoyed many people, more than the actual changes. Already the main shopping-street, formerly clogged with through-traffic, has become a precinct with benches and flower-pots, and Geordies are happy with it. I cannot feel that the urban motorway was a mistake, for without it the city would be plagued with traffic-jams. And whatever the other errors, Newcastle since 1960 has at least tackled its replanning with a forward-looking vigour not always found in Geordieland, nor easily matched in my other towns.

Formidable progress has also been made with housing. Newcastle's old slums were never quite the worst in Britain: that honour went probably to Glasgow or parts of Lancashire. But the rows of little tight-packed two-storey redbrick homes, their chimneys breathing smoke into the crab alleys at the back where the children played and washing hung out, were always a disgrace: most dated from the late-Victorian era, with sanitation unchanged since then. Clearance began soon after the war, and by 1970 only 3,000 of the city's 88,000 homes were classifiable as slums. "But of course 'slum' is a vague term," the housing officer told me, "for our standards are rising all the time, so in a sense our renovation work never ends."

Today all over Tyneside are neat new estates of workers' housing – either individual homes with little gardens in the English manner, or blocks of four or five storeys, with here and there a few high-rise towers, always well spaced out. Quality on average is better than in Toulouse or Bologna, if not quite up to Stuttgart levels. The city council is responsible for all cheaper subsidised housing – called "council housing" in Britain – and, with state help, it spends generously enough for this kind of housing to be plentiful, and rents – fixed partly according to means – to be quite low. Some council property can also be bought rather than rented. So the situation facing a worker in search of a home is much better than in Bologna, and better too on the whole than in Toulouse. But of course the very low population growth of Tyneside, compared, say, with Toulouse, has simplified the problem.

The policy behind all rehousing is not only to improve quality but as far as possible to retain the sense of community that is so important on Tyneside. "When we move people," the housing officer told me, "we try to keep friends and neighbours together in the same new block as far as we can. We must retain the old corner-shop spirit that means so much to people." Hence the emphasis, in many new estates, on the Swedish concept of traffic-free piazzas and long low blocks with "deck-access". The city's housing policy is admirably humane: where possible people have been rehoused close to their old homes, and this is much valued by the Geordie working class with its strong sense of *genius loci.* But slum clearance has also involved overspill building in new areas, and many council tenants have been moved – willingly or not – into "new towns" on the edge of the conurbation. Some Leftist radicals have angrily made an issue of this.

One of the more interesting of the "new towns" is a small one, Killingworth, just north of Newcastle. Today it has 10,000 inhabitants. It was conceived as a "model" town, with ideal planning and amenities, and a mixture of council and private housing that would encourage social integration. Its planner-in-chief and inspiring force, Roy Gazzard, an architect from London, spoke to me of it in the apocalyptic tones that Smith seems to have made fashionable among local pioneers: "I am a social engineer, with spiritual aims, and here at Killingworth we are seeking to preserve a spiritual continuity, to use the early industrial wagonways as our modern footpaths. Today the industrial revolution has come full cycle, and if we do not keep to the signposts of ecology and history we shall lose our way". Along with these high-flown thoughts, Gazzard produced some original practical planning. He put up housing in a variety of designs: deck-access flats, snug little black-and-white weatherboard houses looking like Dutch barns, and some strange flat-roofed brown houses that look as if made of mud and earned Killingworth the nickname "Gazzard's wog village" (he once worked in Uganda). Ghostly at night under its strange green street-lighting, the town has a certain appeal. It won official awards for its design and its amenities.

The new inhabitants, now they have settled in, are mostly happy with their cosy homes and new community life. But Geordies can be stubbornly conservative, and will often object initially to being uprooted to new surroundings, whatever the material improvements. Sometimes, the worse the slums, the more they cling to them. And this has become an ideological issue. Is it right to uproot people from their homes against their will? This was the question asked by Jon Davies, a passionate young Leftist sociologist at the university, when in 1969 the council began tearing down the dismal Ryehill district of Newcastle. He claimed that the humane solution was to modernise existing homes rather than transfer people to hygienic but soulless new blocks. And he wrote a book * describing the intense and colourful social life of the Ryehill slums, to prove that this was worth preserving *in situ* and that everywhere the council should concentrate on improving property rather than pulling it down. The Tory council called Davis a sentimental Leftist dreamer. He lost his immediate battle, and today Ryehill is rebuilt. But when Labour recaptured the city, Davis himself became a councillor, and his ideas gained ground, helped by new Government rules allowing grants for "revitalisation" of old housing. So today the accent is on improvement rather than demolition, where possible. In the past few years the city has modernised 10,000 council homes, putting bathrooms and indoor toilets into the older ones, and so on. The right to be rehoused *in situ* is now recognised.

In some places, however, housing has deteriorated too much for "revitalisation" to be physically possible. This is true of Byker, an archetypal slum-suburb of eastern Newcastle where in the past few

---

* *The Evangelising Bureaucrat,* Tavistock, London, 1972.

years one of the most exciting and unusual housing projects in Europe has been taking shape. Architects, planners and sociologists have flocked from all over the world to see the famous Byker wall.

The old slums of Byker, row upon row of tiny Victorian houses with grey slate roofs, sloped down from a hilltop towards the Tyne. Plans to renovate 200 acres were entrusted in 1969 to the British architect Ralph Erskine who has worked for over twenty-five years in Stockholm, and he came up with a scheme that today is nearing completion: along the crest of the hill there now winds for nearly a mile the Great Wall of Byker, a serpentine construction claiming to be the longest housing block in the world (or rather, it will be when its two main sections are finally joined). The wall is not monolithic: varying from five to nine storeys, its is a crazy-pattern of studied irregularities and its two faces, north and south, are as different as night from day. Approaching from the north, from the wasteland of the Shields Road, what you see *is* a kind of blank wall, a curving façade of polychromatic brick – ochre, reddish-brown and dark grey – with only tiny chinks of windows between red and yellow vents. There is colour and variety, but not much sign of life or light. Erskine built the north face like this to protect against the winds and against the noise from the (then) planned motorway to the coast. And to vary the skyline he has studded the roof of the wall at intervals with a bizarre series of blue peaked turrets, looking like the tails of aircraft.

But penetrate through the passages at the foot of the wall and you enter a different world, on a fine day almost Mediterranean in its brightness (though the design is essentially Swedish). Here the curvaceous façades are painted white, and the flats have big south-facing windows, and wooden balconies and verandahs all green or pink. "Deck-access" is carried so far that it will soon be possible to walk the entire length of the wall along one of these verandahs, at four- or five-storey height, climbing a stairway here and there. Below the wall on this side is a wide traffic-free zone of piazzas and walkways, with benches and greenery, where the new little houses are arranged in groups, their roofs and weatherboard façades painted green, red, blue or yellow. The effect is ingenious, gay and intimate, strongly influenced by the work that Erskine and his mainly Swedish team have carried out in Sweden. Some local purists have criticised this New Byker for breaking so sharply with Tyneside urban tradition: but polls have suggested that 97 per cent of the new inhabitants are pleased with it. By 1977 there were some 2,500 of them, half in the wall itself and half in the housing below it, and finally this total will rise to 7,500. Not all the old slums are yet cleared.

One of the innovations has been that the people of old Byker were consulted in advance at every stage. The architects and the city council showed them the first blueprints of the wall and the other housing, and they were invited to comment on lay-out and colour schemes, even on the interior design of their new homes. Not all their requests were accepted, needless to say, but at least they were given a sense of involvement in the project: and they were not moving into the unknown. Perhaps because of the very grimness of its housing conditions, old Byker has always had an especially strong sense of community, and the aim of the planners has been to preserve this in the comparative luxury of the new Byker. No one is supposed to have to move more than 1,000 yards from his old home, and old neighbours are kept together as far as possible: in one case a whole street of families was transplanted to the same section of the wall. This has not always been feasible and building delays have meant that in many cases people have had to be rehoused for a year or two in another part of Tyneside. But as soon as they can, they always come back to Byker, where demand for the new housing far exceeds supply. The project is an undoubted success – far more so than the more grandiose Le Mirail at Toulouse, or any other new housing development I saw in my other towns, where civic planners rarely show the same inspired human concern. A dustman and his family in Byker, with an income of less than £50 a week, showed me their pretty little house with its fitted carpets, intelligent open-plan design and all mod. cons., and the wife said, "We feel reborn. These homes are palaces compared with the old ones, where there was no bathroom, the toilet was in the back yard, and everything was dirty all the time from the coal-fires. I was continually cleaning, and boiling kettles. And there was nowhere for the children to play in safety: even the back-alleys were invaded by delivery vans. Here the traffic stays the other side of the wall." They felt too that Byker was managing to retain its sense of community – and that, on Tyneside, is what life is all about.

5
The compassionate community

"Here our aim is to build a compassionate community," Roy Gazzard told me in Killingworth; "the first school to arrive in this town was one for sub-normal children." And the dustman I met in Byker, who runs a civic association in his street, said: "There's such a hell of a lot one can do here – for example, organising volunteer home-helps for the old folks." Their words could apply to the whole of Tyneside with its fervent creed of "communi-care", the slogan so repeatedly brandished in public – usually with the sincerest of intentions.

This community concern for the weak – the elderly, lonely or handicapped, frustrated teenagers and others – is a common feature of life in Britain with its envied "civic spirit", and especially here in the north-east with its tradition of mucking-in to face adversity. The concern is manifest at every level – in the services run so enthusiastically by the city council's staff, in the numerous volunteer organisations, and down in street and suburb where people group spontaneously to help each other. This social action is much more marked than in my other towns, where it either tends to be politicised or else (as in Stuttgart) is shrugged off by the citizen as the duty of the authorities. On Tyneside, all is participation and involvement. In fact, the more voluntary the service the better it works, very often: in Britain recently it is the official state-run welfare bodies that have deteriorated, notably the Health Service, plagued by budgetary cuts, creeping bureaucracy, and strikes and go-slows by dispirited, underpaid staff who are losing their sense of public service. Newcastle's hospitals are not immune. But the malaise has not yet spread to the council's own welfare services.

It is impressive, this citizen involvement in the well-being of the whole community, this real ambience of caring and kindness. Yet it may raise one or two question-marks. Is too much welfare making the British soft? – a question often asked. Is Tyneside's obsession with "communi-care" and "serving the community" not related to the area's introspection and fear of other values, and thus a kind of defence? Is it not even a reflection of local narcissism?

Local social workers will hotly deny any such thing. They will point proudly to all that the city is doing. The Labour council since 1973 has increased the accent on social services, and in a period of spending cuts has even managed to keep its budget for these (£8.9 million in 1977) moving well ahead of inflation. It runs seven schools for handicapped children, 16 foster-homes, and 22 old people's homes. In nearly every case the buildings are modern and the care individual, with little of the institutional flavour once associated with such places. I visited one small foster-home for nine children – a neat private house where the matron was looking after orphans, "battered babies" and kids from unhappy homes, as if she were their real mother. A welfare officer told me, "Our policy is to re-create a normal home atmosphere for these kids." The council also runs an elaborate home-help service for about 7,000 old people, bringing them pre-cooked hot meals in their homes – "meals on wheels" the British call it. And since 1976 the council has designated some poorer parts of the city as "stress areas" and is spending some £500,000 a year on improving their amenities and providing special help for the young, the elderly, and the unemployed.

The city housing director took me to see a block of council flats lived in mainly by older people. It had a *concierge* – unusual in English flats at this modest level. "You see," said the director, "we need this care-taker in case someone is ill. His job is to notice whether they've taken their milk-bottles in: if they haven't, he knows something may be wrong." Not quite the main role of the average French *concierge* – but there's communi-care!

The council also runs ten "adventure playgrounds" for children, each with a paid guardian. A new and most original scheme is to create what is called an "urban farm" under Byker Bridge, where a stream flows through wasteland to the Tyne. Here a few acres will be land-scaped to provide scope for riding-stables, canoeing, poultry and even sheep-breeding. The council will appoint a farmer as manager: but the aim is less to promote agriculture than "quality of life" – by bringing nature closer to the lives of poorer city-dwellers.

The work of the voluntary organisations is as remarkable in its way as that of the council. Some 27 of these are now grouped in a smart new headquarters specially built for them near the City Centre, and here volunteers deal with alcoholics, would-be suicides, marriage guidance, the aged and disabled, and other social problems. There is a large shop full of intricate home equipment for the disabled; an old folks' club,

Pop In, where the cronies come for a gossip and maybe a tea-dance; and a day-centre for the less able-bodied, some suffering from chronic arthritis or angina. Here they are brought by bus or ambulance, to be given a bath and hair-cut and a meal, have their clothes laundered, and then be entertained with some simple cabaret where they join in the sing-song. The volunteer staff overflow with friendly concern, in the local manner, and all creeds work together. On the same floor is a Citizens' Advice Bureau, where 36 volunteer helpers on a rota basis deal with hundreds of queries each day, one of the commonest being, "I'm sixteen: how soon can I leave home?"

Daily life in the new towns and suburbs is infused with much the same communal spirit. In the early years of Killingworth, Roy Gazzard, a committed Anglican, took the lead in providing his burgeoning townlet with a "communi-care centre" housed at first in make-shift premises. Here he united doctors and social workers, priests both Anglican and Catholic, factory personnel officers, policemen, teachers and others, to work as a team for the welfare of the newly-arrived and still rootless inhabitants. The team would meet for weekly snack-lunches to pursue their strategy of what he called "whole-man health, spiritual and physical". This was his "compassionate community" and he told me, "All caring agencies, of whatever belief, come together here. This quality of caring is lacking in many new towns, which too often are transit camps: 90 per cent of the first arrivals in British new towns move away because not enough is done for them. We are changing that." He has had some success. Killingworth today has a large permanent Communi-Care Centre.

From the first years also the inhabitants took the initiative of forming their own Community Association. Its chairman, a local Gas Board employee, told me: "The authorities were slow to install some of the amenities we needed, so we badgered them – successfully – to provide telephone kiosks, adequate bus services, and money to buy a hall for social functions." The numerous pressure-groups of this kind on Tyneside are noticeably less politicised than in, say, Toulouse. And social activity develops much more easily than in the new suburbs of either Toulouse or Stuttgart: Killingworth was soon humming with Mothers' Union meetings, beetle and whist drives, mums' morning coffee-parties and amateur drama. Not that all has been perfect. The ideal of class integration has not really been achieved, and a young professional couple told me, "We've been here three years but have made no real friends, there are few people of our kind. This place is all very well if you're gregarious, but in these little houses all facing each other we lack privacy. We go to the coffee-parties, but all that people talk about is their little Johnny and the colour of their curtains. Anyway, our working-class neighbours find the place a luxurious delight after their old slums – and that's the main thing." The Geordies have also brought with them their spirit of kindness, which they extend to friend and stranger alike. Once my car broke down in Killingworth, and a young worker nearby spent two hours helping me to get it going, while his wife administered cups of tea.

In new Byker, the inhabitants have responded to the efforts of the planners to provide them with the environment for a community life. Residents have formed their own Byker Community Centre, animated by a young shipyard worker and his energetic Scottish wife, Jim and May Hodgkinson. She told me, "We persuaded the city council to let us take over a big disused building beside the Wall, and we use it as a social centre – we run ballroom and old-time dancing, a weekly disco for the young, art and drama workshops, sewing groups and keep-fit classes, and a sitting-room for the old folk where they can watch colour TV, play dominoes, and get a meal for 10p. I also run a club for teenagers, sometimes the most neglected members of a community. This helps keep them out of trouble, and maybe it's why we have so little vandalism here." Had Byker people managed to transfer their famous spirit of solidarity to their new surroundings? – Jim answered: "I've lived in Byker all my life and we moved from our slum house two years ago. Of course a few older people nostalgically regret the old days; but nearly all of us, at least the younger ones, do feel that we've kept the old feeling going – with the bonus of good housing. We still all know each other, we still live close together, we're glad we can still live in Byker." The old spirit of mutual aid remains, even if the goods shared in common have changed: in pre-war days, if a family was near starvation, neighbours would rally round with kned cakes, pease pudding, maybe a pot of sheephead broth, while today, as May told me, "Five of us in this street have clubbed together to buy a diesel lawn-mower for our gardens. We own it jointly, with no problems" – not easy to imagine in Toulouse.

Byker has its own two-week festival in July, with a carnival and street concerts and plays. And all summer, on fine evenings, the old people sit out on their balconies on the Wall or in the piazzas, gossiping across at each other, like the old days in Toulouse. It is true that some remain too emotionally attached to "old Byker" to be able to get used to the Wall – like the veteran who wrote in the homespun broadsheet, *Byker Phoenix*: "Life before the war was a hard and bitter struggle, yet for us it was a golden age. We remember. . . .doing the family wash in the old poss tub, baking bread . . . there was always a broth pan on the hob, and a basinful was sent to a sick person . . . you can't beat the old Byker." Yet the old people today can hardly complain they are neglected. Sid Jones, the dustman I quoted earlier, told me: "Our street association has held jumble-sales and charity coffee-mornings to raise money for hampers of food to give to the old folk. I've got £3,200 out of the city council as this is a stress area, and we'll use it to build a leisure centre. No, rehousing has not destroyed the we'll use it to build a leisure centre. No, rehousing has not desroyed the old spirit." This spirit, so especially strong in Byker, can be found all over the working-class north, and these British qualities of neighbourly caring are justly the envy of many foreigners. But sometimes I wonder if there is not another side to the coin. When set beside tougher and less caring Continental societies, is this degree of cossetting with care and welfare, both official and communal, entirely a good thing for Geordies, or other Britons? Does it not weaken their drive, lull them into easy-going cosiness? And why, when the flame of civic spirit still burns so bright, has so much petty egotism and conflict been creeping into factory and other work relations in Britain? Mrs Thatcher, who came to power in May 1979, has firm answers to these questions. Her tough, anti-cossetting approach is the antithesis of the Geordie ethos. Will she shake up Geordieland?

Newcastle's middle-class society – the world of the Tory suburbs of Jesmond and Gosforth – may not share Byker's life-style but has the same very English quality of gregarious casualness. It is a bit like the tribal society of Bologna minus the *bella figura,* and far removed from the formality of Stuttgart. People are cheerfully vulgar, no one stands on ceremony or tries to impress with rank or title, and social life revolves less round family ties than easy open acquaintanceship. There is much harmless bitchy gossiping, and promiscuity veiled in hypocrisy. Jesmond, as seen by the working class, is "where the ladies wear fur-coats and no knickers". I even heard reports of wife-swapping parties and key-parties in some suburbs: this latter event is an erotic lottery where car-keys are pooled, then each female guest draws a key out of a hat and is driven off by the appropriate owner. I was never invited to any such Californian *soirées,* but I did penetrate the Gosforth cocktail world. At one big party where everyone appeared to know everyone, sexy-eyed Jewish girls in low-cut dresses were handing round cubes of cheese and pineapple on sticks, and after an hour or so most of the guests were pissed on gins and dry martinis and were necking with each others' spouses. A group of us then went on to dinner where the talk was mainly about who was having an affair with whom and why so-and-so's husband had just left her. "I'm on my little-boy kick," said my hostess in front of her husband, and then they began to discuss a fat man they knew who'd had an operation to remove his fat and now he had a crinkly tummy with loose folds of skin and he showed it to Leila by taking down his trousers. This was not the party talk I had been used to in Stuttgart, though I had sometimes caught echoes of it in Toulouse.

The gradations of the English middle class are subtle. Except in a few fringe *milieux* – among immigrant executives or university teachers – Newcastle's middle-class society is not of the "U" or public-school kind that survives in the south. The flavour is nearer to that of John Braine's Yorkshire world (*Room at the Top*) though less ambitiously money-conscious. There are few London-style trendy private dinner-parties, but a great many semi-public functions such as charity balls and club dinners. And though people seldom flaunt their wealth or compete in dressy fashionability – few would know how – yet they do like to be in the local social swim. Hence the success of *Newcastle Life*, a glossy monthly magazine that is an imitation of the London *Tatler* with its photographs of society gatherings. It is part of a nationwide group of similar provincial glossies, such as *Leeds Graphic, Glasgow Illustrated, Birmingham Sketch.* Each of them carries the same routine syndicated material of historical and travel articles, plus its own local pages of social photographs and gossip. It is a clever appeal to local snobberies. Flip through a copy of *Newcastle Life* and you will see exactly the same kind of grinning groups in their glad-rags as in the *Tatler*, save that the setting is not Mayfair or Belgravia but Jesmond or the Gosforth Park Hotel and the social tone is lower. "A Jesmond Charity Party – Mr. David Harbottle with Mrs. McDonald-Squires"; "Variety Club Dinner-Dance – Miss Delila Numadia talks to His Worship the Lord Mayor"; "A Gosforth Coffee Morning"; "The Scroggie/Hunter-Aylesford Wedding", are typical entries. A new-rich provincial middle-middle class, wanting to be somebodies, fell for this kind of thing in a big way during the years of rising affluence – above all in snobbish get-ahead places like Leeds and Nottingham. But even Newcastle was not immune.

Some of the smiling groups on these pages, especially the wedding groups, are not inhabitants of Newcastle but members of the superior "county" set, far more "U", who live out in rural Northumberland. This county is a stronghold of the English landed gentry, philistine, well-meaning, mildly absurd, guyed in so many films from *Kind Hearts and Coronets* onwards. I once went to dine in the home of a typical member of this tribe, a bluff, amiable young buffoon who owned and managed a factory outside Newcastle. He hated the theatre and music, went to the cinema only to see Westerns, adored his children and his big shaggy sheepdogs, spent much of his time duck-shooting, and would not hear a word said against the north-east: "No need to change it, everything's splendid up here, all we need is a spot more industry." He talked in feudal tones about his Geordie workers, rather as the British in colonial Africa used to discuss the Bantu: "Your Geordie's a first-rate chap really, honest and direct: treat him straight, and he'll treat you straight. I say to him, 'Geordie, you work hard and I'll pay you well - OK?' - and he responds." He then promised to introduce me to his friend the Duke of Northumberland, but never did. This keeping-up-with-the-Duke set, as I heard it called, comes to Newcastle only for shopping and hair-dos, and tends to hide away in its own exclusive little corner there, the Great Northern Club. I went there once, and overheard two young men in cavalry-twill trousers, warming their bums in front of a big log fire, one saying to the other, "What disinfectant do you use for your stables?" Perhaps they should be recruited for Byker's urban farm.

6
Do-it-yourself dramatics and populist poetry

I am sure my friend Klaus Hübner would be thrilled by Tyneside. He would find here gloriously realised the ideal he has been struggling against the odds to promote in Stuttgart, of a do-it-yourself culture for all the people, to counter the establishment's "temple culture", as he calls it. Here the cultural life is just as vital and varied as Stuttgart's, but the manner and underlying values are very different. The two towns are at opposite poles, representing two philosophies of what culture is all about. Who is right?

"Temple culture" does exist here; but it lies in the shadow of a diversity of other activities, more spontaneous and participatory. Local populist poets recite their earthy verse at public readings; amateur companies offer Chekhov and *Kiss Me Kate,* while groups of strolling players bring newly written Geordie dialect dramas to the workers' clubs. Bearded idealists, preaching "community art", open art-workshops and ciné-clubs in makeshift studios. Jazz swells out from cellars; local TV presents new ballads about old Geordie woes. And much else.

Is it strange that culture should thrive in an area I have suggested is wary of metropolitan standards and in some ways wedded to the mediocre? It depends what you mean by "culture" – a term that the British flee as an abstract concept. They prefer the more concrete "the arts". And above all, the borderline between entertainment and culture (whether classical or *avant-garde*) is far less rigid than on the Continent. The British do not share the view that *Kultur – la culture –* is some sacred tabernacle of enlightenment that only the initiate can hope to enter: "the arts" are there to be widely enjoyed, rather than dutifully swallowed as spiritual medicine, and "intellectualism" is a dirtier word than "amateurism". This is especially true in this age of "popular" art, and nowhere more so than on Tyneside. A visitor from Toulouse or Stuttgart might be scornful of the intellectual and aesthetic level of much of the jolly activity, yet Tyneside has played a leading role in the post-war revival of the arts in the provinces, both in theatre and poetry and in "pop". Just as Yorkshire has produced its working-class "realist" writers such as Stan Barstow, and Liverpool its mighty Beatles and other groups, so from Tyneside there has emerged a small army of new writers, poets and actors. Some have stayed, some have migrated. But Geordieland in its turn has become the magnet for a number of creative people from other areas, who see it as fertile territory for putting their populist ideals into practice. One of them, the Scottish playwright Cecil Taylor, thinks Tyneside has "one of the richest creative climates in Britain".

The organisation that has done as much as any to encourage this climate is Northern Arts. This was the pioneer among a number of arts associations set up by the regions in the 1960s and '70s and is a typically

British institution, public but non-governmental, with no real parallel in my other towns. Its role is to sponsor and subsidise the region's culture – of all kinds, both "temple" and "popular", for it does not take sides in this debate. It was first sponsored by Dan Smith in 1961 as a key element in his grandiose strategy – "We looked to Venice and Florence, to see what made them great," he told me – and today it continues to be used as a weapon in the campaign "to make the north a better place to live in". Northern Arts covers all the far north, including Cumbria. Its Medici are a committee of local worthies with a small paid staff, and their slim budget comes from civic purses and from the Arts Council in London (England's para-governmental "ministry of culture"): in 1978 the Arts Council provided £650,000, local authorities £250,000, and local industry £10,000. Town councils are not obliged to contribute and some refuse to do so, while others continue their own direct patronage too: thus in 1978 Tyne-and-Wear council devoted £90,000 to Northern Arts and £300,000 in direct subsidy to the area's two main theatres.

These sums added together are derisory compared with the official support for culture in my other towns (even allowing for the fact that Newcastle alone among them does not bear the cost of its own opera but relies on touring companies). Even Toulouse council, not the most generous of them, spends over £8 million a year. But in Britain there is simply no tradition of municipal arts patronage on this scale. This makes Tyneside's cultural vitality all the more remarkable: no wonder it must rely so heavily on do-it-yourself.

The Labour leader of one council told me, "We spend thousands on parks and sport – who needs art? Young people want to go outdoors, not sit in concert halls. And it's high-falooting to think culture just means Mozart: here we have one of England's best footballers and he's a great artist too." And Lord Matthew Ridley, Tory leader of Northumberland council, said to me, "Northern Arts is trying to ram culture down people's throats when they prefer football. It's too *avant-garde* and esoteric, doling out cash to fuzzy-wuzzies from the technical college who make sculptures out of baked-bean tins." Amusing, but unfair. Northern Arts has used its shoestring budget to make a wide contribution, within its brief of "encouraging higher standards of performance, helping local talent, and bringing in the best from outside". It cannot subsidise lavishly, but it provides stimulus and publicity, and supports amateurs as well as professionals. It has, for instance, taken music and drama to rural areas, given grants to individual artists, helped small local theatre groups to survive, as well as backing bigger full-time bodies such as orchestras. Among its 500 or so recent beneficiaries, the humbler ones included: Newcastle Big Band (£192), a jigsaw magazine (£192), a writers' local tour (£220) and the Durham Light Infantry Museum (£500).

Professional theatre is the most controversial of the main subsidised activities: as in all my towns, it has been frequently in crisis of one kind or another – a crisis that spotlights the debate about the nature of culture. Tyneside has four permanent theatres, all in Newcastle: a civic repertory house; two theatres used by amateur societies; and the stately Theatre Royal in Grey Street, built in 1837, which has no company of its own but takes tours mainly from London. Crisis number one concerned this Theatre Royal: by 1970 its London-based owners and managers, Howard & Wyndhams, found they were making declining profits with their tours, and they threatened to turn the place over to Bingo * (as was by now the fate of many cinemas) or else tear it down and build shops and offices. There was a public outcry, and a lobby of "Friends of the Theatre Royal" finally persuaded a reluctant city council to buy the place (for £250,000) and run it. Tyne-and-Wear council duly took over this duty in 1974; and today, helped by its annual subsidy of some £150,000, the theatre is enjoying a new lease of life. It has a Christmas pantomime, always popular; it takes pre- or post-London tours of West End productions of modern plays; and for a substantial part of the year it imports quality cultural programmes which draw good audiences. The Royal Shakespeare Company from Stratford came for six weeks in 1977, and played *Much Ado* and *Romeo and Juliet* to full houses. The Royal Ballet from Covent Garden, the Royal Festival Ballet, the English Opera Group (alternating Puccini with Britten, and Gilbert and Sullivan) and the Scottish Opera (with Mozart, Donizetti, Henze, etc) are other frequent and popular visitors. Thus Newcastle, though it lacks its own opera or ballet company, is probably better provided for in these respects, over the year, than Toulouse or Bologna, and the quality is sometimes higher than in Stuttgart. Centralised though it may be, there is something to be said for this British system of tours by the best national companies. They draw audiences from a wide catchment area (including Newcastle and Durham universities) and there is always a large and faithful

---

* See page 253.

attendance for the more popular operas, ballets and Shakespeare plays. It is the modern or difficult works, and the intellectual dramas, that tend to scare a provincial public away.

This is the problem that the repertory company has faced. The old Playhouse, which existed till 1970, used to do fairly well with a mixed policy of musicals, historical dramas, "safe" plays in the Maugham/Rattigan range. In 1968 it scored a big hit with *Close the Coalhouse Door,* which indulged Geordies' cosy prejudices about themselves and even - rarity - drew some working class into the theatre. "But we failed with Wesker's *Roots,* " the former manager told me, "because people here don't like being preached at, they'd rather be amused. They don't like being provoked or made to think - we'd never risk Brecht or Beckett." However, when the Playhouse was torn down to make room for the motorway, the company was transferred to an impressive new civic theatre beside the university, and a new director was appointed, Gareth Morgan, an assertive young Welshman with more ambitious ideas. This provoked crisis number two. On the one hand, he held fashionable populist views about "taking drama into the streets"; on the other, he felt that Newcastle could sustain a relatively highbrow diet inside his University Theatre. He put on English premières of Dürrenmatt and Anouilh plays, he tried *Peer Gynt,* Chekhov and minor Shaw - and his audiences fell away. His productions were often brilliant, but his choice of plays was thought too serious and political. In his turn he tried specially written local plays, but failed to hit the authentic note of *Coalhouse*: *Byker-Byker,* a musical satire, was written by a non-Geordie who had only once been to Byker, and it was found patronising. Like many gifted producers, Morgan was also a poor administrator and began to pile up a heavy deficit which annoyed his main backers, Tyne-and-Wear and Northern Arts. In 1976 he tried a come-back, which ironically was quite successful in box-office as well as critical terms: he staged a "Brecht festival" that attracted London's attention and even drew the locals. But it was too late: his sponsors had lost patience with him, he was sacked and his company disbanded. For nearly two years, the theatre was closed most of the time and its future lay in doubt. Finally, late in 1978, local bodies agreed to back a new repertory venture, which promises to be less eclectic and more conventional.

A possible reason for this failure has been the competition the "rep" has always faced from its amateur rival, the People's Theatre. This is the most distinguished amateur company in Britain and can have few equals in Europe. It was founded in 1911 by local Socialists who took eagerly to Shaw and other new radical writers: Shaw himself was fond of the place and praised it publicly. In more recent years the company has become less radical and more *bourgeois,* but is still as likely to be presenting Genet's *Le Balcon* as *Salad Days,* and in March 1977, for example, was doing Chekhov and Stoppard. How it succeeds in drawing better audiences for such plays than a professional theatre may be something of a mystery: it may be something to do with the unpretentious club-like all-our-own-work ambience, whereas Morgan was seen as a "foreigner", an intellectual from the south, trying to dictate taste to Tyneside. The People's Theatre's enthusiastic troupe are most of them teachers, students, executives, typists, with the odd manual worker. Their theatre is a large ex-cinema in Jesmond which they run also as an arts centre and social club, with exhibitions, films, music recitals, and a lounge and bar where people come to meet friends. It may be middle-class Jesmond, but is also the kind of informal, pally community enterprise that is so typical of Britain, and harder to imagine in Stuttgart.

The acting is often close to professional quality. Tyneside has many other amateur companies too, for drama and music, most of them with far lower performing standards – and this can be a point of controversy. A Northern Arts officer summed up the dilemma as he saw it: "Many of these amateurs take themselves so seriously. We get members of The Tyneside Operatic Society really believing they *are* as good as Sadler's Wells, and so they come to us expecting help. But our priority must be to instill a sense of quality. Of course this amateur activity is of value in itself, it's good for individual and social self-expression. But we have to be careful not to confuse two sets of standards, especially in this region that so often fails, or refuses, to prefer the really good to the mediocre. Northern Arts' task, and it's not easy, is on one level to encourage amateurs and on quite another to set professional standards as high as our means allow and help people to recognise and expect the best."

A typical English dilemma, in this land enamoured of amateurism. Another issue that on Tyneside has attracted even more attention is the familiar one: should theatre be taken out of its middle-class ghetto and brought to the workers, and if so, how? Attempts to answer this have led to some interesting experiments. Only a fraction of the Geordie working class ever sets foot inside the so-called People's or the professional theatres: workers feel theatre is not for them, especially when it is so tactless as to call itself The University Theatre. Alex Glasgow, well-known Geordie song-writer and revolutionary Leftist, put an extreme view to me, referring constantly to "the people" as if the middle class are non-people: "Morgan has no right to use the theatre for plays by Ibsen, Chekhov, or even Brecht, that appeal only to the educated and so perpetuate the people's sense of exclusion, of Us v. Them. I'd like to expel the *bourgeois* from the theatre *for ever*! I'd draw in the people, with new plays that would amuse them and at the same time *tell their own life-stories back to them.*" Glasgow has not tried to put this into practice: but others with roughly similar view have tried the different tactic of taking the theatre to the people. First, in the wake of the global ferment of 1968, a group of art students claiming to be "situationists" staged a kind of political parody of Newcastle's official annual festival. One shaggy youth explained to me: "We objected to the festival as a masturbatory explosion by the City fathers who were trying to sell art as a commodity. We thought it wrong to spend all that money on culture when there's still so much slum housing. So we went down to the Ryehill slums and did street-theatre there: we did a piece on Vietnam, also a play on slum-housing using dustbins as houses. It was all very angry and *engagé,* and we think it did go down well with the people, there was real student/worker empathy."

All very self-consciously intellectual-Leftist and 1968-ish, too. However, this was merely the forerunner of a wider and more coherent professional movement in the 1970s, that has the aim of bringing theatre regularly to working people in their own environment. First Gareth Morgan ran a small unit, attached to his company, that took simple plays round the schools, hospitals, community centres and sometimes workingmen's clubs, with some success. And today Tyneside has six small itinerant professional troupes, each recieving a modest Northern Arts grant, none with its own theatre, but each committed to taking drama to the people. This very trendy movement exists in other British cities too, notably Liverpool, but is especially active on Tyneside, where Geordie community traditions seem to offer promising soil to young idealists in search of this kind of cultural break-through. The troupes go into much the same places as Morgan's unit, with a special accent on pubs and clubs, where they hope to reach the "real" working class. Sometimes they bring existing playlets, even simplified versions of the classics; but more often they take new material with a strong local flavour and even write it themselves. And a new school of Geordie playwrights has sprung up to provide the troupes with material. One of the best known, Tom Hadaway, is a Tyneside fish-merchant who taught himself to write by going to night school: his *The Filleting Machine,* drama of the quarrels in a Geordie fishmonger family, has been a big success in the clubs. An actor in one troupe commented to me: "We find that working people, who've never seen live theatre before, *will* warm to it provided we relate it closely to their own lives." (This is Glasgow's telling the peoples' own stories back to them.) "So the usual dramatic stuff is rarely much use; we must develop our own. And the setting must not only be working class, it must be Geordie: no use giving them a Cockney or Neapolitan drama, they'd find it alien. Parochial, yes, but there it is. So we must use true Geordie accents, and most of us therefore are Geordies." I remain a bit sceptical of the whole venture. The parochialism, as always, upsets me. These new folk-dramas have their own rough vigour, but are not works of art that would transplant to the National Theatre, nor are they meant to be. I suppose they could mark a small tentative first step towards bringing the worlds of Sophocles and Sartre within Geordie horizons.

This issue of educated *versus* popular taste runs through other cultural *milieux* too – music, painting, film, literature. Is culture the expression of popular feeling? Or should it be diluted and simplified, so as to be accessible to all? Or ought it to remain complex, rarefied, uncompromising, to be attained to by the masses only as they become initiated through education? Or can it be all of this at once – as Michael Emmerson, first director of the civic festival held every autumn since 1969, thought that it should? He planned a varied and exuberant community celebration with something for everyone. There were classical concerts, with Menuhin, Schwarzkopf, Richter; and plenty of jazz, folk and pop. Writers gave lectures, poets held readings, there was even singing and dancing in the streets. Most remarkable, hoardings were put up near Eldon Square and paint and brushes provided, for the man-in-the-street to daub his own message. All this went down well, and many people felt a sense of involvement. Under a new director, the festival then became more formal and highbrow, but this caused complaints – "It's far too upper crusty," I was told. The populist policy has now been restored.

The festival's serious concerts always attract good audiences, for classical music has a sizable following on Tyneside, as all over Britain. During the rest of the year, the musical scene may not be as rich as in my other towns (save Bologna). But the 27-member Northern Sinfonia Orchestra, created here in 1958, is regarded as the best chamber orchestra in the provinces, and the 100 or so annual concerts it gives locally are well attended, with Menuhin, Oistrakh and Arrau among its frequent guest performers. The orchestra also tours Britain, Europe and America and has a world reputation. Its main handicap is that there is no good concert hall in Newcastle. It has to make do with the City Hall, a gloomy Victorian building with poor acoustics. Here I heard the orchestra with Tortelier playing Schumann's 'cello concerto to a large and enthusiastic young audience: but the drab auditorium with the look of a Methodist church – and the jerseys instead of jewels – made me feel far from Stuttgart.

The visual arts fare less brilliantly, despite the fact that the university has one of the liveliest art schools in the provinces. It has made little impact on a region whose creative talent is stronger in music, drama and writing than in art. A handful of commercial galleries battle along honourably, but find it hard to make a profit locally. Mick Marshall, owner of the Stone Gallery, told me: "Here, people with money do not buy for investment, nor to be in the fashion, as they might in London or on the Continent. They simply buy what they like. This lack of snobbery is admirable, but it makes my life harder. It's not easy to interest them in modern art. And their taste is oddly undiscriminating – I know people who hang Rossettis and Miros in the same room. I'm a southerner, and increasingly I'm moving my main business back to London. That's where the buyers are: the provincial market is dying."

Mick Marshall today specialises in pre-Raphaelites and aims at a conventional middle-class market. In contrast, Tyneside in the mid-'70s has also been seeing the first signs of an art-workshop trend, more youthful, bohemian and Leftist. Murray Martin, a film-maker from Lancashire, has opened the Side Gallery near the quayside, where he shows ambitious exhibitions of photographs and modern paintings, and runs a small cinema with a "committed" flavour (Wiseman, recent Godard, Cuban films). He has close links with the new theatre groups and shares their ideals. He and a few other local film-makers have also been making documentaries on the life and traditions of Tyneside, helped by grants from Northern Arts. His activities mark a modest but interesting attempt to develop in provincial Newcastle the kind of "counter-culture" that has flourished since the late 1960s in London, Paris and other larger cities.

It is thanks to Martin's cine-club and one or two other ventures that the cinema scene on Tyneside is a little less bleak than a decade ago. Commercial distributors in Britain are almost as timid and philistine as in Germany, and Newcastle's main cinemas rarely show anything but routine American products, dubbed porn, and the few British films that are still made. This is not entirely the cinemas' own fault: public demand for a more adventurous diet is extremely limited in Britain, where even educated people tend to be far less motivated towards "serious" cinema than in France. In Newcastle, most of the people who go readily to Shakespeare or Puccini at the Theatre Royal will seldom look beyond Hitchcock or Peter Sellers in their film-going. For many years a select few have attended the occasional showings of foreign-language or off-beat films at the People's Theatre film society, but when in 1968 the British Film Institute took over a former news cinema and tried to show this kind of film on a regular public basis, the response was poor: by 1974 audiences were down to 12 per cent of capacity, and the cinema closed for a while. Then in 1976 Nina Hibbin, former film critic of the London Communist daily, *Morning Star,* came to Newcastle to try to revive the venture, backed by various grants. After a difficult start, she is making progress. Her little cinema has two auditoria. In the larger (400 seats), she shows the better English-language films, such as *Taxi Driver* or *Annie Hall,* usually as second runs. The smaller house (150 seats) she runs on a club basis, showing foreign-language films including relatively obscure ones from, say, Greece, Spain or Iran. A relative smash-hit, *Cousin Cousine,* she managed to show for all of six performances: "Tynesiders are resistant to sub-titled films, and I have to go slowly," she told me: "even *Cousin Cousine* I would not dare show yet in my larger cinema, though it ran for seven months in London. It's an uphill job, trying to create an awareness of film-culture here." But at least, thanks to her efforts, and Martin's, the choice of serious films is today greater than it is in Stuttgart, where Hübner has faced worse odds and made slower progress.

And Tyneside at least has better television to watch than my other towns, for Britain still manages to justify its claim to possess what Milton Shulman has called "the least worst television in the world". Of course, most of the good programmes are national. But local studios are active too, and of the regular local product the best is certainly the nightly news-magazine, "Look North," produced by the BBC in Newcastle. This, with its ebullient Geordie front-man, Mike Neville, and its lively and sometimes controversial feature items, makes a decidedly more inspired contribution to the local scene than the similar magazines in Stuttgart or Toulouse. Unfortunately, the local BBC studios do not have the brief or the budget to produce longer programmes of their own. This does however fall within the scope of the rival commercial station, Tyne-Tees Television, part of the national ITV network, and it is a pity they do not make more of their chances. When the fourteen regional ITV companies were created after 1955, Tyne-Tees secured the North-East: about half its ownership was local, and it was intended to reflect the region in its programmes. This for a while it did quite well. In the 1960s it produced some lively documentaries on local affairs – one, for instance, criticising the city's housing policies – and several of these were nationally networked. Some even won prizes. But the station then fell into financial doldrums and in 1971 was acquired by a new holding company in which the major partner was its larger neighbour and rival, Yorkshire TV. Since this virtual take-over, Tyne-Tees has shown little of its earlier sparkle. It produces as much as eight hours a week of local material. But its news magazine is poor compared with the BBC's, and its programmes fail to give much encouragement to the arts in the region. I frequently heard many complaints that local orchestras and drama groups are seldom offered the chance to perform on its screens. Probably Tyne-Tees' most interesting recent venture has been in what is known as "access" television, first pioneered nationally by the BBC in London. Local action groups or other minorities are each virtually lent the screen for a few minutes, to express their own views in their own programme, with the station supplying technical help as required but renouncing its usual editorial role. In this field of "community television", Britain is far ahead of the Continent.

Tyneside in the past ten years has also developed its own radio stations, both commercial and BBC, and these too have contributed to the local debate. In some ways they do so more forcefully than the local press, which is efficient but humdrum. The dailies, *Newcastle Journal* (circulation about 100,000) and *Evening Chronicle* (about 200,000), both belong to the world-wide Thomson empire, and are controlled from London. In a country where the press is so much stronger nationally than regionally, the role of these local papers is consequently less important, than, say in Stuttgart. Most Tynesiders prefer to read a national paper, whether it be The *Guardian* or The *Daily Mirror*. So, though Newcastle's papers do give some national and world news, they concentrate on local affairs. This they do in a manner almost as uninspired as *La Dépêche du Midi* of Toulouse. Seldom will they take a strong editorial line, or carry out fearless investigative reporting.

Though they may not admit it, they seem as anxious as we shall see the Toulouse press to be to avoid making enemies with the various local establishments. So their contribution to the local scene is rarely stimulating; yet they are masters of parochialism. A *Journal* reporter, covering a council meeting, once landed the scoop that Stravinsky was to come to conduct a concert of his work: he left it out of his story because, so he said later, "I didn't think it of much interest." The legend also survives that in 1941 a *Journal* night editor spiked the first agency reports of the attack on Pearl Harbour.

In this region of colourful word-spinners, the art that possibly flourishes more than any other, in its idiosyncratic way, is literature. At first you might not think so, from a quick tour of Newcastle's very few bookshops, all of them paltry with the possible exception of one sizeable utilitarian place that caters for students. But then, it is usual in provincial England to find that the bookshops are far worse than the public lending libraries – and *vice versa* on the Continent. If Newcastle has no bookshop anywhere near the size and quality of, for instance, the main bookshop, Privat, in Toulouse, then that city's fusty *bibliothèque municipale* must bow its head beside the splendid Central Library designed by Sir Basil Spence and opened in 1968. It is luxurious and superbly equipped: thick carpets, easy shelf access in the English manner, lots of periodicals both English and foreign, and a big reference room so snug and comfortable that the staff sometimes have a job to prevent it filling up with tramps. This and the 22 branch libraries have a total of one million volumes in stock and a staff of 235; lendings are over 4 million a year – 12 books per inhabitant! The only cloud is that recent spending cuts have been reducing the number of new books acquired. Similar clouds hang over Newcastle's celebrated Literary and Philosophical Society, which despite its name is essentially a library too, the oldest and best private library in the provinces. Tynesiders are rightly proud of it, and are seeking new grants to offset the soaring costs that have recently shut down many other private libraries in England.

As the lending figures show, there are large numbers of people in Newcastle who read and care about books. The town also has its own creative literary *milieu* – not nearly as intellectual as Stuttgart's, nor as passionate as Ljubljana's, but vital in its own way. Indeed, the city has played a dominant role in the curious revival of poetry in the English provinces since the 1950s. I do not say that Tyneside has more or better poets than Slovenia – that would be unimaginable – but for several years until very recently it was the scene of a modern poetry movement that attracted world attention. The doyen was Basil Bunting, born on Tyneside in 1900, an eccentric figure with a curious career. Before the war he became a disciple of Ezra Pound and went to live near him at Rapallo, publishing some volumes of poetry which made little mark. He tried his hand at a number of jobs around the world, then settled back on Tyneside as a local journalist, where to his own surprise at the age of about sixty he was suddenly discovered by English and American critics as a major poet. Cyril Connolly described his autobiographical *Briggflatts* as "perhaps the most distinguished long poem since *The Four Quartets*". Today the aged Bunting lives outside Newcastle and still goes on lecture tours of America, where he is idolised. He is a Northumbrian patriot and separatist: "Most of the things I dislike about Britain are connected with the south," he told me.

Another leader of the movement was Jon Silkin, a bearded London poet who moved here in the 1960s to edit the region's literary magazine, *Stand*. This still exists, subsidised by Northern Arts. A third figure, and the most colourful, was Tom Pickard, the boy-wonder – a plump, shaggy young Geordie who left school at fourteen, spent some time on the dole, declared war on the establishment, then ran a strange poetry bookshop in Newcastle called Ultima Thule, full of pornography and erotic posters of nudes. At the city's 1969 festival, he was invited to recite his poetry in the streets, but his eloquent four-letter words caused an outcry, so the city fathers quickly banned him. A giant slogan then appeared, daubed on one of the outdoor art-hoardings, "GOOD LUCK PICKARD" – but in the night some wag blacked out one of the "O"s of "good" and altered the horizontal lines of the "L". Geordies giggled: Swabians would not have been amused.

There was seriousness alongside the clowning, and Bunting said to me of the movement: "In England, modern poetry now sells more copies, and attracts more attention, than at any time since Tennyson. My books sell 5,000 to 8,000 each, far more than Auden and co. ever did. You see, modern poetry is earthy stuff, appreciated by ordinary people, it's not just for middle-class intellectuals as Auden's was. Good poetry today is rough and instinctive: poems of Pickard's kind are *more* easily understood by ordinary Geordies than by university people who expect 'logic' and 'significance'." Pickard's poems have strong rhythms and an incantatory quality: "Dissolve into the salt upon the sea and still dissolve. . ."

The mid-1960s saw a sudden flowering of this new poetry in Newcastle and Liverpool, and to a lesser degree in some other cities. The phenomenon had some connection with the rise of the Beatles and the youth explosion of that time. Pickard was only eighteen when, in 1965, he persuaded the city council to let him take over an old tower standing empty in the mediaeval walls and run it as a poetry centre. In a small upper room of this Morden Tower, monthly poetry recitals took place in an atmosphere of fervour and discovery. Bunting told me, "We had only two chairs, one with three legs. I was allowed one, as the 'grand old man', and the reader got the other. Everyone else squatted on the bare floor, crammed tight together – we always had more people than the place could hold, a mixed bunch, lots of students but also councillors, barrow-boys, street-whores, you know." Word of this passionate venture spread round the globe, to California and beyond, and Allen Ginsberg and other luminaries of the new poetry were pilgrims to Morden Tower on their European visits. At about the same time Northern Arts instituted an annual writer's fellowship, and this attracted to Tyneside a number of talented non-Geordies. The most notable was the brilliant young Yorkshire poet and dramatist Tony Harrison, who later became famous with his modernised version of *Le Misanthrope* at the National Theatre. He joined the Morden group, and his presence in Newcastle further enriched its literary life.

Today the golden age is over. Morden Tower survives, but has lost its old sparkle: such movements inevitably burn themselves out. Pickard has moved to London; Harrison too is severing his connections with Newcastle and told me in 1977 that he was growing weary of Geordieland's introversions. However, regional writing is still very alive. Nationally known writers, such as novelist Catherine Cookson and playwright Alan Plater, both from Jarrow, still draw inspiration from their native region. So does the best-known novelist living on Tyneside, Sid Chaplin – an archetype. Born in 1916, son of a Durham miner, he left school at fourteen, worked for some years in the mines, then won a scholarship to a workingmen's college and has since earned his living as a journalist with the magazine *Coal* as well as by his fiction. He lives in a *bourgeois* house in Jesmond but emotionally is still in the mines and most of his best work, such as *The Thin Seam,* relates to them. "Like shiny lumps of coal, I picked my stories straight from the pits," he told me. He talks like he writes, with warmth and vividness, but is no intellectual. I found him obsessed with local industrial history: when I mentioned Ljubljana his eyes lit up, and he told me that the highlight of a visit he had once paid there had been to find an old Slovene railway that had used some of Stephenson's early engines.

The school of writing that Chaplin typifies may have its limitations, but its earthy contact with working life has endowed Tyneside with a certain mystique in the eyes of the rest of Britain. Other populist writers have felt the urge to come and live here, for instance the Glaswegian, Cecil Taylor, whose dramas have titles such as *Ae Went Te Blaydon Races* and who is lyrical about the vitality of Tyneside life. And so Tyneside has become the New Jerusalem of a new popular social-realism. As much as the Lancashire of *Coronation Street,* it is *the* most trendy setting in Britain for networked TV soap-operas.

Some Geordies are busily reviving local folk-culture. Every mining village once had its own sword-dance, but the tradition was dying out until some enthusiasts founded the Northumbrian Traditional Group in 1962. Besides sword-dancers, this has local bagpipers, clog-dancers and ballad-singers. They are all amateurs, mostly miners, shipyard workers and housewives. They perform at local functions and take part in folk festivals across Europe, thus linking with the European folk-culture revival that I came across also in Toulouse and Ljubljana. The chief sword-dancer is a retired miner whose wife told me, "My father was killed in a mining accident before the war, leaving a widow and seven children, and the mine-owners promptly evicted us from our colliery house. Life was terrible in those days." She showed me photos of the sword-team's tours and trophies and said angrily, "There's real tradition for you - not in your fancy colleges!"

To attempt to keep a folk-culture alive, even artificially, seems to me admirable. But I am less happy about the way that aspects of Geordie tradition are harped on to the point of morbidity by some local poets, and exploited by the Leftist polemicists among them. Once I heard Alex Glasgow singing his ballads at a late-night revue. One was a lament for the old miners' lamps, now being fabricated commercially for hanging in *bourgeois* homes in Surrey; another, a savage satire about a London deb who thinks it would be so jolly-super to open a miners' boutique in Kensington. Then in London I saw a networked BBC TV programme about the arts on Tyneside, produced by a Leftish Geordie, and much of its material too was poetry on the theme of miners or railwaymen victimised in the bad old days: Chaplin's own contribution was to script a gloomy little film about a museum built to commemorate the martyrdom of a Victorian miner. Finally I saw *Close the Coalhouse Door,* the musical play that was a smash-hit with Geordie audiences and later went to London too. It is by Alan Plater, based on stories by Sid Chaplin, with songs by Alex Glasgow, and it is a more-or-less Brechtian saga, unashamedly sentimental and partisan, of the miners' struggle since 1860. One song begins:

"A is for Alienation that made me the man that I am
and B's for the boss who's a bastard, a bourgeois who don't give a damn.
C is for Capitalism, the boss' reactionary creed
and D's for Dictatorship, laddie, but the best proletarian breed."

Glasgow is entitled to his views. Few Geordies would go all the way with them politically, but they do respond warmly to his indulgent celebration of their tribal sufferings. Of course those sufferings were real and must never be minimised. But I am just not sure whether it is in Tyneside's own interests for so large a slice of its culture to be based on this kind of nostalgia (as in Ireland) for battles long ago against "foreign" oppression: and I met a number of officials and others on Tyneside, those who are trying to drag the place into the modern age, who agreed with me that the Glasgow approach is "dangerous".

7

Happy sing-song hedonists in a gastronomic desert

Prosperity is spread more evenly in Newcastle than in my other towns (save Ljubljana). The rich are less rich, and far less numerous: hence the manifest lack of Stuttgartian opulence. But the poor are scarcely any poorer. For some years British wage differentials have been narrower than on the Continent, and since 1974 the Labour Government has reduced them still further by obliging the middle and wealthy classes to bear the brunt of the mild recession: the salary ratio of semi-skilled worker to middle-executive may be 1 to 3 on Tyneside and 1 to 5 in Stuttgart or Toulouse.* Add to this a factor specific to Tyneside:

* See Appendix, page 455.

with a few exceptions, people with money do not live in the conurbation unless they have to. Such local tycoons and big-earners as exist will prefer to live out in the countryside, while much of the private profit from local industry or property is still creamed away to the south by absentee owners.

The working class, it is true, have suffered a little from the very recent ups-and-downs of the British economy. In 1975-77, years of acute anxiety over galloping inflation, the previous upward curve of their living standards levelled off and even fell slightly. By 1978 these problems had eased, but unemployment was still at 9 per cent. However, in most industries, wages have just about kept pace with inflation, and the affluence built up during the 1950s and 1960s has scarcely been eroded. Geordie workers are still cheerful spenders. A sociologist commented to me: "They may lack graces, but in their way they are great hedonists: they have not yet picked up the middle-class habit of saving. Their instinct is still to enjoy their relatively new prosperity for fear it may not last – a gather-ye-rosebuds attitude that's a hangover from the dark days. A sign, if you like, of Tyneside's psychological backwardness."

I visited several workers' families, all living in neat post-war council houses. In one home, father (forty-six) and son (twenty-three) were both semi-skilled workers in an engineering factory, the former earning £55 a week and his son £45. There were fitted carpets, big comfy sofas, a coal fire. Spaciousness and cosiness, if not taste, seemed above most Continental standards. The family owned no car – "We could afford it, but can't stand the traffic" – but they knew how to have fun. The parents went regularly to the plushy local social club where they played Bingo.* Their favourite films were glossy musicals. Father watched football on Saturdays, or pottered in his back-garden, growing giant leeks to compete at prize shows – a traditional Geordie pastime. The son and his bird frequented local pubs and discos. For holidays, the parents would go to the wife's sister's caravan near Bournemouth. This was a typical new-style Geordie worker's family, acquiring a *petit-bourgeois* veneer while retaining some of the old traditions.

In Byker, in a spruce little two-storey house beside the Wall, a manual worker of fifty-four and his wife were bringing up their three

---

* See page 253.

schoolchildren on his weekly income of only £48, plus a mere £5.40 in family allowances (until recently, these were always very low in Britain, though Labour government policy was to increase them; between 1977 and 1979 they were raised from £1.80 to £4 per child). "Money is short," said the wife; "I get through nearly £20 a week on food alone these days, and I eke out as much as I can by home-baking. Luckily, as my husband's income is low we get a council rebate of £6 a week on this house, whose full rent is £14. For our holidays, we blew some savings last year and went to stay with friends in Austria, but this year I doubt if we can afford to go away. We spend little on outside entertainment: our real pleasure is this lovely new home, for which we've made so many sacrifices." Colour television, goldfish in a bowl, a lurid light from red bulbs suffusing the kitschy landscape paintings, the cheap-jack modern furniture and the hideous orange carpet: an aesthete would have squirmed, but there was cosy comfort all right, and an almost Swabian spotlessness. In a similar house across the road, the affluent end of the new working class was represented by a shipyard fitter earning £64, with a wife bringing in £33 for social work. They had to pay the full £14 rent, but could afford good clothes for their children, and seaside outings in the Austin.

Exploring a different social level, I called on the *nouveau-riche* owner of a big building firm, in his expensively converted manor house outside the town. He told me of the villa he owned on the Cote d'Azur, the land he was developing near Paris, and his daughter's Swiss finishing-school. An athletic-looking fifty-year-old, in smart-casual clothes, he looked as if he was well used to stepping on and off yachts. His face grins out regularly from the social pages of *Newcastle Life*. His house was a mixture of good and outrageous taste: pre-Raphaelites next to modern abstracts, and several salons over-furnished with satin-upholstered chairs. The superb open-range kitchen looked like a floor of Heal's, with an exhaustive array of cooking gadgets and in one corner a breakfasting alcove under a striped red canopy to give the feel of a Riviera sun-terrace. The American-style bar in one sitting-room had an equally exhaustive range of drinks, including a blue liqueur that was new to me. "Business is bad," said my host. "This bloody Socialist government is bleeding us dry. I might have to cut down on my monthly visits to Cap d'Antibes."

Such tycoonery is rare here. In between these extremes lies the buffeted professional class, far less able to afford to be "bled dry". A young secondary-school teacher with a wife and two small children, living in a council house, told me their means ran to hiring a baby-sitter once a week, to allow them an outing to pub or movie or ice-skating. A university lecturer, living with a wife and four kids in cultured semi-poverty in Jesmond, said he could not afford the day-fees at the Royal Grammar School for his clever son. * And I heard other tales of middle-class people cutting down on foreign holidays, entertaining, even car-owning. With rising professional unemployment, a tiny courageous minority have even begun to opt out altogether, in favour of the simple life. An executive in Newcastle told me: "A friend of mine was motoring correspondent of a London paper. He got so fed up with the rat-race, and praising cars he disliked, that he quit. Now he and his wife are living simply in a Cumbrian village, near a sort of commune: they have no car, he earns some money from writing – and they're happy. Of course for this you need a happy private life – and guts. I've got a good job, but I've been thinking of doing the same, and so have others. I'm fed up with paying over £2,000 tax on my £7,000 salary. I could go over to free-lancing at half that gross income and still get by, so long as I lived in a country cottage with no car. Why not?" An English tale for the times.

On my visits to Tyneside, I have always been struck by the low level of dress-consciousness as compared with Bologna or Stuttgart, or even Toulouse. It is more a question of lack of interest than lack of money or choice. At all social levels, most older people look dowdy; young ones may look trendy, in the fashions of a trend or two ago. I am no expert on this subject, but can quote a London fashion expert, in an otherwise sympathetic article on Tyneside: "Women here don't seem to adapt their style for summer. They always seem to wear fake fur hats and overcoats." In the 1960s, this like other cities acquired its rash of youth boutiques, with names like *Boy Meets Girl,* blaring out their "pop" and displaying their minis and maxis. In a quieter way they were still active in the less-swinging '70s. But the owner of one successful chain, Joseph Gould, told me, "There's less fashion-consciousness here than in Leeds or Manchester, and new trends catch on about a year late. Young people here are sheep-like, they all go for the same colour at once. It doesn't help my business." Gould was at one point operating 40 boutiques across the north, and he and a men's outfitter, Lionel Jacobson, have been among the few dynamic storekeepers in New-

---

* See page 263.

castle, where until recently the shops were on much the same level as public taste. With few exceptions, visitors from the south found them old-fashioned and ill-stocked, with uninspired window-displays and salesgirls chummy but inexpert. However, since the opening of the Eldon Square complex, stores have made real efforts to improve, spurred maybe by the invasions of bargain-hunting Norwegian tourists. Newcastle is no longer quite such a backwater for shopping. But the Gosforth ladies will still prefer to buy their clothes in London.

Whether or not Geordies lack taste, they do not lack zest, nor a passion for a wonderful range of leisure activities – including those "hobbies" that Continentals regard as so weird an English eccentricity. Go into any public library, and you will see notices of meetings of pigeon-fanciers, stamp-collectors, brass-rubbers, cat-breeders, campanologists, plane-spotters, model-builders, dahlia-growers, and other such devotees. Geordies also have some traditional crazes of their own, such as whippet-racing and the curious leek-growing contests. Like other Englishmen they are keen gardeners, hence their preference for little houses rather than flats; and if they live in a flat with no garden, they may well hire a small patch of land as an allotment (as in Stuttgart), primarily for growing vegetables. The council owns 60 acres of these around the city, divided into thousands of tiny rented plots where at weekends or on summer evenings you see people digging and weeding away. One cold winter Sunday, I found a lorry-driver hacking at his frozen earth: "I'll be planting peas, beans and cabbages to put in my deep-freeze. It helps the wife's budget, what with prices in the shops these days. But above all it's a hobby for me."

Television caught on earlier than on the Continent, and though the craze is now just past its peak it still takes up many Geordie evenings. However, on fine weekends, or during the long light evenings of the brief but often cloudless northern summer, many Geordies prefer to drive out to the long unspoilt sandy beaches of Northumberland, or to the spacious countryside inland – among the loveliest in Britain and such a contrast to the fearful conurbation. In autumn, many people make the pilgrimage across to the Lancashire coast, to see "t'illuminations" at Blackpool – Britain's counterpart, in a sense, to the Nice carnival. Sport is also popular: facilities are not ideal, for those who cannot afford the expensive private clubs, but matters have improved since the opening of the £2 million Eldon Square recreation centre which on a Saturday I found crowded with people playing squash, bowls and volleyball, and learning judo.

One of the most passionate of pastimes is the spectator-sport of watching football – as much of a religion here as rugger in Toulouse. Newcastle United, one of the greatest English clubs, is a major focus for Geordie patriotism. It won the Cup Final three times in the 1950s and the European Inter-Cities cup in 1969. Since then its performance has been chequered, but for its home matches it regularly draws capacity crowds of bellowing fans – "New-cassel! New-cassel!" Happily, Geordies being a gentle people, the fans rarely riot so disgracefully as Glaswegians, Mancunians and others whose hooliganism at matches abroad has done so much damage to Britain's sporting image. But the United club has other problems, connected, alas, with the old problem of acceptance of ugliness. The stadium is one of the most antiquated, unhygienic and uncomfortable in Europe. Three-quarters of the spectator space is standing-room only, and after all the joyous beer-drinking the toilets are often ankle-deep in urine and are not cleared up promptly. In 1969 the city council, owners of the ground, put forward a scheme for rebuilding the stadium as a modern multi-purpose sports centre, with an athletic track encircling the pitch. The aim was for United to share the centre with the university. The club's board turned the scheme down, claiming lack of finance: in fact, they did not want to lose sole control. During the long ensuing tussle, the council first refused to renew the lease, and the club threatened to move to a new stadium outside the city. Finally a compromise was reached: the club got its lease and in return agreed to modernise, which it has now done, in part. But an imaginative opportunity has been missed, and the council considers that the club has been narrow and selfish.

"A gastronomic wilderness" (even by British provincial standards) is how the food guides have often described Tyneside. And indeed a Frenchman coming to stay in a Geordie home might well be faced by a caricature of all he has been taught to fear about English cooking: even in middle-class families, he may find a surfeit of buns, biscuits and stodgy cakes, boiled potatoes, heavy pastries and sugary custards, and that joke-nightmare of the French that oddly bears a French name, blancmange. Through the bad old days, most poorer Geordies lived perforce on a cheap but warming carbohydrate-based diet. With prosperity the range has widened, nutrition has improved, and some better-off people have turned to fancy foreign dishes though usually without understanding them. It may be *à la mode* today in a certain class to dine out on kebabs or *coq-au-vin*: but most Geordies at heart really *prefer* their old stodge, at least when eating at home. Among their pleasures, eating does not secure a high priority.

Tyneside, like the rest of industrial England, has been cut off for well over a century from the traditions of sound peasant cooking that persist in all my other towns. Hence, very few local specialities survive. One is pease pudding, a mash of peas and flour; another is stoffy-cake, a pleasant doughy bread not unlike Scottish "baps". For the rest, Geordie home diet is much as elsewhere in northern England, with the accent on cheap mincemeat patties, batter puddings and so on – "Revolting," said an immigrant London housewife, who complained to me that in the local shops it is still hard to find the garlic, herbs, French cheeses and other delights that in the south have now invaded even the smallest village grocery. "To Geordies," she added, "spaghetti still means a soggy chopped-up mess from a tin, served on toast, and mayonnaise means vinegary salad-cream." She was right. And fish, in this maritime region, though sometimes it will stretch to vinegar-soused mussels or whelks, usually means the ubiquitous fish-and-chip shop where people queue for their supper of fried cod-and-chips, wrapped up in last week's *Mirror*. Housewives are continually baking and frying, or making suet puddings – that is what their families expect, and nutritional surveys conclude that this diet is the main cause of the problem of obesity on Tyneside. Swabians and Bolognese may suffer from it too: their *spätzle* and *tortellini* at least have *finesse*.

Yet Geordies are perfectly hospitable – in their way. Enter a private home, and at once you will get a cup of good tea, or indifferent coffee, and a plate of buns or biscuits. You may well be invited to stay for a meal – of sorts. I well remember one day of Geordie hospitality. I rang a trade-union official and he cordially invited me to lunch – "We'll have it in my office," he said, "we can talk more easily there." He gave me very stale sandwiches of grey overcooked mutton, the dry bread curling at the edges, and very weak instant coffee with a thick skin of milk. Never mind, I thought: tonight I'm dining with a senior grammar-school master. This kindly and erudite gentleman regaled me with more sandwiches, a little less stale, and cocoa. That was my food for the day. All right, I am quoting special cases, and I admit that in some other *bourgeois* homes I was wined and dined as in Wimbledon. But Tyneside middle-class evening hospitality *is* unpredictable, if only because there is a conflict between two traditions. A tiny educated minority dine at 7.30 or 8 p.m. as in the south: but for the vast majority, including much of the middle class, lunch is called "dinner", and the evening meal is "tea" at about 5 or 6 p.m., followed by a late light snack. So, if you are invited for 7 or 8, and dinner is not specified, you may have to guess according to the family's status whether you will be fed or not. You may get it wrong, and find yourself eating two dinners, or none: it is not unlike the *Abendbrot* dilemma I faced in Stuttgart.

A major consideration is that things happen much earlier than in London, or France. Food shops, now so often open in London till 8 p.m. or much later, almost all close at 5.30 sharp. Some restaurants advertise "suppers and teas from 3.30 to 6 p.m." (when they close) and at 4 p.m. are full of people tucking in to their evening meal. And the word "evening" in London is here "night": the secretary to a doctor with a surgery from 5 to 7 p.m. told me she worked "at night". Up here towards the Pole, I suppose it makes sense on the long dark winter evenings – but what about June, when it is light till nearly eleven?

If Newcastle has few good restaurants – fewer than any of my towns save Ljubljana – one reason, allied to public taste, is the lack of any strong restaurant tradition in this kind of English town. Until the 1950s, Newcastle was served only by a few dismal meat-and-two-veg places and the hotel dining-rooms, nearly all closing their doors at 8 p.m. sharp. Then, to this as to other British cities, came the great foreign invasion, and today there must be 30 to 40 Asiatic and Continental restaurants here, many open quite late, since foreign staff will work late. Of the 1976 *Good Food Guide*'s eight entries for Tyneside, none of them very enthusiastic, four are Indian, two Italian, one Chinese, one French – and none English. The Chinese restaurants are mediocre chop-suey joints, but some of the Indian places are worth a visit. Strange as it may seem, if you want to eat out well in Newcastle, a lamb *vindaloo, bhuna gosht,* or some such, is usually the best bet. And a local middle-class minority adapts gladly to these exotic cuisines. But in other respects the dining-out scene is bleak. Simple, honest English cooking of the steak-and-kidney-pie kind, which can be good when it tries, is disappearing: the only good cheap English restaurant I ever found, the Cloth Market Café, closed down in 1976, never again to serve a fresh-made Scotch broth, Lancashire hot-pot and fruit pudding, for a total of less than £1. Instead there have sprung up the new quick-eateries with their plastic furniture, eternal frozen peas and consumer-belt micro-wave non-cooking. Or else, up-market, you find comically pretentious "French" restaurants where the spelling on the menus is as phoney as the *cuisine* – as in Stuttgart. Local tycoons sip their Martells and do not notice. The service is either foreign-insolent or Geordie-luvvy-duvvy-incompetent. In one pseudo-chic place the waitress brought me *courgettes* and looked at them with incredulity: "Would you like. . . er, er. . . .Continental vegetable?"

Yet Newcastle can rise to the occasion when it tries. Once I had the honour to attend a small banquet given by the Lord Mayor in a civic hall: the French cooking was classic and correct – *coquilles St-Jacques, poitrine de veau farcie* – and the wines first-class. More remarkable still, on visiting the leading luxury hotel, the Gosforth Park, I discovered that the French chef came from a town near Toulouse. When I told him of the coincidence, he offered to make me a *cassoulet* if I came back two days later. He telephoned Harrods, who despatched tins of *confit d'oie* by night train, and indeed it was the best *cassoulet* I had ever eaten. *(La Dépêche du Midi,* please copy.) But how often do the locals come in and ask for it?

This hotel serves as a social centre for the *Newcastle Life* crowd, and is usually pullulating with bridge-parties, charity balls, and ladies in pearls swapping gossip over dry martinis. But it is just outside the town, and hardly caters for all tastes. One drawback to Newcastle, I found, is that down-town there is no big pleasant public meeting-place where you can go for a drink in the daytime and expect to meet friends – no equivalent of the large terrace-*cafés* in Toulouse or Schapmann's in Stuttgart. Newcastle is nearly as badly served for this as Bologna. Pubs exist by the score, of course, but they are restricted by the absurd English licensing hours, and many of the more picturesque old ones have been pulled down. Most of those that remain are dirty, noisy and cramped. A few, however, can at least be fun in the evening when the lads and lasses invade in search of togetherness. One big pub in Grey Street has converted its large basement into a "*Bierkeller*", with Holsteiner lager on draught and phoney "German" décor – answer to the "English" pubs in Stuttgart and Toulouse – and here a good-humoured crowd of under-twenty-fives nightly makes as much din as it can, bawling out *Blaydon Races* (not, I hasten to add, *Eins, Zwei, Gsuffa*). And the venerable old Douglas pub near the station has been pulled down, amid regrets, to be replaced by one of those large Victorian-pastiche places now in vogue all over Europe. This one, *Geordie Pride,* goes it the whole hog, with little alcoves tarted-up as Victorian shops and banks, girls in period costume running whelk and mussel stalls, and facsimile posters with lists of hangings in Newcastle in 1550, including seven women hung for witchcraft. A spurious place, but fun, and booming at night with a *jeunesse* quasi-*dorée* having the whale of a time.

This is one facet of Tyneside's varied and remarkable night life. True, the place has quietened a bit since the '60s, which swung as much here as in London: but, in its own indoor style, it is just as lively at night as Toulouse or Bologna. There is not the same downtown street animation as in a warm Latin city with its *piazza* traditions – Newcastle's shopping streets are deserted after dark – but go into side-streets or suburb, and you will hear the music and song blaring out from pubs, clubs and discos. One advantage of the early eating habit is that it leaves the Geordie with a full evening for going out to have fun, whereas the Toulousain after his longer and later dinner may not feel the same inclination: this is a major factor in the difference between English and French social life. And linked to this is the Geordie's urge towards gregariousness rather than family privacy, an urge which drives the young to the trendy pubs and discotheques and the older ones, with or without their wives, to that hallowed institution which I touched on earlier, the workingman's club. These clubs were a Geordie invention, in the 1860s, and have since been exported across Britain where today there are 4,000 of them. Tyneside, with some 250 clubs, is still their heartland. Curiously, the clubs were initiated by the non-conformist clergy, with the aim of keeping workingmen out of bad habits, and in those Victorian days they did not serve drink. The clubs have since become secular – and anything but teetotal. In fact, Tynesiders are today linked as a cooperative which owns the Federation Brewery, and are thus able to sell its beer to their members at well below pub prices – one reason for their popularity, in a region that values cheapness above quality.

Until the 1950s the clubs were simple barrack-like places with sawdust on the floor and bare wooden tables. Then, with prosperity, they began to go in for modernisation. The larger ones, some with 3,000 or 4,000 members, would vie with each other to install the most luxurious fitted carpets, fancy wallpaper, gimmicky lighting, and plushy seating in the "mixed" lounges. Some would spend up to £50,000 on this. On most nights of the week, and especially at weekends, the clubs are crowded with jokey, boozy, matey Geordies. Many have regular sessions of Bingo – the version of the old game of lotto that has swept working-class England as a social craze in the past twenty years. The players sit in a crowded hall, each with his or her numbered card, while a jolly compère calls out the numbers and the first player with a filled-in card wins a modest prize. It is infantile, calling for no intelligence beyond a certain alertness; but it combines the English love of gambling with the love of togetherness, and hence its vogue. In Newcastle, as in other English towns, it is played not only in the clubs but in big public halls, commercially run, many of them former cinemas, killed off by television. Clubs also run concerts with professional pop groups, cabaret artistes, singers of all sorts, some of them nationally famous and receiving sizeable fees. There is also the curious tradition of midday Sunday strip-tease, – men only, of course. Here I cannot do better than quote David Bean: * "There is a whole sub-industry of local singers, dancers, comedians, beat groups, and strippers – or 'exotic dancers' as the workmen's clubs rather coyly bill them. These last are reserved usually for Sunday dinnertime" – i.e. lunchtime – "sessions, an unlikely time for eroticism in most parts of the world, but possibly instituted as a stimulus here for the more traditional working-class Sunday afternoon occupation of marital hearthrug love while the children are at Sunday school – very often the only opportunity for privacy a couple had in overcrowded conditions. Customs die hard even in comparative prosperity."

But back from love-in-the-afternoon to the gaiety-at-night engendered by this prosperity. During the fabulous '60s the boom in night-clubs and gambling clubs was more sudden and dramatic on Tyneside than anywhere else in the English provinces. In 1960, the area still had no night-club and was dead by 11 p.m., after the pubs had closed. A decade later there were at least thirty – nearly all of them non-exclusive, fairly inexpensive places, catering for the young skilled worker with a quid or two to spend. They were not so much imitations of Annabel's as cousins to the plush new-style workingmen's clubs. Stanley Henry, co-owner of the largest chain of night clubs, the Bailey group, told me how it started: "In the late '50s I was getting bored with my job as an engineer, so I decided to promote dances as a sideline. My partner and I hired halls and bands for Saturday hops all over the north-east and were astonished by our success: the young people poured in, they had nowhere else to go to dance. Then the easing of the licensing laws in 1961 enabled us at last to open proper night-clubs with extended hours. We started Wetherall's in Sunderland, one of the first in the provinces, and it was a wow. Then in 1963 the Betting and Gaming Act made it feasible to run gambling too in these clubs. Rather

---

* *Tyneside: a biography,* page 194.

than use men in dull dinner-jackets like the foreign casinos, we borrowed a sexier idea from the Playboy clubs and trained local girls as croupiers. Soon we were running six clubs on Tyneside – most of them with gaming-room, disco, cabaret, bars and restaurant, all combined – and we were expanding into the north-west and midlands too." And the secret of their success? "We brought real night-clubs into the provinces at a price ordinary folk could afford, and gave Geordies a touch of glamour they'd not had before. We appealed to them with thick carpets, sexy lighting, swoony music, and they went overboard. We built up a regular trade, locals who came two or three nights a week – and it wasn't just a youth thing, linked to the Beatles and Carnaby Street, we had lots of married couples too."

By the mid-'60s Tyneside was in a frenzy of hedonism and para-sophistication: people had suddenly woken up to having money to spend and exciting new pleasures to spend it on. This was happening too in places like Manchester and Leeds, but on a less exuberant scale: Geordies make the best hedonists. Parallel to the Bailey group, another entrepreneur opened the Dolce Vita in central Newcastle which for the next few years was the trendiest night-spot outside London, booking cabaret at £3,000 a week, with such stars as Humperdinck, Tom Jones, Jayne Mansfield. And parallel to this was Grey's, Newcastle's one genuinely exclusive night-club, much more expensive than the others, demanding ties and dark suits and careful references, and frequented by the "county" set and richer local businessmen – yes, a mini-Annabel's.

I visited some of these clubs in 1970, when the vogue was still at its height. A typical one was the Cavendish in Newcastle: membership 21s a year, cover charge about 8s at weekends, whisky 3s 6d, beer 3s a pint (remember shillings?). In one room roulette, blackjack and dicing were in progress, supervised by Geordie girl croupiers in tight-fitting black dresses – bunnies without tails. In the main dance-hall was a live group, and a variegated crowd of members. I noticed several hen-parties, girls sitting on their own in big groups, mostly drinking coke or pepsi. "That's usual," said the manager; "girls feel more secure in a group. But this *is* a hunting-ground: they're on the look-out for boys, you can be sure. Also, people use this place virtually as their local pub, they come here several times a week and need only spend a few shillings." The Latino in South Shields, with similar prices and ambience, had 4,000 members and was often at its capacity of 750. In the restaurant I found two big parties, one entirely of men, the other of women. A newly opened disco next door, the Chelsea Cat, had gay décor, good "repro", and was packed with the flower-shirted and mini-skirted youth of this very proletarian corner of Tyneside. Membership was only 5s a year, cover charge 2s 6d on weekdays, and beer 1s 5d a half-pint, so the humblest manual worker and his girl could here share in all the glamour of the golden '60s. Eldorado had arrived, one generation after the hunger march had set off from Jarrow just down the road.

Today the carnival is a little less frenzied. Some clubs of the '60s have closed, others survive but no longer do quite the same roaring business. It is hardly surprising. Yet the night-scene is far from dead, and economic crisis has done little damage to two other notable Geordie entertainments, the mock-Victorian music-hall and the mock-mediaeval banquet. Balmbra's famous little music-hall in central Newcastle claims to be the only surviving place of its kind in Britain, dating back to the 1850s. It was here in 1862 that *Blaydon Races,* composed by an ex-miner and since adopted by all Geordies as their anthem, was first sung in public:

"Ae went tae Blaydon Races, twas on the ninth o' June,
Eiteen hundred an sixty-two, on a sunny afternoon.
We tuik the bus frae Balmbra's, an' she was heavy laden,
Away we went alang Collingwood Street, that's on the way te Blaydon."

The races at Blaydon did not survive beyond 1916. Balmbra's too went into eclipse, but was revived in 1962, the centenary of the song, and nowadays is packed out nearly every night. It is a charming little Victorian theatre, seating about 150: the audience sit at small tables, and can eat and drink during the show, as at a cabaret. I went in 1977: we paid £2.50 each for the show and a light supper. The evening was the expected mixture of exuberance, nostalgia, and harmless pantomime vulgarity. Two of the entertainers led us in rousing choruses of Geordie and other favourites, and a third, very camp, did jolly transvestite acts of the tits-and-arse kind – wearing blown-up balloons inside his dress, or drawing out lollipops and rubber balls from his ample cleavage to pelt the audience. These artistes are only part-time pros, each having a full day-time job too: the drag comedian is a shop-assistant, the chief singer a shipyard crane-driver. The audience, more women than men, mostly lower-middle class, responded fervently to the jokes in Geordie dialect, and by the end of the evening were prancing round the room in a conga, dancing on the tables, waving handkerchiefs, and kissing each other. I was with some French friends, who got kissed in their turn by the lassies, and were agog: "*Impensable, tout ça, chez nous*." Where was Asterix's *anglaise raide supérieure lèvre?*

The "mediaeval banquets" are much the same sort of thing only more elaborate, in a different setting, and with posher nosh. They came into vogue in the 1960s when about 15 banqueting halls opened across the British Isles, the best known being at Bunratty Castle in Ireland. Not surprisingly, they caught on more than anywhere in Geordieland, where there are three. And whereas the Irish banquets, essentially for tourists, are lyrical, romantic, even literary, those up here are, well, very Geordie, and are patronised mainly by the locals, middle class and working class, for many of whom this is *the* night out of the year. Banquets are often booked up months ahead, even though they cost about £6 per person, are held every night and have seating for 100 to 200. In each case, the commercial operators have taken over a genuine historic castle and decked it out with the right mediaeval trappings, including pewter plates and goblets. At Langley Castle,* near Hexham in Northumberland, the ambience is jokey in Butlin's or Club Med style. One member of staff hides in a suit of armour from where he gooses the giggling lady guests. Other entertainers act out in high camp style their roles of King and Jester. They select guests to be put in the stocks, and other guests pelt them with polystyrene balls. When a lady gets up to go to the loo (Damsels' Room), the King says, "Lady, you must bow to my throne and say 'Prithee, can I use your privee?' " After four hours of this kind of thing, respectable ladies are standing on the table yelling.

I did not myself go to Langley, but to Delaval Hall, north-east of Newcastle, where the style is – slightly – more sedate, with madrigals. The lovely grey stone mansion, still the home of Lord Hastings, was floodlit. Mediaeval minstrels summoned us into the refurbished kitchen quarters, hung with old family portraits, where lyre music was playing. A herald announced in a mock-French accent, "My lords, ladees of Northumbria, welcome to Delaval. Now I pree-sent zee First Ladee of zee House – 'ere, oop yer gets, hinny!" Everyone cheered. The process of half-creating a mediaeval atmosphere, and then sending

* Hunter Davies: *Sunday Times Colour Magazine* and *A Walk along the Wall*, Weidenfeld and Nicolson, London, 1974.

it up, was in full swing. Then all hundred of us, the women in their gladdest rags, were ushered into the splendid high-ceilinged kitchen, adorned with crests. Logs blazed in the huge fireplace. The local Delaval Girls, in their mediaeval dress, served us a goodish meal of peppery broth, spare-ribs eaten in our fingers mediaeval-style, chicken with salad and baked potatoes, and a local pudding called "rastons" (a kind of trifle). The manager explained to me that the food was not intended to be genuinely mediaeval – "The dishes of those days would be found quite uneatable now – meat soused in spices and ginger to disguise its putrefaction." We drank Burgundy out of pewter goblets, and Lindisfarne mead which our nudging and winking Falstaffian compère (*see* the first page of this chapter) assured us was a mediaeval aphrodisiac made by monks – "Ooh, look, there's a lady feeding it to'er 'usband!" Giggles. As the meal ended the diners became rowdier: a buxom lady next to me undid my mediaeval bib and thrust pellets of bread down my neck, and led us all in a sing-song – "Three Old Ladies Locked in the Lavatory" and so on. I felt, as so often, that Geordies communicate with each other primarily by singing. There were several boisterous family parties, one of them celebrating a twenty-first birthday. Then, suddenly, the mood changed. The Delaval Girls, no longer waitresses, returned to sing to us – all had been trained as professionals – and very melodiously they went through "Greensleeves", Scottish ballads, arias from Verdi and Richard Strauss. Falstaff then stirred up our Geordie patriotism and soon, tears in our eyes, we were loudly following the girls down the Blaydon Road, ending triumphantly with my favourite of all Geordie songs:

"Keep your feet still, Geordie hinny, let's be happy through the night,
For we may not be so happy through the day!"

I had to admit that, in my private Eurovision Contest for infectious local patriotism, Geordies in the final round had ultimately triumphed even over Slovenes.

8
Sherry with the dons, in the wake of the Oxford ethos

"Life is too comfortable here for student agitation: the armchairs are too deep, our tutors' sherry flows too freely." The student speaking was the son of a metalworker in Hull. We were sitting quietly in his professor's book-lined study, while the sunlight fell on the mellow red-brick of the university gateway. I felt a world away from the discontented broiler-houses of Bologna and Toulouse.

Something of the Oxford and Cambridge tradition and ethos seems to have rubbed off onto most of the other English universities, even a relatively minor one such as Newcastle's. Academically it may not scintillate, yet by many Continental standards it appears a place of dignity and even of privilege. Perhaps we can seek explanations in the highly selective entry system, and also in the relative autonomy. This university was founded in Victorian days as a college of Durham University and did not win full separate status until recently, in 1963. Yet today it is almost entirely autonomous, like most others in Britain. It has two ruling bodies: a senate, drawn from its own staff and sovereign on academic matters; and a council, dealing with finance and administration, its members including some local councillors, industrialists and other public figures. The government, provider of 90 per cent of its budget, is not represented on either of these bodies; and though it can and does seek to guide university policy, it cannot impose on it save by reducing its budget. The university can spend the money without strings, and can decide also on its own curriculum and appointments. So it has much more freedom than any others in this book. This in some ways makes for a more rational use of resources, and certainly for a happier atmosphere. But it cannot, of course, work academic miracles. The university is strong in medicine, agriculture, the fine arts, physics and some applied sciences, but much weaker in literature, history and economics.

The nature of local industry has influenced some specialisations: thus there is a noted school of marine engineering. Collaboration with local firms, for research and field courses, is at least as close as in Stuttgart, and relations with the town council are reasonably smooth. The university lies in the heart of the city and plays an active part in its life. Yet there is one very striking fact: it is hardly any more "Geordie" in character than a local American-owned factory such as Procter and Gamble. This is because the vast majority of teachers and students come from other parts of Britain.

Here lies one of the strongest points of contrast with Continental education: in Britain, it is normal practice *not* to go to your local university. As many as 74 per cent of Newcastle's 6,000 undergraduates are from outside the Tyneside area and many have come from the south. One reason for this migratory habit is that family ties are less close in Britain and an eighteen-year-old will generally seek to live away from home. Secondly, the generous size of the grants makes it possible for a student even from a poor home to live in lodgings. Third and most important factor: the entry system. Each university sets its own entry requirements in each subject, based on results in the senior school-leaving exam known as GCE "A" levels (equivalent of the *baccalauréat* or *Abitur*), and each can fix its own *numerus clausus.* Thus Britain is even farther removed than Germany from the French and Italian open-door systems. Numbers are kept down, competition is intense, and a student must seek the best place he can find, which usually involves moving to another city whether he wishes it or not. Oxford and Cambridge tend to cream off the most brilliant applicants, and the lesser universities compete for the other bright ones. Newcastle will generally come low on a student's order of preferences and thus its intake, except in a few specialised subjects, is not first-rate. This is a subject of grievance: some people feel that the British system, for all its advantages, perpetuates an unfair élitist ranking.

Yet even at Newcastle, once a student has crossed the hurdles of the selection process he enters a modestly privileged world. His relations both social and academic with his teachers are likely to be closer than on the Continent. Most important, he is assigned a "moral tutor", an academic staff member whose role it is to supervise his welfare and help with personal problems, and thus he can feel that the university cares about him as an individual. If he is studying for honours, he sees his supervisor for a tutorial once a week, in a group of two or three at most; if a pass candidate, he attends intimate twice-weekly seminars.

Most students appreciate this. Many are on pub-drinking Christian-name terms with the younger lecturers, while some staff common rooms hold jolly Christmas parties to which students are invited – all such a different ambience from that of Toulouse. Professors will also invite students occasionally to their homes or at least to a drink in their studies. This whole approach marks a consciousness on the part of provincial academic staff that they have some duty to emulate the civilised standards set by Oxford and Cambridge.

Since the 1968 period, here as in other countries students have been invited to play a role in managing the university. Each faculty now has its staff/student advisory committee, and three students have seats on the senate, with full voting rights. The tone is gentlemanly and un-Toulousain, as a student delegate told me: "The Vice-Chancellor is jolly decent about keeping us informed on policy matters and consulting us over changes. Only a tiny minority of idiot Left-wing students want to rock the boat." This is true. Student strikes and sit-ins are rare at Newcastle, where the odd demonstration by a small Leftist group is more often over a general issue such as Apartheid than over local grievances. As the young man from Hull admitted to me, the relatively humane conditions of student life do dampen the urge to agitate, while the low level of politicisation can be explained also – as in Stuttgart – by the scientific character of the university. Very few students are in "dangerous" disciplines such as sociology. In a new university with a stronger bias towards the social sciences, such as Essex or Warwick, unrest is much greater.

The idyllic picture I have drawn should not imply that Newcastle is the preserve of a middle-class élite. Far from it: the percentage of students from working-class homes is higher than on the Continent (where anyway the *bourgeois* ones are usually the most rebellious). The strict *numerus clausus* makes it possible for grants to be fairly generous. For a student from a poorer family, the means-related grant may be more than £1,000 a year, and with this he can live tolerably. If he comes from outside the region, he can find digs through the university's lodgings service, or rent a flat or even a council house, or live in a superior hostel called a "hall of residence". Social life is much more fully organised than on the Continent: there are over a hundred clubs, for wine-makers, ice-skaters, Hellenists, astronomers and so on, and most students belong to several. Music-making and sport are the most popular. Not only are the officially provided amenities above Continental levels, but students are more active in creating their own amusements, and at weekends the bed-sitters and flatlets of Jesmond are loud with bottle-parties. As in other British universities, the Union Society plays a central role – a large six-floor building provided by the university as a social and welfare centre and run entirely by the students. Newcastle's is modest by British standards, but lavish by those of the tawdry student club-rooms I found in my other towns. Besides offices, it has bars where over 2,000 litres of beer are consumed weekly, and formal debates on the Oxford model with the society officers and main speakers in evening dress. "We try to keep up these traditions," said the Union president, "but alas, juke-boxes and pin-tables are being allowed to infiltrate this building." The "Oxbridge" influence is evident too at the principal hall of residence, which has 320 male students and senior staff and is run on the lines of an Oxbridge college. Four nights a week there is formal dining, with a grace in Latin: all students wear black gowns, and the Warden and staff are present. On Sundays, students go to drink sherry with the Warden. "You see how far we go in aping Oxbridge," said one, "even down to the techniques used in smuggling out girls after the midnight curfew."

Whether this gracious living encourages students to work harder for their exams is not certain. Few of them possess the ambitious drive of the Swabian, and it could be argued that the very qualities of English campus life have lulled them into a false security. However, in recent years they have been brought up against reality by the cut-back in career outlets. Fortunately, students receive far more help with finding jobs than on the Continent: the university's Appointments Board, with a staff of five officers, not only gives career advice but acts as an agency for putting the student in touch with possible employers, and many firms both local and national recruit via this board. This helps to suit horses for courses, but cannot create jobs where there are none. Today, anxieties about future careers have come to haunt the student club-rooms and common-rooms of the university.

Secondary schools in Newcastle share some of the features of the university world: the accent is on community and extra-mural activities, on teacher/pupil contact, and not quite so much on the academic grind. Yet Newcastle's schools have also been caught up in the recent lengthy debate in Britain over state secondary education: should it be the same for everyone, or streamed to suit élites? Just as France has been trying to democratise her system, the British have been going a stage further by introducing egalitarian "comprehensive" schools for all children aged eleven to sixteen or eighteen, whatever their ability, in place of the old duality, within the state system, of grammar-schools for the clever and secondary-moderns for the less so.

Tory-led Newcastle in 1967-73 was one of many councils that hotly contested the comprehensives, a Labour government innovation. But it had to back down. For though Newcastle to an extent controls its own education, it must bend to Ministry directives especially where cash is involved, and in this case the Ministry threatened to cut off its subsidies unless the new system was introduced. So the city reluctantly turned its various public-funded secondary schools into comprehensives. But this posed a special dilemma for its proudest institution, the Royal Grammar School (for boys), which for long has had among the finest academic records in the country: in 1967-70 its percentage of sixth-formers winning Oxbridge scholarships was the highest in Britain, ahead even of Winchester and Manchester Grammar School. For many decades it has been *the* great élite school of the north-east, with ten candidates for every place. So what was it now to do? Like other grammar schools, it could refuse to comply with "going comprehensive", but would thereby lose all its public grant and be forced to become the kind of expensive fee-paying place that in Britain goes under the misnomer of "public school". Yet if it went comprehensive, it would be obliged to align its intake on that of other local schools, and say farewell to its academic prowess. It chose the former course. This has obliged it to raise its day-boy fees (there are no boarders) to over £800 a year; and since local councils may no longer provide scholarships to it for clever boys from poor homes, the school has inevitably become, as one teacher put it, "less the ladder for the poor boy with talent, as it used to be, and more the preserve of the rich". The school still has no shortage of applicants, for such is its quality that many middle-class parents are ready to make the financial sacrifices; or they switch to the RGS from some socially smarter but academically inferior public boarding school. But the net result of the comprehensive innovation has been to widen further the damaging gulf between Britain's private élitist and state systems. The grammar schools, which held the middle ground, have been forced into one camp or the other. (Happily Mrs Thatcher's Government is now reversing this process: removing the compulsion on local authorities to go comprehensive.)

This is one argument against the comprehensives, which on Tyneside and elsewhere have also been widely criticised for lowering academic standards and producing worse exam results. On the other hand, plenty of parents and teachers argue that they are leading to fairer opportunities and a more just society. On Tyneside the quality of the new schools varies enormously, and success may depend largely on the personality of the headmaster or headmistress, who in a British school has much more freedom of initiative than on the Continent. One local headmaster told me: "The city council selects the kind of person it wants, but its direct influence then ceases. Once appointed, I can do much what I like. So long as I adhere to public examination requirements, I can change the curriculum as I wish – for instance, decide we should teach Spanish here and not German, or *vice versa.* Within the limits of my budget, I can decide what equipment to buy, what clubs or sports to encourage, or what kind of prefect system to adopt. I have far more power than I would in France, I know. Inspectors come from the Ministry, but they say little: only if there were some scandal, or if our exam results suddenly deteriorated, would they step in."

One of the better comprehensives I visited was Benfield School. Like all others, it is co-educational. Of the 1,800 pupils, about three-quarters leave as soon as they can, at sixteen, while the rest stay to take "A" levels and try for a university or polytechnic place. Academic standards may not be very high, for the cleverest local children still tend to go to the RGS. But in its human spirit, and especially its efforts to help the more difficult or backward children, I found Benfield impressive. I saw a class of academic dullards being trained in expressionist drama: a master was encouraging them to act out the Agamemnon story by improvising their lines, and the children had made their own costumes and sets. The school has language laboratories, good scientific equipment, art and music rooms in active use, a large gym and swimming-pool, and spacious playing-fields next door. The sixth-formers have their own attractive common-room and library. The school's atmosphere seemed to me much more cheerful and human than in the average *lycée* or *Gymnasium.* Like others on Tyneside, it has various extramural club activities. Children can stay on after class if they wish, to take part in drama, music and sport on a club basis: there is a drama workshop, an orchestra, a debating club. As in most British schools, there is also a prefectoral system whereby seniors take responsibility for juniors, and this works smoothly. In junior forms there is some inevitable rowdiness, but politicisation is largely absent from the school.

Benfield may be above average. In some of the rougher districts of

Tyneside, schools are more likely to suffer from hooliganism, though much less than in London or other cities with large mixed immigrant populations. Probably the greatest problem that a teacher has to face is pupil boredom. A high proportion of children, especially from poorer homes, feel that what they are taught does not relate to life, and few of them show much desire to go on and earn qualifications. Tyneside still has about the lowest average age for school leavers in Britain. Kids are anxious to leave – but then do what? They live in an area where youth suffers worst from the high unemployment level, and where industry is still not far from the doldrums – as we shall now see.

9

Are bosses or unions to blame for the dying shipyards?

Once I asked whether Newcastle's museum of local industrial history was worth a visit. "Certainly," I was told, "but the best industrial museum here is the river Tyne itself." *Si monumentum requiris, circumspice.* Take the 15-mile boat-trip upstream, from Tynemouth past the Wallsend shipyards to the now-silent furnaces of Scotswood and Blaydon, and you pass a long line of memorials to a vanished greatness – rusting dry-docks that once repaired the world's grandest ships, sheds where the first steam-engines were born, and the gaunt walls of factories that built the heavy guns that held an Empire together. It is a melancholy, thought-provoking journey. Why is it that the old genius of Tynesiders, who virtually created the industrial revolution, has failed to respond again to the challenge of a new age? While Stuttgart, birthplace of the motor-car, remains in the front rank of world technology, how is it that Tyneside, which invented the railway-engine, the electric lamp and much besides, has slipped right back? Why has it not better succeeded in adapting its industries to new conditions? Is it just bad luck? – or something to do with archaic labour relations, inefficient management, loss of self-confidence, and exhaustion after so long and brilliant an effort? This question is often asked about Britain's industry as a whole: it applies especially to Tyneside.

The industrial revolution was born here in the 1720s, when the first steam-pumps were used to help with deep-level coal extraction. Over the next decades, steam was applied for a number of other uses too, in connection with Tyneside's all-important coal trade. Then in 1814 a local enginewright, George Stephenson, invented the first locomotive, used initially for transporting coal from local collieries. So the railway age was born. And in 1825 the world's first public railway was opened, from Stockton to Darlington on Teesside, using Stephenson's rolling-stock. The next sixty or so years saw an astonishing whirlwind of inventions, as local engineers and scientists managed to exploit Tyneside's natural advantages as a centre of industry, close to the sea and to resources of coal and iron-ore. Shipyards were built along the Tyne for making modern screw-propelled iron ships, and here in the 1890s Charles A. Parsons invented the steam-turbine, while in 1906 Swan Hunter launched the *Mauretania* which for twenty-two years held the Blue Ribband for fast Atlantic crossing. The world's first battleships were built here, and the first lifeboats. Geordie engineers created the most daring heavy bridges; while another local man, W.G. Armstrong, pioneered the hydraulic crane, the rifled gun-barrel and the field-gun, and built up an armaments industry that had no equal in Europe save Krupp. It was even a Geordie, Joseph Swan, who invented the electric light bulb (some years before Edison).

This creative boom continued until 1918. But then, in the changed world conditions of the 1920s, Tyneside began to suffer. It faced growing competition from newer industrial nations who began to invade its markets and entice away some of its best inventive talent: this was the start of the brain-drain, which continues today. More serious, in the 1920s the world demand for coal, big ships and heavy machinery began to fall, and Tyneside found it had put too many of its eggs in those baskets. With a characteristic unawareness of what the rest of the world was doing, local firms failed to diversify at the crucial moment, and so Tyneside was hit especially hard by the slump of the early 1930s. Since the war, it has at least enjoyed some spin-off from the general expansion of the 1950s and '60s. Diversification of industry has at last made a little progress, but not nearly enough to compensate for the effects of the world shipping crisis and the run-down of the coal-mines. Industrial Tyneside is still very near the top of Britain's black-list of depressed areas.

Most of the great coal-mines to the north and south of Tyneside have gradually become exhausted, or have worn so thin that they are no longer competitive and have been run down by the National Coal Board (Britain's mines were nationalised in 1946). More than 70 collieries have closed since 1950, and exports from the Tyne fell from a peak of 21.5 million tons in 1923 to under 3 million by 1971, when there was only one colliery still active within Tyneside itself. Since the 1974 energy crisis, coal has come modestly back into fashion, with moves to develop new open-cast mines up on the Northumberland moors. But this trend cannot go far, nor do much to solve the serious employment problems caused by the earlier closures: the mines' total labour force fell from 160,000 in 1959 to 47,000 by 1974. The older miners cannot easily be retrained, and young and old alike mostly refuse to emigrate to new jobs away from the beloved homeland, a familiar problem in many countries.

The contraction of the mines was unavoidable and at least has been carried out efficiently and rationally. The decline of the shipyards, however, is as much a saga of missed opportunities as of misfortune. For the first years after the war, the Tyne companies did manage to hold their own on world markets and profit from the world shipping boom that lasted until after the Suez crisis. But at the crucial moment in the 1950s they failed to modernise their methods or equipment sufficiently to cope with growing competition, notably from Japan, also from Sweden, Germany and Spain. Whereas in the 19th century Tyne and Wear yards were building over one-third of all the world's shipping, by the 1960s the figure was under 2 per cent. Finally the government prodded the private firms into taking some urgent action and this led in 1968 to a merger of all the Tyne shipyards into one big company led by Swan Hunter, employing 10,000 men on Tyneside. For the next few years, under the cautious, dedicated, if none-too-inspired chairmanship of old Sir John Hunter, this firm managed to stagger through a series of crises with at least a little more resilience than most other British yards, notably those of the Clyde. Someone called it "the least unsuccessful British shipbuilders". Some years it had full order-books and was building 250,000-ton super-tankers; other years the outlook was bleak and men had to be laid off. Swan Hunter was at the mercy of unpredictable fluctuations in world shipping demand, and like all British yards, it was unable to compete effectively against the Japanese and others with their lower costs and greater government aid. Sir John and his executives complained loudly that they were not getting enough state help to face their uphill task.

They had some cause – but the fault lay also with their own poor management. Though they made some progress after 1968 with labour relations, in their marketing, planning and technical innovations they never recaptured the dynamic and courageous spirit that had marked Victorian days. Swan Hunter seemed a weary firm. Finally in 1977 the Labour government nationalised all British shipyards – more for doctrinal than practical economic reasons – and set about restructuring management. But it seemed far from certain that this would bring any greater success than in the case of other state take-overs of British industry, either in terms of policy or, as we shall see, of labour relations and hence productivity.

Not only in shipping but in other branches of heavy engineering, too, a number of Tyneside's classic old firms have fallen on hard times. Clearly the area must diversify into more modern fields, and this the government and local bodies have been trying to encourage for over forty years, with sporadic success. In the 1930s a new light industrial estate was created near Gateshead, today comprising over 100 small factories that make underwear, cheese-spread, steel furniture and so on. Since the war, a few American firms such as Wilkinson Sword (razor blades) and Shulton Old Spice (cosmetics) have set up plant on Tyneside, and the mighty Procter and Gamble has centred its British headquarters and research on Newcastle. Most important, in 1962 International Research and Development installed a major contract and research centre here. And the government has managed to create about 14,000 new jobs in the services sector by decentralising from London some income tax and social security offices. But all this effort has not made up for the jobs lost in the old heavy industries. In the period 1959-74 the Northern Region (from Tees to the Border) suffered a net loss of 41,000 jobs: 170,000 disappeared in the old heavy industries (mainly mining) and only 129,000 new ones were created, 56,000 of them in light industry and the rest in services. The balance was met by emigration – and the dole. None of my other towns has had to face quite this problem, for in all of them industry has been steadily expanding at least till the recent slow-down.

The authorities have deployed various devices to try to attract new industry. They have modernised communications: Tyneside now has a sizeable airport with flights to cities both at home and abroad, and an impressive new road network. They have launched their "better quality of life" strategy. And, as has also been the case in Toulouse, the government has offered various cash grants and other incentives to firms that create new employment. If the response of outside investors has not been more ardent, a general explanation can be sought in the slow growth of Britain's economy as a whole. And within this slow-moving Britain, Tyneside ranks as one of the least favoured venues for new investment (along with Merseyside and parts of Wales and Scotland: Ulster of course fares worse still). What deters new investors? Some are put off by the distances from the south (a little unreasonably, for in this age of jets and motorways, the area's historic "isolation" has become something of a myth). Others shun Tyneside's "grey" image, its climate, buildings, atmosphere of decline. Many foreign industrialists are frightened by Britain's record of labour disputes. And some firms, after making their enquiries, fear they will be short of skilled labour. Odd though it may seem in an area of high unemployment, this last fear has some basis. The unskilled labour tends to stay put, and the skilled to emigrate. This is a common complaint among local factory-owners, one of whom told me, "I have ex-miners of fifty queuing at my gate, but their skills are no use to me. On the other hand, the area turns out too few modern technicians and it's hard to persuade others to move here from the rest of Britain. At the top level, the university produces fine electronic engineers but they soon move off elsewhere."

The national employment crisis since 1974 has added to the various problems. Unemployment on Tyneside is habitually well above the average: since 1974 the national figure of people out of work has risen from 3 to 6 per cent, and Tyneside's from 6 to 9 per cent. Thousands have lost their jobs through closures of textile or electrical firms or lay-offs in other sectors. In 1977 even the illustrious firm of C. A. Parsons, 19th-century pioneer of the steam turbine, was preparing to dismiss 900 men unless the government came to its aid with orders for turbines for a new power-station. But there are limits to what the state can do. As in the rest of Britain, it has been doling out money to shore up firms in trouble and also to make life easier for those thrown out of work. One imaginative scheme is what is called "Job Creation": a national fund, set up in 1975, to provide temporary non-commercial jobs for young people out of work. In Newcastle in 1977, some 200 people were employed by the city council on tasks thus funded – creating gardens, restoring old buildings, even running theatre groups. Many were young graduates. The state allocates a lump sum to a town council or other suitable applicant, for jobs which must be non-profit-making, and each employee receives the average wage for the job and can hold it for a year. The scheme is more constructive than merely leaving people idle on the dole, and it alleviates a little of the frustration of the hordes of young people who cannot find proper jobs. But in economic terms it cannot be more than a minor stop-gap.

Poor management and unruly labour relations are regularly blamed for Britain's post-war industrial problems. In the case of Tyneside, do the facts bear this out? Yes, to an extent, but not quite in the way you might think. For all the famous Geordie solidarity, unions are often in worse dispute with each other than with management, with whom relations are today fairly smooth. The classic conflict that a Marxist expects to find, between angry workers and aloof capitalist bosses, is much less common here than in the big industries of the south and midlands, or in France or Italy. On the other hand, as recently as 1978 a petty quarrel between rival shipyard unions led Swan Hunter to lose a £52 million order.

The relative harmony between workers and employers may seem surprising, in view of the legacy of the past. In Victorian days and even between the wars, the mine-owners and some other companies exploited their staff callously, and this has left scars of bitterness as we have seen. But the old mine tycoons have long departed, and the post-war Coal Board is respected as a fair employer. When a national miners' strike is called for higher wages, the north-east's miners join in but are not among the more militant. And in most of the other industries still in private hands, the bosses have become more liberal and humane than in the old days. A union leader told me: "Most employers here are considerate, and know how to talk to us. We find they are closer to their workers than in other parts of Britain: they are not remote cigar-puffing tycoons." This may be an aspect of the Geordie social climate, where the local middle class is ready to associate with the working-class ethos. There is not the same class gulf as in the south. All this may go some way to explain why in the past ten years the strike level on Tyneside has been at little more than half the national average. The high level of unemployment may be another factor.

The shipbuilding industry provides some vivid examples of the shifts in union-employer and inter-union relations. In the old days, right up until the mergers of 1968, many of the shipyard owners were unscrupulous and would often lay men off in large numbers at short notice, when a yard fell idle for a few weeks, as happened periodically.

A man might expect to be out of work for about three months of the year. The unions were continually warring against the employers over this: in 1961, for example, a strike lasted six weeks. And to make matters worse, the unions were repeatedly engaged in "demarcation disputes" with each other, and these too led to strikes: for unions in Britain are not structured horizontally on political lines as in France and Italy, but vertically on craft lines. Thus there are hundreds of different autonomous unions, each representing a different craft: on the same shop-floor you may find up to 30 or 40, one for electricians, one for welders, one for fitters, and so on, each jealously guarding its vested interests. Thus, say, if some electric wiring has to be fitted to woodwork, the electrician who does the work cannot also drill the holes in the wood or the local carpenter's union would go on strike against this encroachment on its role: however simple the job, the electrician must wait until a carpenter is available to help him. This narrow intransigence is a legacy of pre-war days of high unemployment and fear of redundancy. It has bitten deep into the unions' psychology and of course has led to over-manning and consequent low productivity, as the unions often insist that two or three men be on hand to do a job that could be tackled by one. It has also led to frequent shop-floor disputes over the exact demarcation between one craft's role and another's: the turning on of a tap by the wrong person can bring a whole factory to a halt for days. This whole problem – largely unknown on the Continent – has been a major cause of British industrial weakness, and has especially plagued the shipyards.

However, at the time of the merger of Tyne shipyards in 1968, an official commission of enquiry came up with the solemn warning that the whole industry would face collapse unless management and unions both changed their ways. Sir John Hunter was a realist who saw the writing on the wall; and so, fortunately, was Dan McGarvey, the national president of the leading union confederation in the yards, the Boilermakers' and Shipwrights' Society. After months of tough bargaining, these two men hammered out a kind of social contract whereby (a) management agreed to regular wage increases, bonuses, and far greater job security; and (b) the unions agreed to accept phased redundancies that would increase productivity, and also to use strikes only as a last resort, if all arbitration failed. McGarvey succeeded too in imposing a measure of rationalisation on the labyrinthine structure of unions in the "iron trades" that build a ship's hull; welders and riveters, for instance, agreed to merge their unions. There was now less risk of demarcation disputes, and the next few years saw increased productivity and a relative absence of strikes.

The Boilermakers' Society has its national office on Tyneside, and here McGarvey ruled like a king. This blunt Scotsman was a typical member of Britain's Left-wing para-establishment: before his retirement in 1977 he even accepted a knighthood "for services to industry". He told me once: "Delivery dates were often being held up by labour disputes, before my pact with Sir John in 1969. We knew we faced our last chance. So we sat round the table and thrashed things out, tough but friendly-like. Both sides made concessions, and we got the main thing we wanted: long-term guarantees of employment. The merger has led to greater flexibility, so that if one yard is idle for a while, the men can be transferred to another nearby. That's far better than the old days. Our members are now more aware that their prosperity is tied up with that of the company, and the employers on their side have become more reasonable and humane." It could almost have been a Swabian unionist talking.

Relations on Tyneside between union leaders and management have that curious British ambivalence – outwardly matey, latently suspicious – that foreigners sometimes regard as mere hypocrisy. Sir John and Sir Dan used to joust with each other in a manner possibly reminiscent of Lercaro and Dozza in Bologna. In the old days, their battles were often truly bitter; after 1969, there was something of a wary truce, with cordial lunches and the two men on "John" and "Dan" terms in the usual Geordie manner. Not all Tyneside employers would behave like this, but Sir John was always something of an informal democrat-paternalist. He began life as a shop-floor apprentice in the family firm, and later as chairman would regularly go round his yards chatting to the workmen, knowing how to talk to them in their own terms, without "side". Union leaders on Tyneside will respond to this approach, probably more easily than in Toulouse where the political battle-lines between unions and *patronat* are more sharply drawn, at least in larger firms like Aérospatiale.

Swan Hunter's take-over by the state has made little difference to relations. It has certainly not given the workers any sense of ownership: in fact, McGarvey's former hopeful words to me – that the men now saw how their own prosperity depended on the firm's – began to sound very hollow in the winter of 1977-8 when an absurd crisis showed just how short-sighted inter-union rivalries still can be. Poland placed a valuable order with Britain for twenty-four ships, and seven of these, worth £52 million, were allotted to the Swan Hunter yards which badly needed the work. But 1,700 outfitters there (plumbers, carpenters, painters, etc) were in the sixth week of an overtime ban, in protest against the fact that their traditional rivals, the boilermakers, were earning about £9 a week more. Fearing that the Tyne would thereby fail to meet its delivery dates, British Shipbuilders laid plans to switch the orders to other yards. Finally the outfitters were pacified with a £5.40 pay rise. But this so infuriated the 3,500 boilermakers, who consider themselves "the kings of the yards", that they tore up the flexibility agreements reached previously between Sir John and Sir Dan, and said they would go back to the "one-man-one-job" rule (e.g. a welder would only weld, not rivet, and *vice versa*). This threatened to reduce productivity again, and thus lose the Tyne what chance was left of the Polish orders. National union leaders tried to reason with the men, but local shop-stewards were adamant. "We do the heavy dirty work, we need more pay," said the boilermen; an outfitter retorted, "They've never cared about us, why should we care about them?" The unions refused a compromise, and finally all seven ships were allocated to other British yards. For the sake of pride and a principle, the Tyne men had cut their own throats: 800 redundancy notices were served at once, with the prospect of more to follow unless new orders came in soon (a Royal Navy £100 million order in 1979 for a new aircraft-carrier did, at least, offer a ray of hope). A London official commented, "It's a tragedy of blind selfishness – the kind of thing that makes Britain a sick joke abroad." And all too frequent, nationwide.

It is indeed baffling that Geordies, so generous and community-spirited in other fields, should revert to this narrow egotism in protection of their jobs and wages. Each union has its own fierce team-spirit, but views its rivals with implacable jealousy. It seems that recent inflation and unemployment have revived in the Geordie subconscious the spectre of the 1930s and this has led to a *sauve-qui-peut* panic, exploited by militant shop-stewards. It has been happening in many industries and services throughout Britain. In some hospitals, for instance, voluntary unpaid workers are being squeezed out because the unions insist on priority for their own paid members. All this is the worst social and psychological legacy of the economic crisis, as Britain's proud community spirit is eroded by fear, fuelled by union selfishness. Stuttgart in the 1920s knew worse.

Unions might well develop a broader and more far-sighted sense of their responsibilities if only some kind of German-style co-management were introduced. But British unions, like French ones, are very wary of *Mitbestimmung*. Management feeds policy information to the staff in each firm, via the unions and the works committee, but neither side is keen for partnership to go farther than this. One union leader told me: "If we took part in company decision-making, this would mean conniving at policies we do not like and could not control. It would be a capitalist lure, and we reject it." On the other hand, many Geordies are still ready to accept benevolent paternalism, whether of the new American or the old family style. The former is represented here by Procter and Gamble, the big chemical corporation: the directors of its British headquarters, in Newcastle, provide generous working conditions and a sympathetic ear to personal problems, while the unions are kept firmly in their place – and give little trouble. In the older style, Victor Products is a locally owned electrical engineering firm that in forty years has never had a strike. Roy Mann, managing director and a member of the owning family, told me: "The secret is that we look after our men well and take the trouble to know them personally. So they are loyal: among a staff of 500, we've donated over 80 gold watches for 25 years' service. I make a point of walking round the factory each morning for half-an-hour, chatting to the men, and I know many of them by their Christian names. At Christmas-time, if a man is off sick I visit him in his home. Call it paternalism if you like, but it works, even though some of Britain's most militant unions have shop-stewards here." Geordies generally respond to this approach, more readily than workers in other parts of Britain, but only provided they can feel that the boss is not some stand-offish snob but is able to relate to them in human terms and empathise with their values.

At first sight, these paternalist links may seem to have much in common with the world of Fein or Bosch in Stuttgart. But I think there is one fundamental difference. In Stuttgart, workers and management are united in their dynamic urge to work hard together on the firm's behalf and thus for their mutual profit. On Tyneside, this is more rarely so. Tacitly, the *entente* is more in the nature of a defensive and complacent truce, an alibi for an easy life. Workers will play the game, provided management do not expect them to work too hard. Even in Toulouse, for all their verbal aggressiveness the unions are in practice readier than on Tyneside to cooperate with management in raising productivity. This has long been one of the major weaknesses of British industry.

Who is more to blame, the worker or his boss? One local executive, a southerner, gave me the view: "I've worked abroad a lot, and the contrast with Germany, Japan, even France is striking: the British worker, Geordie or other, just does not feel the same urgent sense of involvement in his work, he expects endless little tea-breaks, he's always seeking excuses for extended sick-leave. Some of them even seem to make it a point of honour to get through as little as possible for the money they earn. They feel they've scored." Too harsh, maybe. Certainly, management too is seriously at fault.* My own impression, after visiting a number of Tyneside firms, was of the mediocre quality of local leadership, and I found this view shared by many experts who know the area much better than I. Frank Harris, former city manager and before that a Ford executive in the south, told me, "The few go-ahead Tyneside factories are subsidiaries of outside firms such as Procter and Gamble, or are in newly imported branches such as electronics or chemicals. With a few exceptions, the local managers of the older heavy-industry firms are lacking in flair and initiative. Complacently they still believe in the supremacy of their old methods and machinery, and are unaware how far technology has changed." Even the younger executives are generally not of the same quality as on the Continent, and this is a national problem: in Britain, manufacturing industry has lower prestige as a career for young graduates than in other countries. The brightest young brains prefer to go into the media or civil service, the professions or finance. Industry, ill-staffed, lives in something of a ghetto.

Tyneside suffers from this more keenly than most areas. It has also been the victim of historical change. The special union of local circumstances, that led here to the 19th-century industrial miracle, no longer exists. Even if the coal were still plentiful, no longer would it be such an asset today to have large reserves of it near a big port. Moreover, technology in those days was a local affair, and it was local industrial necessity that mothered so many inventions and drew out local genius: today, technology is integrated on a world level, and a local firm that wants to use new methods must be on the same instant wavelength as Ohio or Osaka. Too many Tyneside firms retain the parochial

---

* In July 1977, the Hamburg weekly *Der Spiegel* published a round-up of views of German managers running German subsidiaries in Britain. They laid the blame for Britain's woes on British management. They found their own workers skilled and dedicated, but thought that British managers on the whole were class-ridden, amateurish, insensitive to industrial relations, and unready to take investment risks. But the German managers had all set up German-style co-management councils in their British factories, with success – was this not why they found their workers so satisfactory? The workers almost never went on strike.

mentality that once served them so well but is now a handicap.

When Britain joined the EEC, some local experts feared that this would pull the nation's focus even more strongly to the south-east and thus Tyneside's "isolation" would become an even greater drawback. This has not really happened, but nor has entry into the EEC been much of a help. Continental investors have not exactly been flocking to set up new plant on Tyneside; nor have local firms done much to exploit new markets in the EEC, beyond sending a few sales teams round Europe. Tyneside's industry has become a little more Europe-minded, but on balance the EEC has hardly affected its economy one way or the other. Nor has the North Sea oil bonanza provided much of a direct fillip: the new refineries and spin-off activities are all too far to the north, round Aberdeen. Of course, in a more general sense, Tyneside like the rest of Britain is benefiting from the new money that oil brings: living standards are rising again. But will the money be squandered, or spent on intelligent investment? This is a major question for Britain at the end of the 1970s, and for Tyneside especially. As an economic planner for the region told me, "It's a race against time, as many industries are growing daily more obsolete. Up here, we have to run to stand still."

10

Arise, capital of a new Northumbria

Little groups of foreign students; a few Italian and Oriental restaurants; the occasional delegation from a twin-town; Norwegians over on trade missions or shopping-sprees; Geordies returning from package-tours in Spain – that is about the extent of Newcastle's internationalism. In its ambience and the size of its foreign minorities, just as in its attitudes, it is one of the least cosmopolitan of my towns – needless to say. Visiting foreigners are welcome, but must not expect any passionate curiosity about their homeland.

The brighter side of this coin of passive indifference is the relative absence of racial feeling against Tyneside's coloured immigrants. Admittedly, they are too few to pose much of a threat, real or imagined. There have never been the job outlets to attract them here in great numbers: they make up less than 1 per cent of the labour force, compared with 20 per cent or more in some parts of London and other big cities. Yet, even were they more numerous, they might not face the ugly racial tensions that have been disturbing some areas of urban Britain. Geordies are easy-going and it does not worry them to see turbanned Sikhs driving buses or Pakistanis opening corner-shops, nor have they ever molested the long-established Arab and Chinese trading communities in South Shields. In fact the Race Relations Board, whose job in Britain is to act against racial discrimination, recently closed down its Newcastle office because it did not have enough work to do!

Once I was invited to dinner - yes, at 8 p.m. - by a young West African dentist and his Geordie wife. In their elegant little house with its well-chosen modern paintings and sculptures, they gave me pheasant, vintage claret and cognac, against a background of Bach on the hi-fi. My host casually hinted at his cultural superiority to the natives. "Africans here are less discriminated *against* than *for*. Shopkeepers for instance will allow us credit as we have a high reputation for honesty. You see, most of the Africans here are students or professional people, and many of the Orientals are in commerce. There's not much riff-raff." And apart from the students, these people are nearly all permanent residents in Britain, many with British passports, and not insecure and transitory *Gastarbeiter*. Often you see whites and coloureds drinking in pubs together (Swabians please note).

Other foreigners such as Europeans are extremely few. The university has the largest contingent: some 500 overseas students, led numerically by Norwegians and Greeks. They settle down easily and cause no problems. Outside the university, the American and European colonies number a mere handful of businessmen or wives of Geordies. Of the seventeen consulates, all but one are of the "honorary" kind, run by English businessmen, and no one plays the Stuttgart fantasy game. The only country with a full-time career consul is Norway, which lies 400 miles across the North Sea and is the only foreign land with which Tyneside has really close relations. These date back to Viking days and earlier: many Geordie dialect words come from Norwegian, such as "hyem" for "home". Geordies will usually say they feel more kinship with Norwegians than with other Europeans, and the consul reciprocated this: "We Norwegians," he told me, "feel that this is home territory, more than other parts of Britain, even Scotland." For many centuries there has been heavy cargo trade between Tyneside and Bergen and Oslo. Then during the war many Norwegians settled on Tyneside to escape the Occupation and some married Geordies and have stayed. As thanks for this wartime welcome, Bergen still sends a tall Christmas tree each year, which is erected outside the Civic Centre. So warm in fact are these links that when this Centre was completed in 1968, Newcastle invited King Olaf to inaugurate it, rather than any British royal. Today Tyneside has regular air, car-ferry and cargo links with Bergen and Oslo. And since the fall in sterling, Newcastle has become the magnet for Norwegian bargain-hunters who come in thousands each week, looking especially for wallpaper, leather goods, furniture and clothing, all far cheaper than back home. Sometimes a man will come as a buyer for a whole village, bringing an empty van on a ferry and taking it back full the next day: some shops have sold £200 of wallpaper to a single customer. Many of these rural visitors speak no English, so the Polytechnic has been holding crash-courses in Norwegian for shop-girls, who can learn such useful phrases as "*Ja, det er ferdiglimet vinyl*" ("Yes, that is pre-pasted vinyl"). Some shops have notices in Norwegian. And when a French friend and I were looking at some shirts, and discussing them in French, the girl said: "I'll fetch our Norwegian interpreter."

Newcastle is twinned actively with Bergen and also, more half-heartedly, with Groningen, Gelsenkirchen and Nancy. The Nancy link has had its ups and downs over the years – mostly downs. A few mayoral visits have been made and hopeful plans laid for wider grass-roots exchanges, but neither town has shown much energy for activating these (apart from an enterprising venture in mutual TV reporting in 1978, with BBC North East and the Nancy station each making a 60-minute documentary on the other town). It may be that Geordies find the French mentality too remote and feel more at home with their Nordic cousins. Dan Smith once told me that Newcastle's links with Europe were "alas, feeble and irrelevant". Since then, entry into the EEC has brought a little more awareness, at least in business circles. But for the average Geordie of all classes, Europe is still a remote concept. He has little enthusiasm for the Common Market or understanding of it, and does not feel it has impinged on his life (except by putting up food prices, as many people erroneously believe). In the June 1975 referendum on whether Britain should remain in the EEC, Tyne-and-Wear gave a 60 per cent "yes" vote, a little below the national 66 per cent. Today it would certainly be less than 50 per cent. This about sums things up: at best, Geordies accept the EEC as the lesser of evils (a few dedicated "Europeans" apart). And they note that their Norwegian friends, who voted to stay out, have certainly not suffered from their decision.

Geordies' chumminess with Norwegians derives from the atavistic tribal links. But most of the rest of Europe is alien, incomprehensible territory, somewhere out beyond the already menacing London. A local politician told me, in all seriousness, "My wife and I were twice refused rooms in hotels near Lyon – anti-British feeling, I'm sure." Geordies do go in large numbers on package air tours to the Mediterranean, but in search of sun, not of wider human horizons: they stay in English-speaking hotels full of other English, they eat carefully anglicised food and make little contact with the locals beyond jokey exchanges of "*olé*". This fear of the unknown, or lack of desire to explore it, is found also in schools. A teacher told me that in her comprehensive it was hard to persuade even the children of well-off parents, who could easily afford it, to take part in foreign trips. And at Benfield School a Lancastrian teacher told me, "We can usually persuade pupils to go on purely touristic trips, say to the Loire or Rhine: but when it comes to exchanges involving real human contact we have much more difficulty. It's partly the parents' fault. It is harder on Tyneside than in most other parts of Britain to persuade families to have foreign schoolchildren to stay. When we planned an exchange with a German school, we found only one family here ready to co-operate: it was embarrassing, as so many German families were ready to offer us hospitality. Put it down to typical Geordie insularity." Or put it down to the dislike of having to come to terms with other values or be judged by other standards. Some Geordies even seek to justify this. A journalist asked me, "In what way would it 'improve' us to have more contact with foreigners? – for example, on a holiday in Italy to get to know Italians rather than stay with our own kind in a hotel for the English, which is what we want. I see no virtue in cosmopolitanism for its own sake."

However, once the reticences are broken down and human contact established, then Geordie friendliness wins the day. This is true of all kinds of links with foreigners: once Geordies get to know them, they find they like them, and those school exchanges that do finally take place are usually a success. Much the same applies to relations with those other "foreigners" – Londoners and other southerners who come to Tyneside. If they accept, they are accepted. I met plenty of non-Geordies who had arrived initially with misgivings but later had fallen in love with the place and become enthusiastically integrated. Tyneside usually takes you that way: you love it, or hate it. There are plenty of other "posh" immigrants who wilfully remain outsiders. These are mostly the young executives who accept a job in the region – maybe in the local branch of their firm – as a means of earning promotion. Many despise the Geordie way of life and make little attempt to assimilate, but group in the ghettoes of trim suburban estates such as Darras Hall. At one of their parties, I found only two Geordies among thirty guests. Graham Turner * has described the life of these couples who "flock to Darras Hall like beleaguered American pioneers to the safe stockade of a prairie fort. It is the same sort of estate which they might have lived on had they worked in London or Bristol or Norwich. . . . One thing which soon became plain was that many of the migrants had not come to the north-east willingly. Mike for instance had not wanted to move from Essex, but he did want to be promoted, and a stint in the north-east was one way of ensuring that he took a step up the ladder" – as a sales executive with a big national company. Another young executive told Mr. Turner that he and his wife had found the north-east to be just what they had expected it to be – "black and uninteresting. . . a pretty dark hole with very little history". The author compared the couple to RAF families in post-war Singapore, accepting exile as the price paid for a cushier life.

These and other immigrants are far fewer, and make much less impact, than their counterparts in Toulouse. Yet their presence contributes to the vague Geordie feeling that the region, as Basil Bunting put it, "is still colonised territory". Regional awareness has been growing in recent years, as in other parts of Britain and Europe: yet the centralising influence of London, both bureaucratic and commercial, has been increasing too, so the conflict is becoming more intense. It is rather like Toulouse. While Whitehall officialdom seeks to extend its influence over local affairs, so in the economic sphere too the hand of London grows stronger, in this age of mergers and "rationalisation". Swan Hunter is now in national hands; Bainbridge, a leading department store, has joined the London-based John Lewis group; and so on. A local carpet manufacturer told me: "It's increasingly hard to trade on Tyneside without dealing via London. I can no longer sell direct to local stores, since they now do their buying

* Graham Turner: *The North Country*, Eyre & Spottiswoode, London, 1967.

centrally, so I've had to open a London office and showroom." The trend may be economically wise, and inevitable: but it fuels Geordie feelings that they are somehow being manipulated by outside forces.

And yet at the same time what the British call "devolution" has been in the air. It is true that the causes of Scottish and Welsh autonomy suffered setbacks in the referendums of March 1979. But the issue is no more than dormant. And if the two Celtic nations were ever to secure their own elected assemblies, then there would certainly be new demands – led by the north-east – for the major English "regions" to have something similar. Dan Smith in the 1960s had been one of the first to promote the idea of English regionalism. He saw himself as not merely city boss but regional boss: his dream was to build up Newcastle as the metropolis of a semi-autonomous north-east, and this was his thinking when he took over the Northern Economic Planning Council. But this purely advisory body has never developed much influence. For, in fact, political regionalisation in England itself – as opposed to the Celtic lands – is still far from becoming any kind of reality and is set about with obstacles. England is a small, tightly knit country and at present has much less of a formal regional structure even than France. A governmental body set up in Newcastle in the 1960s, the Northern Economic Planning Board, coordinates the work of the various Whitehall departments in five northern counties, while seven other boards do the same in other parts of England: they are vaguely parallel to the regional prefectures in France but with much less importance and prestige. For although England is *more* decentralised than France at other, more local levels – county council, town council – it simply does not have "regions" in any true sense of the term. Nor would it divide naturally into, say, eight or ten areas corresponding to historical realities, as Germany or Italy, or even France in a way. It has not known "provinces" since early mediaeval times – and today "Mercia" and "Wessex" are largely forgotten memories. This is not to say that some parts of England do not have a strong local patriotism and sense of identity, but most of these tend to be peripheral areas – as Cornwall or Devon – too small to make a "region". The only valid entities large enough to form European-scale regions would seem to be Yorkshire, East Anglia, possibly Lancashire – and of course the north-east. By contrast, what sense of regional loyalty do the amorphous midlands inspire?

This lack of a regional basis is hard on the north-east, for this – the ancient Kingdom of Northumbria – is one of the few parts of England where a true regional tradition survives. It is at least as real and self-aware as Languedoc. Of course, no one on Tyneside is seriously advocating separation. But a degree of autonomy for the north-east – as, say, for Wales – would not be unrealistic, and it could bring positive benefits. If Newcastle became the capital of such a region, with its own elected assembly and executive, stretching from the Scottish border to Teesside, then this could give a new and more up-to-date focus for Geordie pride and patriotism. If Geordies took charge of their own regional affairs, they might gain in self-confidence and thus feel readier to come to terms with the outside world. Gradually this might broaden their horizons and break down some of their complexes. If Newcastle became a true political capital, like Stuttgart, this could have a multiplier effect: less of the area's own best talent would emigrate, new talent would more easily be attracted from outside, industry would benefit, local leadership might be strengthened. For the moment, this is little more than a pipe-dream. But it is not impossible that pressures for some English regionalism might one day build up.

Each time I visit Newcastle, I come away with mixed feelings. I am inspired by the vitality, the warmth, the sense of community, and depressed by the acceptance of mediocrity, the physical and mental shabbiness, the chip-on-the-shoulder introversion tainted with self-pity. It is encouraging to find an urban area that retains such individuality and pride in its traditions – but need this inevitably be coupled with such parochialism? The Geordie feeling of geographical isolation may have had some logic in the old days: today it is absurd. Geordies' enduring sense of isolation is now a mere psychological hang-up: they are "isolated" because they want to be. Happily, a small but growing minority of them realise the dangers of this attitude: these are the ones trying to forge a new north-east, with the aim "of raising the sights of a whole community, of bringing them and their standards of life into line with what more fortunate parts of the country have already accepted as normal". * They are making some progress: thanks to Dan Smith and others, there is at least a wider awareness of real needs than there was twenty years ago. The new Conservative government will certainly show no tolerance for self-pitying Geordie lame-ducks. Too many Geordies are still blinkered, and Europe will not stand still for them to catch up. Since the war, they have won a relative new prosperity beyond their dreams, and they know it. But, when

* Graham Turner, *op. cit.*, page 368.

economic squalls blow up again, as today, they seem to relish the nostalgic whiff this brings of the good old bad old days. With inflation still high and unemployment rising, I recently heard one middle-aged jobless Geordie shipyard worker say to another, in a smart new workingmen's club, "Eh, lad, things are getting so bad again, we'll have to stage another Jarrow march. But this time, we'll go in air-conditioned buses." ' am not sure he was even aware of the irony.

V

Toulouse

If you can't defeat Parisian neo-colonialism, join it

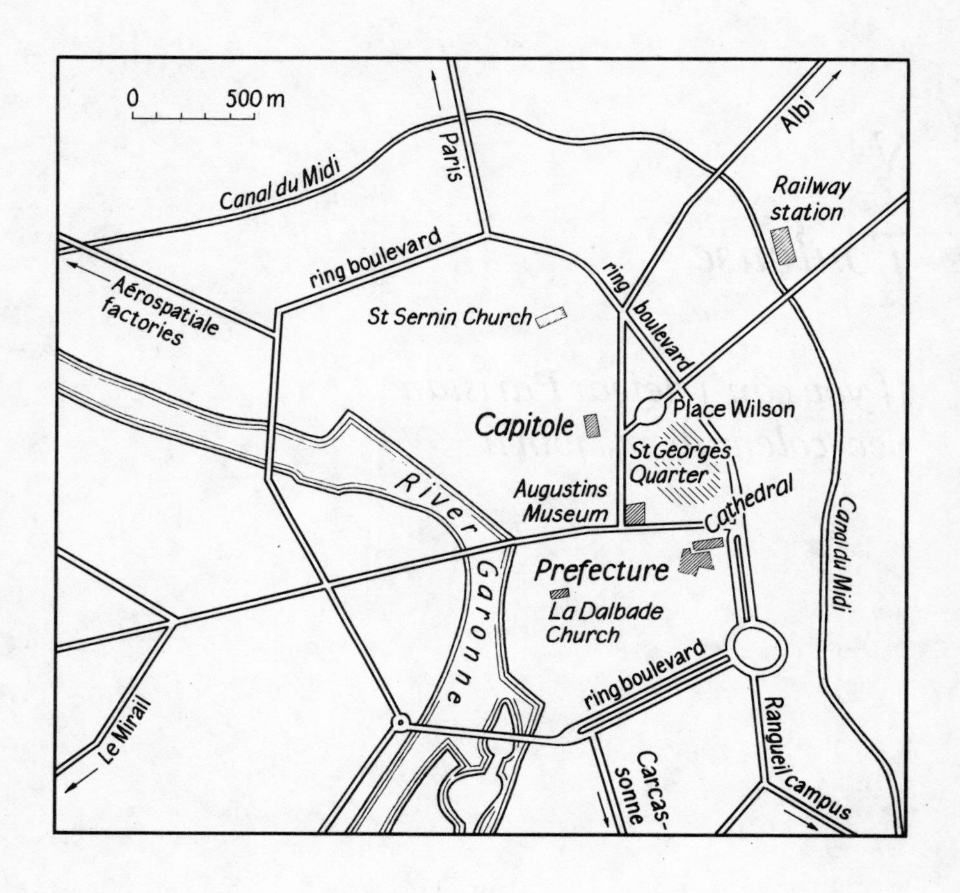
0
500 m
Paris
Albi
Canal du Midi
Railway station
ring boulevard
ring
boulevard
Aérospatiale factories
St Sernin Church
Place Wilson
Capitole
St Georges Quarter
Augustins Museum
Cathedral
River Garonne
Prefecture
La Dalbade Church
Canal du Midi
ring boulevard
Le Mirail
Carcas-sonne
Rangueil campus

1
Introduction

Many times I have made the 400-mile car journey south from Paris to Toulouse and it is always exciting, on the final lap, to cross that mysterious cultural frontier that separates Europe's north from its south. After winding over the lovely western foothills of the Massif Central, the *route nationale* descends at last into the broad valley of the Garonne where suddenly the sun beats stronger, the air is drier, and the ancient villages with their red-tiled roofs have the unmistakable flavour of the Midi. But next I must join the long column of heavy lorries that always clogs up the main road into industrial Toulouse; we crawl for miles past warehouses, hypermarkets, discount emporia selling utility furniture, and high-rise blocks of equally utility flats, till finally I check in at my little hotel in the town centre – to be greeted by the flat twangy accent of the Midi that never ceases to irritate me. "Bong-jourr!"

The weather soon consoles me. Arriving maybe in mid-November from shivering Paris, I find the *café*-terraces filled with sun-bathers enjoying their two-hour lunch-break, while groups of old men are lazily playing *boules* in the dusty squares. And at most times of year the evenings are magical. I take a walk down the narrow old streets of the city centre, where the rose-pink façades of the mediaeval churches and palaces glow under discreet floodlighting. In the unkempt little *cafés* of the main square, students are singing, or arguing politics – this city has the largest student population in the provinces – and even at night the crowds are so thick on the narrow pavements that I am often jostled off the kerb. Toulouse lives late: well past midnight, the big *brasseries* and so-called "drugstores" are full and some boutiques still open. It also lives centrally: the suburbs at night are silent, but this very Latin city has the Latin sense of *agora*, enticing all into its animated centre. And so each time I return I have this impression – in part misleading – of entering a nightly carnival, a confused and exuberant activity against a backdrop of bright lights: so different from sedate Stuttgart.

Is Toulouse a typical French city? No – and yes. In one sense, a town with so fierce an individualism cannot be fully representative of so diverse a nation. This is true of France, as of Italy. Also, Toulouse is essentially a southern city, where much of life is lived outdoors and the temperament is excitable yet easy-going: thus it has much in common with Marseille or Montpellier, but its mood is not that of the sedate and phlegmatic cities of northern France. And yet, in many other ways, Toulouse's experience has been typically and dramatically French. It even provides an ideal case-study for some of the more important transformations in the French provinces since the war. The sudden urbanisation of France, such as Britain knew in the previous century; the transfer from an agricultural to an industry-based economy; the resulting conflicts between tradition and modernism, sharper in France than in most countries; the enduring feud between Paris and the rest of the nation; the current anxieties about industry and youth employment – Toulouse, as much as any French town, exemplifies all of this and more.

France's surge of dynamic new activity and prosperity in the post-war decades has affected Paris and the provinces very differently. It has speeded up the tempo, so that Paris, already a lively city, has become far too hectic and congested for most people's tastes, whereas provincial cities, formerly rather lifeless and enclosed, are now more active, diverse and outward-looking. They have enjoyed the invigoration of living in a time of progress and renewal, yet life still goes at a pace the nerves can stand. There is not only more wealth and industry, but also far more cultural activity than before, and a more open social life. Some towns seem to have achieved a balance between the old-style "*douceur provinciale*" and a new animation; others, such as Marseille, are already reaching the point where they begin in turn to catch the Parisian disease of big-city stress.

Toulouse itself has probably changed more radically in the past thirty years than any other big French town, and has grown faster than any save Grenoble. Fifty years ago it was a sleepy market town, and in 1939 its population was only 180,000: today, with suburbs, it is well over half-a-million. Peasants from the smallholdings of the desolate hinterland have arrived by the tens of thousand, and they have been joined by other immigrants – *pieds noirs* repatriates from Algeria with their pioneering energy, managers and scientists from Paris and other parts of Europe, lacing the city's old parochialism with a new cosmopolitan air. Since the early 1950s the government has used this town as the foremost pilot-zone of its campaign to decentralise the economy and promote new activities in the remoter or less developed provinces, notably in the south-west and west. It has stimulated the growth of technically advanced industries, notably the big aircraft factories which made the Caravelle, Concorde and Airbus here and – at least until about 1974 – were doing quite well. The state has also built up Toulouse into the leading centre outside Paris for scientific education and research, and to staff this vast operation it has enticed cohorts of modern-minded élites to migrate here from other parts of France. Yet this new wave has barely been assimilated by the old Toulouse society – much less, at least, than the Silesians in Stuttgart. The "real" Toulousains, those born and bred here, have looked on the state-directed modernisation of their city with some suspicion. And so today there are two Toulouses: two societies, two mentalities and ways of life, that co-exist uneasily and are only now beginning to mix.

You can notice this contrast, visually. Fly over the city, as it sprawls astride the Garonne on its wide plain, and it looks like some giant vanilla-and-strawberry ice-cream: the old city of mellow brick – truly "a rose-red city half as old as time" – is ringed by a white circle of new flats, factories, colleges and laboratories, a gleaming superstructure grafted onto the old core. Here the two rival élites confront each other: on the one side, the newcomers, the energetic scientists, pilots, professors and managers, together with the *pieds noirs* and other new entrepreneurs; on the other, the "real Toulouse", as it sees itself, a traditional *bourgeoisie* of doctors, lawyers and landowners. They live secluded within their graceful pink palaces in the old city, easy-going and meridional, historically disdainful of industry, patriotically involved in the living past of a city that once ruled the whole earldom of Languedoc as far as the Rhône. No other town in France has a stronger anti-Paris tradition, and tribal memories linger of the brutal colonisation of the city by Paris after the suppression of the Cathar heretics in 1220. So the recent economic and intellectual "colonisation" by Paris, however well-intentioned, is also treated warily. Toulouse thus provides a fascinating example of the paradoxes inherent in the conflict between state regional policies and local aspirations. Are we to see this as government dynamism versus local inertia? – or as local tradition fighting to assert itself against arrogant Parisian centralism? It is all so unlike the situation in Stuttgart!

Toulouse, in its rapid growth, seems recently to have crossed that mysterious threshold where a medium-sized town takes on the atmosphere and life-styles of a modern metropolis. The suburbs grow larger than the main part of the city, townsfolk become commuters, Paris-style quick-lunch bars and night-spots proliferate, and the open country can no longer be reached in a pleasant walk from the centre. This has necessitated a change in mentalities. The old informal street-corner community life has been dying away, and Toulousains have been forced to come to terms with a new kind of suburban living in high-rise estates. Like other Frenchmen, they do not find this easy. In a congested and ill-planned city, they are also facing all the modern problems of ecology and environment. And as the expansion of local industry grinds to a halt, while the universities still swell to bursting, all kinds of new tensions appear. The great era of Toulouse's post-war transformation is now nearly completed, and a new, more uncertain era is opening.

2

Capitouls *and Cathars go into the social melting-pot*

One distinguishing trait of the "old" Toulousains is that they spend much of their time talking and thinking about local history – even more than most Frenchmen. Go to a *bourgeois* dinner-party, and you may hear families solemnly comparing the roles of their ancestors in the mediaeval woad trade or the revolt against Richelieu. "Did your family fight in the First or the Second?" I heard one scion ask another. He was not referring to this century's World Wars, but to the Crusades. Another Toulousain said to me, "We are all deeply marked here by the Roman Conquest, it makes us feel different from Paris," and then added, "We're marked by the Nazi Occupation too" – as if the two events were roughly contemporary.

This telescopic awareness of the past has some basis, for Toulouse's history *is* remarkable. Long before Christ the Romans made it one of the main centres of their empire, and in the Dark Ages it was the capital of the kingdom of the Visigoths. Then from the 9th to 13th century the brilliant dynasty of the earls of Raymond held court in Toulouse, which was capital of their realm of Languedoc and cultural metropolis of the wider area known as Occitania. It was one of Europe's largest cities and also one of the most refined and civilised of its royal courts, attracting troubadours, artists and intellectuals. Some of its finest surviving buildings date from this period, notably the basilica of St-Sernin, largest and possibly the loveliest of romanesque churches in France. But the quarrels of the Church were soon to provoke the city's downfall. The heresy of the Cathars (also known as Albigenses) was imported from the Middle East and in the 12th century flourished widely: in a dissolute age, its believers preached an uncompromising doctrine of piety and asceticism and censured the corruptions of the papacy. Finally Pope Innocent III would tolerate them no more and ordered a Crusade against them, led by Simon de Montfort the Elder (father of the de Montfort who led the revolt of the English barons against Henry III). He carried out his orders with extreme cruelty, burning Cathars alive wherever he could find them. He was killed at the siege of Toulouse in 1218, but soon afterwards the extermination was completed by the armies of Louis VIII of France, acting in the name of the Pope. Count Raymond VIII submitted, and by the Treaty of Paris in 1229 he agreed to bring Languedoc back into full orthodoxy. Fifteen years later the few surviving Cathars were massacred in the *château* of Montségur, in the Pyrenees.

This tragic episode marked not only a religious victory for Rome but also, more unfortunate for Toulouse, a political victory for Paris. The kings of France could now extend their dominion over all the Midi, and in 1271 Toulouse was formally annexed to the Crown. Today the Cathar spirit is long extinct on the religious level – Toulousains are far from ascetic – yet politically and psychologically it remains amazingly present in local minds. There has even been a recent revival of interest: new books on the Cathars are local best-sellers, and features on Cathars in the local media are always popular. Toulousains have neither forgotten nor forgiven that Languedoc's last shreds of autonomy and real identity were torn from it after 1789, when Napoleon carved France into 90 *départements* and Toulouse was reduced to no more than the capital of one of these, Haute-Garonne. The sting still smarts. And

Toulouse's recent post-war elevation, to be capital of the somewhat artificial "region" of Midi-Pyrénées, is seen as no great compensation – a subject we shall return to.

As late as the 17th century Toulouse was still the largest French town after Paris. It flourished as a trade centre, notably for woad (blue dye), cereals and textiles, and it commanded the main east-west routes from Italy into Aquitaine and northern Spain. But with the coming of the railways, and the industrial revolution, Toulouse found itself badly placed. France now became a spider's web with Paris as its focus, and Toulouse was out on a limb, on the wrong side of the Massif Central, less easily linked to Paris than any other big French town. The decline of Spain further limited its trading role: it was now virtually in a cul-de-sac, with the high Pyrenees beyond. This isolation, and sense of neglect, added to local political grievances. It is also one reason why industry never implanted itself here on any scale until very recently, but there is another factor too: Toulousains, and especially the middle and upper classes, have always disdained industry and profit-making. The town is traditionally devoted to law, medicine, arts, commerce, but not to manufacture.

They are a curious people, these Toulousains, instinctive, direct, and less logical than Frenchmen are usually supposed to be. Their temperament is Mediterranean, yet strangely I felt they also have much in common with Geordies – and with my rational Paris/London background I confess I found them almost as alien. A Toulousain will quickly fly into a temper, but without malice, and five minutes later will have his arm round your shoulder and be buying you a drink. He has the quality known as *"bon enfant"*, a good-natured ability to make quick human contact; rather in the Italian manner, he enjoys endless feuding but without taking it entirely seriously, and this helps to explain the complex charade of local politics. Attachment to ideologies is paraded, as usual in France, yet in practice society works more in terms of an elaborate kaleidoscope of human contacts and services rendered, and these count for more than ideas. As in all France and especially in the Midi, inhuman bureaucracy is tamed to human proportion through the famous *Système D:* that is, everyone, including officials, accepts that red tape can be tacitly ignored or twisted from time to time, especially when it is done between pals or over a friendly *verre.* An Englishman with a summer villa near Toulouse once applied for electricity to be installed. He was told this might take years of delay and form-filling – "But," added the village mayor with a smile, "there's some old wiring stacked in the vaults of the *mairie* and the local electrician might fix you up if you ask. But keep it quiet."

In a nation conservative in many of its habits and reflexes, Toulousains are more so than most. Though in 1959 France officially shifted her currency two decimal points, from old francs to new, eighteen years later most Toulousains, including young educated ones, still talk and calculate in old francs – "*deuz mille balles*" means "twenty francs." Often they are vague about time, but no more than is usual in southern Europe. They have a capacity for enjoying life, in their own way, they are sure of their value-system, and one aspect of their anti-Parisianism is that many of them affect to despise the new Paris cult of technocratic efficiency.

When I arrived in Toulouse, friends told me that the man I must meet was Dr André Brouat: he, they said, personifies local character. My encounter was quite an education. I went to his private clinic at the agreed time, and waited half an hour. His staff said they'd no idea where he'd gone but he was probably boozing somewhere. Then he turned up, all charm. A short, stocky, ox-like man in his fifties, with a big square face like a Roman emperor's, he was a rugby champion in his day – a source of abiding prestige in this rugby-mad part of France – and now runs a lucrative private clinic for sporting ailments, such as twisted muscles. Since 1971 he has also been a city councillor, in charge of sport. But this local dignitary is rarely on his municipal dignity. First he took me to his well-cushioned office, full of expensive sculptures, where he turned on a tape-recorder that played his own voice reciting his own erotic Rimbaudesque poems. Then we went to the *brasserie* downstairs, where he offered champagne to me and a swarthy workman in denims, whom he called "*tu*". The barman joined our chat. The scene had a north-of-England kind of earthy informality, and gave me one of my first glimpses of the strange similarities between Toulouse and Newcastle.

"Yes, here in the Midi we are informal," said Brouat, clutching my arm and talking with a bullying directness, almost childlike; "we're not snobs like the people in Paris – or Bordeaux. which is fearfully stuffy-*bourgeois* after all that colonisation by the English. Here, professional people and workers mix easily together, on '*tu*' terms – my kids, for instance, they have money and big cars, but they mix on equal terms with the kids of my chum Marcel here" – and the workman grinned agreement. "We never go to Paris more than we can help," Brouat went on; "Parisians for us are just bloody *couillons*" – and he explained the word by clutching his crotch, a familiar local gesture.

He spoke in the nasal local accent – "*maintenant*" becomes "*mangtenang*" – that I often find hard to follow. Educated people sometimes use it with a touch of affectation. He kept touching me and putting his arm round me, but I did not misinterpret this. He was bragging of his prowess as a lady-killer, which I had already heard about from others. "We're fatalists here," he went on, "we have the *inch'Allah* spirit. And we dislike hard work, I'm glad to say. How I admire a man with private means who's never done a stroke in his life! The aircraft factory-workers here will tell you how they hate their job. Talk to them about nuts and bolts and they'll tell you to fuck off, but they'll happily chat all day about trout-fishing or good *bistrots.*" A teasing exaggeration, I soon learned: Toulouse is not as far removed from the Swabian ethos as all that. "I know a *bistrot* where the owner won't serve you if he doesn't like your face, but if he does, there's *foie gras* on the table and his best bottle out of the cellar. That's the Midi spirit! *Vive le Système D!* We all hate the way Toulouse is changing, we wish it could stay the way it was." He then took me to a *bistrot* for some *cassoulet,* the famous local stew, and we ended the evening at a ramshackle bar in the suburbs, drinking numerous Armagnacs with the fat *patronne,* Mimi. Dr Brouat, I decided, was not my type, but worth appreciating. His non-stop verbiage, though tiring, was instructive. A friend said of him: "When he comes for dinner, he has us laughing for hours with his funny stories and remarks, but then he'll suddenly switch off and sit in a corner with a book. He's got this instinctive, little-boy quality – with a touch of sadness."

Brouat was exaggerating much less about the mix of social classes than about the dislike of work. It is true that class differences are marked in Toulouse, as elsewhere in France: the gulf in income between rich and poor is wide, workers feel alienated from *bourgeois* culture, and there is a strong tradition of antipathy between Left and Right. Yet overlaying these class distinctions is also a kind of complicity between people of very different backgrounds, based on shared local loyalties, habits and temperament. This is typically Toulousain, and much more noticeable than in northern France. Professor Raymond Ledrut, a sociologist from Paris who has lived here many years, told me: "Despite its heavy industry, and its entrenched *bourgeoisie,* this is not really a town divided between the proletariat and the rich – as Lyon is. Mainly it is a town of *petits gens,* not quite working-class. Many workers are ex-peasants who retain their rural links and maybe still own plots of land outside town, and this gives them a different outlook from the true big-city factory-worker." (There is something in common with Stuttgart here.) "Other factors, too, serve to bring the classes together, such as the shared local accent, the anti-Paris solidarity, and the passion for rugby and for local history. And many local *bourgeois,* despite their greater affluence, do have the kind of extrovert life-style, breezy manner and vigorous outdoor interests that humbler local people can easily identify with – Brouat's a perfect example. People here are very sure of their life-style and personality: but if you want to join their society, you must do it on their terms – and a northerner does not always find this easy." (Echoes of Geordieland.) "After more than twenty years here, my wife and I still have few friends in the 'old Toulouse' *milieu.*"

The looks of people as well as their accent betray that this is the Midi. They tend to be short and dark, with sharp, often uneven features – the men a bit rugged-looking, the girls thin-faced, with olive, sometimes sallow complexions. This is not nearly so dress-conscious a town as Bologna, or even Stuttgart; but the latest fashions quickly make their way here from Paris, mass-produced, and the young Toulousaine of today is likely to be wearing what Chelsea or the *Rive Gauche* discovered only three months ago.

In the poorer quarters, many older people still have the looks and dress of peasants, which is what till recently they were. Toulouse has not yet lost its agricultural links: its growth has been so sudden that the old market-town element has not had time to die, and some of its traditions remain. Right in the centre of town there are still regular open-air markets and seasonal "garlic fairs": in the Place du Salin, old peasant women still come in with their bundles to sell hams and sausages, geese and chicken – a mile or so from some of the world's most advanced space-laboratories. And while the town has been spreading its concrete tentacles into the countryside, the new peasant immigrants have also brought the country into the town. At least a quarter of the population of Toulouse is made up of farmers, labourers and their families who in the past thirty years have given up the struggle to make a living, under modern conditions, on the small, unmodernised farms of the region. In the city, they can live in greater comfort and affluence, but often they find it hard to adapt psychologically: they retain not only their rural connections – friends, relatives, maybe a plot of land – but also a certain peasant outlook. Even middle-class people can feel this way. A young building engineer, grandson of a local farmer, told me, "I'm still a peasant in my bones. I'm more at home back in the family's old village than in the block of flats where we live. When it hails in the city, my first thought instinctively is always, 'Will it hurt the vines?' "

The rural links are shared also by the upper crust of "Old Toulouse" society – the nobility and *haute bourgeoisie* whose centuries-old dominance of Toulouse has only recently begun to wane. These families live either in manor houses outside the town or in elegant pink-brick palaces in the mediaeval centre. Most are landowners, merchants, lawyers, doctors. This upper *bourgeoisie* is less ostentatiously wealthy than that of Lyon or Bordeaux, but there is still plenty of affluence, notably among the doctors, who form a special and powerful caste in Toulouse. "A rather unpleasant *milieu,*" one young doctor said to me of his colleagues: "they tend to hold snobbish Right-wing views, and many have made their wealth through exploiting the flaws in the French health service, charging their patients up to three times the rate at which the state reimburses for a consultation."

The aristocracy is different. There are still about eighty titled families in and around Toulouse. Some live in country *châteaux,* devoting their dwindling fortunes to shoring up their estates; others dwell, as they have for centuries, in the old patrician quarter near the Cathedral – in handsome mansions mostly of the 16th or 17th century, giving onto narrow alleys at the front but open at the back onto wide courtyards and gardens invisible from the street. In this noisy city, this is a quiet corner almost Moorish in the secrecy of its charms.

As elsewhere in France, the aristocracy no longer flaunts its titles or asserts itself socially. As in Swabia, it has withdrawn onto the sidelines of public life, and its families tend to cling together discreetly in their own exclusive little world, inviting each other to small informal parties or an occasional ball or banquet with echoes of past glories. And the rest of society tolerates or ignores them: for though the French public adores foreign royalty, or an English *milord,* it cares not a jot for its own nobility. In Toulouse, some of the aristocrats are descendants of the famous *capitouls,* wealthy merchants whom the city's mediaeval rulers appointed to help them administer it. These dozen or so *capitouls* survived right up to the Revolution as a princely oligarchy, as in some Italian cities, and many acquired titles along the way. Each *capitoul* was allowed to build himself a mansion with a special tall tower – and so, in the old town, you can still see these slender pink towers above the rooftops. Again, one thinks of Italy.

Some aristocrats have fallen on what they may regard as hard times. I met a baroness running a children's clothes shop, and a count who was ploughing his own acres outside the town, earning no more than his peasant neighbours. Others have fared better, managing to put their inherited wealth to productive purpose. Toulouse's leading local bank, Banque Courtois, is owned and still actively run by Baron Gilbert Courtois de Viçose, a courteous and civilised old man, with a vivacious Swedish-Austrian wife and a bohemian artist daughter. With the warmth of hospitality that the local nobility show towards foreign (non-Parisian) visitors, they invited me several times to their beautiful mansion in the old quarter. Here, in a curious *salon* that was like an antique-dealer's, crammed with heirlooms, fading photos and assorted ornaments, the Baron offered his best local Armagnac (who in Toulouse drinks the despised rival brandies of Cognac?) and said: "My ancestors were bankers here in the 16th century, and several had English wives. They were *capitouls,* but all that means nothing any more. My grandfather was a baron, but we've never used the title since his day: we're Protestants, anti-royalist and anti-titles too. My family worked hard and managed to keep its wealth, and now we give regular dinner, bridge and cocktail parties, but not just to other nobility: we invite doctors, writers and others too. Toulouse's society may not match the brilliance of the 'silk aristocracy' of Lyon or the 'wine aristocracy' of Bordeaux. But we try to keep the old elegance alive, in this workaday age."

This old Toulouse society, formerly so self-absorbed and self-sufficient, has now been invaded by varied waves of immigrants. The city has exploded into a new diversity, to become a social melting-pot. The first symptoms appeared sixty years ago, when the first modern industries arrived and began to make an impact on local attitudes. In 1939, tens of thousands of Spanish refugees settled here, and were followed, around 1962, by an even greater number of French repatriates from Algeria. Add to these the peasant immigrants from the region, the scientists, teachers and executives from Paris, and the smaller colonies of British, Germans and others, in the new industries, and the "old" Toulousains are now far outnumbered. After Stuttgart, this is much the most cosmopolitan of my towns.

The most influential of the new waves has been that of the many thousands of professional people who have moved here with their families, mostly from Paris, to take well-paid jobs in industry, research, administration. Many were at first dubious about settling here, and especially their wives. Would they not feel isolated and friendless in this remote southern city with its strange ways? By Paris standards, would it not seem monstrously uncultured? However, most of them soon found they liked it, and today few of them want to return to the capital. They have found far more culture than they expected. They have been won over too by the sunny climate, the architecture, the relative nearness of mountains and sea, and other delights of life in the Midi.

In fact, one of the oddest changes that has come over French society in the past two decades is that the traditional Parisian scorn for the provinces is being stood on its head. Life in central Paris has become so tough and hectic that many sophisticated Parisians are gladly moving to the provinces, especially to the south – and Toulouse is one of the most popular destinations. Of course there are still plenty of ambitious young Julien Sorels who leave their little town for the bright lights of the capital: but at least it is now a two-way process. It is now *à la mode* to praise the provinces and find Paris "impossible": amazingly, it can be just as *chic* to say you live and work in Languedoc or Provence as in Montparnasse. That was not so twenty years ago.

These immigrants play a dominant role in the economic and cultural life of Toulouse, but as yet they have made little impact on local politics. The town council remains in the hands of the "old" Toulousains, and it reflects the traditional hostility to the government in Paris. These tensions, and the uneasy balance of power between locally elected mayor and Paris-appointed prefect, have caused difficulties for local government and town-planning in Toulouse since the war – as we shall now see.

3

Mayor and Prefect, uneasy bedfellows

Local politics in this temperamental southern city with its mixture of populations are even more complex than is normal in France. Rivalries between mayor and prefect, and even between government services;

rivalries between new and old Toulousains or between the city and its surrounding communes; antagonisms on the Right between Gaullists and others, on the Left between Communists and others – all this creates a kaleidoscope of intrigues and conflicting loyalties that is more baffling than the political world of Paris, though does not take itself quite so seriously. Witness the paradoxes on the Left. There are plenty of Communists here, but not all their leaders are the solemn intellectuals or union stalwarts you find in northern cities: the best-known local Party man, Jean Doumeng, is a flamboyant and smartly dressed tycoon who lives on a ranch near Toulouse and has made millions through agricultural deals with Eastern Europe, such as selling off the EEC's butter mountain to the Russians or buying oranges from Spain and trading them to the Czechs. In 1975 he was fined 20 million francs for selling wines that did not meet EEC regulations.

Or consider Paul Ourliac, an ex-Pétainist who worked in a Ministry at Vichy (and remains proud of it), then for more than twenty years was a senior Toulouse councillor, cosily teamed up with Socialist mayors who had fought with the Resistance. In fact, trying to understand the effect of the Occupation on post-war local politics is far from easy. At the Liberation, the powerful Communist *maquis* of the south-west (led by non-Toulousains) made a heavy-handed attempt to seize control of the city, and there was a fearful settling of scores which took the form of vendettas between rival Resistance groups no less than of witch-hunts against alleged collaborators. Hundreds of people were killed, mostly by the Communists. This has not been forgotten by the older generation, and helps to explain the Socialists' enduring hostility to the Communists. Yet in other respects the hatreds of the Vichy period seem to have had surprisingly little influence on post-war politics. Pétain once said that the French have short memories, and in an odd way this is especially true of Toulousains, who will continue to brood over mediaeval Crusades and Cathars, yet show a remarkable tolerance and realism when it comes to burying far more recent hatchets and reaching *ententes.* So the case of Ourliac begins to make sense. During the 1950s and '60s the dominant Socialists and Radicals ruled this city in a succession of shifting coalitions with various Gaullist, Centrist and other Right-of-centre forces, including some ex-Pétainists. For local Socialism in that period was no more than the palest shade of pink: it was of the old, conservative, Guy Mollet kind, and most of its leaders were *bourgeois* with business interests.

The most serious friction has generally been that between city council and Paris, that is, between locally elected mayor and Paris-appointed prefect – not surprising, in a town with so strong a resentment of Paris. Things were at their worst in the 1960s when the Socialist mayor was stubbornly anti-de Gaulle. Today the mayor is Giscardian and relations are easier. Yet Toulouse is still suitable terrain for investigating the strengths and weaknesses of the French local government system, based on its uneasy balance of power between the two rival poles, *maire* and *préfecture.*

The two buildings are very different in atmosphere. The *préfecture,* next to the cathedral and formerly the archbishop's palace, is a stately pink edifice round a large courtyard. Here the regional prefect and his family live in a sumptuous flat. He is a high civil servant, equivalent of an ambassador; he wears a blue-and-gold uniform at official ceremonies, and like a diplomat he is moved from post to post every few years – for he must not get too involved with his "subjects". "State control is essential, for we cannot allow disparate local bodies to carry out uncoordinated policies," the Prefect of the Midi-Pyrénées told me loftily, in his office filled with *empire* furniture, its walls hung with colour photos of Giscard *and* de Gaulle *and* Pompidou. His immediate staff are mostly the privileged products of the French élitist system, often *alumni* of the all-influential *Ecole Nationale d'Administration,* youngish, well-dressed, clever, smoothly self-confident. In the planning department, the *"Mission Régionale"*, they flourish their wall-charts and statistics with *brio,* and in the modern French technocratic manner talk eagerly of implanting a motorway or power-station here, an airport or new town there. "Yes, we have a sense of mission," said one; "We've come from Paris to help these people to a better future." He spoke as if he were dispensing aid to some darker corner of Africa.

Each of France's 96 *départements* is governed by a prefect. He still has the political role conceived for him by Napoleon: preserving law and order through control of the police, and reporting to Paris on local political trends. But under modern conditions he has increasingly assumed economic duties too, with the new stress on regional planning. The *départements* are now grouped into 22 "regions", so the Prefect of the Haute-Garonne *département* (capital, Toulouse) is also regional Prefect of the Midi-Pyrénées, comprising eight *départements* from the Spanish border up into the Massif Central. The prefect is charged with coordinating and supervising the work of the local branches of the Paris Ministries and other state services, and to this end he has wide powers over the local spending of state budgets. His scope for initiative is considerable, and he uses it – far more than a prefect in Italy. But, as in Italy, he has a more negative function too, that of exercising tutelage over the hundreds of communes that make up the *département,* most of them mere villages, some big towns – as Toulouse. And here the trouble begins, for although the tutelage has been relaxed recently, it can still irk proud Toulouse and its mayor.

The *mairie* is a large 18th-century palace, Le Capitole (named after the old assembly of the *capitouls*), imposingly handsome from the exterior, less so inside with its high gloomy corridors and air of petty officialdom. When I told one councillor I had just been to the *préfecture,* he asked nervously, "What did they say about us? Were they critical of our lack of cooperation?"

The 49 councillors elect the mayor, who as in all French towns becomes *ex officio* a state servant, responsible to the prefect in many matters. His position is equivocal. The mayor of many big French towns is often a man of power and authority, maybe a national figure (as Chaban-Delmas in Bordeaux, Defferre in Marseille); once elected he frequently rules as an autocrat, and if he has the right qualities he can achieve much for his town. But much will depend on his relations with the prefect. Most of his and the council's decisions require the prefect's formal approval, and as the city's own finances are highly limited, it has to rely on state partnership for most of its projects. Though less cripplingly so than in Bologna, Toulouse can thus be at the mercy of state vetoes and delays.

Another drawback is that, as in Newcastle, the mayor and his councillors are unsalaried, receiving only modest indemnities. Most of them therefore must give much of their time to their regular jobs; and though some are men of ability, others are wheeler-dealing mediocrities who see the town hall as a means of helping along their own businesses (again, as in Newcastle). The city's elected rulers are not the high-calibre professionals one finds in Stuttgart. They are assisted by a team of salaried administrators, from the town clerk *(secrétaire-général)* down to the various technical officers: but few of these men are of the calibre their difficult modern jobs demand. A post in a town hall, even in a big place like Toulouse, offers poor pay, worse prestige and limited prospects, and does not attract the bright graduates of *ENA* or other élite schools. Moreover, prefectoral surveillance does not always prevent abuses: I was quoted the case of an official under the Socialist régime who had two rooms in the *mairie,* one empty and tidy for receiving civic visitors, and one at the back full of papers where he did paid work on the side for a building firm. The councillors turned a blind eye, knowing how little they paid him. All this may explain why civic administration appears less efficient here than in Stuttgart.

The mayor from 1958 to 1971, Léon Bazergue, became a by-word in France for a certain kind of old-style Socialist potentate of the Midi, on bad terms with his Prefect. He was a clever and energetic man who could be charm itself when he wished, but was not liked for his quick temper, cutting insults, arrogance and snobbery. Son of a small factory-owner, he became a lawyer, sedulously courted the upper *bourgeoisie,* and applied his Socialist principles by amassing a private fortune through astute property deals, both before and after he become mayor. When his friends in the property world won contracts for some of his grandiose building schemes, tongues wagged as in the days of Dan Smith on Tyneside.

Bazergue received me one day in his mayoral office – a sturdy silver-haired man in a large room with Victorian décor, thick red satin curtains and bad landscape paintings. He began by rebuking me for writing too little about him in the Toulouse pages of my book on France: "It was I who built this town, I did all the creative thinking. If Louis Bazergue had not been in this seat these past twelve years, Toulouse would be still asleep." Then he waxed apocalyptic about the city's "great destiny as Europe's gateway to Africa". Then I was dismissed.

Bazergue's merit was to recognise that Toulouse must modernise and develop, as his predecessors had failed to do. His mistake was to insist on doing the work on his own terms, without proper consultation. He behaved like an autocrat, as he believed this was how to get things done: but it led to incessant conflicts with the prefect. In lesser matters, where he had the funds to be his own master, he was able to achieve a good deal – for example, in improving the city's pavements, street lighting and drainage, previously a disgrace. But where he needed the state's help, he ran into trouble. When the government set up a town-planning unit for the area, he refused point blank to collaborate, saying it was an intrusion on his own preserve. Yet his own town-planning too often consisted of prestige projects embarked on with inadequate feasibility studies. The largest of these was for a huge new super-suburb to house 100,000 people: Le Mirail. He won government backing, and work began; but after 1965 Paris began to cut funds.

The prefect claimed that the over-grandiose project needed to be trimmed: Bazergue alleged that the new Minister of Construction, a Toulousain, was exacting vengeance for his defeat by the mayor in local elections. Conflicts of this kind were common. "The Gaullists victimise me," Bazergue told me; "Bordeaux under Chaban gets far more aid than we do." There was some truth in this, for during the period of the Fifth Plan, 1966-70, while the government poured money into its own industrial and university expansion schemes for Toulouse, which had nothing to do with the city council, its subsidies for municipal projects amounted to only 130 million francs a year, against 270 million for Bordeaux and 460 million for Lille/Roubaix, towns of comparable size. Paris may have been unfair, but Bazergue himself was quite largely to blame.

During the run-up to the municipal elections of 1971, Bazergue's alliance with the non-Gaullist Right came unstuck and he was forced to rely on Communist support in face of a strong opponent, Pierre Baudis, a local Giscardian. The campaign was intense. The final electoral duo between the two leaders took on the drama of a bull- or cock-fight, and the Toulousains with their love of vivid personality clashes relished the spectacle. In a nation-wide radio debate, Baudis accused the mayor of having appeared on the balcony of the Capitole in May, 1968, surrounded by the red and black flags of bolshevism and anarchy – a reference to an incautious populist gesture by Bazergue when 6,000 Leftist students had surrounded the *mairie* and challenged him to prove his Socialist faith. Bazergue never lived it down. Baudis won the elections comfortably and has been mayor ever since, winning again more narrowly in 1977. Socialists and Radicals had ruled "*la ville rose*" without a break (save under Vichy) from 1904 to 1971, but their long reign was now ended.

Under Baudis, local politics are much smoother. He is very different from his predecessor, a quiet, rather dull man in his early sixties, courteous, prudent, excellent at baby-kissing, anxious to avoid giving offence. What is more, he supports Giscard, so relations with the *préfecture* have improved considerably. Funds are no longer withheld arbitrarily; projects are discussed amicably, and disagreements are kept to a practical level and not inflated emotionally into issues of pride. An example of the new order concerns two disused Army barracks covering 40 acres near the centre of town. Bazergue had been trying for years to secure these useful sites, but the Army's price was excessive. Baudis in 1976 lobbied his friend Raymond Barre, the Prime

Minister, who prevailed upon the Army to drop its price by one-third. At the next local elections, Baudis was able to present this as a great victory (probably Barre had acted deliberately so as to help him retain his marginal seat). And yet, though Baudis' diplomacy may bring results, he is hardly a dynamic mayor. He dislikes taking decisions, he has not innovated or shown imagination. From being aggressively opposed to Paris, Toulouse has merely changed into a town readier to acquiesce in the state's scheme of things.

Baudis at least has done something to improve coordination between Toulouse and its surrounding suburban communes. This has become a familiar problem in France – as in some other countries – where the growth of conurbations has made nonsense of the old municipal boundaries, yet communes have been reluctant to pool services for fear of seeing their precious semi-autonomy dwindle further. The commune of Toulouse is lucky to cover a wide area (larger than the Ville de Paris) with plenty of vacant land, and this at first led Bazergue to believe that he could develop the town without reference to its neighbours. But soon the suburban communes were growing much faster than the city itself. Colomiers in particular, to the north-west near the aircraft factories, was expanding dynamically under its ambitious Socialist mayor, André Raymond. He attracted new factories to his little town, whose population shot up from 3,000 to 25,000 in thirteen years. This infuriated Bazergue, who refused to be even on speaking-terms with his fellow-Socialist colleague. Since a large part of a town's own resources comes from taxes on local industry and commerce, Bazergue saw how much his own over-stretched finances might suffer if new factories and hypermarkets preferred to settle outside his boundaries – exactly Stuttgart's problem.

Bazergue at first retaliated by refusing to help the burgeoning suburbs to meet their growing needs in public services – water, sewage, public transport, and so on, matters where the city itself was already fairly well organised. Grudgingly it sold them water, but would not extend its bus routes outside its boundaries, to serve the new suburbs. The peripheral communes tried to group together for some utilities, but this was barely practicable. Clearly the rational answer was for some voluntary association of communes within the conurbation, of the kind already working well in more enlightened places such as Grenoble. This the prefect suggested, but at first Bazergue refused. Then, in 1969, he took fright that the government might impose the solution recently applied in Lyon and Bordeaux: a *communauté urbaine,* or urban district. Neither he nor the other mayors wanted to be thus swallowed up. Feeling cornered and isolated, with elections approaching, he suddenly changed his tack to one of charming cooperation and accepted the prefect's plan for a joint planning committee, which set to work. Amazingly, it was the first time that Bazergue and his fellow mayors, most of them Socialist, had ever sat round a table together: "At last he shakes hands and says 'good morning'," Raymond told me; "it's he who's changed, not me." Since Baudis came to power in 1971, matters have further improved. A new public transport body now services the whole conurbation rationally, so that no longer do you have to change buses at the city boundaries, as if crossing a national frontier. There is some joint long-term planning too. Raymond told me in 1976: "Toulouse is moving closer to its neighbours, but slowly and piecemeal. There is still no concerted policy." The basic problems remain, and they are much as in Stuttgart, save that Toulouse has more *Lebensraum* so its plight is less acute. Any modern conurbation of this kind needs to pool many resources and services: Toulouse could learn from Tyneside. But French communes, large or small, are so proud of their identity that they will seldom consent to federation, let alone mergers.

So how should we assess the French system of local government, as seen from Toulouse? Clearly the town has less autonomy than Stuttgart and less – in some ways – than Newcastle. This is not only a question of state supervision of civic affairs, but of the fact that many major matters lie outside civic control altogether. Newcastle to quite a degree looks after its own school education, health, and low-cost housing, with backing from the state: in Toulouse, these are run by the state. So the city's range is limited. And on top of this, it has grown increasingly short of finance even for paying for the services that are its responsibility, such as roads, transport, conservation, culture, sport and leisure. Like most French towns, it has run increasingly into debt and has had to push up rates faster than the level of inflation, as well as raise public loans. For its own sources of local taxation are extremely limited, by law: of its overall 1977 budget of 962 million francs, only 205 million was met by local taxes. Municipal budgets in France equal only 15 per cent of the total state budget, against 50 per cent in Britain and 80 per cent in Germany (though adjustment must be made for the fact that cities in these two countries are having to spend on a wider range of services).

The town thus has to rely on financial partnership with the state, for most of its commitments. There are norms here: for main roads, bridges and major new buildings, the state contributes about half the cost; for drains, lighting minor roads, some 20 per cent; for an old people's home or a sports ground, about 20 per cent; for adult education, up to 80 per cent; and so on. But to obtain one franc the council must first secure state approval of the project as a whole, and this gives Paris some leverage: it can veto or delay. Some urban renewal schemes can wait five years or more for the go-ahead – as in Newcastle. Seldom today is Paris being vindictive; more often the factors are bureaucratic caution, parsimoniousness, and sheer muddle and inertia.

Gradually the government has consented to give towns a little more autonomy of execution, if not greater powers of raising finance. Under 1972 reforms the system of tutelage has eased, so that a prefect can no longer demand to scrutinise every detail of a town's annual budget (including matters where the state is not involved) unless he suspects irregularity. Mayors have a little more elbow-room. There is no doubt that a strong mayor can achieve a great deal, if he wins the prefect's cooperation – Fréville proved it in Rennes, Pradel in Lyon, and others elsewhere. The French system of the mayor/prefect tandem can, and does, have its positive side, when the two accept to work together for common goals of development, each providing a salutary check on the other. And, when set beside the British system of honorary mayors, many French towns benefit – as do German ones – from the tradition of the influential local ruler with a strong local power base, often serving for long periods and able to carry through a consistent long-term policy. But it does depend on the individual. And Toulouse has been unlucky since the war in not possessing this kind of mayor. When the local ruler and his council are too passive, too uncooperative, too lacking in any proper development policy, then the state is likely to step in and take the initiative – and this drives the town onto the defensive, as Raymond Ledrut said to me of Toulouse: "Too often the council waits for a Ministry or the prefect to urge it to act, over some matter, then takes up a defensive position to defend what it sees as its interests. This is the heritage of more than a hundred and fifty years of state tutelage: even today, too many of the key decisions affecting Toulouse are taken elsewhere, in Paris. And it's a vicious circle: Toulouse gets more dependent and lethargic, which forces the state to act for it, which encourages further dependence. So there's a sense of mediocrity about this town's civic affairs. It doesn't seem able to seize its chances."

4
A car-clogged city half as old as time

This city of enchanting beauty and sprawling confusion presents the modern town-planner with fearsome problems. How to renovate a decaying fabric, and ease the ever-increasing pressures of traffic, without spoiling the architectural heritage? It is Bologna's problem over again, made more difficult here by the very much more rapid growth of the city. Only belatedly, at the eleventh hour, have the authorities begun to master it with any success.

Let us return to the image of the Neapolitan ice. On the east bank of the Garonne lies the kernel of the old city, about a mile square. Its brick changes colour with the changing light – "pink at dawn, red under the midday sun, mauve at sunset", the local saying goes. Some of its narrow streets, between the cathedral and the river, are quiet, dignified backwaters; others have become furiously commercial and congested, notably those that lead onto the main square, the Place du Capitole, flanked by the town hall. Whatever the failings of those who rule from this building, at least they take pride in showing off the city's architectural splendours: some older buildings are gently floodlit after dark, to magical effect, and some central squares have neat flower-beds and fountains playing. But all day long the traffic never lets up, along main streets rarely broad enough for more than two cars. And outside this central zone sprawls the newer 19th- and early 20th-century town, its railway-sidings, barracks and arsenals, schools, hospitals, cemeteries, workshops, higgledy-piggledy bungalows and flats, creating a chaotic jumble that has few redeeming features of planning save for the Paris-style ring boulevard that is now inadequate for the traffic it bears. This era of the city's growth spreads onto the west bank of the wide Garonne – spanned by six bridges – where a third of the population now live. Farther out again lies the post-war city: to the south-east, the neat white buildings of the new science campus, spaciously planned; to the north-west, the aircraft factories and the busy airport; and on every side, large low-cost housing estates with their grey or off-white high-rise blocks.

Until the 1960s virtually nothing was done to cope with the problems caused by this headlong expansion. Bazergue's predecessor, René Badiou, was a kindly old scholar who wanted Toulouse to remain basically a university and market town: the best way to deal with urban growth, he felt, was to ignore it. So the haphazard private building of *pavillons* continued unchecked, and in their midst blocks of workers' flats were implanted here or there, wherever land was vacant. With the rise in car ownership, traffic jams grew unbearable, since it was difficult to avoid the narrow bridges or the congested city centre. This was the serious situation which Bazergue inherited, and after some delay he drew up a master-plan for the city, and submitted it to the prefect in 1962. It provided for much-needed urban ring-roads, properly planned new suburbs, and renovation of some decaying central areas. The plan was pored over, revised and re-revised, subjected to endless delays – and finally is being applied in parts, spasmodically. In 1977 the town clerk told me proudly, "In 1960 we had a 30-year backlog in infrastructure, but now we've almost made it up." This is an exaggeration. But at least the housing shortage has been solved, and traffic has been eased through new transport schemes and the building (not yet completed) of ring-roads. Toulouse's historically centripetal structure is simply not viable once the city gets beyond a certain size, and attempts are now being made to ease the pressure on the centre by creating a new "multicellular" structure, with the decentralisation to new suburban complexes of certain key services – public offices, TV studios, large parts of the university, and so on.

The least successful aspect of the new planning has been the renovation, or restoration, of the historic centre, which has less grandeur and harmony than Bologna's but covers almost as large an area. On the positive side, at least there has been little desecration. With the backing of the Ministry of Culture, the council has shown a concern for preventing modern buildings from disfiguring the mediaeval zone. Some have crept in, shops and office blocks, but they are kept discreetly apart from the most beautiful buildings. Real eyesores are few. However, large parts of this central zone are in gentle decay, and little is being done for them – through lack of funds or of foresight.

The only major renewal scheme has concerned the St-Georges district, a 15-acre site just north of the cathedral. The buildings were not considered of sufficient historic value to be worth restoring, and the area had degenerated into a slum – a mass of archaic little workshops, and tenements without indoor toilets, crumbling into decay. So the decision was taken to rebuild. In 1956 the council began demolition, and finally a total of 2,424 people, mostly poor or elderly, were evicted and rehoused in the suburbs. The site is now filled with new middle-class flats, smart shops, a big hotel, all built in the local pink brick, around a patio. The result is visually pleasing, but . . . Firstly, the operation took over twenty years to complete, owing to state cut-backs in funds and delays in granting permits. One factor was the anxiety to avoid destroying, by mistake, some historical relic – a policy on which a local contractor gave me his heretical slant: "It's a pity Toulouse wasn't worse bombed in the war. The Allies attacked the aircraft factories in the suburbs, but their aim was too accurate, they never helped us by knocking down parts of the centre. And today the council and the Ministry of Culture are so monument-conscious that they insist on every old building being checked minutely before we can touch a brick. It slows us down, maddeningly, so my workers have agreed to turn a blind eye to what they find. When we unearthed a bit of old Roman bath under one cellar, we just cleared it away." It seems not all Toulousains show overmuch pride in their Roman heritage.

Secondly, the council was sharply criticised on the Left for evicting workers and bringing in *bourgeois*: political motives were alleged. The council's answer was that it could not have afforded low-rent housing in a central area with high costs. Anyway, I was told at the *mairie* in 1977 that St-Georges-type renovation is now out of fashion, and the accent is to be on restoration and conservation – as in Bologna, and even Newcastle. A modest start has been made, in two pilot zones; yet there is no concerted plan, although some of the loveliest parts of the old city are in grave decay. In the ancient Dalbade quarter, close to the river, the streets are lined with classic *bourgeois* mansions, 17th-century or earlier; and while some are still lived in by well-to-do families and beautifully kept up, others have fallen derelict or become slums occupied by poor immigrant workers. Most of these have no modern plumbing. I poked my nose into one, where an old crone told me that "*Madame la propriétaire*" – probably the impoverished sole descendant of some noble family – lived alone on the first floor and let off the rest at low rents. A stench exuded from the earth closet in the filthy courtyard. I was told that the cost of restoring these buildings was such that private buyers baulked. So could they not be turned into picturesque little hotels, of the kind you find in the heart, say, of Arles or Siena? – the hotel industry had thought of it, but decided the rooms were the wrong shape. Nearby were derelict warehouses, tenements, empty plots full of rubbish: a disgrace in the heart of this proud city. The Garonne's right bank at this point is a mess, as neglected as the riverside at Newcastle. Why, I asked, did the council not take the area in hand, and renovate if it could not afford to restore? I was told with a shrug that funds were short and other priorities higher.

One such priority has been the provision of new low-cost housing, for a population that in the 1950s and '60s was growing by 7,000 a year. The post-war housing shortage was as grave as in other French cities, but by the mid-60s it had been largely solved through a crash programme carried out by public agencies (jointly funded by city and state) for the building of HLMs (*habitations à loyer modéré*), the equivalent of Britain's council housing. Blocks of these new flats were thrown up all over the outer districts. They met basic human needs, but their quality, siting and amenities left much to be desired. So Bazergue in the early 1960s decided he would leave his mark on Toulouse by providing it with something far more gracious and coherent: a splendid modern garden-city that would be the wonder and envy of the world. He selected the commune's one large tract of still vacant land, near the *château* of Le Mirail, west of the river. The resulting project – half-success, half-failure – has been more talked about and squabbled over than any other post-war Toulouse venture except for Concorde. Like Concorde, it provides an object-lesson in what happens when inadequate forecasting is made worse by running conflict between two uneasy sponsors – Paris' co-sponsor this time being not Whitehall but the Capitole. It also shows how the French administrative system is not easily suited to coping with a scheme of this size.

Le Mirail was conceived at a time of rapid urban expansion in France when soulless concrete dormitories, such as the notorious Sarcelles, were sprouting in the Paris area. Bazergue wanted to do better. To take charge of the scheme he hired Georges Candilis, the brilliant Greek-born disciple of Le Corbusier, and he came up with interesting designs for wide traffic-free zones, lakes, and long blocks of flats with deck-access, curving round piazzas. Le Mirail was planned for 100,000 inhabitants. It was to have its own apparatus of factories, offices, hypermarkets, *lycées*, university, yet it would not just be another new town in the middle of nowhere: it was to be an integral extension of Toulouse, less than three miles from the centre. So work began. But during the next years it ran into every kind of hazard and fell far behind schedule. On top of the inevitable financial wrangles between city and state, there were some typically French legal and bureaucratic difficulties. The *pont-et-Chaussées* department in Paris had to give approval for every new bridge or roadway, and this often took up to two years. Then, when the first flats came to be sold, the lawyers found that no one had worked out to whom the ground itself belong – land ownership being a crucial issue in property-loving France – and this took eighteen months to sort out. What is more, it soon became clear that private builders and buyers were holding back. The initial aim had been to destroy class barriers and make Le Mirail socially "mixed", half HLM tenants, half middle-class buyers. But the latter were deterred by the delays in providing the promised amenities, while even working families were reluctant to emigrate to Le Mirail, now that housing in the city was fairly plentiful. Soon hundreds of flats were standing empty. There were rumours too that officials in the local HLM office were trying to sabotage the project, out of spite either against Bazergue, or against Candilis because he had been preferred to a local architect. The intrigues and dramas infesting Le Mirail soon became a local laughing-stock: "Toulousains are never capable of finishing their grand projects," one sceptic told me: "look at the Cathedral, incomplete after seven centuries" (true).

However, the first phase at least, the Bellefontaine quarter, was finally completed in the early '70s and today is pleasantly habitable. It consists of a network of polygonal blocks of flats winding round concrete platforms, like some vast honeycomb, a little stark for my taste – less appealing than Newcastle's Byker Wall – but an improvement on the ranks of high-rise rectangles built in France in the '60s. There is a sports and cultural centre, plenty of shops and other amenities, and the socially mixed population is gradually building its own community life. Bellefontaine is a relative success. But under Baudis, who would have no truck with Bazergue's grandiosity, the rest of the project has been scaled right down, and many earlier plans for large blocks are being replaced with low-density individual housing. Le Mirail's final population will be much nearer 50,000 than the original 100,000 forecast. In a time of slower French expansion, the vogue for these mammoth new cities has passed and the accent is on a smaller, more human scale. Bellefontaine will survive as an epitaph to a past era.

With the housing shortage now largely solved, the planners have turned their main attention recently to the fearsome problem of traffic congestion. During the boom '60s the volume swelled rapidly, yet little action was taken and traffic jams became among the worst in Europe, owing to the city's knot-like structure. As there were no ring-roads, most through-traffic including heavy lorries had to churn its way close to the centre where the narrow streets meant for carts and horses came close to asphyxia. At rush-hour, it could take up to an hour to cross the Garonne bridges. French individualism aggravated the problem: France has the highest level of car ownership in Europe after Sweden, and by 1970 in Toulouse there was one car per three people – but would they leave the car at home to go by bus? No. Toulousains more than most Frenchmen dislike using public transport, and this created a vicious spiral: the more cars on the streets, the slower the buses could go, so the less inclined people were to use them, so the less money the bus company had for putting on better services. The number of passengers carried annually decreased from 47 million in 1964 to 33 million in 1971 despite the growth of population. Suburban services were rare: no buses went from the city centre as far as the big new science campus at Rangueil, and one car-less student told me, "The only viable transport in the city is a moped, or one's feet." Bazergue was urged to build a Metro, possibly the best solution for a city of this central density, but he turned it down on cost grounds. Then he created a new sewage system, in such a way as to make a Metro impossible for ever – an example, cited by his critics, of his myopia as a master planner.

In the closing months of his reign, Bazergue made some hurried last-minute efforts to reduce the traffic chaos by embarking on underground car-parks and throwing ugly, precarious-looking single-lane flyovers across certain junctions. But this electoralism won him few votes. It was then left to Baudis to carry through some more effective projects. Today a proper urban ringway at last skirts the city to the west and south, via a new Garonne bridge. This has done a good deal to ease central traffic. It has been opposed by residents' conservationist groups, and so has a newer plan to drive an expressway along the right bank of the Garonne, similar to the one in Paris: the familiar controversy over urban motorways is much the same as in Newcastle, but in this car-mad town, the planners are getting their way. When at last in 1983 or so the state completes its much-delayed national Bordeaux-Narbonne motorway, bypassing Toulouse, heavy through lorries will no longer clog up the city.

Serious efforts have at last been made in recent years to improve the traffic flow. Traffic-lights are regulated by a new computer system. In wider streets, lanes are reserved for buses. The public transport network has been overhauled, improved and extended, with new bus routes serving the outer suburbs, and passenger utilisation is slowly increasing again. New car-parks have been built; and parking-meters, long resisted on aesthetic grounds, have finally made their appearance. But the city council has never found the political courage – as the authorities have done in Bologna and, to an extent, Newcastle – to deter motorists from bringing their cars into the centre: it has even encouraged them, by making parking there much easier. Some 84,000 cars enter and leave the central area each weekday: "To limit them would be electorally disastrous," an official at the *mairie* told me. So the rush-hour jams by the bridges are still maddening, even if less so than ten years ago. Matters would be more tolerable if local drivers were more disciplined. Horns blare in chorus at the slightest hold-up, cars park illegally on pavements, blocking them to pedestrians, and the police are too lax about fines. People tend to jump lights, or turn without indicating. Even Parisians, whose traffic nerves are strong, can be shocked: I have heard tourists with Paris number-plates yelling "*espèce de paysan!*" at locals cutting across their path. France has one of the highest road-casualty rates in Europe, and Toulouse unsurprisingly is above the national average: some 70 deaths a year in the city.

Life may be at risk: but at least Toulousains are now becoming much more concerned about so-called urban "quality of life". This has been a marked trend in Giscard's France of the mid-'70s, and is backed by government policy. The heady years of expansion-for-its-own-sake created urban indigestion, but today the accent, as in so many Western cities, is on environmental improvement. Toulouse has had to make up a lot of lost ground. In the '50s it still had open drains in the streets, and the mess was cleared away only by rain. Bazergue installed a modern drainage system, and did a good deal to tidy up the town, though it still appears dirty compared with spruce Stuttgart or Bologna – especially when the notorious local winds send the litter whirling.

The drive now is for more green parks. Though the tiny central squares with their fountains and flower-beds are carefully looked after, Toulouse is less well served with larger green spaces than most big French towns (not that down-town Bologna or Newcastle do any better, when compared with Stuttgart's delightful Schlossgarten).

And as always in France, it is forbidden to loll on city lawns, even when these exist. Today, at any rate, four new leisure and sports zones are being created in the outskirts, covering 1,800 acres. And Baudis has finally begun to make some attractive use of the Garonne banks, hitherto neglected ("The city has always turned its back on its great river," is a local saying). In 1975 he created a large public garden and open-air theatre by the river, where in summer the council holds free concerts and ballet and folk spectacles – enchanting, on a warm night.

Toulouse is also following, hesitantly, the modern fashion for turning some streets into paved traffic-free walks for pedestrians. The prefect had wanted a little-used canal backwater near the station to be converted into a motor ringway: but Baudis vetoed the plan on environmental grounds, and the tree-lined canal has now been filled in, to be used as a promenade. In the centre, one or two busily commercial little streets near the Capitole have finally been banned to traffic, after years of opposition from shopkeepers who feared it would hit their trade. In the event, it has done nothing of the sort, and the traders are satisfied. However, the council goes prudently, for electoral reasons, and will not impose a pedestrian precinct on a street unless the shopkeepers agree. Not nearly enough has been done. While Bologna, Newcastle and Stuttgart have all of them recently banned private cars from their busiest shopping streets, Toulouse drags its feet, in thrall to the motor-car.

Finally, pollution: since most of the factories are cleanly modern, or out in the suburbs, the city does not suffer from polluted air, save in the vicinity of the smoke-belching state nitrogen plant. Yet there is one curious affliction that the council has never managed to cure: bird-shit. Every winter evening, thousands of starlings settle in the trees of the central squares and *boulevards,* attracted by the warmth and light. And these Hitchcockian terrorists spray their yellowish fertiliser on pavements, cars, clothes and hair. Dry-cleaners do a roaring trade, but petrol-stations under trees claim serious loss of business. Once a woman with her car inch-deep in the stuff went to a garage advertising a cheap, quick six-franc car-wash: "Sorry, Madame," said the owner, "that'll cost you twenty." The council has tried various methods of removing the birds, including a curious screeching *musique concrète* to scare them away. But they seemed to enjoy the sound. Poison has even been considered, but was thought likely to lose votes. Some older Toulousains believe that the birds are exacting nature's revenge for the wicked modernisation of the city.

5

Political squabbles in a lonely new suburbia

Does the Toulousain's strong emotional attachment to his town translate itself into an active civic spirit? Does he feel any day-to-day involvement in the work of the council he has elected? Not very often. In France, more than in Britain, a gulf separates rulers from ruled, and public opinion is passive. The government, once chosen, becomes "them", the resented authorities, while the citizen is a mere *administré:* he will grumble, and maybe publish formal protests *(prises de position),* but rarely does he feel he has the power to influence his rulers' actions, save to vote them out at the next election. This is true in national affairs and often in municipal ones too. Toulouse under Bazergue was a star case. The council made little effort to inform or convince people of its policies, it seldom held press conferences or public enquiries, and there was noticeably less of a regular civic dialogue than, say, in Newcastle. The council was isolated from the public, who in turn were passive. They would grumble, but rarely band together spontaneously for civic action.

Under Baudis there has been a certain change. Encouraged by the civic participation campaign of Hubert Dubedout, the go-ahead mayor of Grenoble, the new council set about trying to create a dialogue. Belatedly it appointed a city PRO and began to publish a newsletter. It set up a few local annexes, for dealing with routine matters and even holding public discussions (but without ward councils, as in Bologna). All this marked a modest step forward. But alas, in the politically polarised France of the mid-'70s, things soon became disrupted by politicisation. A number of *comités de quartier* (impromptu neighbourhood associations) sprang up around town, as in other French cities – partly a result of the 1968 spirit of contestation. But these were a far cry from the kindly community welfare bodies of Newcastle, or the orderly civic ward councils of Bologna. They were anti-*mairie* pressure-groups, mostly Left-wing. And Baudis threw the weight of his own new local infrastructure into countering their influence. Genuine community action degenerated into political dog-fighting.

Part of the trouble lay with the absurd and undemocratic French municipal electoral system prior to 1977. This was "winner-takes-all": the victorious party or coalition was allocated every seat and their opponents got none at all. In Bazergue's day, the ruling coalition at least covered a wide spectrum. But Baudis' team was homogeneously Right-of-centre, leaving the Parties of the Left unrepresented on the council. So they could hardly be blamed for channelling their opposition into other action. However, as from the 1977 elections, Toulouse and some other cities have returned to something nearer proportional representation, giving the Left opposition about a third of the seats. So, politically, the *comités de quartier* now have less *raison d'être.* But they are still active, and some of the residents' defence groups have achieved results, for good or ill. One of them has secured indefinite delay of the plan for a throughway beside the Garonne. On another occasion, in the new suburb of Rangueil, when the council announced plans for high-rise flats on a site previously scheduled to be a park, the inhabitants united, put barricades of tree-trunks across the road in the classic French style, and forced the council to back down. But, without any such specific target or strong Left-wing motivation, many other associations have withered away. A housewife told me of her efforts to start a civic action group in a poorer district: "The housing is new, and people hardly know each other. We decided to bring them together, just for human contact, and also so that jointly we could lobby the *mairie* to improve our services – we've no bus shelter, and no public 'phone box. We canvassed everyone, but only a handful turned up to our first meeting. We started an informal citizens' advice bureau, but it's hardly ever used. People seem suspicious, they want to deal with their own problems separately, they don't want alliances with neighbours." A familiar French phenomenon – and so unlike Tyneside.

In the old days, when Toulouse was smaller, the sense of civic or community loyalty was stronger. But it seems to have been diluted by the new immigrations, and disrupted by the changes in the town and the transfers from old to new districts. Older inhabitants feel the town has become amorphous; and few of the new ones yet feel involved. Almost all councillors and other local leaders are native Toulousains: the newly arrived élites have not yet entered local politics but remain in their own circles, academic or industrial, critical of the city but not yet ready or able to come out and grapple with it. Toulouse contrasts significantly with Grenoble, where the immigrants dominate and the social mutation has gone a stage farther. Debedout himself is a "new" Grenoblois, as are other councillors, and the fusion of populations has virtually taken place. A Toulousain said: "Grenoble has completed its revolution; we are still in bewildered transition."

The transition is patent not only in local politics but in day-to-day social life, at all levels. As suburbs grow and Toulouse ceases to be "the biggest village in France", so an old style of human contact, warm and friendly, if narrow in its horizons, is pressured aside. And people are forced to grope for a new one. It is the drama of many French cities, including Paris.* People move from their old friendly slums to big new estates where they know no one, and the adaptation is not made easier by the usual French wariness of neighbours. In Toulouse, where the past is so powerful and the present so perplexingly different, this is especially so.

Many older people regret the changes. One said to me, "In the old days, in the poorer quarters near the centre, we'd sit on chairs outside our front doors on fine evenings, knitting, chatting, calling across the street to each other. We all knew each other. But today there's too much traffic for that kind of life. Or the houses have been pulled down or turned into shops, and people have moved off to the new suburbs. Everyone's in a hurry nowadays – *on n'est plus heureux à Toulouse.*" Yet this intimate, informal style of life does persist in a few older districts. A teacher told me that in his narrow street, in the old city, the postman got to know him after two days, the baker's wife found time to chat with every customer, and life still had a friendly, gossipy, Pagnolesque village quality. In some squares, you still see groups of friends playing *pétanque* (a kind of *boules*) on Sunday mornings, as their forebears have for centuries. And in some older quarters, young people still hold *baloches* in the little squares – open-air "hops" with *bal musette* bands, and rows of coloured lights hanging from the trees. But these dances are slowly dying out, or transferring to the new suburbs where they go over to commercial "pop".

At least one Toulousain in three lives on a new housing estate, amid the usual French problems. During the worst of the housing shortage, the flats were put up with such haste that little forethought was given to

---

* *The New France,* Penguin, Harmondsworth, 1977, pages 335-53.

the provision of amenities, and many estates have only recently acquired the needed transport, schools, shops, or social centre. Yet even when cultural or other amenities are provided, do the inhabitants flock to them to forge a brave new community life? I visited Empalot, beside the Garonne, built in the 1950s and now with 10,000 inhabitants. The ranks of high-rise HLM blocks with austere concrete corridors were uninviting, and the flats were poky. But at least the estate was well kept up, with tidy lawns and roads. A hypermarket blazed its huge red neon sign into the twilight, turning the whitish façades of the nearest flats a Toulouse pink. Youths were playing with pin-tables (*"le baby-foot"*) in the drab utilitarian *café.* In the youth centre, a dance-hall had been decorated pleasantly in Canadian log-cabin style, and a few young people were milling around aimlessly. Notices advertised photo and drama clubs, PT classes, ski outings. But despite these signs of life, the young resident who showed me round was gloomy: "Despite the amenities provided, this suburb is really dead, it's too big and impersonal. In its early days, people would stroll up and down in the evening as in any southern town, but now they stay home and watch TV – that's killing what social life we had. People stay with their families, they don't care about making new friends. In summer they play *pétanque,* but that's about all, and at weekends they clear off in their cars to the country or seaside, leaving the place deserted. The clubs are badly attended: people are too individualistic. And this big suburb has only one *café.* Except in the centre of town, *café*-going is declining."

Empalot may be a bad example, for in one or two other suburbs, community life is a little more active. At Les Mazardes, a smallish and prosperous estate, partly middle-class, the HLM office has provided an impressive civic and cultural centre, with library, gymnasium, tennis-courts, photo-workshop. The night I called, the amateur drama society was rehearsing a Priestley play, the handsome marble-floored foyer was taken up with a modern sculpture exhibition, some men were playing billiards in one room, and the gym was full. I was told that the gym instructors gave their time free of charge, and so did the exhibition organisers – the kind of Anglo-Saxon style voluntary work that is rare in France unless politically motivated, as here it was not. Yet Les Mazardes has its problems. I found that the big room set aside as a youth club was locked and empty. Why? – "The youngsters wouldn't take responsibility for looking after the place themselves," said the centre's elderly president; "they let it get in a mess, they broke the ping-pong table, and we haven't the funds for a paid monitor. So we've had to close it."

It is the same in many French towns: the *maisons des jeunes* do not work, for these reasons. Most Toulouse youth clubs are run by the *mairie,* and many have run into trouble, either through hooliganism, or else for political reasons. At Empalot, the *maison des jeunes* first fell prey to a gang of hooligans who frightened more serious young people away, so that the carefully planned programme of lectures and film-shows was ill-attended. Then a defrocked Franciscan with Leftish views took charge of the place. He got rid of the trouble-makers, and started progressive discussion-groups on moral and social problems, such as free love and worker-management. These were a great success. But the council under Baudis soon decided that this Leftism in one of its own centres was dangerous. They tried to close it. There was a local outcry, and finally the *mairie* backed down – a rare example in Toulouse of successful spontaneous public action of this kind. Over at Bellefontaine, in Le Mirail, there has been similar trouble. Here the well-equipped new "socio-cultural centre" has appealed mainly to teenagers on the loose after school, whose parents do not want them home, or else to elderly card-players, two groups with time to kill and no place else to meet. When the centre's young staff *animateurs* tried to promote some more purposeful events of a cultural nature, such as showing "underground" films, the *mairie* reacted as at Empalot. In this case it won, and the staff kept quiet on pain of dismissal. In many parts of Toulouse, since Baudis came to power in 1971, there has been this running battle between local Leftish groups and a council determined to assert its own control. Yet these political squabbles are secondary to the wider problems of the new suburbs: the reluctance of the inhabitants to put down new roots and make new friends, or to take the initiative in improving their own environment. Adaptation to the new suburbia is more traumatic in Toulouse than in any of my other towns, and it may take another generation for the psychological mutation to be completed.

Even among the affluent *bourgeoisie* and professional classes, with their servants and elegant homes, and their supposedly wider horizons, social life has some of the same inhibitions. The men lead hectic working lives; but their leisure lives are noticeably more private and less gregarious than in either Newcastle or Bologna. This does not apply so much to the older local *bourgeoisie,* surrounded by relatives and close friends they have known for decades; but it is very true of the "new" Toulousains, who though now in the majority have not yet been fully accepted into the social life of the local establishment. This remains largely in the hands of the "old" Toulousains: few of the "new" ones are to be seen at Rotary or similar club meetings. The newcomers stick to their own little groups, by professions – university teachers in one circle, aeronautic engineers in another, and so on. A professor from Alsace told me: "We've lived here for some years, but have little contact with such party-going life as exists. How do I spend my time? Well, I have to go to Paris about once a week, where I see my real friends. Here in Toulouse, I spend the odd evening with university colleagues, but most of my free time is for my family, in this lovely old converted farmhouse." In fact the French of all classes, despite their loquacity and readiness to talk to strangers in trains or *cafés,* are socially much more reserved than Anglo-Saxons when it comes to making friends. They distinguish much more sharply between real friends (whom they will probably have known for many years) and mere acquaintances, who mean little to them. The Anglo-Saxon style of easy, chummy friendship they consider superficial and indiscriminate. So, arriving in a new town, even the most gregarious couple may spend years before they accept it, or are accepted by it, and thus many "new" Toulousains still feel in a kind of exile. In the old days, when France was a sedentary society and professional people seldom moved outside their native region, this problem was less common: today, with the new mobility caused by a modern economy, it is causing some traumas of adaptation.

People are often hospitable within their own little circle; but there is not much sense of a social limelight, save on a boring official level. It is hard to imagine here a magazine such as *Newcastle Life,* * full of glossy photos of hunts balls and garden fêtes, angled at readers avid for gossipy details of the latest social goings-on. In Toulouse, no one could care less: "society" is not like that. Lyon, Bordeaux, Nice and one or two other towns may have their party-going *milieux* that modestly parallel "*le tout-Paris*", the fashionable world of the capital: but not Toulouse. An older local family, titled or *bourgeois,* will sometimes throw a large party for its own kind, on an occasion such as a wedding. But apart from this, most big social functions are semi-official, with obligatory appearances by *Monsieur le Président* of this or that. And

* See page 228.

parties of the *vernissage* type tend to be stiff and boring, because people do not seem to know each other. Once I was invited to a large reception by the leading local publisher, Pierre Privat, to celebrate the opening of his splendid new bookshop. Hooray, I thought, at last I shall see *le tout-Toulouse* in all its glory. But what a let-down. There were hundreds of guests, not talking much, waiting around stiffly as if for something to happen. Most of them kept their overcoats on the whole time, which did not add to the sense of chic. Many wore dirty old raincoats. There were a number of priests – and in one corner a trio of nuns eagerly reading copies of *Astérix.* I was with a university couple who said they knew no one, nor did they try to meet anyone. Tables were laden with *canapés, petits-fours,* whisky, champagne, but no one touched any of it until the prefect arrived and he and Privat made formal speeches. Then everyone drank a dutiful glass or two, and went home. Not exactly swinging.

Yet in a private context these same people are often full of wit and warmth. The local *bourgeoisie* are not inhospitable to each other, nor indeed to an inquisitive intruder like myself, who comes from abroad and flatters them by showing an interest. At any rate, they flooded me with invitations to lunch or dinner-parties in their homes – the French reputation for not entertaining in their homes may be true of Parisians, but not of provincials – and the style was less formal than I might have expected. The old French tendency to entertain with high ceremony or not at all is on the decline in the provinces, where younger people especially will often issue a casual dinner invitation "*à la fortune du pot*". The dinner-parties I attended were most of them unpretentious and civilised affairs, with better conversation and better food than in Newcastle, and less sartorial snobbery and status-consciousness than in Bologna or Stuttgart. There were, it is true, some formalities by Anglo-Saxon standards: for example, my host and hostess would call me "*Monsieur*" unless they knew me quite well, and today I remain on surname terms with a number of Toulousains whom I consider friends. Younger people may be picking up the Christian-name habit under British or American influence, but among older ones it is rare – though far less rare than in Stuttgart. Women especially are the formal ones: I know two married couples in their forties, where the husbands are firm friends and use Christian names and *tu,* while the wives, though they know each other quite well, say *Madame* and *vous.* It is another aspect of French reserve towards new acquaintances. On the other hand, where ideas and opinions are concerned the French are anything but reserved, and I found that most Toulouse dinner-parties had an atmosphere of stimulating intellectual outspokenness.

One party was in the home of a successful doctor and his wife, daughter of a leading local industrialist: moneyed people, with a lovely old mansion near the cathedral, but not pretentious – their daughter of ten helped serve the meal. The usual ritual was observed: aperitifs including the finest Scotch whiskies (*de rigueur* in every French *bourgeois* home), then an excellent five-course meal, followed by coffee and a good selection of local Armagnacs. My host shared the Toulouse passion for local history and proudly showed me his ancient maps of the city, hung on his walls. The other guests were three middle-aged couples, mostly in business, and conversation was serious: for instance, about how to improve housing conditions or allow workers more say in running factories. They struck me as thoughtful liberals with social consciences, maybe sheltering a shade too complacently behind their money and comfort, yet concerned with France's problems.

Another dinner-party in a rich doctor's home showed me a less pleasant side of the *haute bourgeoisie.* The food was delectable, including *confit d'oie*; the conversation less so. One guest was a senior technocrat from a local factory, assertive and arrogant, guffawing at his own bad jokes with loud horse-laughs, viciously anti-American (though his vulgarity seemed American in style). Another guest, a young doctor, treated us to a succession of anti-Arab stories and extreme-Right opinions ("De Gaulle was a Communist"), talking fast in a rasping Midi accent. He poured forth an egotistical, irrational patter of anecdotes and absurd prejudices – sometimes funny, often hard for an outsider to follow – of a kind I was quite used to in Toulouse. My host and hostess seemed to find him terribly amusing. And while the maid served the meal, the party swapped obscene jokes as if she were not present – a vulgarity common in the English provinces, but rare in France where the *bourgeoisie* enjoys its smut but *pas devant les domestiques.* Buñuel would have relished such indiscreet charmlessness.

At the first party, conversation had turned to the gulf between "new" and "old" Toulouse. My hostess told me that not all the "old" Toulousains wanted to exclude the newcomers; in fact, she and some of her women friends were making efforts to welcome them and help them to integrate. Following the lead of Lyon and some other towns, they had created a voluntary body, "*Toulouse Accueil*": "Firms give us the names and addresses of new arrivals, and we then write a personal letter to each of their wives, inviting them to join us – we hold lectures, socials, bridge-parties, tours of old Toulouse. Few working-class wives reply – maybe the bridge-parties put them off – but we get some response from the wives of *cadres* in industry and the civil service. We wish we could call on the newcomers in their homes, as you would in Britain, but such an 'invasion of privacy' is not possible in France. But the town council has lent us premises, and we do feel we are answering a human need. When we started the work, we were amazed and shocked at the number of cases of extreme loneliness and distress among newly arrived wives. Their husbands had their jobs, but the women were bored and seemed to have no idea how to make new friends." One guest then added that the local Samaritans, known here as *"SOS Amitié"*, were inundated with suicidal distress calls, often due to loneliness. So much for the sociable French.

Day-to-day community action and participatory democracy might be richer and fuller, if only the local press, television and broadcasting were to make a more vital contribution. But they are uninspiring, more so than in most of my other towns. To be fair, local television is at least a good deal less awful than a few years ago. Regional TV made a very late start in France, and until the early '70s Toulouse's embryonic studios were no more than a minor outpost of the much-criticised state-run networks, putting out a few feeble local programmes. But since 1974 French TV has been partially liberalised: one of the three main networks is now run on a regional basis, and the Toulouse station is one of its key production centres. It has decent modern studios and serves a wide slice of southern France. It puts out a nightly magazine programme for its own region, plus a number of longer documentaries each year, some of which are nationally networked. In theory it has a good deal of autonomy, but in practice it is subject to all kinds of local political pressures, and the editorial and production staff – few of them of high calibre – tend to fight shy of controversy. A typical news-magazine might be made up of such items as an exhibition of playing cards, a trip down local canals, an amateur jazz group, some shots of goats, an interview with a local festival director, and a long boring account of the umpteenth visit of Paris journalists to Aérospatiale. There is a lot of live rugby and *bel canto,* but few hard-hitting local political interviews. It is true that, since the 1974 reforms, some producers have begun to tackle more delicate issues, such as union/employer relations, or the role of the prefect in dealing with local councils. Toulouse's television is certainly more lively and competent than five or six years ago, and gone are the days when a telephone call from a Ministry could cancel a programme. But habits of prudent self-censorship linger. And the station is entirely dependent on funding and ultimate control from Paris. It has none of the organic links with its own region that are found in Stuttgart or Ljubljana, or to an extent in Newcastle.

Toulouse's one daily newspaper, *La Dépêche du Midi,* at least has its roots deep in its region and is locally owned and run. It used to be one of the great provincial dailies of Europe, almost a *Manchester Guardian*: today, though still prosperous, it has lost its influence and seems little more than a fusty relic of the Third and Fourth Republics, a venerable but cobwebby institution, typical of the city's nostalgia for its past. For a hundred years it was a major force behind the Radical Party, powerful supporter of its leaders from Clemenceau to Mendès-France, and a key element in Toulouse's reputation as a bastion of the Left. Before the War, so fierce was its anti-clericalism that it was actually excommunicated, some priests would refuse its readers the sacraments, and as recently as the 1960s in some villages old women would throw stones at its vans, shouting "Clear off, Bolsheviks!" In the war, so strong was its opposition to Vichy that one of its editors was killed by the militia and others were deported. Then, under the Fourth Republic, it would make and unmake the Radical-led governments of Bourgés-Manoury and others, so that its owner, the mighty Jean Baylet, became known as a kingmaker – "*El Glaoui* of the South-West". He hated de Gaulle so much that he would even write pro-American or pro-*Algérie Française* editorials just to annoy him; and such a thorn in their side did the Gaullists find his paper that they made efforts to buy it up or launch a rival to sink it. But they never succeeded.

After Baylet's death in a car crash in 1959, his widow courageously took over. But she has not proved an inspired manager, and the paper has steadily lost influence. One factor has been the serious decline and split in the Radical Party itself, which of course has affected *La Dépêche* too. Another, paradoxically, has been the paper's rise in sales. Like other big French provincial morning dailies, it has gone from strength to strength since the war, widening its sales area and killing off or absorbing little local competitors, to the point where it now has a virtual monopoly in the Midi-Pyrénées, with 20 local editions and sales of about 300,000 – high for France. It has held the Paris press at bay, too. For in France, as in Germany, there is virtually no big-selling national Press on the English model: *Le Monde* sells a mere 3,000 copies in Toulouse. Big popular papers are regional. But *La Dépêche*'s monopoly has editorial drawbacks, for it makes it feel obliged to appeal to all readers, of all tastes, and not offend them. It has even begun to publish religious news and articles! Evelyne Baylet, a severe-looking schoolmistressly lady in thin steel-rimmed spectacles, told me she was convinced that local news, not politics, sold her paper. *La Dépêche* does still carry rather more foreign and national news than most provincial dailies, and often has long, erudite articles on local history, which are popular. But its sales *forte* is local tittle-tattle – flower-shows, Rotary dinners, local worthies' speeches reported in full, and minor accidents – what the French call "*chiens écrasés*". A teacher told me: "My maid reads the paper avidly for news of her village. I just read *Le Monde.*"

Until today, the paper has been edited and printed at gloomily shabby offices unaltered since 1900, a monument to Third Republic fustiness – "We're nostalgic about this dear old building, we want to keep it just as it is," said Mme Baylet. Over the front entrance, a pre-war plaque reads, "*Pour une France renouvellée!*" France has since renewed itself, without waiting for *La Dépêche.* However, the unmerry widow is now retiring, and the paper moved in 1978 to modern premises at Le Mirail – will this give it a new lease of life? Its great weakness at the moment, editorially, is that it fails to take any strong line on local issues, just like the dailies in Newcastle andBologna. Being still more-or-less Left-wing, it dislikes the Baudis régime, but will not come out with this openly, for it dare not make enemies of the local establishment. It reports municipal affairs in tones of dull neutrality, and will rarely conduct searching enquiries into local problems. Even more than the local television programmes, it shuns controversy. And so its columns do little to encourage Toulousains to take a more eager or active part in civic matters.

6

Multi-million-pound opera, and Marxist Shakespeare

An average spring evening . . .. an American chamber group is playing Mozart in the floodlit courtyard of a pink Renaissance palace, the *cinémathèque* is showing Eisenstein, Verdi is at the opera house and Sartre at the civic repertory theatre, while the *Centre Culturel* has a "trad" jazz concert and a modern sculpture exhibition. . . . Whatever the limitations of their neighbourly social life, Toulousains in some sense make up for it by being dedicated culture-goers, and culturally this city is today one of the three or four liveliest in the French provinces. Despite some failures and ups-and-downs, the all-the-year-round diversity is stimulating, from classical to *avant-garde*.

It used not to be so. For many decades, Toulouse like other towns suffered from the cultural stranglehold of Paris, which sucked the provinces dry of most of their talent and activity. Almost any ambitious creative artist, in any field, would make for the limelight of the capital, and only in opera was Toulouse able to hold something of its own. But since the 1950s, the tide has been slowly turning. The cultural revival of the provinces has been a general French trend, and Toulouse exemplifies it. The arrival of the new élites and the rise in student numbers have vastly increased the potential audience, while the growth of prosperity – at least till recently – has made new funds available. It is true that Paris still exerts its lure. Much of the best culture on offer in Toulouse is still imported from Paris or elsewhere rather than being home-grown, and the local product is not always of high quality. But, increasingly, talented creators are prepared to make their careers here, rather than move to Paris. In music, for instance, Michel Plasson and Georges Auriacombe have built a world-wide reputation based on Toulouse.

During an average month in season you may find some twenty to thirty different art exhibitions, a dozen or so concerts, eight or ten theatre and opera productions, scores of films in the cine-clubs, and so on. It is a diversity that compares honourably with most of my other towns. As in Stuttgart or Ljubljana, most of the culture is officially organised or sponsored, and whether classical or modern it is considerably more highbrow than in Newcastle: not much attempt is made to cater for the less educated. But, as in many other European cities, the public is tending to polarise: on the one hand, an older middle-class audience wanting the known classics; on the other, a new generation, mostly students, searching for the new, the experimental, maybe the politically provocative. In a provincial city such as this, some cultural bodies have trouble trying to cater for both tastes, which can lead to tensions, as it has in Stuttgart.

The city council spends generously on the arts, far more so than any British town. Of its total 1977 budget, it devoted 7.7 per cent or 75 million francs to culture, a figure as high per capita as in Stuttgart (46m DM, or 99m francs), a larger and wealthier town. As is the rule in France, theatre, music, museums and some other arts are subsidised jointly by state and city, with the latter paying the larger share: thus in 1977 the opera house and its regular company received 3 million francs from the state, a mere 2.3 million from box-office takings, and the balance of its deficit – 17.3 million! – from the city. For the regional orchestra, box-office brought in 763,000 francs, the state contributed 2.3 million francs, leaving the council to make up the balance of 3.1 million. These are astonishing figures, especially when you consider that the opera plays to 98 per cent capacity. Some councillors may themselves be philistine, but their pride in their city is such that they are glad to spend millions on keeping its cultural renown alive (in the Middle Ages, was it not one of the great artistic centres of Europe, "*Toulouse la Palladienne*"?). Of course the odd voice is raised today that the funds could be better devoted to new schools or hospitals; but generally speaking, as in Stuttgart, the spending of ratepayers' money on the arts is not the electoral suicide that it can be in Britain.

The lavish investment in music seems to be paying off, for the city's once-so-glorious operatic tradition is now reviving, after a period of decadence. One of Toulouse's dearest *idées reçues* about itself is that it is among the great operatic capitals of Europe, the citadel of what is called locally "*le bel canto*". And so until 1914 it more-or-less was. Many leading singers would come to the opera house – the ornate Théâtre du Capitole, in the same palace as the town hall – where local high society in evening dress would throng to hear them. But, as in other big French cities, two world wars helped to spell decline. In the 1960s the opera house was still gamely trying to keep up the old ceremonial standards as if time had stood still: heavy Victorian fittings with plush red carpets, and a fleet of elderly ushers in white-tie-and-tails even for a *matinée* on a sweating summer Sunday. The quality of productions was fair-to-middling; audiences were mostly middle-aged, and not very large.

In 1974 the council handed over management of the opera house to Michel Plasson, the gifted young Parisian who was already conductor of its orchestra. He was given a hugely increased budget, while some 10 million francs were spent on modernisation. As was hoped, Plasson has managed to improve quality quite considerably, and has attracted new and younger audiences so that performances are almost always packed out. His *corps de ballet* of 30 remains poor, but his permanent chorus is adequate, and his 80-man orchestra, which he still conducts, is excellent. Directors and lead singers are hired from Paris or abroad, while in order to reduce costs, many productions are staged jointly with the Bordeaux company, who provide costumes and stage sets. The repertoire is centred on the classics which correspond to popular taste – Verdi, Puccini, Bizet, Berlioz (Plasson's own favourite), occasional Mozart – but with sorties into modern opera. And Plasson insists that works be sung in the original language: the chorus even managed a passable darkie accent for *Porgy and Bess* in English. Plasson is a difficult, arrogant man; but by raising standards, and attracting the attention of the Paris critics for so doing, he has made himself into a local hero. Toulousains feel he has given them back their *bel canto.* When he took his company to perform *La Traviata* at the Opéra Comique in Paris, and *Romeo and Juliet* in Verona, thousands of local fans went with him – by hired coach and charter flight – so as to sit in the stalls and cheer him on! "The company's being treated like a football team, a focus of local patriotism," said one sceptic. Even Stuttgart's ballet fans do not go to quite such lengths.

This euphoria does not mean that Le Capitole has suddenly become La Scala or the Met. The productions I saw were of decent provincial standard, no more – better than Bologna if not quite equal to Stuttgart. The Toulouse company now ranks as one of the two or three best in the French provinces, and at least France is trying seriously to keep opera alive outside Paris: nine cities have active opera houses with permanent companies, whereas English opera thrives in few places outside the London area. In orchestral and chamber music too,

Toulouse as much as any French town has been the scene of a renaissance of public interest – in a France that Malraux once wrote off as "not a musical nation". The great classics used to be performed here only intermittently: but recently a former market, the *Halle aux Grains,* has been converted into a large concert hall where Plasson's orchestra regularly plays Bach, Beethoven, Stravinsky, etc., to crowded audiences of mainly young people. Another innovation is a summer outdoor festival, with concerts in parks or floodlit courtyards. And Toulouse's famous chamber orchestra is still regarded as one of Europe's best, though its quality has dropped a little since its founder, the great Georges Auriacombe, was forced by illness to retire. Both he and Plasson have done a lot to educate local taste, which suffers from the disgraceful neglect of music teaching in French schools. The one advantage of this *lacuna* is, arguably, that as young people have little grounding in classical music they are thereby more open to modern atonal or polyphonic music. At any rate, audiences for contemporary music are larger and more enthusiastic than in my other towns. Plasson's concerts of Hindemith, Berg, Webern and others have been popular, while Xenakis and Messiaen have been eagerly received on their visits in person.

Theatre in Toulouse has suffered from fluctuating fortunes just as much as opera. In every town in this book, civic repertory theatre has been the centre of a storm, usually because a Leftist or *avant-garde* company has clashed with its cautious council sponsors, worried about conventional theatre-goers' reactions – and nowhere more so than in Toulouse, which presents a microcosm of the triumphs and tribulations of post-war French provincial theatre. By 1939, provincial drama was almost dead, killed by the slump, the cinema, the motor-car: in Toulouse, of the five theatres active in 1900, only the opera house remained open. But then, after 1945, a number of young actor/managers in various towns courageously decided to forgo the bright lights of the Paris boulevards and devote their talents to reviving provincial theatre. Encouraged by generous government subsidies, they succeeded remarkably in a number of places, so that today scores of theatres throughout France are playing to new audiences. The best-known pioneer of this movement has been Roger Planchon, in the Lyon suburb of Villeurbanne: but close behind him ranks the provocative Maurice Sarrazin, in Toulouse. Not the most modest of men, he told me: "It was I who started the trend, before Planchon, in 1945 when I was only twenty. I was born here, and at first like others I thought that Paris was the only place for an actor. But there were ten thousand of us out of work there then, so I came back here, formed a troupe, and decided to prove that serious creative work of Parisian standard could be possible in the provinces, provided new popular audiences could be found." And he succeeded. Many of his early productions of Shakespeare, Brecht, etc., were brilliant, and gradually he built up a new regular audience, mostly students. A Left-wing idealist, he also tried hard to attract workers, and like Planchon he would send groups of actors round works canteens or schools in popular districts, to explain theatre to people who had never seen it. The working-class share of his audience never rose above 7 or 8 per cent, but this was probably better than similar more recent efforts in Newcastle and Stuttgart.

For many years, state and city smiled upon his work, despite his Leftism. The city in 1963 even built him a new theatre, the Daniel Serano. And under Malraux' reign as Minister of Culture, Sarrazin was one of several Left-wing producers in France who benefited from his liberalism, continuing to receive large state grants despite their blatant anti-Gaullism. But in the later 1960s relations with the council deteriorated: Bazergue and others accused Sarrazin of wilful provocation, of filling his repertoire with plays by modern Leftists such as Armand Gatti, and thus alienating decent *bourgeois* audiences (and embarrassing the mayor electorally). Bazergue pointed out, not unreasonably, that Sarrazin was entitled to his political views, but that as his was the only regular drama company in town, and publicly subsidised, he ought to restrain his bias and cater for all tastes. And when Sarrazin began tampering with the classics, civic tempers rose higher: he produced a "*Hamlet gauchiste*", altering some scenes so as to give the hero's revenge a political edge, and introducing an angry crowd of Danes as a Brechtian chorus of revolutionaries. Soon after this came the watershed of May 1968 whose backlash toppled so many radical producers in France, including Barrault in Paris, and Bazergue at this point lost patience and threw Sarrazin and his company out of the civic theatre. But this action boomeranged, for a large part of Sarrazin's young regular audience proved so faithful to him that they virtually boycotted the second-rate touring productions that the council found to fill its theatre in his place. The Daniel Serano became more than half empty. For the next few years there was stalemate, with Sarrazin refusing to leave his beloved Toulouse and staging modest productions in makeshift premises. Finally in 1974 he reached a compromise with Baudis, whereby he could use the civic theatre for two months a year, provided he behaved himself. And that is roughly the situation today. It has been a saga entirely typical of the political battles that flare up over theatre in France: in Caen, Bourges, St-Etienne and other towns, Leftist directors have suffered similar fates to Sarrazin's, or worse. And whereas in civic theatre disputes of this kind in Britain, the director is usually accused of being too highbrow, in France his alleged crime tends to be Leftism.

Sarrazin is now ageing and calming down. He will still stage the occasional experiment – for instance, a *gauchiste* version of *Julius Caesar* with Mark Antony as a Marxist ("Comrades, Romans, fellow-fighters in the glorious struggle of the proletariat"), and a "structuralist" *Don Juan* (Molière) which *lycéens* went dutifully to see as it was a set play for the *bac,* but came away bewildered. However, most of his productions nowadays are more conventional, with himself in all the main roles. He is on good terms with the municipality and has faithful audiences, even though artistically he is well past his prime. On the insistence of the Ministry, Sarrazin recently had a co-director foisted on him: Bruno Bayen, a gifted young Parisian intellectual with a taste for reflective, highbrow plays with a social "message", staged with the minimum of décor. He and Sarrazin fell out, and their company was virtually split into two. It was an ironical situation: the ageing *prima donna*-like autocrat, tamed now and complacent, his truce made with the *bourgeoisie,* found himself politically and artistically up-staged by the kind of pioneering radical he was himself a generation ago. In 1978, Bayen, fed up, left Toulouse.

The theatre scene is quite lively and diverse. In addition to the "serious" plays at the Daniel Serano, the Capitole itself when it is not staging opera is used to house touring *boulevard* comedies of the André Roussin type: these generally do good box-office with conventional audiences, so long as there is a star name or two in the cast. And on the fringe, one or two small experimental theatre troupes struggle along in make-shift premises, shored up by modest Ministry grants. They are more intellectual, less populist, than the parallel groups in Newcastle; but at least they mark an attempt at spontaneous, do-it-yourself cultural activity, rather than reliance on official spoon-feeding.

As in Stuttgart, however, the prevailing philosophy is that culture is a civic responsibility, and people of all views work together under this civic umbrella: the curator of the leading museum, for instance, is a well-known Communist. Despite the individualistic local temperament, there is very little in the way of an autonomous counter-culture. People expect culture to be officially organised, and the only point of controversy is over the role of the state. Here, Toulouse's answer is clear: as far as it has the funds, it wants to do things itself. When in the early 1960s André Malraux proposed that towns should join with his Ministry in partnership for building multi-purpose arts centres – the famous *Maisons de la Culture* – this city refused, characteristically. Instead, it went ahead and built its own modest *Centre Culturel.* And the result has been a reasonable success, at least compared to many of the larger *Maisons de la Culture,* which have proved over-expensive cathedral-like monuments to Gaullist *folie de grandeur.* Toulouse's little centre, in a quiet street near the cathedral, is on a more human and inviting scale, better suited to its purpose, and its varied activities are mostly well attended, while its annual subsidy of about a million francs is easily within the city's means. A compact suite of rooms includes small theatre, library, bar, exhibition hall. Here there are low-budget drama productions, classical films, weekly chamber concerts or recitals, and frequent art exhibitions: one recent monthly programme included a season of films by Pabst, a modern Japanese sculpture display, a new American play, and three concerts – by a Japanese baritone, a Parisian chamber quartet playing Schönberg, and a violinist from Paris playing Mozart and Bartok. Inevitably, much of the material is what is available on tour from Paris, but some productions are local – I saw an excellent double-bill of Schisgal's *The Tiger* and Albee's *Zoo Story* played by local actors. The programmes, though variable, maintain a fairly high average of professional quality; and the centre does seem to have disproved the scornful forecasts of Parisian critics that, locally run without Ministerial supervision, it would fall far below the *Maisons de la Culture* in its standards.

Moreover, the programme policy is noticeably more highbrow than it would be in a comparable British provincial arts centre. This is to be expected in France: but does it really correspond to French public taste? The director until 1971, Christian Schmidt, was a gentlemanly autocrat from Strasbourg who believed passionately in modern art and music, did a great deal to introduce them to Toulouse, and to his credit persuaded the city fathers to give him a free hand with this ambitious *avant-garde* policy. This mandarin felt that he had a sense of mission to introduce the true secrets of art to a fortunate populace, without consulting them, and he ran his centre rather like a school under a strict headmaster. Since his departure, the centre is now managed in a somewhat more easy-going and less highbrow vein by a culture-minded city councillor – but the spoon-feeding still goes on. The French, like the Germans, are quite used to accepting this. It springs from their education. Attitudes to culture may not be quite as reverential as in Stuttgart, yet they are closer to this than to the English ethos, found especially on Tyneside, where culture approximates to jolly entertainment. Of course, in so large a university town there is a sizeable audience for a relatively highbrow diet, large enough to provide the *Centre Culturel* and other local activities with a steady following. Yet, as in Stuttgart, there are grumblings on the Left against the concept of a "temple" culture. Complaints have been growing that this élitist or *bourgeois* definition of culture requires so high a level of education that it deters the vast majority – and of the centre's 20,000 subscribing members, only some 2 per cent are from the working class.

The French have the reputation of being a highly cultured people. Certainly they are culture-goers, as we see in Toulouse, and in the case of younger people the enthusiasm is patently sincere. Yet the gulf between this minority, educated into cultural values, and the vast mass of early school-leavers from poorer homes is as wide as in any European country. Though their methods may not be those used on Tyneside, several Left-wing idealists have been trying to break down these barriers and coax the masses into the temples. Sarrazin tried it in his earlier days. And Denis Milhau, the charming Communist who runs the leading civic museum, the Augustins, told me of his more recent efforts: "During a Picasso exhibition here, I invited the works committees of some local factories to organise visits. It was a success: we expected 250 and 1,000 turned up. The workers entered the place timidly as if it were a church, but then they began asking really critical questions about Picasso – they were far more frank and direct than my *bourgeois* public, who approach a genius such as Picasso with abject veneration, whether they really like him or not. It was strange – the workers seemed to want to be assured first that there were no *bourgeois* lurking about who might laugh at them and speak a different, educated language: but once I'd put them at their ease, they were very outspoken. They criticised Picasso for 'mocking' the public with his distortions. And they launched into me for evangelically trying to dispense divine wisdom – they accused me of betraying my own ideals by showing works that appealed just to an élite. So I feel in the same dilemma as, say, Sartre – how at the same time do you pursue difficult intellectual truth *and* be at one with the proletariat?" It is the dilemma I found also on Tyneside: do you try to "enlighten" the masses? Or do you go humbly to speak to them in their terms, creating a new, non-intellectual, populist art?

Modern art is not the strongest feature of the town's cultural life. The council occasionally buys contemporary paintings, for housing in the Augustins museum (alongside the treasured Delacroix and Toulouse-Lautrecs). And once or twice it has dared to stage open-air shows of *avant-garde* French sculpture, by César and others. But the dozen or so private art galleries in town tend to be as ephemeral as discothèques, for they have to struggle against odds to make a living: they are handicapped by the general decline in modern French painting, giving them little good material to offer. And serious collectors of modern art are very few: "I sell only about fifteen modern paintings a year," the owner of one of the better galleries told me; "so I'm forced to do most of my trade in pottery and ornaments. Toulouse is isolated from the main art-world circuits and is years behind the times. The fashionable French artists and dealers, all in Paris or Provence, refuse to exhibit in a town like this – can you blame them?"

Yet if we turn to another visual art, the cinema, we find a brighter picture. The commercial cinemas, it is true, are entirely undistinguished: for a mass public they show the expected Hollywood product (dubbed) and routine new French films, with a strong dosage of porn. But Toulouse also has the best *cinémathèque* in the provinces (remarkably, a private venture), as well as several cine-clubs and one cinema showing "serious" films subtitled. Between them these outlets provide a fuller range of good films, old and new, French and foreign, than is found in any of my other towns. And they get good audiences, for the educated French have a strong cinema culture and (unlike most British and Germans) they take film as seriously as any other art.

I wish I could be as enthusiastic about the municipal library system, which as usual in France is far from adequate. It is a strange lapse, on the part of a city council that takes its other cultural duties so seriously. The central lending library is gloomily old-fashioned, run on bureaucratic lines by elderly females; some of the newer branches in the suburbs are more attractive, but very small. Shelf access is limited, most books are stored away, and borrowing figures are far below Newcastle or Stuttgart levels. In fact, things are little better than in Bologna. And yet – as in the rest of France – though public libraries are poor by British standards (or even German ones), bookshops by contrast are far better and more numerous. Is it that the French, lacking good libraries, have little option but to go out and buy a book when they want one? Or is it another aspect of French unneighbourliness, that they shy away from anything as communal as sharing a used book with strangers and must have their own copy? I suspect a bit of both. Anyway, Toulouse has as many as fifty bookshops, mostly small but a few large and modern. The recently extended Privat bookstore is the largest in southern France and far better than any I know in the English provinces: with its spacious open-plan lay-out on three floors, photocopier, hot drinks dispenser, and piped classical music, it has more the atmosphere of a modern fashion boutique than of a traditional bookshop, and the lively young staff actually seem to know and care about what they are selling. Poetry and books in foreign languages do well. The ambience and facilities are vastly superior to those of the public library: in Newcastle, vice-versa.

Of course there are plenty of serious *literati* in this town, and a scattering of creative writers and artists. But even more than in Stuttgart they remain isolated from each other, perhaps deliberately: when an attempt was made to develop a well-known *café* near the Capitole as a meeting-place for artists and writers, it failed through lack of response. Outside strictly university circles, there is no creative intellectual social *milieu* here, in the Paris Left Bank sense, or corresponding to what I found in Ljubljana or even Newcastle. It is true that vestiges remain of an elegant literary tradition, claiming lineage back to the troubadours: an ancient local society, the *Académie des Jeux Floraux,* co-opts members in the manner of the *Académie Française* and meets ritually to discuss *belles-lettres* in a beautiful mansion, the Hôtel d'Assézat. But these ageing historians and poets are pursuing themes far removed from modern concerns, and their fusty gatherings merely reflect the more negative and narcissistic side of Toulousain nostalgia.

In fact, when we turn from the lively scene of the performing arts to the world of solitary creation – writers, artists, composers – we find that nothing much seems to be happening in Toulouse. The few local painters are unremarkable: the better ones prefer to go off and live in Paris or Provence, where they feel less isolated. The same applies to many writers, for whom the lure of life in the capital is far stronger than it is in Britain. Possibly the future may lie with a revival of the Occitan tradition. Dotted around the region are a few capable novelists and historical writers – Kléber Haedens, José Cabanis and René Mauriès spring to mind – who deal with local themes and in some cases are writing in the ancient *langue d'oc* which has given its name to this part of France. And if Toulouse is to become again a centre of creativity, as it was in troubadour days, then it must probably build round this tradition, in order to distinguish itself from Paris. In the performing arts, it has staged a splèndid revival and broken the stranglehold of Paris. But a culture with genuine regional roots and flavour remains to be developed. So what is the future for Occitania, for Languedoc? – a theme to be examined at the end of this chapter.

7

From cassoulet *to "drugstores"*

In their daily lives, at work and leisure, Toulousains are struggling to reconcile the traditional French ways with a newer, more international style of consumer living. Are the evenings still for long, leisurely talkative meals, or for a quick snack followed by thrillers and quiz-games on television? Does an employee still make his way home every noon for the ritual family lunch, despite commuter problems that make this habit ever less realistic? – or will he opt for the canteen? Does his wife hold out for fresh farm produce, or stock up with tins and frozen packets from the new hypermarket down the road? In these and many other ways, Toulousains are torn between old and new.

Their living standards rose steadily in the 1945-75 period, especially in housing. Twenty or so years ago, the average family ate well and knew how to enjoy itself, but accepted a low level of home comfort. In 1954, only 44 per cent of homes had inside flushing lavatories and a mere 11.4 per cent had bath or shower. This latter figure has now risen to well over 50 per cent, since for some years all new homes have been built with modern plumbing. But most lower-income flats are still equipped with no more than a shower or hip-bath, and their living-rooms are very small: despite the improvement, Toulousains remain noticeably less comfortably housed than Swabians, or even Geordies. Yet they manage to fill up their cramped little dwellings with every kind of modern gadget – levels of ownership of washing-machines and refrigerators are higher than in Britain. Toulousains are finally becoming more house-proud, and their patterns of domestic budgeting are gradually moving closer to those of northern Europe with a relative decline in the high percentage devoted to food and entertainment.

It was claimed to me by Dr Brouat that the true Toulousain disdains hard work and lives for his pleasures, but I think that today this is only partially true. Much of the city's working life has become infected by the new work mania of the French, imported here by the newcomers, notably the Parisian executives and the energetic *pieds noirs. Cadres* and businessmen work with more eagerness and dynamism than in Newcastle, and for longer hours, often staying at their desks till 7 or 8 at night: if they were better at teamwork, the results might reach Swabian levels.

One management consultant told me that he and all his staff work from 8 a.m. to 7 p.m., though this does include the two-hour lunch break that is still the norm in Toulouse despite its growing impracticability. "Many of us," he said, "would like to move over to the Anglo-Saxon short break and go home an hour earlier in the evening. But this would be hard to adopt unless other firms did the same: many of my clients do their busiest work after six and expect me to be here at the end of the 'phone." Most shops, banks, offices, hairdressers, still close from 12 till 2 – "By staggering my staff, I could easily stay open," said the owner of one big store, "but there's not the public demand for it. My customers are not used to shopping at midday, they expect to be home eating a big lunch." This is still the main meal of the day for most families. Schoolchildren as well as their fathers go home for it, even though the growth of the city is making it less convenient: as people move out to new suburbs, they may have to spend half their two-hour lunch break on travel, and rush-hour traffic-jams occur four times a day. In Paris and many northern French cities, there has been a steady move towards the Anglo-Saxon system, which the French call "*la journée continue*": but Toulouse, conservative in so many things, has been slow to follow this trend, and only in the past few years have some larger stores and banks begun to remain open over lunchtime. On the other hand, supermarkets stay open till 8 p.m., often later, whereas in Newcastle they close at 5.30 or 6. This English practice is also tiresome, though in a town of commuter proportions it seems more logical.

Since they stay at work so late, Toulousains set less stress than

Geordies or Swabians on evening leisure activities during the week. They have few hobbies, they are not great club-joiners. But they live for their weekends and their holidays - the French take the longest holidays in Europe. Most families now own a car, and their first aim at the weekend, summer or winter, is to get out of town, for Toulousains adapt little better than Parisians to the new tensions of urban living, and they feel an urgent need to regain contact with nature. Since many are ex-peasants, or the children of peasants, at weekends they go to relatives in the country, or else they retain the old family farmstead for use as a weekend and holiday cottage. People of all classes, including workers, spend money on buying some little rural *résidence secondaire*. Or else they go walking or skiing in the Pyrenees, or for trips to the Mediterranean or Atlantic. And the vast traffic-jams on the roads into Toulouse every Sunday evening bear witness to a weekly migration that is largely responsible for the dearth of social and community life in the city. In the old days, before mass car ownership, most Toulousains were forced to rely on each others' company at weekends: the new mobility has encouraged privacy, hence unsociability. In addition, the average family takes at least four or five weeks' holiday a year, and in the wealthier classes it may be much more. They go to the sea or their country cottage, or they tour abroad, mostly to nearby Spain.

Toulousains spend more time on outdoor sports than most Europeans. All classes go hunting, shooting and fishing on their country weekends; in town, they play tennis or *pelote* (a kind of outdoor fives or squash, Basque in origin) or, above all, *boules*. So popular are sports that the city council has recently built four large new recreation centres in the outskirts, complete with lakes for boating, swimming-pools and playing-fields. The latter are essentially for rugby, which was imported here by the English in the last century and is today more popular than association football throughout the south-west. In Toulouse, rugby is a proud tradition almost on a par with *bel canto* and *cassoulet*: the town has 30 teams, two of them of international class. One of these, the Stade Toulousain, has seven times won the French national championship. When it plays at home to one of its major rivals, such as Bordeaux, the crowd gets almost as excited as Newcastle soccer fans when their team is at home to Liverpool.

An important part of local leisure is good eating, as much as in Bologna and far more than in my other towns. Toulousains may care less for gastronomy than in former days, yet the tradition remains in their bones: they eat well as a matter of course, without thinking twice, and with the innate good taste that a Bolognese, for instance, shows over dress or a Stuttgarter over music. A housewife will spend time and care on choosing just the right cut of meat, or cheeses of perfect ripeness, or the correct fresh vegetable to go with a certain dish, and even an ordinary weekday family lunch is a carefully planned affair. A middle-class family might start with some neat array of *hors d'oeuvres* including *crudités* and *terrine* of duck, then go on to garlicky roast leg of lamb with properly-dressed salad, followed by a cheese tray including the local Roquefort, then a home-made *clafoutis* (a kind of sweet Yorkshire pudding filled with cherries), a regional speciality. Wines are also likely to be local – say, a red from Cahors or Gaillac – for only on special occasions will Toulousains drink a more expensive wine from another region.

Admittedly, the gastronomic tradition is now under pressure, as younger housewives find less time for careful home cooking, as a new generation turns its attention to other things, and as the French food industry begins to adopt the mass-processing habits of other countries. Much later than in Britain or Germany, frozen foods made a cautious appearance in northern France in the 1960s and are now percolating to conservative Toulouse. Some hurried housewives may now accept to buy frozen or tinned vegetables rather than fresh ones, or put some processed ingredients in their soups, casseroles and cakes. Or they may as soon toss a steak under the grill as spend hours preparing some local stew such as *cassoulet* or *boeuf en daube* as their mothers would have done. Gastronomy suffers. Yet there are some bright signs – one, that when the French do go over to processed foods, they often ally them to their own complex classic dishes. Go into a Toulouse hypermarket, and you will find the deep-freeze full of packets of pre-cooked *cassoulet, coq-au-vin, bouillabaisse,* and so on, as well as frozen snails, quail and frogs' legs; and the French are more ready to buy these costly delicacies than staple frozen items such as peas or fish-fingers, so popular in Britain. In fact, many experts believe that the French, after a difficult transition phase, may succeed in preserving their traditional quality within the context of modern techniques. Already one finds instances of how modern mass catering can retain gastronomic flair: in the canteen of the Motorola factory in Toulouse (American-owned!) I had a delicious *cassolette des fruits de mer,* the *plat du jour.* I found no such refinement in the works canteens of Stuttgart or Newcastle.

Toulouse's restaurants are in much the same transitional phase as home cooking, and many have lowered their standards, as they struggle with rising costs, staff shortages, and the temptation to cut corners by using tins and packets. It used to be possible in almost any *bistrot* to find for a modest price an honest *cassoulet,* the famous rich stew of haricot beans, port, mutton, Toulouse sausage and preserved goose. I know a few places in Toulouse where the *cassoulet* is still superb, but in most others the vital ingredient, *confit d'oie,* will have come straight out of a tin and the dish will lack flavour. Another local speciality, as in all the south-west, is truffled *foie gras,* often served hot in a sweet sauce with tiny grapes – delicious, but pricey.

Toulouse has fewer really distinguished restaurants than most larger French cities: one clue, it musters a total of only four stars in Michelin, fewer than Lille (six) or Strasbourg (seven), or indeed Bologna (five). But this judgement is relative, for any of the city's better restaurants easily outclasses anywhere in Newcastle, or even Stuttgart. And scattered around town are plenty of simple, traditional places, crowded at lunch, generally quieter at night, where an adequate three-course meal with wine still costs only 25 francs or so: as anywhere in France outside Paris, this city still offers value for money. Its eating-out scene has also diversified hugely in the past decade or so, not always in the interests of quality, but indicating perhaps that Toulouse is no longer a sleepy market town but, for better or worse, a metropolis. You can find romantic student cellars with candlelight and guitarists; modern fast-food and self-service places (mostly awful); imitation "ye olde pubs" and "drugstores"; restaurants in hypermarkets, on canal barges, in converted manor-houses. There are even one or two foreign restaurants, Vietnamese, Spanish and Italian, for the French provinces are at last discovering that French is not the only cuisine.

Les Nouvelles Galeries, the best department store, has a top-floor restaurant with views over the pink rooftops where you sit on stools at a long zig-zagging counter: while shoppers and typists queued up for me to vacate my seat, I devoured in thirty minutes flat an excellent 20-franc lunch of *terrine,* duck with chestnuts, peach melba. L'Entrecôte, La Grillothèque and La Grillière are modernised *brasseries* successfully offering a set formula meal with no choice: lettuce-and-walnut salad, tender pink sliced *entrecôte* with mustard sauce, dessert, house Beaujolais. Their popularity suggests that many younger French people today are less interested in complex gastronomy than in simpler meals of good quality. Or else they want atmosphere: one popular new pseudo-*bistrot* in the heart of the mediaeval city serves basic fodder of lettuce-and-bacon salad, toughish chops with chips, supermarket plonk; but with its cheery student service, modest prices and candles dripping romantically down their bottles, it is always packed till late with a *jeunesse* more-or-less *dorée.* You could well be in Chelsea or St-Germain-des-Prés – ten years ago.

Inevitably, Toulouse has its "Le Grill-Pub", pseudo-smart, with expensive hybrid menu and plush décor hopefully imitating some imagined Victorian pub – one of scores of such places in France today. For a few years recently it also had "Le Drugstore". So-called "drugstores" first appeared in Paris in the early '60s and soon spread to the provinces, Toulouse's being one of the first. They adopted an American name because of the naïf fashion for *franglais* words: but the French "drugstore" is a purely French invention, owing little to American ones. In France, a drugstore is a modernised *brasserie* with a ritzy Paris/New York air and a number of boutiques attached, all open till late: Toulouse's sold books, newspapers, cosmetics, sweets and tobacco, till about midnight, and very useful it was too. Its two restaurants served rather good food. It was a favourite haunt of the younger affluent society, and on a small scale had something of a metropolitan Champs-Elysées air. Unfortunately it lost money, and closed in 1976, to re-open as a simple steak-bar. One or two newer places also call themselves "drugstores", but they have no boutiques, and entirely lack the old ambience.

These "drugstores" are inheritors of a *café* and *brasserie* tradition that has changed radically since the war – and for the worse, older Toulousains will say. In the days before television, some eight or nine of the big terrace-*cafés* on the main *boulevard* each had its own live orchestra, and they were packed till midnight with regulars for whom this was the staple evening entertainment. I remember on my own first visit to Toulouse, in 1953, sitting in a large *café* where a spirited all-woman orchestra was pounding out a French version of "Let's all sing like the birdies sing – tweet, tweet-tweet, tweet-tweet!" But the last *café*-orchestra vanished in 1961, killed by television. And the leading *café-brasserie,* Les Américains, once the focal point of the city's *café* life, was pulled down in 1970 to make way for a trendy shopping and leisure centre, all boutiques, cinemas and fast-food snack-bars. Many Toulousains were horrified: it was like chopping down La Coupole and Le Dôme, at Montparnasse. Plenty of large, brightly-lit terrace-*cafés* still exist, and often they are full before lunch and in early evening; but, save in student quarters or during the tourist season, they grow quiet at night as customers creep home to their small screens.

Cafés and *brasseries,* bars, "pubs" and night-clubs have a complex sociology all their own. The *cafés* round the Place Wilson are *bourgeois,* those in the Place du Capitole more studenty or bohemian. Some others are haunts of *pieds-noirs,* or Leftish political groups, or inveterate card-players, while the bars of the larger hotels are often meeting-places for foreign cliques such as the British and German aircraft engineers. Some *cafés* are even open all night, for despite the new telly-watching suburban trends, the tradition of living late persists – as in Bologna – in this southern Latin city with its warm summer nights. There are no licensing hours, and in the city centre and around the station at two or three in the morning certain little bars are still crowded with bohemians, late revellers, and members of the city's thriving semi-criminal underworld.

Night-clubs proliferate – they number at least thirty. Few have a long life-expectancy, they flourish briefly, then wilt and die like flowers at the end of spring, and others take their place. Scores of sleazy discothèques sprang up in the late '60s when the youth prosperity boom set Toulouse, like many cities, in frantic imitation of "swinging London" and the Quartier Latin. But only one or two night-clubs are established, well-managed and sophisticated: Bub, the smartest, has a genuine chic that would not disgrace Mayfair or Montparnasse, and caters for young businessmen, *fils-à-papa* students and their Courrèges-dressed girls. For other tastes, there are dim-lit cavernous dives where you drink beer or cheap wine and join in the choruses as some bearded guitarist goes through the repertoire of French bawdy songs, *Jeanneton-prends-ton-fauchon* and the rest. Or, in the outskirts, you find big modern dance-halls with loud pop-groups, crowded out on weekend nights. In short, Toulouse has its own diversified night-life, far gayer than staid Stuttgart's and almost as lively as Newcastle's, in a different style. There may not be much of the home-based or club-based community life of residential suburbs that you find in Tyneside as in other Anglo-Saxon cities; yet in a more anonymous way Toulousains are gregarious. They like to go with a small group of friends to a public place where they can listen to a lot of noise and help to make it. Or at least, the young do – and of this city's teeming crowds of students, not all are quiet stay-at-homes all the time.

8
Some students have more égalité *than others*

Toulouse as a university city is today both a glory and a shambles, a place where the chosen few receive a brilliant technological training, and the hapless many limp along in pursuit of pass degrees of little practical value. Founded in 1229, the university is one of Europe's oldest, almost as old as Bologna's. Its fall from past glory has not been as catastrophic as Bologna's, nor is its present crisis so acute: but many of the problems, of over-crowding, under-funding, and political feuding, are comparable.

With almost 50,000 students in full-time higher education – 42,000 at the three universities and the rest in smaller colleges – Toulouse is one of the three largest university centres in the French provinces, on a par with Lyon and Marseille. And it *is* very much a student-infested city, as Stuttgart and Newcastle are not. Students are everywhere, not only in their sprawling campuses in the suburbs, but thronging the down-town *cafés* and daubing the street-walls with their posters advertising jazz-sessions, poetry readings, dances (*surboums*) or Maoist revolution. Yet these students are not all equal. A great gulf separates the privileged few of the *Grandes Ecoles* (engineering colleges), assured of fine careers, from the "student proletariat" in the swollen, amorphous universities, struggling on poor grants to glean what crumbs of learning they can in the overcrammed lecture-rooms, many of them cynical and dispirited in face of a system that may end them up as bank-clerks or sales-touts, if not in the dole queue. A visitor to Toulouse is shown the vast and vaunted scientific campus, where specialised institutes are doing some of the most advanced research in Europe, with some of the world's best equipment: but there is another side to the coin, which he may not always see.

In my book *The New France* I tried to analyse the complexities of the French education system, and here I shall simply give a general impression of the current situation in Toulouse, fairly typical of France as a whole. As elsewhere, the government's bid, since May 1968, to restructure the university on new lines has been working out only indifferently. It has fallen victim to shortages of funds, also to the conservatism of the teaching corps, whatever their politics. First, the attempt to create inter-disciplinarity has largely failed. Under the 1969 Faure reforms, Toulouse was invited to split itself into three smaller universities each embracing a wide range of disciplines, the aims being to achieve a more human scale and to break down the rigid barriers between faculties. But the professors at the head of the faculties refused to make the necessary compromises. The professors in the Law faculty, mostly Right-wing, rejected plans to co-habit with their Left-inclined colleagues in the Arts faculty, and vice versa. "We do not want to be contaminated by *gauchistes,*" said the Dean of the Law faculty publicly. Similarly the Medical school preferred to keep its apolitical purity and not associate with the Arts departments. The Ministry tried every persuasion, but failed, and the three new universities that emerged at the end of 1969 were little more than the old faculties under a new name: law, arts, and science (including medicine). It is true that within each of these universities there has been some small progress towards inter-disciplinarity: thus, in arts, a student can now combine mathematics with economics as he could not before 1968, and all science students must now study foreign languages. But the broad exchange of courses and ideas across disciplines, such as you find in the newer English universities, has failed to materialise. The three universities have little contact with each other: Paul Sabatier (science and medicine), on its wide new campus in the south-east suburbs, relatively calm, hard-working and well-organised; Le Mirail (arts and human sciences), on a new campus out to the west, much more politicised, and frequently in chaos; and "Toulouse I" as it is called (law and economics), still in old buildings in the centre of town, dominated by Right-of-centre conformism both at staff and student level.

The universities at least have more autonomy than in pre-1968 days. The 1969 reforms did away with the old highly centralised system whereby each university was fully controlled by the Ministry in Paris, whose permission was needed even for the staging of a dance in a student hostel. Today, each university elects its own governing council made up of one-third students and two-thirds teachers and other staff (including even floor-sweepers). The council can also co-opt delegates from the world outside, such as industrialists, trades-unionists and city councillors, and this innovation has done something to bridge the notorious gulf between French universities and the rest of French life. Each teaching department also elects its ruling council. These and other changes, made in the wake of the 1968 explosion, have at least brought French universities nearer to Anglo-Saxon or north European standards of autonomy, and have made it possible for each to develop its separate personality as is happening in Toulouse. Its three universities today have decidedly more practical independence than Bologna's, and in many respects as much as Stuttgart's – though they still lag well behind Newcastle. For example, though each university can now decide how to use its working budget, it is still dependent on the Ministry for its allocation and has no other resources; and the Ministry still decides on, and pays for, all major building and equipment projects. It also still awards national degrees and diplomas and sets the exams for them, whereas Newcastle sets its own exams. However, a Toulouse university is now almost as free as Newcastle to decide on its own teaching and exam methods leading to the diplomas, and it can vary the syllabus so long as it satisfies the Ministry that standards are being kept up. Thus some departments in Toulouse have virtually abolished lectures and interim exams and gone over to a credit system, while others have not.

At the law and science universities, the new system has finally taken root and is working quite well. But at Le Mirail, many Left-wing professors have staged lengthy rearguard actions against the reforms, which they oppose on principle as they come from a government they hate. Also, the teachers' innate conservatism is often strongest among those on the Left who claim loudest to be "revolutionary"! Frequently there have been strikes and sit-ins at Le Mirail, led by the teachers and supported by *gauchiste* students. But the *gauchistes* are few in number: student effervescence has died right down since the 1968 period, and today the mass of students betrays an equally alarming symptom, that of inertia. So few have come forward as candidates for the university elections that the student quotas on the new self-governing bodies have in many cases not been filled, and "participation" has not acquired much reality.

Today it is the teachers, not the students, who are the most angry and militant: their main grievance is the grave shortage of funds from the Ministry for coping with the huge student numbers. Budgets have not been keeping pace with rocketing costs, and in every teaching department I heard the same litany of complaints: staff reductions, and freezing of funds for badly-needed new equipment and premises. A geography professor told me that his department could no longer afford to fund his students' field research, or provide them with photocopied material, or supply the library with new books.

The strain on resources would be less if only there were a *numerus clausus,* as in Britain and Germany. But in France, as in Italy, anyone with the senior school leaving certificate (*baccalauréat*) retains the automatic right to university entry, so numbers have swelled uncontrollably. The students, though the chief victims of the situation, remain rigidly opposed to a *numerus clausus,* which they claim would be undemocratic: only in medicine have the authorities, even in the face of student strikes, had the courage to impose a selective system, and this only after the first year. Elsewhere, a certain natural process of selection does operate in practice, since many students find they are not suited to the academic grind and drop out in mid-course. But this is a wasteful solution, and leads often to frustration and a lasting sense of failure.

Students on the campus are left to fend for themselves, with inadequate amenities, rather than being cosseted as individuals, as they are at Newcastle. A teacher at Le Mirail told me, "Many feel lost, and seem to wonder what they're doing here. The libraries are overcrowded, and many students unless they live nearby are reduced to studying in noisy *cafés*" – as happens in Bologna. At least the overcrowding has eased a little since the new out-of-town campuses were completed. And the May 1968 upheaval seems to have narrowed, once and for all, the notorious gulf that existed between students and teachers. A junior lecturer told me, "The younger or more liberal teachers are now more accessible to the students; many are now on their side against the system. The tyranny of the older professors has been broken too. Some of the old dodderers in the Law university now have their lectures booed and interrupted." Yet the sheer weight of numbers still makes it hard for teachers to get to know their students personally, at least at undergraduate level. Nor is it in the French tradition for a professor to invite students to his home, as at Newcastle. An open-minded senior professor told me, "My staff would be outraged if they felt expected to entertain their students in this way. 'Our job,' they'd say, 'is to teach them, not give them apéritifs.' There'd be complaints of favouritism too – you just can't do this sort of thing in France. Nor do we have 'moral tutors' as in England. I do manage to get to know personally a few of my senior or post-graduate students, for at that level numbers are smaller. But in the junior years there must be many poor bastards who know none of their teachers at all. No wonder they feel so lost."

Students suffer too from understandable fears that their study courses are not geared to the needs of the world outside, for the university is still too much an ivory tower. Students of literature and languages have few possible career outlets except to be teachers of future students – an absurd hermetic circle. Even in physics and biology the problem is much the same: "The science teaching," I was told, "is too theoretical to be much use to industrial firms, who prefer to recruit from the élitist *Grandes Ecoles* or, at a lower level, from the new vocational technical colleges. Our young graduates just become teachers." And a student of English complained, "The teaching is far too literary. We study Shakespeare and Chaucer, but learn nothing of modern commercial English, so we'd be useless in industry or business. Nor do we feel fitted for jobs like advertising or television. We shall end up as teachers. The whole system needs changing." His professor later commented to me, "The problem of career outlets does not interest me. My duty is to preserve a high level of culture, and ensure that the students imbibe it." My mouth fell open.

The economic crisis since 1974 has worsened the situation. Not only are jobs in industry harder than ever to obtain, but cut-backs in education budgets have reduced even the number of teaching posts available to young graduates. There are no equivalents of Newcastle's Appointments Board, and graduates must fight their own battles on the labour market. Those who take only the shorter two- or three-year degree courses (leading to DEUG or *licence*) are liable to land up as check-out girls in a supermarket or ushers in a town hall.

In 1975, with graduate unemployment rising dangerously, the government finally came out with a project for bringing degree courses closer to job realities. It instructed each university to devise its own new courses for the *maîtrise* (master's degree) in various disciplines, "taking account of job possibilities on the local and national level", and what is more, it invited members of the industrial and business world to sit on the Ministry's commissions that were to approve the new courses. This caused a storm of protest from teachers and students alike, throughout France, with Toulouse in the forefront. Universities were angry at the way the reform was foisted on them without consultation, and threatened to apply their own *maîtrise* courses without ministerial approval. Students then panicked in turn, fearing that these "local" degrees, lacking national validity, would be of little value. And

Left-wing teachers and students were united in their fury at the invitation to the *Patronat*: "It's a sell-out to capitalism," said their leaders, "we shall be brainwashed to suit the needs of the boss class!" All very typical of the perverse French Left: the same people who for years had been protesting at the lack of job outlets were now in arms against a reform aimed to remedy just that. At Le Mirail in February 1976, strikes broke out that lasted ten weeks. Later the movement fizzled out, and by 1977 the reforms were being tentatively applied, with some hope that they might eventually remedy the situation. But Leftist disgruntlement continued: "I'm not really interested in getting a job," one student told me, "I just want to overthrow the régime. Better starve than be used to prop up a dying capitalism."

Nearly all students come from Toulouse itself or within an 80-mile radius: except at *Grande Ecole* level, in France there has never been the English tradition of moving to another provincial university away from one's home region. About half of all students therefore live with their families; or else they rent rooms, or stay in utilitarian hostels where they must study against incessant noise. They receive grants, rated according to their parents' means, but even the largest of these allow for no more than subsistence living, and about 40 per cent of students have to pay their way through college with part-time jobs which are now increasingly hard to find. It follows that there is not much *dolce vita* about the average student's leisure life. A small minority, children of indulgent well-to-do parents, have a jolly time: you can see them dashing about in sports cars, or in the discothèques. But for the majority there is hard-working drudgery, and a sense of isolation. A number of clubs and other such activities do exist, some run by the students themselves: there is a student theatre group, as well as cine-clubs and various other cultural societies, and sports clubs, while in summer and at Christmas the students organise *boums* (impromptu dances). But communal activities are noticeably less well patronised than in Newcastle. Is it that students lack the time, or the money? "Most of all it's a question of habit and temperament," the director of a student welfare body told me; "the French of all ages are too individualistic, they're not club-joiners. I've tried to start various discussion-groups and other activities, but people won't turn up. They have their little knots of friends and they sit around in *cafés* or each others' rooms, but they won't take part in anything more organised. No wonder so many students feel so lonely and fail to find any sympathetic *milieu.*"

Maybe I have drawn too harsh a picture of Toulouse's university problems. At least, as compared with Italy, some real constructive attempt at overall reform has been made in France in the past decade; and at least the new semi-autonomy of the universities is an improvement on the old centralisation. Steadily they are now developing their own personalities. Left-wing student extremism has lost much of its influence, even if it can still occasionally flare into action as happened in 1976 over the "*maîtrise*" affair. But the universities are still bedevilled by the seemingly insoluble problems of too many students and too little money. This could be partly resolved overnight, with the introduction of selective entry. But there would remain another serious obstacle to progress: the ghetto-mentality of so many teachers. Toulouse's universities, despite their size, have less contact with the rest of the life of the city and the nation than I found to be the case in any other of my towns, even Bologna. Most of the teachers I met were living in their own tight little social cliques, meeting few people except their own colleagues, obsessed by their own sectarian feuds and endless political dog-fighting between their rival unions. Everything that went wrong they would simply blame on the government, and as a matter of principle made no efforts to supply their own remedy. "Yes, I know we live in a ghetto, cut off from the rest of French life," one of the more open-minded teachers told me, "but what can we do about it? It's society's fault."

The *Grandes Ecoles* and the various state-backed scientific institutes in Toulouse exist on a different planet from the universities. While the latter show little enthusiasm for research links with local industry and tend to spurn applied science, the former associate actively with local firms, especially in aeronautics and electronics. It was the presence of these industries that encouraged the government to develop Toulouse as a metropolis of scientific research; and so it is that so many laboratories and study centres, dealing in electronic optics, space satellites, and so on, are spread across the wide campus beside the science university. Hither the government also transferred from Paris in the 1960s two of the most prestigious of those élitist engineering colleges known as the *Grandes Ecoles*: the *Ecole Nationale de l'Aviation Civile,* and the *Ecole Nationale Supérieure de l'Aéronautique et de l'Espace* (known for short as "*Sup'Aéro*"). Each *Grande Ecole* operates its own rigorous selective entry, highly competitive; and once admitted, the lucky student leads a relatively privileged existence. He has close contact with his teachers; and so high-powered and so practical is his training that he is virtually assured of a worth-while career in private or public industry, at a high starting salary. At *Sup'Aéro,* the 350 students come from all over France and live as boarders in elegant halls of residence. They despise the university "proletariat" and lead a separate social life, sometimes slipping off to Paris for the weekend in an aircraft placed at their disposal. A director of the college showed me round the spacious premises – such a contrast with what I had seen at Le Mirail: smooth lawns and patios with modern sculptures, impressive language-laboratories and closed-circuit TV systems, and a reading-room that looked like the lounge of a luxury hotel. "We've never had student unrest here," said my guide: "what is there to protest about?" But plenty of Frenchmen today believe that somehow the gulf must be narrowed between these élitist little *milieux* and the university broiler-houses – if worse student explosions are to be avoided.

The French school system I analysed at length in *The New France,* and here I shall make a few remarks about one Toulouse school, the Lycée Fermat, the town's best-known State *lycée* for boys. Despite a huge increase in numbers, it still occupies its original premises in the centre of the city where it has no room to expand physically; and it is bursting at the seams. Some 3,250 boys are crammed into buildings intended for a thousand. A history master told me, "The school has grown so big that it's completely lost all atmosphere and sense of being a living community. It's just a teaching factory. The staff is so large that we hardly know each other. Two masters met by chance on holiday abroad, and were surprised to learn they both worked at Fermat. They did not even know each other by sight."

The May 1968 explosion had a dramatic influence on this school as on so many in France. The old order is now gone for ever. An immediate effect of the crisis was to split the staff into two camps, liberals and diehards: a leftish Catholic teacher told me, "For the next year or so, at least half my colleagues would not shake my hand, and this because I had sympathised openly with the rebellious students." Since 1968 the school has now settled down again, in a new mould, with slightly more autonomy and spirit of democracy than before. The headmaster, instead of being the dictatorial agent of the Ministry in Paris, is now flanked by an elected administrative board that includes staff and pupil delegates and some outsiders. This at least marks a gesture towards "participation", even if it is the head who still takes the main decisions. A few extra-curricular activities have also been introduced, of the type hitherto so strikingly absent from French schools: there is now a drama group and a sking club, and a roneoed magazine produced by the pupils under staff supervision – the kind of things that any Newcastle secondary school has long taken for granted and does on a far more ambitious scale. The *lycée* has not been granted any extra funds from the Ministry for such activities, and the pupils lack even a proper reading or recreation room, since there is neither the space for it nor the money to equip it. The pupils – almost all are day-boys – arrive in the morning for their lessons, play around in the yard and the corridors during their breaks, and then go home. And nearly all teachers still see their role as simply to stuff the boys' heads with academic wisdom: few of them take the trouble to get to know the boys personally, or help them with their problems, or encourage out-of-class activities. No wonder the school has so little "soul", compared with those I visited in Newcastle and even in Stuttgart.

Before 1968 the school had no autonomy: in every detail of its time-table and curriculum it had to adhere to the uniform national pattern imposed by the Ministry in Paris. The headmaster is now granted a little more leeway, and since 1973 this school like others in France is actually allowed to spend 10 per cent of working hours any way it pleases, preferably on non-academic activities – another tiny step towards the informality that any British school takes for granted. But the experiment has met with only patchy success. No new funds have been made available for it; and at least half the teachers at Fermat have opposed the scheme, either through fear it would lead to a lowering of academic standards, or out of inertia and dislike of having to think up new ideas, or else through rejection on principle of any innovation coming from the government. "It's the usual French problem," one liberal teacher told me; "they complain about state control, but then have no idea how to use freedom when they are given it. They lack any initiative, save that of protest." He summed up the present situation in the school: "The old pre-1968 austerity is gone. The place is untidier than before, with slogans around the place, but at least it's a bit more free and lively. The present generation of schoolboys are less rebellious than those of 1968, they work hard and behave quite well – but they don't show enthusiasm, or respect for the teaching they are given, as many of the brighter ones did before 1968. The old ethos of a *lycée,* as a temple of truth and wisdom, seems to have gone for ever. In the old days, the boys came to the *lycée* to seek something. Today, they attend their classes dutifully, but grudgingly, and give the impression that what they really get out of life is elsewhere – via television, travel, relationships, political activity. I find it sad. It makes me feel useless."

9
Textiles turn trendy as Concorde flounders

In the countryside round Toulouse, it is not hard to find peasant families where the parents are still farming, the daughter has a job making transistor parts at Motorola's factory, and the son is helping assemble jet aircraft at Aérospatiale. Toulouse can thus be seen as a typical and vivid example of France's transformation since the war from a mainly agricultural to a prosperous industrial nation. Yet the town's industrial revolution, product less of local initiative than of state prompting, is still precariously based, as the post-1974 crisis has shown. And it seems ironical that, just when a number of older local firms are at last waking up to modern ideas of progress, the newer and larger industries installed here so triumphantly by Paris (in aeronautics and electronics) are the ones proving most vulnerable to the new conditions.

Toulouse has little of the manufacturing tradition of Stuttgart or Newcastle. Its prosperity in the past was based on commerce and agriculture; its *bourgeoisie,* cultivated and easy going, scorned the hard-working dedication that industry demanded, preferring to invest in land and property. Geographically remote and without mineral resources, the Toulouse area was also ill placed to benefit from the industrial revolution, which largely passed it by. So during the 19th century its local firms, producing textiles, pottery, farm implements, remained small in size and closed to ideas of expansion and profit.

It was almost by accident that Toulouse finally began to assume a modern industrial role, during and just after the 1914-18 war. The geographical isolation that had formerly been a handicap now became an asset: aircraft and munitions firms were transferred here, so as to be as far away from the Germans as possible, and between the wars Toulouse became the leading aircraft-making centre in France. Then in the 1950s the Government embarked on a policy of planned regional development, entirely new for France. The whole of the south-west was scheduled for special aid, an area with far too little industry and too large a population of inefficient small farmers. And Toulouse in particular, with its established nucleus of aircraft firms, was selected as the principal French testing-ground of the new policy of industrialising the regions. But this decision to decentralise was taken in the true centralised French manner, in Paris: local people were barely consulted.

In the 1950s the emphasis was initially on rebuilding France's aircraft industry, virtually dismantled during the war. Toulouse was already the site of the main factory of the state-owned Sud-Est Aviation company (later known as Sud-Aviation, after various mergers, and today as Aérospatiale), and this first pioneered the Caravelle, later Concorde, then Airbus. In the 1950s the Government also began to complement the aeronautics industry with two other activities. First, Toulouse was to be developed as one of the leading French centres for advanced scientific research, mainly in space communications, aeronautics and electronics. Several important state-backed research bodies were founded or transferred here, notably the *Centre Nationale des Etudes Spatiales.* Second, Toulouse was to be given an "electronics vocation", as the official jargon put it: electronics firms were to be encouraged to settle here, and to collaborate with the research centres and the aircraft industry. By way of enticement, the government deployed the full battery of its regional incentives: Toulouse was a "priority" zone, and new firms could receive grants of up to 25 per cent of investment costs. Two electronics companies in particular seized the bait. Motorola, of Phoenix, Arizona, set up its first French plant here, in 1967. And a French-owned firm, the Compagnie Internationale pour l'Informatique (CII), was established for the manufacture of computers.

By about 1970 this policy was bearing dividends. Motorola and CII were expanding fast; the Caravelle had been a huge success and Concorde, despite the delays, was at least airborne. But one weakness of the overall strategy was that all this new industry had been imposed on Toulouse artificially from outside: the town had not yet acquired any industrial dynamism of its own. Most larger firms depended on Paris (or indeed Arizona) for their decisions, and this remains true today. When I telephoned Aérospatiale's Press office in Toulouse, after my arrival, I was told that I could not be received until I had submitted my request in writing to the firm's chief Press officer in Paris!

While Aérospatiale was preparing Concorde, at the other end of the scale Toulouse's own little local firms remained many of them in the cottage-industry stage of the 19th century. In 1954 the town had 6,089 manufacturing enterprises of which 2,729 were family craft firms with no employees, while the others averaged only 11 workers each. Yet many of them were turning out a range of hundreds of different products, and then wondered why they could not make a profit. I visited one factory, with 48 employees – huge, by Toulouse standards – making material for the packaging industry. It was filthy, ramshackle and ill-lit, and the machinery looked as if it had not been changed for decades. The owner, an elderly Toulousain, told me, "I see no reason for us to expand. We just about make a profit, we tick over, that's enough for me. I don't like working too hard. For me this place is just a job, not a way of life." They see things differently in Stuttgart.

Hundreds of little firms of this kind were gradually forced out of business under pressure of new competition, during the boom years of France's modernisation. And finally, in the late 1960s, there began to emerge a new generation of Toulousain entrepreneurs for whom "expansion" and "productivity" were no longer dirty words. At last the old mediaeval city opened its ears to the message so urgently preached by the planners in Paris: France must modernise or perish. Some local success-stories were remarkable. At Ramonède, a sleepy little family-owned clothing firm in Colomiers, the father handed over control to his three young sons who brought in a new outlook, attacked the export market, and increased turnover twelvefold between 1965 and 1969. François Castaigne, a local doctor, patented a drug called Solvestorol in 1956, and from this he built up a pharmaceuticals firm that expanded dynamically, took over laboratories in other parts of France, and by 1970 was exporting as far afield as Argentina and Japan. And in 1969 a thirty-year-old Moroccan Jewish *pied noir* set up a little workshop making trendy leather trousers and jackets, to which he gave the suitably Carnaby-Street-sounding name of Perkins. Within two years he had 130 employees and was exporting 50 per cent of his output, most of it to Germany – "The Germans really dig leather," he told me. "My clients fly in from Frankfurt and take away suitcases full of samples. The Common Market has helped us a lot. But the secret of our success is that we have the right flair and self-confidence, as compared with most of the local textile firms here. I do all the designing – I taught myself."

The culmination came in 1971 when this new generation won control of the Chamber of Commerce and Industry. The sitting president of this body was an old fogey worthy of the local folklore museum, a Toulousain cobwebbed in the trappings of the Third Republic: when I called to see him, he extolled to me the glories of the city's past and reeled off the associations of which he was president, but showed no concern for current economic realities. Finally he was ousted and replaced by Claude Duffour, manager of a local oxygen firm, a whizz-kid in his late forties who immediately set about preaching a new gospel of dynamism and expansion. He shook the Chamber of Commerce out of its old apathy, secured the funds for building a modern business centre at the airport, and persuaded the airlines to create new international flights. In 1974 he told me: "Toulouse is at last becoming industry-minded and export-minded in its own right, instead of letting Paris call the tune. The new spirit may not yet have infected more than a handful of firms, but it's spreading fast – you'll see. A new, very different generation is emerging." But unfortunately, just when the local firms were making this belated transformation, the newer and larger ones implanted from outside began to suffer seriously from the world recession. Motorola's world-wide retrenchment obliged its Toulouse plant to cut back on staff and cancel plans for expansion; CII fared even worse and had to abandon some of its ambitious computer projects, as these were no longer viable in face of American competition. French schemes for an independent European-backed computer industry were tumbling in ruins, and CII fell with them. And – as the world knows well – much worse still befell Aérospatiale and its Concordes, affecting in turn scores of local sub-contractors. By 1975-6 unemployment was becoming a serious problem in Toulouse for the first time since the war.

The story of Aérospatiale is one of triumph turning to tragedy. At the end of the war France's aircraft industry was at such a low ebb that the factory at St-Martin-du-Touch, in the western suburbs of Toulouse, was reduced to making gas-generators and refrigerators. But the government put in charge of the firm an exceptionally vigorous young manager, Georges Hereil, one of the ablest of France's famous post-war technocrats. He was given the brief of rescuing the industry.

He drew round him a team of gifted designers and engineers who conceived the Caravelle medium-range jet, then built it in record time, long before Boeing could bring onto the market its rival, the 727. A total of 280 Caravelles were sold, and in 1963 they were accounting for 77 per cent of all jet traffic in Europe. This aircraft was one of the supreme successes of the French post-war industrial "miracle". Then the Toulouse factory turned its efforts to building the Anglo-French Concorde, in partnership with the British Aircraft Corporation at Bristol – a technological triumph but an ultimate commercial disaster – and too many tons of ink and tears have been shed over this saga for me to wish to add any more. Concorde was followed by the four-nation Airbus, its components built in various parts of France, Germany, Holland and Britain, then assembled in Toulouse. Airbus has proved a relative success, under the difficult world conditions since 1974, but it has not saved the fortunes of Aérospatiale. This vast state-backed consortium, with factories all over France, makes a steady profit on its ballistic missiles and helicopters, but its civil aircraft division (based essentially on Toulouse) has been running ever deeper into the red and by 1977 was reckoned to be losing 1.5 million francs a day. There are various reasons for this failure, some not the company's own fault, notably governments' vacillations and misjudgements over Concorde, and then the barely foreseeable slump in the world aviation market since the oil crisis. But Aérospatiale does suffer from the excessive bureaucracy and civil-service rigidities that encumber so many large nationalised firms; and since Hereil departed in 1962 his frequent successors have none of them shown the same flair, not even General Jacques Mitterrand (brother of the Socialist leader) who was appointed in 1975 to attempt a rescue operation. It is a sad situation, for the brilliant engineers and other experts working on the prototypes have always shown exceptional enthusiasm, dedication, and technical pride. They feel they have been let down by the politicians, as an Englishman on the Airbus team told me: "We are being sabotaged. All of us working on this 'plane, English, French, Germans and others, have little sense of national difference. We simply take pride in our job. It's only governments who are over-conscious of national interests." The result of the failures, notably of the run-down of Concorde's production, was that Aérospatiale had to reduce its work-force at Toulouse from 8,500 in 1972 to 7,500 in 1976. The unions grew restive, and were pacified only when the firm agreed to transfer part of its helicopter production from a plant near Marseille.

Despite these particular difficulties of Aérospatiale, Toulouse's overall industrial achievement has been far from negative, and it illustrates dramatically some of the changes in post-war France. While on Tyneside, a great industrial heritage has been falling into decay, in Toulouse a new tradition has been forged out of next to nothing. As in the rest of France, various factors have contributed: the drive and enthusiasm of executives, at least in larger and newer firms; the relative docility of trade unions (for all their verbal militancy); pride in craftsmanship, a virtue equally common in Germany but diminishing in Britain; the adaptability of the French, especially those from a peasant background, to new kinds of work; and a readiness to work hard. It is true that Toulousains like others in the Midi have the reputation of being slower and lazier than most French: I met industrialists who claimed that their productivity was up to 20 per cent below that of northerners. But I think it is largely a question of the lead set by management. In the older-style local firms, where the boss lacks energy and enterprise, his workers are the same: but the *cadres* in many newer firms, such as Motorola, seem to be able to infect their staff with their own hard-working dynamism and enthusiasm.

The story of Motorola in Toulouse is intriguing and instructive. It is true that the factory has recently run into difficulties, owing to Motorola's world-wide retrenchment. Nonetheless, since the plant was first built at Le Mirail in the late 1960s it has provided a fascinating example of the pioneering of a style of work relations new to France, and of the adaptability of the French when faced with a challenge. Motorola decided on Toulouse for its first French factory for two main reasons: the kind of semi-skilled labour it needed was plentiful, and the university was already strong in electronics and likely to be of use for research. Motorola then hired an entirely French team of senior executives and scientists and sent them for a year to head office in Phoenix, Arizona, for indoctrination in American work methods. The company also made a daring choice of manager. Instead of taking a man from industry, it did something rare in France: it chose a university man, E. J. Cassignol, a teacher at the science faculty. A Toulousain with a cocky and informal manner, he set about creating an enterprise not at all in the usual French hierarchical mould. He picked a very young staff: the average age of executives is only about thirty, while nearly all shopfloor workers are under twenty-five, most of them girls from country areas with no previous factory experience. Cassignol broke with the normal rigid French chains of command, and applied the more flexible

American system of group work and shared responsibility – and the staff responded. Each time I have visited this pleasant modern factory, the atmosphere has seemed to me relaxed and relatively egalitarian. Senior executives and scientists join the queue in the canteen and take lunch in their shirt-sleeves next to their secretaries (a practice rare in France, hard to imagine in Germany, and unusual even in Britain). An engineer who had previously worked at Aérospatiale said to me, "The set-up here is entirely different. Aérospatiale has four separate canteens, each for a different level of staff; and in any group, you can see at once who is the boss. Not so at Motorola, where everyone is arguing democratically." This group system seems to work. Sitting shirt-sleeved beside his dark-eyed secretary as we ate the canteen's excellent *cassolette de fruits de mer,* Cassignol explained to me, "There's no mystique about this American-style management, it's mere common sense. And we find that French employees of all grades will adapt to it readily and easily, provided they have not already worked too long in the older type of firm." Of course, a discreet American-style paternalism lurks in Motorola, and I did notice that although Cassignol called his secretary by her first name, she replied "Monsieur". Motorola has even tried to keep the Left-wing unions out of the factory, and has succeeded largely because most workers are young girls, not yet union-minded. Other factors may also play a part – the above-average wages, working conditions and welfare amenities. Motorola even organises staff parties and picnics – unusual in France – and in true American style encourages its staff to develop a corporation loyalty. It seems to bring results.

Labour relations in Toulouse and the role of the unions fit approximately into the national pattern which I analysed in my book on modern France. If anything, the unions are weaker and a little more docile than in other big French industrial cities, and a visitor from, say, Newcastle or Stuttgart, might judge that their bark is worse than their bite. The local level of union membership, around 23 per cent of employees, is even lower than the low national figure of 25 per cent, for the Toulousain is even more of an individualist and less of a club-joiner than most Frenchmen, nor is this an area with any strong heritage of exploitation by heartless employers. Labour relations have generally been easy-going, and it is significant that the most moderate and "collaborationist" of the three main French unions, *Force ouvrière,* is relatively stronger in industries here than elsewhere in France.

As in Italy, unions are structured on political lines: *Confédération générale du travail* (Communist-led), *Confédération française et démocratique du travail* (radical Socialist), *Force ouvrière* (moderate Socialist). There are not the multiple craft divisions found on Tyneside, hence the virtual absence of demarcation disputes. Union rivalry, though intense, is thus not a matter of petty jealousies between guilds but of normal competition for influence and membership, and unions often unite for joint action. CGT and CFDT are verbally militant, ever denouncing the Government or employers; but in practice they have instigated very few major strikes in Toulouse since the 1968 national uprising. Government concessions after 1968 brought French labour relations closer in line with those of socially "advanced" countries such as Britain or Germany, so that today any Toulouse firm of more than 50 employees has a complex apparatus of works committees, staff delegations (a channel for grievances) and statutory profit-sharing schemes, while unions finally have a right to offices on the premises.

Since 1968, most employers have shown themselves more understanding of workers' problems and readier to share information. This may be one factor behind the relative absence of strikes. Moreover, Left-wing unions have been anxious to avoid rocking the boat during the various pre-electoral periods of 1973-8; and the workers themselves have been reluctant, as anywhere, to jeopardise their jobs by going on strike in a time of high unemployment. Much of their industrial action has been purely defensive: led by the unions, they have frequently staged factory sit-ins or other demonstrations against threatened closures or redundancies. These have sometimes succeeded in reducing the size of lay-offs, but rarely have they prevented closures. A CFDT leader told me: "When a local paper factory announced plans to close down, we and the CGT staged a sit-in of all 250 workers. We occupied the premises and seized stocks of paper. This went on for three months, until July 1975, but it seemed to be getting us nowhere: the firm was doomed. Finally the workers got bored with the sit-in and went off on their paid holidays."

Both the CGT and CFDT consider themselves "revolutionary" and they firmly reject any German-style formal collaboration with management. And yet, *ad hoc* day-to-day collaboration is a great deal more frequent than the attitudinising and the adamant *prises de position* might suggest. Workers accommodate to new productivity schemes and labour-saving innovations; they do not cut their own throats with the kind of pig-headedness seen in the Tyne shipyards in 1977-8. They seem to have a basic common sense and realism, accepting that willy-nilly they have a stake in the employer's goals of profitability and would do well not to obstruct too much. And though some union leaders might wish for a tougher line, the unions cannot easily impose it when less than one worker in four is unionised. "Personalities and human contact count for more, here in the Midi, than ideologies," said one official; "passions may flare up, but just as quickly they die down again, people shake hands on it and forget." In an area where most industry is so recent, shopfloor workers tend to come from artisan or peasant families and are not yet schooled in the hard proletarian attitudes of older industrial towns. But as the industrial tradition deepens, will Toulouse tend towards the British or the German pattern of labour relations?

10

Fading dreams of Algiers, new hopes for Occitania

In the Place Wilson, groups of elderly Spanish exiles in drab suits are gossiping under the warm April sun. In a bar nearby, done up as a mock English "pub", aero-engineers from Bristol are playing a regular game of darts, to remind them of home. Down the *boulevard,* three Negro students chat up a German blonde, beside a street-stall run by a *pied-noir* advertising *"le vrai merguez comme à Sidi-Bel-Abbès".* A corner of the Drugstore des Américains is full, suitably, of hirsute American youth, arguing about Carter and *détente.* And everywhere are young Moroccans and Algerians, hawking carpets and leatherwork, shouting at each other in their rasping staccato tongue, or strolling listlessly, lonely-looking and celibate. So many home-thoughts, from so many varied exiles.

This was an average downtown Sunday scene, in a city that ranks as the most cosmopolitan in this book after Stuttgart. And though the foreigners are fewer than in Stuttgart, they seem to make their presence felt as assertively, in this outdoor-living town. In a French geographical context it may appear peripheral, yet its links with the world have been increasing fast, thanks to such factors as the international nature of the aircraft industry, the appeal of the universities (where 3,000 students are foreign), and the southerly situation on routes to Spain and Africa. Almost as much as Marseille, Toulouse is a polyglot Latin melting-pot, the venue for scores of thousands of exiles, political or other, from all over the western Mediterranean.

Spaniards, Portuguese and Italians are numerous. But the largest and most influential immigrant community is actually made up of French nationals, who arrived around 1960-2 feeling every bit as alien as the Iberians, and still cling together. These were the settlers who fled from Algeria at the time of its independence (their nick-name of *pieds noirs* dates from the early days of French colonisation when the barefoot Muslims called them after their black shoes). Of the 800,000 or so who settled back in France, 60,000 came to Toulouse and half of these have stayed in the city while others have moved on to nearby towns and farms. They are mostly from the Oran district; many are Jews, or of Spanish blood. Like so many colonisers, they are dynamic and resourceful; and though in Algeria they produced the thugs and diehards of the OAS, back in France those same traits of toughness and perseverance have shown the brighter side of their medal: they bought up dying businesses and have made them buzz. Their hardworking vitality has given a healthy shot-in-the-arm to the local economy, especially in commerce where they took over small shops, *cafés* and restaurants by the hundred, running them with gusto and winning Toulousains over to their dishes such as *couscous* and *merguez* (spiced sausage) which they had inherited from the Muslims. One Toulouse street today has ten *pied-noir* shops within 100 yards; about one-third of all local trade is in *pied-noir* hands, much of it Jewish. In agriculture, in a region notorious for the primitivism of much of its peasant farming, the repatriates took over hundreds of properties and imported a new outlook as well as the modern techniques they had used on their much larger estates in North Africa. Someone said, "They see the Midi as offering them the same kind of challenge as Africa in the last century."

Many arrived virtually penniless, forced to leave their possessions behind. They were helped by government indemnities, while the Toulouse city council made real efforts to help them find homes and jobs. This would hardly have been possible under today's economic conditions: but it is a testimony to the elasticity of the fast-growing French economy of the 1960s, as well as to the tolerance and good sense of the French, that this huge population was able to be absorbed into France with relatively little friction. True, as late as 1970 there were still occasional *pied-noir* demonstrations in Toulouse against alleged delays in the government's indemnity programme. And some older people failed to adapt: there were suicides, and I was told of the widow of a landowner who, ten years later, aged sixty-five, was working as a charlady. But the vast majority rapidly found their feet. A dentist from Algiers told me, "Life was tough for the first year. We slept on the floor, as we had no money even for a bed or mattress. But within three years I was earning as much as in Algiers."

And yet, though materially the adjustment has been made, socially and psychologically many *pied noirs* still feel "different" – more French than the French. Northern France they find alien, and cold in every sense, and most have preferred to settle in the Midi. But they often complain that even their Mediterranean cousins, the easy-going Toulousains, are too *fermés* and reserved by their standards. They are an odd lot, these *pied noirs,* exuberant, extrovert, optimistic: if you come across an especially noisy *café,* the odds are it is a haunt of theirs, and in some of these places they still hold regular meetings of their old *amicales,* such as the *Cercle Mostagenem.* One *café* is the headquarters of the Sidi-Bel-Abbès football team, still active in exile in Toulouse. And poorer *pied noirs* have appropriated a whole working-class quarter, scornfully nicknamed "Bab-el-Oued" by Toulousains, after the notorious poor-white slum in Algiers that furnished the OAS with its bloodiest fanatics.

Not that daily relations between Toulousains and *pied noirs* are hostile. They live and let live, but most repatriates still prefer to cling together socially. Most astonishingly, over fifteen years later even some younger *pied noirs* who never knew Algeria save as children still keep alive a tribal loyalty to this lost homeland, like the Jews of the old diaspora yearning for Zion. For me it was an experience both alarming and moving to call on one family that epitomised this. They were charming, vivacious, cultured people, with a comfortable life-style: the father was a *lycée* teacher from Oran who had found a similar job in Toulouse. The son, a student, and the daughter, a young lawyer, both lived and breathed their tragic Algerian past as if no other cause mattered. The son produced his guitar and sang me nostalgic laments for the "homeland", spiced with bitter anti-de Gaulle jibes – "Ah, what we innocent people suffered from that traitor!" He showed me the *pied-noir* student paper he edited, full of similar comments and praise for former *Algérie Française* champions such as Salan. I was offered *pied-noir* brands of *pastis* and cigarettes, both made in France, and was treated to diatribes about how shockingly the government had treated the repatriates, how the Toulousains had victimised them after 1962, how the *pieds noirs* hated and feared the local Arab immigrant workers, and how the present situation in southern Africa proved just how tragically wrong de Gaulle had been to sell out French Algeria to the coloured "Commies". The daughter, pretty, sharp-minded, persuasive, said: "We know we have no hope of recovering our homeland. But we have formed a committee whose aim is to set the record of history right, to counter the wicked lies now creeping into the history books about how *we* were the villains of the Algerian war and the FLN its heroes. We want 'psychological indemnity'. And we want to keep alive the sacred flame of our French Algerian spirit, so that our children may come to share it. Also we must convince people that we *are* fully French." It seemed an odd emotional logic that led her to couple this fierce *pied-noir* identity with an equally fierce Frenchness – "We are more truly French than the France that betrayed us," she seemed to be saying. It was odd, too, to hear this fiery attachment from a family whose Algerian roots were not deep: the parents' parents had gone there from Dunkerque and the Pyrenees. It was bewildering to hear such charming and civilised people uttering views that far outdid Ian Smith, and above all it was incredible to hear such bitterness, and loyalty to a dead cause, from a young generation that had known Algeria only as children. They had all the passionate fire of young Israeli nationalists – but without a nation to defend. It was historical surrealism. Luckily, this family was an extreme case and such views no longer have political influence. Few younger *pieds noirs* sit down to weep quite so bitterly by the waters of the Garonne, when they remember thee, O Oran. They assimilate. But the scars will still take some time to heal.

The 15,000 Spaniards in Toulouse, the biggest non-French group, present a different picture. Their homeland, far from being lost, has suddenly been restored to them since Franco's death – or so it seems to many of the 5,000 or so Republican refugees from the Civil War, who constitute the first of two distinct waves of Spanish immigrants here: political, from the late 1930s, and economic, from the post-war period.

Of the first wave, some succeeded in carving out lucrative careers for themselves, like the *pieds noirs*: I met one who was running a large building firm. But the majority were simple workers who had fought against Franco, while some were from the liberal professions and these found it hardest to adapt, for seldom were their Spanish diplomas valid in France. Thus a Barcelona lawyer turned to hairdressing, and a leading Madrid architect ended his days as a draughtsman. Socially, these people and especially their children have gradually integrated into local society over the past forty years and many have become naturalised. The Toulousains accept them easily: but at heart they have remained profoundly Spanish. After the political amnesty many of them began to return to Spain on short visits, but until Franco's death they continued to edit a Republican paper in Toulouse, in Spanish.

The second Spanish immigrant wave is today the more numerous. These are people who arrived in search of work, often encouraged by the Spanish government, during the years of rapid French expansion. Many brought their families with them. They have their own social circles, but they do not face nearly the same degree of ostracism as their *Gastarbeiter* compatriots in Stuttgart: after all, a Spaniard seems much less alien to a Toulousain than to a Swabian. Some of these immigrants have done well economically – I heard of a building worker who had bought a Peugeot 404, and I met a foreman from Galicia who told me, "Back home, we were almost starving, but now I earn as much in a week as I used to in a month. Our kids are doing well in French schools, they're now bilingual, and the French accept us quite easily. Of course, there are some things we miss – in the suburbs, the streets are so dead at night, there's no friendly *paseo*. Yet I doubt we'll ever go back to Spain." However, since about 1974 the picture has been changing. First, rising unemployment in France has virtually put an end to new immigration, and a few Spaniards have taken advantage of the French government's recent policy of paying grants to foreign workers to go back home. Secondly, a few hundred of the earlier, political wave of émigrés have returned to live in Spain since the restoration of democracy in 1976. But the vast majority, of both waves, are now too deeply settled in the Toulouse area to want to leave.

The city's coloured population comprises about 1,000 students, mostly from francophone Africa, and some 8,000 North African workers, who usually come without their families, live dismally in shanty-towns, work hard so as to send remittances back home, and do the menial jobs that the French and Spanish refuse. Though open friction is rare, they are generally scorned and ignored by the Toulousains: racism is not as blatant as in Stuttgart, or some parts of Britain, yet it smoulders discreetly, and Negro and Asian students sometimes have trouble finding lodgings. A Lebanese told me, "I am pale and can pass for French. I found a nice room, but when I told my landlord-to-be my name, he said, 'Sorry, it's let after all.' " There are even some *cafés* that illegally practise a tacit colour bar. At one modish place in the town centre, if you go in with a black, you are asked politely not to bring him again; if blacks go in alone, they are told, sorry, the place is full, even when it is half-empty. Yet within student circles this kind of racism does not exist. Left-wing French students in particular go out of their way to be friendly to the coloureds, and I was told that the Communists have a strategy of trying to win Third World students to their cause by instructing girl Party zealots to sleep with them. Whether or not the young *camarade* considers this combining duty with pleasure, she obeys.

Toulouse's active association with other Common Market countries has a lot to do with the presence of Italian, German and British communities, and almost nothing to do with formal town-twinnings. The parochial-minded former mayor, Léon Bazergue, was not interested in such things. He half-heartedly fixed up twinnings with two non-EEC towns, Tel Aviv and Saragossa, but exchanges have remained minimal despite the nearness of the latter. Pierre Baudis, mayor since 1971, has been far more outward-looking. He has formed twinnings with towns as far-flung as Kiev and Atlanta, Georgia. The Kiev link engendered a Soviet cultural festival in 1977, while the Atlanta link has led to student and mayoral exchanges: its origin is that Atlanta's mayor, a Negro, is the son of a former student at Toulouse. Georgia's most famous citizen has not yet paid a visit here, as he did to Newcastle in 1977; but Toulousains live in hopes.

Owing to Bazergue's attitude, Toulouse has missed out on its chance to find suitable twins in Germany or Britain: all bigger towns are already paired off. However, Baudis has been building up links of other kinds. His town council sponsored a German cultural festival in 1975, and a highly successful British one in 1976. Through Airbus and Concorde, the town has unofficial civic links with Munich and Bristol.

There is little of the cocktail-party diplomatic life – real or fantasy – of Stuttgart. Italy and Spain keep full-scale consulates; honorary consuls represent Germany, Belgium and a few other countries; the British Council flies the flag of culture; that is about all. However, in other ways Toulouse is more directly involved with the rest of Europe than any of my towns save Stuttgart, as you can observe by the constant to-ing and fro-ing of scientists and businessmen, or by a visit to the airport with its flights to London, Frankfurt and Geneva, and its imposing new international business centre. Of the various EEC communities, the Italian is the largest and oldest: about 5,000 Italians live in Toulouse, some of them immigrant workers like the Spaniards, some refugees from the Fascist era who have stayed on here because they like it. The building industry is dominated by Italian entrepreneurs.

The German colony, a few hundred strong, includes school and university teachers and a number of engineers and executives working on the Airbus. Mostly these Germans enjoy living in Toulouse: some display an effusive francophilia that can be almost embarrassing. At weekends you see organised groups of them touring the Pyrenees region, guide-books in hand, digesting the culture and history. Germany also exports its culture through the local *Goethe Institut*, which runs language classes, lectures and exhibitions. In 1976, the day after Ulrike Meinhof's suicide (in Stuttgart), its building was burnt down – but this was believed to have been the work of German extremists, not of Toulousains, whose attitudes to the Germans today are largely friendly. Among the older generation, notably those who fought in the Resistance or were deported. of course there is still some hostility: a professor aged sixty told me, "I'm pro-EEC, and I know we should feel sympathy for the Germans today, but I do find it hard. Deep in my heart I fear they will never change and I still hate them." Sometimes this attitude is bound up with the old French internal feuds that survive from the Occupation, and the director of the *Goethe Institut* told me of a revealing incident: "Once we showed a film on the German Resistance to Hitler, to which we invited local ex-Resistance groups. At the party afterwards, all they did was squabble amongst themselves, Gaullists versus Communists and so on, about wartime France, and showed no interest in the film. That's typical. My impression is that the germanophobia of that generation has little to do with Germany today but is mainly a facet of their own historical complexes. Younger people feel quite differently. Recently I went to Germany with a party of young Toulousains, mostly girls, and we were entertained by a *Bundeswehr* unit: with a lot of giggling they put on German helmets and uniforms and thought it all a great joke. They hardly seemed to know who Hitler was."

My own conversations with young people have tended to confirm these impressions. German students at Toulouse told me they did not sense any anti-German feeling among their French colleagues, while a number of young Toulousains said they would rather go on exchange visits to Germany than to Britain. Young Germans, they said, might sometimes be arrogant, but were always outward-going, generous, interested, eager to get to know the French: the British were usually reserved and self-absorbed.

Witness the difference between the local British and German colonies. The British – aircraft constructors, plus a few teachers, businessmen and others – are about as numerous as the Germans. At the height of the work on Concorde, the aircraft contingent with their families totalled about 500, but by 1976 the figure was down to some 150, mainly engaged on Airbus. With a few notable exceptions, these people adapt less well to Toulouse than their German counterparts. A Hawker Siddeley engineer told me, "I personally love this place and the French way of life, and I've made many French friends – but I'm not typical. Most of my colleagues accept a posting here for a year or two solely as a means of getting experience and promotion. They can't wait to get back home, and their wives even more so. They make little effort to come to terms with France: instead of exploring the fresh food markets, they go on buying the things they're used to at home, such as English brands of cereals and biscuits, and then complain that food is three times English prices. They're crazy. Many of these aircraft people have been used to living on RAF compounds in, say, Singapore or Cyprus, and they retain the same kind of ghetto spirit, isolated from the natives." The bachelors and grass-widowers spend their evenings in the bars of the larger hotels, or they go to one of the English-style "pubs" which they have virtually made their own, driving out the natives and installing darts-boards.

Some Britons do make more effort to adapt, I am glad to say. I met a young BAC engineer and his wife who came from Newcastle – of all places! – they had bothered to learn good French, and were on friendly dropping-in terms with their suburban neighbours. "We admire the French," said the girl; "they work hard and fully deserve their greater prosperity. As for Newcastle, it's a dump, we're glad to have left. It has nothing in common with Toulouse – I can't think why you're comparing them." Untypical Geordies. Nor can the example of another family I met be called typical, but I found it inspiring. John Prince, from Birmingham, is a lecturer in English at Le Mirail, and he and his English wife Jenny and their five children all fell in love with Toulouse and wanted to settle there. But under French law he could not, as a non-Frenchman, move higher up the hierarchy than non-established junior lecturer. So he faced a hard choice between returning to England or staying in Toulouse with a low grade and low salary. Finally the family opted for a third solution: they all took out dual nationality, which was easy after five years' residence. Today this "Anglo-French" family live happily in a converted farmhouse on a hillside south of the city: John will soon be a professor, and the children – *les petits Princes* – are all in local schools and speak better French than English. I have rarely met such a pure case of an entire English family becoming French by osmosis, voluntarily, without any previous ties of blood: a small victory for the beleaguered cause of a United Europe. Is it too much to hope that, as the EEC progresses haltingly towards the breaking down of national barriers in the professions, transplants of this kind will become easier and perhaps less rare?

So what are the prospects for Toulouse, as a regional capital within the European Community? The vast majority of Toulousains have long accepted the EEC as part of the landscape and today they take it for granted, if without great enthusiasm: it is no longer a subject of controversy, as in Britain. The only opposition comes from some Left-wing Socialists and Communists, who consider the present EEC too capitalist, too much dominated by a Germany in league with American interests. But the average local attitude was summed up to me by one young graduate: "We recognise that the EEC has helped France economically, and Toulouse has shared in that. Most of my generation are still vaguely in favour of a united Europe, but less enthusiastically than our parents after the war. We've grown sceptical. The EEC has become too technical, it's lost its idealism, and that's largely the fault of the politicians, especially the British. What's more, here in Toulouse we do feel a bit remote from the main EEC centres of power."

Less keenly maybe than Danes or Bretons, the Toulousains do feel aware of being out on the periphery, and therefore economically handicapped. So, for commercial and other reasons, they are much in favour of Spanish entry into the EEC – all except local farmers, who fear being undercut by low Spanish prices. But businessmen welcome the boost that Spain could bring to trade. "Toulouse, gateway to Iberia", has long been a catchphrase of local publicists, yet during the decades of Spain's semi-isolation it had little basis in reality, and at the time of

Franco's death in 1975 the city still had astonishingly few economic links with the big country on its doorstep. And this despite the cultural affinities, the large Spanish colony, and the popularity of Spain for holidays. Even today, communications are still poor. The Pyrenees are a powerful barrier: Spain's main links with France are on the coast at either end, and Toulouse, in the middle, is linked to Barcelona and Madrid by long, tedious train journeys involving changes. There are some direct air flights to Barcelona, but still none to Madrid. Today, with the return of democracy and the opening-out of the Spanish economy, matters are beginning to improve: trade is increasing, some Spanish firms are investing in Toulouse. The city's hope is that it will at last discover a more central role in Europe, when Spain joins the EEC.

There is another equally important question, political rather than economic. In a French context, will Toulouse ever be allowed to become a true regional capital, with a power and influence that accord with its size and history? It is a question facing all French towns of its kind – Bordeaux, Nantes, Strasbourg, even Lyon. And the answer depends on the will of the centralised French state, whose approach to regional development is a little two-faced. Toulouse has been encouraged to expand and modernise, but without receiving any more power. It is still a long way from being a true regional centre of decision-making, like Stuttgart, or even (tentatively) Bologna. And this adds fuel to the ancient fires of Cathar resentment against Paris.

From Napoleon's day until 1964, Toulouse was no more than the seat of a *préfecture* governing the Haute-Garonne, and thus administratively had no higher status than neighbouring capitals of departments, tiny towns such as Foix and Auch. Then de Gaulle grouped the ninety-odd departments into 22 "regions", solely for economic planning purposes (in other respects the former have kept their functions). Thus Toulouse is now the seat of a regional prefecture for the Midi-Pyrénées with its eight departments. After 1964 the Government also transferred from Paris certain ministerial services and placed them under the authority of the prefect, giving him powers to take decisions formerly taken in Paris. This was hailed as a feat of decentralisation, whereas it was no more than an administrative reshuffle: there are certain advantages in having decisions now taken on the spot, but they are still being made by state officials and not by locally elected bodies. However, after the 1968 ferment, pressure built up for a more genuine regionalisation, and in 1972 Pompidou's

Government carried through a reform setting up two new indirectly chosen bodies in each region. One is purely consultative, an economic and social council of local delegates; the other has more substance, being made up of the deputies and senators for the region, plus some other co-opted worthies. This new assembly has a small budget of its own, derived mainly from local taxes, to a ceiling of 20 francs a year per capita, and from this it can finance some local projects on its own initiative. The regional prefect must also consult it on all planning matters. The Midi-Pyrénées assembly regularly has a left-wing majority, its president being Alain Savary, a deputy for Toulouse and a leading French Socialist.

The 1972 reform does mark a small step forward. At least the "region" has finally been legalised as a political institution: previously it was a mere planning convenience. But as the assemblies' powers are limited to the use of their minuscule budgets, the prefects in practice keep the authority, and they will always look to Paris. Within each region it is the prefect who has the staff and facilities for drawing up detailed projects, and he tends to present them as a *fait accompli* to the assembly, which has neither the resources nor the know-how for this kind of work. In the Midi-Pyrénées, the Socialist-led assembly has managed on a few occasions to stand up to the prefect and push through it own projects, for new local roads and buildings, using its own budget: but its range of action is extremely limited. Moreoever, it does not have the moral authority of a direct popular mandate. It is merely a college of existing dignitaries, most of them elderly and cautious by temperament. French regionalists therefore believe that no reform can have much effect until, first, the assemblies are directly elected – as now in Italy – and, secondly, their powers and budgets are increased. In 1975 Giscard spoke in favour of direct elections, but was soon obliged to backtrack under pressure from his Gaullist allies, scared by the separatist flare-ups in Corsica, Brittany and some other places. Gaullists and other "Jacobins" have two main fears: that devolution would encourage secessionist tendencies in some areas; and that directly elected Left-controlled assemblies in certain regions – such as Midi-Pyrénées – would increase the influence of the opposition. They fear the trend could lead to a break-up of the state. So immediate prospects for further regionalisation are not bright.

This angers Toulousains. As in some other areas, the economic and cultural revival since the war has helped to promote the new regional awareness which in turn has stimulated new political claims against the state, which are not being answered. Toulouse feels like a teenager whose father has given him a new car but will not let him drive it. There has been a great deal of government-sponsored physical decentralisation from Paris: two *Grandes Ecoles* and several scientific bodies have moved here, the universities have grown far faster than Paris', the state has greatly expanded its regional television services; and so on. But this is not the same as devolution of power. Paris still controls the puppet-strings. And in many subtle ways, commercial as well as political, the city's dependence on the capital is as great as ever. Big firms such as Aérospatiale are managed from Paris. Local branches of major banks and credit bodies are run from Paris too, and Toulouse's tiny stock exchange is a mere toy. Local businessmen must continually be running to Paris to seek clients, even local ones: one consultant engineer told me, "Most big employers here are state-backed bodies, whether aircraft firms, hospitals or universities, and it's my Parisian rivals who get their contracts unless I'm careful. I'm even thinking of opening a Paris office in order to get *local* orders – it's crazy." (Not unlike the carpet-maker in Newcastle.)* Many people also believe that the rapid growth of air links and other modern transport, while opening up the remoter provinces has at the same time brought the controlling hand of Paris closer to them. Toulouse is less isolated than before, but also more subject to centralisation, linked to Paris by nine daily one-hour flights.

None of this has lessened the Toulousains' obsessive irritation with Paris, which is less chip-on-the-shoulder than the Geordie's view of London, and more like the arrogant fury of a colonised race that feels itself to be just as good as its occupier. Toulousains dislike going to Paris for pleasure, or affect to do so. Yet they discuss its influence endlessly, almost neurotically. "This could be a great city, if it weren't for Paris," was the kind of remark I often heard.

These local attitudes are bound up with the much wider Occitan regionalist movement that has gained ground recently in this part of France, not only in the Toulouse area but more especially in the lower Languedoc to the east, around Narbonne and Montpellier. Here the ancient Cathar spirit of anti-Paris dissidence burns even more fiercely than in Toulouse, and merges with the vinegrowers' violently-expressed grievances against current government wine policies. A few romantic hotheads have even launched an Occitan separatist

---

* See page 280.

movement: they dream, not very realistically, of creating an independent province out of that wide stretch of southern France known in mediaeval times as "Occitania", the land of the "oc" language (*langue d'oc*). You see their "OC" slogan daubed on walls. Their heartland is the coastal area, and their half-baked political ideas have little real influence. Up in Toulouse, on the fringe of Languedoc, the Occitan current is less political, more disciplined, more intellectual and cultural – and in some ways thus more meaningful. It represents a serious attempt to rediscover the region's authentic cultural roots, obscured in recent centuries. Some new poets are writing in Occitan, the old language of the troubadours, fairly similar to Provençal. Each year, over 1,000 Toulousain pupils take Occitan as an optional subject for the *bac*; Occitan "pop" singers draw eager audiences; and so *à la mode* is the trend that supermarkets have even launched publicity slogans in Occitan. More seriously, a group of semi-amateur enthusiasts have created a folklore group of some artistic quality, the *Ballets Occitans,* and this receives a municipal subsidy and often tours abroad. It has carefully reproduced the old costumes, songs and dances of the region, many of them colourful and elegant. The *Ballets Occitans* is entirely apolitical. Its dances celebrate a vanishing rural way of life, the seasons, the harvest festivals, and it has a strong appeal for the new city-dwellers nostalgic for their peasant roots.

This cultural revival is in some ways artificial. There is very much less contemporary creativity with a regional flavour than in Newcastle or Ljubljana, and most of the new culture in Toulouse – plays, operas, concerts – does of course rely on material drawn from outside. And yet, the search for Occitan roots is based on historical realities: this is an authentic region, culturally, that needs to rediscover itself in modern terms. There is a growing popular desire for a new regional identity, but one problem is that present official boundaries do not always help people to focus their loyalty. This again can be blamed on Paris. While many of France's 22 new regions correspond roughly to the old provinces – Brittany, Alsace, Burgundy, etc. – and thus to some reality, others are mere hybrid groupings of departments. Midi-Pyrénées – part Gascony, part Languedoc, part Rouergue – is one of these. In itself, it inspires no emotions: it is artificial. And many of France's leading advocates of regionalism believe that 22 regions are too many, when set beside the *Länder:* they should be reorganised, and reduced to eight or ten in number. If this were done, Toulouse could revert to its historical role as capital of a Languedoc stretching from Gascony to

Provence. On this basis, it could become the true capital of a politically authentic region – like most of my other towns. Giscard, among others, is believed to be in favour of some such national regrouping. For the moment, French political pressures are such that further effective regionalisation seems unlikely: and yet, for how much longer can the French government set its face against a devolutionary trend that so much of Europe is following, including, so recently, Italy, Spain and Britain?

Toulouse has come a long way since the war. It has expanded and changed – from sleepy market-town to industrial and scientific metropolis – more radically than any of my other towns. But it is like an adolescent who has shot up to six-foot too rapidly. It is still in the process of coming to terms with its growth; its diversified society is still atomised and partly rootless; its new suburbs are still in the trauma of adaptation to big-city living. And now, in the new economic climate, its era of heady expansion seems to be ending; some of its big industries are in difficulty; anxieties hang over its future. Where will Toulousains find the answers? In a revival of their Occitan past? In new links with Spain? Or, finally, in a more generous new deal by Paris to the troublesome old city of the Cathars and *capitouls*?

VI

Ljubljana

At last, Socialism with a human face – and human failings

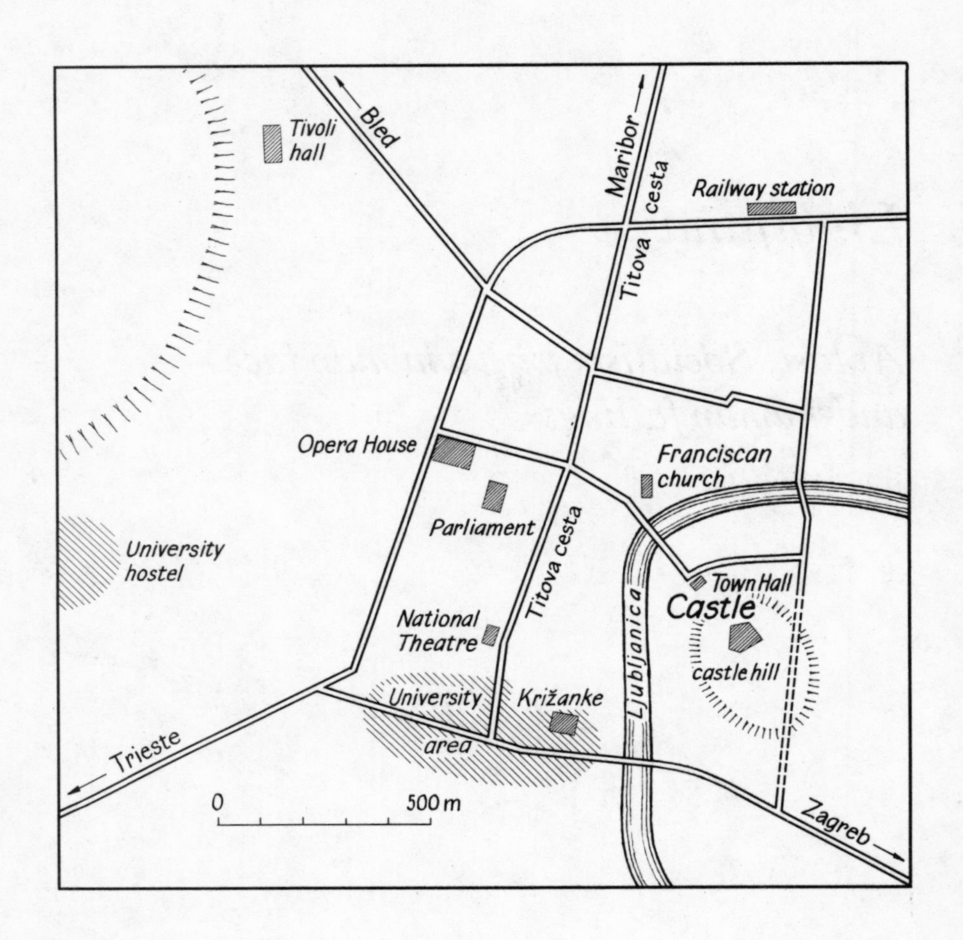
Bled
Tivoli
hall
Maribor
cesta
Railway station
Titova
Opera House
Franciscan
church
Parliament
University
hostel
Titova cesta
Town Hall
Castle
Ljubljanica
National
Theatre
castle hill
University
Križanke
area
Trieste
0
500 m
Zagreb

1
Introduction

A few weeks before I began my travels for this book, I wrote an article in a London monthly, *Modern English,* that circulates among teachers and students of English on the Continent. I explained my plans and choice of towns, and invited any readers living in them to contact me. I got virtually no replies of any interest from Stuttgart, Toulouse or Bologna. Perhaps significantly, the only two useful contacts, and both turned out to be very useful, came from Ljubljana. A schoolteacher wrote, "If I can be of any help, please let's meet . . . I'm in love with my Ljubljana, yours sincerely, Lučka P." And a schoolgirl of eighteen sent a long letter in near-correct English. "Everyone in England who don't know much about us think that it's just the same situation here as in Russia. But people are mistaken. . . . When I spent three months in London this year, and I told to some of my English friends that there is no soldiers with guns in streets, no more policemen as anywhere else, they wouldn't believe me. But there is no need to be afraid. . . . Students life is very interesting here. . . . Some of them are from rich parents, some are very poor. Those rich are spending money for beautiful dresses in so-called 'boutiques'. We have some nice, modern shops of high fashion as you find in London or Paris. . . . You really must come and see it yourself! I am sure nobody can be disappoint about life of young, about new ideas, about opposition to the established order, etc. I would like you to arrive, not just I, everybody here would like it. So don't hesitate too much, be guest of our nice town Ljubljana! I can help you by showing you everything. Beautiful regard from Irene N."

That was an offer I could not refuse. I came, and was not "disappoint". From Lučka and Irene, and from hundreds of other Slovenes, I received an exuberant welcome – alike from high Party officials and Catholic priests, from dissident students and self-managing factory-workers, and from Slovenia's legions of poets with whom I would debate over cheap brandy in the crowded Writers' Club till 3 a.m. There are some aspects of Ljubljana that have not ceased to irritate me – the outward shabbiness of buildings, for example, and certain limitations on freedom – yet I have come to like this the best of my five towns. I could give four main reasons, and hope they do not sound too patronising. First, there is that knock-out charm, vitality and expressiveness that always attracts me in Slavs and today burns more brightly in semi-autonomous Slovenia, as elsewhere in Yugoslavia, than in the lands to the north and east under Soviet tutelage. Secondly, the unique Titoist model of "liberal" Communism seems to be tolerably popular and, within limits, a success: I am no Marxist and might not choose to live under this system myself, but it has produced a society that a visitor may find intriguingly and constructively different. Next, Slovenes combine a fierce national pride with a warm involvement in the outside world, so theirs is a less introverted local patriotism than some others in this book. Finally, educated Slovenes are cultured and often well travelled, yet retain an unpretentiousness, even a kind of innocence by certain jaded Western standards. Perhaps all this has something to do with belonging to a tiny nation of less than two million, a nation that has some traits in common with the Irish. Ljubljana – poets, folk-patriots, booziness, loquacity, unpunctuality, shabbiness and all – kept reminding me in curious ways of Dublin.

The capital city of this subalpine Marxist Ruritania is not at first sight a very prepossessing place. It has little of the mediaeval grandeur of Bologna or Toulouse, or the shiny opulence of Stuttgart. It lies in a flat, open valley between low hills, within sight on a clear day of the Karawanken Alps on the Austrian frontier. On the higher hill stands the mediaeval castle that dominates the town, and below it along the curving banks of the river Ljubljanica are a number of baroque churches and mansions, witnesses to the long centuries of Austrian rule that ended in 1918. Ljubljana – then Laibach – used to be thought of in Hapsburg days as "a typical Austrian provincial town", a bit like Graz. Little of that ambience now remains, save in some older architecture: the modern spirit of the town is not at all Austrian. It has few interesting post-1918 buildings save a curious group of palaces, monuments and bridges designed in the 1920s by the noted Slovene architect Jože Plečnik, who drew on a native Slovene folk tradition and added neo-Italianate flourishes. The result is unusual and appealing. But away from the river there stretches drably the modern post-1945 town, astride the main artery, Titova Cesta. Its public buildings – the Slovene Parliament, ministries and so on – are in the typical socialist-austerity style of the late '40s and '50s, flanked today by a number of newer towers in steel and concrete that could be in Paris, London or anywhere.

The shabbiness is disconcerting. It is an odd reflection on Socialism that although Slovenia today is more prosperous and more keen to display itself at its best than ever before in its history, yet its towns look much scruffier than they did under the Hapsburgs. The old Laibach, despite its severe poverty beneath the surface, was a spruce and tidy place, as most of Austria's towns still are. Today matters are reversed. Ljubljana has acquired a modest affluence: go inside a flat or office and you will often find it neatly and smartly furnished. But down on the street, the façades of public buildings and the entrances of office and apartment blocks are as gloomily unkempt and unpainted as elsewhere in Communist Europe. And the style of graphic design, in the signs outside shops and other places, seems to belong in some unaesthetic limbo left behind by the worst of the early 1950s. It is all curious, in a society otherwise so cultured, so eager to be modern, so proud. Is it simply that the easy-going pleasure-loving Slovenes do not share the Germanic obsession with spruceness? Or is it some flaw in the workings of Socialism, so that public ownership of property leads to a lack of incentive to look after it properly? We shall see.

However, there are few other visual signs that one is outside the capitalist world, apart maybe from the absence of Shell or Esso stations. Here are no red banners, no street slogans proclaiming the onward march of the proletariat, as you still find in Dresden or Sofia: Slovenes would ridicule such crude hectoring. On my last visit, the only big posters in the streets were advertising a concert by American pop stars. Of course, portraits of President Tito are *de rigueur* in public premises, and statues to him and other wartime heroes stand all over town. But here in Slovenia the Tito personality cult is seriously rivalled by that of the early 19th-century poet-patriot France Prešeren, who to Slovenes is Shakespeare, Burns, Bolivar, Dante and Joan-of-Arc rolled into one. His stanzas are on every cigarette packet. An American visitor commented to me, "In the States, cigarettes carry Government health warnings: here, love-poetry. A contrast of two civilisations."

On the day of my first arrival, one March, it had been snowing and grey slush lay unswept-away in the streets. I had been warned to expect Ljubljana's violent changes of climate, as it lies uneasily between the balm of the Adriatic and the rigours of inland Central Europe. I drove down streets of drab-looking little shops and *cafés* and into the centre, where with some trouble I found a parking-space amid the fleets of locally made Renaults, and the Mercedes imported by those thousands of Slovenes who have earned foreign currency from jobs in West Germany. I went for a stroll. The faithful were pouring out of a large church: at the kiosk opposite, *Playboy* and *Der Spiegel* were on sale, also *l'Unità.* Everywhere were posters for concerts, opera, plays – for example, Stoppard's *Rozenkranc in Gildenstern sta mrtva.* Some of the bigger stores' window displays were almost Dickensian, but I saw also a few of the small, chic boutiques that Irene had promised; and in the middle of a piece of waste ground stood a large smart new-looking department store, "Maxi-Market" (sic), that would not have disgraced Stuttgart. It was full of Nescafé made in India, Italian toys, Johnnie Walker, Tampax imported from France, and other necessities of the good life. The large bank next door was far more modern than anything in Bologna.

Pedestrians waited obediently at crossings for their light to go green, even when there was no traffic near – as in Stuttgart. Was this Socialist discipline? – I enquired later. "No," an Englishman told me, "it's an orderliness that must be a hangover from Austrian rule. Down in Serbia, no one pays attention to lights, and a motorist must beware the Serb on the kerb."

I took coffee, the usual Turkish of the Slav lands, in an elegant little *slaščičarna* (tea-cum-pastry-shop) next to the Slon Hotel. It was full of some of the prettiest girls I had ever seen, evidently a social centre of such *jeunesse dorée* as existed – and a civilised contrast to near *café*-less Bologna. Later I queued up with the Slovenes on the kerb for a dinar's worth of chips fried in cheap oil. As evening fell, the streets were busy. The younger people in particular looked noticeably happy and animated. Some were showily dressed with an eye to current youth fashion. But most people wore nondescript clothes without much style or colour or attempt to impress. It was like Newcastle.

Ljubljana is very different from my other four towns in two essential respects: in its political and economic system, obviously; and also because it is the capital of a real nation with its own culture and language (no mere dialect, as *bulgnais* or Swabian) and its own sense of nationhood developed across a thousand years. Slovenia thus has a more precise identity than Northumbria or Languedoc, or indeed Emilia-Romagna or Baden-Württemberg. Tito, while retaining strong reserve powers, has wisely and boldly granted a high measure of internal self-government to the six nations that make up the Yugoslav Federation, so that Slovenes today not only feel themselves emotionally to be a nation but find they can also act like one, in many political respects. Belgrade seems remote not only physically (it is farther away than Munich or Milan) but in other ways too, and makes little direct impact on their lives: few of them visit it often. Moreover, 1,850,000 is a small enough population (less than that of Wales) to encourage a sense of kinship and community that many larger nations lack; and the focus of loyalty here is very much the Slovene nation rather than the city of Ljubljana (in contrast to the strong emotive pull of Bologna and Toulouse). So eager are Slovenes to possess the full attributes of nationhood that they spend huge sums on decking themselves out with all its insignia – a national library, national ballet, national institutes of this and that, national TV and radio, national publishing houses translating much of the world's literature into Slovene, and so on. A French resident commented to me, with French disdain, "It's a shade comic, this twee little Lilliput, trying to be so metropolitan about everything and not quite succeeding because of lack of resources and first-class talent: but it's stimulating." Personally I found this authentic, full-blooded cultural nationalism rather attractive, and it increased my sympathy for other aspiring autonomist movements.

This might not have been so, had I not also found the Slovenes so pleasantly un-insular. Not the least of the merits of the liberal Titoist system is that it imposes virtually none of the foreign travel restrictions usual under Communist régimes, save for a few currency limitations that hardly anyone obeys. Italy and Austria are each a mere hour's drive from Ljubljana, and most educated Slovenes have travelled widely in the West. Most of them also speak English and/or French and other languages. This has always been the most un-Balkan, westernised and prosperous part of Yugoslavia: consumer affluence has been rising steadily (at least until the recent world slow-down), and though there is still poverty in rural areas, Ljubljana's own living standards are little below the Austrian level. Various Western influences have been creeping in, including Western-style consumer habits and even some semi-disguised forms of capitalism that are the subject of anxious debate among Party loyalists. Slovenes thus exist in a strange middle world, titillated by Western consumer affluence but not yet made spoilt or blasé by it; half attracted and half repelled by the Western way of life which they see on their doorstep but is not quite theirs; proud, if critical, of their homespun Socialism with its strange mixture of schoolroom Marxist ruthlessness and anarchic *laisser-faire*; and still trailing the clouds of glory of a peasant Ruritanian naïvety from the mountain valleys whence they sprang.

I should add that as a visiting journalist I had the same liberty to move and talk freely, and to meet whom I wished, as in a Western country. Before I arrived I had contacted the Slovene authorities, who were helpful and provided numerous contacts but without trying to dictate who I should or should not see. I also made a large number of my own contacts, mainly through friends in London. And I found nearly everyone ready to talk to me openly, and often critically, as in France or Italy. I mention this because sometimes there are misconceptions about Yugoslavia. Only on one occasion – with a Catholic priest who had been in trouble, as I shall relate – did I sense serious reticence. Of course restrictions, and major ones, do exist on freedom of political expression; but some personal freedoms are greater than in the West, perhaps too great for society's own good. I found an endless debate in progress on the rights and wrongs of this system and how to improve it: everywhere people were eager to explain Slovenia and its Socialism to a foreign visitor, and often the talk would go on late into the night in some tavern, over bottles of cheap local wine, usually turning before long to bawdy jokes and much folk-singing.

This is a very informal, tolerant, self-satirising society. As in France, rules are made to be broken: once I went to visit a sick friend in a large public hospital and found it was well after visiting-hours, but no nurse or orderly stopped me and asked my business and the wards were full of other visitors. People are also vague about time, often forgetting appointments or arriving hours late but then, once you have met, thinking it churlish if you do not stay to chat and drink for several hours. Like most Slavs, Slovenes are moody, full of gay conviviality one minute, then heavy with sudden despair: the suicide rate, especially among the young, is one of the highest in Europe. In short, Ljubljana is at an opposite pole from Stuttgart with its greater opulence and tidiness, also its greater pomposity, formality and phlegmatism. Once I drove direct from the first town to the second and suffered severe cultural shock from the contrast; my notebook records a jotting during some solemn interview at the *Rathaus,* "Fearfully lacking in Slovene lightness of touch, *diese Schwaben.*"

2

The Party rule, O.K. – a paradox of discipline and laisser-faire

The dominant feature of the Slovenes' history is that they have remained on the same spot for fourteen centuries but during nearly all this period were under foreign subjugation and used their cultural unity as their chief weapon of survival against assimilation. This is the basis of their pride.

Ljubljana itself has existed since pre-Christian times, first as an Illyrian settlement, then as a Roman colony. Among the earliest inhabitants of the area were the Celts, and when this race were driven to the western fringes of Europe by later invasions, some of them managed to retreat up into the isolated mountain valleys of Slovenia where they have stayed ever since, finally assimilating with the later Slovene immigrants. So the Slovenes have a dash of Celtic blood in their Slav veins, and even a few Celtic words in their Slav tongue: a Slovene friend told me that on a visit to Wales he found some of the place-names oddly recognisable.

The Slovenes arrived from the north-east in the 6th century AD. After a short phase of independence in the Dark Ages, they fell under the rule of south German feudal lords and remained so throughout the mediaeval period. In the 15th century the central Slovene lands, known as Carniola, became a province of the House of Hapsburg, and this and the surrounding Slovene regions were to continue under the Austrian crown until 1918. There were repeated revolts and national upsurges, which kept the national spirit buoyant but never managed to set it free. A series of peasant revolts in the 16th century were followed by the arrival of the Reformation in Slovenia, which gave some encouragement to Slovene culture. But soon afterwards the counter-Reformation crushed these gains: Slovenia became fully Catholic, and from then on her Church leaders were dutifully loyal to the Austrian rulers (this is one reason for the Church's unpopularity today with Slovene Communists).

During the Napoleonic period Slovenia came for a while under the rule of the French, but after 1815 was restored to Austria. Throughout the 19th century nationalist resentment against the Austrians grew, and Slovenia played its part in the European risings of 1848. During all this time German was the official language and that of the nobility, but Slovene was the language of the people, and the Slovenes went on quietly developing their folk traditions and their literature, with leaders such as the poet Prešeren. The astonishing tenacity of the Slovene character is shown in the way they managed to preserve this culture despite all the pressures to germanize them. After 1848 they at last won the right to teach their own language in schools, alongside German. But they remained indignant at their under-representation in the Austrian Parliament and at Vienna's refusal to allow them any university: Ljubljana's was not founded until after independence, in 1919.

The Austrian rulers and the Franks before them had virtually wiped out the Slovene ruling class during the Middle Ages and imposed their own: so Slovenia for centuries has been basically a peasant nation, with only a small urban middle class and no nobility of its own. This is an important key to its character today. Peasant traits, of tenacity, roughness and simplicity, are found even in the most metropolitan *milieux* of Ljubljana.

In the last century there was widespread rural poverty, leading to mass emigration: by 1910, 100,000 Slovenes were in America. But the Slovene peasantry were also hard-working and found ways of developing craft industries such as lace and woodwork, and of educating themselves. This was always the most literate and advanced of the south Slav lands, and so the Slovene leaders were able to play a full part in building the new free Yugoslavia after 1918. But 1918-41 proved a fragile period. Slovenia was less horribly poor than the rest of Yugoslavia, and some progress was made with industry and education; but Slovenes suffered like others from the corruption and instability of Yugoslavia under the monarchy. Then the Nazis marched in, and the western part of Slovenia was put under Mussolini's rule. Very quickly the Slovenes, like other Yugoslavs, began to take to the hills against the enemy. For reasons of terrain, Slovenia never became so important a centre of Titoist Resistance as the mountainous heartland further south, in Croatia and Bosnia; yet Slovenes fully played their role as Partisans, many fought heroically and many, including girls, were tortured and shot as hostages.

From the survivors of this Partisan generation there emerged the Communist rulers of post-war Slovenia - and it was their towering prestige as Slovene patriots and freedom-fighters that made it possible for them to win popular acceptance for the new Socialism in which they believed. As in the five other Republics, the early post-war years were tough. A Stalinist police state was set up, attempts were made to push the peasants into collectives against their will, and priests, landowners, *bourgeoisie* and others were generally branded as "Nazi collaborators" - whether they had been or not - and either were liquidated or fled into exile. But after Tito's break with Stalin in 1948, things began gradually to change for the better - and they have gone on changing ever since, not always for the better, sometimes forwards, sometimes backwards, in a bewildering succession of new federal constitutions, economic reforms and counter-reforms, and periods of liberalisation followed by ideological tightenings-up. The basic system of self-management is still in a phase of fluid experiment, and recently a Ljubljana official was able to say to me: "We are still pioneering here, unlike France or Britain which are so traditional. Let's hope this reformist mania will die down soon, for it's a bit tiring. But at least our Yugoslav system is all home-grown."

The basis of the system is a duality, whereby power operates on two entirely different levels at once. On the one hand, there has been a steady process of devolution of responsibility and practical decision-making, so that all local units - schools or hospitals as well as factories, hotels or stores as well as town councils - are expected to manage themselves with a minimum of interference from the state. On the other, the centralised guiding role of the Party has been repeatedly reasserted: it is this that provides the cement holding the federation together. Between these two structures - the Party hierarchy, and the network of self-managing bodies - the state itself is supposed slowly to wither away, as Lenin intended. And this it has been doing, more at least than in other Communist countries. The aim is to avoid the heavy bureaucracy and centralism of the Soviet system, and through self-management to produce a Socialism that is popular because everyone can contribute directly.

Belgrade keeps control of foreign affairs, defence, central economic planning, and constitutional changes including those that affect self-management. From this central point, the first step in a tiered devolution is from federal level to the republics, thus making Slovenia autonomous – within some federal guidelines – in such matters as education, culture, welfare, taxation, local economic planning and transport. This has something in common with the West German or American systems – save that here, if a dispute arises between the two tiers of government, it tends to be settled behind the scenes at top Party level. Within each republic, devolution then goes on down through the local self-management bodies, as I shall describe: the aim is to spread responsibility as widely as possible.

The influence of the Communist Party is equivocal. It has a monopoly, in that no other political force is allowed under the Constitution. But during the years of liberalisation it gradually shifted its role from rule by authority to leadership by precept. It became less secretive and its name was changed officially to "the League of Yugoslav Communists" which is supposed to sound more friendly and voluntary than the word "Party". Its membership in Slovenia is about 100,000. Its aim is to retain its position by popular persuasion rather than intimidation: its activists seek to convince by discussion and personal example and are discreetly present in all workers' councils and other local bodies, setting the pace, advising, admonishing, seeing that "Socialism" is correctly applied. Most of the older members are ex-Partisans, men and women with a warm humanism and a practical approach, and talking to them I found little trace of the defensive dogmatism and double-think that characterises Communists in many countries.

For electoral purposes the Party operates through a wider "front" body, the Socialist Alliance of the Working People, which puts up candidates, not all of them Party members but all subject to approval by the Party. In civic affairs, in industry, education and other services, a majority of the senior executive jobs go to Party members but by no means all: in the liberalising period up until 1973 a growing number of non-Communists entered key jobs and it became increasingly hard to tell who was a Party member and who was not. A Ljubljana office worker told me, "In our *milieu,* being a Communist or not has ceased to be an issue. The Communists are simply the most dynamic and active element in society: the rest of us are not necessarily anti-Communist but are just more passive. I have one or two friends whom we tease a bit for being Party members: I'm not a member, but I'm not against. I suppose it's a bit like being a church-goer or not in your country, at least in the old days." This rather lax state of affairs began to worry the Party, and after Tito's crack-down on the Croat dissidents in 1972, it moved to a more assertive role again, in Slovenia as elsewhere. Some of the more rigorous Marxist-Leninists moved back into key jobs, at the expense of those suspected of being too pro-Western. This is the position today, dictated as much as anything by the anxieties over the post-Tito future.

But there has certainly been no return to the dark days. Restrictions on free political expression still go hand-in-hand with a high degree of tolerance in private living. You may not criticise Tito in public, nor his foreign policy, nor advocate a return to capitalism or to a multi-party system: but, if you are discreet, you can embrace a certain capitalist life-style and get away with it. Freedoms include unrestricted foreign travel, the right to run a small private business, the right to build your own house more-or-less where you like, and a remarkable permissiveness in the arts. In reaction, a number of younger idealists have even accused the authorites of hypocrisy, complaining that the pure ethos of Socialism, bred of the Resistance, is being corrupted by consumer values and private greed. But these are minority voices. If the majority of Slovenes today accept and like the system they live under, it is much more *because* of its *laisser-faire* loopholes than despite them. It would be hard to put the clock back.

The older generation of diehard *bourgeois* anti-Communists has by now nearly all emigrated or died away. The Slovenes I met expressed all kinds of criticisms of the way that Socialism works in practice, but almost all of them felt that the system was basically right for their country. And this is not the picture that a visitor rapidly acquires in other parts of Eastern Europe. Slovenes do feel free, and are largely unaware of the ways in which, by our standards, they are not. A French resident summed up his feelings: "I am no Communist, and I often find this place maddening. But at least, after the blasé West with its self-doubts about capitalism, it is refreshing to live in a society where people still have some faith that Socialism can be improved." We should now look in more detail at how the self-management works in practice, and what are the actual limits on freedom – in working life, local government, the arts, education, religion and the media.

3

Worker-management theory and moonlighting practice

Ljubljana has always been an important commercial centre, but is not primarily an industrial town. However, since the war it has played its part in Yugoslavia's drive to become a modern industrial nation. Slovenia's industrial output increased fourfold in the period 1949-69, and today Ljubljana has factories that turn out electrical goods, textiles, chemicals and food products: the largest, Litostroj, employing 3,000 people, assembles Renault cars under licence and also makes turbines. It would be pleasant to be able to report that these firms are as modern and successful as those, say, in Stuttgart or Toulouse. Alas, this is not quite so. Not only is there a serious lack of up-to-date equipment, but productivity nearly everywhere is low by Western standards. Are we to infer that the self-management system, whatever its successes in democratic terms, has not quite proved that it can also promote economic efficiency?

The system dates from 1950, when Tito admitted the failure in Yugoslavia of Soviet-style centralism and staged the *volte face* of setting up workers' councils. At first these applied just to industry but were later extended to every kind of work organisation, so that today schools, hospitals, government offices, even art galleries, theatres and restaurants, are each run like a cooperative, by a council elected by its entire staff. The original aim of the system has been well defined by Phyllis Auty,* writer on Yugoslav affairs: ". . . to prevent a dichotomy and hence hostility developing between management and workers. Through serving on the Councils, workers were to become educated and experienced in the multifarious problems of management. This it was hoped would produce industrial harmony and break the cultural barrier that in the past had separated qualified, educated managers

* *Yugoslavia,* Thames and Hudson, London, 1956.

from less educated, often ignorant workers. . . . It was also hoped that it would lead to greater productivity . . ."

The system has been repeatedly modified since 1950 and today, in industry, works roughly as follows. The staff of each enterprise elects its council for a two-year term. The council varies between about 20 and 120 members, according to the size of the firm (in very small firms, the entire staff make up the council). The council, many of whose members may be junior or unskilled workers, then appoints a management board of competent specialists to run the firm's affairs, and a director to preside over the board. The relationship of council to board is roughly that of parliament to cabinet, with the director as prime minister. The council meets once a month, when the board must report to it fully on the firm's financial and technical affairs. The council can veto the board's decisions or impose plans of its own, and in extreme cases can even dismiss the board or director if it thinks they are incompetent. In practice however, when a firm is running well, the council will leave major policy decisions to the professional management and will concentrate on welfare matters and working conditions, also on fixing salary levels.

A firm does not belong to its staff, but neither does it belong to the state: in law, its owners are "the community", and its staff do not have the right to sell it, nor are they its shareholders. After wages and other overheads have been met, profits go into a reserve fund to be used partly for productive investment, partly for welfare and improved conditions. Each firm is independent, and in theory – though not always in practice – Slovene government and Party do not interfere in its affairs unless it gets into serious economic difficulty. Under a free market system, firms compete with each other much as in the West: indeed, the 1960s saw a rapid development of modern advertising techniques. In one company, the advertising manager enthused to me in Madison Avenue tones about the beauties of his trade: "When I studied economics after the war, we were taught that advertising is the wicked product of capitalism – but now we've all adopted it. And I do not see that it conflicts with Socialism."

One typical Ljubljana firm is Kolinska. Formerly in private hands, it was "socialised" at the Liberation, and today produces a wide range of foods, from baby cereals to puddings and chewing-gum. The manager told me proudly that they had recently reached agreement with Knorr of Zurich, an American affiliate, to produce their soups under licence. He showed me round the plant, where I noted the out-of-date-looking machinery, shabby, unmodernised offices, and seemingly lackadaisical though cheerful atmosphere. But the Slovene charm was in full flood and the brandy flowed freely as the manager and the president of the workers' council explained to me the virtues of self-management. The manager was a neatly-dressed executive who had been with the firm nearly forty years, since its capitalist days; the president was a rough working man who had begun as stores assistant. He told me that his four-year term of office was honorary, involving many hours of unpaid committee and paper work in his spare time, on top of his regular job. "Our staff is 720 and the council 25, two-thirds of them women. At the meetings, the women tend to complain about trifles, as women do, rather than raise policy issues. But management/council relations are generally good, for we trust our management. Our role is mainly as watchdog: we scrutinise the board's budget and sometimes we veto its plans – for example, we refused to let them go ahead with a proposed merger with another firm, which we thought ill-advised." I then asked how the League of Communists fitted into this picture. They exchanged glances, and the president said, "I'm not a Party member, but the manager is – it's a matter of chance. The Party plays little role in decisions." The company secretary added, "When I was appointed, I was not even asked whether I was a member." (But in some firms, especially in the past five years, matters can be less simple.) The manager explained that each firm draws up its own statute, which fixes minimum wage levels for different jobs and these are supplemented by bonuses that vary according to the firm's annual profits. So there is a kind of profit-sharing. I was told that the differential between the manager's salary and that of a junior worker was as high as six and a half to one. This firm, like all others, has a trade union which defends the workers *qua* earners against the workers *qua* self-managers, but this Alice-in-Wonderland situation is not as odd as it sounds and indeed in some firms can lead to strikes and confrontations. The union also looks after welfare and social matters: Kolinska has a holiday camp on the coast, a sports club, and elaborate further education schemes. And so we parted, amid high conviviality. I noted that everyone was on free-and-easy first-name or "*tovariš*" – so unlike Stuttgart.

So how are we to assess the results of self-management, after nearly thirty years of it? There is little doubt that, in human terms, it has reduced the workers' sense of alienation and given them more feeling of involvement. At least one employee in three has served on a council at one time or another. "It's our best safeguard against autocracy," said a Party leader to me as we sat in the bar of a big hotel; "see that young barman over there, he may well be the company president." And most workers I met told me they felt the system was steadily improving, as people became more used to it. Of course, there is a negative side too. One price paid is the time spent on palaver. Though a council meets formally only once a month, there are also numerous *ad hoc* or sub-committee sessions, and a key man may spend twenty to thirty hours a month at these, much of it in his spare time. "What a waste, all this chat, it simply holds up *work*," said one dynamic business lady. The capitalist world, too, suffers from the committee disease: but it concerns only an executive minority, who are paid.

A far more serious drawback is that many workers' councils, lacking the business expertise or education, tend to put short-term self-interest ahead of the real interests of the firm and hence indeed of their colleagues. Where there are profits, they will often vote for higher wages rather than new equipment. This goes some way to explain Yugoslavia's high inflation rate and low productivity, and most politicians and economists will talk frankly about this problem. One official told me: "Too many worker delegates lack training in economics and misunderstand the advice of their management. For example, if a merger with another firm is recommended, they may veto it on selfish grounds, fearing for their jobs. Workers' councils are splendidly democratic, but their efficiency is not yet proven. The best answer may be to strengthen the role of professional management, but that's not easily compatible with our ideology." (I commented that trade unions in Britain have created a parallel kind of problem.)

This is not Mao's China, and the Yugoslav self-management system has not destroyed ordinary human self-interest or the spirit of personal incentive. Mercifully, maybe. Employees may feel rather more involvement in their firm than in the West, but they still want to feather their own nests. Hence the prevalence of a kind of moon-lighting, a further cause of industrial inefficiency. As in a number of countries outside Western Europe, the normal working day is from 6 or 7 a.m. to 2 or 3 p.m., when all offices close (some factories have a later shift too). This leaves most of the afternoon free, and many people of all grades use it to supplement their earnings with a private free-lance job. Many a factory worker will spend, say, from 5 to 8 p.m. as odd-jobbing electrician, plumber, carpenter, car repairer, or suchlike. In the earlier post-war years this was often a necessity, for supplementing the very low wages, but with greater affluence the practice has continued, since people now feel they need the extra cash for their new consumer luxuries. And there is a heavy client demand for this kind of free-lance work, for service industries such as plumbers and garages win a low priority in the official economic structure. The result is that many a worker will conserve his energies during his secure regular job, in order to be strong and fresh for his lucrative free-lancing. The effect on firms' productivity is inevitable. Politicians are aware of the problem, but the practice is so widespread and deep-rooted (many Party leaders have their own stake in it, for example by lecturing or running some small business) that to limit it would cause a major outcry.

Though productivity has been rising, it remains below the levels in my other towns, even Newcastle. Ljubljana's largest factory, Litostroj, was founded in 1947 to make turbines, at the height of the Stalinist heavy-industry-at-all-costs epoch. Later it tried to diversify into other mechanical goods but found it lacked the capital to make the investment economic. Losing money, it turned in 1969 to assembling Renault cars under licence, for the growing Yugoslav consumer market. But it still found it hard to make a profit, and when I visited the grimy old foundries, little changed since 1947, I was not so surprised. "We lack the money for renewing our equipment, and this limits our output," said the manager; "there's a forty-two-hour week, but we cannot persuade workers to do overtime since it would interfere with their free-lance jobs. So the plant is under-utilised." And when I asked an economist the reasons for Yugoslavia's very high inflation levels, he said, "The usual factors – low productivity, high costs leading to poor competitivity on world markets, under-use of industrial capacity, too many small firms that fail to integrate rationally when they merge . . . and so on." "Comrade," I said, "a Tynesider might not feel too out-of-place here."

As in the case of the Tyneside shipyards, there has been a certain ideological confusion as to the best way to tackle the problems. Does the answer lie in better professional management, capitalist-style, or in stronger official control? In the early post-war years factory managers tended to be political appointees, as in Russia – Party zealots or former Partisan heroes. Then in the 1950s came the rise of the technocrat, as workers' councils began to be encouraged to choose a manager for his abilities rather than for political reasons. Posts were advertised publicly, and managers became able to dictate their salaries or move to another firm offering more, as in the West. However, since the tightening-up in 1973 the pendulum has swung back against the apolitical technocrat and the Party has recovered its influence in the choice of managers. Recent appointees have mostly been Party men. This latent but pervasive influence of the Party, in industry as in other sectors, is especially important when a firm runs into serious financial trouble. Legally, the government has little power to interfere in the running of a firm – less, say than in *étatiste* France – and if an enterprise faces insolvency, then it must go to its supporting bank and discuss a loan, a merger, redundancies, or some other solution, just as in the West. In practice, the Party does often intervene behind the scenes in a mediatory role, and this helps to explain why so few firms do actually close, despite the frequent insolvencies. I was told of a large food products firm near Trieste which was doing so badly that the workers' council sacked the management *in toto* for incompetence: the Party then intervened, a new management was chosen, and funds were somehow found to get it going again. All very symptomatic of Yugoslavia's mysterious compromise between market capitalism and Soviet-style centralism.

So how are firms to be made more efficient and productive, without sacrificing the self-management system? It is a difficult dilemma. Several Slovene economists told me they felt the best solution to under-capitalisation was massive Western investment. This has in fact been sanctioned since 1967, after some ideological heart-searching, and a foreign partner may now own up to 49 per cent of the capital of a Yugoslav company and draw 25 per cent of the profits: German and Italian firms in particular have taken advantage of this. The debate continues in the Party as to the wisdom of this reliance on Western capitalism.

Some purists also feel that the government ought to take steps to limit the brain-drain that deprives the economy of some of the skilled top talent that it needs. Hundreds of engineers and scientists move off, if only for a few years, to better-paid jobs in the West. But to restrict this would cause an outcry: Slovenes value liberty of movement as one of the most precious of their freedoms. So what other ways can be found of increasing industrial efficiency? Since 1974 the government has set out to supervise the investment programmes of workers' councils a little more closely, even at the risk of infringing on self-management. Yet it also seems to have been moving in the opposite direction by breaking self-management down into yet smaller units so as to give the individual an even more direct sense of involvement. Each department in each firm now has its own little workers' council, with a certain autonomy. One aim is to give each employee a greater awareness of the need to restrain excessive wage rises or other abuses. But it can also lead to a certain anarchy. I visited a publishing and printing firm, where the production department was now free to decide on its own printing contracts and could as well award them to an outside company as to its own. Several observers of modern Yugoslavia have commented that the mania for decentralisation has led to "a mood of cheerful chaos" and that collective responsibility for management means that no one is prepared to assume final authority. "Go into a shop, and complain of a defect in the goods you have bought," said a foreign resident. "and the store manager will send you away with a shrug, saying it's not *his* fault." A flaw in the welfare-state ethos that is not the monopoly of Communist countries?

On the margin of this Socialised world, small-scale private enterprise is sanctioned and even flourishes. Foremost are the peasants, who after the war rejected Tito's collectivisation attempts with the true stubbornness of Balkan peasantry. Today 85 per cent of the land is still privately farmed, though holdings may not exceed 10 hectares. In some upland parts of Slovenia there is still poverty, but in the fertile plains around Ljubljana most farmers make a fair living; and, as around Stuttgart and Toulouse, some factory workers retain their smallholdings – *their* contribution to the national moonlighting industry!

Then there are the numerous owners of small inns and restaurants, craft workshops and boutiques, garages and other service firms – owners running these as a full-time business, not as moonlighters. The government forbids them more than five employees each, so as to prevent "exploitation", and it assuages its muddled Marxist conscience by taxing them heavily. Yet these mini-capitalists are often among the wealthiest people in Slovenia – and the most efficient. Sometimes they expand discreetly by running two firms under different names, thus getting round the five-employee limit – "It's so easy to dodge the rules in this country," a building contractor said to me.

In Ljubljana I was introduced to the family owners of a boutique, making and selling real-leather handbags. The shop was full of Italian fashion magazines, and had a modish décor and ambience very different from that of the average utilitarian publicly owned store. The attractive young owner and her Mastroianni-like brother were dressed with ostentatious elegance: I felt I was back in Bologna. The girl told me: "My father was the rich owner of a large handbag factory in Ljubljana before the war. The new régime then kept him on as technical director, as he was the only person who knew the business. Now I run this workshop, selling about 20 quality bags a day for 500 to 600 dinars each. We can't sell other firms' bags, only our own, for private retail shops are illegal: you must run a workshop, selling your own goods. I find it easy to get good staff, since I pay more than the average factory. Of course," she lowered her voice, "I don't advertise or put bright lights outside the shop or do anything like that to attract attention. It could make the tax inspectors tougher than they are already: we pay 19.5 per cent tax on our sales and about 4,000 dinars a month on each employee. Private firms like ours are tolerated, even discreetly encouraged, and they are more numerous than a few years ago. But they are still a source of debate within the Party, and it might clamp down again, you never know. Best to keep a low profile." But she and her family earned enough to afford an Alfa-Romeo, a weekend seaside villa and foreign holidays. Had I met a last relic of the old Yugoslavia, or the vanguard of the new?

4

Democratic innovation – but no one keeps the place tidy

Like industry, the system of local government in Slovenia follows the principles of self-management and decentralisation. The result is a curious and complex three-tier structure that has gradually evolved. The most important unit is the commune: each has about 30,000 inhabitants, it bestraddles urban as well as rural zones, and has a certain autonomy. The second and overlapping tier is the city council, which may group several communes or parts of communes, or lie within one commune, according to the size of the town. And the third tier is a series of autonomous corporatist bodies for specific matters such as health and education, operating parallel to the other local government units. All very complicated.

Ljubljana is made up of five communes of roughly equal population: a central one, purely urban, and four others each embracing suburbs and surrounding rural areas. This mixing of town and country is usual in Slovenia, but I was surprised to be given two divergent reasons for it. One official told me it was an attempt to apply the Marxist ideal of abolishing the historic antipathy between city-dwellers and peasantry. But others said that Edvard Kardelj, a leading Slovene politician and close friend of Tito, had borrowed the idea from England's rural district councils. Perhaps both versions are true.

The republic allots each commune a budget, which comes direct from a tax on companies in proportion to their wage bill. The commune can spend the budget as it likes, save that it must not neglect its responsibility for infrastructure such as new roads and school buildings. If it is short of money, it can levy an extra local purchase tax: thus the Ljubljana communes put a new tax on cars, whereupon the inhabitants went off and bought their cars in other towns, the local dealers raised an outcry, and the tax was taken off again!

The Ljubljana urban area, comprising four-fifths of the five communes' population but only a small part of their surface, is a separate unit: it has its own mayor and city assembly, its own budget and responsibilities. It has to pay for public services and utilities, adult education, and so on; but its budget is only about two-thirds of that of the five communes together, and there are many difficulties of liaison and arguments over who should pay for what. A problem familiar to many of my towns.

The third tier, set up more recently, is what is known as the "Communities of Interest" – one for education, one for scientific research, one for culture, one for health and social care. These operate roughly in the same way as the health service in Britain, save that there is a greater degree of self-management at local level and less *étatisme.* Each community has its budget fixed by the republic and, like the communes, it derives this direct from company taxes. The community is then run by a board of delegates drawn from workers at all levels in the given sector – from hospital managers to junior nurses, from professors to primary teachers and cleaning staff – with some government representatives too. But the Ministries play little more than a supervisory role, or one of liaising with Belgrade or foreign countries. The communities are self-managing: thus culture, education and health are run neither by the state nor by local authorities, but by themselves – rather like broadcasting in Britain. And the self-management goes down the line, so that each hospital or school has its own workers' council (pupils are represented, but not patients). As in industry, the result is a great deal of chat, a certain amount of muddle, and a happy sense of democracy. Shortage of funds is the main problem, leading at least till recently to a serious shortage of hospital beds in Ljubljana. But finally a large and splendid new hospital has been built, equipped to the best Western standards, with a free-and-easy atmosphere and a foyer where a visitor can buy his sick friend a bunch of roses or a copy of *Playboy*.

The communes and the city each have their own directly elected assemblies which are bicameral: a House of the People, a House of Producers. The former are elected by the citizens as a whole, and the latter by employees within factories, shops and offices – the aim of this House of Producers being "to reinforce the role of the workers in decision-taking". So some citizens are a little more equal than others, in their franchise; and most civic decisions require the approval of both houses. Local elections are for four-year terms. In theory, anyone can be a candidate so long as he can muster ten signatures: in practice, virtually all candidates are selected and sponsored by the Socialist Alliance of the Working People, a broadly-based body within which the League of Communists lurks as guide and animator. Many successful candidates are non-Communists: but they will have been screened by the League. In city council debates, there is genuine free discussion on practical issues, and not too much invoking of Marxist dogma. But inevitably League members tend to get most of the key jobs. At the time of my last visit, the mayor and one of his two deputies were Communists, but not the other.

The town hall, at the foot of the castle, is a charming old 15th-century building with a pretty courtyard and smart modern additions. On my last visit, an OECD delegation was in session. The mayor, elected by the assembly for four years, is full-time and fully salaried, as in Stuttgart: his deputies are part-time, with small indemnities, while other councillors are unpaid. The mayor greeted me jovially, offered me apricot juice (alcohol is forbidden in government offices, or the budget and work-schedules would be ruined) and lit my cigarette from one of those square Italian boxes of tiny matches, this one with a picture of Ljubljana Castle. He was a burly man in his late thirties, a metallurgist and economist by training, who had been a senior Communist official in Maribor and then a federal deputy in Belgrade. He took me out to a good lunch, and talked non-stop about the city's planning and economic problems, the shortage of telephones, the need to improve sewage systems, the virtues of the consumer boom: not a word about politics or ideology. He seemed the complete technocrat, an unassuming little man, entirely different from the demagogic ego-boosters so common in Western Europe and America – the Dan Smiths and Bazergues. Mayors and other elected officials are forbidden to serve in the same post for more than two terms (a total of eight years), the aim being to ensure a rotation of responsibility and prevent individual power-building based on personality cult (only Tito is allowed *that*). This succeeds, to the extent that I found no dominant personalities in Ljubljana to correspond to the Zangheris and Rommels of my other towns: power resides in the hands of a shifting oligarchy of cautious and unpretentious public servants.

Ljubljana, like other Slovene towns, is chronically short of funds for essential new projects, but one ingenious means used to combat this is the system of voluntary *ad hoc* levies. If a city or commune feels that it needs a new school, clinic or swimming-pool, it can organise a referendum to ask the citizens if they will each provide a fixed sum from their own pockets to pay for it (new building is the concern of the local authority, not of the Communities of Interest). I saw an impressive new primary school in a town near Ljubljana, for which the inhabitants had each contributed 0.5 per cent of their salary over three years. And in a suburb of Ljubjana that needed a nursery school, the commune agreed to put up two-thirds of the money provided the inhabitants raised the rest themselves, paying 40 dinars per family. They agreed.

So does this mean that the citizen's active interest in local community affairs is greater than in the West (and we have seen how low it can be in Toulouse and Stuttgart)? Not necessarily: people will vote in elections, or will pay money for something of practical value to them, but they do not flock to join residents' associations or cultivate an American-style neighbourliness, any more than the Germans or French. This has nothing to do with a reaction against Socialism: it is not in the Slav individualist temperament. A young executive and his wife on a new high-rise housing estate told me there was no organised communal life in the place, such as clubs or social centre – "and we personally feel no need for it: we have plenty of friends elsewhere in the city." The Slovenes, like the Toulousains, are convivial in public yet devoted to their privacy. A local sociologist told me that, while self-management in factories and offices was a relative success because people's livelihood and status were at stake, in the everyday *milieu* of the civic community they preferred to leave affairs to the elected assemblies, and few had direct experience of civic matters. "We are losing the traditional style of village community life," he said, "where people made their entertainments together: now, with their cars and television, they have retreated into more private pleasures, leaving a vacuum in the community." It could have been a Toulousain talking.

Town-planning is the city council's concern. In the late 1960s it drew up a master-plan which is slowly being applied: ring-roads are being built, and zones have been marked out for preservation or renovation. On paper, it is all very strict and precise; but in practice it is casual and flexible, more so than in the West, and sanctions are inadequate: this was very strongly the view of an American I met, a consultant to the city planners. Because the land is neither privately owned nor municipal but vaguely "public", anyone thinks he can do anything with it. And a serious lack of capital has held up many re-development projects. For example, by the late 1960s the castle had fallen into serious disrepair and parts of it had become a slum tenement. So a project was drawn up for rehousing the slum-dwellers elsewhere and turning the castle into a municipal centre for leisure and culture. Foreign investment was found, but later vetoed during one of Slovenia's various ideological about-turns. Only by the end of 1974 did restoration work begin. Delays of this kind are typical, though it should be added in fairness that when new projects *are* finally completed they are often architectually impressive. This is true of the new hospital, and of the Tivoli Hall, one of the biggest and most up-to-date sports and leisure stadiums in this part of Europe.

An architect said to me, "We're amazingly free here to build what we like, how we like: there's little bureaucracy. But we find it hard to raise the capital. In Austria, it's the other way round – which is worse?" And the town clerk commented, "Just as in France, or the United States, we are getting to the stage of public-squalor-amid-private-wealth: people are selfishly not prepared to sacrifice their personal living standards for the public good, even if that is their good too."

Lack of public funds is also one of the causes of the most striking visual characteristic of Ljubljana: its horrifying shabbiness. If you arrive from Italy or Austria, this hits you like a blow between the eyes – not so, coming from Zagreb, which is even shabbier. I am not referring to the relative absence of brightly decorated shopfronts or gaudy neon advertising, inevitable in a Socialist country where there is little commercial competition. I speak of something more pervasive. Enter any office block more than a few years old, and the foyer, the stairs, the courtyard, will be drearily unkempt: then open the front door of some firm within the block, whether private or public, and you may well find thick new carpets, cheerful modern paintings and the sprucest furniture and décor. Pay a call at a private villa, and you may have to pick your way through potholes and muddy pavements, past weeds and builders' rubble outside their front door, before finally you can sink into their luxurious sofa and admire their hi-fi. Government or university buildings, unless brand new, tend to look like gaunt survivors from the Berlin of the late 1940s. And yet in monarchist Hapsburg days this town was known as "*Laibach die weisse*" – white and clean.

I asked many Slovenes about this phenomenon, and finally pieced together the reasons. Above all, it is due to the nature of land ownership, or rather, non-ownership. You may own a building or part of one (a flat or villa), but not the land on which it stands, for legally this is free like the sky or high seas. The communal parts of blocks of flats or offices, such as the entrances, also belong to "the public", e.g. to no one – so no one has any responsibility or incentive for their upkeep, any more than for that of his own front path. The city and communal authorities are supposedly responsible for keeping pavements and public buildings in good repair, but their overall lack of funds leads them to give this a low priority. As was explained by the American planner I met: "The cost of redevelopment is very high, owing to the high compensation that must be paid to the owners of property pulled down. So it is cheaper to build on a new site than expropriate and rebuild. Redevelopment is considered economic sabotage: it's thought wrong to pull down buildings that can still find some practical use. The result is general mess and ugliness, with new high-rise towers next to old hovels that are still occupied but no one would think of repainting."

It is a curious flaw in the Socialist system, not only in its property laws but in the community conscience. There is also the influence of an ethos that holds it all right to acquire wealth but bad form, ideologically, to flaunt it. Keeping-up-with-the-Pavlovičs must be done discreetly or it appears anti-Socialist: so you do not make your house or shop look too smart from outside. Nor do the Slavs tend to share the Germanic obsession with orderliness or the Italian passion for elegance. An English resident told me: "The average Slovene would give painting his house a low priority compared with boozing or travelling. I even think they get so used to this shabbiness that they cease to notice it."

When I asked a Party official why the authorities did not enforce some rules for tidying doorways or front gardens (as de Gaulle had imposed *ravalement des façades* on the shabby Paris of 1960), he said: "In pre-war days, you were legally obliged to clean the pavement in front of your property, just as in Germany today. But the principle of government by consent has now become so rooted that if any Minister proposes stricter measures he's denounced as 'Stalinist'." I laughed: so Slovenes cannot copy tidy *bourgeois* Swabians because it might lead back to Stalinism!

The housing industry and the property market are equally full of anomalies. In the post-war years, when the accent was on the growth of productive industry, housing was desperately short and mostly of poor quality, even though Ljubljana had been little damaged in the war. Since then housing has gradually improved, though it is still below Western standards. And since about 1965 there has been a sharp switch of emphasis, officially encouraged, from rented publicly owned flats to private ownership - leading to crypto-capitalist abuses.

For the building of cheaper housing for rent by lower income groups, the official system puts the onus on the tenant's employer. Of the tax which each firm pays to the authorities, proportionate to its wage bill, a fixed part is syphoned off to a development bank which uses it for building flats for the firm's employees, helped by official subsidies. Thus many firms own blocks of flats which they rent off cheaply to their staff. I met a railway worker with a wife and two sons, living in a pokey three-room flat barely big enough to contain their large TV set, washing-machine and other mod cons: the tenement block, owned by the railways, was grim, but they paid only 250 dinars rent a month and so were reluctant to move. This block was built in the 1950s, when rented housing was cheap but not plentiful. Today there is still a shortage, as the levies on firms are pegged too low. While private consumption has been rising fast, the money officially put into housing has been kept low, so that workers are not as well housed as they could afford to be. As someone put it, "They have larger cars than flats."

From the early 1960s, the official solution to this problem was to encourage private ownership, which was formally recognised in the 1963 Federal constitution. A campaign then began to urge people to save up to buy their own flats or houses, helped by easy mortgage terms from banks or employers. This soon bore fruit: whereas in 1950 only 760 new dwellings were built in Ljubljana, by 1967 the rate was over 3,000 and has been kept up since. Today 95 per cent of all new house building in the city is for private ownership, and some 70 per cent of all homes are already owner-occupied. Building for speculative resale or for letting is forbidden, for this *is* Socialism: but so long as a family can produce part of the cost of the home from their savings, their employer or bank will usually make up the rest (up to 70 per cent) with a 20 to 30 year loan at as little as 1 or 1½ per cent interest, a tiny fraction of the inflation rate. So the *bourgeois* property-owning instincts of the Slovenes are not only encouraged but actively subsidised by the Communist régime – and a Geordie or Toulousain with his 10 to 12 per cent mortgage rates may feel green with envy.

Much new private building is in the form of flats, but much, too, is individual. Many people will get permission to build a new house in their garden, and then use their old home as a barn or garage. If they do not have a garden, but want to build a house, then they will probably have to look outside the city, in nearby rural areas where there is more land available. This creates problems, for the land outside the town is either ownerless, or it belongs to a farmer, and there are no clear planning rules. A family will simply appropriate some little plot, or lease it hurriedly from a farmer, and without seeking a planning permit will throw up a house in a few weeks with the help of a private builder. Hence the rash of new bungalows and villas all round Ljubljana, higgledy-piggledy, often without proper drainage or other services – a little like the inter-war suburban sprawl of outer Paris. It is one more result of the anomaly of land being "free". The authorities could if they wished stop the abuses, by enforcing the planning permission which has been flouted. Sometimes they do step in and pull the houses down, *pour décourager les autres* – but this simply causes an outcry. Too many influential middle-class people have a vested interest in the *status quo,* too many Party leaders have built such houses or are planning to do so. The authorities thus turn a blind eye. And this "black housing", as it is called, is one more intriguing feature of Yugoslavia's laisser-faire Socialism.

5
Slavonic exuberance and Western consumer values

Slovenia since the war has come some way – but not all the way – towards creating an egalitarian society. Class divisions and antagonisms of a West European kind have been disappearing. But within a new supposedly classless society, differences of income and cultural level, hence also of life-style, persist strongly. Recently they have even been on the increase.

The narrowing of the old extremes of wealth and class, a process that has slowly been taking place in most of Europe, here happened much more suddenly and radically after 1945. Today there are no more big landowners, no more private fortunes or extreme privileges of birth: the peasantry and workers are not only better off than before but feel they have more of a stake in society. Between citizens there is some real sense of equality of rights – stimulated by the self-management system – so that people of very different rank or social origin mix without inhibition. When a friend of mine, a woman schoolteacher, rang up on my behalf a leading Slovene politician, whom she had never met, he at once called her by her Christian name, and when we all met they talked like equals. In some ways Slovenia seemed to me closer to the open, informal societies of the United States or Australia – where there may be status snobberies based on income, but where dustman and chairman chat like mates – than to the hierarchic formalities of France or Germany or the uptight class prejudices of southern England. It is a little like Geordieland, too, in its ethos.

This is evident especially among the young. In the secondary schools, the sons and daughters of manual workers and professional people will make close friends, have love-affairs, visit each others' homes, go on holiday together, without complexes. The differences are felt not as social but financial, and thus maybe cultural too. A doctor or professor will not only earn much more than a factory worker, he will probably also have wider cultural horizons and his home, though it may not be much larger, will have more books and may be furnished with more taste. These variations tend to be passed on to the next generation, since opportunities for higher education are not as equal as they should be. Student grants are small and Slovenia has only one full university: so in practice it is easier for a prosperous Ljubljana family to send its children there than it is for workers or peasants living maybe miles away. About half the students at the university are from Ljubljana itself; and while the total student body has increased hugely since the war, the percentage from working-class or peasant homes is said to be no larger than in pre-war days – 19 per cent, better than in France or Germany but below what one might expect of Socialism. This inequality is a big talking-point today, especially among younger people whose Socialist idealism tends to be warmer than that of their elders.

Many are also indignant about the growing wage differentials. In the earlier post-war years these were pegged low, and a manager might earn only twice as much as an unskilled worker. But, with the move to a market economy, it was found necessary to raise differentials in order to improve incentives. Firms, so long as they did not pay below the agreed basic rates, could now fix their own salary scales by virtue of their profitability, and this has led to anomalies. I met a graduate executive in a factory whose wages were 20 per cent below those of a friend of his, a mechanic in a more successful firm. Such things are common; and with skilled technicians and good managers in short supply, salaries at the upper level have tended to spiral as firms compete for the best men. Today in an average Slovene firm the monthly wage for an unskilled woman worker is 3,000 dinars, for a heavy manual worker 3,900, for a mechanic 4,800, while the company secretary may earn 13,000 and the manager 19,000. This six and a half to one differential may rise to ten to one in some firms, with managers earning 30,000 dinars. Of course they are quite heavily taxed, as are many professional people such as surgeons and, as I described earlier, the prosperous owners of private enterprises. "It's not easy to reduce these disparities," one official told me, defensively: "you see, firms are competing not only with each other but with foreign countries. We have to ensure a good standard of living for our top talent or they'd simply emigrate to the West with its higher salaries – as some of them do. This brain-drain menace is the price we pay for our open-frontier policy. But it's worth it."

It is not easy to compare Ljubljana's living standards accurately with those of my other towns. For one thing, an employee's take-home pay can be a misleading guide. His income tax and social insurance are paid by his firm, his wife probably works, he may have a second unofficial job himself, and he enjoys a number of facilities which are much cheaper than in the West, such as very low rents and mortgages and relatively cheap fuel charges. On the other hand, many consumer goods such as clothes are dearer than in the West. According to OECD statistics, the average annual per capita income for all Yugoslavia is $1,500, for Slovenia $1,900, while for Ljubljana it must be well over $2,500. This puts the city roughly on a level with many Austrian or Italian towns, and shows that economically as much as geographically it is closer to the West than, say, to Montenegro. At a guess, I would say that Ljubljana's standard of living is not far from that of Newcastle and perhaps 20 to 25 per cent below that of Toulouse or Bologna. From a very low post-war level it has been rising fast, though inevitably has levelled off since about 1974. Consider the consumer statistics. The number of TV sets in Slovenia, 500,000 or 2 for each 4 people, is only a little below British or West German levels. And car ownership in Ljubljana rose from 1 per 24 people in 1961 to 1 per 6 in 1976. A Slovene told me: "When I was in New York some years ago, and saw the sea of red car-lights along Park Avenue, I felt, 'that will never happen back home'. But now, on Sunday evenings, the lines of cars crawling back into Ljubljana, bumper to bumper, are just as in the West."

As I have indicated, housing standards are still appreciably below Western levels. At the top end of the market especially there is a levelling-off: no luxurious penthouses or villas with swimming-pools. Higher-salaried people, senior executives and others, live in comfortable but not very spacious homes, rarely of more than four or five rooms, and nowhere are there large or sumptuous dwellings in private hands. Middle-income people live in neat but small new flats, or else in ramshackle older ones for which they pay next to no rent: it is rather as in Paris twenty-five years ago. The newer flats built for workers have improved in quality and are barely distinguishable from middle-income ones.

The railway worker I mentioned earlier, living with his wife and two teenage sons in a small but neat three-room flat, could be regarded as typical of the new working class, their ambitions, possessions and life-style. The father told me he had fought with the partisans, was now fifty-four and earned 2,200 dinars a month and would retire at sixty. The elder boy was studying nuclear physics at the university, with a grant of 400 dinars a month; the younger boy was at a *gymnasium.* The family said they had recently managed to buy a second-hand Yugoslav-made Fiat for 12,000 dinars – six months of the father's salary! There was a large refrigerator in the hall, a gas cooker, a hip-bath, a big TV set. Their recreations were watching TV, going sometimes to the theatre (seats are very cheap), playing cards with friends, and belonging to a gardeners' club where they had an allotment. The boys occasionally frequented a local youth club, while the father preferred to drink at home with his friends. They were not churchgoers; but granny, who lived in the country, was. For their holidays (the father had five weeks a year), they would spend some of the time on the grandparents' farm, helping with the harvest, and some time at a cheap holiday camp by the sea, owned and run by the railways and reserved for staff. On occasions they had been to Trieste and Austria. The boys, polite and good-looking, both talked perfect English; the father, a plump, jolly man, talked Italian and German – a usual situation. "Slovenia is happier than before the war," said the father; "Socialism's not perfect, but at least we're all much better off." I felt the family was little different from its counterparts I had met in my other towns – save that I doubt you could find many workers' families in Newcastle or Bologna speaking three foreign languages, or many railway workers in Toulouse with sons studying nuclear physics.

With affluence, Slovenes' leisure and holiday activities have been developing much as in the West. They have a beautiful and varied country, and in summer the roads out of Ljubljana are packed with cars going for the day or the weekend to nearby beauty spots such as Bled and Bohinj, to the Adriatic beaches, to Trieste for shopping, or in the winter to the Alpine ski-slopes near Bled. Many people now have weekend country cottages. Within Ljubljana, facilities for sport are much better than, say, in Bologna. There are five public swimming-pools, as well as plenty of scope for volleyball and football. Everyone works a five-day week, and the hours for all offices are 7 a.m. through without a break to 3 p.m.: shops stay open later, and often stagger their staff. When he gets home at three, the Slovene has an enormous family lunch, then a siesta (even in winter), then probably does his bit of moonlighting or some recreation, then has the light, casual type of cold supper that is common to all central Europe, then enjoys himself, often drinking and talking late into the night although his working day begins early – Slovenes, like the French, seem to manage on nervous energy rather than sleep. This curious 7-to-3 working day takes a bit of getting used to, for a foreign visitor. And the Slovene authorities even tried to change it in 1968. Their economists discovered that productivity was higher in countries with a 9-to-5 day, so the Slovene Parliament passed a law accordingly, which was actually implemented for two months or so. But there was a popular outcry – not only from moonlighters, but from working mothers with kids in nursery school, from others who felt that family life would be threatened, and from heavy eaters who found it impossible to work after their customary large lunch. So, in true Slovene democratic style, the law was rescinded under popular pressure.

This particular move towards a Western life-style may have failed, but others have not. Western consumer influences have been sweeping in, most of them officially condoned. The Slovene State TV, alongside its homilies on Marxism-Leninism, carries Western-style consumer ads in the Slovene equivalent of *franglais* – "Golden Kiss" shampoo, Bebimiks (a Croatian baby food), Coca Cola, "pure new wool" Shetland jerseys, and Dry Gin (*all* of these Yugoslav products, announced with English names) were a typical selection I culled from one evening's viewing. And in one firm I met an advertising manager who told me his hero was David Ogilvie, and how wonderful it was that Young and Rubicam were now setting up in Yugoslavia and that already ten Yugoslav firms were each spending more than $1 million a year on advertising. Nor is this eyewash, for the goods do exist in the shops. Ljubljana's newer department stores and supermarkets I found better than those of Bologna, and fairly close to Newcastle standards. Much of Yugoslavia's own output is still of poor quality – for instance, pharmaceuticals – but there is a wide range of imported stuff, from Old Spice after-shave to Australian canned fruit, from Finnish cut glass to French liqueurs. And since the dinar is in many respects convertible, all goods can be purchased at their face value in any currency: there is nothing like the officially run black market that flourishes so cynically in Prague and Warsaw where prostitutes are the chief beneficiaries of the hard-currency shops.

A Ljubljana publishing firm has had a big success with publishing a Slovene edition of the French magazine *Elle,* called *Ona* (which also means "she"). Some of the features are syndicated from *Elle,* others are locally produced, and so are the glossy advertisements. The fashion photos show pretty models in a wide range of elegant outfits – and in the streets and *cafés* of Ljubljana you see the same kind of pretty girls wearing the same kind of clothes. The new generation has a definite sense of style, not up to Bologna standards but comparing favourably with Newcastle or Toulouse.

Yet despite all this consumer modishness, the style of social life and entertainment in Ljubljana remains noticeably unsophisticated by most Western standards. There is no "society" *milieu* of people competing to give the smartest parties – the kind of activity that, provincial or pretentious though it might seem, I found in one style or another in all my Western towns. In Ljubljana, people rarely give formal lunch or dinner-parties, they just expect their friends to drop in, and then everyone sits round eating open sandwiches and drinking. Only once or twice did I catch a glimmer of any local jet-set, and that was among the young artisan/*boutiquiers,* people who dress fashionably, go on foreign holidays in their sports cars, sometimes even dare to build a swimming-pool, in short behave more like Italians than Slovenes. But they are few, and their *dolce vita* is lived circumspectly for it is contrary to the local ethos. If they want to splash their money, they do it abroad.

This is not to say that Slovenes fail to enjoy themselves or be hospitable. Quite the reverse. Pay a call at someone's home, and at once you will be offered a drink and snack – unlike France – and often be invited to stay for an impromptu cold supper. It is all very casual and simple. Young people from well-to-do families will drive off in groups in the evenings for a boisterous time in some country inn, but they are not blasé about their social life. There is an unpretentiousness too about the animated night-life of Ljubljana's bars and restaurants, in this provincial world where everyone knows everyone and gossip is a thriving pastime. Men and girls are all together: there is not the *machismo* element that you find on Tyneside and even in Bologna. Gossip and cultural chit-chat soon turns to singing or, even in mixed company, to sexual badinage, a Slovene speciality. Verbally and visually at least, this is a permissive society: just as many old Slovene folk-songs have obscene words, so today almost anything goes on stage or screen. The extent of actual physical promiscuity is harder to assess. In Slovene peasant communities there is a tradition of sexual tolerance, and for a girl to become pregnant is no disgrace. But in Ljubljana, as in many cities, the cramped housing situation puts restrictions on young people, most of whom live with their families. For this reason, if for no other, it may be that Ljubljana girls have less pre-marital sex than in some Western countries. But Slovenes at least like to think of themselves as erotic and full-blooded, as in many ways they are. There is a *mot* that when a girl of sixteen or seventeen starts a love-affair, her elders mutter, "So young, and already a Slovene."

The Slovenes' attitude to food is unsophisticated, like their social life. Theirs is a rough, peasant-based style of cooking, with Austrian and Bosnian influences and a bias towards *Schnitzel*, spicy sausages, smoked cold meats. The quality of the meat is often poor and the cooking in restaurants variable, and I fear that for my taste Ljubljana runs Newcastle a close second as the least gastronomic town in this book. Swabians too have unrefined palates, but in Stuttgart at least the ingredients and the presentation are far superior. The chief merit of Ljubljana restaurants is their cheapness.

One or two newer restaurants are trying to woo the new affluent classes with a conscious effort at smartness and quality – Vitez (The Knight) is perhaps the best – but if you go into the average hotel dining-room or larger eating-house, the drabness of the décor, the poor presentation of the food and the sluggishness of the service might remind you of some north of England town in the late 1950s. These places are "socialised". If you want to eat better, in a congenial setting, you must visit one of the dozen or so old country inns outside the town, nearly all of them privately-run, and increasingly *à la mode*. Some have antique furniture, dim lights, soft classical music, French as well as other foreign dishes, and are the kind of places where Slovenes will take foreign visitors. Others are simpler, with a jolly tavern atmosphere. In nearly all, the service is far better than at the more utilitarian socialised places in town. Some local officials told me they were worried at this contrast, and wondered how public catering could be improved and brought nearer to Western standards. As in some Communist countries, lack of incentive and true competition seems to be at the heart of the problem.

If Ljubljana's restaurant scene is uninspiring, its coffee-house and *Konditorei* world still thrives in the grand Central European tradition. There are several of those big classical Vienna-style *cafés,* with the day's newspapers on rods, and sometimes live musicians. Younger people prefer to go to newer, smaller, smarter places, most of them splendidly animated in the early evening. Students would take me to the Bar Juliya, an elegant *café* behind a flower-shop, where they would order sweetish Albanian brandy or Ballantine's whisky. Intellectuals would ask me to meet them at the Europe coffee-house or a drugstorish place called Ferent, where we would drink local brandy or *šlivovica* or one of the many good local wines. Or I would meet my friends at one of the numerous pastry-shop-*cafés* called *šlaščičarna,* where in true Central European style we would gorge ourselves on sticky cakes over a cup of coffee. Whenever I wanted a pleasant place to sit in and read or write notes for an hour or two, between interviews, I found Ljubljana as well supplied with *cafés* as Toulouse – in stark contrast to Bologna.

Later at night the scene changes. There are several large, inexpensive discothèques and dance halls with live pop bands, popular with students. Or if you go to the bigger hotels, the Lev and the Slon, you can find cabarets with live sex-shows that would not be out of place on the Reeperbahn: they are almost exclusively for foreign visitors, notably Italians who come for the kind of provocative strip-tease that is still banned in Italy. Slovenes are not interested in such things. They would rather go to a tavern, drink a lot, and sing their folk songs in lusty chorus – at midnight, when Stuttgart is fast asleep, the streets of Ljubljana are merry with drunkards untunefully ruining some old local love-ballad. An English girl told me: "Slovenes when they meet, like to talk for an hour, then sing for three." Especially on a Saturday night, the town is awake till nearly dawn. I remember one evening when a young poet took me first to the bar of the Union Hotel, crowded with young people at midnight or so, where we met another poet with a withered arm and his tiny plump blonde mistress, and a man who was celebrating not having got married that day (he was with another girl, not his ex-fiancée), and off we went for a round of drinks to the arty-smarty Vitez restaurant, still packed at 1 a.m. with what passes for the local *jeunesse dorée,* and then we ended up at the delightful Writers' Club, an intense social centre for the artists, actors, intellectuals and other cultural layabouts in town – a place that has no equivalent in any of my other towns – and there we discussed whither Slovene poetry and whence Socialism and whether peasant girls were as passionate as they were beautiful, till the light was breaking over the hills towards Croatia. My Dublin ancestry made me feel totally at home.

6

"We all write poetry – it's the national disease"

The first fact about culture in Ljubljana is that there is one hell of a lot of it – far more, in proportion to the size of the place, than in any of my other towns. This little city has six theatres and an opera house, three full-time orchestras, three choirs, a ballet company, all of them going full tilt and playing mostly to full houses, not to mention an international festival every summer. And, this being so assertively a national capital, there is every kind of institute such as the National Library and the Slovene Academy of Science and Art. The publishing houses turn out 1,200 new titles a year in Slovene, and so great is the appetite for literature that some books written in English sell more copies in their Slovene translation than they do in Britain! Slovenia claims to be the nation with the highest proportion of writers in the world, ahead even of Iceland: one of them said to me, "We all write poetry here, it's the national disease."

While some of this activity is highly nationalistic, Slovenia is also so avid for outside influences that it gives itself indigestion in trying to mirror the full range of latest world creation, as if it were London or Paris. On an average summer evening, you might have a choice between, say, Smetana at the opera house, plays by Arrabal, O'Neill and Pinter at the theatres, an exhibition of modern Italian abstract art, concerts ranging from Britten or Shostakovich to the German classics, dance troupes from Bulgaria or Senegal at the Festival, and various new foreign films, mercifully undubbed.

But is this quantity matched by the *quality* of the locally produced culture? "It's not as good as it thinks it is," was the comment of a French resident, the one whose views on the local Lilliput syndrome I quoted earlier. "On this tiny stage, everyone thinks he is Hamlet, or Shakespeare, everyone supposes he is a 'great' singer or artist. There's a lot of mediocrity that is truly provincial. Musical standards, for instance, are not as high as in Graz, where I used to live. On the other hand, I think there's more genuine enthusiasm and appreciation here, among performers and public: Austrian audiences are snobs" – as in Stuttgart. Of course, standards in Ljubljana are variable, and there are not often the resources for lavish new productions which must thus make do with second-rate sets. But my general impression was of vitality and competence among actors, singers and music-makers – a fair provincial quality, not as metropolitan as it is aiming to be, but better than in my other towns, except Stuttgart. The mediocrity that does exist is not so much a matter of amateurism or wilful pursuit of the middlebrow, as in Newcastle, but rather the small-town second-rateness that I suppose one also finds somewhere like Oslo.

The culture both modern and classical draws large audiences mostly of young people, who go out of genuine interest rather than status-snobbery. The opera plays to 82 per cent capacity, six nights a week. Seats it is true are very cheap (often 20 dinars or less) since the official policy, as in most Socialist countries, is that culture should be available to all the people. This succeeds, to the extent that the percentage of workers among audiences is higher than in the West. But it involves heavy subsidies – "All this culture is a costly burden for a small nation, yet we must have it," said a theatre director. Sometimes voices are raised that the money could be better spent on more schools or improved public utilities, but these carry little weight. Culture is seen as an essential national asset, like the defence forces. There is however some feeling that a saturation point has now been reached in the amount of culture provided, and I also heard the fear expressed that as new consumer tastes develop – cars, dining out, TV, more comfortable homes – this might affect the level of culture-going as has sometimes happened in the West. But there is little sign of it as yet. Nor can it be said that the theatres or concert-halls are full partly for the same reasons as in Prague or Moscow, that is, because there are not many other outlets for enjoyment and "pop" culture is officially frowned on. Here there are no limits on travel, and there is plenty of "pop" available too, which is also enjoyed.

The Slovenes have poetry and theatre in their blood like the Irish, and music in their blood like the Welsh. The enthusiasm for culture is also an expression of nationalism. Pride in Slovenia's orchestras, museums, artists, singers, writers, runs high among all sections of the people. "Culture formed our nation," I was often told: in a country so long occupied, it was for centuries the secret agent of national unity and awareness, and even more recently many Slovene Communists have seen their role less as political than cultural – the building up of Ljubljana as a shrine of the Slovene spirit, a New Jerusalem. Not only France Prešeren of the 19th century but also some modern poets of the Partisan era, such as Matej Bor, are revered as national patriot heroes. And this public attitude gives the contemporary writer a different role in society from that in Britain or France. A poet told me, "It's because we are a small and newly free nation that we of the Writers' Association feel we have a mission to spread Slovene culture. Often when we visit schools or clubs we are formally greeted, 'Welcome to the guardians of our national heritage.' It can be almost embarrassing."

I cannot see Graham Greene or Philip Larkin being welcomed like that at an English school – even though, on a regional level, this *is* how Sid Chaplin and Alan Plater are tacitly regarded in Geordieland. There are many parallels between Tyneside and Slovenia, despite their very different environments, and it may be no coincidence that conscious attempts to revive or maintain folk traditions – industrial in the one place, rural in the other – are more vigorous in these two regions than in the others in this book.

In Slovenia, modern art and architecture have frequently drawn inspiration from old local designs. An ethnological institute today collects local folk art, and another assembles old folk tales and customs. But the biggest effort, in this land of song, goes on preserving the nation's rich heritage of folk music and dance. This began in the 1930s, when a folk institute was founded privately. Today it is national. Its director, Valeus Vodušek, a musicologist, told me that he and his staff had taped 14,000 different songs or variations of songs in the villages. When I asked him whether folk activity still survived spontaneously in country areas, he said, "Not much folk-dancing, but a great deal of folk-singing everywhere, for that is our speciality. In the villages, old religious ballads are sung all night at wakes before funerals. And in some places young men will sit under the linden trees in the centre of a village, after dark, and sing love-serenades in elaborate part-song. Alas, that's dying out." He played a cassette – a slow, melancholy melody that recalled Clare and Galway to me. "In the vineyard areas around Maribor," he went on, "they still sing wine-songs at harvest time, in the taverns and in the fields. And on winter evenings in the countryside, several farming families will gather round one fireside to sing together as they do their craftwork, making baskets, or cushions from goose-feathers, and then they will dance" – just as in Auvergne and Brittany before the war. "But this is disappearing, as industry changes the way of life. In the towns, there's still a lot of folk-singing in the taverns, but often drunken and debased. However, at least they sing local songs rather than imported ones. Some ballads are sung endlessly, night after night" – Slovenia's *Blaydon Races,* he told me, begins, "In the winter the flowers are not blooming: where shall I gather new flowers for you?" I asked whether there were conscious efforts to revive the traditions now menaced by changing life-styles. "Yes! the radio and TV are helping us. Until a few years ago, all the light radio music was imported pop or jazz, but now there are several professional ensembles that have re-arranged the old folk tunes, fitting new words to them, trying to adapt traditional melodies to themes relating to modern life. They broadcast a good deal, and also play 'live' in the taverns – it's a popular new fashion. Some of the words are banal, but I can't disapprove of the trend." There is also a semi-amateur Slovene folk-dance group, mostly university students, who perform frequently and have toured Europe. Dr Vodušek took me to see them rehearse, as they were about to take the night train to Cannes to entertain an IBM congress. They performed some energetic dances, with high-pitched singing and stamping on the floor; then an elegant chain-dance that reminded me of something I had once seen from the Shetland Isles, and reels with whooping cries that seemed equally Scottish. "Of course," said my learned host – "it's all from the same Celtic source. Ask any anthropologist."

Until the reforms of 1973, the arts in Ljubljana were subsidised jointly by the city council and the Slovene Government, rather as in Stuttgart. The subsidies were impressive: the city was spending more each year on the arts than on water, gas, street-lighting, street-cleaning and town-planning combined, and this unusual order of priorities was all too apparent. The city was like some cultured old tramp who can recite Shakespeare by heart but never takes a bath. Now that culture, since 1973, has become a Community of Interest, like health and education, its funding is organised differently but is still just as lavish. From the tax on companies it receives an overall budget, at a level fixed by the Republic, and decisions on how this should be shared out between the bodies needing subsidy (theatres, etc.) are taken by a board of delegates from all cultural fields plus one or two government and Party representatives. "This is certainly more democratic than the old system," said a delegate representing writers; "previously the main decisions were taken privately by a group of officials connected with the Ministry of Culture. Now, our board of 96 delegates holds open meetings and it's much easier for the rank-and-file to put across their views. The Ministry simply has a supervisory role. But the drawback is that we waste a lot of time in verbose sub-committee meetings, and each theatre, orchestra, art gallery and so on is lobbying for its own interests rather than looking at overall cultural needs. We are each grubbing for money all the time. This, I can assure you, plays a far greater part in our debates than matters of ideology, even in these days when the Party loyalists on our board are trying to impose a more 'correct' Marxist line in artistic policies."

The theatre scene in Ljubljana is wonderfully lively, varied and adventurous, but also stormy: disputes over box-office, or ideology, or both at once, are frequently in the headlines. Just as in Stuttgart, the National Theatre has two buildings, one the opera house, the other a "straight" theatre with two auditoria; and in recent years the latter has been going through much the same kind of upheaval as subsidised theatres in *all* my other towns. The crisis here, oddly enough, has less to do with politics than with the eternal quarrel between high- and middlebrows over what audiences to aim at. The theatre's director in the late 1960s was a highbrow who imposed a diet of Arrabal, Sartre, Beckett and the like, and succeeded in alienating much of the older audience and reducing attendance in the larger hall from 80 to 55 per cent of capacity. There was a blazing row within the theatre's self-management council, which spread into the press and created a national crisis. Many of the older star actors accused the director of various crimes, such as wasting public money, flouting public taste, and flirting with the decadent Western *avant-garde*: a few neo-Stalinists among them even demanded a return to popular realism. A new director was found, and since 1970 a compromise policy has been worked out, where safe classics such as *Twelfth Night* alternate with new Slovene plays and the occasional experimental piece. The variety is impressive: in the 1974-5 season it ranged from the *Oresteia* via Molière to Panizza's *Council of Love,* Peter Barnes' *The Ruling Class,* and a pro-Dubček play by the Czech dissident Pavel Kohout - a discreet blend of the anti-Christ and the anti-Kremlin. Attendance has risen again, but box-office covers only 30 per cent of revenue, and the National Theatre is supported by a 9 million dinar annual subsidy from the Cultural Community. In his choice of plays the theatre director is now more responsible than before 1973 to the staff self-management council and the latter in turn to the Community. So the debates are endless – "So tiring, this democracy," sighed one dramaturge, "it's like the Athens of Pericles, with everyone talking at once."

The other and smaller theatres in the city have fewer problems, if only because they are not national sanctuaries obliged to try to satisfy all tastes. The City Theatre does good box-office with a "*boulevard*" repertory policy on the level of Coward, Feydeau and Axelrod, plus sometimes a new Slovene play: I saw an interesting social satire, *Zlata Mladina* ("Golden Youth"), full of jibes about Stalinism and the excesses of modern Slovene youth. There is a charming puppet theatre, also two new experimental theatre companies which have developed from a former student Leftist fringe group:* both operate on a shoestring in make-shift premises, but draw eager young audiences for their way-out shows, which are part surrealist "happening", part disguised political satire, part anthropological research *à la* Peter Brook. They consider Brecht and Wesker old hat, and are closer to Brook, Handke, Vitez and the Living Theatre.

The city's theatre audiences are polarising in just the same way as in Toulouse and Stuttgart: on the one hand, a growing audience of young people for experimental work and anything modern or provocative; on the other, a declining but still reliable older clientèle, with much the same tastes as in the West for "*boulevard*" or classic plays. The National Theatre is still in the dilemma of trying to satisfy both these trends. Nor is this the only problem facing Slovenia's producers and actors. The profession is overcrowded, but they do not like to emigrate if only because – even in Zagreb or Belgrade – this would involve using another language, and they want to act in Slovene. So they stay in this intense and adored little world, but sometimes admit to claustrophobia. However lively the theatre scene, the amount of work available is inevitably limited in so small a place, so most actors have to eke out a living with free-lance jobs in films and broadcasting. Few are other than poor.

The city's musical life is also varied and active, but more conventional. Nearly every evening there is a classical concert of some kind, especially during the summer festival period: the obvious classics such as Beethoven are the basis of the repertoire, but modern composers such as Berg and Stockhausen also draw audiences, mostly younger people. The Slovene Philharmonic Orchestra is the oldest in

---

* See page 422.

Central Europe, dating back to 1701. Today it plays to 88 per cent capacity in its elegant concert hall, and travels over Europe. The performance I attended was of decent provincial standard, not up to the best in Stuttgart but as good as Newcastle's Northern Sinfonia. The Slovene radio orchestra, which I did not hear, is said to be better.

The national opera company maintains a wide repertoire that is arguably a little too ambitious for its resources. In one average fortnight during my visit, it was offering *La Traviata, Madame Butterfly, Turandot, The Bartered Bride, Carmen, The Queen of Spades* and *Aïda,* in repertory: I saw the *Turandot,* a lively and colourful production that outclassed the *Il Trovatore* I had seen in Bologna. The company sings only in Slovene and puts the emphasis on Slav and Italian operas, which are the most popular – "Few people like modern opera," the musical director told me, "nor do we often try Wagner. People here think he smacks of fascism. Also, you need special voices."

Ljubljana has a firm place on the international music circuits. The opera company travels abroad regularly, recently winning a Grand Prix in Paris, while in return the opera house receives leading foreign touring companies. And the three-month annual festival has an incredible range: an average season might include six or seven ballet and folklore groups, from Senegal and Romania, London and Leningrad, opera from Berlin and Italy, and the Vienna Boys' Choir. Concerts are usually held in the open courtyard of the beautiful Križanke building, a former monastery renovated after the war by Jože Plečnik. The festival's quality may not rival that of Salzburg or Edinburgh but nor, to say the least, do its prices. Thanks to the large subsidies, many seats are only 20 or 30 dinars each. This is true of the city's musical life all through the year, with the result that numerous students and working people are regular concert-goers. Like their Austrian and Hungarian neighbours, the Slovenes have a passion for music, and this is encouraged by their education: the playing and appreciation of music is given as high a place in primary and secondary schools as it is in Germany, and much more so than in France or Italy. The opera's director told me: "As in Hungary, the manufacture of musicians is a national industry, and a major export too, perhaps too much so. Our musicians are tempted by the higher salaries they earn in the West: the opera has lost many of its best singers to the voice drain, and it affects our standards. But it's a free country."

The visual arts may not flourish with the same intensity as music or drama, though the artists' *milieu* includes a number of talented primitives and abstract painters, who can work untroubled by the ideological pressures towards realism that are found in Soviet countries. Their main handicap is the city's lack of private art galleries and dealers who could help them earn a better living. Ljubljana is internationally known however for its *Biennale* of prints and engravings. As for cinema, Slovenia actually makes a few of its own feature films, with studios in Ljubljana. This is not an art at which Slovenes shine, and there are no directors with the talent to win a reputation abroad. However, in the showing to the public of imported films, the range compares favourably with that of any of my other towns, even Toulouse. From *Star Wars* to Fassbinder, most of the world's better-known new films arrive fairly promptly in one or other of the town's nine cinemas, where they are shown sub-titled rather than dubbed. Rarely is any foreign film banned for political reasons.

Literature is as lively as theatre and music. The publishing industry is phenomenal, especially considering that little more than two million people in the world have Slovene as their mother tongue. As in most Socialist countries, publishing is subsidised and books are cheap: new hardbacks often cost a mere 60 to 80 dinars. But this is not the only reason for the high sales, in this nation of avid readers. Tastes are far from uniformly highbrow, and light romantic novels come top of the best-seller lists as in any country: but even Unesco's cultural history of the world sold 8,000 copies per volume, almost as much as the London edition with its vastly greater world-wide market in English. And a new edition of the poems of Prešeren sold 100,000 copies – a symptom of Slovenes' patriotism, yes, but also of their real love for poetry. Most workers' homes have at least a shelf or two of books. And people read as well as buy, as the library figures prove: Ljubljana's large and impressive municipal library has 800,000 borrowings a year, nearly four books per inhabitant.

A writer in Slovenia is thus, understandably, a person of some public importance. As many as 20 Slovene writers manage to earn a full living from creative work: a new novel will usually sell at least 2,000 to 3,000 copies, which even in Britain with 30 times the population would be a respectable figure. New novels and poetry come under intense public discussion, and the headquarters of the Writers' Association with its 200 members is the liveliest cultural meeting-place in Ljubljana, with the ambience of a literary *café*.

It is a facet of the corporatist element in the Yugoslav political system that this Association tends to think of itself as a pressure-group and is officially encouraged to do so. It has a state subsidy and owns villas at Bled and on the coast where its members can go for holiday or to work in peace. In some respects it acts as a kind of self-protective body to check non-conformist writing; but in others its influence has often been liberal. This brings us to the whole question of freedom of expression – in literature and the other arts, in the media, in religion – to which we will return after looking first at education.

7

Education: Alpha for languages, Gamma for student conditions

The Slovenes inherited their educational system from the Austrians. They have done little to change the pedagogic methods, which to an Anglo-Saxon still seem formal and encyclopaedic. But since the war they have remodelled the structures to suit their self-management principles. Thus schools and colleges are today run by a Community of Interest, made up largely of delegates from within the profession. This body appoints headmasters and other principals and decides on general policy, while each school has its staff council that elects new teachers and holds the usual endless debates. So although the teaching itself may seem a little old-fashioned, the atmosphere of schools is a good deal more free-and-easy than in Stuttgart, and a school has far more autonomy than in Bologna or Toulouse.

There is a remarkable eagerness for education, among all social groups. The school leaving age is fifteen, but 60 per cent of pupils stay on till at least eighteen – a high figure for any country. In the senior secondary schools, the *gymnasia,* there is little specialisation: everyone has a fair dose of science, arts and modern subjects right up to the university entrance exam, the *matura.* Thus in one *gymnasium* I found sixteen-year-olds all doing some five hours a week of Slovene, four of maths and five of physics, six of foreign languages, seven of history, geography and sociology (Marxist-based) and two hours of pre-military education (cadet training for the boys, first aid for the girls).

This very general education is under criticism for leading to low academic standards, but it also has its advantages, and one is the emphasis it places on the living arts and languages. In junior forms there is far more teaching of music and art than you find in Italy, and in many *gymnasia* two foreign languages are compulsory: usually English plus either French, German or Russian. Slovenes have an even stronger flair for languages than most other Slavs, and this is stimulated by the lively teaching methods: in ordinary schools I found kids of thirteen or fourteen talking easily and fluently in English with their teachers. On the other hand, when it comes to the more intellectual teaching of ideas in senior forms, in subjects such as history and literature, the pupils tend to be crammed with facts and forced to learn concepts parrot-wise rather than being encouraged to evaluate for themselves. This is a common complaint by foreign teachers on assignment, but as one young English lecturer said to me, "This is more the legacy of Austrian methods than the result of Communism. You could make the same criticisms of teaching in Germany."

Schools are short of funds. The buildings tend to be shabby and unkempt in the usual Slovene manner, and there is little modern equipment. Shortages of classrooms and of teachers often necessitate a double-shift system, as in Italy, with pupils attending either in the morning or afternoon. But as compared with Bologna, or Toulouse, I was impressed by the amount of extra-curricular activity that is added to an already heavy schoolwork programme. Schools are living communities, not mere academic factories. I visited one small *gymnasium* that had a lending library with 7,000 books (many in English or French), rooms with music and painting classes in progress, and two "gyms" (in the English sense of the word) where girls were cheerfully engaged in basketball and jumping exercises, with no supervision from a teacher. I was told that the school had weekly dances, as well as concerts, film-shows and a film-making club. A bust of Tito stood in every room. At a large *gymnasium* in the town centre, I found a photography club, and a school newspaper where the pupils published poems urging Slovenia towards a more idealistic Socialism. There were school concerts and fêtes, where pupils recited their poems, and a debating society where they decided on their own subjects: recent debates were on student unrest, suicide, Soviet policy and the role of religion in the modern world. The views expressed fell within a broad Titoist orthodoxy, but with some room for clashes of opinion. I felt that the school, with its accent on community and general culture, was in many ways closer to the British system than to that of France or Italy.

Yet at Ljubljana University, similarities with France and Italy appear at every turn. Many of its problems are the familiar European ones – overcrowding, a high drop-out rate, complaints of too much *ex-cathedra* teaching and of over-formal studies ill adapted to today's needs. Again, the Austrian legacy bears some responsibility, for although the university was not founded until 1919, it has derived many of its academic methods from the former Occupiers.

The university is a group of unlovely buildings near the town centre, where 14,000 students work in unenviable conditions. They have some voice in administration, for there are student delegates on the self-management council that runs this semi-autonomous university. But as in France and Italy there is no *numerus clausus* (except in medicine and architecture) and anyone with the *matura* can enrol. This aggravates the overcrowding caused by lack of funds and is also a cause of the high drop-out rate, for many students are arguably unsuited to university. Since Yugoslavia's liberalisation in the 1950s, students are free to choose their branch of study, without the compulsions found in some Communist countries. As a result, more of them opt for arts subjects than the career market can cater for, and graduate unemployment has been rising. Liberal Slovenia faces exactly the problems of the West.

Methods of continuous assessment and oral examination have been introduced, as well as attempts to develop seminars rather than lectures. But the shortage of teachers is such that few seminars, at least in arts subjects, have less than 30 students. They complain that, although human contact with their teachers is amicable enough, it is impossible for a professor to get to know more than a handful of them individually. And they complain even more about what they see as old-fashioned teaching methods: "It's like at school: we're filled up with facts and not made to think for ourselves," said one student. Another added, "We're still too close to the old Austrian system. And the 'profs' teach just the same things as a generation ago." But professors, as anywhere, are slow to accept change.

Only a minority of students receive grants: many take part-time jobs to pay for their studies. There are many bright children from workers' families who miss out on university because their parents feel they cannot afford it, and according to one estimate the percentage of students from this social category is no higher than in Britain. This alleged failure of Socialism to create equal opportunity is widely criticised by the younger generation. Apart from a minority of *jeunesse dorée* from the new élite classes, many students live in near-poverty, either in lodgings or on a campus where conditions are spartan: many students must share a room, and at the time of my visit the hostels were shiveringly under-heated, though I am told this has since improved. The campus does not even have its own swimming-pool. It seems that the university authorities, short of cash, do little to provide for the welfare or social needs of their students.

Yet the students at least, within their means, show some enterprise in organising these things for themselves – more so than in any of my other towns, save Newcastle. They have a body called Forum, which runs skiing parties, regular dances, medical care, even an employment service: it has handsome new premises and is the nearest equivalent I found on the Continent to the British student unions. There is a student choir and folk-dance society, and all kinds of clubs, sporting and cultural. In short, despite their austere environment, students in Ljubljana struck me as probably having more fun and a livelier social life than, say, the lonely crowds on the Toulouse campuses. And this is largely because they help themselves. They have even created their own student radio service, something they claim to be the first of its kind in Europe. It is financed by a university grant and by advertising – "We are like Radio Luxembourg," I was told proudly. There are four professional technicians, while the journalistic work is done by students – it is the radio equivalent of a student newspaper. They broadcast for four hours a day on a 100-volt transmitter with a 20-mile range: music, news, and discussion programmes including interviews with politicians. The initiative for founding the station came from the students after the 1968 period of unrest.

In the early 1970s there was also a provocative experimental theatre group, *Pupelija,* run by some radical students of literature with the shaggy hair and hippy dress of the day: "We are all poets," they told me, "and we moved into this kind of theatre to seek poetic expression. We devise all our own material." I attended one of their rehearsals, and was startled. In the first scene, they tore piles of newspapers into shreds, some actors began eating the paper and tearing it from each others' mouths while others recited gibberish items from the press. This was supposed to be a comment on the mass media. Then, in a scene called "Necking", couples writhed on the floor in mock-copulation while others recited letters from agony columns: "I am fourteen and have slept with two boys – what do I do now?" or "I can give myself orgasms but cannot get them during intercourse – what should I do?" Then a man and a girl took all their clothes off and had a bath together. Then one actor sucked at the breast of a naked girl while another recited nursery rhymes. Then the whole cast linked their bodies and imitated a computer. Other scenes included a skit on a bad Italian novelette, done in the style of a comic strip; a satire on Christ, with a bearded man talking drivel to his disciples, as in Buñuel's *La Voie Lactée*; and for good measure, a send-up of Titoist Partisan songs. Finally, while the cast imitated a brood of hens, an actor writhed on the floor holding a globe to his penis – a theatre metaphor, so he explained to me, for the Slovene expression, "Fuck the world."

Pupelija had obvious affinities with other anarchic movements of the period, such as America's *Living Theatre,* Fassbinger's *anti-teater* in Munich, or even Liverpool's The Scaffold. But the students claimed to me they had not seen these groups, they did not feel influenced from outside, they were simply in tune with the spirit of the times. A scene where they slaughtered a live hen on stage caused protests in Ljubljana, and eyebrows were raised too at the sexuality and the skits on the Partisan tradition. But in the liberal Slovene climate of that period *Pupelija* was able to get away with its provocations. Most of its members saw themselves as Leftists, critical of the complacent Communist establishment. Whether they would survive in today's stricter times is uncertain: but the group has since disbanded for other reasons. Its leaders are no longer students, and some of them are now professionals, running the city's new *avant-garde* theatres.

Student unrest in the 1968 period was never as marked as in Belgrade or Zagreb, or many Western cities. Or at least, it was less political than in Belgrade (where Tito clamped down on the Maoists and Trotskyists) and mainly took the form of demands for better living and study conditions. For the next few years, small groups of radical students continued to agitate discreetly, usually through underground magazines, against a régime they thought too conservative. But this unrest gradually exhausted itself and died away, as elsewhere in the student world, in Europe and America. The next generation was less political. However, in Yugoslavia there was also the factor of tightening of Party discipline after 1972, and this brings us to consider the general issue of freedom of expression in Ljubljana today.

8
Subtle restrictions on Catholics and intellectuals

The degree of tolerance afforded to practising Christians is probably as good a guide as any to the real state of freedom in Ljubljana. Slovenes have long been regarded as second only to Poles, among the Slavs, in the fervour of their Catholicism. But during the war, though many rank-and-file Catholics joined the Resistance, including some priests, the pro-Nazi record of the Church hierarchy was little less disgraceful than in Croatia. And at the Liberation the reckoning was heavy: some clergy were executed, some put in prison, while others fled abroad, including Bishop Rožman of Ljubljana.

In the early post-war years many lay Catholics too were persecuted. The new Communist rulers used their understandable vengeance against collaborators as a pretext for a wider crusade against the rival ideology of Christianity. But attempts to eradicate it failed dismally, and in the more liberal 1950s the attitude changed to one of acceptance: freedom of religion was guaranteed by successive federal constitutions. Today, the Church is tolerated provided that it "keeps out of politics" in the official definition of that term, which in practice means keeping out of cultural, social and welfare matters too. The Communists are wary above all of the Church developing a rival structure that it could try to use for temporal ends, and their attitude to it is two-edged: *qua* government they leave it alone, so long as it obeys the tacit rules; but *qua* Party they perpetually harry and criticise it, in their press, in speeches, in self-management debates, as if it were a political opposition group. Many priests accept this as normal competition, even salutary: their handicap is that they cannot, in public, answer back. And the resulting situation is highly equivocal, with apparent Party leniency and correct relations going hand-in-hand with subtle behind-the-scenes pressures against individual Catholics. There seems to be no clear central policy, and much depends on the vagaries of individual Communists' initiatives.

The initial post-war Communist view was that Catholicism, an outworn superstition, would wither away of its own accord as the new ideology of Socialist brotherhood took root. But the churches today are fuller than ever. There are twenty in Ljubljana, many in bad repair but somehow kept going by donations from parishioners and funds from exiles abroad. At one big parish church a priest told me that 13 masses were celebrated each Sunday for a total of 7,000 communicants, and that regular attendance in Ljubljana was 25 per cent of the population, twice the figure for Paris. According to an independent survey, 60 per cent of Slovenes call themselves practising Catholics. And the young are attracted as much as the old: witness that 70 young Slovenes enter the priesthood each year and the city's seminary has 300 novitiates. It seems that many young Slovenes go to church as a reaction against what they see as the growing materialism of their society: they are not rejecting Socialism for capitalist values, far from it, they want more equality and idealism.

The state fights against this revival by excluding religion from schools and from broadcasting. There has been no religious teaching in state schools since the war, nor are pupils allowed to invite Church leaders onto school premises. In history textbooks, "AD" and "BC" are replaced quaintly by "Our Era" and "Before Our Era", and children are not invited to ask what this means. On radio and TV, the ban is even more severe – to the extent that one producer was penalised for allowing a priest to appear for three minutes in a programme unconnected with religion, while a girl TV announcer, who by mistake had allowed a crucifix on her necklace to become visible, was condemned by a Party congress as "provocative" and banned from the screen.

Religion is subject to apartheid, yet within its allotted tribal reserves the Church does have a fair amount of freedom. It can run Sunday schools on its premises, and these are twice as numerous as before the war: in Ljubljana 40 per cent of children attend, and more in rural areas. The Church can also publish its own periodicals on religious and cultural subjects (these are even printed by the presses of the Party's newspaper group!). A weekly, *Druzina* ("Family"), sells 113,000 copies, and a monthly youth magazine 80,000. These and other papers are supposed to steer clear of any criticism of Marxist values, though during the liberal era around 1970 *Druzina* managed to get away with an article about how a girl with atheist parents was converted to

Christianity. *Družina* has since been obliged to be more circumspect. Nor has the Church ever been allowed to step into welfare: it is forbidden to run its own youth organisations, and if it takes a group of young people on an excursion, there are tirades from Party officials that it is meddling in "politics". A priest commented: "But what is politics? – we and the Party do not agree. They fear we are aiming to create a rival focus of loyalty which they could not control. We simply want to give young people some fun."

Disputes of this kind are usually provoked by Party zealots and not by the government which rarely risks any direct confrontation with the Church. All is equivocal, in the mild Slovene manner: there is no police terror. Formal relations between bishops and the authorities are polite and businesslike, if cool, and the Church is even invited to official ceremonies as in Bologna. But on an intellectual level there is little of the Catholic/Marxist debate that you find in France or Italy: the Party does not seek it. The basic difference is that, in Bologna, Don Camillo and Peppone are free and more-or-less equal rivals, whereas here Peppone is in the saddle and Don Camillo, whatever his following, must toe the line. The Party feels no need to compete with the Church, electorally or intellectually. And, again unlike Bologna, very few people are both Catholic and Communist.

The state authorities will give money to help with the restoration of old churches of architectural value. But the Ljubljana communes have repeatedly turned down requests for permission to build new churches: they claim there are no sites available. So it was something of a breakthrough when finally, in the mid-1970s, the clergy managed to get a new church built in a prosperous suburb. But, to avoid being thought provocative, they put no cross on the building which outwardly does not resemble a church at all.

Some Catholics similarly disguise themselves, for in many jobs they are liable to be subtly discriminated against. Education is the most sensitive area. A primary teacher told me that in the hard years after the war she was officially warned that she would lose her job if she went on taking her children to church. So she stopped. Today, these pressures have eased, but many Catholics still feel the need to be prudent. "I go to church secretly in another district from where I live and work," a young teacher told me. No identifiable churchgoer has much chance of promotion to the rank of university professor or headmaster, just as no practising Catholics are mayors or deputies (though in rural areas some are municipal councillors). And in schools, many Communist teachers seek to exclude Catholic children from joining organised school exchanges with foreign countries, lest they "contaminate" the others or give a "wrong" impression of Yugoslavia to their foreign hosts.

I got to know one teacher, a courageous and devout girl, who told me she takes all this with a big pinch of salt. "I've given up trying to be discreet, it's hypocritical. They know I go to church, let them sack me if they want to!" – and she laughed boisterously. She also edits English textbooks for schools: "I was hauled over the coals by a man from the Ministry of Education because in one book I put a drawing of a church against the song, 'The bells are ringing', and because I referred to Christmas and Easter festivals – but it was a book about England. Luckily his boss, a more sensible man, stuck up for me. You see, it's all very personal and arbitrary. There's no clear line from the top, it just depends who you are dealing with. Anti-Catholic campaigns come and go here: one just has to be philosophical."

In the early 1970s the Church was on the offensive, encouraged by its rising popularity, and began lobbying to get its own radio and TV programmes. The Party grew worried at its growing influence among young people. So when Tito in 1972-3 gave the cue for the Party to reassert itself in public life, Slovene Communists renewed their attacks on the Church. In 1974 state officials raided the offices of *Družina* and accused its editor, a priest, of illegally hoarding foreign currency and of being in contact with hostile émigré groups in the West. The affair was exploited by the Communist press and there seemed a danger of *Družina* being closed down. When I visited its offices late in 1974, I found a scared and furtive atmosphere, very different from the outgoing self-confidence of two years previously. But the axe did not fall, and *Družina* today continues, discreetly. It appears that the raid was instigated by a few neo-Stalinists for their own purposes and was not necessarily sanctioned by the government. Even so, the Church is still regarded with some suspicion, as a potential political threat, even by some of the younger and otherwise liberal Communists. One of them told me: "Many priests would like to create a clerical party, like the Christian Democrats in Italy. This is alien to our system: so the Party is right to put a check on the Church's surreptitious attempts to move back into politics." These fears are certainly exaggerated. A handful of older priests may hanker after some political power, but the vast majority of younger Catholics want no more than fuller personal freedom and an end to petty discriminations against them in public life – such as being banned from the screen for wearing a cross on a necklace. Probably these pinpricks will continue. But there will be no putting back of the clock to Stalinist days: Communists, as much as Catholics, are certain of that. So strong is its popular support that the Church is likely to retain its own kind of freedom, as in Poland.

The degree of the régime's tolerance can also be tested by the amount of freedom it allows in literature, the arts and the media. Here too there is plenty of ambivalence. Western newspapers are freely on sale, authors such as Solzhenitsyn are published in Slovene, while in moral and sexual matters, permissiveness in the arts goes a long way. But politically, clear limits are set. The basic tenets of the régime cannot be criticised directly, or not at least in the mass-media. This is less a matter of formal government censorship than of a discreet self-censorship, whereby the Party sees to it that its own trusted men control the key editorial positions.

Consider broadcasting. Slovenia is autonomous in the running of its state radio and TV services, and in some respects policy is liberal and Western-orientated – indeed, until 1973 the second TV channel relayed Italian television for several hours each evening, by agreement with RAI. This anomaly is now ended, and the channel now relays Zagreb and Belgrade programmes, which seems only reasonable. But the networks are not under the control of Belgrade, and they freely buy many programmes from the BBC and elsewhere in the West. The Ljubljana papers daily print details of Austrian and Italian programmes, which anyone is free to watch. And like the other Republics, Slovenia belongs to Eurovision and not to the Soviet bloc's Intervision – an interesting sidelight on Tito's stance astride the iron curtain.

Some 25 per cent of revenue comes from advertising – those glossy commercials I described earlier – and the rest from licence fees. Slovenes are keen viewers, and the number of sets, 500,000, is as high *per capita* as almost anywhere in Europe. Not that the quality of the locally produced programmes is any higher than you might expect in a small country with limited resources. There are humane and honest documentaries on social subjects such as divorce and handicapped children, but also rather too many swoony self-admiring features on local landscape and folklore. Series on recent Slovene history are predictably orthodox – for the senior programme planners are nearly all dedicated Party men, who supervise the editorial line.

Much the same is true of Ljubljana's principal newspaper and magazine group, Delo, which the Party's "front" body, the Socialist Alliance of Working People, founded during the war and still controls, appointing its main executives in consultation with the works council. The group comprises the leading local daily, *Delo* (circulation, 90,000), and several weeklies and popular magazines. *Delo* is in many ways a good newspaper, with far fuller international coverage than you find, say, in the *Newcastle Journal* or *La Dépêche* at Toulouse. It has its own staff correspondents abroad, in Paris, Bonn, Rome and Moscow; it reprints articles on Yugoslav affairs from such papers as *Le Monde*; and it has a guest opinion column where divergent views can be expressed. It genuinely encourages free discussion on domestic issues, but this must be within the framework of official policy. Thus its columns will reflect outspokenly the controversies on such matters as the theatre crises, housing scandals, or the role of the workers' councils: but it will not allow its contributors to question the basic tenets of Socialism. And certain subjects are taboo, notably any direct criticism of Tito and his leadership, or of Yugoslav foreign policy, or indeed (for obvious reasons of national security) of the Soviet Union. "If I want to know what is really happening in Yugoslavia at the top level," said one Slovene, "I must read the Western Press. Luckily, we can."

Yet turn to the arts, and you find erotic provocations in the experimental theatres and highly suggestive stills outside cinemas showing sex films. The theatre critic of *Delo,* an elderly Communist, told me: "For my taste, it's all gone too far. When the National Theatre puts on an Arrabal play about a man changing sex, it's obscene. Yet I'm against any official censorship: public taste must be the only arbiter." The authorities are reluctant to intervene in matters of taste and morality. When a student magazine published some poems that were pornographic and also satirised the Partisan tradition, there were public protests: but the authorities simply handed the matter over to the Writers' Association, saying in effect, "You please deal with these young people: we do not want to appear repressive by interfering."

The fact that writers and intellectuals are organised as a kind of trade union provides their more outspoken members with a certain protection, for a tacit self-censorship can be operated. The Writers' Association has nearly always pushed for more liberalisation and on some occasions has succeeded in defending members in trouble with the authorities. This is easier in tolerant Slovenia than in the severer *milieux* of Serbia and Croatia. A leader of the Slovene PEN Club told me: "I am not a Party member, but this is no drawback to me. Matters may be a little stricter here than before 1973, but we can still invite any Western writers we like to our meetings here, without reference to the authorities. We just pray each day that it will stay that way and not get worse." Writers are free to tackle personal and aesthetic themes as they wish, and sometimes they can get away with criticisms of the political system if these are suitably oblique or if the setting is the past. This is notably true in the theatre, where recent Slovene plays have criticised the excesses of the Stalinist period, and in the case of the various "little magazines" that are privately run. These are allowed much more licence than the dailies or popular magazines, but are liable to lose their official subsidies if they go too far.

The political tightening-up since 1973 has largely by-passed the world of theatres, poetry, novels, art, or other areas judged to be relatively of minority appeal or not too close to politics. But the impact has been far greater in the media, especially television. Political satire allowed in the small magazines is forbidden on the screen: a producer told me, "Some little papers can get away with a joke or cartoon such as 'The comrades leading us into Socialism have lost their way in their smart cars', but when we repeated that same joke on the screen, the Party – *touché,* maybe – were furious and the programme director lost his job." Since 1973, the regular broadcasting output of discussions and lectures on Marxism, self-management and related topics has been greatly stepped up – "It's the equivalent, you could say, of Religious Broadcasts in Britain," one cynic told me, "save that, alas, it tends to be at peak hours." Slovenes take all this with a pinch of salt. So long as the official ideology is respected in its outward forms, in private discussion anyone can say what he thinks without fear. I have been in Slovenes' homes where convinced Catholics and senior Party leaders have held long and friendly arguments about the roles of Church and state. Each has respected the other's views, they have drunk to each other's health and parted cordially. The difference with the West is that this kind of debate cannot be held in public.

9

A Lilliput that loves the rest of the world

"Be happy and prosperous with us!" proclaimed the street banners, in English and Slovene, during international ice-skating championships. Slovenes' devotion to their homeland may have an element of narcissism, yet this Lilliput is not closed or hostile to the outside world: in fact, I found a keener awareness of the world than in any of my other towns. People are more welcoming to foreigners, more eager to learn about other cultures, far better at languages. This mixture of local pride and international spirit I found attractive. Maybe it has something to do with being so small a nation in so central a position, assertively self-aware yet historically subject to outside influences.

In 19th-century days of poverty, Slovenes emigrated massively to America. Today, Cleveland (Ohio) still has 60,000 people of Slovene origin, which makes it the world's biggest "Slovene" city after Ljubljana and Maribor. There are still plenty of transatlantic family contacts, and some Slovene-Americans return to the old country for their retirement. A further exodus, mainly middle-class, took place after the war, for political reasons. Today, permanent emigration is entirely legal, but it is rare: partly because of this *bourgeois* post-war exodus, emigration is considered a little shameful not only by officialdom but also by ordinary Slovenes who believe that patriotism demands they spend most of their life in their homeland. However, many do go to the West for a few years, to earn money or improve their skills, and this temporary expatriation is even encouraged by the government as a means of improving technological expertise. Plenty of young engineers, doctors, architects, go to study or work in the more advanced Western countries. A few unskilled workers have also followed the *Gastarbeiter* trail to Germany, but at this level Slovenia is sufficiently advanced to be herself a net importer of migrant labour, most of it Bosnian.

Thousands of Slovenes take their holidays in the West. Among a school class of sixteen-year-olds I met, all but two had been abroad, most of them to nearby Austria or Italy, some to Hungary – and none to Russia. At the weekends, the streets of Trieste and Klagenfurt are full of Slovene cars: in the days of Yugoslav consumer austerity, people went for shopping, but today goods are almost as varied in Ljubljana as across the border, so they go merely for the fun of it. Ljubljana is, after all, nearer to Trieste than to Zagreb and five times nearer than to Belgrade. Passport formalities are minimal – much the same as, say, between France and Spain. The only serious restriction on travel is that Slovenes are not supposed to carry more than 1,500 dinars out of the country: but few of them take much notice of this. They regularly smuggle out dinar notes, which they can then change in the West virtually at parity (there are not the artificial multi-level exchange-rates which provoke black-marketeering in Soviet bloc countries). Or else they can legally take out money they have earned abroad. If a Slovene brings foreign money into the country, he has the right to keep it in an external bank account and use it as he pleases. And as many Slovenes work abroad at one time or another, there is always a lot of this "external" money in circulation. The government does not bother to tighten up: it even turns a blind eye on the banknote smuggling. The reasons? – first, the revenue from foreign visitors is so much greater that the outflow hardly matters; more especially, most Party leaders and senior officials are themselves regularly involved in these practices. Only when someone exploits the situation a little too blatantly is a public example made: one woman bought six foreign cars with the money she had earned abroad, imported them and resold them, and was then hauled up in court. But such instances are rare.

Ljubljana is not cosmopolitan in the sense of having large resident foreign communities, like Stuttgart: but its spirit is international, in other ways. As I have said, the people are excellent linguists. Once I went into a chemist's for shaving-soap and began miming my request: "Oh, you want a shaving-stick?" said the shopgirl, in English. On other occasions, lost with my "GB" car in the remoter suburbs, I found polite youths coming up to offer detailed directions in good English. I met no educated person who did not speak at least one foreign language fluently, and often two or three. With the older ones, it is usually German; with the young, firstly English, sometimes French or Italian, but rarely their fellow-Slav language, Russian.

Ljubljana is twinned formally with two Italian towns, Parma and Pesaro (both Communist-run) and informally with several towns in both East and West: Nottingham, Wiesbaden, Bratislava, Karl

Marzstadt (GDR), Tiflis and Sousse (Tunisia). I even found a *gymnasium* that conducts regular youth exchanges with the United States. In this whole field of twinning, Ljubljana is certainly more active than Newcastle or Bologna. It also takes pride in being host to frequent international events – sports championships, scientific conventions, the annual festival. When I called on the university students' international committee (its office decked with posters discreetly critical of Moscow), I found them organising a European seminar on "national minorities" (Basques, Scots, etc) – as if to prove that Slovenia has plenty to teach the rest of Europe on this subject!

Except during the festival, Ljubljana is not a town that attracts tourists for any length of time, though scores of thousands – notably Germans – drive through it each year on their way to the Dalmatian coast or to Greece. And Italians and Austrians come in hordes on day or weekend excursions. In order to attract more of these visitors, the authorities have created casinos and strip-tease night-clubs, in Ljubljana and the resorts, and these entice many Italians by offering risqué entertainments they are still denied at home. But Yugoslavs are banned from gambling in the casinos. I heard plenty of criticism of what could be regarded as a cynical and hypocritical operation, unworthy of Slovene Socialism: one moral code for exploiting the foreigner, another for the locals.

The resident foreign colony is tiny – just a few score students, mainly from the Third World, and handfuls of British, French, Americans, etc., mostly in technical or teaching jobs. There is no diplomatic community, apart from a small Austrian consulate and official French and American cultural centres. The British Council operates out of Zagreb. The French centre opened in 1967 and the American (USIS) one in 1972, after much hesitation by the Federal Government which feared that these moves would give the Russians a cue for demanding a centre too. This does not seem to have happened. But the French and Americans have to be careful, and face certain restrictions. They are not allowed to do language teaching, for this by law is a Slovene monopoly: however, the French get round this by sending their teachers to hold classes on Slovene premises, at the university or in adult education centres. Similarly, the foreign institutes must seek advance approval of any film they want to show – "It's a nuisance, when we need to change a programme at the last moment," a French official told me, "but we generally just show the film and then apologise afterwards. No one minds. Things are free-and-easy here, so long as you're tactful to the right people. You see, *le Système D français* is very much a Slovene practice too!"

Another restriction, more rigidly enforced, is that no Yugoslav may lecture in these foreign centres. This is the result of an incident in Belgrade in 1969, when a Serb made an embarrassing pro-Soviet speech about the Czech affair in the Russian cultural centre there. In fact, most of the limitations imposed on foreign centres are *not* aimed against the Western ones but at preventing the spread of Soviet influence; and the Yugoslavs must treat all alike, to avoid provoking Moscow. Apart from this, the French and American centres in Ljubljana work well and are popular. They have libraries, lectures and film shows. The USIS director told me: "The Slovenes were keen for us to open here, but of course they keep an eye on us. I have to report the titles of the new books I get for the library. At the time of the Allende affair, some youths daubed anti-American slogans in red paint on our outside walls – the police had failed to protect the building. But when I protested, they came and wiped it clean."

Apart from rare outbursts of this kind, Americans, French and British are all popular in Ljubljana. Italians, too – for the Trieste dispute and the Occupation are largely forgiven, if not forgotten. Against Germans and Austrians there is expectedly more resentment, especially among older people: one hears stories of rude treatment of German tourists in country areas, though in the city itself there are seldom any problems. As for the Russians, they rarely appear except in formal delegations, and the Slovenes prudently hardly ever mention them: the Soviet menace, like any private nightmare, is not a topic that a Slovene will readily discuss in public, certainly not with a foreigner.

Attitudes to Belgrade and to the rest of Yugoslavia are much like Swabian attitudes to the rest of Germany, only more so. "We are in Central Europe, the rest of Yugoslavia is Balkan," said one Slovene, reminding me that the old gateway astride the road to Zagreb, in the eastern suburbs, is known as *"Porta Balkanica"*. Slovenes consider themselves the most sophisticated of the Yugoslavs (perhaps rightly, though Croats run them a close second). Belgrade seems remote, and impinges little on their daily lives – far less than London impinges on a Geordie, or Paris on a Toulousain – while the semi-primitive Muslim south is vaguely despised. Most Slovenes have never even been to the south, which seems far more distant to them, culturally as well as physically, than north Italy. They have little direct contact with it, except through the presence of immigrant workers, mostly from Bosnia, who make up 18 per cent of the Slovene labour force and do many of the more menial jobs.

Beneath the surface there is some resentment over the money that has to be paid into the federal budget for the development of the south – just as in north Italy, over the *Casa del Mezzogiorno*. And, as you might expect, Slovene officials are frequently irked by Belgrade bureaucracy: but these tensions rarely get aired in public or in the press, for federal Party discipline forbids it. A corner-stone of Tito's policy has always been the avoidance of quarrels that might disrupt national unity and so play into Soviet hands. Slovenia once sought a loan from the World Bank for building a motorway, and for a while there was a lively debate on this in the press. Then Belgrade vetoed the project, as it had a right to do (international loans being a federal matter). The Slovene press abruptly went silent on the issue, evidently on Party orders from on high. That is how things work. However, Slovenia is genuinely autonomous in so many matters that points of friction of this kind are fewer, far fewer than in France or Britain. Seen from Ljubljana, Belgrade is another world. Rare is the Slovene who wants to go and live there, unless he is aiming at a top political career (the federal Ministries are staffed largely with Serbs and Bosnians). A mere 50,000 Slovenes live in the whole of the rest of Yugoslavia, an incredibly low figure, and most of them are people from eastern Slovenia living in nearby Zagreb. When I asked a university class what careers they were planning, not a single student wanted to work in Belgrade: a few were hoping to find jobs in the West, for a few years, while the general chorus was, "Slovenia is best, here's where we want to spend our lives."

"Yes, I admit we are too self-contained and self-satisfied a little community here," said one Party official, echoing a common view. "Yugoslavia ought to develop more of the social mobility that is common in America and increasing in Western Europe. If more of us were prepared to go and live elsewhere, it would lend more strength to Tito's policy of welding these six disparate republics into a solid nation. But our autonomy is still so new, we are still busy consolidating ourselves." This lack of mobility may contain dangers for Yugoslavia, politically; yet the virtues of her decentralised structure shine brightly when set in the wider context of the European regionalist debate. I feel that Slovenes are lucky to belong to a nation authentic enough and small enough to give them a real sense of community; and they enjoy enough autonomy not to feel the same resentments as, say, the Bretons. I came away from Ljubljana with the certainty that centralised countries could learn a good deal from Yugoslavia, as from West Germany.

My final impression of this city is that its inhabitants are on the whole contented with the unusual system under which they live. But is this because of, or despite, its Communism? Self-management may be liked and accepted: but would people put up so happily with the political restrictions, were not the pill so sugared with *laisser-faire* and crypto-capitalism? That is the paradox.

In the years before 1973, *laisser-faire* was on the increase and it led to various abuses. One heard stories of the profits of self-managed firms finding their way into private pockets. But the official line remained liberal, and in 1971 the Slovene premier, Stane Kavčič, advocate of a mixed economy, even proposed the setting up of a kind of stock exchange for private investment, so that the large sums earned abroad by some Slovenes could at least be ploughed into the nation's economy rather than squandered abroad. But this was greeted as heresy by orthodox Marxists, and when the tighter line was introduced, Kavčič and some other liberals lost their posts. In many firms, leading figures suspected of capitalist sympathies were quietly ousted, and Party watchdogs began to play a stronger role in supervising factory management. It has now become harder to advance in one's career, if one is not a Party member. But there has been no reign of terror. No one has been put in prison, or even on trial: people are simply shifted to other jobs. "It's the ordinary musical-chairs of power in any country," said one Slovene, "and not so very different, say, from Heath being ousted from the Tory leadership in favour of Margaret Thatcher." Though the Party is now more assertive, it still seeks to lead by persuasion rather than compulsion. I met a young writer who in 1968 had been a student rebel with Maoist leanings: "I've now joined the Party," he said; "I've realised that it's sterile to campaign from outside it, for the radical reforms of society I believe in, when the Party itself offers us scope for our views." You could say he had little option, but he went on, "Within the Party at all levels there is free discussion and democratic decision-taking. Then, at the self-management meetings, the Party spokesmen put forward their ideas, which are accepted or not, on their merits, like those from non-Party people. Things are still quite liberal." It is not always so simple. Yet the tightening-up has certainly been less marked than in Croatia, habitually more extremist, or even Serbia. A French resident told me, "In all my talks with Slovene officials, I get little feeling of living under what one thinks of as Communism. It's not like, say, Bulgaria, where red banners in the streets proclaim Socialism. People here are too sophisticated for that."

Slovenia's "Socialism with a human face" is based on a tacit compromise between Marxist principle and the acceptance of human selfishness. As such, it just about hangs together. Self-management may be a disappointment in terms of economic efficiency, since it falls foul of human nature: but in its way it offers real grass-roots democracy, and thus is popular. For the moment, it seems to be not incompatible with the steady growth of consumerism. More and more people are owning their own properties, or finding ways of feathering their nests, and I heard it predicted that Slovenia would become steadily more *petit-bourgeois,* a kind of semi-Marxist Switzerland. As in the West, it is a section of the young generation that rejects this spread of middle-class values and demands greater equality and a truer Socialism. But the ruling classes, senior Party members and others, have become as dependent as anyone on the new consumerism. As for the future, much of course will depend on outside factors, notably on how Yugoslavia survives after Tito. For the moment, Ljubljana is a happy place, though a little anxious. Its balancing-act between rival ideologies provides the rest of Europe with some intriguing lessons.

VII

Conclusion

"I'm so lucky to have been born in our town, 'cos it's the best town in the whole wide world!" So speaks the six-year-old youngest child of the family (played by Margaret O'Brien) in the film *Meet Me in St Louis,* set in the serene 1890s.

In America today, a relatively mobile society, such innocent conviction may no longer be so common even among tiny tots. But in old Europe, where roots go deep and so many people stay close to them, plenty of adults feel about their town just as that St Louis girl did. Mobility in Europe may be increasing, yet few of the natives born and bred in the towns in this book have any urge to go and live somewhere they think might be better; or if they do, then they leave when still young. And this is the essence of provincialism, in towns of this kind: a satisfaction with one's spot on the map, if not with all the other conditions of life. The rest of the nation is treated with complacent disdain; the capital city is resented, and ignored as far as possible.

A visitor from the world outside may be dismayed, as often I was, by the parish-pump mentalities, the inflated regard for the second-best: but he may also find that life in a community of this size has its attractions. The town is still just small enough to preserve a human scale, a sense of belonging, and most significant, a fellow-feeling that cuts across social divisions. In each of these towns, the local patriotism seems to have resulted in a softening of the class hostilities found in some other areas, notably in the national capitals. There is a certain matey, democratic spirit in these towns, varying between Swabian paternalism, Geordie populism and Bolognese intramural complicity. This sense of belonging may in some cases be on the wane, as new populations spill out into new distant suburbs; but especially in Bologna, Newcastle and Ljubljana it is still strikingly alive, while even Stuttgart and Toulouse still like to call themselves "the biggest village in Germany", "the biggest village in France".

And yet, at the end of this long journey, I am left facing the question: beyond their similar pride and provincialism, what do these towns have in common that adds up to "Europe"? Do the four Western ones share enough common ground, in their civilisation, their way of life, their values, for the ideal of EEC unity to make sense? Some readers may have been struck most by the similarities, others by the differences. The latter are perfectly obvious, in many matters of taste and daily life-style, partly dictated by local resources or by the climate. But in real human terms these differences may often be superficial, even irrelevant. If a Geordie enjoys beer and darts, and a Toulousain wine and *boules,* so what? – more important is whether the nature of social contact is the same. In fact, it may not be. Some of the divergences in temperament and social outlook certainly run deep, for example those between Geordie casual chumminess and Swabian formality and status-seeking. But time and again I have been made aware of the similarities that lie behind contrasting façades, and notably by the kinship between certain Geordie attitudes and those of the faraway Latin societies. Few towns could look more different than grey Victorian Newcastle and mediaeval Bologna; yet their stubborn inbred patriotism, their gregarious tribalism, their preference for compromise and human proportion, have much in common. Newcastle is in physical contrast to Toulouse as well; yet the political intrigues and wheeler-dealing of the one sometimes reminded me of the other, despite the differing government structures; and an earthy, loquacious, un-Cartesian eccentric such as André Brouat is not so far in spirit from a Geordie such as Arthur Grey – nearer, at least, than *cassoulet* is to pease-pudding.

The "specialness" of each of these three towns is in part auto-suggestion. Each is different because it feels itself to be different, like some introverted adolescent who regards his problems as unique, unaware that they are the problems of all adolescence. In many practical respects the towns are less different from each other, and from the rest of their nations, than they suppose. All five cities are today being drawn closer by the same modern consumer trends – for good or ill – and are facing many of the same problems of adaptation. How are the new dormitory estates to become lively local communities? How is the citizen best to participate in civic affairs? What should be the structural links between a city and its surrounding townships that tend to lure away its population and resources? How to reconcile the imperatives of the motor-car and of urban conservation? Should subsidised culture be for the few or the many? How can a classical education system be best adapted to a more egalitarian age, when funds are short? How can the desire of workers for more shop-floor democracy be equated with the needs of industrial competitivity? These and other issues recur in every town, and in many cases the popular responses to them are remarkably similar – for, after all, a student in Ljubljana or Toulouse, a factory worker in Bologna or Newcastle, a housewife in Stuttgart or anywhere, share much the same aspirations. And the arguments in the local debates on each issue are often similar too. It is the solutions proposed or applied that most frequently vary: but in very many cases this is due to decisions (or lack of decision) at central governmental rather than city level. If Bologna had its own way, might not its school system move much closer to Newcastle's? If Toulouse had the opportunity, might it not follow some of Stuttgart's methods in civic administration?

And suppose I were asked which of these towns comes nearest to being an ideal community? Or in which are the citizens happiest? An answer would not be easy. Happiness is a matter of temperament, as much as circumstance. The serious Swabians appear to have less capacity for enjoyment than the Toulousains, yet they are probably more contented. The Geordies, like other Englishmen, have some reason to be anxious about their future, yet they possess a greater readiness for accepting life placidly than the more exigent Continentals. For what it is worth, a world-wide Gallup survey published in 1976 showed that to the question, "Do you feel very happy with your life?", 38 per cent of the British sample answered "yes", against only 22 per cent of French, 12 per cent of West Germans, and a mere 8 per cent of Italians! (Yugoslavia was not included.) Yet this was a time when Britain was supposedly facing economic collapse. If we take these figures at all seriously, what are we to make of them? They may not relate accurately to the towns in this book, for there is no doubt that the Bolognese are happier (with cause) than most other Italians, while sedate Stuttgart may be a more contented place than some of the more frenetic German cities. But I think the high British response is revealing. The British on the whole complain and agitate less than most Continentals, they demand less of life, nowadays, and you could say they accept lower standards, or at least that their expectations have risen less sharply. Greater British egalitarianism may be a factor too: wage differentials are narrower than on the Continent. In Newcastle, working-class families probably get as much fun out of life as the struggling professional classes. In Bologna, Toulouse and especially Stuttgart, money-values count for more, and at least in theory the rich are happier. But the rich are few. Does this help to explain why so very few Italians and Germans tell Mr Gallup they are "very happy"?

Other statistics, which I do not possess, would almost certainly indicate that a Toulousain feels happier than a Parisian, a Bolognese than a Roman, and probably a Geordie than a Londoner. Nor do I have statistics to show whether people feel happier than, say, ten years ago, though my impression is that they do not. The inhabitants of all these towns have been influenced by the malaise in Europe since the 1973-4 energy crisis, by rising unemployment and inflation, and by the political uncertainties that shadow all these countries, chronically or intermittently. Maybe this anxiety has not been very clearly reflected in these chapters, for it is often an intangible thing, and living standards have fallen only marginally and in some cases are picking up again. But in several *milieux* I was made aware of the malaise – notably among teachers in Bologna and Toulouse, the middle-classes generally in Newcastle, and young people and students almost everywhere as they struggle with antiquated education systems and dismal job prospects. I have found it impossible to compare accurately the living standards of these towns, other than subjectively and impressionistically, for floating currencies and varying inflation rates destroy much of the value of comparative statistics, and moreover most of the useful statistics are at national or regional rather than city level. However, the tables of national figures in the appendices may give some indications.

Each community has much it could learn from the others. Stuttgart in many respects sets a standard for what can be achieved through systematic hard work, initiative and self-confidence, in public affairs and in business. And Stuttgart's industries best illustrate what workers can gain, within a capitalist framework, when their unions agree to collaborate with management. Ljubljana's system offers an ingenious alternative to capitalism, but has not yet solved the problem of how to combine worker-control with incentives to work harder. Bologna and

Toulouse have only recently emerged from the first vigorous flush of industrialisation, and despite union politicisation, staff at most levels are still fired with a degree of energy, ambition and work-motivation – less than in Stuttgart, but more than on Tyneside where a century-and-a-half of industrial effort has led to a certain collective weariness. Geordies have half turned their backs on the Continental rat-race: theirs is a less competitive society, in some ways less materialistic. They want an easy life, but are not always prepared to face the consequences: they seem to think they have a right to a high standard of living without working hard for it, and this applies to executives as much as workers. They should come to take a look at Stuttgart.

Yet it is Newcastle that provides the best example of a generous participatory democracy – followed by Bologna and Ljubljana, in their fashions. The Bolognese Communists have had some success – by Italian standards – in involving the citizen in civic affairs and extending welfare amenities. But they are held back by their own cautious compromising, and by the heavy hand of Rome which limits their scope and runs so very badly the main welfare services such as hospitals. In Ljubljana, the intensive self-management system is a real victory for a certain style of democracy, though it does seem to lead to more talk than action; and the earnest nanny-knows-best role of the Party can be counter-productive. In Newcastle, by contrast, community action is more spontaneous. All the waffle about "communi-care" and "building a compassionate society" is more than empty words; and the communal activity of the new Tyneside council estates points a contrast with the lonely Toulouse suburbs.

It is possible to argue, as some people do, that too much welfare and protection, given by the state or local bodies, has been making the British soft; and that life on Tyneside, once so cruel for the workers, is now too cushioned and comfortable, lacking the necessary challenge of a harder society such as Stuttgart's. Many British people themselves feel this, and there may be some truth in it. The Geordies set high store on such matters as care for the weak and lonely, but what about their standards in other areas? Here we enter a delicate zone of subjective value-judgements, where it may be hazardous to choose between Geordie and Swabian civilisations: in the one case, a warm easy-going kindliness mixed with vulgarity, amateurism and an acceptance of mediocrity; in the other, a certain formality, intolerance and lack of neighbourly concern, mixed with a much higher perfectionism and zeal for progress, in many matters.

The contrast is apparent also in the differing cultural scenes of the two cities. Which model is to be preferred, Stuttgart's spoon-fed "temple" culture, or the anti-highbrow, do-it-yourself, something-for-everyone approach of Tyneside? Toulouse and Bologna lie in between, but nearer to Stuttgart. The model I most enjoyed myself is that of Ljubljana, where culture is neither diluted and vulgarised for the masses, nor put on a pedestal of *bourgeois* status-snobbery, but corresponds to the enthusiasm and taste of a widely civilised people. Yet if we turn to look at education, we see that Ljubljana has been no more successful than capitalist societies in bringing its education system in line with modern needs. In all these towns – except Newcastle – I found near-identical problems of over-crowded and under-funded universities, where students struggle through out-of-date exam courses and lack contact with their teachers; and fusty secondary schools that stuff their pupils with facts but do little to encourage them to think for themselves or to develop their full personalities outside the classroom. Matters are worst in Bologna, much less bad in Stuttgart. In Newcastle, as elsewhere in Britain, at least university and schools are run with more humanity: but in academic terms, standards are often lower than on the Continent, and it is the pseudo-egalitarian bias against intellectual excellence that is at the heart of Britain's educational crisis.

Education is not (except in Newcastle) a municipal concern. Town-planning is: and here these towns have muffed many of their chances. They have all had to face much the same basic dilemma: as population, traffic and commercial activities all multiply, do you facilitate this trend by tearing down to rebuild (*à la* Haussmann), or do you conserve the old, and put limits on growth? The solutions vary, and are hard to compare since the towns' physical structures vary so much too. Bologna's council is obviously right to try to preserve the historic centre and limit traffic there. Yet in the newer parts of the town it has done little towards imaginative redevelopment – and the two need not be incompatible. Its overall approach seems a little Malthusian. Toulouse has expanded far more rapidly than Bologna, and has only recently begun to come to terms with the problems this causes. It is still far too indulgent towards city-centre traffic, and is allowing some parts of its historic centre to fall into ruin. But at least, as in Bologna, the main public buildings are beautifully kept up, fountains play, flowers bloom. It is sad that the proud Slovenes do not show the same civic pride in keeping their city spruce and tidy. In Newcastle, the grandiose schemes for central redevelopment have at least largely solved the traffic problem; but the indulgence here has been towards ugly speculative building in the centre. In Stuttgart, matters are much the same. The hurried post-war rebuilding of the blitzed central areas was done without much regard for aesthetics; and although the more recent road and subway schemes are keeping traffic jams at bay, the city's modern metallic core fits unhappily within its gentle girdle of wooded hills.

Nearly all these towns are now taking environment more seriously, though they may be finding that their earlier building schemes, or neglect, have made the task harder. Stuttgart, Newcastle and Bologna have each of them recently closed their main shopping-street to private cars; new leisure zones and other amenities are being created, such as Newcastle's "urban farm" under Byker Bridge and Toulouse's open-air riverside theatre. This corresponds to a growing public concern for better "quality of life", now that the basic needs of new housing have been largely answered. In these towns, as in many others in Europe, the fashion is now moving away from high-rise buildings, huge office complexes, and measures that encourage private cars in city centres. Town-planning is becoming more human. But most towns are severely hamstrung by lack of finance, lack of *Lebensraum,* and the bureaucratic encroachments of central government.

This applies even to Stuttgart, whose record in local government is in many other respects the best of these towns. It gains from having an *Oberbürgermeister* and team of assistant mayors who have a popular mandate yet are also full-time fully paid professionals. The result is a technocratic style of rule that may not encourage civic participation. But it makes for efficiency and honesty: Stuttgart is probably the best administered of these towns. England might benefit from a similar system: if the Dan Smiths were allowed to run local politics as fully salaried professionals, they could be less prone to temptation. Stuttgart's weak point – hardly its own fault – is that it has not yet managed to come to terms with the surrounding townships which are draining it of resources: unless the *Land* steps in to insist on a wider joint authority for the conurbation, the city council will be in serious economic trouble. And here it is Britain's turn to provide a model, for the new Tyne-and-Wear metropolitan county, though far from ideal, does ensure some coordination of funds and planning decisions within the urban area. Toulouse and Bologna, like Stuttgart, face problems of coordination with the rapidly growing peripheral communes that entice away their sources of revenue. But the greater perennial headache for them is the issue of relations with the prefect, satrap of a central government that imposes its will on them more forcibly than in the case of Stuttgart, or even Newcastle. In Italy, with its succession of ineffectual and over-bureaucratic governments, the influence of the Rome administration on a city such as Bologna has been largely negative: prefects and ministries have repeatedly vetoed local projects or withheld funds, preventing the city from making progress with its conservation plans. In Toulouse the balance is different, for governments in post-war France have been far more dynamic and fertile in ideas, and much of the initiative for the development of the city has come from Paris. There are some useful safeguards in the system whereby mayor and prefect can veto each others' plans, but the uneasy division of power can prove negative when the mayor is hostile to Paris; and Toulouse, like Bologna, really deserves more autonomy especially in its financing. Newcastle too, and even Stuttgart, suffer in different ways from the growing bureaucratic pressures of a higher level of government (Whitehall in one case, *Land* and *Bund* in the other). In all these nations, even federal Germany, there is a case to be made for some rethinking of the relations between local councils and the remote bureaucrats of the capital (in Slovenia, the problems are not comparable).

In some countries, a solution might come through a strengthening of the intermediate tier, that of regional government. Today Europe needs more regional decentralisation, in order to counter the impersonal centralising tendencies of modern states and of the EEC itself. And regionalism is no artificial growth: it relates to cultural realities. The common factor of local pride that links these towns is in many cases regional as much as civic. Bologna may be the exception in preserving the mentality of a walled city-state, but even here there is a burgeoning new loyalty to Emilia. And elsewhere, notably in Newcastle and Ljubljana, love of city is part of a wider patriotic loyalty to the region of which the city is the headpiece. Each of these towns or regions has preserved its own language or dialect, in some cases the vehicle of daily speech. Most of the towns are striving, self-consciously or not, to revive or retain the old regional cultural traditions, through the creation of folklore groups such as the *Ballets Occitans*. And in all the towns there is strong popular awareness of regional ancestries, stretching back unbroken to the days of the Cathars, the kings of Northumbria, the dukes of Württemberg, the patricians and scholars of 12th-century Bologna, and the Slovenes preserving their culture against mediaeval foreign overlords. Regionalism, Europe's past, can also be its future.

Paradox though it may seem, regionalism can also help to combat narrow parochialism. The two towns I have come to like and admire the most – Stuttgart and Ljubljana – are also the ones that are true capitals of regional government under a federal structure. And this may not be a coincidence. One of the features I like best about each is that a strong local pride is combined with an outward looking spirit. And an explanation of this may be that if a society's aspirations for some political identity and autonomy are satisfied, then it is more likely to acquire the self-respect and sense of security that will encourage it to go out and communicate with the world. Of course there is plenty of the parish-pump in Stuttgart and Ljubljana, but in each there is also an openness to outside influences, a lack of complexes in its readiness to meet the world on equal terms. And this has something to do with its regional status. In Newcastle and Bologna, and to an extent in Toulouse, the local pride is more inward-looking and insular, and seems to reflect atavistic resentments against the capital for "colonisation" and refusal of devolution. I sincerely believe that if the north-east were to become a semi-autonomous region with Newcastle as its capital, then the narcissistic Geordie inferiority complex would be forced to occupy itself with more constructive tasks than the contemplation of its navel and grousing against London. And the same could happen in Toulouse and Bologna. If the embryonic new Italian regionalism were to be allowed to develop properly, and if Emilia-Romagna were in practice to acquire the status of Baden-Württemberg, then the Bolognese might be encouraged to look beyond the horizon of their arcades. Perhaps I am being naïvely optimistic. But I did return from Slovenia with a certain envy for this kind of small nation and with added sympathy for, amongst others, the Scottish and Basque nationalists.

Of course the super-metropolis such as London or Paris will always have a major part to play, internationally as much as nationally. It provides a focus for intellectual and cultural exchange and advance, without which all the world is provincial. As I suggested, there are some disadvantages to Germany in no longer having such a metropolis. But the need is to find a balance: after all, Stuttgart was already powerful even in Berlin's heyday. In the case of France and Britain, although Toulouse and Newcastle have each achieved a notable cultural revival since the war, the pull exerted by Paris and London still seems too strong. Toulouse may have attracted immigrant executives and academics from Paris, but they are uneasily integrated, and the town remains noticeably weaker than Stuttgart in sophisticated local talent and leadership. Newcastle, all the more so. On average, the quality of local politicians, of senior management, intellectuals, artists, and others, is higher in Stuttgart than in my other towns, and not surprisingly. Hence there is sound sense in the campaigns carried out by the promoters of Tyneside and Toulouse, to try to attract more executives and other talent from the capital by improving cultural and other amenities and vaunting the local "quality of life". The campaign has met with a great deal more success in the case of Toulouse, perhaps inevitably. Toulouse in the sunny south with its tradition of easy living is a saleable commodity. By comparison, far fewer ambitious young men and women have accepted to take the grey road north to Newcastle.

Tyneside, like Bologna, strikingly lacks an infusion of new blood from outside, and I think that both places suffer from this, psychologically and – in Tyneside's case – economically too. Stuttgart, by contrast, has been hugely invigorated by the thousands of Silesian and other immigrants from the East and – though it may not always admit it – by the *Gastarbeiter*. Toulouse, even more, has been enriched by the waves of *pieds noirs,* Spaniards, Parisians and others, even if it has not assimilated these newcomers too well. But Bologna has expressly set its face against large-scale immigration from outside its area; and Tyneside, for economic and climatic reasons, has not had much other choice. The result has been to intensify parochialism and, in Tyneside's case, to inhibit industrial renewal too, for local firms are short of new talent. Newcastle suffers worst of all my towns from a brain-drain, for not even Geordie patriots always want to stay in the area. Many of the brightest have hitched their wagons to the great trails of the new European mobility. In the past decades, many European nations have begun to follow the American pattern of the mobile society: French and Germans in particular are far readier than before the war to move from their native province to a new home hundreds of miles away, especially in the executive classes. The trend has not yet reached the proportions found in some parts of America and it might be harmful if it did, for a rootless society can be even less happy than a stagnant one. But – Little Englanders please note – a community that rejects infusions of new blood will wilt of anaemia. A vigorous regionalism, with deep roots, is not at all incompatible with a creative mobility.

So, if I had to live the rest of my life in one of these towns, which would I choose (assuming I could find a suitable job)? Stuttgart, definitely. True, I feel closer to the French than to the Germans, and there are aspects of Swabian life that might not cease to madden me. But I admire Germany, and find it an endlessly fascinating enigma. And in Stuttgart I would feel least cut off from the European mainstream: it is the most centrally situated of these towns, as well as the most metropolitan, intellectually sophisticated, and so on. In short, I am a metropolitan at heart: provincialism has its charms, but not for too long at a stretch. My ideal might be to find a city of metropolitan character but moderate size.

Toulouse I like for its vitality, its stimulating contradictions, plus the pleasures of sunlight and countryside and a certain *douceur de vivre*. But the wayward temperament of the Midi irritates me, and so does that insistent twangy accent. Toulouse is a town of cliques, a compartmentalised society where family privacy is rated high and it is not easy to make real friends outside one's own little *milieu*: a lonely place in a way, beneath the surface chatter and animation. In Ljubljana, I adore the people and love to visit them; but I think its small-town unsophistication might annoy me in the long run, and so could the subtle pressures and restrictions of a political system that does not allow full liberty of dissent. Bologna has a more generous warmth and gregariousness than Toulouse, and a greater social coherence; but it is hard to penetrate unless you share its unusual wavelength. Many English visitors do: I could never find it other than claustrophobic. Unlike most people, I unashamedly prefer serious, efficient Germany to capricious Italy. And being the person I am, a middle-class Oxford-educated Londoner, I could never come to terms happily with alien Newcastle, either. It remains in several respects the odd-man-out of my four Western towns – indeed, of all five, political systems apart. It is the only truly northern town in this book, far to the north of that crucial line that divides the Europe of vineyards from the Europe of beer. It is the only town deeply marked by the industrial revolution. It is the least conscious of belonging to the European heritage. Ljubljana, by contrast, feels itself to be at the very heart of the European tradition, as geographically and culturally it is.

I have said little in these chapters about people's attitudes to the

EEC and to European unity: generally I have found their views self-evident, or too vague. In all the Western towns there has been a decline of European idealism in the past five or so years, and a creeping pessimism or apathy about the future of the EEC even among many of its champions. But this does not mean there is actual opposition to the general concept of the EEC or the prospect of European unity – save among Geordies, quite a number of whom feel that Europe is irrelevant to Britain. Elsewhere, the case of Bologna is indicative. The Bolognese think themselves wonderful and disdain the Ferrarese or Milanese: but, unlike Geordies, they are fully aware of being part of the mainstream of Europe. For many of them, it is still a kind of Renaissance Europe of federated city-states. Asked if they believe in a united Europe, they will reply sincerely, "Yes, of course" – like most Italians. Bologna-style parochialism, then, is not incompatible with a general pro-European feeling: the hostility is directed more against the national capital, Rome or Paris, than against foreigners. If the peoples of my towns are largely unaware of each other, and moreover expressed little interest in each other when I told them of this book, may it not be because they have rarely allowed themselves the opportunity to meet each other? If they met, given patience and a little linguistic help, they would in most cases discover they like each other and even find a fellow-feeling. I repeat: what they have most in common is the unawareness of what they have in common.

My pessimism about the future of Europe – and who these days can be easily optimistic? – is therefore tempered. "Only connect", E. M. Forster's dictum about human relationships, applies equally to peoples. All they need do is take the trouble to make real contact: their common humanity will then transcend supposed enmities and prejudices, as Renoir's *La Grande Illusion* dared to suggest. Certainly in Toulouse and Stuttgart I found few remaining vestiges of Franco-German hatred, save among some older Frenchmen. In recent years I have also attended a number of town-twinning activities, not so much mayoral visits as grass-roots exchanges between families and sporting or other groups, and I have found that when ordinary people go to stay in each others' homes, the Germans in France, the French in Britain and so on, they quickly become friends. At a meeting in 1976 between the amateur football teams of Crowborough (Sussex) and Montargis (near Orléans), the young French captain said in his speech: "A United Europe will not be created by the politicians in Brussels, fighting over the price of butter, but by the peoples, getting together to dance, drink and sing" – and we roared applause, and danced, drank and sang. It is the young especially who feel, when they travel, that the old frontiers no longer make much sense, and who readily discover a comradeship across those frontiers. But first they have to make the effort to stir off their backsides (Bolognese and Geordie teenagers, please note).

The future of Europe depends on many factors far outside the scope of this book. As I write in the spring of 1979, the outlook is not too bright, despite the modest innovations of a new monetary system and direct elections. National economies are still diverging, and this drives many governments back towards defence of self-interest, just when they had been on the point of closer integration. Frequently it is the politicians who are more nationalistic than the general public. They hurry to the protection of individual pressure-groups – Grimsby fishermen or Languedoc vinegrowers – whose militant discontent could lose them precious votes. But they take less account of the larger silent majority that rarely feels so actively menaced by EEC measures. The public, even the British public, is not so much hostile to Europe as baffled and indifferent, and it needs to be led. If the politicians were to present it convincingly with a new European ideal, then the public would not reject it. But at present we are caught in a vicious circle, especially in Britain: public coolness to the EEC causes vote-minded politicians to be cool too and therefore to do nothing that would coax the public out of its coolness. To break away from this stalemate will require political courage, the courage of the great pioneers of previous years, Monnet, Brandt, Spaak, Heath and others. Will the national leaders of the 1980s be able to rediscover the idealism of Europe's founding fathers?

In the meantime, the peoples little by little *are* discovering each other. At one twinning exchange between small French and German towns, I heard a French shopkeeper say to his German host, a schoolmaster, "Why do you silly Germans prefer your pickled cucumbers sweet? Anyone with taste knows that a gherkin should be sharp and sour." And the German said, "Because that's the way we are, my friend – and we'll stay that way." And they laughed, and slapped each other on the back. *Vive la différence!* – how awful it would be if we moved into a uniform conveyor-belt Europe where tastes were standardised. Long live Europe's cultural diversity: the click of *boules* in a dusty square as the churches glow gold in the sunset along the Garonne, the piles of home-made *ravioli* and *tortellini* in the little shops beside the Palazzo del Podestà, the stout matrons in hats drinking chocolate and whipped cream under the chandeliers of the *cafés* in the Königstrasse, the roar of a hundred voices singing *Blaydon Races* in a dockland pub beside the cranes of Wallsend, the young poets arguing about socialism and pornography in the Writers' Club off Titova Cesta at two in the morning. But long live also the day when French, Germans and others have nothing more destructive to quarrel about than whether pickled baby cucumbers should be eaten sweet or sour.

Statistical Appendix

In the preceding chapters, comparisons of such matters as standard-of-living and consumer spending have been no more than approximate and impressionistic. This is because the relevant statistics do not exist for the towns as such. However, the table below gives some figures for the five nations as a whole, though the reader will have to bear in mind that Stuttgart is even more prosperous than the West German average; Bologna is about average for North Italy but well above average for all Italy; Newcastle is below average for Britain; Toulouse is about on the French average; and Ljubljana is far above the Yugoslav average. Thus Ljubljana is not nearly so far behind the four Western towns as these figures might suggest, while Bologna in practice is at least as prosperous as Newcastle, and the gap between Newcastle and Stuttgart is even greater than national statistics might indicate.

	W. Germany	Italy	UK	France	Yugoslavia
Gross domestic product per capita, 1976 (dollars)	7,250	3,040	3,910	6,550	1,510
Private consumption per capita, 1976 (dollars)	4,010	1,960	2,350	4,080	821
Passenger cars, per 1,000 people	290	257	249	289	72

Telephones, per 1,000 people	317	259	379	262	61
TV sets, per 1,000 people	305	213	315	235	131
Doctors, per 1,000 people	1.9	2.0	1.3	1.5	1.4
Percentage of young people entering higher education	24.2	31.0	21.8	31.4	16.6
Infant mortality (deaths in first year per 1,000 live births)	19.7	20.7	16.0	13.6	39.7
Deaths in road accidents, 1976	14,820	8,927	6,570	13,577	-
Average monthly salaries (in £ sterling):					
Managing director	2,260	1,926	974	2,235	-
Sales manager	1,344	1,155	615	1,267	-
Skilled worker	563	237	338	418	-
Unskilled worker	457	185	290	321	-
National spending on social security, as percentage of GDP	23.8	21.4	16.6	19.5	-
Registered unemployed, as percentage of working population, July 1978	3.6	6.8	6.2	5.3	-
Inflation rate, July 1977 to July 1978	2.2	12.0	7.8	9.2	13.9

Sources: OECD, EEC, Confederation of British Industries.
For Yugoslavia, some statistics are either not available, or not relevant owing to the different economic system.

Acknowledgements

In each of these towns, scores of kind people gave me help and hospitality of various sorts and talked to me freely. They are too numerous for their names all to be mentioned, but I wish to thank them all. My special thanks go to the following:

In Stuttgart: Werner Schloske and his wife, who were unfailingly helpful and generous; Ian Bell, former British Consul-General, and his wife Ruth; Michael Maegraith; Mayor Manfred Rommel and his predecessor, the late Arnulf Klett, and their councillors and staff in the *Rathaus*.

In Bologna: Mayor Renato Zangheri, his councillors and staff at the *Municipio*; Gabriella Nardi; Professor Federico Mancini and many others at the university; Dr Vittorio Cervi.

In Newcastle: Dan Smith, Arthur Grey, Donald Gilbert, Ken Galley, and other councillors and officials, past and present, at the Civic Centre; David Dougan, director of Northern Arts; the late Dr Henry Miller and others at the university; Estrella and Geoffrey Fox.

In Toulouse: Catherine and Pierre-Yves Péchoux, who have been especially kind and hospitable; Michel Valdiguié, and his colleagues at Motorola; Paul Ourliac, André Brouat, Jean Krynen, François Lafont, and other councillors and officials at the *mairie*, past and present; Bernard Kayser, John Prince, and others at the universities; René Recouly and his fellow-Rotarians.

In Ljubljana: Lučka Pilgram, Irene Novak, Veno Taufer, Veseljko Simonovič, Tomo Martelanč; Boštjan Barborič and other Slovene Government officials; Andrej Skerlavaj and other municipal officials.

I should also like to thank: Dr Brigitte Lohmeyer, former cultural counsellor at the West German Embassy in London; Sandy Dunbar, former director of Northern Arts; Professor Vincent Wright and other experts on local government; as well as the directors and staff of Secker & Warburg; my American publisher, Cass Canfield, jnr, of Harper & Row; and my long-suffering wife, Jenny.

Bibliography

These are some of the books, both specifically about the towns or more generally about their countries or regions, which I found helpful as sources of background information:

Thaddäus Troll: *Stuttgart* (Belser, Stuttgart, 1969)

Robert H. Evans: *Coexistence: Communism and its practice in Bologna, 1945-65* (University of Notre Dame Press, Notre Dame, Ind., 1967)

Max Jäggi, Roger Müller, Sil Schmid: *Red Bologna* (Writers and Readers, 1977)

Dominique Schnapper: *L'Italie Rouge et Noire: les modèles culturels de la vie quotidienne à Bologne* (Gallimard, Paris, 1971)

Peter Nichols: *Italia, Italia* (Macmillan, London, 1973)

David Bean: *Tyneside, a Biography* (Macmillan, London, 1971)

Jon Davies: *The Evangelising Bureaucrat* (Tavistock, London, 1972)

Dan Smith: *Autobiography* (Oriel, Newcastle-upon-Tyne, 1970)

Graham Turner: *The North Country* (Eyre, London, 1967)

Christian Béringuier, André Boudou, Guy Jalabert: *Toulouse Midi-Pyrénées: La Transition* (Stock, Paris, 1972)

Jean Coppolani: *Toulouse XXe Siècle* (Privat, Toulouse, 1963)

Phyllis Auty: *Yugoslavia* (Thames & Hudson, London, 1965)

Frederick Singleton: *Twentieth-Century Yugoslavia* (Macmillan, London, 1976)

Stevan K. Pavlovitch: *Yugoslavia* (Praeger, New York, 1971)

Jean-Marie Domenach and Alain Pontault: *Yugoslavia* (Vista Books, London, 1962).